M/B	Market to book ratio
MCC	Marginal cost of capital
NPV	Net present value
P	Price of a share of stock
	P_0 = price of the stock today
P/E	Price/earnings ratio
Pmt	An annuity
PV	Present value
r	(1) Rate of return
	(2) The IRR on a new project
	(3) Correlation coefficient
R_F	Rate of return on a risk-free security
ROA	Return on assets
ROE	Return on equity
ROI	Return on investment
S	(1) Sales
	(2) Stock, total market value
Σ	Summation sign (capital sigma)
σ	Standard deviation (lower case sigma)
t	(1) Tax rate
	(2) Time, when used as a subscript
	(for example, D_t = the dividend in Year t)
TIE	Times interest earned
V	Value
YTM	Yield to maturity

Introduction to
Financial Management

Introduction to Financial Management

B.J. Campsey
San Jose State University

Eugene F. Brigham
University of Florida

The Dryden Press

Chicago   New York   Philadelphia   San Francisco   Montreal   Toronto
London   Sydney   Tokyo   Mexico City   Rio de Janeiro   Madrid

About the cover:
The cover shows a
graphic representation
of the skyline of
Chicago, financial hub
of the Midwest.

Acquisitions Editor: Elizabeth Widdicombe
Developmental Editors: Susan Meyers, Nancy Moudry
Project Editor: Nancy Moudry
Managing Editor: Jane Perkins
Design Director: Alan Wendt
Production Manager: Mary Jarvis
Permissions Editor: Doris Milligan

Copy Editor: Mary Englehart
Indexer: Sheila Ary
Compositor: The Clarinda Company
Text Type: 10/12 Palatino
Cover Photo: © Eric Sutron, Gartman/Hilstrom Agencies

Library of Congress Cataloging in Publication Data

Campsey, B. J.
  Introduction to financial management.

  Includes bibliographies and index.
  1. Corporations—Finance. 2. Business enterprises—
Finance. I. Brigham, Eugene F., 1930– II. Title.
HG4026.C23   1985   658.1'5   84-10284
ISBN 0-03-059666-1

Printed in the United States of America
567-016-987654321

Address orders:
383 Madison Avenue
New York, NY 10017

Address editorial correspondence:
One Salt Creek Lane
Hinsdale, IL 60521

CBS COLLEGE PUBLISHING
The Dryden Press
Holt, Rinehart and Winston
Saunders College Publishing

Preface

The theory and practice of financial management have changed greatly in recent years. Strong inflationary pressures have pushed interest rates to unprecedented highs, and the resulting high and volatile cost of capital has led to profound changes in corporate financial policies and practices. Academic researchers have made a number of significant theoretical advances. At the same time, business practitioners have been making increasing use of financial theory.

While theory is an important factor in developing financial practice, this book focuses on the practitioner, particularly one who will own or manage a small- to medium-size business. The book is designed for the general business student, not just for the finance major. It is our opinion that many so-called introductory texts are designed specifically for finance (and accounting) majors. These are excellent textbooks, but in their efforts to include theory—some of which seems to contain little practical usefulness—or detailed models of financial concepts, the non-finance major is often lost or "turned off" to the study of finance. This is unfortunate, because financial planning affects and in turn is affected by marketing, production, and other business decisions. Thus all business students must have a thorough knowledge of finance. It is our hope that this book will provide that knowledge in a manner that is interesting and enjoyable to all business students, regardless of major.

Intended Market and Use

By its title one can be assured that this book is intended for use in an introductory course in financial management. The main parts of the text can be covered in a one-term course, but supplemented with cases and some outside readings, *Introduction to Financial Management* can also be used over two terms.

If the book is to be used in a one-term course, the instructor will probably want to cover only selected chapters, leaving the others for students to examine on their own or to use as references in conjunction with work in other courses. In our own courses, we seldom are able to complete an entire book. The material we tend to omit is contained in Chapters 22 through 25. Our students cover these topics in subsequent finance courses. Other instructors have indicated that they often save material in Chapters 16, 19, and 21 for an advanced course. Where a money and banking course is required, instructors may wish to omit parts of Chapters 3, 4, and 5; in schools that do not require such a course, instructors may wish to expand the material covered in these chapters. Still other instructors may wish to utilize the material in Chapters 14, 17, and 18 earlier in the course than the chapter sequence indicates. Thus many other course structures are possible, and we trust that it will be quite easy to cover chapters in a sequence different from the one in the book. The Glossary and Appendix F (which summarizes the equations contained in the text) make alternative sequences easy to follow.

Special Features of This Text

1. *Streamlined Quantitative Material*
A conscious effort has been made to streamline as much of the quantitative material as possible without lowering the quality of the text. Thus, where possible, very detailed mathematical formulas or concepts have been simplified or deleted. For example, our chapter on risk in capital budgeting assumes no previous statistical knowledge. Further, the chapters on the diverse areas of bankruptcy, international finance, mergers, and changes in credit policy have received a practical orientation.

2. *Decisions in Finance*
Each chapter begins with an actual financial decision faced by business-people. The actual resolution to the decision is given at the end of the chapter. For example, Chapter 21 begins with Ford's dilemma over whether or not to offer a dividend in the face of substantial losses. We hope in these sections to challenge the student to consider how knowledge of the material contained in the chapter would help the financial decision maker.

3. *Industry Practice*
In several chapters we present a real-world industry practice section that highlights or expands key issues in the chapter. For example, the Industry Practice in Chapter 2 explains why certain industries pay little in taxes while others receive few tax breaks. These illustrations also help to enliven the material in the chapter.

4. *Focus on Small Business*
Several chapters also contain a small business practice section, written by Professor Christopher Barry of Southern Methodist University. For example, the small business section in Chapter 3 explains in detail how emerging new firms raise venture capital. These sections are especially

useful in giving the student a view of finance from the standpoint of the smaller firm.

5. *Running Glossary*

A brief definition of important terms appears in the margin of the text. Additionally, the key terms in each chapter are highlighted as they occur and are listed for review at the end of the chapter.

6. *Self-Test Problems*

A set of fairly difficult self-test problems, with detailed solutions, is given at the end of the more difficult quantitative chapters. These problems serve (a) to test the student's ability to set up problems for solution and (b) to explain the solution set-up for those who need help.

7. *Range of Problems*

The end-of-chapter problems have been revised significantly in relation to other Brigham finance texts. The number of problems has been increased, and their range of difficulty has been expanded.

8. *New Chapters*

Significant additions to the previous Brigham texts include chapters on the banking system, breakeven analysis and operating leverage, and working capital policy. Additionally, most chapters have been substantially revised to bring them in line with the goal of streamlining the book while maintaining the Brigham quality and readability of prior texts.

Ancillary Materials

1. *Study Guide.* This supplement, coauthored by Linda E. Pepple, outlines the key sections of the text, offers students self-testing questions for each chapter, and provides a set of problems and solutions similar to those in the text.

2. *Instructor's Manual.* A very complete manual is available to instructors who adopt the book. The instructor's manual also includes lecture notes that are keyed to the acetate transparencies.

3. *Test Bank.* A test bank, revised to fit the material in *Introduction to Financial Management*, with questions and problems in objective format, is available to adopters of the text. We feel that the test bank is especially suitable for mid-term and final examinations.

4. *Overhead Transparencies.* A set of acetate transparencies is available from your Dryden Press representative to instructors who adopt the text. These transparencies focus on key areas of difficulty in the text and can be used as the basis for lectures to both large and small classes.

5. *Computerized Test Bank.* A computerized version of the test bank will be available to adopters for use on the IBM PC and Apple II microcomputers.

6. *Supplemental Problems.* Additional problems, organized according to topic and level of difficulty, are also available to instructors from The Dryden Press.

7. *PROFIT.* This software supplement by James Pettijohn of Southwest Missouri State University contains 18 user-friendly programs that include the time value of money, forecasting, and capital budgeting. The program includes a user's manual and is available for the IBM PC and Apple II microcomputers.

8. *Casebook.* A revised edition of *Cases in Managerial Finance,* fifth edition (Dryden Press, 1983), by Eugene F. Brigham and Roy Crum, is well suited for use with this text. The cases show real-world applications of the concepts developed in the text.

9. *Readings Books.* A number of readings books, including *Issues in Managerial Finance,* second edition (Dryden Press, 1980), edited by Eugene F. Brigham and Ramon E. Johnson, can be used as supplements.

10. *Lotus 1-2-3 Book.* A new book, *Financial Management with Lotus 1-2-3* (CBS College Publishing), by Paul D. Cretien, Susan E. Ball, and Eugene F. Brigham, is available to explain how many commonly encountered problems in financial management can be analyzed with electronic spreadsheets.

Acknowledgments

A great many people participated, directly or indirectly, in the preparation of this book, and we would like to acknowledge their help.

First we would like to thank the professors who formally reviewed the manuscript and made many excellent suggestions as to ways in which the finished product could be improved. Their contribution has made a significant impact on the quality of the final book, and we appreciate their input. Those professors were:

Christopher Barry, Southern Methodist University
Joseph H. Black, San Jose State University
Faramarz Damanpour, James Madison University
Zane Dennick-Ream, Miami University
George L. Granger, East Tennessee State University
David J. Johnston, Northeastern University
Donald Nast, Florida State University
Clarence C. Rose, Radford University
Gary Simpson, Oklahoma State University
Les Strickler, Oregon State University
John M. Wachowicz, Jr., University of Tennessee
James W. Walden, Sinclair Community College
Howard R. Whitney, Franklin University
Sally Jo Wright, Sangamon State University

In addition, thanks are due to those who helped with earlier Brigham texts that served as a model for this book. Those individuals are Art Herrmann (bankruptcy chapter), Hai Hong (international finance chapter), Steve Vinson (lecture notes), Lou Gapenski (*Test Bank*), and Dilip Shome. Their input to earlier Brigham texts served as a guide for this book.

Special thanks are due to those who had a direct impact on this text, particularly Christopher Barry for his fine work on the small business sections and Linda Pepple for her assistance in coauthoring the *Study Guide*.

To our colleagues at The Dryden Press—especially Liz Widdicombe, Susan Meyers, Nancy Moudry, and Cate Rzasa—we couldn't have done it without your exceptional patience and guidance.

We want to thank Cynthia Fostle for her valuable work in developing the pedagogy and Mary Englehart and Nancy Maybloom for their meticulous copyediting and proofreading.

Finally, to our friends and colleagues at the University of Florida, San Jose State, and around the country, thank you for your suggestions and support.

Conclusion

Finance is, in a real sense, the cornerstone of the free enterprise system, so good financial management is vitally important to the economic health of business firms and hence to our nation and the world. Because of its importance, finance should be widely and thoroughly understood—but this is easier said than done. The field is relatively complex, and it is undergoing constant changes in response to economic conditions. All this makes finance stimulating and exciting but also challenging and sometimes perplexing. We certainly hope that *Introduction to Financial Management* will meet these challenges by contributing to a better understanding of the financial system.

B.J. Campsey   Eugene F. Brigham
San Jose, California   *Gainesville, Florida*
January 1985   *January 1985*

About the Authors

B.J. Campsey (Ph.D., University of Texas; MBA, University of Houston) is a Professor of Finance at San Jose State University, San Jose, California. He has also taught at the University of Virginia and was a Visiting Professor at the University of Texas–Austin. He has taught undergraduate and graduate courses in managerial finance and investments. He has served as a consultant for financial and industrial firms as well as having been the Director of Candidate Programs for the Chartered Financial Analysts, 1979–1980.

A native of Fort Worth, Texas, Professor Campsey is a member of the Financial Management Association, the American Finance Association, and the Western Finance Association. His research interests are in managerial finance, investments, and financial education. He has written articles for several professional journals.

Eugene F. Brigham (Ph.D., Cal-Berkeley; B.S., North Carolina) is Professor of Finance and Director of the Public Utility Research Center at the University of Florida. He has also taught at Cal-Berkeley, San Jose State, UCLA, Wisconsin, and Connecticut and has lectured in numerous executive programs in the United States and abroad. He is past president of the Financial Management Association, and he has held offices in a number of other finance organizations.

Professor Brigham has served as a consultant to many firms and government agencies, including AT&T, Texas Power & Light, Commonwealth Edison, Shell Oil, Bank of America, and the Federal Reserve Board. He has published articles on various financial issues in *Financial Management*, the *Journal of Finance*, and other journals, and he has authored or coauthored several leading textbooks and casebooks in finance and managerial economics. Professor Brigham currently teaches graduate and undergraduate courses in financial management.

Careers in Finance

While some students take an introductory course in financial management because they wish to pursue a career in some area of finance, most take the course because it is required. Whatever the original motivation for taking the course, many students enjoy the topic's material to the extent that they begin to consider the field of finance as a career opportunity. We are often asked, "What kinds of jobs are available to finance majors?"

The answer is that there is a broad range of job opportunities in the area of finance. If one had to categorize this book, it would be considered a business or managerial finance text. Even so, we still study topics in this text related to the other two major sources of employment for finance students—financial institutions, especially banks, and the investment profession.

Working Capital Management. The bulk of this text is concerned with the duties of a financial manager in a corporate or business setting. Most students entering the finance department of a business begin in some area of working capital management. A typical first assignment would be in the credit department. Here credit analysts review initial credit applications and supervise ongoing accounts for signs of deteriorating creditworthiness. More senior assignments would be concerned with the supervision of the firm's cash account. Here the manager is concerned with the rapid receipt of customer payments, probably through lockbox banking arrangements and the timely disbursement of funds to creditors. This manager will also be responsible for the maintenance of a positive relationship with all of the company's banks.

Capital Budgeting. As the novice financial manager gains experience, even more challenging job opportunities may be found. For example, in the area of capital budgeting a manager must analyze appropriation requests, forecast cash flows from projected capital budgeting projects, and review the progress of current projects. Such a job requires careful coordination with other functional areas such as marketing for sales information and production engineering for cost figures. The manager in charge of capital budgeting must also project future financing needs which arise from the acceptance of capital budgeting projects.

The manager of capital budgeting would probably elicit the help of the manager for project finance (titles may vary) in planning a project's financing. Generally, the manager for project finance will be responsible for obtaining the lowest-cost funds within the parameters of the firm's target capital structure. To do so this manager must be familiar with current financial market conditions and have a close working relationship with the firm's investment bankers.

Vice President of Finance. The vice president of finance oversees all of the functions of the subordinate financial managers. If the company is a small one, the vice president of finance will probably perform all the functions that have been discussed. Thus this financial manager must plan for future expenditures, evaluate past decisions, and execute the capital structure, capital budgeting, and dividend policy decisions of the firm.

Banking and Investment. Many of the topics covered in this text are also important in other areas of financial employment. For example, a banker would use the analytical tools discussed in Chapters 7 and 8 to analyze the financial statement of a loan applicant for creditworthiness. Similarly, the techniques of security valuation indicated in Chapters 17 and 18 would be used by investment analysts in brokerage firms.

For further information on career opportunities in finance see:

Jack S. Rader, *Careers in Finance* (Tampa, FL: Financial Management Association, 1983). Your instructor may order copies of this brochure by contacting: Financial Management Association, College of Business Administration, University of South Florida, Tampa, FL 33620.

Frank K. Reilly, "Career Opportunities in Investments," in *Investments* (Hinsdale, IL: Dryden Press, 1982). Second edition due for publication in January 1986.

The Dryden Press Series in Finance

Brigham
Financial Management:
   Theory and Practice, *Fourth Edition*

Brigham
Fundamentals of Financial
   Management, *Third Edition*

Brigham and Crum
Cases in Managerial Finance,
   Fifth Edition

Brigham and Gapenski
Intermediate Financial Management

Brigham and Johnson
Issues in Managerial Finance,
   Second Edition

Campsey and Brigham
Introduction to Financial
   Management

Clayton and Spivey
The Time Value of Money

Fama and Miller
The Theory of Finance

Gitman
Personal Finance, *Third Edition*

Greer and Farrell
Contemporary Real Estate:
   Theory and Practice

Greer and Farrell
Investment Analysis for
   Real Estate Decisions

Harrington
Case Studies in
   Financial Decision Making

Johnson and Johnson
Commercial Bank Management

Kidwell and Peterson
Financial Institutions, Markets,
   and Money, *Second Edition*

Lorie and Brealey
Modern Developments in
   Investment Management,
   Second Edition

Mayo
Investments: An Introduction

Mayo
Finance

Myers
Modern Developments in
   Financial Management

Pettijohn
PROFIT

Reilly
Investment Analysis and Portfolio
   Management, *Second Edition*

Reilly
Investments

Tallman and Neal
Financial Analysis and
   Planning Package

Weston and Brigham
Essentials of Managerial Finance,
   Seventh Edition

Weston and Copeland
Managerial Finance, *Eighth Edition*

Contents

Part I Introduction 1

Chapter 1 Defining Financial Management 3
Decision in Finance: Kennecott Copper 3   Increasing Importance of
Financial Management 5   The Place of Finance in a Business
Organization 7   The Goals of the Firm 9   *Industry Practice: Social
Proxy Fights Spice Up Annual Meetings* 13   Organization of This
Book 16   Summary 17   *Small Business: Goals and Resources in the
Small Firm* 18   Resolution to Decision in Finance: Kennecott
Copper 20

Chapter 2 How Business Is Organized and Taxed 23
Decision in Finance: Where Did Baldwin-United's Millions Go? 23
Alternative Forms of Business Organization 24   The Federal Income
Tax System 27   *Industry Practice: Corporate Taxes: Why Some Firms
Pay Less* 32   Summary 38   *Small Business: Organizing the Small
Firm* 38   Resolution to Decision in Finance: Where Did Baldwin-
United's Millions Go? 42

Part II The Financial Environment 47

Chapter 3 Capital Markets 49
Decision in Finance: NYSE versus AMEX versus OTC: A Bitter
Triangle 49   **Role of Financial Markets 50**   **Role of Financial
Intermediaries 52**   *Industry Practice: The Supercompanies Emerge* 52
The Stock Market 58   **Market Efficiency 66**   **Summary 67**
Small Business: Risk Capital for Growth Businesses 68   Resolution to
Decision in Finance: NYSE versus AMEX versus OTC: A Bitter
Triangle 71

Chapter 4 The Commercial Banking System 75
Decision in Finance: The Perils of Paul: Volcker's Scary Choices 75
The Banking System 76   *Industry Practice: Why So Many Banks Go
Belly Up* 78   **The Federal Reserve System 84**   **Summary 91**
Resolution to Decision in Finance: The Perils of Paul: Volcker's Scary
Choices 92

Chapter 5 Interest Rates 95
Decision in Finance: Who Says the Price Is Right? 95   Interest Rate
Determination 96   *Industry Practice: The Interest Rate Business
Ignores* 97   Interest Rates and Business Decisions 110   Interest
Rates and Stock Prices 112   Summary 113   Resolution to
Decision in Finance: Who Says the Price Is Right? 113

Part III Financial Statements and Financial Planning 117

Chapter 6 Examining a Firm's Financial Data 119
Decision in Finance: Letters from Chairman Buffett 119   The
Annual Report 120   The Income Statement 121   *Industry Practice:
"Take Your Report and . . ."* 124   The Balance Sheet 125   The
Cash Flow Cycle 129   The Statement of Retained Earnings 131
The Statement of Changes in Financial Position 131   Summary 136
Resolution to Decision in Finance: Letters from Chairman Buffett 137
**Appendix 6A: The Effects of Depreciation and Inventory Valuation
on Reported Income** 142

Chapter 7 Interpreting Financial Statements 153
Decision in Finance: Cooking the Books 153   Importance of
Financial Statements 154   Ratio Analysis 154   *Industry Practice:
Light in Dark Corners* 155   Sources of Comparative Ratios 171
Limitations of Ratio Analysis 172   Summary 173   *Small Business:
Financial Analysis in the Small Firm* 174   Resolution to Decision in
Finance: Cooking the Books 176

Chapter 8 Determining Future Financial Needs 189
Decision in Finance: AT&T Conquers the Fear of Forecasting 189
Sales Forecasts 190   Forecasting Financial Requirements: The
Percentage of Sales Method 190   *Industry Practice: What Does the
Future Hold?* 194   Forecasting Financial Requirements When the
Balance Sheet Ratios Are Subject to Change 203   Computerized
Financial Planning Models 204   Summary 205   Resolution to
Decision in Finance: AT&T Conquers the Fear of Forecasting 206

Chapter 9 Analyzing Operations 217
Decision in Finance: Menpower versus Penpower 217   Breakeven
Analysis 218   *Industry Practice: Detroit Gets Lean and Mean* 221
Business Risk 225   Operating Leverage 226   Summary 231
Resolution to Decision in Finance: Menpower versus Penpower 232

Part IV Working Capital 237

Chapter 10 Working Capital Policy and Management 239
Decision in Finance: Not a Minute Too Soon 239   Defining
Working Capital 240   Impact of Current Assets on Risk and
Return 241   Alternative Strategies for Financing Working
Capital 243   Combining Current Asset and Liability Decisions 249
Summary 250   *Small Business: Growth and Working Capital Needs* 251
Resolution to Decision in Finance: Not a Minute Too Soon 253

Chapter 11 Managing Cash and Marketable Securities 259
Decision in Finance: The Race Is to the Slow Payer 259   Cash
Management 260   *Industry Practice: The Perils of Cash
Management* 264   Marketable Securities 274   Summary 280
Resolution to Decision in Finance: The Race Is to the Slow Payer 281

Chapter 12 Accounts Receivable and Inventories 289
Decision in Finance: The King of Scrap Mountain 289   Accounts
Receivable 290   Credit Policy 290   *Industry Practice: How to Spot a
Professional Debtor* 292   Inventory Management 300
Summary 308   Resolution to Decision in Finance: The King of
Scrap Mountain 309   **Appendix 12A: Establishing a Credit Policy:
An Illustration** 316

Chapter 13 Financing Current Assets: Short-Term Credit 319
Decision in Finance: A Bank That Looks at More than Numbers 319
Accrued Wages and Taxes 320   Accounts Payable, or Trade
Credit 320   Short-Term Bank Loans 326   Commercial Paper 333
Use of Security in Short-Term Financing 335   Summary 335
Small Business: Financing Receivables Directly 336   Resolution to
Decision in Finance: A Bank That Looks at More Than Numbers 338
Appendix 13A: The Use of Security in Short-Term Financing 345

Part V Capital Budgeting: Investment in Fixed Assets 353

Chapter 14 Time Value of Money 355
Decision in Finance: Reenlisting with the Generals 355   Future
Value (or Compound Value) 356   Present Value 360   Present
Value versus Future Value 362   Future Value of an Annuity 364
Present Value of an Annuity 366   Present Value of an Uneven
Series of Receipts 368   Determining Interest Rates 370
Amortized Loans 371   Review of Chapter Concepts 372
Summary 376   Resolution to Decision in Finance: Reenlisting with
the Generals 377

Chapter 15 The Process of Capital Budgeting 385
Decision in Finance: Jack Welch's New GE 385   Steps in Capital
Budgeting 386   Ideas for Capital Projects 387   Project
Classification 388   Estimating the Cash Flows 389   Methods
Used to Evaluate Proposed Projects 392   An Expanded Case in
Capital Budgeting 400   The Post-Audit 403   Summary 404
Resolution to Decision in Finance: Jack Welch's New GE 405
Appendix 15A: Conflicts between NPV and IRR 413

Chapter 16 Evaluating Risk in Capital Budgeting 417
Decision in Finance: Gambling on a State-of-the-Art Refinery 417
Replacement Decisions 418   Effects of Inflation on Capital
Budgeting Analysis 422   Risk and the Capital Budgeting
Decision 425   Portfolio Theory and the Capital Asset Pricing
Model 432   The Relationship between Risk and Rate of Return 439
Risk Analysis in Capital Budgeting 441   Summary 446   *Small
Business: Capital Budgeting in the Small Firm* 447   Resolution to
Decision in Finance: Gambling on a State-of-the-Art Refinery 450

Part VI Long-Term Financing 457

Chapter 17 Bonds and Preferred Stock 459
Decision in Finance: U.S. Steel 459   Funded Debt 460   Term
Loans 460   Bonds 461   Types of Bonds 464   Bond Ratings 468
Industry Practice: Junk Collecting 474   Valuation of Bonds 477
Preferred Stock 482   Advantages and Disadvantages of Bonds and
Preferred Stock 484   Summary 485   Resolution to Decision in
Finance: U.S. Steel 485

Chapter 18 Common Stock 493
Decision in Finance: Fred Adler's Big Giveaway 493   Legal Rights
and Privileges of the Common Stockholders 494   Common Stock
Valuation 497   Issuing Common Stock 503   Summary 507
Small Business: Raising Equity Capital for the Small Firm 508
Resolution to Decision in Finance: Fred Adler's Big Giveaway 510
Appendix 18A: Warrants and Convertibles 519

Chapter 19 The Target Capital Structure 533

Decision in Finance: Is Cities Service Worth the Price? 533   Types of Risk 534   Financial Leverage 534   Taxes, Bankruptcy Costs, and the Value of the Firm 546   Liquidity and Cash Flow Analysis 547   Capital Structure and Mergers 549   Checklist of Factors That Influence Capital Structure Decisions 550   Variations in Capital Structures among Firms 552   Summary 553   *Small Business: Capital Structure in the Small Firm* 554   Resolution to Decision in Finance: Is Cities Service Worth the Price? 556

Chapter 20 The Cost of Capital 565

Decision in Finance: The New World of Corporate Finance 565   The Logic of the Weighted Average Cost of Capital 566   Basic Definitions 567   Minimum Required Return 568   Cost of Debt 570   Cost of Preferred Stock 571   Cost of Retained Earnings, k_s 572   Finding the Basic Required Rate of Return on Common Equity 573   Cost of Newly Issued Common Stock, or External Equity, k_e 575   Combining Debt and Equity: Weighted Average, or Composite, Cost of Capital, k_a 576   Changes in the Cost of Capital 581   Combining the MCC and the Investment Opportunity Schedule (IOS) 586   Summary 588   *Small Business: Cost of Equity Capital for Small Firms* 589   Resolution to Decision in Finance: The New World of Corporate Finance 591

Chapter 21 Determining the Dividend Policy 603

Decision in Finance: Generous to a Fault? 603   The Residual Theory of Dividends 604   Factors That Influence Dividend Policy 608   *Industry Practice: Dividend Achievers of 1983* 609   Dividend Payment Procedures 615   The Actual Dividend Payment 617   Dividend Reinvestment Plans 618   Stock Repurchase 619   Stock Dividends and Stock Splits 620   Establishing a Dividend Policy: Some Illustrations 624   Summary 626   Resolution to Decision in Finance: Generous to a Fault? 627

Part VII Selected Topics in Financial Management 633

Chapter 22 Mergers 635

Decision in Finance: The James River Paper Chase 635   The Economic Implications of Mergers 636   Types of Mergers 637   Procedures for Combining Firms 637   Financial Analysis of a Proposed Merger 640   *Industry Practice: Do Mergers Make Sense?* 642   Effects of Accounting Practices on Reported Profits 649   Holding Companies 653   Summary 655   Resolution to Decision in Finance: The James River Paper Chase 656

Chapter 23 Bankruptcy and Reorganization 663

Decision in Finance: Don Lennox's Tough Decisions 663
Failure 664   Causes of Failure 665   The Failure Record 666
Industry Practice: The Big Bankruptcy Scare 668   Extension and
Composition 671   Reorganization 672   Federal Bankruptcy
Laws 673   Financial Decisions in Reorganization 674   Liquidation
Procedures 679   Liquidation in Bankruptcy 680   Summary 683
Resolution to Decision in Finance: Don Lennox's Tough Decisions 684

Chapter 24 Leasing 691

Decision in Finance: Sandy's Gamble 691   Sale and Leaseback 692
Service Leases 692   Financial Leases 693   *Industry Practice: Why
Sale-Leasebacks Are Booming* 694   Internal Revenue Service
Requirements for a Lease 695   Effects of Leasing on a Firm's
Balance Sheet 696   Evaluating Lease Proposals 698   Factors That
Affect Leasing Decisions 702   Summary 703   Resolution to
Decision in Finance: Sandy's Gamble 704

Chapter 25 International Financial Management 709

Decision in Finance: Sri Lanka: Playing the Incentive Game 709
Exchange Rates and the International Monetary System 711
Procedures for Analyzing Potential Foreign Investments 718
Industry Practice: The World Woos U.S. Business 719   Management of
Foreign Assets 727   International Capital Markets 731
Summary 733   Resolution to Decision in Finance: Sri Lanka:
Playing the Incentive Game 733

Appendix A: Future Value of $1 at the End of n Periods 742

Appendix B: Present Value of $1 744

Appendix C: Sum of an Annuity of $1 per Period for n Periods 746

**Appendix D: Present Value of an Annuity of
$1 per Period for n Periods** 748

Appendix E: Answers to Selected End-of-Chapter Problems 750

Appendix F: Selected Equations 752

Glossary 756

Index 769

Introduction

The goal of financial management is to maximize stockholders' wealth. It is a simple goal to state, but this entire book is dedicated to investigating how such a goal can be implemented.

Chapter 1 contains an overview of financial management, including the duties of a financial manager and the role of finance in a business organization. The forms of business organization and highlights of current tax information, vital to financial decisions, are covered in Chapter 2.

Defining Financial Management

Decision in Finance

Kennecott Copper

Several years ago the board of directors of Kennecott Copper faced a dilemma. By selling off Peabody, its coal subsidiary, the company had generated a huge amount of cash. Keeping the cash, management feared, would make Kennecott an attractive target for a corporate raider.

Because Kennecott's recent performance had been poor, the managers could expect to be fired if a takeover occurred. It is alleged they proposed a plan that would make Kennecott a less attractive acquisition target and, in the process, save their jobs.

Management asked the board of directors to use the newly acquired cash to buy Carborundum Company. Many observers felt that the price was several hundred million dollars above Carborundum's actual value, but this was part of management's strategy. Once the deal went through, Kennecott would be rid of its cash and burdened with an overvalued acquisition. As a result, the managers believed, corporate raiders would lose interest.

As you read this chapter, think about how you would have voted if you had been a member of Kennecott's board of directors. What should have been the company's primary goal? What factors would you have considered in addition to the interests of management?

The resolution to this Decision in Finance is given at the end of the chapter.

finance
Evaluation and acquisition of
productive assets, procurement
of funds, and disbursement of
profits.

The function of financial management is to plan for, acquire, and utilize funds in a way that maximizes the value of the firm. More specifically, **finance** is concerned with evaluating and acquiring productive assets, procuring the least expensive mix of funds, and disbursing profits in a manner consistent with the best interests of the firm's owners. Of course, this is a vast oversimplification of the duties of a financial manager, since we will need to spend the remaining chapters expanding on this operating definition of finance.

The study of financial management has undergone significant changes over the years. When finance first emerged as a separate field of study in the early 1900s, the emphasis was on legalistic matters such as mergers, consolidations, the formation of new firms, and the various types of securities issued by corporations. Industrialization was sweeping the country, and the critical problem firms faced was obtaining capital for expansion. The capital markets were relatively primitive, making transfers of funds from individual savers to businesses quite difficult. Reports of earnings and asset values in accounting statements were unreliable, while stock trading by insiders and manipulators caused prices to fluctuate wildly. Consequently investors were reluctant to purchase stocks and bonds. In this environment it is easy to see why finance in the early 1900s concentrated so heavily on legal issues relating to the issuance of securities.

The emphasis remained on securities through the 1920s. However, radical changes occurred during the depression of the 1930s, when an unprecedented number of business failures caused finance to focus on bankruptcy and reorganization, on corporate liquidity, and on government regulation of securities markets. Finance was still a descriptive, legalistic subject, but the emphasis shifted from expansion to survival.

During the 1940s and early 1950s finance continued to be taught as a descriptive, institutional subject, viewed from the outside rather than from the standpoint of management. However, methods of financial analysis designed to help firms maximize their profits and stock prices were beginning to receive attention.

The evolutionary pace quickened during the late 1950s. Whereas the right-hand side of the balance sheet (liabilities and capital) had received more attention in the earlier era, the major emphasis began to shift to asset analysis. Mathematical models were developed and applied to inventories, cash, accounts receivable, and fixed assets. Increasingly the focus of finance shifted from the outsider's to the insider's point of view, as financial decisions within the firm were recognized to be the critical issue in corporate finance. Descriptive, institutional materials on capital markets and financing instruments were still studied, but these topics were considered within the context of corporate financial decisions.

The 1960s witnessed a renewed interest in the liabilities-capital side of the balance sheet with a focus on (1) the optimal mix of securities and (2) the cost of capital. At the same time the theory of asset selection by individual investors, or "portfolio management," with its implications for corporate finance was being developed. These trends have continued during the 1970s, and the result has been a merging of investments with corporate finance. As for the 1980s, new and innovative means must be found to manage business firms' resources in an environment of high inflation, high interest rates, and increased competition from abroad.

Increasing Importance of Financial Management

These evolutionary changes have greatly increased the importance of financial management. In earlier times the marketing manager would project sales, the engineering and production staffs would determine the assets necessary to meet these demands, and the financial manager would simply raise the money needed to purchase the plant, equipment, and inventories. This mode of operation is no longer prevalent. Today decisions are made in a much more coordinated manner, with the financial manager having direct responsibility for the control process.

Northeast Utilities can be used to illustrate this change. A few years ago Northeast's economic forecasters would project power demand on the basis of historical trends and then give these forecasts to the engineers, who would then proceed to build the new plants necessary to meet the forecasted demand. The finance group simply had the task of raising the capital the engineers told them was needed. However, inflation, environmental regulations, and other factors combined to double or even triple plant construction costs, and this caused a corresponding increase in the need for new capital. At the same time rising fuel costs caused dramatic increases in electricity prices, which lowered demand and made some of the new construction unnecessary. Thus Northeast found itself building plants that it did not need and unable to raise the capital necessary to pay for them. The price of the company's stock declined from $20 to $5. As a result of this experience, Northeast Utilities (and other utilities and industrial companies) now places a great deal more stress on the planning and control process, and this has greatly increased the importance of the finance staff.

Certainly no business can prosper unless all functions—accounting, finance, marketing, personnel, and so forth—are fully staffed with competent individuals. In times of abundant financial resources, the role of the financial manager whose duty it is to acquire external financing may decline in importance. However, Professor Gordon Donaldson of Harvard contends that ". . . in harder times and with expensive money, the importance of the financial function grows."[1]

---

[1]"Why the Finance Man Calls the Plays," *Business Week*, April 8, 1972, 54.

In 1976 an article in *Fortune* indicated that corporations seemed to be turning to financial executives to fill top management positions. After commenting that well over half of the top executives at that time had majored in business administration in college, versus approximately 25 percent a few years earlier, the author continued:

Career patterns have followed the educationai trends. Like scientific and technical schooling, nuts-and-bolts business experience seems to have become less important. The proportion of executives with their primary experience in production, operations, engineering, design, and R. and D. has fallen from a third of the total to just over a quarter. And the number of top officers with legal and financial backgrounds has increased more than enough to make up the difference. Lawyers and financial men now head two out of five corporations.

It is fair to assume the changes in training, and in the paths that led these men to the top, reflect the shifting priorities and needs of their corporations. In fact, the expanding size and complexity of corporate organizations, coupled with their continued expansion overseas, have increased the importance of financial planning and controls. And the growth of government regulation and of obligations companies face under law has heightened the need for legal advice. The engineer and the production man have become, in consequence, less important in management than the finance man and the lawyer.

Today's chief executive officers have obviously perceived the shift in emphasis, and many of them wish they had personally been better prepared for it. Interestingly enough, a majority of them say they would have benefited from additional formal training, mainly in business administration, accounting, finance, and law.[2]

Recent trends in the business world, including high inflation, tight money, and limited resources, have reinforced the fact that finance is the most direct route to the top in many firms. As one executive noted, "The fastest way to the top in any company is to develop and implement a cure for the company's most severe problem and be widely recognized as the individual responsible for solving the company's toughest problem."[3] Thus, although there is no universal way to the top, in hard times when capital is expensive and scarce, the importance of the finance function grows for the firm.

We have been "beating the drum" for finance, but we hasten to note that there are no unimportant functions in a business firm. Our point, rather, is that there are financial implications in virtually all business decisions, and nonfinancial executives must know enough about fi-

[2]C. G. Burck, "A Group Profile of the Fortune 500 Chief Executive," *Fortune*, May 1976, 173.
[3]G. A. Weimer, "Finance Favored as Key to the Executive Boardroom," *Iron Age*, April 16, 1979, 35.

nance to incorporate these implications into their own specialized areas of analysis. The importance of finance to all areas of a business is reflected by the fact that most executive development programs report that their most popular course is "Financial Analysis for the Nonfinancial Executive."

Thus it is becoming increasingly important for people in marketing, accounting, production, personnel, and other areas of business to understand finance in order to do a good job in their own fields. Marketing people, for instance, must understand how marketing decisions affect and are affected by financial decisions. When marketing efforts successfully increase sales, for example, additional funds must be found to support increases in inventory, accounts receivable, plant capacity, and so on. Accountants, to cite another example, must understand how accounting data are used in corporate planning and viewed by investors. The function of accounting is to provide quantitative financial information for use in making economic decisions, whereas the main functions of **financial management** are to plan for, acquire, and utilize funds in order to maximize the efficiency and value of the enterprise.[4]

financial management
The acquisition and utilization of funds to maximize the efficiency and value of an enterprise.

The Place of Finance in a Business Organization

No single organizational structure will serve for all businesses. A huge, worldwide corporation would need an extremely large finance department. For example, Du Pont's Finance Department contains 9 divisions with a total of 29 sections as well as separate areas of Investor Relations, Personnel Relations, Accounting Policy, and International Finance. A small firm, of course, will not need as much specialization as a vast, multinational corporation like Du Pont. In fact, in a small firm all the necessary financial functions may be handled by only a few persons whose other duties may include such diverse areas as market planning or production management. The smaller the organization, the more the financial duties will be shared among individual managers or perhaps between the accountant and the president.

A fairly typical picture of the role of finance in the organizational structure of a firm is presented in Figure 1-1. The chief financial officer, who has the title of vice-president–finance, reports directly to the president. The controller and the treasurer are the finance VP's key subordinates.

The dividing line between the functions of the controller and the treasurer is neither exact nor absolute. The position of the treasurer is most closely associated with the topics discussed in this text. This of-

---

[4]American Institute of Certified Public Accountants, *Statement of the Accounting Principles Board No. 4* (New York, October 1970), 17.

Figure 1-1
Place of Finance in a Typical Business Organization

In a typical business organization such as that shown here, most general financial management functions fall to the treasurer. The treasurer is responsible for overall financial planning, selection and management of the firm's assets, and management of working capital, accounts receivable, and inventory. To plan and manage effectively, the treasurer needs constant input from the sales and manufacturing areas of the business. The controller oversees all accounting, auditing, and tax matters of the firm.

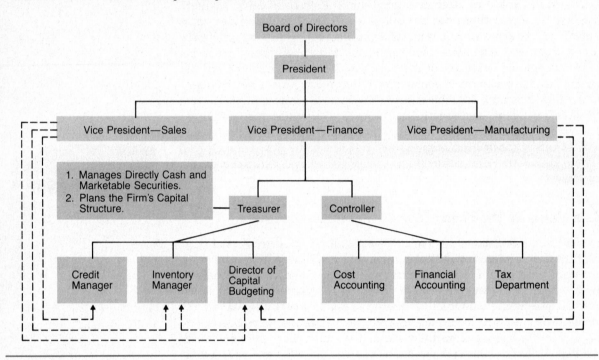

ficer has direct responsibility for planning the capital structure and maintaining relationships with all sources of financing such as banks, shareholders, and other suppliers of funds. The treasurer's office must also keep in contact with the capital markets, generally through an investment banker.

The treasurer is also responsible for the selection and management of the firm's assets. Financial managers must evaluate all capital projects and determine if the investment opportunities should be undertaken. Furthermore, these projects must be monitored for continuing profitability. The management of working capital, which consists of short-term assets, is no less important. The treasurer must insure that enough cash is on hand to cover all checks and invest any excess in money market securities. Management of accounts receivable and inventory is yet another important function of the treasurer's office (although occasionally the controller handles this asset management task).

In larger firms the employee benefits area, including the pension fund and insurance section, is included in the treasurer's office. In smaller firms these services are generally handled externally by independent pension managers or insurance agents.

Thus the traditional duties assigned to the treasurer's office can be briefly summarized as selection and continuing evaluation of productive assets, forecasting financial needs arising from current and new operations, financing those operations, and establishing dividend policy for the disbursement of the returns of those operations.

The traditional functions of the controller's office include the generation and interpretation of accounting reports and the monitoring and control of accounts. In other words, the controller generally has responsibility for all elements of accounting and auditing in the firm. Additionally, the controller is often responsible for all tax matters as well as other information required by government agencies. To a large extent, we leave a discussion of the controller's function to accounting courses.

The Goals of the Firm

Decisions are not made in a vacuum—they are made with some objective in mind. *Throughout this book, we operate on the assumption that management's primary goal is to* **maximize the wealth of its stockholders.** As we shall see, this translates into *maximizing the price of the common stock.* Firms do, of course, have other objectives—managers, who make the actual decisions, are interested in their own personal satisfaction, in employees' welfare, and in the good of the community and society at large. Still, for the reasons set forth below, *stock price maximization is probably the most important goal of most firms (except public utilities)*, and it is a reasonable operating objective upon which to build decision rules in a book such as this one.

stockholder wealth maximization
The appropriate goal for management decisions; considers the risk and timing associated with increasing earnings per share in order to maximize the firm's stock price.

Why Managers Try to Maximize Stockholders' Wealth

Stockholders are the owners of the firm and, in theory at least, control management by electing the members of the board of directors, which in turn appoints the management team. Management, in its turn, is supposed to operate in the best interest of the stockholders. We know, however, that because the stock of most large firms is widely held, the managers of such firms have a great deal of autonomy. This being the case, might not managements pursue goals other than maximization of stockholder wealth? For example, some argue that the management of a large, well-entrenched corporation could work to keep stockholder returns at a fair or "reasonable" level and then devote part of its efforts and resources to public service activities, to employee benefits, to higher management salaries, or to golf.

Similarly, a firmly entrenched management might avoid risky ventures, even when the possible gains to stockholders are high enough to warrant taking the gamble. The theory behind this argument is that stockholders are generally well diversified, holding portfolios of many different stocks, so if one company takes a chance and loses, the stockholders lose only a small part of their wealth. Managers, on the other hand, are not so well diversified. A manager's salary represents his or her largest wealth asset, even if such factors as stock options are considered. Thus a potential setback, which might result in the manager's demotion or dismissal, is probably more devastating to the manager than it would be to a diversified stockholder. Accordingly, corporate managers may be less motivated to take risks that, if successful, would benefit stockholders (and to some extent managers, if they own or have options to own the firm's stock) by increasing the value of the firm's stock. Managers might also receive a bonus as part of their reward for success in a risky venture. However, if the venture is unsuccessful, it may well result in the manager's rebuke, demotion, or removal from the firm. Therefore some maintain that managers are not well compensated for their successes and incur disproportionate penalties for their failures. If this is true, would a manager risk his or her job in order to maximize the stockholders' wealth rather than provide a less risky but still acceptable rate of return?

It is extremely difficult to determine whether a particular management team is trying to maximize shareholder wealth or is merely attempting to keep stockholders satisfied while pursuing other goals. For example, how can we tell whether or not voluntary employee or community benefit programs are in the long-run best interests of the stockholders? Are relatively high management salaries really necessary to attract and retain excellent managers who, in turn, will keep the firm ahead of its competition? When a risky venture is turned down, does this reflect management conservatism, or is it a correct judgment regarding the risks of the venture versus its potential rewards?

It is impossible to give definitive answers to these questions. Several studies have suggested that managers are not completely stockholder-oriented, but the evidence is cloudy. It is true that more and more firms are tying management's compensation to the company's performance, and research suggests that this motivates managers to operate in a manner consistent with stock price maximization.[5] Additionally, in recent years tender offers and proxy fights have removed a number of supposedly well-entrenched managements; the recognition that

---

[5]Wilbur G. Lewellen, "Management and Ownership in the Large Firm," *Journal of Finance*, May 1969, 299–322. Lewellen concludes that managers seem to make decisions that are largely oriented toward stock price maximization.

GULF SHAREHOLDERS— LET'S KEEP OUR MOMENTUM GOING!

Dear Fellow Shareholder:

Gulf Oil Corporation is moving forward rapidly with a soundly conceived program to **enhance the long-term value of its assets.** This program is designed to build on your Company's greatest strengths — its substantial resources as well as its economies of scale which stem from Gulf's position as a major integrated oil company.

Gulf is pursuing a coherent, positive, results-oriented business strategy to enhance its value to share-holders. Over the last several years your Company has:

● **Redirected its exploration strategy** to concentrate on frontier prospects for oil and gas. In our opinion, today we have some of the most promising hydrocarbon prospects in years;

● **Invested $500 million to modernize its refineries** — which has increased our ability to process lower cost crude oil;

● **Focused its marketing efforts** toward high volume/low cost areas to improve profit margins;

● **Implemented a cost reduction program** that we expect will reduce overhead expenses by $100 million annually; and

● **Sold off more than $2 billion worth of marginal assets.**

These actions are having positive effects on your Company's financial results:

● In the most recent quarter ended September 30, 1983, **Gulf achieved a 74% increase in profits over the same period for the year before and an 87% increase in earnings per share.** The percentages would be 29% and 40%, respectively, if nonrecurring items are excluded for the same periods.

● **Gulf has repurchased 30 million shares since mid-1981,** or approximately 15% of its common stock then outstanding. Thus, each share of Gulf stock you hold is supported by approximately as many barrels of U.S. domestic petroleum reserves today as it was in 1980.

● Gulf has reduced its debt by over $300 million, since the beginning of this year.

● In our opinion, **Gulf has the financial strength to fund a capital expenditure program of $3 to $3.5 billion in 1983** and for the next several years, without any large, new borrowing.

● Gulf increased its dividend last month to $3.00 per share per year. **This is the tenth consecutive year in which the annual dividend payments have been increased over that of the prior year.**

Consistent with the goal of enhancing shareholder value, **your Board of Directors has recommended unanimously that Gulf Oil Corporation be reorganized as a holding company in Delaware.**

We believe that the planned reorganization best serves your investment in Gulf. This reorganization will remove the ability of a minority shareholder to disrupt our program.

LET'S KEEP OUR MOMENTUM GOING!

I urge you to vote <u>FOR</u> your Company's proposed reorganization. **Abstaining from voting is the same as voting against the proposal,** since it is necessary that more than 50% of the Company's out-standing shares be voted <u>FOR</u> the proposal for it to be approved.

Please express your support of Gulf's proposal by signing, dating, and mailing the <u>WHITE</u> proxy card. If you have previously signed a Blue opposition proxy, you have every right to change your mind. **Remember, your latest dated proxy is the only one that counts.**

The management and Board of Directors thank you for supporting your company.

James E. Lee
James E. Lee
Chairman of the Board and
Chief Executive Officer

November 23, 1983

In this public notice to shareholders, Gulf Oil Board Chairman and CEO James E. Lee attempts to sway votes in a proxy fight by asking shareholders to support the company's proposal to be reorganized as a holding company in Delaware.
Source: Courtesy of the Gulf Oil Corporation.

such actions can take place has probably stimulated many other firms to attempt to maximize share prices.[6] Finally, a firm operating in a competitive market, or almost any firm during an economic downturn,

---

[6]A *tender offer* is a bid by one company to buy the stock of another company, whereas a *proxy fight* involves an attempt to gain control by getting stockholders to vote a new management group into office. Both actions are facilitated by low stock prices, so self-preservation can lead management to try to keep the stock values as high as possible.

will be forced to undertake actions that are reasonably consistent with shareholder wealth maximization. Thus, although managers may have other goals in addition to stock price maximization, there are reasons to view this as the dominant goal for most firms.

What Can Managers Do to Maximize Stock Prices?

Assuming that the financial manager's goal is to maximize the shareholders' wealth, what decisions are important in this task? The financial manager must determine, along with the rest of the management team, the investment, financing, and dividend policies of the firm. However, these decisions often have many ramifications. For example, management must consider not only the timing and risk of the income stream from the investment, but also the form of the returns. That is, will **profit maximization** result in stock price maximization, or should the financial manager be concerned with some other form of return, such as **earnings per share (EPS)**?

profit maximization
The maximization of the firm's net income; does not consider risk or timing of earnings and thus is not an appropriate standard for financial decisions.

earnings per share (EPS)
The net income of the firm divided by the number of shares of common stock outstanding.

Suppose Company X had one million shares outstanding and earned $2 million, or $2 per share, and you owned 100 shares of the stock. Now suppose the company sold another one million shares and invested the funds received in assets that produced $1 million of income. Total income would have risen to $3 million, but earnings per share would have declined from $2 to $3,000,000/2,000,000 shares, or $1.50. Now your own earnings would be only $150, down from $200. You (and the other original stockholders) would have suffered an earnings dilution, even though total corporate profits had risen. Therefore, other things held constant, *if management is interested in the well-being of its stockholders, it should concentrate on earnings per share rather than on total corporate profits.*

Will maximization of expected earnings per share always maximize stockholder welfare? The answer is *no:* other factors such as timing and risk must also be considered. Think about the *timing of the earnings.* Suppose one project will cause earnings per share to rise by $0.20 per year for five years, or $1.00 in total, while another project has no effect on earnings for four years but increases earnings by $1.25 in the fifth year. Which project is better? The answer depends on which project adds the most to the value of the stock. This, in turn, depends on the time value of money to investors. In any event, timing is an important reason to concentrate on wealth as measured by the price of the stock rather than on earnings alone. We consider the important topic of the time value of money in Chapter 14.

risk
The probability that actual future earnings will be below the expected earnings.

Still another issue relates to **risk.** Suppose one project is expected to increase earnings per share by $1.00, while another is expected to raise earnings by $1.20 per share. The first project is not very risky; if it is undertaken, earnings will almost certainly rise by about $1.00 per share. The other project is quite risky, so while our best guess is that

Industry Practice

Social Proxy Fights Spice Up Annual Meetings

When proxy resolutions addressing social issues were first presented to corporations, they were laughed out of the house. At first, companies refused to put them on the ballots sent to shareholders. After the Securities and Exchange Commission ruled in 1972 that resolutions germane to a company's business could not be excluded arbitrarily, proposals raising a variety of issues were routinely added to proxy statements—and were routinely voted down by overwhelming majorities. They are still being added and they are still being voted down, but they keep attracting more and more support.

In 1982, according to the annual survey conducted by the Washington, D.C.-based Investor Responsibility Research Center, 109 resolutions were voted on by corporate shareholders—and eighty-one, or 74 percent, received more than 3 percent of the vote. That's the highest percentage recorded since the IRRC began keeping track of resolutions in 1973. In that year, as a point of contrast, forty resolutions were brought to votes—and only seven, or 17.5 percent, managed to garner more than 3 percent of the votes cast. Three percent is a key level because a resolution needs to receive at least that much support the first year to be presented again. The second year it needs 6 percent for re-presentation and the third year, 10 percent. In 1982, there were seven antinuclear resolutions that needed 10 percent support for re-presentation—

and two of them got it. The following were the 1982 resolutions that racked up the greatest support:

A resolution submitted by Accuracy in Media asking that RCA appoint an independent ombudsman to investigate the accuracy and balance of NBC news programs. It received nearly 14 percent of the vote.

A resolution presented to Long Island Lighting Company asked that utility to develop additional conservation and alternative energy programs, report on such progress to shareholders every quarter, and halt further development of nuclear facilities. It got 11.5 percent of the vote.

A resolution asking Philadelphia Electric to stop nuclear plant development gained over 10 percent of the vote.

A resolution asking Xerox not to expand its operations in South Africa and to cease all sales to police and military forces in that country received 10 percent of the vote.

A resolution submitted to Wells Fargo asking the bank to give shareholders a report on its lending activities in Chile received over 9 percent of the vote.

earnings will rise by $1.20 per share, we must recognize the possibility that there may be no increase whatsoever. Depending on how averse stockholders are to risk, the first project may be preferable to the second.

The riskiness inherent in projected earnings per share also depends on *how the firm is financed.* As we shall see, a large number of firms go bankrupt every year, and the greater the use of debt, the greater the threat of bankruptcy. Consequently, *while the use of debt financing may increase projected EPS, debt also increases the riskiness of these projected earnings.*

Still another issue is the matter of paying dividends to stockholders versus retaining earnings and plowing them back into the business, thereby causing the earnings stream to grow over time. Stockholders like cash dividends, but they also like the growth in EPS that results from plowing earnings back into the business. The financial manager must decide exactly how much of current earnings should be paid out as dividends rather than retained and reinvested—this is called the **dividend policy** decision. The optimal dividend policy is the one that maximizes the firm's stock price. We see, then, that the firm's stock price is dependent on the following factors:

dividend policy
Determination of percentage of current earnings to be paid out as dividends to stockholders.

1. Projected earnings per share
2. Riskiness of projected earnings
3. Timing of the earnings stream
4. Manner of financing the firm
5. Dividend policy

Every significant corporate decision should be analyzed in terms of its effect on these factors, and hence on the price of the firm's stock. For example, a coal company may be considering opening a new mine. If the mine is opened, can it be expected to increase EPS? Is there a chance that costs will exceed estimates, that prices and output will fall below projections, and that EPS will be reduced because the new mine was opened? How long will it take for the new mine to start showing a profit? How should the capital required to open the mine be raised? If debt is used, how much will this increase the firm's riskiness? Should the firm reduce its current dividends and use the cash thus saved to finance the project, or should it finance the mine with external capital? Financial management is designed to help answer such questions as these, plus many more.

Social Responsibility

social responsibility
The concept that businesses should be responsible to some degree for the welfare of society at large.

normal profits
Those profits close to the average of all firms within an industry.

Another point that deserves consideration is that of **social responsibility:** should businesses operate strictly in the stockholders' best financial interest, or is the firm in some sense responsible for the welfare of society at large? In tackling this question, consider first those firms whose rates of return on investments are close to **normal profits,** that is, close to the average for all firms. If such companies attempt to be social do-gooders, thereby increasing their costs over what they otherwise would have been, and if the other businesses in the industry do not follow suit, then the socially oriented firms will probably be forced to abandon their efforts. Thus any socially responsible acts that raise costs will be difficult, if not impossible, in industries subject to keen competition.

What about firms with profits above normal levels—can they not devote resources to social projects? Undoubtedly they can; many large, successful firms do engage in community projects, employee benefit programs, and the like to a greater degree than would appear to be called for by pure profit or wealth maximization goals.[7] Still, publicly owned firms are constrained in such actions by capital market factors. Suppose a saver who has funds to invest is considering two alternative firms. One firm devotes a substantial part of its resources to social actions, while the other concentrates on profits and stock prices. Most investors are likely to shun the socially oriented firm, thus putting it at a disadvantage in the capital market. After all, why should the stockholders of one corporation subsidize society to a greater extent than stockholders of other businesses? For all these reasons, even highly profitable firms (unless they are closely held rather than publicly owned) are generally constrained against taking unilateral cost-increasing social actions.

Does all this mean that firms should not exercise social responsibility? Not at all—it simply means that most cost-increasing actions may have to be put on a *mandatory* rather than a voluntary basis, at least initially, to insure that the burden of such actions falls uniformly across all businesses. Thus, fair hiring practices, minority training programs, product safety, pollution abatement, antitrust actions, and the like are more likely to be effective if realistic rules are established initially and then enforced by government agencies. It is critical that industry and government cooperate in establishing the rules of corporate behavior and that firms follow the spirit as well as the letter of the law in their actions. Thus the rules of the game become constraints, and firms should strive to maximize stock prices subject to these constraints. Throughout this book we shall assume that managements operate in this manner.

If firms attempt to maximize stock prices, is it good or bad for society? In general, it is good; in fact, the same legal actions that maximize stock prices also benefit society. First, stock price maximization requires efficient, low-cost operations that get the most value out of a given set of resources. Second, since price maximization also requires

---

[7]Even firms such as these often find it necessary to justify such programs at stockholder meetings by stating that they contribute to long-run profit maximization.

the development of products that consumers want and need, the profit motive leads to new technology, new products, and new jobs. Finally, stock price maximization requires efficient and courteous service, adequate stocks of merchandise, and well-located business establishments because these things are all necessary to make sales, and sales are certainly necessary for profits. Therefore the types of actions that help a firm increase the price of its stock are also directly beneficial to society at large. This is why profit-motivated enterprise economies have been so much more successful than other types of economic systems.

Organization of This Book

This introductory chapter has described, in broad terms, the duties of the financial manager and the goals of the firm. Someone once said, "Any road will do if you don't know where you're going." We have therefore carefully charted our destination—the goal of shareholder wealth maximization—and attempted to indicate how this goal influences the duties and actions of the financial manager. The next chapter explores both the types of business organization under which firms can be structured and the federal tax system.

The chapters in Part II investigate the economic environment in which the financial manager operates. First, the general purpose of financial markets—to transfer savings to firms and individuals with attractive investment opportunities—is analyzed. Then, the principal institution in financial markets, the commercial bank, is described. Finally, the role of interest rates in the economy is explored.

Since both long- and short-run plans are analyzed in terms of financial statements, Part III first reviews how these statements are constructed. Then, in the chapters concerning the use of accounting data, we first concentrate on analyzing reports of past operations, and then on projecting financial statements into the future under different strategic plans and operating conditions.

In Part IV we move into the execution phase of the financial management process. Here we examine current, ongoing operations, looking first at the role of finance in insuring that cash, inventories, and other current assets are used effectively, and then we consider the question of how current operations should be financed.

In the first chapter of Part V we introduce the concept of the time value of money. This chapter plays a key role in most of the subsequent chapters. The first application of the time value of money concept comes in the analysis of fixed asset acquisitions, or capital budgeting. Since major capital expenditures take years to plan and execute, and since decisions in this area are generally not reversible and affect operations for many years, their impact on the value of the firm is obvious.

Part VI focuses on raising long-term capital. The questions of the principal sources and forms of long-term capital, the cost of each type, and how the method of financing affects the value of the firm—are all addressed in this section. Part VI also describes the means by which the investor evaluates the firm's debt and equity instruments. The interrelationships between value, cost of capital, capital structure, and dividend policy serve to integrate the book and show how the parts meld into a cohesive whole.

Finally, in Part VII, we consider some subjects that, while important, are best studied within the basic framework of the preceding material presented in the text. Included in this section are mergers and acquisitions, bankruptcy, leasing, and international financial management.

Summary

This chapter has provided an overview of financial management. We began with a brief review of the evolution of finance as an academic discipline, tracing developments from 1900 to the present. We next examined the place of finance in the firm and saw that the financial manager has been playing an increasingly important role in the organization. We also considered the goals of financial management and concluded that the key goal in most publicly owned firms is stock price maximization. Managers do have other goals, both personal and social, but in a competitive economy, where managers serve at the pleasure of stockholders, stock price maximization must be the dominant goal.

Financial capital is the major resource for any firm. The duty of the financial manager is to implement the acquisition, allocation, and management of this resource. Therefore finance permeates all segments of the firm's activities. Because of its broad impact, managers, marketers, and long-range planners, along with chief executive officers (CEOs), must be aware of how their functions influence financial requirements. Thus all managers in the firm must understand the finance function.

Small Business $\quad \$ \quad \$ \quad \$ \quad \$ \quad \$ \quad \$ \quad \$ \quad \$ \quad \$

Goals and Resources in the Small Firm

Small business is key to the vitality of the American economy. The Small Business Administration (SBA) points out that 98.2 percent of all nonfarm businesses are considered small by SBA standards, and 99 percent of all farm businesses are considered small. Small nonfarm businesses provide 58 percent of U.S. business employment and the vast majority of *new* jobs in American industry. Finally, the SBA reports that "more than half of all the product and service innovations developed in the United States since World War II" have been developed by independent small business entrepreneurs.[1]

Although small business is a vital contributor to the financial health of our economy, the businesses themselves are often fragile and especially susceptible to failure owing to poor management, particularly poor financial management. Financial management, then, is a subject of great importance to the small business.

Significant differences exist between small businesses and big businesses: the way they are owned, the way they are managed, and the financial and managerial resources they have at their disposal. These differences affect the financial management function in smaller firms and make it difficult to apply unmodified standard financial management principles to these firms. Two especially important differences are resource poverty and goal conflicts.

Resource Poverty

John Thompson is the owner of 75 percent of the stock in Board Products Corporation, a small but growing manufacturer of products based on semiconductor components. The remainder of the stock is owned by his various friends and relatives. The company began operation with about $250,000 in cash and has developed a series of promising products that it has recently begun to market. The firm has used up nearly all of its original capital.

In addition to Thompson, the company has 12 employees, all but two of whom are engineers or technicians involved in the development and testing of new products. The other two are clerical and secretarial personnel. Thompson uses the services of an outside accounting firm to process the company's monthly statements, which typically are completed approximately six weeks after the end of the month.

Thompson has full responsibility for the management of Board Products with the exception of product development, which is run by vice president Roland Smith. Smith is a technical whiz with no interest or background in business management, but he does have an impressive list of technical credentials. He recently left a senior engineering position at a large electronics company to join Thompson's company.

Thompson's responsibilities include making contacts with large potential clients, handling all personnel decisions, giving final approval to all planned products presented by the technical staff, overseeing investor relations, handling legal issues both in the patent area and in the issuance of the firm's stock, managing the firm's relations with the bank, and managing the firm's finances. He hasn't taken a day off in six months and doesn't expect to do so for several more months.

Thompson is not unusual. Management in small firms is often spread very thin, and one or two key individuals end up taking on far more responsibility than they can handle reasonably. Thompson, for example, may feel that other priorities in the business are too important to let him spend time putting together a budget or checking regularly to see how well the company is doing against such a budget. He argues, "I have a pretty good feel for how we're doing cash-wise, and I really don't have the time to go into any more detail. Making budgets doesn't make money."

Given a request by the technical staff for some new and expensive testing equipment for development purposes, Thompson may make the decision to buy or not to buy the equipment with little or no formal analysis but proceeds on the basis of his "gut feelings." He may see the analysis as being too time-consuming in that he must put together a presentation for a potential customer or talk with a venture capital firm about providing Board Products with new capital to get the products into the market.

Not only is it often the case that management is spread thin in small firms, but it is also frequently true that smaller firms cannot readily acquire new funds needed for business expansion or they can get funds only under very difficult conditions. Until Board Products achieves a fairly substantial size, say, $15 million or so in sales, the company is not likely to be able to sell stock or bonds successfully in public markets. Furthermore, if the company did have a public stock of-

fering, it would be very expensive for the firm by comparison to the cost of stock issuance by a larger firm. Thus Board Products may have only very limited access to public capital markets.[2] Banks may also be reluctant to loan Board Products very much money because of the firm's lack of a track record.

Small firms are thus limited both in their access to managerial talent and in their ability to muster adequate financial resources. It is no wonder that small firms often fail either because of poor (or overworked) management or because of undercapitalization.

Goal Setting

Small businesses also differ from large firms in that the goals in a small firm mày be different. We pointed out earlier that share price maximization is taken to be the goal of all firms. Thompson, however, is a good example of an owner whose life is tied up in his company. He depends on the firm for his livelihood, and he has bet his future on the success of the company. His personal wealth portfolio is probably not at all diversified: he has perhaps put everything he owns into the company. Given his level of commitment to the company and his lack of a fallback position, Thompson might take a very different posture toward risk-taking in his firm than would a typical investor in a public company. Such an investor is likely to hold a number of other investments, all contributing toward a well-diversified portfolio of holdings, and his or her personal income may come from a job in an altogether separate industry.

It cannot be denied that the owner-manager of a small firm is interested in the value of the firm, even if the value of the firm cannot be readily observed in the market. He or she may have in mind "taking the firm public" or having it merged into a larger firm at some future date—hopefully at the highest possible value. But the motives of small business owners are complex, and they may even be dominated by such considerations as the desire to be their "own boss" even if it means not letting the firm grow at the fastest rate possible or be as profitable as it could be. In other words, there is value in being in control, and that value is not easily discernible. As a result, we often observe small businesses taking actions that do not make sense when judged on the basis of value maximization but that do make sense when seen in the light of the true objectives of the owners.

To the extent that the goals of the small firm differ from value maximi-

zation, some of the prescriptions in this text may not be entirely applicable. Most of the tools will be useful for the small business even if its objectives are different, but they may need to be modified. In any event, these brief "Small Business" sections will serve as a vehicle for exploring special issues of importance to small firms.

[1]Extracted from Small Business Administration, *Facts about Small Business and the U.S. Small Business Administration* (Washington, DC: U.S. Government Printing Office, 1981).

[2]The ability of small firms to acquire equity capital in public markets and the costs of doing so are explored in Hans R. Stoll, "Small Firms' Access to Public Equity Financing," forthcoming in *Financing Small Business*, eds. Paul M. Horvitz and R. Richardson Pettit.

Resolution to Decision in Finance

Kennecott Copper

Kennecott Copper's board of directors voted to accept management's proposal and bought Carborundum Company. This touched off a vicious fight for corporate control led by a group of stockholders who believed that the company had not acted to maximize shareholders' wealth. The dissidents thought that the cash from Peabody's sale should have been distributed to them as dividends instead of used to buy Carborundum. Although the group lost their fight for control, they won three seats on the board.

Some experts contend that this is a prime example of American business's greatest flaw: it is afflicted by selfish, number-crunching managers who care only about short-term profit goals and are blind to the real world of people and products. These experts believe that other objectives besides maximizing shareholders' wealth should be added to a manager's performance evaluation. And these should pertain to the welfare of employees, the community, and the economy.

Others believe that managers have too much freedom. Says Harvard's David Mullins, "Managers can't be fired at the annual meeting, or, really, anywhere else. If shareholders don't like what you're doing, they yell at you at the annual meeting. So you hold the meeting in Singapore. If the stockholders sue, you sue back—with their own money. The freedom of the modern executive is really awesome."

In the end, most experts believe that the real problem isn't short-term management versus long-term management but how to teach future executives that, in the long run, it is in their self-interest to be less selfish. All agree that American managers are too selfish and unaccountable. But they disagree over whether we need a new definition of the firm or stricter enforcement of accepted definitions.

Source: Thomas Friedman and Paul Solman, "Is American Management Too Selfish?" *Forbes*, January 17, 1983, 75–77.

Key Terms You should be able to define the following terms:

Finance; financial management	Risk
Profit maximization; stockholder	Dividend policy
wealth maximization	Social responsibility
Earnings per share (EPS)	Normal profits

Questions

1-1 Would the "normal rate of return on investment" be the same in all industries? Would "normal" rates of return change over time? Explain.

1-2 Would the role of the financial manager be likely to increase or decrease in importance relative to the other executives if the rate of inflation increased? Explain.

1-3 Should stockholder wealth maximization be thought of as a long-run or a short-run goal—that is, if one action would probably increase our stock price from a current level of $20 to $25 in 6 months and then to $30 in 5 years, but another action would probably keep our stock price at $20 for several years but then increase it to $40 in 5 years, which action would be better? Can you think of actual examples that might have these general tendencies?

1-4 What is the difference between stock price maximization and profit maximization? Would profit maximization not lead to stock price maximization?

1-5 If you were running a large, publicly owned corporation, would you make decisions to maximize stockholders' welfare or your own? What are some actions stockholders could take to insure that your interests and theirs coincided?

Selected References

For a good summary of financial management, see:

Pogue, Gerald A., and Kishore Lall, "Corporate Finance: An Overview," *Sloan Management Review*, Spring 1974, 19–38.

For alternative views on firms' goals and objectives, see the following articles:

Anthony, Robert N., "The Trouble with Profit Maximization," *Harvard Business Review*, November–December 1960, 126–134.

Donaldson, Gordon, "Financial Goals: Management versus Stockholders," *Harvard Business Review*, May–June 1963, 116–129.

Elliot, J. W., "Control, Size, Growth, and Financial Performance in the Firm," *Journal of Financial and Quantitative Analysis*, January 1972, 1309–1320.

Findlay, M. C., and E. E. Williams, "A Positivist Evaluation of the New Finance," *Financial Management*, Summer 1980, 7–17.

Lewellen, Wilbur G., "Management and Ownership in the Large Firm," *Journal of Finance*, May 1969, 299–322.

For a general reivew of the state of the art in academic finance, together with an extensive bibliography of key research articles, see:

Beranek, William, "Research Directions in Finance," *Quarterly Review of Economics and Business*, Spring 1981, 6–24.

How Business Is
Organized and Taxed

Decision in Finance

Where Did Baldwin-United's Millions Go?

Between 1968 and 1983 Cincinnati-based Baldwin-United Corporation changed from a staid old piano manufacturing firm into a high-flying financial conglomerate. The mastermind of this transformation was Morley Thompson, who started with the company as a door-to-door piano salesman in Alaska and eventually became its chief executive officer.

While he was president of Baldwin, Thompson was an avowed "taxophobe": he deferred or avoided taxes with great resourcefulness. He claimed to have no secret tax tricks. He merely knew the tax codes inside out and exploited them ruthlessly.

Baldwin's income statement for the nine months ending September 30, 1982 seemed to indicate that the company enjoyed strong financial health. Reported profits rose to $91 million—a 68 percent increase over profits for the same period in 1981. But in fact Baldwin was in deep financial trouble. The company had actually suffered an operating loss of $28 million. Of the earnings gain it had claimed, $83 million consisted of tax credits. And when $440 million that it owed to banks fell due, Baldwin was unable to pay.

As you read this chapter, look for ways in which Morley Thompson could have used the tax laws to Baldwin's benefit. Why didn't Baldwin's tax credits do it more good? What would you do if you were a Baldwin-United shareholder? If you were one of Baldwin's bankers? If you sat on Baldwin's board of directors?

See end of chapter for resolution.

Financial management cannot be studied in a vacuum—if the value of a firm is to be maximized, the financial manager must understand the legal and economic environment in which financial decisions are made. Accordingly, this chapter presents some background information on forms of business organization and on the federal income tax system.

Alternative Forms of Business Organization

There are three major forms of business organization: the sole proprietorship, the partnership, and the corporation. In terms of numbers, about 80 percent of business firms are operated as sole proprietorships, while the remainder are equally divided between partnerships and corporations. By dollar value of sales, however, about 80 percent of business is conducted by corporations, about 13 percent by sole proprietorships, and about 7 percent by partnerships.

Sole Proprietorship

proprietorship
A business owned by one individual.

A **proprietorship** is a business owned by one individual. To go into business as a single proprietor is very simple—one merely begins business operations. However, most cities require even the smallest establishments to be licensed, and occasionally state licenses are required as well.

The proprietorship has key advantages for small operations. It is easily and inexpensively formed; no formal charter for operations is required; and a proprietorship is subject to few government regulations. Furthermore, the business pays no corporate income taxes, although all earnings of the firm are subject to personal income taxes, whether they are reinvested in the business or withdrawn.

The proprietorship also has important limitations. Most significant is its inability to obtain large sums of capital. Also, the proprietor has unlimited personal liability for the business's debts. Finally, the life of the proprietorship business is limited to the life of the individual who created it. For all of these reasons, the individual proprietorship is restricted primarily to small business operations. However, businesses are frequently started as proprietorships and then converted to corporations whenever their growth causes the disadvantages of the proprietorship form to outweigh its advantages.

Partnership

partnership
An unincorporated business owned by two or more persons.

A **partnership** exists whenever two or more persons associate to conduct a business. Partnerships may operate under different degrees of formality, ranging from informal, oral understandings to formal agreements filed with the secretary of the state in which the firm does business. In a partnership, each partner contributes a certain amount of funding to support the business and does a certain amount of the work needed to run it. Of course, each partner then is entitled to a comparable share of the business's profits (or losses). The major advantage of a partnership is its low cost and ease of formation. The disadvantages are similar to those associated with proprietorships: (1) unlimited liability, (2) impermanence of the organization, (3) difficulty of transferring ownership, and (4) difficulty of raising large amounts of capital. The tax treatment of a partnership versus that of a corporation can be either an advantage or a disadvantage, depending on the situation; this point is discussed later in the chapter.

Regarding liability, the partners must all risk their personal assets as well as their investments in the business, for under partnership law the partners are liable for the business's debts. This means that if any partner is unable to meet his or her pro rata claim in the event the partnership goes bankrupt, the remaining partners must take over the unsatisfied claims, even having to draw on their own personal assets when no other sources are available.

Some of the problems of a general partnership, which we have just described, may be reduced by the formation of a **limited partnership.** In a limited partnership certain partners are designated *general partners* and others *limited partners*. The general partners have the same unlimited liability as with any general partnership, but the limited partners' liability extends only to the amount of their investment in the partnership. Limited partners are often termed "silent partners" since they have no active voice in management. Limited partnerships are quite common in the area of real estate investment, but they have not worked well in many other types of business ventures. Limited partnerships constitute only 10 percent of all partnership businesses.

limited partnership
An unincorporated business owned both by general partners having unlimited liability and by other partners having liability limited to their investment in the firm.

The first three disadvantages of a general partnership—unlimited liability, impermanence of the organization, and difficulty of transferring ownership—combine to cause the fourth, the difficulty partnerships have in attracting substantial amounts of capital. This is no particular problem for slow-growing businesses, but if a company's products really catch on so that it needs to raise large amounts of capital to expand and thus capitalize on its opportunities, the capital attraction situation becomes a real drawback. Thus companies such as Hewlett-Packard and Apple Computer generally begin life as proprietorships or partnerships but at some point find it necessary to convert to corporations.

Partnerships are responsible for only five percent of the total dollar volume of American business; they are common in small professional firms, such as medicine, law, accounting, and, recently, consulting.

Corporation

corporation
A legal entity created by a state, separate and distinct from its owners and managers, having unlimited life, easy transferability of ownership, and limited liability.

A **corporation** is a legal entity created by a state. It is separate and distinct from its owners and managers. This separateness gives the corporation three major advantages: (1) It has an *unlimited life*—it can continue after its original owners and managers are dead; (2) it permits *easy transferability of ownership interest* in the firm, as ownership interests can be divided into shares of stock, which can be transferred far more easily than can partnership interests; (3) it permits *limited liability*. To illustrate, if you invested $10,000 in a partnership and the partnership went bankrupt owing a considerable sum of money, you could be assessed for a share of these debts. Thus an investor in a partnership is exposed to unlimited liability. On the other hand, if you invested $10,000 in the stock of a corporation, your potential loss on the investment would be $10,000—your liability would be limited to the amount of your investment in the business.[1]

While a proprietorship or a partnership can commence operations without much paperwork, setting up a corporation is a bit more involved. The incorporators must prepare a *charter* and a set of *bylaws*. The **charter** includes the following information: (1) name of proposed corporation, (2) type of activities it will pursue, (3) amount of capital stock, (4) number of directors, (5) names and addresses of directors, and (6) duration (if limited). The charter is filed with the secretary of the state in which the firm will be headquartered, and when it is approved, the corporation is officially in existence.

charter
A formal legal document that describes the scope and nature of a corporation and defines the rights and duties of its stockholders and managers.

bylaws
A set of rules for governing the management of a company.

The **bylaws** are a set of rules drawn up by the founders of the corporation to aid in governing the internal management of the company. Included are such points as (1) how directors are to be elected (all elected each year or, say, one third each year); (2) whether the existing stockholders shall have the first right to buy any new stock the firm issues; and (3) what provisions there are for management committees, such as an executive committee or a finance committee, and their duties. Also included is the procedure for changing the bylaws themselves, should conditions require it.

The value of any business other than a very small one will probably be maximized if it is organized as a corporation. The reasons are outlined below:

1. Limited liability reduces risk to investors, and the lower the risk, other things held constant, the higher the value of the firm.

2. Value is dependent on growth opportunities, which in turn are dependent on a firm's ability to attract capital. Since corporations can

---

[1]In the case of small corporations, the limited liability feature is often a fiction, as bankers and credit managers frequently require personal guarantees from the stockholders of small, weak businesses.

attract capital more easily than unincorporated businesses, they have superior growth opportunities.

3. The value of an asset also depends on its **liquidity,** which means the ease of selling the asset and converting it to cash. Since an investment in the stock of a corporation is much more liquid than a similar investment in a proprietorship or partnership, this too means that the corporate form of organization can enhance the value of a business.

liquidity
The ability to sell an asset at a reasonable price on short notice.

4. Corporations are taxed differently from proprietorships and partnerships. In some instances the tax laws favor corporations. This point is discussed in the next section of the chapter.

Since most firms are indeed managed with value maximization in mind, it is easy to see why most business is conducted by corporations.

The Federal Income Tax System

The value of any financial asset, including stocks, bonds, or even whole firms, depends on the stream of *usable* income produced by the asset. Usable income means income *after taxes.* Proprietorship and partnership income must be reported and taxed as personal income to the owners. Most corporations must first pay taxes on their own income, and stockholders must then pay taxes on corporate after-tax income distributed to them as dividends. Therefore consideration must be given to both *personal* and *corporate* income taxes.

Federal income tax rates for individuals may be as high as 50 percent, and when state income taxes are included, the marginal tax rate on an individual's income can approach 70 percent. Business income is also taxed heavily. The income from partnerships and proprietorships is reported by the individual owners and taxed at their own rates, while corporate profits are subject to federal income tax rates of up to 46 percent, in addition to state income taxes. Because of the magnitude of the tax bite, taxes play an important role in many financial decisions.

Taxes are so complicated that university law schools offer master's degrees in taxation to practicing lawyers, many of whom also are CPAs. In a field complicated enough to warrant such detailed study, we can only cover the highlights. This is all that is really necessary, because business people and investors should and do rely on tax specialists rather than trust their own knowledge. Thus this chapter is intended to show how taxes apply to business and personal decisions, using recent tax facts as examples. At the time you read this chapter, many of the details may have changed, but the basic importance of taxes in our business and personal lives remains unchanged.[2]

---

[2]It should be noted that Congress changes the tax laws fairly often. Some of the details of this chapter may be changed by the 1984 Tax Reform Act, which is being discussed in Congress as this chapter is written. However, while the details may change, the importance of taxes in business decisions is unlikely to change.

Table 2-1
Tax Rates under the Tax Act of 1981

a. Single Individuals

If Your Taxable Income Is	1982		1983		1984	
	You Pay This Amount on the Base of the Bracket	Plus This Percentage of the Excess over the Base (Marginal Rate)	Tax on Base	Marginal Rate	Tax on Base	Marginal Rate
Up to $2,300	No tax	—	No tax	—	No tax	—
$2,300 to $3,400	$ 0	12%	$ 0	11%	$ 0	11%
$3,400 to $4,400	132	14	121	13	121	12
$4,400 to $6,500	272	16	251	15	241	14
$6,500 to $8,500	608	17	566	15	535	15
$8,500 to $10,800	948	19	866	17	835	16
$10,800 to $12,900	1,385	22	1,257	19	1,203	18
$12,900 to $15,000	1,847	23	1,656	21	1,581	20
$15,000 to $18,200	2,330	27	2,097	24	2,001	23
$18,200 to $23,500	3,194	31	2,865	28	2,737	26
$23,500 to $28,800	4,837	35	4,349	32	4,115	30
$28,800 to $34,100	6,692	40	6,045	36	5,705	34
$34,100 to $41,500	8,812	44	7,953	40	7,507	38
$41,500 to $55,300	12,068	50	10,913	45	10,319	42
$55,300 to $81,800	a	a	17,123	50	16,115	48
Over $81,800	a	a	b	b	28,835	50

a. In 1982 all income over $41,500 was to be taxed at a 50% rate, so the tax is $12,068 + 50% of the excess over $41,500.
b. In 1983 all income over $55,300 was to be taxed at a 50% rate, so the tax is $17,123 + 50% of the excess over $55,300.

Individual Income Taxes

progressive tax
A tax that requires a higher percentage payment on higher incomes. The personal income tax in the United States, which goes from a rate of 11 percent on its lowest increments of income to 50 percent on the highest increments, is progressive.

marginal tax rate
The tax applicable to the last unit of income.

average tax rate
Taxes paid divided by taxable income.

Individuals pay taxes on wages and salaries, on investment income (dividends, interest, and profits from the sale of securities), and on the profits of proprietorships and partnerships. Our tax rates are **progressive;** that is, the higher the income, the larger the percentage paid in taxes. Table 2-1 gives the scheduled tax rates for single individuals and married couples filing joint returns as established in the Economic Recovery Tax Act of 1981. Here are the highlights of the table:

1. Taxable income is defined as gross income less a set of deductions which are spelled out in the instructions to the tax forms people must file (Forms 1040 or 1040A).

2. The **marginal tax rate** is the tax on the last unit of income; marginal tax rates are zero on the first units of income and rise to 50 percent. Prior to 1982 marginal tax rates went up to 70 percent on unearned income such as interest and dividends. Beginning in 1982, no distinction is made between earned and unearned income.

3. One can calculate **average tax rates** from the data in the table. For

b. Married Couples Filing Joint Returns

If Your Taxable Income Is	1982		1983		1984	
	You Pay This Amount on the Base of the Bracket	Plus This Percentage of the Excess over the Base (Marginal Rate)	Tax on Base	Marginal Rate	Tax on Base	Marginal Rate
Up to $3,400	No tax	—	No tax	—	No tax	—
$3,400 to $5,500	$ 0	12%	$ 0	11%	$ 0	11%
$5,500 to $7,600	252	14	231	13	231	12
$7,600 to $11,900	546	16	504	15	483	14
$11,900 to $16,000	1,234	19	1,149	17	1,085	16
$16,000 to $20,200	2,013	22	1,846	19	1,741	18
$20,200 to $24,600	2,937	25	2,644	23	2,497	22
$24,600 to $29,900	4,037	29	3,656	26	3,465	25
$29,900 to $35,200	5,574	33	5,034	30	4,790	28
$35,200 to $45,800	7,323	39	6,624	35	6,274	33
$45,800 to $60,000	11,457	44	10,334	40	9,772	38
$60,000 to $85,600	17,705	49	16,014	44	15,168	42
$85,600 to $109,400	30,249	50	27,278	48	25,920	45
$109,400 to $162,400	c	c	38,702	50	36,630	49
Over $162,400	c	c	d	d	62,600	50

c. In 1982 all income over $85,600 was to be taxed at a 50% rate, so the tax is $30,249 + 50% of the excess over $85,600.
d. In 1983 all income over $109,400 was to be taxed at a 50% rate, so the tax is $38,702 + 50% of the excess over $109,400.

example, if Sally Heck, a single individual, had a taxable income of $30,000 in 1984, then her tax bill would be $5,705 + 0.34($30,000 − $28,800) = $5,705 + 0.34($1,200) = $6,113. Her *average tax rate* would be $6,113/$30,000 = .204 = 20.4% versus a *marginal tax rate* of 34 percent. If Sally received a raise of $1,000, to $31,000, she would have to pay $340 of it as taxes, so her net raise would be $660.

4. Tax rates declined for individuals from 1982 to 1984. For example, if Sally's 1982 income had been $28,800, she would have paid $6,692 in taxes. If her income were still $28,800 in 1984, her tax bill in that year would be only $5,705. Note also that marginal rates at all brackets also decline, so if Sally were to receive a raise, she would get to keep more of it.

5. Between 1982 and 1984 the income at which the top marginal tax rate applies rises from $41,500 to $81,800 for singles and from $85,600 to $162,400 for couples.

6. Although not shown in the table, Congress committed itself (though it could change its mind) to **indexed tax rates** beyond 1984 to avoid the

indexed tax rate
Provision which ties tax rates to inflation (or other index) to prevent bracket creep.

bracket creep
Situation that occurs when progressive tax rates combine with inflation to cause a greater portion of each taxpayer's income to be taxed.

bracket creep that occurred during the 1970s and de facto raised tax rates substantially.[3]

Taxes on Dividend and Interest Income. Dividend and interest income is fully taxed at rates going up to 50 percent.[4] Since corporations pay dividends out of earnings that have already been taxed, there is *double taxation* of corporate income. To partially offset double taxation, the first $100 of dividend income ($200 for married couples with jointly owned stock) is *excluded* from personal income taxes.

capital assets
Assets with a life of more than one year that are not bought or sold in the ordinary course of business, such as stocks, bonds, and real estate.

capital gain
The profit from the sale of a capital asset for more than its purchase price.

Capital Gain versus Ordinary Income. Assets such as stocks, bonds, and real estate are defined as **capital assets.** If you buy a capital asset and later sell it for more than your purchase price, the profit is defined as a **capital gain.** If you suffer a loss, it is called a **capital loss.**

An asset sold within six months of the time it was purchased produces a **short-term gain or loss,** while an asset held for more than six months produces a **long-term gain or loss.** Thus, if you buy 100 shares of GM stock for $70 per share and sell it for $80, you make a capital gain of $100 \times 10, or $1,000. If you sell the stock for $60, you have a $1,000 capital loss. If you hold the stock for more than six months, the gain or loss is long-term; otherwise it is short-term.[5]

capital loss
The loss from the sale of a capital asset for less than its purchase price.

short-term gain or loss
Gain or loss from the sale of an asset within six months of the time it was purchased.

long-term gain or loss
Gain or loss from the sale of an asset held for more than six months.

---

[3]*Bracket creep* is the situation that occurs when progressive tax rates combine with inflation to cause a greater share of each taxpayer's income to go to the government. For example, if you were single and had a 1984 taxable income of $10,000, your tax bill would be $1,075. Now suppose inflation causes prices to double, and your income, being tied to a cost of living index, rises to $20,000. Because our tax rates are progressive, your taxes (at 1984 rates) would jump to $3,205. Your after-tax income has thus increased from $8,925 to $16,795, but, since prices have doubled, your real income has declined from $8,925 to $8,398 (calculated as one half of $16,795). You are in a higher tax bracket, so you are having to pay a higher percentage of your real income in taxes. If this happens to everyone, and if Congress fails to change tax rates sufficiently, then the federal government gets a larger share of the national product. This is exactly what happened during the 1970s, but President Reagan's tax program, and especially the plan to index rates, is designed to stop it.

[4]However, interest on state and local government bonds is not subject to federal income taxes. Thus a taxpayer in the 40 percent bracket would receive as much after-tax income by owning a 6 percent state bond as by owning a 10 percent corporate bond:

$$\text{Tax-exempt yield} = \text{Taxable yield} (1 - \text{Tax rate})$$
$$= 10\% (0.6)$$
$$= 6\%.$$

The primary purpose of this provision is to help state and local governments borrow at lower rates than would otherwise be available to them.

[5]The holding period needed to qualify for long-term capital gain treatment has been shortened to six months, from one year, for property acquired after June 22, 1984. This change will remain in effect until September 30, 1988, when the holding period is scheduled to revert to one year.

Long-term capital gains are generally taxed at much lower rates than short-term gains (or other ordinary income). As a rule, 60 percent of any long-term gain is deducted, so taxes are paid on only 40 percent of long-term gains income. Thus, if one individual has $1,000 of short-term capital gains (or dividends) and is in the 30 percent marginal tax bracket, the gains tax would be $300, while if another individual in the same bracket had $1,000 of long-term gains, the tax would be only 0.3 ($1,000 − $600) = $120. As a percentage, the tax rate for long-term gains is 40 percent of the ordinary tax rate. Of course, there are certain complexities to this general rule that are not discussed here.

The fact that capital gains income is taxed at a lower rate than dividend or interest income has an important bearing on financial management. As we shall see, most businesses have at least some flexibility in providing returns to investors in the form of dividends or capital gains. Since the tax treatment of income from an asset has a significant effect on the value of the asset, personal income taxes must be taken into account by a firm seeking to maximize the value of its stock.

Corporate Income Taxes

The corporate tax structure is relatively simple. In 1984 corporations were required to pay 15 percent on the first $25,000 of taxable income, and the rates progressed up to 46 percent on all income over $100,000:

1st $25,000	15%
2nd $25,000	18%
3rd $25,000	30%
4th $25,000	40%
Over $100,000	46%

Therefore, if a firm had $220,000 of taxable income, its 1984 tax bill would have been

$$\begin{aligned}
\text{Taxes} &= 0.15(\$25,000) + 0.18(\$25,000) + 0.30(\$25,000) \\
&\quad + 0.40(\$25,000) + 0.46(\$120,000) \\
&= \$3,750 + \$4,500 + \$7,500 + \$10,000 + \$55,200 \\
&= \$80,950.
\end{aligned}$$

Thus the corporate tax is very progressive up to $100,000 of income, but it is constant thereafter. Also, note that the marginal tax rate is 46 percent if a firm earns over $100,000.

Interest and Dividend Income Received by a Corporation. Interest income received by a corporation is taxed as ordinary income at regular corporate tax rates. However, 85 percent of the dividends received by one corporation from another is excluded from taxable income. The

Industry Practice

Corporate Taxes: Why Some Firms Pay Less

While it may make sense to tax corporations, the way they are taxed is hard to justify, in the opinion of many experts. For starters, the tax burden falls unequally—some industries are favored with special breaks while others are not. And whatever the tax bite, it's argued that consumers end up paying for it in the form of higher prices.

As things now stand, the statutory 46 percent rate on corporate income is virtually a sham. Actual tax rates range from below zero to 39.7 percent on an industry-by-industry basis, depending on what tax breaks—such as accelerated depreciation, the investment tax credit, or the offset for foreign taxes—apply to a particular line of business (see table). Even within industries, there is a surprising difference in the tax rate individual firms end up paying in a given year. For example, aerospace giant Northrop Corp. reduced its rate to a negative,

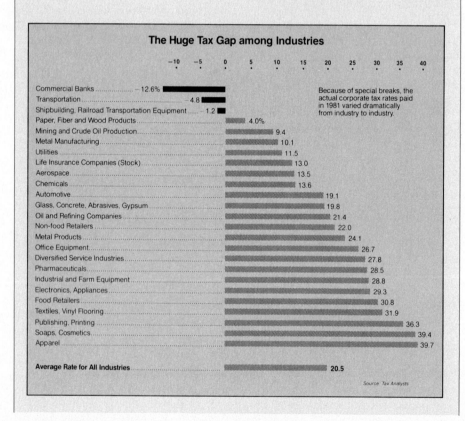

The Huge Tax Gap among Industries

Industry	Rate
Commercial Banks	−12.6%
Transportation	−4.8
Shipbuilding, Railroad Transportation Equipment	−1.2
Paper, Fiber and Wood Products	4.0%
Mining and Crude Oil Production	9.4
Metal Manufacturing	10.1
Utilities	11.5
Life Insurance Companies (Stock)	13.0
Aerospace	13.5
Chemicals	13.6
Automotive	19.1
Glass, Concrete, Abrasives, Gypsum	19.8
Oil and Refining Companies	21.4
Non-food Retailers	22.0
Metal Products	24.1
Office Equipment	26.7
Diversified Service Industries	27.8
Pharmaceuticals	28.5
Industrial and Farm Equipment	28.8
Electronics, Appliances	29.3
Food Retailers	30.8
Textiles, Vinyl Flooring	31.9
Publishing, Printing	36.3
Soaps, Cosmetics	39.4
Apparel	39.7
Average Rate for All Industries	**20.5**

Because of special breaks, the actual corporate tax rates paid in 1981 varied dramatically from industry to industry.

Source: Tax Analysts

−103.1 percent (which can be carried forward and applied against future tax liabilities), while Lockheed Corp. paid a 36.8 percent rate on U.S. income in 1981.

It's obvious that industry rates vary wildly—and that there are clear winners and losers. Generally speaking, capital-intensive industries that can take advantage of investment credits and accelerated depreciation get the biggest breaks. Some of the lowest effective rates on U.S. income in 1981 were paid by firms in transportation (−4.8 percent), shipbuilding (−1.2 percent), paper and wood products (4.0 percent), and mining and crude oil production (9.4 percent). Commercial banks had the lowest rates of all, −12.6 percent, in large part because banks have become capital-intensive too.

Less fortunate are companies that must rely heavily on human skills. All of the industries with the highest effective rates are labor-intensive—apparel (39.7 percent), soaps and cosmetics (39.4 percent), publishing and printing (36.3 percent), and processors of meat and other foods (33.6 percent). Indeed, such firms get a double whammy because they are being hit by higher and higher Social Security levies without getting much from accelerated depreciation and other breaks voted by Congress. Corporate taxes as a percentage of total federal revenues fell from 23.2 percent in 1960 to 8 percent in 1982, while payroll taxes rose from 15.9 percent to 32.6 percent, according to the Office of Management and Budget.

The tax-break chisels that are used to chip away at the basic 46 percent corporate rate vary from industry to industry, notes Richard Kaplan, a professor of tax law at the University of Illinois. "Public utilities lean heavily on depreciation and investment-tax credits because of their massive investments in plants," he says. "Timber and lumber companies, for their part, are able to take capital gains (on trees, for example), which really should be their ordinary business income." Drug companies, Kaplan adds, get tax savings through a special provision that applies to Puerto Rican operations, which is an advantage open to other industries but mostly used by pharmaceutical firms.

Because of these various escape hatches, the Treasury will lose more than $80 billion in corporate tax revenues in fiscal year 1984, according to Congress's Joint Committee on Taxation. Almost half of this amount stems from investment credits and accelerated depreciation, which is why capital-intensive firms end up paying the lowest rates.

One solution might be to reform or abolish the corporate tax, but the roadblocks are substantial. Killing the corporate tax or eliminating most special breaks would be a drastic change. Some companies would receive a windfall; some would be devastated.

And as Congressional Budget Office Director Alice Rivlin notes, the national sport of tax avoidance may be the ultimate reason for keeping some form of corporate income tax. "If it's eliminated or reduced sharply, how will you keep individuals from incorporating themselves to avoid personal income taxes?" she asks. "That's a problem not to be sneezed at."

Source: Adapted from "Corporate Taxes: Why Some Firms Pay Less" by Marilyn Wilson. Reprinted with the special permission of *Dun's Business Month* (formerly *Dun's Review*), May 1983. Copyright 1983, Dun & Bradstreet Publications Corporation.

remaining 15 percent of dividends received is taxed at the ordinary tax rate. Thus a corporation earning over $100,000 and paying a 46 percent tax rate would pay (0.15) (0.46) $= 0.069 = 6.9$ percent of its dividend income as taxes. If this corporation passes its own after-tax income on to its stockholders as dividends, the income is ultimately subjected to *triple taxation*—the original corporation is first taxed, then the second corporation is taxed, and finally the individual who receives the dividend is taxed. This is the reason for the 85 percent exclusion on intercorporate dividends.

Notice that if a corporation has surplus funds that can be invested in marketable securities, the tax factor favors investment in stocks, which pay dividends, rather than bonds, which pay interest. For example, suppose a firm had $100,000 to invest and it could buy bonds that pay interest of $10,000 per year or stock that pays dividends of $10,000. If the firm is in the 46 percent tax bracket, its tax on the interest would be 0.46 $($10,000$) = $4,600$, and its after-tax income would be $5,400. If it bought stock, its tax would be (0.15) $($10,000$)$ $(0.46) = 690, and its after-tax income would be $9,310. Other factors might lead the firm to invest in bonds, but the tax factor favors stock investments when the investor is a corporation.

Interest and Dividends Paid by a Corporation. A firm's operations can be financed with either debt or equity capital. If a firm uses debt, it must pay interest on this debt, whereas a firm generally pays dividends to equity investors (stockholders). The interest paid by a corporation is deducted from operating income to obtain taxable income, but dividends paid are not deductible. Thus interest is paid with before-tax dollars, while dividends are paid with after-tax dollars.

To illustrate, suppose a firm's assets produced $25,000 of earnings before interest and taxes (operating profit) in 1984. If the firm were financed with debt that had interest payments of $25,000, then, as we see in Table 2-2, taxable income to the firm would be zero, taxes would

Table 2-2
Cash Flows to Investors under Debt and Equity Financing

	Debt Financing	Equity Financing
Operating Income	$25,000	$25,000
Interest	25,000	0
Taxable income	0	25,000
Taxes (15%)	0	3,750
After-tax income	$ 0	$21,250
Income to debt investors	$25,000	$ 0
Income to equity investors	0	21,500

be zero, and the debt holders would receive the entire $25,000. If, however, the firm had no debt and was therefore financed only by equity, the $25,000 would be taxable income to the corporation, the tax would be $25,000(0.15) = $3,750, and the equity investors would receive only $21,250 compared to the $25,000 the debt investors would receive under the debt-financing alternative. Although no firm is financed exclusively with debt, this example emphasizes that *interest is a tax-deductible expense which has a profound effect on the way businesses are financed—our tax system favors debt financing over equity financing.* This point is discussed in more detail in Chapters 19 and 20.

Corporate Tax Loss Carry-Back and Carry-Forward. Ordinary corporate operating losses can be carried back to each of the preceding 3 years and forward for the following 15 years, and used to offset taxable income in those years. For example, an operating loss in 1984 could have been used to reduce taxable income in 1981, 1982, or 1983 and then any remaining losses carried forward and used in 1985, 1986, and so on to the year 1999. If the firm elects to carry back its losses, the loss is applied first to the earliest year, then to the next earliest year, and so on; or the firm may elect not to carry back its losses, but rather may elect to use the losses to lower future tax liabilities.

To illustrate, suppose the Detroit Dolphins, Inc. had a $1 million pre-tax profit in every year except 1984, when they had a bad season and lost $6 million. Now suppose the Dolphins decide to use the carry-back feature to recompute taxes for 1981, using $1 million of the operating losses to reduce the 1981 reported profit to zero. This would permit them to recover the amount of taxes paid in 1981, so in 1985 the Dolphins would receive a refund of 1981 taxes because of the loss experienced in 1984. Since $5 million of unrecovered losses would still be available, the Dolphins would repeat this procedure for 1982 and 1983. Then in 1985, 1986, and 1987 they would apply the loss carry-forward to reduce profits to zero in each of these years. The purpose of permitting this loss averaging is, of course, to avoid penalizing corporations whose incomes fluctuate from year to year.

Improper Accumulation to Avoid the Payment of Dividends. Corporations could refrain from paying dividends to permit their stockholders to avoid personal income taxes on dividends. To prevent this, the tax code states that earnings accumulated by a corporation are subject to penalty rates *if the purpose of the accumulation is to enable stockholders to avoid the personal income tax.* Of income not paid out in dividends, a cumulative total of $250,000 (the balance sheet item "retained earnings") is by law exempted from the improper accumulation tax. This is a benefit primarily to small corporations.

Although there is a penalty rate on all amounts over $250,000 *shown to be unnecessary to meet the reasonable needs of the business,* many com-

tax loss carry-back and carry-forward
Corporate losses that can be carried back or carried forward to offset taxable income.

improper accumulation
Earnings retained by a business for the purpose of enabling stockholders to avoid personal income taxes.

panies do indeed have legitimate reasons for retaining earnings over
$250,000 and are thus not subject to the penalty rate. Earnings during
a given year may be retained and used to pay off debt, to finance
growth, and to provide the corporation with a cushion against possible
cash drains caused by losses. How much a firm should properly accumulate for uncertain contingencies is a matter of judgment. We shall
consider this matter again in Chapter 21, which deals with corporate
dividend policy.

Consolidated Corporate Tax Returns. If a corporation owns 80 percent
or more of another corporation's stock, it can aggregate income and file
one consolidated tax return. Thus losses in one company can be used
to offset profits in another company. (Similarly, one division's losses
can offset another division's profits.) No business ever wants to incur
losses (you can go broke losing $1 to save 46 cents in taxes), but tax
offsets do make it more feasible for large, multidivisional corporations
to undertake risky new ventures or ventures that will suffer losses during a developmental period.

depreciation
The systematic distribution of the
cost or value of equipment
charged off over its estimated
useful life or IRS determined tax
life.

Depreciation. Suppose a firm buys a piece of equipment for $100,000
and uses it for five years. The cost of the goods and services produced
by the firm must include a charge for the machine, and this charge is
called **depreciation.** Depreciation reduces profits as calculated by the
accountants and reported to investors. It also reduces taxable income
and hence the firm's tax bill.

A given piece of equipment can be used for a longer or shorter time
depending on the intensity of its use, on the firm's maintenance policy,
and on the firm's replacement policy. Therefore the appropriate period
over which to depreciate assets has always been a controversial issue,
as has been the proper method used to calculate the annual depreciation.

Since depreciation affects taxable income and consequently taxes, it
is an important element in federal tax policy. Over the years Congress
has varied both the methods and the asset lives which companies are
permitted to use when calculating depreciation for tax purposes. We
defer a discussion of depreciation procedures to Chapter 6, where we
actually calculate depreciation, and in Chapter 15 we use it in the capital budgeting process. We can note at this point, however, that under
the 1981 law most equipment acquired after 1980 is depreciated over
either three or five years, while buildings are generally depreciated
over eighteen years.

investment tax credit (ITC)
A specified percentage of the
cost of new assets that business
firms can deduct as a credit
against their income taxes.

Investment Tax Credit. The **investment tax credit (ITC)** is designed to
stimulate business investment. The ITC is figured as a percentage of
the cost of certain new assets used in any corporation, partnership, or
proprietorship. Congress varies the ITC depending on economic con-

ditions. Beginning in 1981, it was 10 percent for an asset with a depreciable life of 5 years or more, 6 percent for an asset with a life of 3 years, and zero for an asset with a life of less than 3 years under federal tax law. However, for property placed in service after 1982, an important modification to the ITC rule was enacted. Under the new provision, if a firm uses the full ITC, the basis for the asset's depreciation falls by 50 percent of the ITC. In other words, for 5-year (or greater) class property the depreciable basis for the asset would be 95 percent of the purchase price plus any installation and shipping charges.

However, a business firm may take the full depreciation allowance if it reduces the amount of the ITC by 2 percentage points—that is, from 10 to 8 percent for 5-year (or greater) class property or from 6 to 4 percent for 3-year property. Since the ITC produces an immediate tax reduction that is larger than the tax shield provided by depreciation, most firms will choose the ITC when given the option.

The ITC is a direct reduction of taxes. Suppose a firm estimates that its taxable income next year will be $100,000 and that its tax bill will be $25,750. Now it decides to buy equipment that costs $50,000 and has a 5-year life. The company's tax bill will be reduced by (0.10) ($50,000) = $5,000. *Thus the ITC reduces the effective cost of fixed assets, and this stimulates investment.*

Taxation of Small Businesses: Subchapter S Corporations

Subchapter S of the Internal Revenue Code provides that small businesses which meet certain restrictions as spelled out in the code may be set up as corporations and thus receive the benefits of the corporate form of organization—especially limited liability—yet still be taxed as proprietorships or as partnerships rather than as corporations. There are several reasons for a small firm's electing to be taxed under the Subchapter S procedures, including the following:

1. If the firm is profitable, its income is reported on a pro rata basis by its owners. This avoids the double taxation that occurs when a corporation reports income, pays taxes, and then pays dividends that are taxable income to the stockholders.

2. If the firm has operating losses, these losses can be claimed on a pro rata basis by the stockholders as deductions against their ordinary income. This is an especially attractive feature for a new business that incurs heavy start-up costs and whose stockholders are in high marginal tax brackets because of income from other sources.

3. If the firm has investment tax credits, these credits can be passed along to the stockholders. Again, this is especially important for small, new firms that are making heavy capital investments yet whose income is insufficient to fully utilize the tax credits generated by these investments but whose owners have outside income that can be offset by the firm's tax credits.

Subchapter S
The section of the Internal Revenue Code that allows certain small business corporations to be taxed as either proprietorships or partnerships rather than as corporations, yet allows investors to retain the limited liability feature of the corporation.

Many factors other than taxes bear on the question of whether or not a firm should be organized as a corporation. However, the existence of Subchapter S makes it possible for most small businesses to have the benefits of a corporation yet be taxed at the owners' personal tax rates.

Summary

This chapter has presented some background information on forms of business organizations and on income taxes. First, we saw that firms may be organized as *proprietorships*, as *partnerships*, or as *corporations*. The first two types are easy and inexpensive to form. However, corporations have a major advantage in terms of risk reduction, growth possibilities, and investment liquidity. These features make it possible to maximize the value of any business except very small ones by using the corporate form of organization. Accordingly, corporations are the dominant form of business.

The value of any asset is dependent on the usable income it produces for its owner. *Effective income* means *after-tax income*. Since corporate income is taxed at rates up to 46 percent, and since personal income is subjected to additional federal and state taxes of up to 70 percent, the tax consequences of various decisions have a most important impact on a firm's value. It is not necessary to memorize everything about taxes—indeed, this would be impossible. However, you should know the basic differences between corporate and personal taxes, that interest is a tax deduction to the payer of the interest, that capital gains and operating income are taxed differently, and what the investment tax credit is. These matters will come up throughout the book as we examine various types of financial decisions.

Small Business $ $ $ $ $ $ $ $ $

Organizing the Small Firm

As discussed in Chapter 1, small firms are often at a disadvantage in competing for funds in capital markets. However, the federal government has made some special tax provisions to encourage the flow of equity capital into smaller firms.

These are not tax "loopholes" but rather measures purposefully designed to aid small business. In addition, other tax provisions encourage the acquisition of funds to stimulate research and development, and these provisions may be especially meaningful to the small high-technology firm in the early stages of development. This section considers three provisions that stimulate growth businesses: Subchapter S tax status, Section 1244 stock, and the R&D Limited Partnership.

Subchapter S Tax Status

Subchapter S of the Internal Revenue Code allows a small business to enjoy the limited-liability benefits of the corporate form of organization while obtaining the possible tax benefits of being taxed as a partnership. To enjoy Subchapter S status, a corporation must be a small business, must be a domestic corporation, and must be owned by no more than 25 individuals. The corporation and its shareholders must elect Subchapter S status at the beginning of the tax year; it cannot be elected after the fact. Other restrictions apply as well.[1]

Owners of Subchapter S corporations are taxed as if they were partners in a partnership. This tax treatment can be especially beneficial in the early stages of a firm's development when the firm is making heavy investments (and incurring investment tax credits) and anticipating operating losses. A firm often plans on having one or more unprofitable years in its early life while it is developing new products or trying to gain a foothold in a market. If the firm were not a corporation, the tax benefits of the ITCs would be passed on directly to the owners, and the losses would be used to offset other income that the owners may have. Subchapter S status allows the corporation to pass on those benefits as if the firm were a partnership, with the shareholders sharing in the benefits on a pro rata basis in accordance with their fractional ownership of the firm's equity.

If the firm is profitable during a year in which Subchapter S status has been elected, the earnings are added to the individual owners' ordinary incomes and taxed at their marginal personal tax rates. This feature of Subchapter S tax treatment can be either an advantage or a disadvantage. If the corporation plans to distribute all of its earnings to shareholders, then Subchapter S allows the firm to avoid double taxation. The earnings are taxed only at the personal level and not at the corporate level. On the other hand, if the owners wish to retain all earnings in the firm to finance continued growth, then Subchapter S status may be a disadvantage. If the corporate tax rates are lower than the tax rates of the individual owners, then more capital might be freed up by allowing the income to be taxed at the corporate level. When the owners have substantial incomes apart from their income from the corporation, their marginal tax rates may be as high as 50 percent. Since corporate tax rates are lower than 50 percent, taxes may be lower without Subchapter S status when the corporation is profitable.

Section 1244 Stock

Subchapter S status gives the corporation certain tax benefits in the treatment of the corporation's operating income. However, it does not apply to capital gains or losses. Capital gains enjoy favored treatment under the Internal Revenue Code when they are long term: the maximum tax rate under current law is 20 percent for long-term capital gains. However, investment in a new venture involves a high risk of failure and loss of capital. The Internal Revenue Code allows capital losses to be used only to offset capital gains or to offset up to $3,000 in ordinary income. That is not very encouraging to prospective investors in new high-risk ventures and may deter other investors. Section 1244 of the code contains a provision that gives favored tax treatment to capital losses to small businesses that qualify.

Stock issued under 1244 gives the holder benefits in the event of losses of capital from the purchase of the stock. The losses can occur because the corporation liquidates at a lower value than it had at the time of stock issuance, because the stock of the corporation is later sold at a lower price than that initially paid for it, or because the corporation goes "belly up." The losses in such events are treated as ordinary losses. For an individual in a high tax bracket, this feature essentially reduces the downside risk of investment. For example, if the investor is in the 50 percent tax bracket and has made a $10,000 investment in 1244 stock that becomes worthless, the investor gets back $5,000 in the form of reduced taxes. With 1244 stock, then, the investor gets the favored tax treatment of capital gains if the venture does well and gets substantial benefits if the venture does badly. This treatment acts as a significant enhancement to the value of an investment in a small high-risk firm and hence encourages investment.

As was the case with Subchapter S status, the issuance of 1244 stock is subject to certain limitations. Since the provision was established to help small firms compete for investment capital, it is restricted to small firms—firms with less than $1,000,000 in invested capital. It applies only to the original holders of the stock, and then only to individuals or partnerships—corporations and trusts cannot obtain 1244 benefits. The aggregate losses that qualify as ordinary losses are limited to $50,000 in any taxable year. Some other restrictions apply as well.[2]

Since Subchapter S status can be selected for corporations that have issued 1244 stock, investors can enjoy the benefits of favored tax treatment both on the operating income of the firm and on their equity position in the firm.

R&D Limited Partnerships

The past ten years have witnessed rapid growth in the formation of new high-technology businesses. Typically in such a business there is a start-up period in which considerable funds are expended for research and development, leading to a new product. The R&D Limited Partnership is a form of organization set up to permit the partners to treat the early losses in the project as ordinary losses while converting future gains from the commercial use of the product into capital gains.

The R&D Limited Partnership is a complex legal entity that should be established only with the help of an attorney who has specialized experience in its creation. The legal documents and prospectus involved may easily run in excess of 100 pages. However, the organizational structure is not difficult to describe since the principles are straightforward. There will be a set of general partners and a set of limited partners, with the limited partners enjoying limited liability and typically putting up the majority of the funds for the development activities.

To illustrate, suppose High Tech Electronic Software, Inc. (HTES) wishes to develop a new software product that runs on the IBM PC. It will cost $1,000,000 to develop the product, and HTES doesn't have the cash to support its development. HTES creates an R&D Limited Partnership in which the company acts as the general partner and sophisticated investors act as the limited partners, putting up the full $1,000,000. The partnership contracts with HTES to develop the product, which remains the property of the partnership.

During the first year the only activities are in product development. No revenues are earned. The partnership loses $1,000,000, having spent all of the initial cash, and the limited partners all write off their pro rata shares of the loss. This write-off effectively reduces the cost of product development to $500,000 if the investors are all in a 50 percent marginal tax bracket. On December 31, however, the product is ready to be marketed.

The partnership agreement gives HTES an exclusive right to market the new product. In exchange for this right, HTES pays the partnership royalties from the sale of the product. If the attorney handled all of the arrangements correctly and a variety of legal conditions are met, the income from the product might receive capital gains treatment for the limited partners. The limited partners then receive both a favorable tax treatment on the losses incurred in product development and a possibly favorable tax treatment on the income received from the marketing of the product.

The R&D Limited Partnership can be used on relatively small development projects, such as the one just described, or on very large projects. For example, Gene Amdahl, the inventor of the famous Amdahl computer, was able to raise $55 million in a public offering of an R&D Limited Partnership to start Trilogy Systems Corporation, and the DeLorean automobile was initially funded with $20 million from such an arrangement. Nevertheless, the R&D Limited Partnership can also be an important alternative for the entrepreneur needing even relatively limited funds to develop products from emerging technology.

---

[1]Conditions that must be met in qualifying for Subchapter S status are described in Ernest W. Walker and J. William Petty II, *Financial Management of the Small Firm* (Englewood Cliffs, NJ: Prentice-Hall, 1978), Chapter 2.
[2]An interesting presentation of the advantages of 1244 stock and the conditions for qualifying for 1244 treatment is given in Dick Levin, *Buy Low, Sell High, Collect Early and Pay Late* (Englewood Cliffs, NJ: Prentice-Hall, 1983), Chapter 4.

Resolution to Decision in Finance

Where Did Baldwin-United's Millions Go?

Morley Thompson created an ingeniously complex financial empire at Baldwin-United. During his tenure he acquired 13 insurance companies, a savings and loan, some mortgage-banking companies, two trading-stamp companies, and assorted other firms, and he started a leasing business. His goal was to create shareholder wealth through two primary tactics: acquiring cash at little or no cost and avoiding or deferring income taxes.

For example, the insurance companies provided low-cost cash from the premiums they collected. And the savings and loan brought in cash from low-interest passbook accounts. At the same time the leasing company generated tax credits, as did the acquisition of companies with large unrealized losses.

Baldwin's biggest revenue producer also turned out to be the greatest drain on its income. Between 1979 and 1982 Baldwin raised over $3 billion in single-premium deferred annuities (SPDAs). SPDAs allow investors to earn tax-deferred interest on a lump sum payment made to an insurer. To attract buyers, Baldwin offered high interest rates to investors and high commissions to salespeople. The commissions could be used as tax credits, and Baldwin could afford to pay the annuities' high interest rates as long as the company itself could invest at higher rates. But a fall in interest rates wiped out Baldwin's high earning power.

Thompson's virtuoso deal making made some Wall Streeters uncomfortable and scared off more conservative investors. And his elaborate construction of tax credits eventually gave way. As one security analyst pointed out, "Tax credits are fine for impressing shareholders, but they are not real money. You can't pay the bills with them."

In fact, one serious limitation of tax credits is that they translate into spendable money only if a company has taxable profits. Then the credits can be used to reduce the tax liability. But in 1982 Baldwin had no tax liability. And the $83 million tax credit it reported as current income was, in fact, merely a credit against future income.

Shareholders expressed their anxieties by selling millions of Baldwin-United shares as soon as the company's troubles came to light. But the bankers couldn't bail out that easily because they didn't want to push Baldwin into default. In May 1983 sales of annuities were halted, and Victor H. Palmieri replaced Morley Thompson as president of Baldwin.

In July, under court order, the six Baldwin insurance companies that sold SPDAs were taken over the by state insurance commissioners in Arkansas and Indiana. And the following September Baldwin filed a Chapter 11 reorganization.

Due to tax loopholes, companies may be able to manipulate their books to make their earnings look better, but Thompson took a risky route when he built an entire company on loopholes. The realization that reported earnings are merely the result of shrewd bookkeeping can alarm lenders, investors, and customers. In addition, the government may close the loopholes at any time, leaving the company on even more perilous financial footing.

Sources: "Where Have Baldwin-United's Millions Gone?" *Fortune*, April 18, 1983, 99–100; and "The Smart Taxophobe," *Fortune*, March 8, 1982, 52–59.

Key Terms   You should be able to define the following terms:

Proprietorship; partnership; limited partnership; corporation
Charter; bylaws
Liquidity
Progressive tax
Marginal tax rate; average tax rate; indexed tax rate
Bracket creep
Capital assets

Capital gain; capital loss
Short-term gain or loss; long-term gain or loss
Tax loss carry-back and carry-forward
Improper accumulation
Depreciation
Investment tax credit (ITC)
Subchapter S

Questions

2-1 What are the three principal forms of business organization? What are the advantages and disadvantages of each?

2-2 Suppose you owned 100 shares of General Motors stock and the company just earned $6 per share. Suppose further that GM could either pay all its earnings out as dividends (in which case you would receive $600) or retain the earnings in the business, buy more assets, and cause the price of the stock to go up by $6 per share (in which case the value of your stock would rise by $600).
   a. How would the tax laws influence what you, as a typical stockholder, would want the company to do?
   b. Would your choice be influenced by how much other income you had?
   c. How might the corporation's decision with regard to dividend policy influence the price of its stock?

2-3 What does *double taxation of corporate income* mean?

2-4 If you were starting a business, what tax considerations might cause you to prefer to set it up as a proprietorship or a partnership rather than as a corporation?

2-5 Explain how the federal income tax structure affects the choice of financing (debt versus equity) used by U.S. business firms.

2-6 How can the federal government influence the level of business investment by adjusting the ITC?

2-7 For someone planning to start a new business, is the average or the marginal tax rate more relevant?

Problems

2-1 In 1984 Nevada Industries had $150,000 in taxable income.
   a. What federal income tax will the firm pay?
   b. What is its average tax rate?
   c. What is its marginal tax rate?

✱ 2-2 The Dyl Pickle Company had a 1984 income of $200,000 from operations after all operating costs but before (1) interest charges of $10,000, (2) dividends paid of $20,000, and (3) income taxes. What is Dyl Pickle's income tax liability?

2-3 Moses Manufacturing had an operating income of $3,500,000 and capital gains of $400,000 this tax year. Additionally, the firm received $200,000 in interest from a loan repayment from Benton Industries and dividend income of $300,000 from Wofford Electric. Assuming that ordinary income is taxed at 46 percent and the capital gains rate is 18 percent (roughly 40 percent of the ordinary income tax rate), compute Moses's tax bill for the year.

✱ 2-4 **a.** The Thomas Corporation had $200,000 of taxable income from operations in 1984. What is the company's federal income tax bill for the year?
   b. Assume Thomas receives an additional $20,000 interest income from some bonds it owns. What is the tax on this interest income?
   c. Now assume that Thomas does not receive the interest income but that it does receive an additional $20,000 as dividends on some stock it owns. What is the tax on this dividend income?

2-5 Bob Kemp is reaping the rewards of many years of careful investing. If Bob is in the 40 percent tax bracket, what tax would he pay on:
   a. $1,000 ordinary income?
   b. $1,000 gain on the sale of an investment held for 5 months?
   c. $1,000 gain on the sale of an investment held for more than 1 year?
   d. $1,000 dividend received?
   e. $1,000 interest received?

2-6 The Columbus Construction Company has made $200,000 before taxes for each of the last 15 years, and it expects to make $200,000 a year before taxes in the future. However, this year (1984) Columbus incurred a loss of

---

*Refer to Appendix E for check answers to problems with asterisks.

$1,200,000. Columbus will claim a tax credit at the time it files its 1984 income tax returns and will receive a check from the U.S. Treasury. Show how it calculates this credit, and then indicate Columbus's tax liability for each of the next 5 years. Assume a 50 percent tax rate on *all* income to ease the calculations.

Selected Reference

There are a number of good reference books on taxes. One is: Prentice-Hall, *Federal Tax Course* (Englewood Cliffs, NJ: updated annually).

The Financial Environment II

The financial manager does not make decisions in a vacuum. Part II of this text describes the financial environment in which we all work.

The job of financial intermediaries is to efficiently transfer funds from surplus economic units to deficit economic units. Chapter 3 introduces the processes and the institutions involved in successfully converting savings to productive investments. Although large business firms deal with a variety of financial intermediaries, all businesses utilize at least some of the services provided by one type of intermediary—the commercial bank, which is discussed in Chapter 4. The chapter also describes the means by which the Federal Reserve System influences the economy. The economic health of the country is measured by interest rates; Chapter 5 examines the components which determine those rates.

Capital Markets

Decision in Finance

NYSE versus AMEX versus OTC: A Bitter Triangle

Within the past few years, the competition for new listings has been heating up among the New York Stock Exchange, the American Stock Exchange, and the over-the-counter market. The stakes are high because much of the three markets' revenue comes from companies' listing fees and member brokers' fees based on the volume of trades.

The competition takes many forms. The NYSE and AMEX mount extensive advertising campaigns, develop elaborate marketing proposals, and keep in frequent personal contact with prospective companies. Meanwhile, all three institutions constantly upgrade their automated trading systems to help satisfy both companies and brokerage houses that trades are being handled as efficiently as possible.

Given the heated rivalry, the LIN Broadcasting Corporation wasn't surprised that both the NYSE and AMEX had been pounding on its door for several years. New York-based LIN traded over the counter, but it qualified to be listed on both exchanges. Finally, the company decided to invite the NYSE to present its case. Afterwards, LIN's directors faced a decision: Should they stay with the OTC or switch to the Big Board?

As you read this chapter, look for the factors that LIN's directors probably considered as they mulled over the NYSE's presentation. Do you think the company would be better off listing with one of the exchanges? Why or why not?

See end of chapter for resolution.

The duties of a financial manager, discussed in Chapter 1, can be distilled (with some imagination perhaps) into two basic decisions regarding (1) the firm's investment in assets and (2) how those assets are to be financed. In this chapter we discuss the means by which necessary funds are made available to businesses and specifically the role of the stock and bond markets in raising money for business.

Role of Financial Markets

At the risk of oversimplification, it can be said that financial markets exist to convert savings into productive investments. In other words, without financial markets each economic unit[1] would have to be self-supporting. An individual business could not invest in additional means of production unless it were financed with the firm's own current savings. Thus without financial markets every opportunity to invest would be predicated on the individual economic unit's ability to save.

Unfortunately, most economic units that have productive investment opportunities often do not have all the savings required to finance their projects. For example, suppose Tampa Electric Company forecasts an increase in the demand for power in its service area and decides to build a new power plant. Because it almost certainly will not have the $500 million necessary to pay for the plant, it will have to raise this capital in the market. Or suppose Mr. Jones, the proprietor of a local hardware store, decides to expand into appliances. Where will he get the money to buy the initial inventory of TV sets, washers, and freezers? Similarly, if the Smiths want to buy a home that costs $60,000, but they have only $20,000 in savings, how can they raise the additional $40,000? Also, if the city of Sacramento wants to borrow $20 million to finance a new sewage plant, and if the federal government needs some $180 billion to cover its projected 1984 deficit, they each need sources for raising this capital.

On the other hand, because some individuals and firms have incomes that are greater than their current expenditures, they have funds available to invest. For example, Edgar Rice has an income of $36,000 but his expenses are only $30,000, and in 1981 Xerox Corporation had accumulated about $500 million of excess cash that it could make available for investment.

Entities wanting to borrow money are brought together with those having surplus funds in the *financial markets*. Note that "markets" is plural—there are a great many different financial markets in a developed economy. Each market deals with a somewhat different type of

---

[1]The most important economic units within the domestic economy are business firms, individuals (often referred to as households), and governments (local, state, and national). While our comments are directly concerned with business firms, the statements are valid for the other economic units as well.

security, serves a different kind of customer, or operates in a different part of the country. Different kinds of **securities** include stocks and bonds, or any claim to ownership or debt. Some of the major types of markets follow:

securities
Financial assets, such as stocks or bonds, that are claims to ownership or debt.

1. Physical Asset Markets and Financial Asset Markets. These terms must be distinguished. Physical assets (also called "tangible" or "real" assets) include wheat, autos, real estate, computers, and so on. Financial assets are stocks, bonds, notes, mortgages, and other *claims on assets*.

2. Spot Markets and Futures Markets. These are terms that refer to whether the assets are being bought or sold for "on the spot" delivery (or within a few days) or for delivery at some future date such as six months or a year in the future. The futures markets (which could include the options markets) are growing in importance, but we shall not discuss them until much later in the text.

3. Money Markets. These markets are for short-term (less than one year) debt securities. The New York **money market** is the world's largest, and it is dominated by the major U.S. banks, although branches of foreign banks are also active there. London, Tokyo, and Paris are other major money market centers.

money market
The financial market in which funds are borrowed or loaned for short periods.

4. Capital Markets. These are markets for long-term debt and corporate stocks. The New York Stock Exchange, which handles both the stocks and the bonds of the largest corporations, is a prime example of a **capital market.** The stocks and bonds of smaller corporations are handled in other segments of the capital market.

capital market
The financial market in which funds are borrowed or loaned for long periods.

5. Mortgage Markets. These markets deal with loans on residential, commercial, and industrial real estate, and on farmland.

6. Consumer Credit Markets. These involve loans on automobiles and appliances, as well as loans for education, vacations, and so on.

7. World, National, Regional, and Local Markets. These types of markets also exist. Thus, depending on an organization's size and scope of operations, it can borrow all around the world or it may be confined to strictly local, even neighborhood, markets.

8. Primary Markets. These are markets in which newly issued securities are bought and sold for the first time. If AT&T were to sell a new issue of common stock to raise capital, it would be a **primary market** transaction.

primary markets
The markets in which newly issued securities are bought and sold for the first time.

9. Secondary Markets. These are the markets in which existing, outstanding securities are bought and sold. The New York Stock Exchange is both a primary and a **secondary market** for securities. However, the

secondary markets
The markets in which stocks are traded after they have been issued by corporations.

majority of the sales on the NYSE deal with "used" as opposed to new stocks and bonds. The firm receives no money when the stock sells in the secondary market, yet its existence insures an active market for the stock if more is issued.

While savings must equal investment, financial markets allow the savings and investment process to be separated. Thus savers do not necessarily have to have their own productive investment opportunities. Since savings and investment are rarely equal for individual economic entities, a healthy economy is dependent on efficient transfers of funds from savers to firms and individuals who need capital, that is, on *efficient financial markets*. Without efficient transfers the economy simply could not function: Tampa Electric could not raise capital so Tampa's citizens would have no electricity; the Smith family would not have adequate housing; Edgar Rice would have no place to invest his savings; and so on. Obviously, our level of productivity, and hence our standard of living, would be much lower. It is therefore absolutely essential that our financial markets function efficiently—not only quickly but also at a low cost.

Role of Financial Intermediaries

We have indicated that savings must equal investment, but we have not indicated how the process is implemented. Basically, the transfer of funds from saving units to those units with productive opportunities

Industry Practice

The Supercompanies Emerge

For years, industry observers have used the future tense when talking of financial supermarkets that would serve the consumer's every need in banking, credit card services, insurance, investments, real estate, and so on.

Well, the future has arrived. A handful of financial services supercompanies has clearly emerged: Sears, Roebuck and Co., Prudential-Bache Securities, BankAmerica Corp., American Express, Citicorp, and Merrill Lynch & Co. Each of these super-

companies (they don't like to be called "supermarkets") can already serve customers in at least three of the five major financial areas, and they are all working to extend their reach and penetration. Meanwhile coming on strong are Travelers, Transamerica, Aetna, and Security Pacific Bank, among others.

These financial conglomerates have come along much faster than expected because of profound changes in insurance, banking, and securities wrought by the interplay of high interest rates, technology, and deregulation.

Mesmerized by high rates, consum-

Company	Assets (Billions of Dollars)	Revenue (Billions of Dollars)	Net Income (Millions of Dollars)	Degree of Financial Services Activity				
				Banking	Credit Cards	Insurance	Real Estate	Securities
American Express	$30.0	$8.1	$581	None domestic	High	Moderate	Low	High
BankAmerica	122.5	4.0	451	High	High	Low	High	Moderate
Citicorp	130.0	5.2	723	High	High	Low	High	None
Merrill Lynch	20.7	5.0	309	None	Low	Moderate	Moderate	High
Prudential-Bache	76.5	18.5	2,130	None	Low	High	Moderate	High
Sears, Roebuck	36.0	30.0	861	Low	High	Moderate	Moderate	High

ers grew disenchanted with their historical investments. They took money out of passbook savings, borrowed on insurance policies, cashed in whole-life insurance policies, and stopped leaving free credit balances with brokers.

Deregulation—legislated and de facto—gave rise to a slew of investment alternatives, and computers and 800 telephone numbers made it possible to buy them easily and cheaply. Faced with these changing consumer preferences, bankers, insurers, and brokers are being compelled to find new revenues and profits centers.

There is plenty to be had. Americans spent $200 billion for financial services in 1983, and the suppliers of these services earned an estimated $42 billion—a mouth-watering 25 percent margin. Moreover, consumers have some $4 trillion in financial assets. The potential for consumer financial business and profits, says Vice Chairman John Reed of Citicorp, is "larger than corporate banking."

While they're already on the scene, the financial services supercompanies still haven't evolved into the final form, or forms, they will take. For one thing, legal barriers still hinder the entry into some businesses. Banks are barred from insurance (except for credit policies), from investment banking, and from interstate branching. Securities brokers that own investment banking operations are barred from banking. (To compare their activities in key areas see the Table). Moreover, since there hasn't been a model supercompany to learn from, no one is sure what combinations of businesses will prove to be the winning ones.

It is generally agreed, however, that the learning experience is going to be expensive. The financial giants are already sinking wads of money into marketing, product development, and technology—$1 billion just for automated teller machines (ATMs), for example. Citicorp's Reed estimates that to mount an ad campaign in an effort to establish a national image, a company must spend $60 million a year. Yet money alone won't guarantee success. The companies will also need a sharply defined strategy and a savvy organization to execute it.

The upcoming battle over their investment dollars is good news for consumers. They will be swamped with an avalanche of new products and services. ATMs, central assets accounts, such as Merrill Lynch's Cash Management Account, and universal life insurance are just the first wave.

Source: Adapted from "The Supercompanies Emerge," by Arlene Hershman. Reprinted with the special permission of *Dun's Business Month* (formerly Dun's Review), April 1983. Copyright 1983, Dun & Bradstreet Publications Corporation.

financial intermediaries
Specialized financial firms that facilitate the transfer of funds from savers to those who need capital.

but not enough savings to initiate the investment process (we call these deficit economic units "borrowers") is facilitated by **financial intermediaries.** Financial intermediaries include commercial banks, savings and loan associations, credit unions, pension funds, life insurance companies, and mutual funds. These intermediaries aid the capital allocation process in several ways.

By way of explanation, let's consider an economy devoid of financial intermediaries. Further, let's assume that a businesswoman, Ms. Rossi, has discovered a cure for the common cold but requires $400,000 to obtain the proper productive assets for manufacture and distribution of the product. She must find someone with savings to invest in her project.[2]

Ms. Rossi has several problems if no financial intermediaries exist. First, she must find someone with savings. Through family and friends, she finds a saver, Mr. Chapman. Ms. Rossi's problems are not over, however. In persuading Mr. Chapman to invest, Ms. Rossi will encounter several obstacles. First, Mr. Chapman may not have enough savings to cover the entire $400,000 investment. Therefore Ms. Rossi must search for more investors. Second, Mr. Chapman realizes that by putting all of his money into a single project, he is facing more risk than he would if he diversified by investing in several projects.[3] With this higher risk Mr. Chapman may require a greater return than Ms. Rossi wishes to pay. Third, Mr. Chapman may need to withdraw his funds for retirement or a financial emergency before the project is completed, causing refinancing problems for Ms. Rossi. Any or all of these problems—search for investors, divisibility of savings (a saver may wish to invest more or less than a project requires), risk (which will drive up the investor's required return), and liquidity—may end the investment project before it begins. We see, then, that if productive investments cannot be financed, economic growth could stagnate.

In a developed economy such as our own, many of the problems encountered by entrepreneurs like Ms. Rossi are alleviated by financial intermediaries. Of course, not all transactions, even in a complex, developed economy, require the services of an intermediary. Transfers of capital between savers and those who need funds can take place in three different ways, as diagrammed in Figure 3–1:

1. *Direct transfers* of money and securities may be made without intermediaries.

2. Transfers may take place through an **investment banking house,** such as Merrill Lynch, Pierce, Fenner & Smith, which serves as a middleman and facilitates the issuance of securities. Although they may serve as financial intermediaries in many respects, investment bankers

investment banking house
Financial firm that underwrites and distributes new investment securities and that helps businesses obtain financing.

---

[2]For the purposes of our example, the investment may be in the form of either an equity share or a loan.

[3]We discuss diversification and how it reduces risk in Chapter 16.

Figure 3-1
Diagram of the Capital Formation Process
There are three traditional ways of transferring capital between savers and those who
need funds. Direct transfers without intermediaries are possible, but lack efficiency and
security. Investment banking houses serve as intermediaries in indirect transfers, and thus
technically do not create their own financial claims. Financial intermediaries actually
create new financial products by transferring savers' funds to borrowers through such
instruments as mortgages, stocks, and bonds. They then issue their own securities, such
as checking and savings accounts, mutual fund shares, and life insurance policies, to the
saver.

1. Direct Transfers

2. Indirect Transfers through Investment Bankers

3. Indirect Transfers through a Financial Intermediary

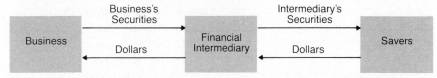

are technically not intermediaries since they do not create their own
financial claims.

3. Transfers may occur through a *financial intermediary,* such as a bank
or mutual fund, which obtains funds from savers and then issues its
own securities in exchange. Intermediaries literally transform money
capital from one form to another, which increases general market efficiency.

Direct transfers between businesses and savers are possible and do
occur on occasion, but it is generally more efficient for a business to
obtain the services of a specialized financial institution called an investment banking house. Merrill Lynch, Dean Witter, and E. F. Hutton are examples of investment banking houses. Such organizations (1)
help corporations design securities with the features that will be most
attractive to investors, (2) buy these securities, and then (3) sell them
to savers in the primary markets. Thus the investment bankers are *mid-
dlemen* in the process of transferring capital from savers to businesses.

The financial intermediaries shown in the third section of Figure 3-1 do more than simply transfer money and securities between firms and savers—these intermediaries literally create new financial products. For example, an individual saver may not have the capital or the inclination to finance a new home mortgage for a borrower. A loan of this type would be quite risky since the borrower could default and since, once the loan was made, the savings that were lent could not be withdrawn and would not be repaid for many years. However, a saver who deposits money in a savings and loan association is actually making an indirect loan to a home buyer. By opening a savings account instead of loaning money as an individual, the saver enjoys several advantages: he or she does not have to evaluate borrowers, the money is available on demand, and it is insured, within limits, by a government agency. Thus intermediaries repackage the original financial claims of borrowers into financial claims on the intermediary. Financial obligations of intermediaries are also called "indirect securities," since they represent a rearrangement of the borrower's original promise to pay into one that is more compatible with the needs of the saver. These indirect claims include checking accounts, mutual fund shares, money market accounts, passbook savings, and life insurance policies.

Additionally, the cost of the intermediary's funds to the borrower will be lower than if a direct loan from the original saver could have been negotiated. Since intermediaries are generally large institutions, they gain economies of scale in analyzing the creditworthiness of potential borrowers, in processing and collecting loans, and in pooling risks and thus helping individual savers avoid "putting all their financial eggs into one borrower's basket." These factors allow intermediaries to lend at lower rates than could individual savers. Further, intermediaries are better able to attract funds, since a system of specialized intermediaries can enable savings to do more than just draw interest. Thus people can put money into banks and get both interest and a convenient way of making payments (checking), put money in life insurance companies and get both interest and protection against early death, and so on.

In the United States and other developed nations, a large set of specialized, highly efficient financial intermediaries has evolved. The following are the major classes of intermediaries:

1. Commercial Banks. These are the traditional "department stores" of finance, serving a wide variety of savers and those with needs for funds. Historically, the commercial banks have been the major institutions that handled checking accounts and through which the Federal Reserve System expanded or contracted the money supply; today, however, some of the other institutions that will be discussed also provide checking services and significantly influence the effective money supply. Since commercial banks and the Fed play such an important role in the overall economy, their functions are discussed separately in Chapter 4.

2. Savings and Loan Associations (S&Ls). Generally serving individual savers and residential mortgage borrowers, S&Ls take the savings of many small savers, then lend the money to home buyers and other types of borrowers. The savers are provided a degree of liquidity that would be absent if they bought the mortgages or other securities directly. Therefore one major economic function of the S&Ls is to "create liquidity" which would otherwise be lacking. Also, the S&Ls have more expertise in analyzing credit, setting up loans, and making collections than individual savers could possibly have; hence the S&Ls reduce the cost and increase the feasibility of making real estate loans. Finally, they hold large, diversified portfolios of loans and other assets and thus spread risks in a manner that would be impossible if small savers were making direct loans. Because of these factors, savers benefit by being able to invest their savings in more liquid, better managed, and less risky accounts, while borrowers benefit by being able to obtain more capital, and at lower costs, than would otherwise be possible.

3. Mutual Savings Banks. These operate primarily in the northeastern states, accept savings primarily from individuals, and lend mainly on a long-term basis to home buyers and large corporations. Mutual savings banks are very similar to S&Ls.

4. Credit Unions. These are cooperative associations whose members have a common bond such as being employees of the same firm. Members' savings are loaned only to other members, generally for automobile loans and the like.

5. Pension Funds. These are retirement plans funded by corporations or government agencies for their workers and administered primarily by the trust departments of commercial banks or by life insurance companies. Pension funds invest primarily in bonds, stocks, mortgages, and real estate.

6. Life Insurance Companies. These take savings in the form of annual premiums, then invest the funds received in stocks, bonds, real estate, and mortgages, and, finally, upon the deaths of the insured parties, make payments to their beneficiaries.

7. Mutual Funds. These are corporations that accept dollars from savers and then use these dollars to buy stocks, long-term bonds, or short-term debt instruments issued by businesses or government units.

mutual fund
Corporation that invests the
pooled funds of savers, thus
obtaining economies of scale in
investing and reducing risk by
diversification.

money market fund
A mutual fund that invests in
short-term, low-risk securities
and that allows investors to write
checks against their accounts.

**financial service
corporations**
Institutions whose services
include a wide variety of financial
operations, usually including
banks, S&Ls, investment
banking, insurance, pension
plans, and mutual funds.

These organizations pool funds and thus reduce risks by diversification. They also gain economies of scale, which lower the costs of analyzing securities, managing portfolios, and trading in stocks and bonds. Different **mutual funds** are designed to meet the objectives of different types of savers. Hence we have bond funds for those who desire safety; stock funds, whose owners are willing to accept significant risks in the hope of very high returns; and still other funds that are used much the same as interest-bearing checking accounts (the **money market funds**). There are literally hundreds of different mutual funds with dozens of different goals and purposes.

The financial institutions have been heavily regulated, with the major purpose of this regulation being to insure the safety of the institutions for the protection of their savers. However, this regulation—which has taken the form of prohibition of nationwide branching, restrictions on the types of assets the institutions can buy, ceilings on the interest rates they can pay, and limitations on the types of services they can provide—has tended to impede the free flow of capital from surplus to deficit areas and thus has hurt the efficiency of our capital markets. Recognizing this fact, Congress has authorized some significant changes, and more will be coming along.

The major result of the developing changes is a blurring of the distinctions among the different types of institutions. Indeed, the trend in the United States today is toward huge **financial service corporations,** which own banks, S&Ls, investment banking houses, insurance companies, pension plan operations, and mutual funds and which have branches across the country and, indeed, around the world. Sears, Roebuck is, interestingly, one of the largest financial service corporations. It owns Allstate Insurance, Dean Witter (an investment banking firm), Coldwell Banker (the largest real estate brokerage firm in the United States), a huge credit card business, and a host of other related businesses. Other major companies, most of which started in one area and have now diversified to cover the full financial spectrum, include Transamerica, Merrill Lynch, American Express, Citicorp, and Bank-America.

The Stock Market

As has been noted, secondary markets are the markets where outstanding, previously issued securities are traded. By far the most active market—and the one of most importance to financial managers—is the *stock market*. It is here that the price of each stock, and hence the value of a business firm, is established. Since the primary goal of financial management is to contribute to the maximization of the firm's stock price, a knowledge of the market in which this price is established is clearly essential for anyone involved in managing a firm.

The Stock Exchanges

There are two basic types of stock markets—the **organized security exchanges,** which are typified by the **New York Stock Exchange (NYSE)** and the **American Stock Exchange (AMEX),** and the less formal **over-the-counter markets.** Since the organized exchanges have actual physical market locations and are easier to describe and understand, we shall consider them first.

The organized security exchanges are tangible, physical entities. Each of the larger ones occupies its own building, has specifically designated members, and has an elected governing body—its board of governors. Members are said to have "seats" on the exchange, although everybody stands up. These seats, which are bought and sold, represent the right to trade on the exchange. In 1968 seats on the NYSE sold at a record high of $515,000, but in 1979 they sold for as little as $40,000. They were back up to $210,000 in 1982, and the price had risen to $360,000 in March 1984.

Most of the larger investment banking houses operate *brokerage departments* that own seats on the exchanges and designate one or more of their officers as members. The exchanges are open on all normal working days, with the members meeting in a large room equipped with telephones and other electronic equipment that enable each bro-

**organized security
exchanges**
Formal organizations having
tangible, physical locations and
conducting auction markets in
designated ("listed") securities.

**New York Stock Exchange;
American Stock Exchange**
The two major U.S. security
exchanges.

over-the-counter markets
All facilities that provide for
trading in unlisted securities—
those not listed on the organized
exchanges.

The trading floor of the New York Stock Exchange is the central location where registered members of the exchange meet to buy and sell shares for customers.
Courtesy of the New York Stock Exchange, Edward C. Topple, photographer.

kerage house member to communicate with the firm's offices throughout the country.

Like other markets, security exchanges facilitate communication between buyers and sellers. For example, Merrill Lynch, Pierce, Fenner & Smith (the largest investment banking firm) might receive an order in its Atlanta office from a customer who wants to buy 100 shares of General Motors stock. Simultaneously E. F. Hutton's Denver office might receive an order from a customer wishing to sell 100 shares of GM. Each broker communicates by wire with the firm's representative on the NYSE. Other brokers throughout the country are also communicating with their own exchange members. The exchange members with *sell orders* offer the shares for sale, and they are bid for by the members with *buy orders*. Thus the exchanges operate as *auction markets*.

Special procedures are available for handling large blocks of securities. For example, if General Motors, whose stock is already listed on the NYSE, plans to sell a new issue of stock, the exchange has facilities that make it easier for the market to absorb the new issue. Similarly, if a large mutual fund or pension fund wants to sell a large block of a listed stock, procedures are available that facilitate the sale without putting undue pressure on the stock price.

The Over-the-Counter Market

In contrast to the organized security exchanges, the over-the-counter market is a nebulous, intangible organization. An explanation of the term over-the-counter will help clarify exactly what this market is. The exchanges operate as auction markets—buy and sell orders come in more or less simultaneously, and the exchanges are used to match these orders. But if a stock is traded less frequently, perhaps because it is the stock of a new or a small firm, few buy and sell orders come in, and matching them within a reasonable length of time would be difficult. To avoid this problem, brokerage firms maintain an inventory of the stocks. They buy when individual investors wish to sell, and sell when investors want to buy. At one time the inventory of securities was kept in a safe, and when bought and sold, the stocks were literally passed over the counter.

Today over-the-counter markets are defined as all facilities that provide for security transactions not conducted on the organized exchanges. These facilities consist primarily (1) of the relatively few dealers who hold inventories of over-the-counter securities and who are said to "make a market" in these securities and (2) of the thousands of brokers who act as agents in bringing these dealers together with investors. The dealers who make a market in a particular stock will, upon request, quote a price at which they are willing to buy the stock (the **bid price**) and a price at which they will sell shares (the **asked**

bid price
The price a dealer or specialist in securities will pay for a stock.

price). The spread between bid and asked prices represents the dealer's markup, or profit.

In terms of numbers of issues, the majority of stocks are traded over-the-counter. However, because the stocks of larger companies are listed on the exchanges, it is estimated that two-thirds of the dollar volume of stock trading takes place on the organized security exchanges.

asked price
The price at which a dealer or specialist in securities will sell shares of stock out of inventory.

Some Trends in Security Trading Procedures

From the NYSE's inception in the 1800s until the 1970s, the vast majority of all stock trading occurred on the Exchange and was conducted by member firms. The Exchange established a set of minimum brokerage commission rates, and no NYSE member firm could charge a commission lower than the set rate. This was a monopoly, pure and simple. Finally, in the 1970s, the **Securities and Exchange Commission (SEC),** with strong prodding from the Antitrust Division of the Justice Department, forced the NYSE to abandon its fixed commissions. Commissions declined dramatically, falling in some cases as much as 80 percent from former levels. These changes were a boon for the investing public but not for the brokerage industry. A number of brokerage houses went bankrupt, and others were forced to merge with stronger firms. Many Wall Street experts predict that, once the dust settles, the number of brokerage houses will have declined from literally thousands in the 1960s to perhaps 20 large, strong, nationwide companies, all of which are units of diversified financial services corporations.

Securities and Exchange Commission (SEC)
The U.S. Government agency that regulates the issuance and trading of stocks and bonds.

Stock Market Reporting

Information on transactions both on the exchanges and in the over-the-counter market is available in daily newspapers. We cannot delve deeply into the matter of financial reporting—this is more properly the field of investment analysis—but it is useful to explain the basics of the stock market reporting system.

Table 3-1 represents a section of the stock market page for stocks listed on the NYSE taken from a daily newspaper published on January 25, 1983. For each stock listed it provides specific data on the trading that took place on the previous trading day, January 24, 1983, as well as other, more general information. Similar information is available on stocks listed on the other exchanges and on stocks traded over-the-counter. Stocks are listed alphabetically from AAR Industries to Zurn Industries; the data in Table 3-1 were taken from the top of the page. The two columns on the left show the highest and lowest prices at which the stocks have sold during the year; AAR, the first company shown, has traded in the range from 10⅛ to 5¾ (or $10.125 to $5.75) during the past 52 weeks. The figure just to the right of the company's

Table 3-1
Stock Market Transactions, January 24, 1983

52 Weeks High	Low	Stock	Div.	Yld. (%)	P/E Ratio	Sales (100s)	High	Low	Close	Net Change
10⅛	5¾	AAR	.44	4.9	21	31	9¼	8⅝	9	− ⅜
38	27½	ACF	2.76	8.4	6	108	33¾	32⅝	32¾	−1¼
24⅛	12¼	AMF	1.36	8.1	5	464	16⅞	16⅜	16¾	− ¼
25¾	9¼	AMR Cp		…	…	2372	20⅝	18½	20⅝	+1¼
12⅜	3½	AMR wt		…	…	939	9⅜	8	9⅜	+ ¾
17⅞	12¾	AMR pf	2.18	12.0	…	108	17¾	17⅝	17⅝	…
5⅛	2½	APL		…	18	20	3⅝	3½	3½	− ⅛
38	23½	ARA	2	5.9	10	109	35⅝	33¾	34⅛	−1⅜
79⅞	24½	ASA	3.00	4.3	…	2607	70¾	67	69¾	−3
26⅞	12	AVX	.32	1.5	33	207	21¾	21¼	21⅜	−2
41⅝	26	AbtLab	.84	2.1	17	1307	39⅝	38¾	39¼	− ½

abbreviated name is the dividend; AAR had a current indicated dividend rate of $0.44 per share and a dividend yield (which is the dividend divided by the stock price) of 4.9 percent in 1983. Next comes the ratio of the stock's price to its annual earnings (the P/E ratio), followed by the volume of trading for the day; 3,100 shares of AAR stock were traded on January 24, 1983. Following the volume come the high and the low prices for the day and then the closing price. On January 24 AAR traded as high as $9.25 and as low as $8.625, and the last trade was at $9.00. The last column gives the change from the closing price on the previous trading day. AAR was down ⅜ (or $0.375), so the previous close must have been 9⅜ (since $9⅜ − ⅜ = $9.00, the indicated closing price on January 24). Essentially the same information is given for stocks that are traded on the other exchanges and in the over-the-counter markets.

The stock market page also provides financial quotations for other equity instruments. AMR Corporation (a holding company that was formerly known as American Airlines, Inc.) has quotations for its common stock and two other securities. The first security is a warrant that allows the purchaser to obtain one new share of AMR's common stock for $14 per warrant. These warrants expired on April 1, 1984. We shall discuss the use of warrants in equity financing in Appendix A of Chapter 18. AMR's other equity issue is its preferred stock. Preferred stock is discussed in detail in Chapter 17.

Bond Markets

Corporate bonds are traded much less frequently than common stock, and over 95 percent of the bond trading that does occur takes place in the over-the-counter market. The reason is that, unlike stocks, most bonds are owned by and traded among the large financial institutions (for example, life insurance companies and pension funds, which deal in very large blocks of securities). It is relatively easy for the over-the-counter bond dealers to arrange the transfer of large blocks of bonds among the relatively few holders of the bonds. It would be impossible to conduct similar operations in the stock market among the literally millions of large and small stockholders.

Information on bond trades in the over-the-counter market is not published. However, a representative group of bonds is listed by the bond division of the NYSE and is traded on that exchange. Information on NYSE bond trades is published daily, and it reflects reasonably well the conditions in the larger over-the-counter market.

Table 3-2 gives a section of the bond market page in the January 25, 1983, issue of the *Wall Street Journal* reporting trading on January 24, 1983. A total of 1,230 issues were traded on that date, but we show only the bonds of Alabama Power Company. All of Alabama Power's bonds had a par value of $1,000—this is how much the company borrowed and how much it must someday repay. Looking at the first bond listed, we see that there is a 9 just after the company's name to

Table 3-2
NYSE Bond Market Transactions, January 24, 1983

Company	Coupon Rate	Maturity Year	Current Yield	Volume	High	Low	Close	Net Change
AlaP	9	2000	12.	2	74	74	74	− ¼
AlaP	8½	01	12.	2	70	70	70	−1
AlaP	7¾	02	12.	35	65⅝	63	63	−3¼
AlaP	8⅞	03	13.	12	69¾	69⅛	69⅛	−2¾
AlaP	8¼	03	12.	1	66½	66½	66½	−1½
AlaP	9¾	04	13.	20	75⅞	75⅞	75⅞	−1⅛
AlaP	10⅞	05	13.	2	86½	86½	86½	+1½
AlaP	8⅞	06	13.	6	69⅛	69⅛	69⅛	−2
AlaP	8¾	07	13.	2	69	69	69	− ¼
AlaP	9½	08	12.	27	76¼	75	76¼	+ ⅞
AlaP	9⅝	08	13.	18	74⅜	74	74	…
AlaP	12⅝	10	13.	35	97	96⅞	96⅞	− ⅛
AlaP	15¼	10	14.	25	109	108	108⅛	−1⅜
AlaP	14¾	91	14.	18	106⅞	106½	106½	− ¼
AlaP	17⅜	11	15.	45	118	116⅛	116⅛	− ⅞

Notes:
1. This listing contains only those Alabama Power bonds that were actually traded on the NYSE on January 24, 1983. The company has a total of 38 separate bond issues; however, only those listed above were traded on January 24.
2. Of the Alabama Power bonds traded on January 24, 1983, all the bonds had 30-year maturities except the 14¾s of 1991, which were issued in 1981 with a 10-year maturity.

coupon rate
The stated rate of interest on a
bond.

indicate that the bond is of the series that pays 9 percent interest; thus
0.09($1,000) = $90 of interest per year.[4] Nine percent is defined as the
bond's **coupon rate**. The *2000* indicates that the first bond must be repaid in the year 2000; it is not shown in the table, but this bond was
issued in 1970 and hence had a 30-year maturity when it was issued.
The *12* in the fourth column is the bond's current yield, which is defined as the annual interest payment divided by the closing price of
the bond: current yield = $90/$740 = 12 percent approximately. Only
two of the 9s of 2000 were traded on January 24, 1983. The prices
shown are expressed as a percentage of par, so the high, low, and
close of 74 mean the price of the bond remained unchanged for the
day at $740 (74 percent of $1,000 par). As with the common stock, the
net change refers to the change in price from the closing price on the
previous trading day.

Alabama Power has been growing, and it has been selling bonds
almost every year to finance its growth. As we see in Chapters 5 and
17, interest rates vary over time, and companies generally set their coupon rates at levels that reflect the "going rate of interest." If rates were
set lower, investors simply would not buy the bonds, and the company
could not borrow the money it needed. The fact that the coupon rates
shown in the table rise as we move down the list indicates the general
rise in interest rates after 1970.

Bond prices reflect how much investors are willing to pay for bonds,
given their riskiness, as well as the interest they pay and interest rates
available elsewhere in the economy. Alabama Power's 9s of 2000 were
worth $1,000 when they were issued in 1970, but people were not will-
ing to pay $1,000 in 1983 for a bond that would provide only $90 of
interest per year when $1,000 would buy a newer bond that would pay
$120 or $130 of interest annually. Thus the 9s of 2000 had fallen in price
from $1,000 in 1970 to $740 in 1983 because competitive interest rates
had risen.

Regulation of Security Markets

The operations of investment bankers, exchanges, and over-the-
counter markets are regulated by the Securities and Exchange Commission (SEC) and, to a lesser extent, by each of the 50 states. Certain rules
apply to new securities, whereas others apply to securities traded in
the secondary markets:

1. **Elements in the Regulation of New Issues by the SEC:**
   a. The SEC has jurisdiction over all interstate offerings to the public
   in amounts of $500,000 or more.

---

[4]The Alabama Power bonds, like most in the United States, pay interest semiannually;
therefore the company would send a check for $45 each six months to the holder of one
of the 9s of 2000.

b. Securities must be registered at least 20 days before they are publicly offered. The registration statement provides financial, legal, and technical information about the company. A prospectus summarizes this information for use in selling the securities. SEC lawyers and accountants analyze both the registration statement and the prospectus, and if the information is inadequate or misleading, the SEC will delay or stop the public offering.

c. After the registration has become effective, the securities may be offered if accompanied by the prospectus. Preliminary or "red herring" prospectuses may be distributed to potential buyers during the 20-day waiting period.

d. If the registration statement or prospectus contains misrepresentations or omissions of material facts, any purchaser who suffers a loss may sue for damages. Severe penalties may be imposed on the issuer, its officers, directors, accountants, engineers, appraisers, underwriters, and all others who participated in the preparation of the registration statement.

2. Elements in the Regulation of Outstanding Securities:

a. The SEC regulates all national securities exchanges. Companies whose securities are listed on an exchange must file reports similar to registration statements with both the SEC and the stock exchange and must provide periodic reports as well.

b. The SEC has control over corporate **insiders.** Officers, directors, and major stockholders of a corporation must file monthly reports of changes in their holdings of the stock of the corporation. Any short-term profits from such transactions are payable to the corporation.

insiders
Officers, directors, and major stockholders of a company who might be able to take advantage of their positions to profit in their company's stock at the expense of other stockholders.

c. The SEC has the power to prohibit manipulation by such devices as pools (aggregations of funds used to affect prices artificially) or wash sales (sales between members of the same group to record artificial transaction prices).

d. The SEC has control over the proxy machinery and practices.

e. Control over the flow of credit into security transactions is exercised by the Board of Governors of the Federal Reserve System. The Fed exercises this control through the **margin requirements,** which stipulate the maximum percentage of the purchase price of a security that can be borrowed. If a great deal of margin borrowing has been going on, then a decline in stock prices can result in inadequate coverage, which forces the stockbrokers to issue "margin calls," requiring investors either to put up more money or to have their margined stock sold to pay off their loans. Such forced sales further depress the stock market and can set off a downward spiral. To prevent this, the Fed controls the volume of margin borrowing.

margin requirement
The maximum percentage of the purchase price of a security that can be borrowed.

3. State Regulations:

a. States have some control over the issuance of new securities within their boundaries. This control is usually exercised by a "Corporation Commissioner" or similar official.

Blue Sky Laws
State laws that prevent the sale
of securities that have little or no
asset backing.

b. State laws relating to security sales are called **"Blue Sky Laws"** because they were put into effect to keep unscrupulous promoters from selling securities that offered the blue sky but actually had little or no asset backing.

In general, government regulation of securities trading is designed to insure that investors receive information that is as accurate as possible, that no one artificially manipulates (that is, drives up or down) the market price of a given stock, and that corporate insiders do not take advantage of their position to profit in their companies' stocks at the expense of other stockholders. Neither the SEC nor the state regulators can prevent investors from making foolish decisions or from having "bad luck," but they can and do help investors obtain the best data possible for making sound investment decisions.

Market Efficiency

Over the last decade and a half, financial research has centered on the question of capital market efficiency. These studies of efficiency have been concerned with how effectively stock prices reflect value. Efficiency in this context refers to the ability of stock prices to (1) react quickly to new information and (2) reflect, at any point in time, all available information regarding the securities.

efficient capital market
Market in which securities are
fairly priced in the sense that the
price reflects all publicly available
information on each security.

Requirements for an **efficient capital market** are relatively few and realistic in today's investment world. First and perhaps foremost, there must be a reasonably large number of profit-seeking individuals engaged in security analysis who operate independently of one another. Second, the investors should have quick and full access to any news regarding present and potential investments. Announcements of new information will be disseminated as soon as the news breaks; thus new information will come to the market in a random fashion. Finally, the efficient market hypothesis assumes that investors are rational in that they will act quickly to adjust security prices in light of new information.

One of the critical requirements for an efficient market is the free flow of reliable information to analysts and investors. The SEC and other government agencies have labored to insure that accurate information is quickly disseminated and that no special interest group is able to profit from special access to nonpublic information. The vast majority of academic studies, found in summary form in most textbooks on security analysis, agree that our financial markets, while not perfect, are very efficient. An efficient market is therefore one in which security prices adjust rapidly to new information, reflecting all available information including the risk associated with a particular security. Thus, in an efficient market securities will be priced to reflect the risk involved, with higher-risk issues providing the larger expected return.

Figure 3-2
Risk and Expected Returns on Different Classes of Securities
The risk/return trade-off in our financial markets is shown in this figure. An investor willing
to invest in the most risky security, common stock, has the potential to earn the highest
rate of return. Investing in the least risky security, Treasury bills, will provide the lowest
return. This risk/return trade-off hypothesis has been empirically demonstrated in a study
of a 50-year period by Ibbotson and Sinquefield.

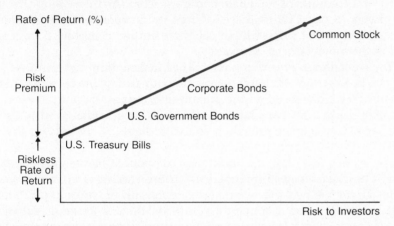

The risk/return trade-off is depicted in Figure 3-2, which is based on
a study of risk and return covering a 50-year period.[5] The securities
with the least risk (Treasury bills) were found to have furnished the
lowest return, while the class of securities with the most risk—common
stock—provided the highest return.[6] Thus both through the efforts of
several government agencies to provide accurate financial information
quickly and through the competition provided by many analysts, the
financial markets appear to be efficient indeed.

Summary

Financial markets exist in a dynamic economy because the investment
opportunities and the savings of individual economic units are seldom
equal. Since few economic units are fully self-supporting, financial
markets must transfer savings from surplus units to deficit units that
have productive investment opportunities.

Financial intermediaries facilitate the transfer of funds from savers to

---

[5]Roger G. Ibbotson and Rex A. Sinquefield, *Stocks, Bonds, Bills, and Inflation: The Past
(1926–1976) and the Future (1977–2000)* (Charlottesville, VA: Financial Analysts Research
Foundation, 1977).
[6]A word of caution is probably necessary at this point. Remember that this and other
studies were based on past data for many securities over long periods of time. A selected
high-risk security may not provide superior returns over any time period. After all, if
high-risk securities *always* provided the highest returns, there would be no risk.

firms and individuals who need capital. Financial intermediaries perform several services, including (1) bringing savings and deficit units together and (2) reducing the saver's risk by converting the ultimate borrower's financial promises into the intermediary's own financial claims, which are more consistent with the saver's requirements for investment amount, risk (including liquidity), and return.

For business firms retained earnings represent corporate savings from year to year. When these savings are insufficient for investment needs, corporations must either sell more equity or borrow from lenders in the money or capital markets.

The capital market is the market wherein long-term debt and equity capital is acquired. Although some direct financing exists, most transactions take place on either the organized exchanges or in the over-the-counter market. Primary market sales raise new capital, and sales in the secondary market provide a source of liquidity for current investors.

The money market is the short-term component of our financial system. The chief financial intermediary in this market is the commercial bank. In the next chapter we investigate the role of banks in our financial system. We also examine the role of the Federal Reserve System in its attempt to control the economy by manipulation of the money supply, principally through the banking system.

Small Business $ $ $ $ $ $ $ $ $

Risk Capital for Growth Businesses

The public markets for common stock and debt provide massive amounts of funds to larger businesses. Small businesses do not ordinarily have access to those markets for funds, however. In order to sell an issue of common stock in the public equity markets successfully, several conditions have to be met. For one, the issue must be large enough to capture the attention of the markets; otherwise it is likely to be ignored. The size of the issue also has an effect on the marketability of the stock. Investors buying common stock in public mar-

kets can expect to be able to sell their stock with little delay because the stock is liquid. A very small issue would have only a limited market, would experience little trading, and would therefore be difficult for an investor to sell quickly.

Second, information about the firm must be available. Because many small firms seeking funding for the first time have no historical track record of sales and earnings for evaluation by potential investors, it is difficult for investors to determine a fair value for the shares. Furthermore, much of the information that management does have is important to the company's competitive position in the industry and cannot be released without jeopardizing the company's prospects for success. As a result, a large part of the information needed by the public cannot be made available by management.

Third, it must be possible for investors to make reasonable analyses of the riskiness of the firm. The rewards for making a successful investment in a small firm can be enormous; the annals of small firms contain many stories in which an investor or entrepreneur invested a few thousand dollars that led in a few years to a payoff in the millions. High returns, however, are usually accompanied by high risks. An investment in a small firm, and especially a new small firm, is likely to be very risky. Analysis of each investment therefore requires great care and expertise in order to avoid making a series of investments in firms that fail. The general public is not equipped to make such evaluations.

For the above reasons, the public debt and equity markets do not supply adequate risk capital to support the development of new small businesses. An industry known as the **venture capital** industry has been developed to fill the void and to supply both capital and managerial expertise to growth businesses. The venture capital industry does not supply capital to all small businesses, however. Venture capital firms try to limit their investments to firms that are likely to grow to a very profitable size, eventually selling their stock in a public market or perhaps being acquired by a public corporation.

The venture capital industry consists of firms that manage a substantial amount of capital for other investors or perhaps for larger firms, such as banks, that own the venture capital firms. Some venture capital firms are private partnerships or corporations with limited ownership that obtain funds from a variety of private sources and manage those funds for a fee. Others are public companies. Whether public, private, or captive (owned by another firm), the venture capital firms are run by experienced managers who are able to evaluate very risky investment prospects. Some of the venture capital firms specialize in investments in start-up companies; others refuse to invest in any venture that has not already established a record of sales and earnings. Many of the venture capital firms specialize in certain industries. For example, some invest only in energy-related companies and others limit their investments to high-technology companies.

The venture capital industry has grown from an industry with $2 billion under investment in 1970 to an industry that by 1980 had almost $11 billion under investment.[1] This extraordinary growth has been associated in part with the development of the microelectronics industry and with promising technologies in the medical and biological fields. The needs for risk capital have increased greatly, and with them have come outstanding opportunities for high returns on the part of venture capital investors. The result has been a huge increase in the availability of venture capital to support American industry. In fact, many of the newer members of the venture capital industry have themselves been successful managers of companies funded by venture capital firms. They eventually became wealthy when their firms went public and they invested their funds in yet other small companies.

venture capital
Risk capital supplied to small companies by wealthy individuals, partnerships, or corporations, usually in return for an equity position in the firm.

[1]"The Growth of an Industry: Venture Capital, 1977–1982," *Venture Capital Journal*, October 1982, 6–11.

A Venture Capital Company: Sevin Rosen Partners

Sevin Rosen Partners illustrates the workings of a venture capital firm very well. The company is a partnership formed by L. J. Sevin, the former chief executive officer of Mostek, Inc., and Ben Rosen, a well-known figure in the electronics industry. Having raised $25 million in funds from a combination of families, corporations, insurance companies, a foundation, and a university endowment, they began operations in 1981. Because of its founders' backgrounds, Sevin Rosen has tended to specialize in high-technology businesses, particularly in the electronics field, and has emphasized investment in start-up ventures and in firms working with emerging technologies.

Sevin Rosen has been unusual among venture capital firms in that a number of its investments have proven themselves, either successfully or unsuccessfully, very quickly. For example, three of the firm's best-known investments have been in Compaq Computer Corporation, Lotus Development Corporation, and Osborne Computer Corporation. Sevin Rosen invested $727,000 in Compaq, a firm that manufactures portable computers that are compatible with the IBM personal computer as a start-up venture in the spring of 1982. It is common for a venture capital firm to make an initial investment and later increase its investment if the firm progresses well. Accordingly, in the fall of 1982, Sevin Rosen added another $1,200,000 to its investment in Compaq as a co-investor in Compaq's $8,500,000 second-round financing. Then, in the fall of 1983, when Compaq went public with an offering of $100 million in common stock, Sevin Rosen profited very handsomely from its investment.

Sevin Rosen also invested in a computer software company, Lotus Development Corporation, that has been one of the greatest success stories in this young field. Lotus developed a package called 1-2-3 that lets the user build financial models, develop graphs quickly, and manage data. Sevin Rosen invested $590,000 in the firm at the start-up stage in the spring of 1982, followed up with an investment of $1,500,000 in late 1982, and saw the company go public in August 1983 with an offering of $35 million. Although Lotus's success was no greater than Compaq's, it was truly remarkable for a software company to achieve such a high value in such a short time.

With such a record of success, it may appear that venture capital is indeed an attractive business. But with such high returns, there is usually great risk. A third investment made by Sevin Rosen was in Osborne Computer Corporation. Osborne developed the first portable personal computer and grew from a new company to an annual sales level of nearly $100 million in just two years. Sevin Rosen invested $300,000 in the firm in the summer of 1982, but in the summer of 1983, Osborne filed for bankruptcy. Sevin Rosen has likely lost all of its investment in Osborne, illustrating that very high returns do indeed entail very high risks.

Like most venture capital firms, Sevin Rosen contributes more than money to its portfolio companies. The venture investor firms will frequently put a member on the board of directors of the company in which it has made a substantial investment, and the venture firm will frequently assist the company in locating management personnel or scientific talent. The venture firm thus takes on the role of advisor to the small business and may provide very useful advice and experience.

In order to find four or five attractive investment opportunities each year, a firm like Sevin Rosen may review literally hundreds of business plans a year from prospective companies. The experience the venture capitalists usually have is extremely valuable in sorting out attractive investments from those that are likely to fail. Even with their careful analysis and years of experience, the venture capitalists will make numerous investments in which all or part of the investment is lost. In fact, it has been estimated that of all venture capital investments made in the decade of the 1970s, 40 percent of them were partial or total losers. Venture capital is indeed risk capital.

Resolution to Decision in Finance

NYSE versus AMEX versus OTC: A Bitter Triangle

In their competition for companies, both the NYSE and the AMEX place strong emphasis on the advantages of listing with an organized exchange. They point to the national market and the high visibility that their operations can offer. The NYSE also likes to emphasize the prestige that accompanies a listing on the Big Board.

The NYSE is always on the prowl for new listings and has been quite successful in luring companies away from the AMEX and the over-the-counter market. Among the big names it has attracted are Anheuser-Busch from the OTC and Carnation from the AMEX. In an attempt to become even more competitive, the NYSE asked the Securities and Exchange Commission to lower the eligibility standards for listing on the Big Board. This would make it easier for young, fast-growing companies to join.

The AMEX is pursuing an equally ambitious strategy in its search for new listings. Feeling pressured by both the NYSE and the OTC, the AMEX decided it had to distinguish its services from those of its competitors. Thus it bills itself as the market for mid-sized growth companies that have matured enough to benefit from the prestige and visibility of listing on an organized exchange. The AMEX tries to appeal to companies that believe they are too big for the OTC but too small to compete with the crowd on the Big Board.

The OTC seems to be winning the contest, however. Between 1978 and 1983, the number of OTC companies grew by 50 percent while the rosters of the AMEX and the NYSE shrank. Much of the OTC's growth was attributable to a booming new issues market and the development of automated trading. OTC dealers once set prices using the scant information on "pink sheets," which recorded the previous day's price action. But today, thanks to the Automated Market System, dealers can quickly obtain up-to-the-minute data on the last price and trading volume of the 682 most active OTC stocks. Automation had vastly improved communication within the network of OTC dealers and greatly facilitated trading. As a result, many companies that in the past might have moved on to the NYSE or the AMEX now stick with the OTC.

The LIN Broadcasting Corporation is one of the companies that prefers the OTC. LIN's board of directors listened patiently to the NYSE's presentation but remained unimpressed. They were put off by the Exchange's bureaucracy and the high penalties it charged for delisting. Furthermore, they felt that the OTC provided a better marketplace for growth companies like their own. They briefly considered the AMEX but decided that it had little more to offer than the NYSE.

Adapted from "NYSE vs AMEX vs OTC: A Bitter Triangle," *Financial World*, January 11–24 1984, pp. 16–19.

Key Terms You should be able to define each of the following terms:

Securities	Bid price; asked price
Money market; capital market	Securities and
Primary market; secondary market	Exchange Commission (SEC)
Financial intermediary	Coupon rate
Investment banking house	Insiders
Mutual fund; money market fund	Margin requirement
Financial service corporation	Blue Sky Laws
Organized security exchanges; NYSE; AMEX	Efficient capital market
	Venture capital
Over-the-counter market	

Questions

3-1 What would happen to the standard of living in the United States if people lost faith in the safety of our financial institutions? Explain.

3-2 How does a cost-efficient capital market hold down the prices of goods and services?

3-3 In what way does the secondary market contribute to the efficient functioning of the primary market?

3-4 What is the financial intermediary's primary role in our economy?

3-5 What are the most important services provided by financial intermediaries?

3-6 What would happen to required rates of return if no financial intermediaries existed?

Problems

3-1 Look up IBM's common stock in the *Wall Street Journal* or another appropriate financial publication.
  a. On what exchange is the stock listed?
  b. What is the dividend per share based on the latest quarterly payment?
  c. What is the stock's dividend yield?
  d. What is the price/earnings ratio based on the closing price and the most recent 12 months' earnings?
  e. Based on the P/E multiple, what is the most recent 12 months' earnings for the firm?
  f. How many shares were sold on the trading day you investigated?
  g. How much did the stock's price rise or fall from the close of the previous day's trading?
  h. Is the stock's closing price closer to the stock's high or low for the year?

3-2 Look up General Motors Acceptance Corporation's bonds in the *Wall Street Journal* or another appropriate financial publication. The firm's bonds are identified by "GMA" in the *Wall Street Journal*'s bond listings. Specifically, answer the following questions based on GMA's 8⅞ percent bond.
  a. On what exchange is the bond listed?
  b. In what year will the bond mature?
  c. How much interest will the investor receive during the year?
  d. If an investor purchased the bond at the end of the trading day, what price would be paid?
  e. What was the bond's price at the close of the previous day's trading?
  f. Was the bond selling above, below, or at par?
  g. If General Motors Acceptance Corporation were to sell a new issue of bonds, approximately what coupon rate would be required for the issue to sell at par?

Selected References

There are several excellent texts on financial markets and the role of financial intermediaries. They include:

Gup, Benton E., *Financial Intermediaries: An Introduction*, 2nd ed. (Boston, MA: Houghton Mifflin, 1980).

Gurley, John G., and Edward S. Shaw, *Money in a Theory of Finance* (Washington, DC: Brookings Institution, 1960).

Kidwell, David S., and Richard L. Peterson, *Financial Institutions, Money, and Markets,* 2nd ed. (Hinsdale, IL: Dryden Press, 1984).

Light, J. O., and William L. White, *The Financial System* (Homewood, IL: Irwin, 1979).

Van Horne, James C., *Financial Market Rates and Flows*, 2d ed. (Englewood Cliffs, NJ: Prentice-Hall, 1984).

Many texts describe the stock and bond markets. One excellent text is:

Reilly, Frank K., *Investments* (Hinsdale, IL: Dryden Press, 1982).

The Commercial
Banking System

4

Decision in Finance

The Perils of Paul: Volcker's Scary Choices

Paul A. Volcker is Chairman of the Federal Reserve Board. When he
delivers one of his semiannual reports before the Senate Banking Committee, it's standing room only. Reporters grab all the seats, while
bankers, bond traders, and lobbyists stand for hours along the sides
and back of the hearing room.

Since becoming Chairman of the Fed in 1979, Volcker has built him-
self an imposing power base. He has also been a constant source of
controversy. In May 1983 he seemed to have little chance of being reappointed to his job as Chairman. But less than a month later, due to a
combination of political and economic events, Volcker seemed more
indispensable than ever.

Although President Reagan would have preferred to name his own
person to run the Fed, pressure from both at home and abroad made
it clear that only Volcker—or someone with the same views—would be
acceptable to the financial markets. Unable to find another candidate
of equal stature, President Reagan reappointed Volcker for four more
years, much to the relief of Fed watchers.

As you read this chapter, think about the kinds of decisions that Paul
Volcker and the Fed's Board of Governors must make. How do the
Fed's decisions and policies affect our economy? Why might the Fed's
choices be considered scary?

See end of chapter for resolution.

In the previous chapter we evaluated the role of financial intermediaries, especially those who serve to channel long-term funds from ultimate lenders to ultimate borrowers. As important as these intermediaries are, if the single most important group of financial intermediaries were to be identified, it would be the commercial banking system. Unlike the financial intermediaries discussed in Chapter 3, commercial banks tend to lend for periods of one year or less, although they also provide intermediate-term loans of from three to five years, and in some cases even longer.

Beyond a discussion of the commercial banking system's role as a critical component in providing needed financing for business, this chapter emphasizes the attempts of the Federal Reserve System (Fed) to regulate the economy, which it does largely through the banking system. We therefore review the tools available to the Fed for influencing the availability and cost of money and credit in the national economy.

The Banking System

The commercial banking system is the largest of all financial intermediaries. In fact, the financial assets of the banking system are almost as large as the assets of all other financial intermediaries combined. Furthermore, the bulk of all deposits in our financial system reside in commercial banks.

Banks have become, especially after the Depository Institutions Deregulation and Monetary Control Act of 1980, virtual financial supermarkets, offering wide ranges of savings certificates, IRA and Keogh retirement plans, trust and leasing departments, and, of course, a wide variety of short- and medium-term loans for individuals, businesses, and state and federal governments. Banks are also important providers of mortgage loans.

Nevertheless, banks probably enjoy their lofty status in our financial system not so much because of the above-mentioned impressive array of services, but rather because of two other very important factors. First, the commercial bank is important to the economy because demand deposits are money, and the bank can create demand deposits through the extension of credit in the form of loans. Recently other financial intermediaries have gained the right to expand money and credit, but these efforts are *quite* limited when compared to the banking system. Second, banks are important because the Federal Reserve System works principally through the banking system to affect the money supply and thus interest rates.

Table 4-1
Balance Sheet of a Typical Commercial Bank

Assets		Liabilities and Capital	
Cash	11.3%	Demand deposits	20.8%
Investments	23.8	Savings deposits	15.2
Loans	58.2	Time deposits	36.5
Other assets	6.7	Borrowed funds	18.3
Total assets	100.0%	Other liabilities	2.9
		Capital	6.3
		Total liabilities and capital	100.0%

Sources and Uses of Bank Funds

A review of a typical commercial bank's balance sheet (see Table 4-1) provides information regarding the sources of bank funds and the uses to which those funds are put.[1]

Demand deposits, at one time the major source of bank funds, are deposits made by individuals, businesses, and government units that are available on demand, usually through a check. Thus demand deposits are the major source of liquidity for all economic units.

Today the most important source of bank funds is savings and time deposits. *Passbook savings accounts* are deposits evidenced by entries in a passbook. Although banks retain the legal right to require 30 days' notice of withdrawal, they seldom insist on advance notice, allowing funds to be withdrawn on demand. In fact, a recent variation of the passbook account, the **NOW (Negotiable Order of Withdrawal) account** allows withdrawals by check.

A **certificate of deposit (CD)** is a receipt for funds deposited in an institution for a specified time and interest rate. Generally, the interest rate on CDs increases with the term to maturity. Certificates of deposit were known but not widely used until Citibank of New York announced in 1961 that it would issue CDs in negotiable form. The negotiability feature allows the funds to be utilized before maturity. These CDs were specifically designed to attract business funds and other deposits in large denominations beginning at $100,000. Other, much smaller-denomination certificates are available to individuals and other small savers. Unlike the larger $100,000 CDs, these savings certificates are not redeemable prior to maturity.[2]

demand deposits
Noninterest-bearing transaction deposits at commercial banks that are available on demand, usually through a check.

NOW (Negotiable Order of Withdrawal) account
A form of savings account that allows withdrawal by check.

certificate of deposit (CD)
A time deposit evidenced by a negotiable (for large-denomination CDs, generally $1 million or more) or nonnegotiable (usually denominations under $100,000) receipt issued for funds left with the financial institution for a specified period of time; rates of interest generally depend on the amount of deposit and time to maturity.

---

[1]Although this presentation of the items that comprise a bank's balance sheet is not technical, some readers may wish to refer to Chapter 6, Examining a Firm's Financial Data, before continuing with this chapter.
[2]If a saver must redeem a certificate, the interest rate paid reverts to the passbook level less an early-withdrawal penalty, generally three months' interest.

Industry Practice

Why So Many Banks Go Belly Up

A financial thunderbolt struck the tiny farm community of Danvers (pop. 920) in west-central Illinois one Friday. The First National Bank of Danvers, the only bank in town, with 2,560 accounts and about $11 million in deposits, was declared insolvent by federal authorities and shut down until new owners could reopen it under another name. That same day 2,000 miles away, the Oregon Mutual Savings Bank in Portland also closed its doors before being taken over by an Idaho holding company. The bank had seen its net worth fall nearly 20 percent in just six months.

Bank failures used to come in isolated outbreaks. During the 1960s and 1970s, they averaged fewer than ten a year. But despite the stronger-than-expected economic recovery, they are now occurring at a worrisome rate. In 1983, across the United States, more than one bank a week was failing.

Many banks are now teetering on the brink of collapse. Recently, the Federal Deposit Insurance Corporation listed 540 "problem" banks, ranging from small state-chartered ones with too many weak agricultural loans to nationally chartered banks with bad business loans. Among the 540 the FDIC secretly lists dozens as likely to fail unless they are soon merged with healthier financial institutions. Says John Downey, chief national bank examiner for the Comptroller of the Currency: "The number is the highest I've ever seen it."

No longer does a bank failure result in angry customers milling outside locked doors, or widows and orphans being stripped of their life savings. Closings have become so routine that agencies like the FDIC perform them with robot-like precision. Typically, authorities move in after business hours on Friday and freeze accounts. By the following Monday, they have either paid off the depositors or allowed another bank to assume control.

Part of the blame for the rising number of failures belongs to the recession that occurred in the early 1980s and its complement of bankruptcies and defaulted loans. But increasingly, the problems are due to poor bank management.

Some examples involve mismanagement or the failure to make a move at the right time. Two weeks before First National Bank of Danvers failed, its officers filed a suit against former President Terry Winterland, claiming he had made loans without adequate collateral. The collapse of the United American Bank of Knoxville, Tennessee in February 1983 resulted in the closing of five other financial institutions. The FDIC identified in these six financial institutions bad loans totaling hundreds of millions of dollars. The banking authorities alleged that many of the loans had been made to family friends, relatives, and business associates. In far fewer cases bank failure involves criminal misconduct, such as intentional fraud or dishonesty, by bank officials.

Bank failures are one effect of the growing deregulation of financial institutions. Since interest rate ceilings on savings deposits were lifted in

1982, banks have been cut off from easy sources of cheap money and have had to increase sharply the rate of return they pay on deposits. In addition, deregulation has made banking more competitive. In California, the number of banks has surged from 242 four years ago to 387. They must now also compete with such firms as Shearson/American Express, Merrill Lynch, and Prudential-Bache, which offer accounts that operate much like the savings and checking accounts once offered only by banks. With everyone striving for more business, risks grow and profit margins shrink.

A banker's job has not been made any easier by rapid and unpredictable changes in the economy. Banks that gambled on interest rates going down when they actually went up find themselves paying out more for de-posits than they are charging for loans. Real estate investments turned sour after mortgage rates hit 17.5 percent; oil and gas deals fell apart when energy prices dropped. Other loans that looked profitable when the rate of inflation was expected to be running at 15 percent became disasters when the rate dropped below 5 percent and stayed there.

Despite the hard times and high risks, the number of new commercial banks being started still outnumber failures 10 to 1. A bank is still a good place to make money.

Source: Adapted from "Why So Many Banks Go Belly Up" by Alexander L. Taylor III, *Time,* August 29, 1983, p. 47. (Copyright 1983 Time Inc. All rights reserved. Reprinted by permission from *Time.*)

In addition to deposits, banks may choose to finance a part of their assets with borrowed funds. A portion of these borrowings may be from the Federal Reserve System itself. As we shall see, however, banks are restricted as to the purpose and term of loans from the Fed. Therefore a large proportion of bank borrowing takes place in the **federal funds market.** The federal funds market essentially involves a bank with excess reserves lending funds to a bank that has a temporary need for reserves.

A bank's **capital account** is similar to a business firm's net worth or common stock equity account. This account reveals the owners' contribution to the bank's financing, both through the purchase of the common stock and through the undistributed profits which are retained by the bank. One should note that the total assets of the bank less all liabilities equals the bank's capital.

The bank's capital provides a cushion to protect depositors from losses. Losses to banks generally occur from loans that cannot be repaid or from poor investments. These losses cannot be borne by depositors (customer deposits are liabilities to the bank), so they are charged against the bank's capital. Thus if a bank had 25 percent capital, up to 25 percent of the bank's loans could be uncollectible and there would still be sufficient funds to pay depositors. Of course, banks do not have capital accounts equaling 25 percent of assets. The

federal funds market
The market in which depository institutions lend reserve funds among themselves for short periods of time.

capital account
The account that represents a bank's total assets less its liabilities.

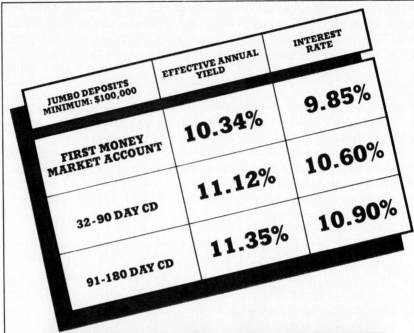

JUMBO DEPOSITS MINIMUM: $100,000	EFFECTIVE ANNUAL YIELD	INTEREST RATE
FIRST MONEY MARKET ACCOUNT	10.34%	9.85%
32-90 DAY CD	11.12%	10.60%
91-180 DAY CD	11.35%	10.90%

FIRST RATE JUMBOS

Y our jumbo deposits deserve jumbo rates. And that's exactly what you'll get at The First National Bank of Chicago.

Our Jumbo CDs give you a wide variety of maturity dates, as well as a guaranteed rate for the term you select.

A First Money Market Account offers you high rates and access to your cash—by check, or through any Cash Station or CIRRUS® automatic teller machine.

Just call The First Team at 1-800-828-SAVE (in Chicago call 732-1981).

FMMA interest compounded daily for actual days on a 365-day basis. 91 to 180-day CD interest compounded quarterly on a 365-day basis; yield shown assumes interest added to principal quarterly. Effective annual yield for 32-day CD shown; yield assumes interest added to principal at maturity. (Yields for 33-90 day CDs will be lower, minimum 11.02%.)

Rates effective through 8/10/84 and subject to change weekly. A substantial interest penalty is required for early withdrawal from CDs.

FIRST CHICAGO
The First National Bank of Chicago

Member FDIC

To attract business deposits, banks offer such lures as guaranteed high interest rates and various maturity dates for "jumbo" deposits of $100,000 or more.

Source: Courtesy of The First National Bank of Chicago. Prepared by Foote, Cone & Belding.

typical commercial bank has only 6 to 7 percent of its assets financed by the capital account. Thus the traditional banker's conservatism is well founded since loans or investments can decline by only 6 to 7 percent before the bank becomes insolvent. This low level of bank capitalization has also led banking to be among the most regulated of all industries.

On the left-hand side of the balance sheet, the first asset one encounters is cash. Actually the account includes more than just vault cash. Part of the **cash account** includes "items in process of collection," which is the value of checks drawn on other banks but not yet collected. The cash account also includes funds that are required by law to be kept on deposit at the district Federal Reserve Bank.

Of the three components of the cash account, actual cash kept at the bank for daily transactions would be the smallest in size for most banks. First, banks are able to maintain relatively small amounts of vault cash since normal transactions generally result in approximately the same amount of cash deposits as cash withdrawals. Second, like other businesses, banks wish to keep their funds invested in productive, high-return assets. Excess cash is therefore channeled into more productive loans and investments.

A second use of funds is the purchase of securities for investment purposes. These securities are required by law to be of the highest investment quality. Typically, the majority of these securities are issued by the state and other political subdivisions in the bank's geographic area. U.S. Treasury securities also account for a large proportion of the bank's investment portfolio.

Investments provide a rate of return for a bank, but that is not their principal role. Banks are required by law to hold reserves equal to a certain percentage of their deposits. These required reserves must be kept as vault cash or as deposits at the district Federal Reserve Bank. The bank's investment portfolio serves to provide liquidity in case more required reserves are needed. The investments must be of high quality so that they may be converted into cash quickly, with little chance of loss. The primary responsibility of banks is to lend money in support of economic growth in their area. Fortunately, loans also represent an investment of funds with the highest rate of return. If there is not enough demand for loans or if the quality of demand is low, however, banks turn to investment in securities as a source of revenue.

Banks are the major source of short-term credit for the business sector. Historically, banks have preferred to make "self-liquidating" loans. In our agrarian past a farmer would borrow money to buy seed and upon harvest repay the loan with the proceeds of the crop's sale. A modern equivalent of a self-liquidating loan would be a merchant's borrowing to increase inventory before Christmas. After Christmas the merchant repays the loan from the proceeds of the holiday sales. These short-term loans were the historical rule for banks because their pri-

cash account
The account that represents a bank's vault cash and funds required to be kept on deposit with the Federal Reserve.

mary source of funds was short-term demand deposits. However, with the greater proportion of funds now coming from time and savings deposits, banks are increasingly willing to provide intermediate, 3- to 7-year term loans. Some loans, such as real estate loans, are for even longer periods.

Approximately 80 to 85 percent of a bank's revenue is generated from interest on loans. Much of the remainder accrues from investment in state, local, and federal government securities. Service charges and earnings on other assets provide the smallest source of revenue for the bank.

Demand Deposit Creation

In the United States the most important form of money is demand deposits, not currency. This means that commercial banks are at the heart of the nation's financial system. This status is not due simply to their role as conservators of the financial system's demand deposits, but rather to the banking system's ability to create money.

As we shall see later in this chapter, the Fed requires a bank to maintain a stated portion of its demand, time, and savings deposits on reserve at the Fed or in vault cash. This means, of course, that the bank is not required to keep the remaining deposited funds at the bank and that therefore these funds may be lent to others. For example, if the overall reserve requirement were 25 percent, a $1,000 deposit would result in a required reserve of $250 against the deposit liability. However, $750 of the deposit is considered to be excess or free reserves, and may be lent or invested by the bank. It is through its loans and secondarily through its investments that the bank makes a profit.

By lending excess reserves banks create money. Assume for a moment that there are currently no excess reserves in the banking system and that the Fed's reserve requirement for deposits is 15 percent.[3] Suppose further that a customer deposits $1,000 in the bank. For that single transaction the bank's balance sheet would be increased by $1,000:

Assets		Liabilities	
Reserves	$1,000	Customer deposits	$1,000

However, since the bank must maintain only 15 percent of the deposit as required reserves, $850 represents excess reserves. Since banks are in business to make a profit, they will wish to lend the money. Of course, the bank does not lend cash; rather it simply credits the ac-

---

[3]Actually, reserve requirements depend on the size and type of deposits at a commercial bank. See Table 4-3 for a more complete explanation.

count of the borrower with $850. Thus the bank has created money through the granting of the loan, and its balance sheet would appear as follows:

Assets		Liabilities	
Reserves	$1,850	Customer deposits	$1,850

This is the first stage of a potentially large deposit-expansion process. At each stage in the process, both total loans and total deposits for the banking system increase by an amount equal to the excess reserves before the loans were made. The increase in required reserves based on the deposit expansion of $850 is $128. Thus:

Total reserves gained from initial deposit		$1,000
Required reserves for initial deposit	$150	
Required reserves for first loan	$128	
Excess reserves after first loan		$ 722

Now these excess reserves of $722 may be lent to another customer seeking to borrow from the bank.

When the borrowed funds are used for purchases, the borrower will write a check that may be deposited in another bank. However, the movement of excess reserves from one bank to another will not end the expansion process in the system. Whichever bank receives the deposit also acquires an equal amount of reserves, of which all but 15 percent will be "excess." In theory this process can continue through several stages until there are no excess reserves remaining.

The process of deposit expansion is presented in Table 4-2. It is theoretically possible for the commercial banking system to expand the original $1,000 deposit into $5,667 in loans, since banks need to maintain only 15 percent of each deposited dollar in reserves. We can determine the maximum possible expansion in deposits by using the following ratio:

$$\text{Total deposit expansion} = \frac{\text{Initial excess reserve}}{\text{Reserve requirement}}.$$

In our example:

$$\text{Total deposit expansion} = \frac{\$1,000}{.15} = \$6,667,$$

which includes the $5,667 in loans and the initial $1,000 deposit.

Table 4-2
Deposit Expansion—Commercial Banking System

	New Loans	Reserves Required	Reserves Excess	Total Demand Deposit
New demand deposit: $1,000		$ 150	$850	$1,000
Expansion stage: 1	$ 850	128	722	1,850
2	722	108	614	2,572
3	614	92	522	3,186
4	522	78	444	3,708
5	444	67	377	4,152
6	377	57	320	4,529
7	320	48	272	4,849
8	272	41	231	5,121
	.	.	.	.
	.	.	.	.
	.	.	.	.
Final stage of expansion	$5,667	$1,000	$ 0	$6,667

Realistically, however, several factors prevent the full limit of credit expansion. First, if customers decide to keep portions of their newly created demand deposits in the form of cash rather than in the bank, there will be less available excess reserves to lend. Second, the bank may decide, as a matter of policy, to keep some excess reserves in the bank in case of unexpected contingencies. These excess reserves would be invested in high-quality, short-term marketable securities. These securities, often called **secondary reserves**, provide the bank with both income and liquidity. Third, the bank may have excess reserves that it wishes to lend but cannot find sufficiently qualified borrowers. Any or all of these factors create "leakages" that reduce the deposit-expansion potential within the commercial banking system.

secondary reserves
Excess reserves invested by banks in marketable securities.

The Federal Reserve System

Federal Reserve System
The central banking system in the United States; the chief regulator of the banking system.

Since commercial banks are at the center of the nation's financial system, a number of regulatory agencies have been developed to control the banking system and its ability to create credit. The most important of these agencies is the **Federal Reserve System.** The Fed attempts to influence the ability of banks to create credit (and hence influence the money supply) principally by increasing or reducing the reserves available to the banking system. Later in the chapter we shall review the three major tools that the Fed may use to exercise control over reserves.

Organization and Structure

The Federal Reserve Act of 1913 allowed the country to be divided into 12 Federal Reserve Districts. The districts' operations are conducted through a Federal Reserve Bank located in each district. These banks are located in Boston, New York, Philadelphia, Cleveland, Richmond, Atlanta, Chicago, St. Louis, Minneapolis, Kansas City, Dallas, and San Francisco. Branches of the district banks are located in 24 additional cities.

The real decision-making authority in the Federal Reserve System is given to its **Board of Governors** in Washington, DC. The seven members of the Board are appointed by the President and confirmed by the Senate. Even so, the framers of the Federal Reserve Act wished to keep the Board as free from political influence as possible. For example, the seven Board members are appointed for terms of fourteen years, and their terms are arranged so that one expires every two years. Thus it would, in theory, take a president almost a full two terms to appoint a majority to the Board. However, resignations or deaths can create a faster turnover on the Board. For example, President Carter appointed five members of the Board in slightly more than three years. Thus, although the Fed has legal independence from the executive and legislative branches of government, great influence is still exerted on the Fed's policies by the political sector of our government.[4]

Another component of the Federal Reserve System is the organization of member banks. All national banks are legally required to be members of the System. Additionally, approximately 10 percent of all state banks voluntarily joined the Federal Reserve System. One reason that more state banks did not join the System is that the Fed's reserve requirements were generally higher than the state-imposed reserve requirements. The **Depository Institutions Deregulation and Monetary Control Act of 1980** opened the Fed's services to all depository institutions for a fee. The same legislation removed the impediment of differing state and federal reserve requirements. After an initial phase-in period, the reserve requirements will be the same for all depository institutions regardless of membership in the Federal Reserve System.

Another important element of the Federal Reserve System is the **Federal Open Market Committee (FOMC),** which has responsibility over **open-market operations.** Open-market operations are the purchase and sale of U.S. Government securities conducted through the Federal Reserve Bank of New York. As we shall see, open-market operations

Board of Governors of the Federal Reserve System
Seven-member decision-making authority of the Fed.

Depository Institutions Deregulation and Monetary Control Act of 1980
Act that eliminated many of the distinctions between commercial banks and other depository institutions.

Federal Open Market Committee (FOMC)
Committee of the Federal Reserve System that has responsibility over open-market operations.

open-market operations
The purchase and sale of U.S. Government securities.

---

[4]Even though the designers of the Fed attempted to shield it from political influence, it is difficult to believe the members of the Board of Governors are immune to political pressures. After all, Nixon designed plays for then Redskins coach George Allen; and it's an even bet that "the Gipper" will provide Joe Gibbs with some "strategy" before one of their terms in office is over.

are the most effective monetary tool available to the Fed. Thus the FOMC is at the heart of the Fed's power. It consists of twelve members: the seven members of the Board of Governors and representatives from five of the twelve Federal Reserve District Banks. One of the five is always the president of the Federal Reserve Bank of New York, since this bank is responsible for the transaction of the open-market operations. The other four members rotate among the presidents of the remaining eleven Federal Reserve Districts.

Tools of Monetary Policy

The Board of Governors of the Federal Reserve System cannot dictate its monetary objectives to the banking system. However, by affecting reserves in the system, it influences the money supply and hence interest rates.[5] The principal tools of control are: changes in the reserve requirements, changes in the discount rate, and open-market operations. Reserve requirements refer to the percentage of each type of deposit that deposit institutions must hold as reserves. Discount policy refers to the terms under which deposit institutions may borrow from the Fed. Open-market operations involve the purchase or sale of U.S. Government securities.

Reserve Requirements

The Federal Reserve System requires all depository institutions to hold reserves against their deposits. The way in which these reserves are determined changed in February 1984. Previously, for example, banks were required to compute their reserve positions based on a weekly average determined from average deposits two weeks earlier. Because of the delay, the system was called the "lagged reserve requirement."

required reserves
The minimum reserves that a bank must hold as vault cash or reserve deposits with the Federal Reserve.

Under the new system, called the "contemporaneous reserve requirement," the amount of **required reserves** will be based on the two-week average of checking account deposits ending on the second Monday of the period. Banks must settle their reserve requirements every other Wednesday, as before. However, with contemporaneous reserves the maintenance period begins after two days rather than after two weeks as before.

The new system applies only to checking accounts. Other nontransaction deposit accounts continue to have their reserves computed on a lagged basis. Two-thirds of the nation's 40,000 depository institutions are exempt from the contemporaneous reserve requirement owing to their small size. Nevertheless, 96 percent of all checking account deposits will still be covered by the new method.

---

[5]The interrelationship of reserves, money supply, and interest rates is not a simple one and is open to much debate and controversy. The interested reader should refer to any of the many excellent money and banking or economics texts for further details.

Table 4-3
Reserve Requirements of Depository Institutions

Type of Deposit and Deposit Interval (Millions of Dollars)	Member Bank Requirements before Implementation of the Monetary Control Act		Type of Deposit and Deposit Interval	Depository Institution Requirements after Implementation of the Monetary Control Act	
	Percent	Effective Date		Percent	Effective Date
Net Demand			*Net Transaction Accounts*		
$0–$2	7	12/30/76	$0–$28.9 million	3	12/29/83
2–10	9½	12/30/76	Over $28.9 million	12	12/29/83
10–100	11¾	12/30/76			
100–400	12¾	12/30/76	*Nonpersonal Time Deposits*		
Over 400	16¼	12/30/76	*by Original Maturity*		
			Less than 1½ years	3	10/6/83
Time and Savings			1½ years or more	0	10/6/83
Savings	3	3/16/67			
			Eurocurrency Liabilities		
Time			All types	3	11/13/80
$0–$5, by maturity					
30–179 days	3	3/16/67			
180 days to 4 years	2½	1/8/76			
4 years or more	1	10/30/75			
Over $5, by maturity					
30–179 days	6	12/12/74			
180 days to 4 years	2½	1/8/76			
4 years or more	1	10/30/75			

Source: *Federal Reserve Bulletin*, February 1984, p. A7.

It would appear that the reserve requirement could serve as a powerful, direct tool in the management of banks' reserve position. In truth, however, the reserve requirement is seldom used. From 1963 to the implementation of the Monetary Control Act, reserve requirements on demand deposits were changed only five times, and those on savings deposits were changed twice. A summary of reserve requirements as of February 1984 is presented in Table 4-3. Reserve requirements are scheduled to change slowly over the next few years to the levels set by the Monetary Control Act. Note, however, that even after the phase-in period ends there will still be different reserve requirements for large and small institutions, for time and transaction accounts, and for personal and nonpersonal time deposits.

The major tools of the Federal Reserve System are used to influence depository institution reserves. Yet the Fed appears to be less willing to fully utilize a tool that directly changes required reserves. Why? Basically, the Fed's reluctance to use reserve requirements as an active tool of monetary policy stems from the fact that it is too powerful an instrument to be used in "fine tuning" the economy. Consider the effect of an increase in the reserve requirements in a "tight money" period. Even a 1 percent increase in the reserve requirements would increase required reserves by hundreds of millions of dollars. Furthermore, just as we have noted with the multiple expansion of credit when reserves increase, a decrease in excess reserves could further reduce demand deposits by a multiple many times larger than the original 1 percent decline in reserves as banks are forced to call in outstanding loans. Such a radical decline in money and credit would be potentially damaging to the economic system. Thus the potential impact of even a modest change in the reserve requirements makes it a tool that is seldom used by the Federal Reserve System.

The Discount Rate

discount rate
The interest rate charged by the Fed for loans of reserves to depository institutions.

The **discount rate** is the rate of interest that the Fed charges to institutions that borrow reserves. Institutions may find themselves temporarily short of reserves when there has been a large or unexpected shift in reserves, perhaps due to a large withdrawal. Institutions may also borrow from the Fed during times of tight money to relieve temporary reserve imbalances.

It is important to note that the Federal Reserve System views these loans as a temporary mechanism for the adjustment of the specific institution's reserve position. The Fed discourages the use of these funds for profit making. Moreover, these borrowings are considered to be a privilege and not a right. Thus the Fed can and does exert pressure on institutions to curtail their borrowings. While the privilege of borrowing offers a safety valve to relieve temporary strains on reserves, there are strong incentives to repay borrowings quickly. For example, if a particular institution shows a borrowing pattern that is characterized by frequent or continuing indebtedness over an extended period, the Fed may press for repayment, even if it means that the bank must call in some loans or liquidate some investments. Thus banks are reluctant to use the Fed for other than temporary needs. In fact, some banks, particularly large banks, avoid the Fed altogether as a source of temporary credit.

When the Federal Reserve System was established in 1913, the discount rate was considered to be the principal instrument of monetary control authorized by Congress. However, such has not been the case. As Figure 4-1 shows, the discount rate has lagged behind other short-term rates, such as the Treasury bill rate. Obviously, an effective instrument of monetary policy would lead, not follow, market rates.

Even though the discount rate is not the active tool of monetary policy that the Fed's founders envisioned it to be, announcements of changes in the discount rate have an important psychological effect in

Figure 4-1
The Discount Rate and the Treasury Bill Rate, 1975–1983
The Federal Reserve System makes loans to banks to correct temporary imbalances in
their required reserves at a rate of interest known as the discount rate. First envisioned as
a major instrument of monetary control, the Fed's discount rate has proven instead to lag
behind other short-term rates. This figure, for example, shows how the Treasury bill rate
led the discount rate from 1975 to 1983.

Source: *Economic Indicators*, February 1984, 30.

the financial community. Increases in the discount rate are thought to
signal a movement toward tight money policies, for example. If such
an announcement causes financial institutions to become more stringent in loan policies or causes businesses to reconsider expansion
plans, the discount rate, in a roundabout fashion, has done part of
its job.

Open-Market Operations

The ability to change reserve requirements and the ability to change
the discount rate remain important tools of Federal Reserve monetary
policy. However, the infrequency of change in the reserve requirements and the lagging nature of the discount rate indicate that they are
not the most important tools in the Fed's arsenal. The purchase and

sale of U.S. Government securities, called open-market operations, is the most useful instrument of monetary policy available to the Federal Reserve. Unlike changes in the reserve requirements, which could trigger massive changes in bank reserves, securities may be bought and sold in any quantity to fine-tune the economy. Changes in the discount rate may have little effect on bank reserves since a bank may seek funds elsewhere, but open-market operations are an effective means of increasing or decreasing bank reserves since the bank's customers write or receive checks that affect reserves when the securities are bought or sold. Thus open-market operations are effective in changing bank reserves, even if the bank does not directly participate in the securities transaction.

Assume that the Federal Open Market Committee (FOMC) has determined that an expansion in the money supply is desirable to stimulate a depressed economy. The FOMC will direct the Federal Reserve Bank of New York to buy government securities through government securities dealers.[6] The Federal Reserve Bank pays for its purchases with a check drawn on itself. The securities dealer deposits the check in a bank, which now has an increase in excess reserves. It is important to note that this increase in reserves does not take away from the reserves of any other bank; rather it comes from funds that the Fed has created by drawing a check on itself. This action obtains the desired results in two ways. First, as the Fed purchases securities, demand will exceed supply and the price of securities will rise. The increase in price has the effect of reducing the securities' yield.[7] This interest rate effect will spread to other sectors of the financial markets, reducing yields on other interest-bearing securities, including the rates charged for loans. Concurrently, the bank will wish to lend the excess reserves which were generated by the government securities dealer's deposit of the Fed's check. To stimulate borrowing, the bank will further lower the interest rate it charges on loans. Thus the purchase of government securities by the Fed has increased the money supply and put in motion events which will serve to lower interest rates. These lower interest rates will encourage additional borrowing and spending, providing benefit to the depressed economy.

During a period of excessive expansion or inflation, the FOMC will sell securities to reduce bank reserves. Of course, as the supply of securities increases relative to demand, their price will fall, resulting in an increase in interest rates. However, this is only the first stage in the

---

[6]The Fed does not buy or sell securities directly from individuals or banks. The government securities dealers supply the securities to the general public and banks.

[7]The inverse relationship between prices and rates of return will be discussed in Chapter 17.

Fed's attempt to slow economic growth. As the government securities dealers' checks for the purchased securities clear, banks will lose reserves. The effect of reserve deficiencies for individual banks will quickly spread through the banking system. Banks may attempt to replenish reserves by borrowing through the interbank federal funds market. As the demand for excess reserves increases, the rate charged for these funds will increase and these reserves will become less easily obtained. Banks will be forced to sell securities and reduce their loan portfolios to generate needed reserves. The sale of securities by banks along with those sold by the Fed further increases interest rates since an oversupply relative to demand depresses their price. Because banks have fewer excess reserves, the availability of credit is affected, further increasing interest rates. Thus the sale of securities by the Fed reduces the ability of banks to lend to some and results in higher interest rates, which discourages others from borrowing. The resulting reduction in debt-financed spending is desirable for an economy faced with excessive, inflationary expansion.

Summary

This chapter opened with a discussion of financial intermediaries and the services they perform in our economic system. It has concentrated on the largest of all financial intermediaries, the commercial banking system.

The banking system's power to create money via the creation of demand deposits sets banks apart from most intermediaries. The shift in their sources of funds from shorter-duration demand deposits to longer-term time and savings deposits has allowed banks to increase the maturity schedule of their loans. Short-term loans of less than a one-year maturity still dominate the banks' loan portfolios, however.

The Federal Reserve System attempts to monitor the economic health of the nation principally through affecting the reserves of commercial banks. Its central instrument of monetary policy is open-market operations. Purchase of U.S. Government securities by the Fed has an expansionary effect on the money supply, whereas sales of securities has a restraining effect. The Fed does not change the reserve requirements often since open-market operations accomplish the same task without the potentially severe consequences of changes in reserve requirements. Similarly, the Fed does not rely on discount rates as a major instrument of monetary policy. In part, the discount rate is a less effective tool because banks can avoid borrowing at the Fed by borrowing in the federal funds market.

The ability of the Fed to increase or decrease bank reserves is only a part of the equation in the determination of interest rates. In the next chapter we explore how interest rates are determined.

Resolution to Decision in Finance $$

The Perils of Paul: Volcker's Scary Choices

The Federal Reserve System is the most important of the government agencies created to regulate the U.S. banking system. Its purpose is to promote orderly and stable growth in the money supply by regulating commercial banks' ability to create credit. This is a very powerful responsibility because the results of a Fed decision to expand or contract credit extend far beyond the banking community.

The Fed's open-market operations have their first impact on commercial banks' reserves and the prices and yields of U.S. Government securities. But the effects soon spread to other capital markets and eventually influence the markets for goods and services, as well as income, employment, and prices. The Fed's monetary policy must therefore encourage economic expansion without leading to either inflation or recession.

The U.S. economy has grown so complex that this is no simple task, and few experts agree on how it can be best accomplished. In addition, politicians pressure the Fed to find quick and painless fixes for economic problems that actually require long-term—and possibly painful—solutions.

Under Paul Volcker the Fed has dared to make some difficult decisions and enforce some unpopular policies. In an effort to beat inflation, the Fed kept money growth extremely tight from the fall of 1979 until the summer of 1982. Inflation dropped from 11 percent to 5 percent annually, but the economy was benumbed by the high cost of credit. To compensate, the Fed reversed itself and started pumping money back into the economy. Most agree that this paved the way for the stronger than predicted economic recovery of 1983.

Each time the Fed tightens the money supply, there is the threat of recession; and each time it lets the money supply grow, there is the threat of inflation. Managing those two conflicting forces while coping with pressure from politicians whose reelection is tied to the nation's economic health would be a difficult job for anyone.

Sources: "Why the White House Likes Volcker Better Now," *Business Week*, June 27, 1983, 24–25; "Is Inflation Coming Back?" *Fortune*, March 21, 1983, 60–63; "The Perils of Paul: Volcker's Scary Choices," *Fortune*, July 25, 1983, 36–38.

Key Terms You should be able to define each of the following terms:

Demand deposits

NOW account

Certificate of deposit (CD)

Federal funds market

Capital account; cash account

Secondary reserves

Federal Reserve System; Board of
  Governors of the Federal Reserve
  System

Depository Institutions Deregulation
  and Monetary Control Act of 1980

Federal Open Market Committee
  (FOMC); open market operations

Required reserves

Discount rate

Questions

4-1 What are the three principal tools that the Federal Reserve System uses in affecting the nation's money supply?

4-2 When the Fed buys government securities, is it attempting to increase or decrease the money supply?

4-3 Why is the Fed reluctant to use the reserve requirement as an active tool in monetary policy?

4-4 From the standpoint of a commercial bank's balance sheet, evaluate the statement: "One financial unit's asset is another's liability."

4-5 If the primary goal of the financial manager is to maximize shareholder wealth, what is the bank manager's primary goal?

4-6 Why do banks attempt to minimize their investment in excess reserves?

4-7 What are the characteristics of securities that banks would obtain for their investment portfolios?

4-8 Why have banks, among financial institutions, historically been the major suppliers of short-term funds to borrowers?

4-9 What is the importance of the Depository Institutions Deregulation and Monetary Control Act of 1980? (Note: This question requires investigation of sources outside this text.)

Problems

4-1 The Fed sells $5 million in government securities.
  a. Will the money supply expand or contract?
  ✶b. If the reserve requirement is 10 percent, what is the potential increase (decrease) in demand deposits?

4-2 The Fed buys $80 million in government securities.
  a. Will the money supply expand or contract?
  ✶b. If the reserve requirement is 12.5 percent, what is the potential increase (decrease) in demand deposits?

4-3 Obtain the financial statement of a local bank. Compare the bank's balance sheet with that of a manufacturer (or see Carter Chemical Company's balance sheet in Chapter 6). What major differences are apparent?

---

*Refer to Appendix E for check answers to problems with asterisks.

Selected References

Among the many excellent books on banks and banking are:

Crosse, Howard, and George H. Hempel, *Management Policies for Commercial Banks*, 3rd ed. (Englewood Cliffs, NJ: Prentice-Hall, 1980).

Hempel, George H., Alan B. Coleman, and Donald G. Simonson, *Bank Management: Text and Cases* (New York: Wiley, 1983).

Kidwell, David S., and Richard L. Peterson, *Financial Institutions, Markets, and Money*, 2nd ed. (Hinsdale, IL: Dryden Press, 1984).

Ritter, Lawrence S., and William L. Silber, *Principles of Money, Banking, and Financial Markets*, 4th ed. (New York: Basic Books, 1983).

Several important publications are available from the Federal Reserve:

Board of Governors of the Federal Reserve System, *The Federal Reserve System: Purposes and Functions* (Washington, DC: Federal Reserve Board, 1974).

Federal Reserve Bank of New York, *A Guide to Federal Reserve Regulations* (Washington, DC: Federal Reserve Board, 1978).

The federal government also provides banks and other financial institutions with data from a wide variety of sources. Nationally, the best known is:

Board of Governors of the Federal Reserve System, *The Federal Reserve Bulletin* (Washington, DC: Federal Reserve Board, published monthly).

Each Federal Reserve district bank publishes financial data and articles of interest both nationally and regionally.

Interest Rates

Decision in Finance

Who Says the Price Is Right?

At 11:00 A.M. on Wednesday, October 3, 1979 a small group of financial executives from International Business Machines met with investment bankers from Salomon Brothers and Merrill Lynch. Their task was to price the largest public borrowing in corporate history to date. IBM, which had never before issued public debt, was about to offer $500 million in 7-year notes and $500 million in 25-year debentures, for a grand total of $1 billion.

Tension filled the room. IBM was anxious to make a wildly successful debut in the debt markets, but it also wanted to keep its interest rates as low as possible. Salomon Brothers and Merrill Lynch were anxious too. They saw this as a golden opportunity to prove their acumen as investment bankers, but they feared the losses they would suffer if the offering failed.

Adding to the pressure were alarming financial signals: interest rates had been rapidly rising, stock and bond prices had been falling, gold was selling at record highs, and the dollar was sinking in the foreign exchange markets.

As you read this chapter, look for the factors that IBM and its investment bankers should consider as they set the interest rates on the new notes and debentures. Given the uncertainty of the financial climate, should IBM proceed as planned? Why or why not?

See end of chapter for resolution.

interest rate
The price paid by borrowers to lenders for the use of funds.

Interest rates are extremely important to finance, because they are the price paid for borrowing capital (or money). Investors, thus, earn interest on *debt* (money they have loaned to businesses). If, on the other hand, investors have bought *stock* in a business, rather than loaned it money, they expect compensation in another form: dividends and, eventually, capital gains. The factors which affect the supply of and the demand for investment capital, and hence the level of interest rates, are discussed in this chapter.

Interest Rate Determination

As we discuss at length in Chapter 20, the firm's cost of capital is determined by the rate of return required by its investors. That return is dependent, in part, on factors specific to the firm itself: its financing, product innovation, competition, and management skills—to name a few. However, the firm's cost of capital is not determined in a vacuum. The basis for the required return is shaped by market forces: the supply and demand for funds, risks such as inflation, and investor perceptions of the future. The ways in which these economic forces combine to determine the interest rate are analyzed in the following sections.

Production Opportunities and Time Preferences for Consumption

production opportunities
The return available within an economy from investment in productive (cash-generating) investments.

time preferences for consumption
The preferences of consumers for current consumption as opposed to saving for future consumption.

To understand how two fundamental factors, **production opportunities** and **time preferences for consumption,** interact to affect interest rates, consider first an isolated island community where the inhabitants live on fish. They have a certain stock of fishing gear that permits them to survive in reasonably good shape, but they would like to have more fish. Now suppose Mr. Crusoe were to have a bright idea for a new type of fishnet that would enable him to double his daily catch. However, it would take him a year to perfect his design, build his net, and learn how to use it efficiently, and Mr. Crusoe would be likely to starve before he could put his new net into operation. Therefore he might suggest to Ms. Robinson, Mr. Friday, and several others that if they would give him one fish each day for a year, he would return two fish a day during all of the next year. If someone accepted the offer, then the fish which Ms. Robinson or one of the others would give to Mr. Crusoe would constitute *savings;* these savings would be *invested* in the fishnet; and the extra fish caught would constitute a *return on the investment.* Obviously, the more productive Mr. Crusoe thought the new fishnet would be, the higher would be his expected return on the investment and the more he could offer to pay Ms. Robinson or the others for their savings.

In the example we assumed that Mr. Crusoe would be able to pay, and would offer, a 100 percent rate of return—he offered to give back two fish for every one he received. Quite possibly he could have decided to offer only 1.5 fish next year for every one he received this year, which would be a 50 percent rate of return to Ms. Robinson or the other potential savers. Mr. Crusoe might even be able to attract savings for less. For example, Ms. Robinson might be thinking of retirement, and she might be willing to trade fish today for fish in the future on a one-for-one basis. On the other hand, Mr. Friday might have a wife and several children and need his current fish, so he might be unwilling to "lend" a fish today except in exchange for three fish next year. Mr. Friday would be said to have a high *time preference for consumption,* Ms. Robinson a low time preference.

In a more complex society there are many businesses like Mr. Crusoe's, many products, and many savers like Ms. Robinson and Mr. Friday. Furthermore, people use money as a medium of exchange rather than barter with fish. Still, the interest rate paid to savers depends in a basic way on (1) *the rate of return producers can expect to earn on invested capital* and (2) *consumers'/savers' time preferences for current versus future consumption.* Producers' expected returns set an upper limit on how much they can pay for savings, while consumers' time preferences for consumption establish how much consumption they are willing to defer and hence to save at different levels of interest offered by producers.[1]

Industry Practice

The Interest Rate Business Ignores

Real interest rates—market interest rates adjusted for inflation—are for economists the only adequate way of measuring the true cost of borrowing or the actual return that lenders receive on their investment. During a period of inflation, borrowers pay back in cheap dollars. The opposite is true when prices are falling, as they have been doing during the last few months.

Nevertheless, a *Business Week* survey shows that, by and large, business executives react mainly to the nominal, or market, interest rate in making borrowing and investment decisions. Says Stephany Titelbaum, a business forecaster at Crown Zellerbach Corp.: "We look at the nominal rate of interest; only economists look at real interest rates."

One reason nominal rates are more important to business is that they are more understandable. "The real interest rate is too sophisticated a con-

---

[1]The term "producers" is really too narrow. A better word might be "borrowers," which would include home purchasers, people borrowing to go to college, or even people borrowing to buy autos or to pay for vacations, in addition to business borrowing.

cept," says Colorado real estate developer William H. Schechter. "Businessmen need something they can hack."

Complex Calculations

Moreover, the severity of the past recession has made short-term market rates more important than real ones. With their balance sheets still fragile and cash flow still squeezed, executives are forced to concentrate on market, not real, rates to keep their companies afloat. As Robert S. Miller, Jr., executive vice-president for finance at Chrysler Corp., puts it: "The nominal rate is the one you have to pay."

Executives also downplay real rates because there is so much confusion even among economists on how to measure them. Economists at Brown Bros. Harriman & Co., for example, calculate real long-term rates by deducting the past year's change in prices from the long-term nominal interest rate. Thus they subtract 4% inflation from the rate on 20-year Treasury bonds, which yields a real rate of about 7%.

But most economists say that such an approach is wrong. The correct inflation adjustment, they argue, is the rate of price increases expected over the life of the security. "People buying long-term bonds are not interested in the next year's inflation," notes Alan Greenspan of Townsend-Greenspan & Co. "What's relevant is the next 20 to 30 years' inflation."

Forecasting inflation for the next 20 to 30 years is obviously risky. Almost all executives expect inflation to accelerate. But they differ widely on exactly how much it will speed up. A major Western oil company, for ex-

ample, thinks inflation will spurt to 6% by next year. That is the figure many corporations are using for intermediate and long-term forecasts, according to Joel Popkin, a Washington consultant who helps companies forecast their costs and prices. Crown Zellerbach, however, sees inflation moving up to 7% by 1985. And Westinghouse Electric Corp. is even more pessimistic, forecasting that inflation will average approximately 10 percent annually over the next 10 years.

"I'm Lost"

Such different inflation forecasts produced wildly different estimates of real rates, ranging from 4.5% to a mere 0.5%. And many executives are wary about long-run inflation forecasts anyway. Says John S. Blue, treasurer for Frontier Airlines, Inc.: "Anything beyond a year or two is pure speculation."

Getting a fix on the short-term real rate is easier. Yields on three-month Treasury bills are a bit higher than 8.5%. Deducting an inflation rate of around 2.5%—which is commonly expected over the next 90 days or so—leaves a real rate of 6%, well above the historic norm of 3%. But corporate officers, frustrated by how wrong inflation forecasts have been in the past, have doubts about predicting even a few months out. Says one executive: "There are too many scenarios you can build into this thing. I'm lost."

Figure 5-1 graphs the production/consumption situation in a sup-
ply/demand framework. Savers will save more if producers offer higher
interest rates on savings, and producers will borrow more if savers will
accept a lower return on their savings. There is an equilibrium rate, k*,
which produces a balance between the aggregate supply of and demand for capital in the economy. The term **k*** is often called the **real
rate of return** on savings, or the *real rate of interest*.

The real rate, k*, is not static—it changes over time, depending on
conditions. For example, if a major technological breakthrough occurs
and raises the rate of return on producers' investment, then the "investment" curve in Figure 5-1 will shift to the right, causing both k*
and S* = I* to increase. Similarly, if consumers' attitudes change and
they become more thrifty, the "savings" curve will shift to the right,
causing k* to decline but S* = I* to increase.

real rate of return (k*)
The real, default-free rate of
interest that produces a balance
between the supply of and
demand for capital.

Figure 5-1
Supply of and Demand for Savings
This figure shows how the supply/demand system works to determine the real rate of
interest (k*) on savings. The investment curve indicates that borrowers (producers) will try
to attract more savings from savers as interest rates decrease. Conversely, the savings
curve shows that savers will try to save more only as interest rates increase. These
conflicting desires of savers and borrowers come together at some equilibrium point, k*
(called the "real rate of interest"), creating a balance between supply of and demand for
savings. At that point savings will equal investment (S* = I*).

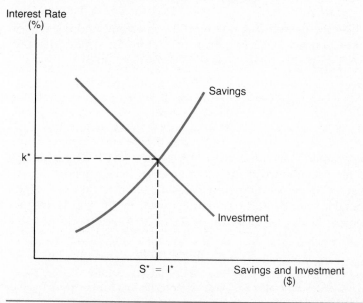

Default Risk

The risk that a borrower will not pay the interest or principal on a loan, or that the borrower will go into *default*, also affects the interest rate built into the transaction: the greater the **default risk,** the higher the interest rate lenders charge. Treasury securities have no default risk; hence they carry the lowest interest rates in the United States.[2] Corporate bonds are ranked from AAA, which is the rating for the very strongest of companies, down to D, which is applied to a company that is already in bankruptcy; the higher the **bond rating,** the lower its risk and consequently its interest rate. Here are some representative interest rates on long-term bonds during January 1984:[3]

U.S. Treasury	11.75%
AAA	12.20
AA	12.71
A	13.13
BBB	13.65

The difference between the interest rate on a Treasury bond and that on a corporate bond is defined as a **default risk premium (DP).** Therefore

$$\begin{matrix} \text{Actual rate of interest} & & \text{Treasury} & & \text{Default} \\ \text{on a corporate} & = & \text{bond} & + & \text{risk} \\ \text{security} & & \text{rate} & & \text{premium} \\ k_{\text{corp bond}} & = & k_{\text{T-bond}} & & + \text{ DP}. \end{matrix}$$

In January 1984 the default-free rate was 11.75 percent, and the rate on AAA corporate bonds was 12.20 percent; therefore the default risk premium on AAA corporate bonds was 0.45 percentage points:

$$\begin{aligned} k_{\text{AAA}} &= k_{\text{T-bond}} + \text{DP} \\ &= 11.75 + 0.45 \\ &= 12.20. \end{aligned}$$

The default premium on more risky AA bonds was 0.96 percentage points, and the premium rose still more on even riskier bonds.

Notice that we have *not* defined a Treasury bond to be riskless. All long-term bonds, even default-free bonds issued by the U.S. Treasury, have an element of risk because the prices of long-term bonds decline

default risk
The risk that a borrower will not pay the interest or principal on a loan.

bond ratings
Ratings assigned to bonds based on the probability of their firms' default. Those bonds with the smallest default probability are rated AAA and carry the lowest interest rates.

default risk premium (DP)
The difference between the interest rate on a Treasury bond and that on a corporate bond.

---

[2]Some state and local government bonds have a lower interest rate than Treasury bonds, but this is because state and local bonds are tax exempt. On an after-tax basis, Treasury bonds provide the lowest returns.
[3]*Federal Reserve Bulletin,* February 1984, p. A26.

if interest rates rise. Thus Treasury bonds with a coupon rate of 7⅝ which were issued for $1,000 in 1972 sold 10 years later for only $592. Clearly, there was some kind of risk to investors who bought these bonds, even though they had zero default risk. This point will be amplified shortly.

Inflation

Inflation also has a major impact on interest rates. To illustrate its effects, suppose you saved up $1,000 and invested it in a Treasury bond which matures in 1 year and which pays 5 percent interest. At the end of the year, you would receive $1,050—your original $1,000 plus $50 of interest. Now suppose the rate of inflation during the year was 10 percent, and it affected all items equally. If beer had cost $1 per bottle at the start of the year, it would cost $1.10 at the end. Therefore you could have bought $1,000/$1 = 1,000 bottles at the beginning of the year, but only $1,050/$1.10 = 955 bottles at the end. Thus, in *real terms*, you would be worse off—you would have received $50 of interest, but it would not be sufficient to offset inflation. You would have been better off having bought and held 1,000 bottles of beer (or some other storable asset such as land, timber, apartment buildings, wheat, or gold) than having bought bonds.

Investors are well aware of all this, so when they lend money, they add an **inflation premium (IP)** to the rate they would have charged in the absence of inflation. For a default-free U.S. Treasury bond, the actual interest rate charged ($k_{T\text{-bond}}$) would be the real rate (k^*) plus the inflation premium (IP):[4]

$$k_{T\text{-bond}} = k^* + IP.$$

Therefore, if the real equilibrium rate of interest for default-free investments were $k^* = 4\%$, and if inflation were expected to be 11 percent (and hence IP = 11%), the actual rate of interest on Treasury bonds would be 15 percent. The interest rate on a corporate bond would be

$$k_{corp\ bond} = k^* + IP + DP.$$

It is important to note that the rate of inflation built into interest rates is the *rate of inflation expected in the future*, not the rate experienced in the past. Thus reported inflation rates (which are always for some past period) might show an annual rate of 8 percent, but people on the

inflation
An increase in the volume of money and credit relative to the available supply of goods, resulting in a rise in the general level of prices.

inflation premium (IP)
A premium for anticipated or expected inflation that investors add to the pure rate of return.

---

[4]This equation is called the Fisher Equation, after the great economist Irving Fisher, who first set forth the relationship between inflation and interest rates. It is an approximation to the true theoretical relationship. For a more complete discussion, see Appendix 2A to Eugene F. Brigham, *Financial Management*, 3rd ed. (Hinsdale, IL: Dryden Press, 1982).

average might be expecting a 6 percent inflation rate in the future. If so, it is 6 percent that will be built into the current rate of interest.

Note also that the inflation rate reflected in the interest rate on any security is the *average rate of inflation expected over the security's life*. Thus the inflation rate built into a 30-year bond is the average rate of inflation expected over the next 30 years.

Expectations for future inflation are closely related to, but not perfectly correlated with, rates experienced in the recent past. Therefore, if the inflation rate reported for the past few months increases, people tend to raise their expectations for future inflation, and this change in expectations causes an increase in interest rates.

Figure 5-2 illustrates how inflation and interest rates have tended to move together. From 1960 to 1964, when the average rate of inflation

Figure 5-2
Relationship between Annual Inflation Rates and Long-Term Interest Rates
There is a close, although not perfect, correlation between interest rates and rates of inflation, as shown in this figure. Over a 30-year period, the two rates tended to fluctuate together. The inflation premium built into long-term interest rates is based on expectations of future inflation, with these expectations arising largely from past and present experiences of inflation rates.

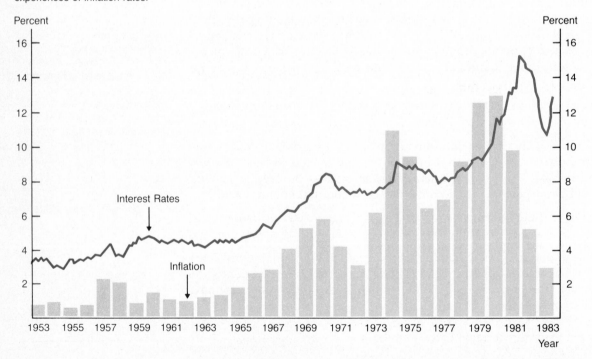

Notes:
1. Interest rates are those on AAA long-term corporate bonds.
2. Inflation is measured as the annual rate of change in the consumer price index (CPI).

was 1.4 percent, interest rates on AAA-rated bonds ranged from 4 to 5 percent. As the war in Vietnam accelerated in the mid 1960s, the rate of inflation increased, and interest rates began to rise. The rate of inflation dropped after 1970, and so did long-term interest rates. However, the Arab oil embargo in 1973 and a quadrupling of oil prices in 1974 caused a spurt in the price level, which drove interest rates to new record highs in 1974 and 1975. Inflationary pressures eased in late 1975 and 1976 as a result of a severe recession, but then rose again after 1976. In early 1984, as this is written, inflation rates are down sharply from recent levels, but fears of returning double-digit inflation have kept interest rates from falling at a faster pace.

It should also be noted that when economists speak of the real rate of interest, k*, they typically define this term as the rate of interest that would exist on a default-free U.S. Treasury security if the expected rate of inflation were zero. Henceforth, we shall follow this convention. Therefore we shall hereafter define k* as a **real, default-free rate of interest**. Also, we should note that although it is very difficult to measure k* precisely, many experts think that in the United States in recent years it has fluctuated in the range of 2 to 4 percent.

real, default-free rate of interest
The rate of interest on default-free U.S. Treasury securities less the expected inflation rate.

Liquidity Premiums

As noted earlier, a security which is highly **liquid** can be sold and converted to spendable cash on short notice. Active markets, which provide liquidity, exist for government bonds, the stocks and bonds of the larger corporations, and the securities of certain financial intermediaries. If a security is *not* liquid, investors will add a **liquidity premium (LP)** when they establish the equilibrium interest rate on the security. Thus the interest rate formula, including liquidity premium, is as follows:

liquid asset
An asset that can be readily converted to spendable cash.

liquidity premium (LP)
A premium added to the equilibrium interest rate on a security that cannot be converted to cash on short notice.

$$k = k^* + IP + DP + LP.$$

It is very difficult to measure liquidity premiums, but a differential of at least one and probably two percentage points exists between the least liquid and the most liquid financial assets.

The Term Structure of Interest Rates

U.S. Treasury securities are free of default risk in the sense that one can be virtually certain that the government will pay interest on its bonds and will pay them off when they mature; therefore their *default risk* premiums should be close to zero. Furthermore, active markets exist for Treasury securities, so their liquidity premiums are also very close to zero. Thus, as a first approximation, the rate of interest on a

Treasury bond should be equal to the real rate, k*, plus the inflation premium, IP:

$$k_{\text{T-bond}} = k^* + IP.$$

Now note (1) that the Treasury can borrow on a short-term basis such as 90 days, on a long-term basis such as 30 years, or anywhere in between, and (2) that the inflation premium built into any bond's interest rate is the *average inflation rate* over the bond's life, or its *term to maturity*. Therefore, it is appropriate to add a subscript, t, to the inflation premium, depending on its maturity. Thus $IP_t = IP_3$ is the inflation premium for a 3-year bond, and it is equal to the average inflation rate expected over the next 3 years.

To illustrate, suppose that in late December 1984 the real rate of interest were $k^* = 2\%$, and expected inflation rates for the next 3 years were as follows:

	Expected Annual (1-Year) Inflation Rate	Expected Average Inflation Rate over the Indicated Period	
1985	9%	9 ÷ 1	= 9.0%
1986	6%	(9 + 6) ÷ 2	= 7.5%
1987	3%	(9 + 6 + 3) ÷ 3	= 6.0%

Given these expectations, the following pattern of interest rates would be expected to exist:

	Real Rate (k*)		Inflation Premium, Which Is Equal to the Average Expected Inflation Rate (IP$_t$)		Treasury Bond Rate (k$_{\text{T-bond}}$)
1-year bond	2%	+	9.0%	=	11.0%
2-year bond	2%	+	7.5%	=	9.5%
3-year bond	2%	+	6.0%	=	8.0%

Had the pattern of expected inflation rates been reversed, with inflation expected to rise from 3 percent to 9 percent, the following situation would have existed:

1-year bond	2%	+	3.0%	=	5.0%
2-year bond	2%	+	4.5%	=	6.5%
3-year bond	2%	+	6.0%	=	8.0%

yield curve
The graph of the relationship between the yields and maturities of a security.

term structure of interest rates
The relationship between yields and maturities of securities.

These hypothetical data are plotted in Figure 5-3. The lines are called *yield-to-maturity curves*, or **yield curves** for short, and the graphs are said to depict the **term structure of interest rates**. Whenever the annual

Figure 5-3
Hypothetical Example of the Term Structure of Interest Rates
The inflation premium built into the interest rate for any security is the average inflation
rate expected over the life, or term to maturity, of the security. The term structure of
interest rates is depicted by the hypothetical yield curves shown in this figure. If inflation is
expected to decline, short-term securities will yield more than long-term securities, as
shown with Yield Curve a. Conversely, if inflation is expected to increase, as in Yield
Curve b, short-term securities will yield less than long-term securities.

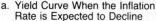 a. Yield Curve When the Inflation
     Rate is Expected to Decline

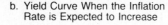 b. Yield Curve When the Inflation
     Rate is Expected to Increase

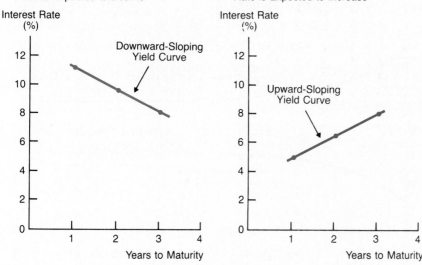

rate of inflation is expected to decline, the yield curve "points down."
Conversely, if inflation is expected to increase, the yield curve
"points up."

If you refer to Figure 5-2, you will see that the actual inflation rate
was relatively low in 1976. The United States was just coming out of a
recession, and people expected the inflation rate to remain low for a
while but to increase as the economy picked up steam. Therefore in
March 1976 interest rates on U.S. Treasury securities with different maturities were as shown in the lower curve of Figure 5-4. Here the yield
curve is *upward sloping*, signifying that in 1976 investors expected inflation to increase in the future from the then-current rate of 6 percent.
Now refer again to Figure 5-2 and note that inflation was quite high in
both 1979 and 1980. People were clearly worried about inflation, but
the consensus view was that inflation rates would drop below the
then-current level of 12 percent in 1981 and beyond. Therefore in
March 1980 the yield curve was downward sloping.

Our graphs show yield curves for U.S. Treasury securities, but we
could have constructed them for corporate bonds. For example, we

Figure 5-4
Actual Examples of the Term Structure
This figure shows the actual yield curves for various term Treasury bonds in two recent years. In 1976 investors expected inflation to rise from the then-current 6 percent; this produced an upward-sloping yield curve, meaning long-term bonds offered a higher interest rate than did short-term bonds. By 1980 inflation was expected to decline, creating a downward-sloping yield curve; that is, in 1980 the Treasury was not willing to sell long-term bonds at the same high rate at which it was selling short-term bonds. The 1976 situation was favorable to the long-term saver, whereas 1980 favored the short-term saver.

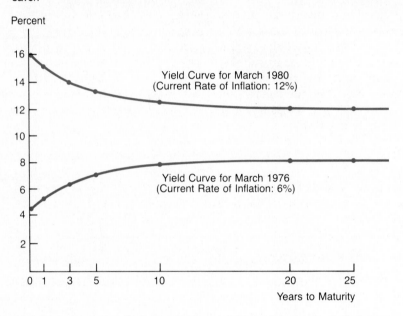

could have developed yield curves for AT&T, Exxon, General Motors, Chrysler, or any other company that borrows money over a range of maturities. Had we constructed such curves and plotted them on Figure 5-4, the corporate yield curves would have been above those for Treasury securities, but they would have had the same general shape as the Treasury curve for the same period. Also, the more risky the corporation, the higher its yield curve; thus Chrysler's curve would have been above that of General Motors.

Maturity Risk Premiums

If investors in general expected the inflation rate to remain constant in the future, it would seem at first glance that the yield curve should be horizontal. For example, if k* were 2 percent, and if inflation were expected to remain constant at a rate of 6 percent on into the future, then Treasury bonds of all maturities might be expected to yield 8 percent.

However, this is not completely correct. For instance, the prices of long-term bonds decline sharply whenever interest rates rise; since interest rates can and do occasionally rise, all long-term bonds, even Treasury bonds, have an element of risk called **interest rate risk.**[5] As a general rule, the bonds of any organization, from the U.S. government to Chrysler, have more interest rate risk the longer the maturity of the bond.[6] Therefore a **maturity risk premium (MP),** which is higher the longer the period to maturity, must be included to determine the actual interest rate.

interest rate risk
The risk to which investors are exposed due to changing interest rates.

maturity risk premium (MP)
A premium for the risk to which investors are exposed due to the length of a security's maturity.

The effect of maturity risk premiums is to raise interest rates on long-term bonds relative to those on short-term bonds. For example, with two given sets of expectations about inflation, the yield curves on Treasury securities might be shown by the solid lines in Figure 5-5. However, with maturity risk premiums added, the actual yield curves would be shown by the dashed lines. In recent years the maturity risk premium on 30-year Treasury bonds has generally amounted to about one percentage point.

The "Risk Premium"

In this book, and in finance generally, the term **risk premium (RP)** is used to denote the sum of the default risk premium and the maturity risk premium:

risk premium (RP)
The difference between the required rate of return on a particular risky asset and the rate of return on a riskless asset with the same expected life.

$$\text{Risk premium} = \frac{\text{Default}}{\text{risk premium}} + \frac{\text{Maturity}}{\text{risk premium}}$$

$$RP = DP + MP.$$

Here are some observations about this overall risk premium:

1. The DP is zero on Treasury securities, but the MP increases the longer the maturity. Therefore, other things held constant, the longer the maturity of a Treasury bond, the higher its $RP = MP$, and hence the higher its interest rate.

2. Very-short-term Treasury securities have zero default risk and zero maturity premiums. Therefore very-short-term U.S. Treasury securities are essentially riskless. Often the term R_F, for **risk-free rate**, is used to describe short-term Treasury securities.

risk-free rate (R_F)
The rate of return on short-term Treasury securities, which have no default risk and no maturity premiums.

3. Generally, it is easier to predict that a corporation will be able to pay off its short-term debt than its long-term debt. Therefore, as a rule,

---

[5]For example, if you had bought a 30-year Treasury bond for $1,000 in 1972, when the long-term interest rate was 7⅜ percent, and held it until January 1982, when long-term rates were about 13.5 percent, the value of your bond would have declined to $592. Had you invested in short-term bonds in 1976 and subsequently reinvested your principal each time the bonds matured, your investment would have still been worth $1,000.
[6]Corporate securities also have more default risk the longer the maturity.

Figure 5-5
Effect of Interest Rate Risk on the Yield Curve
Because values of long-term bonds decline sharply when interest rates rise, all such bonds have an element of risk called "interest rate risk." To provide some protection against this risk, a maturity risk premium is built into interest rates. The longer the term of the security, the higher this premium will be. Thus, whether the pure expectations yield curve slopes up or down, the interest rate will be increased by the maturity risk premium.

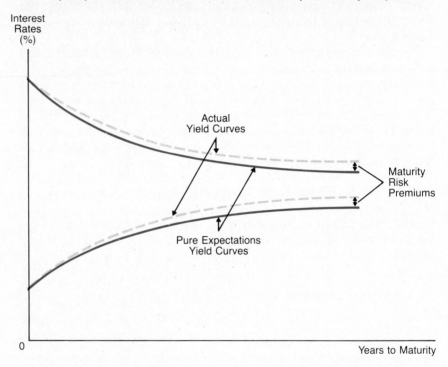

default premiums rise along with maturity premiums the longer the life of a corporate bond. Hence RPs for corporate bonds increase with maturity at an even greater rate than do those for Treasury bonds.

Federal Reserve Policy

The growth in the money supply has a direct impact on both the nation's level of economic activity and the rate of inflation. In the United States the Federal Reserve System controls, or at least attempts to control, the money supply.[7]

---

[7]For a more complete discussion of the role of the Fed in monitoring the money supply and the nation's economic activity, refer to Chapter 4.

When the Fed tightened the money supply, as it did in late 1981, short-term rates increased sharply. At the same time the fact that the Fed was taking strong action to reduce inflation caused expectations for long-run inflation to fall. Generally, when the Fed is actively intervening in the markets, the yield curve will be distorted. Short-term rates will be temporarily "too high" if the Fed is tightening credit, and "too low" if it is easing credit. Long-term rates are not affected as much by Fed intervention, except to the extent that such intervention affects expectations for long-term inflation.

The "Normal" Yield Curve

In a stable economy such as we had in the 1950s and 1960s, where (1) inflation fluctuated in the 1 to 3 percent range, (2) the expected future rate of inflation was about equal to the current rate, and (3) the Federal Reserve did not actively intervene in the markets, the yield curve was relatively low, and it generally had a slight upward slope to reflect maturity effects. People often speak of such an upward-sloping yield curve as being a **"normal" yield curve,** and a yield curve which slopes downward is called an **inverted** or **abnormal yield curve.** Since the mid 1960s the actual curve has sloped down about as much as it has sloped up, so it is hard to say what is normal and what is abnormal.

"normal" yield curve
An upward-sloping yield curve.

inverted yield curve
A downward-sloping yield curve.

Interest Rates and Recessions

Figure 5-6 shows how long- and short-term rates have fluctuated over time and how recessions have influenced rates. Here are the key points revealed by the graph:
1. Because inflation has generally been increasing since 1953, the general tendency has been toward higher interest rates.
2. Until 1966 short-term rates were almost always below long-term rates. Thus in those years the yield curve was almost always "normal" in the sense that it was upward sloping.
3. The shaded areas in the graph represent **recessions.** During recessions the demand for credit falls, and at the same time the Federal Reserve tends to increase the money supply in an effort to stimulate the economy. As a result, there is a tendency for interest rates to decline during recessions.
4. In recessions short-term rates fall much more rapidly than long-term rates. This occurs because (1) the Fed operates mainly in the short-term sector, and hence Federal Reserve intervention has its major effect here; and (2) long-term rates reflect the average expected inflation rate over the next 20 to 30 years, and this expectation does not change radically during a relatively short recession.

recession
A period of slack economic activity usually having two or more consecutive quarters in which real output declines.

Figure 5-6
Long- and Short-Term Interest Rates, 1953–1984
This figure depicts the fluctuation of long- and short-term interest rates over the past 30 years and shows how these rates have responded to business recessions. Recessions have caused sharp drops in short-term rates due to Federal Reserve intervention and falling demand for money. Long-term rates are much less affected by recessions, since these rates are based on long-range expectations not significantly changed by relatively temporary recessions.

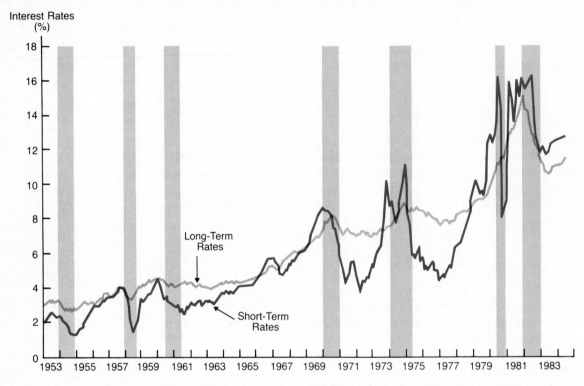

Note:
The shaded areas designate business recessions. Short-term rates are measured by four- to six-month loans to very large, strong corporations, and long-term rates are measured by AAA corporate bonds.
Source: *Federal Reserve Bulletin,* various issues.

Interest Rates and Business Decisions

Turn back to Figure 5-4 and focus on the yield curve for March 1976. That curve shows how much the U.S. government had to pay in 1976 to borrow money for 1 year, 3 years, 5 years, 10 years, and so on. A business borrower would have had to pay somewhat more, but assume for the moment that we are back in 1976 and the yield curve shown for that year also applies to your company. Now suppose you have decided (1) to build a new plant with a 20-year life that will cost $1 million and (2) to raise the $1 million by selling an issue of debt (or bor-rowing) rather than by selling stock. If you borrowed in 1976 on a short-term basis, say, for 1 year, your interest cost for that year would be only 5.8 percent, or $58,000, whereas if you used long-term financ-ing, your cost would be 8 percent, or $80,000. Therefore, at first glance, it would seem that you should have used short-term debt.

However, with 20-20 hindsight, we can see that this would have been a horrible mistake. Had you used short-term debt, you would have had to renew your loan every year, and the rate charged on each new loan would have reflected the then-current short-term rate. Inter-est rates have been rising since 1976, and by 1980 you would have been paying over 16 percent, or $160,000 per year. These high interest pay-ments would have cut into and perhaps eliminated your profits. Your reduced profitability could easily have increased your firm's risk to the point where your bond rating would have been lowered, causing lend-ers to increase the risk premium built into the interest rate they charged you, and forcing you to pay 20 or even 25 percent. These su-per-high interest rates would further reduce profitability, worrying lenders even more and making them reluctant to renew your loan. If the lenders refused to renew the loan and demanded payment, as they have every right to do, you might not be able to raise the cash—high interest rates may have caused a recession, in which case it would be difficult for you to convert your physical assets to cash without making drastic price cuts, which would mean heavy operating losses or even bankruptcy.

On the other hand, had you used long-term financing back in 1976, your interest costs would have remained constant at $80,000 per year, and the increase in interest rates would not have hurt you. You might have even been able to buy up some of your bankrupted competitors at bargain prices—bankruptcies increase dramatically when interest rates rise.

Does all this suggest that firms should always avoid short-term debt? Not necessarily. For example, in December 1981 the yield curve for corporate borrowers was slightly upward sloping—long-term money to a strong company cost 15 percent versus 13 percent for short-term funds. If a company borrowed at 15 percent, it would be paying a great deal more in interest than a competitor who used short-term debt until December 1983, when comparable interest rates had fallen to approxi-mately 11 percent. Of course, we are blessed with hindsight in this example. But should we wait for rates to drop lower still before we borrow? In December 1983 financial managers were faced with this same forecasting problem. If President Reagan's economic programs continued to work and inflation continued to fall in the next few years, so would interest rates. On the other hand, President Reagan's pro-grams might not continue to work, and the large tax cut and conse-quent federal deficits could drive inflation and interest rates up to new record levels. In that case the financial managers would wish they had borrowed long-term at the end of 1983.

Finance would be easy if we could predict future interest rates accurately. Unfortunately, predicting future interest rates with consistent accuracy is somewhere between difficult and impossible—people who make a living selling interest rate forecasts say it is difficult; many others say it is impossible.

Even if it is difficult to predict future interest rate *levels*, it is easy to predict that interest rates will *fluctuate*. This being the case, sound financial policy calls for using a mix of long- and short-term debt, as well as equity, in such a manner that the firm can survive in most interest rate environments. Furthermore, the optimal financial policy depends in an important way on the nature of the firm's assets—the easier it is to sell off assets and thus to pay off debts, the more feasible it is to use large amounts of short-term debt. We will return to this issue later in the book.

Interest Rates and Stock Prices

Interest rates have a direct effect on corporate profits: interest is a cost, so the higher the rate of interest, the lower a firm's profits, other things held constant. Interest rates also affect stock prices because of their effects on profits and, more important, because of competition in the marketplace between stocks and bonds. If interest rates rise sharply, investors can get a higher return on their money in the bond market. This can induce transfers of funds from the stock market to the bond market and consequently can depress stock prices.

To illustrate, suppose you had $100,000 invested in Midwest Power stock, which provided dividends of 12 percent, or $12,000, per year. At the time, Midwest Power's bonds returned 9 percent, so you could have switched and received $9,000 per year, but you chose not to do so because you wanted to earn the $3,000 more that the stock paid. (The $3,000, or 3 percent, differential reflects a risk premium.) Now suppose interest rates doubled and Midwest Power's bonds yielded 18 percent. If the stock were still yielding 12 percent, then you could switch to bonds, increase your income from $12,000 to $18,000, and be exposed to less risk than you were with the stock. You (and other stockholders) would call your broker and try to sell the stock and buy the bonds. However, the influx of sell orders would depress the price of the stock relative to that of the bond before you could complete the transaction.

We examine the relationship between interest rates and stock prices in more detail in later chapters, but you should recognize at this point that rising interest rates tend to depress stock prices and therefore that the level of interest rates in the economy has a major effect on any firm's stock price.

Summary

This chapter has described how interest rates are determined and some of the ways in which interest rates affect business decisions.

The basic, or real, interest rate (k*) is determined as a joint product of (1) the returns on investment available to producers and (2) consumers' time preferences for current consumption as opposed to saving for future consumption. To establish the interest rate for a given loan, we must add to the basic interest rate some premiums which reflect (1) expected inflation over the life of the loan (IP), (2) the default risk inherent in the loan (DP), (3) the degree of liquidity of the loan (LP), and (4) the maturity of the loan (MP):

$$k = k^* + IP + DP + LP + MP.$$

Interest rates fluctuate over time. Long-term rates change primarily because of changes in the rate of expected inflation, whereas short-term rates reflect both expected inflation and Federal Reserve intervention in the markets.

The yield curve describes the relationship between long- and short-term interest rates. When inflation is expected to continue at the current rate, the yield curve tends to slope upward because of maturity effects; such a curve is called "normal." However, in recent years the yield curve has been "abnormal," or inverted, about as much as it has been normal.

Resolution to Decision in Finance

Who Says the Price Is Right?

In pricing the new notes and debentures, IBM, Salomon Brothers, and Merrill Lynch took as a benchmark the yield on Treasury securities of comparable maturities. Their goal was to price their issues close enough to Treasury rates to keep IBM's borrowing costs down but high enough to attract investors and sell quickly. Because IBM held a high credit rating—AAA from both Moody's and Standard & Poor's—the default premium could be low. Given IBM's high standing in the business world, the bonds were expected to enjoy a lively market, so the liquidity premium could also be small. All parties agreed that the maturity premium on the 25-year debentures should be slightly more than the premium on the 7-year notes. But problems arose when the group tried to consider the rapidly rising rates in the money markets.

At one point IBM suggested that Salomon price the notes and debentures at only .05 percent above Treasury rates. But because the investment bankers stood to lose millions of dollars if interest rates continued to rise, they resisted. Finally the word came down from IBM headquarters: the company would agree to a yield of .07 percent above Treasury notes for the 7-year notes and .12 percent above Treasury bonds for the 25-year debentures. Thus IBM in effect contracted to pay 9.62 percent on the notes and 9.41 percent on the debentures. (Note that although IBM agreed to pay a higher maturity premium on its longer-term debt, the total interest rate is lower than the rate on the shorter-term debt. This indicates that an inverted yield curve existed at the time. Although interest rates were rising rapidly, the rate of inflation was expected to fall in the long run.)

At 12:40 P.M. the meeting adjourned and the investment bankers snapped into action. But that very afternoon things started to unravel. First the yield on Treasury bonds rose by .05 percent, wiping out almost half the difference between the T-bond rate and that of the IBM debentures. The next day 4-year Treasury notes similar to the IBM issue sold at 9.79 percent—a shocking .17 percent *above* the IBM rate.

Salomon, Merrill Lynch, and their partners in the deal were left holding the bag. If they tried to sell the bonds at the agreed-upon price, the interest rates would be too low to attract investors. But if the underwriters allowed the bonds' prices to adjust to the market, they would lose millions of dollars due to the higher interest rates. In the end they had no choice; they let the issues' prices adjust to the market and took an estimated loss of $15 million.

Financially, IBM could be viewed as a winner because it managed to lock in such low interest rates. Based on the yields of similar AAA-rated corporate debt at the time, IBM's estimated savings amounted to $10,450,000 per year. On the other hand, it is difficult to measure the amount of glitter IBM traded in order to realize this financial gain. The offering created headlines and chaos that neither Wall Street nor IBM will soon forget.

Source: "The Bomb I.B.M. Dropped on Wall Street," *Fortune*, November 19, 1979, 52–56.

Key Terms You should be able to define each of the following terms:

Interest rate
Production opportunities; time
  preferences for consumption
Real rate of return (k*); real, default-
  free rate of interest

Default risk
Bond ratings
Default risk premium (DP)
Inflation; inflation premium (IP)

Liquid security; liquidity premium (LP)

Yield curve; term structure of interest rates

Interest rate risk; maturity risk premium (MP)

Risk premium (RP)

Risk-free rate (R_F)

"Normal" yield curve; inverted yield curve

Recession

Questions

5-1 Suppose interest rates on residential mortgages of equal risk were 14 percent in California and 16 percent in New York. Could this differential persist? What forces might tend to equalize rates? Would differences in borrowing costs for businesses of equal risk located in California and New York be more or less likely than mortgage rate differentials? Would differentials in the cost of money for New York and California firms be more likely to exist if the firms being compared were very large or if they were very small?

5-2 Which fluctuate more, long-term or short-term interest rates? Why?

5-3 You feel that the economy is just entering a recession. Your firm must raise capital immediately, and debt will be used. Would it be better to borrow on a long-term or a short-term basis? Explain.

5-4 Suppose the population of Area A is relatively young, while that of Area B is relatively old, but everything else about the two areas is equal.

    a. Would interest rates be the same or different in the two areas? Explain.

    b. Would trends toward nationwide branching by banks and S&Ls and toward the development of diversified financial corporations affect your answer to Part a?

5-5 Suppose a new and much more liberal Congress and administration were elected, and their first order of business was to change the Federal Reserve System and force the Fed to greatly expand the money supply. What effect would this have

    a. On the yield curve at the present time?

    b. On the yield curve that would probably exist two or three years in the future?

5-6 The federal government (1) encouraged the development of the S&L industry; (2) forced the industry to make long-term, fixed interest rate mortgages; and (3) restricted the S&Ls' capital largely to deposits that were withdrawable on demand.

    a. Would S&Ls be better off in a world with a "normal" or an inverted yield curve? Explain.

    b. If federal actions such as deficit spending and expansion of the money supply produced a sharp increase in inflation, why might it necessitate a federal "bailout" of the S&L industry?

5-7 Assume that the yield curve is horizontal. Now you and other investors receive information that suggests the economy is headed into a recession. You and most other investors think that the Fed will soon relax credit and that this will lead to a decline in short-term interest rates. Over the long run (the next 5, 10, or 15 years) people expect a fairly high rate of inflation, and they expect that this will keep long-term rates fairly high. Explain what all of this will probably do the the yield curve. Use a graph to illustrate your answer.

5-8 Suppose interest rates on Treasury bonds rose from 12 percent to 17 percent. Other things held constant, what do you think would happen to the price of an average company's common stock?

5-9 Why are Treasury bills popular short-term investments for corporations and commercial banks?

Problems

5-1 Suppose you and most other investors expect the rate of inflation to be 10 percent next year, to fall to 5 percent during a recession in the following year, and then to run at a rate of 8 percent thereafter. The real rate, k*, is 2 percent. Maturity risk premiums on Treasury securities rise from zero on very-short-term bonds (those that mature in a few days) by 0.30 percentage points for each year to maturity up to a limit of 1.5 percentage points on 5-year or longer T-bonds.

***a.** Calculate the interest rates on 1-, 2-, 3-, 4-, 5-, 10-, and 20-year Treasury securities, and plot the yield curve.

b. Now suppose AT&T, an AAA-rated company, had bonds with the same maturities as the Treasury bonds. As an approximation, plot an AT&T yield curve on the same graph with the Treasury bond yield curve. (Hint: Think about the risk premium on AT&T's long-term versus its short-term bonds.)

5-2 Look in the *Wall Street Journal* or some other paper which publishes interest rates on U.S. Treasury securities. Identify some Treasury bonds which mature at various dates in the future, record the years to maturity and the interest rate for each, and then plot a yield curve. (Note: Some of the bonds—for example, the 3 percent issue which matures in February 1995—will show very low yields. Disregard them—these are "flower bonds" which can be turned in and used at par value to pay estate taxes, so they always sell at close to par and have a yield which is close to the coupon yield, irrespective of the "going rate of interest." Also, the yields quoted in the *Journal* are not for the same point in time for all bonds, so random variations will appear. An interest rate series that is purged of flower bonds and random variations, and hence one that provides a better picture of the true yield curve, can be obtained from the *Federal Reserve Bulletin*.)

5-3 Look in the *Wall Street Journal*. Examine the interest rates for comparable maturity dates of U.S. Treasury securities and government agency securities.

a. Which group of securities carries the slightly higher interest rate?

b. Why do you think this relationship exists?

Selected References

Much of the material referenced in Chapters 3 and 4 is also applicable to this chapter. For current empirical data and a forecast of monetary conditions, see the most recent edition of this annual publication:

Salomon Brothers, *Supply and Demand for Credit* (New York).

---

*Refer to Appendix E for check answers to problems with asterisks.

Financial Statements and Financial Planning

III

A company's financial statements tell an important story about the firm. However, the financial manager or financial analyst must be able to interpret these statements in order to completely understand them. Chapter 6 discusses the four basic financial statements—the *income statement,* the *balance sheet,* the *statement of retained earnings,* and the *statement of changes in financial position.* Financial analysis, explored in Chapter 7, allows the analyst to predict future conditions and allows management to use this knowledge to plan actions to meet future challenges. Predicting future business conditions is an important requisite to effective financial management. Chapter 8 provides useful tools for this necessary financial forecasting. The section's final chapter continues the concentration on techniques of evaluation and forecasting by emphasizing the relationships between cost, volume, and profit in an environment containing business risk.

Examining a Firm's Financial Data

6

Decision in Finance

Letters from Chairman Buffett

Savvy readers of corporate annual reports usually check three elements: the auditor's opinion, the financial results, and the footnotes. Few give more than a glance to the chairman's letter, which they assume will be pure puffery.

But even the most jaded analysts settle back in their chairs and prepare for a good read when the Berkshire Hathaway report arrives. It invariably contains two things they look forward to: good news about the company's financial performance and a long, insightful, and entertaining letter from Chairman Warren Buffett. In fact, the letters are so popular that Berkshire Hathaway often receives requests for reprints and, to meet demand, has assembled an anthology of the last five.

Most chairmen's letters try to paint a rosy corporate picture, regardless of the reality of the situation. But Buffett believes that stockholders are too smart to buy such an approach. Describing his attitude toward his readers, he says, "I assume I've got a very intelligent partner who has been away for a year and needs to be filled in on all that's happened." Consequently, in his letters he often admits mistakes and emphasizes the negative. In 1979, for example, he wrote, "We continue to look for ways to expand our insurance operation, but your reaction to this intent should not be unrestrained joy. Some of our expansion efforts—largely initiated by your chairman—have been lackluster, others have been expensive failures."

Buffett also uses his letters to educate his shareholders and help them interpret the data presented in the rest of the report. In one letter he lamented the complexities of accounting and observed, "The Yāno-mamö Indians employ only three numbers: one, two, and more than two. Maybe their time will come."

119

As you read this chapter, think about the kinds of information that corporations provide their stockholders. Do the four basic financial statements provide adequate data for investment decisions? What other information might be helpful?

Also consider the pros and cons of Chairman Buffett's decision to include long, frank, and frequently self-critical letters in his company's annual reports. Would you suggest that other companies follow suit? Why or why not?

See end of chapter for resolution.

Any analysis of a firm, whether by management or investors, must include an examination of the company's financial data. The most obvious and readily available source of these financial data is the company's *annual report*. In this chapter we examine the *basic financial data* that are available in the firm's annual report. In following chapters we discuss the *techniques of financial analysis* used to evaluate financial data in the determination of the firm's relative riskiness, profit potential, and general management competence.

The Annual Report

annual report
A report, issued annually by corporations to their stockholders, containing basic financial statements and management's opinion of operations and future prospects.

Of the various reports corporations issue to their stockholders, the **annual report** is by far the most important. Two types of information are given in this report. First, there is a verbal statement that describes the firm's operating results during the past year and discusses new developments that will affect future operations. Second, the report presents four basic financial statements—the *income statement*, the *balance sheet*, the *statement of retained earnings*, and the *statement of changes in financial position*. Taken together, these statements give an accounting picture of the firm's operations and financial position. Detailed data are provided for at least the two most recent years, along with historical summaries of key operating statistics for the prior five to ten years.

The quantitative information and the verbal information are equally important. The financial statements report *what has actually happened* to earnings and dividends over the past few years, while the verbal statements represent an attempt to explain *why* things turned out the way they did. For example, suppose earnings dropped sharply last year. Management may report that the drop resulted from a strike at a key facility at the height of the busy season, but then go on to state that the strike has now been settled and that future profits are expected to bounce back. Of course, this return to profitability may not occur, and investors will want to compare management's past statements with subsequent results. *In any event, the information contained in the annual report is used by investors to form expectations about future earnings and div-*

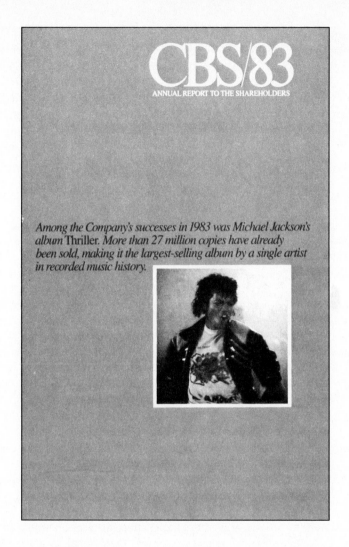

Among the Company's successes in 1983 was Michael Jackson's album Thriller. *More than 27 million copies have already been sold, making it the largest-selling album by a single artist in recorded music history.*

It was appropriate that CBS chose a photo of Michael Jackson for the cover of its 1983 annual report. The cover tells shareholders about one of the company's most successful operations during the year. Jackson's *Thriller* album was the best-selling in the history of the CBS/Records Group.
Source: CBS, Inc. 1983 Annual Report.

idends and about the riskiness of these expected cash flows. Therefore the annual report is obviously of great interest to investors.

The Income Statement

An **income statement** summarizes a firm's revenues and expenses over an accounting period—generally one year. Table 6-1 presents the income statement as it might appear in an annual report. This financial statement records the 1983 and 1984 profits and disbursements of Carter Chemical Company, a major producer of industrial and consumer chemical products.

Reported at the top of the statement are net sales, from which various costs, including income taxes, are subtracted to obtain net income

income statement
A statement summarizing the firm's revenues and expenses over an accounting period.

Table 6-1
Carter Chemical Company: Income Statement for Year Ending December 31
(Millions of Dollars, except Per Share Data)

	1984	1983
Net Sales	$3,000	$2,850
Costs and Expenses		
Labor and materials	$2,544	$2,413
Depreciation	100	90
Selling	22	20
General and administrative	40	35
Lease payments on buildings	28	28
Total costs	$2,734	$2,586
Net operating income, or earnings before interest and taxes (EBIT)	$ 266	$ 264
Less Interest Expense		
Interest on notes payable	$ 8	$ 2
Interest on first mortgage bonds	40	42
Interest on debentures	18	3
Total interest	$ 66	$ 47
Earnings before tax	$ 200	$ 217
Federal income tax (at 40%)	80	87
Net income after taxes available to common stockholders	$ 120	$ 130
Disposition of Net Income		
Dividends to common stockholders	$ 100	$ 90
Addition to retained earnings	$ 20	$ 40
Per Share of Common Stock		
Earnings per share (EPS)[a]	$ 2.40	$ 2.60
Dividends per share (DPS)[a]	$ 2.00	$ 1.80

[a]Fifty million shares are outstanding: see Table 6-2. Calculations of EPS and DPS for 1984 are as
follows:

$$\text{EPS} = \frac{\text{Net income after tax}}{\text{Shares outstanding}} = \frac{\$120,000,000}{50,000,000} = \$2.40.$$

$$\text{DPS} = \frac{\text{Dividends paid to common stockholders}}{\text{Shares outstanding}} = \frac{\$100,000,000}{50,000,000} = \$2.00.$$

available to common shareholders. Although this is the general form
for income statements, several variations exist. For example, rather
than deducting all operating costs from sales, as in Table 6-1, some
income statements deduct cost of goods sold from sales to produce
gross profits. Gross profits are then reduced by all operating expenses
to obtain operating profits.

The most important continuing source of revenue for a business is *sales* or *operating revenues*. For a manufacturer like Carter, the sales account is the accumulation of total units sold multiplied by their respective prices.

Operating Costs and Expenses

In a typical manufacturing firm, the operating costs and expenses accounts include all costs required to obtain raw materials and convert them into finished products, the costs of selling, and the costs associated with overseeing operations. *Cost of goods sold* represents costs associated with raw material acquisition and direct production costs. Salesmen's travel expenses and salaries or commissions, promotion, and advertising are generally the most significant items in *selling expenses*. Staff and executive salaries and office expenses are the major items in *general and administrative expenses*. Of course, expenses attributable to assets used in the production, selling, and supervision processes must be accounted for through these direct costs, through *depreciation*, or through *lease payments*.

Even though the computation of these expenses appears to be unambiguous, several of them have a wide latitude of expression. Great discretion is allowed managers in calculating depreciation and valuing inventory (as part of cost of goods sold).[1] Since these calculations have a large impact on reported income, we investigate alternative means of calculating each in Appendix 6A.

Remaining Disbursements

The *earnings before interest and taxes*, or *operating profits*, are further reduced by interest payments on debt—which must be paid whether the company is profitable or losing money. Payment of principal is not indicated on the income statement but is reported, as we shall see, on the balance sheet.

All firms have a partner, some might say an "uninvited partner," who demands a predetermined percentage of the profits. This partner is, of course, the U.S. government, which requires that a portion of the firm's profits be paid in the form of income taxes. State and local governments require tax payments as well. Certain accounting conventions allow the firm to postpone these tax payments, as we see in Appendix 6A.

---

[1]These are not the only areas of managerial discretion in financial reporting. Such items as the determination of pension fund liabilities and the decision between expensing or capitalizing certain costs also have a significant impact on reported profits.

The Bottom Line

Financial managers often refer to net income as "the bottom line," denoting that of all the items on the income statement, net income draws the greatest attention. One manager even noted, "Net income is so important that we underline it twice!"

The net income of the firm is either paid to the shareholders in the form of dividends or retained by the firm to support the firm's growth. These divisions are reported in total dollars. The dividends to shareholders are reported on a per share basis, as well. Similarly, net income is also reported on a per share basis. Carter earned $2.40 per share in 1984, down from $2.60 in 1983, but it raised the dividend from $1.80 to $2.00.

Industry Practice

"Take Your Report and . . ."

Futility, thy name is Annual Report. Beyond perhaps poetry and first novels, few pieces of writing get so much care and attention from their authors as a company's annual report—and so little from the public. Corporate relations people sweat over them, lawyers tear them to pieces, art directors fuss, the chairman's family has veto power over the photography. And the intended recipients? A large majority casually dispatch the reports, unread, to the garbage.

But hope springs eternal. Four New York Stock Exchange companies in recent months decided to do a shareholder survey to see not only how the firm's annual and quarterly reports were being received, but to determine the company's image in the minds of shareholders as well. Two of the surveys were conducted on the telephone, the other two by mail. The firms are in electronics, metals and mining, computers, and financial services.

The results were hardly flattering. Typical comments from shareholders: "I don't read it. It's a waste of money sending it to me." "Feel free to take me off the annual report mailing list. Besides, it costs more than the dividends I receive." Many of the responses were touchingly candid: "I would like to save you the expense of writing to me. Please don't misunderstand. I like you, but I don't know a thing about stocks and never will." A note written for one shareholder read: "Mr. Edwards is in his 95th year and isn't able to digest much data anymore."

Many shareholders indicated that they felt guilty about shirking the reading but justified their lethargy by criticizing the report. What did most find to criticize? Above all, the report's lavishness—its glossy pages and color photos. "This must have cost a fortune" was a typical reply. Others said: "Couldn't this money have been better spent on something else?" And: "The slick annual report tells me that the executives at the company are on nothing but a huge ego trip."

Is this fair to the executives who slaved over the reports, hoping against hope to put the company's best foot forward? Probably not. But it proves a point: Lavish presentation in annual reports is self-defeating. Far from getting the stockholders to read, it gives them an added excuse not to read.

Who does study the reports? Analysts, of course. And, interestingly, people who don't own the stock. As long as they haven't yet bought any shares, an attractive—and even lavish—annual report is something that they state helps make a good impression on them. As one, who is the president of a small firm, put it: "I like to see visible evidence that the company is doing well."

Once they have bought the stock, however, they become penny pinchers, convinced that the company is squandering its—or more accurately now, their—money trying to tout its virtues. A representative remark: "Don't these clowns know I already *own* the stock."

At bottom there is a clear feeling among shareholders that annual reports are so utterly self-serving that reading them is a waste of time. The same people who tell me that they spend hours weekly reading the *Wall Street Journal, Forbes,* and other business publications barely look at annual reports.

Under ordinary circumstances only approximately 3 percent would read the report. But when these companies included a query card, about 15 percent of the respondents said they studied the reports. One shareholder in Southern California summed up the situation nicely: "I probably wouldn't have read the report had you not sent the questionnaire." Isn't that curious? On second thought, maybe it isn't. By including the query card, the company was at least asking the stockholders what *they* thought about something, instead of just telling them what *it* thought.

Apparently, what we need is a new approach to annual reports.

Source: "Take Your Report and . . ." by Dr. Srully Blotnick, *Forbes,* August 15, 1983. Reprinted by permission.

The Balance Sheet

The income statement reports on operations *over a period of time*—for example, during the calendar year 1984. The **balance sheet**, on the other hand, may be thought of as a snapshot of the firm's financial position *at a point in time*—for example, on December 31, 1984.

The left-hand side of Carter's balance sheet, which is shown in Table 6-2, shows the firm's assets, and the right-hand side of the statement shows claims against these assets. These claims are divided between funds supplied by the owners (stockholders' equity) and money the company owes to nonowners (liabilities).

balance sheet
A statement of the firm's financial status at a specific point in time.

Table 6-2
Carter Chemical Company: Balance Sheet as of December 31
(Millions of Dollars)

Assets	1984	1983	Claims on Assets	1984	1983
Cash	$ 50	$ 55	Accounts payable	$ 60	$ 30
Marketable securities	0	25	Notes payable	100	60
Accounts receivable	350	315	Accrued wages	10	10
Inventories	300	215	Accured federal income taxes	130	120
Total current assets	$ 700	$ 610	Total current liabilities	$ 300	$ 220
Gross plant and equipment	$1,800	$1,470	First mortgage bonds	$ 500	$ 520
Less depreciation	500	400	Debentures	300	60
			Total long-term debt	$ 800	$ 580
Net plant and equipment	$1,300	$1,070	Stockholders' equity:		
			Common stock		
			(50,000,000 shares, $1 par)	$ 50	$ 50
			Additional paid-in capital	100	100
			Retained earnings	750	730
			Total stockholders' equity		
			(common net worth)	$ 900	$ 880
Total assets	$2,000	$1,680	Total claims on assets	$2,000	$1,680

Assets

The **assets** are listed in the order of their liquidity, or the length of time it typically takes to convert them to cash. The current assets, or working capital, of the firm consist of assets that are normally converted into cash within one year. Temporary stores of liquidity are *cash* and *marketable securities*. Examples of securities used for temporary investment purposes are identified in Chapter 11. *Inventories* are both raw materials used in the production process and finished goods awaiting sale. *Accounts receivable* result when the firm sells a product on credit. When the customer pays, the account receivable is converted to cash.

Assets with a useful life of more than one year are referred to as *fixed assets*. These assets typically include the plant, equipment, office furniture, and other assets which may be used repeatedly in the production process. With extended usage these assets will eventually wear out. *Depreciation* was at one time supposed to reflect the decline in an asset's useful productive value. However, since depreciation is a noncash expense which postpones the firm's taxes, the actual relationship between an asset's productive value and its book value is low.

Liabilities

Money supplied by the owners of the firm is called **equity**. Those funds provided by nonowners are called **liabilities**. These claims on the assets of the firm are listed in the order in which they must be paid. Current liabilities are those debts that mature within one year.

Accounts payable represent the amount the company owes to business creditors for purchases of goods on open account. Each of these purchases is recorded on the seller's balance sheet as an account receivable. Notes payable are more formal evidence of short-term debt owed to banks or other lenders. Accruals are current expenses which have not yet been paid as of the date of the balance sheet. Accrued wages and accrued federal income taxes are payable on a periodic basis—weekly or monthly for wages and quarterly for taxes, for example. These accounts build as the wage and tax liabilities increase during the period. Once paid, they are reduced by the amounts paid, and then begin to build again as the process resumes.

Long-term liabilities are debt obligations with more than a single year remaining until maturity. The debt may have been incurred from any source, such as financial intermediaries, for example, or through the sale of bonds. Table 6-2 indicates Carter Chemical Company has two bonds outstanding, a first mortgage bond issue and a debenture issue.[2]

The bond's principal may be repaid either at maturity in a lump sum or in periodic repayments. The provision for the orderly repayment of a bond issue is known as a sinking fund. Carter is required to pay off $20 million each year. Accordingly, its outstanding mortgage bonds declined by $20 million from December 31, 1983 to December 31, 1984. The current portion of the long-term debt is included in notes payable here, although in a more detailed balance sheet it would be shown as a separate item.

Stockholders' Equity

The equity, or **net worth**, is a residual, that is,

$$\text{Assets} - \text{Liabilities} = \text{Stockholders' equity}$$
$$\$2,000,000,000 - \$1,100,000,000 = \$900,000,000.$$

Suppose assets decline in value—for example, suppose some of the firm's inventory is obsolete and is written off at a loss. Since liabilities remain constant, the value of the net worth declines. Therefore the risk of asset-value fluctuations is borne entirely by the stockholders. Note,

equity
Financing supplied by the firm's owners.

liabilities
All the legal claims held against the firm by nonowners.

net worth
The capital and surplus of the firm—capital stock, paid-in capital, and retained earnings, also called equity or stockholders' or owners' equity.

---

[2]We discuss differences in bond indentures (debt contracts) in Chapter 17.

par value
The nominal or face value of a stock or bond.

however, that if asset values rise, these benefits accrue exclusively to the stockholders.

The equity section of the balance sheet is divided into three accounts—*common stock, paid-in capital,* and *retained earnings.* The first two accounts arise when the firm issues new common stock to raise capital. A **par value** is generally assigned to common stock—Carter's stock has a par value of $1. Now suppose Carter were to sell 1 million additional shares at a price of $30 per share. The company would raise $30 million, and the cash account would go up by this amount. On the right-hand side of the balance sheet, the transaction would be reflected by an increase of $1 per share, or a total increase of $1 million in the common stock account. The remaining $29 per share would be added to the **paid-in capital** account. This account is occasionally referred to by its more descriptive title, *capital-in-excess-of-par.* The results of a sale of new common stock are shown below:

paid-in capital
The funds received in excess of par value when the firm sells stock.

	Before Sale of Stock
Common stock (50,000,000 shares, $1 par)	$ 50,000,000
Paid-in capital	100,000,000
Retained earnings	750,000,000
Total stockholders' equity	$900,000,000

	After Sale of Stock
Common stock (51,000,000 shares, $1 par)	$ 51,000,000
Paid-in capital	129,000,000
Retained earnings	750,000,000
Total stockholders' equity	$930,000,000

Thus, after the sale, common stock would show $51 million, paid-in capital would show $129 million, and there would be 51 million shares. Naturally, the retained earnings account is not affected by the sale of new common stock.

The common stock and paid-in capital accounts provide information about external sources of equity funds. Self-generated, or internal, equity comes from the undistributed profits of the firm. The retained earnings account is built up over time by the firm's "saving" a part of its net income rather than paying all of its earnings out as dividends.[3] Thus, since its inception, Carter has retained, or plowed back, a total of $750 million—$20 million was added just this year.

---

[3]A word of caution is in order here. The retained earnings account does *not* represent a pool from which funds may be withdrawn. The retained earnings account simply indicates the source from which some of the firm's assets were originally procured.

The Cash Flow Cycle

Figure 6-1 shows the **cash flow** cycle within a firm. Rectangles represent balance sheet accounts—assets and claims agains assets—and cir-

cash flow
The actual net cash that flows into or out of the firm during a specified period.

Figure 6-1
Cash and Materials Flows within the Firm
The focal point of a firm's cash flow cycle is its cash account, whose balance is influenced by the firm's other accounts (rectangles) and activities (circles). The lower portion of this diagram shows how the cash account is increased through stock issues and borrowing. The cash is then used to purchase raw materials and acquire fixed assets, both of which feed into the production of goods and eventually replenish the cash account through sales. Note that cash flows continuously through this cycle, so that lags in any one portion will influence all portions and will ultimately affect the cash account.

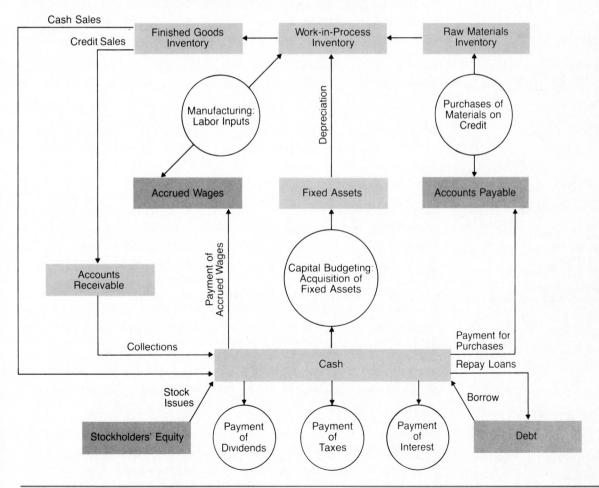

cles represent actions taken by the firm. The diagram is by no means a complete representation of the cash flow cycle: to avoid undue complexity, it shows only the major flows.

The cash account is the focal point of the graph. Certain events, such as collecting accounts receivable or borrowing money from the bank, will cause the cash account to increase, whereas the payment of taxes, interest, and so on will cause the cash account to decline. Similar comments could be made about all the balance sheet accounts—their balances rise, fall, or remain constant depending on events that occur during the period under study, which for Carter is December 31, 1983 through December 31, 1984.

Projected sales increases may require the firm to raise cash by borrowing from its bank or selling new stock. For example, if the firm anticipates an increase in sales, it will (1) expend cash to buy or build fixed assets, (2) step up purchases, thereby increasing raw materials inventories and accounts payable, (3) increase production, which causes an increase in accrued wages and work-in-process, and (4) eventually build up its finished goods inventory. Some cash will have been expended, and the firm will have obligated itself to expend still more cash to pay off its accounts payable and accrued wages. These events will have occurred *before* any cash has been generated. Even when the expected sales do occur, there will still be a lag in the generation of cash until receivables are collected. Depending on how much cash the firm had at the beginning of the buildup, on the length of its production-sales-collection cycle, and on how long it can delay payment of its own payables and accrued wages, the firm may have to obtain significant amounts of additional cash by selling stock or bonds.

If the firm is profitable, its sales revenues will exceed its costs, and its cash inflows will eventually exceed its cash outlays. However, even a profitable firm can experience a cash shortage if it is growing rapidly. It may have to pay for plant, materials, and labor before cash from the expanded sales starts flowing in. For this reason, rapidly growing firms often require large bank loans or capital from other sources.

An unprofitable firm will have larger cash outlays than inflows. This, in turn, will typically cause a slowdown in the payment of accrued wages and accounts payable, and it may also lead to heavy borrowings. Thus liabilities build up to excessive levels in unprofitable firms. Similarly, an overly ambitious expansion plan will be reflected in an excessive buildup of inventories and fixed assets, whereas a poor credit/collection policy will produce bad debts and reduced profits that first show up as high accounts receivable. Financial analysts are well aware of these relationships, and they use the analytical techniques discussed in the remainder of this chapter and in the next chapter to help discover problems before they become too serious.

Table 6-3
Carter Chemical Company: Statement of Retained Earnings for Year Ending
December 31, 1984 (Millions of Dollars)

Balance of retained earnings, December 31, 1983	$730
Add: Net income, 1984	120
Less: Dividends to stockholders	(100)
Balance of retained earnings, December 31, 1984	$750

The Statement of Retained Earnings

Changes in the equity accounts between balance sheet dates are reported in the **statement of retained earnings**; Carter's statement is
shown in Table 6-3. The company earned $120 million during 1984,
paid out $100 million in dividends, and plowed $20 million back into
the business. Thus the balance sheet item "retained earnings" increased from $730 million at the end of 1983 to $750 million at the end
of 1984.

Note that the balance sheet account "retained earnings" represents a
claim against assets, not assets per se. Furthermore, firms retain earnings
primarily to expand the business. This means investing in plant and
equipment, inventories, and so on, *not* in a bank account. *Thus retained
earnings as reported on the balance sheet do not represent cash and are not
"available" for the payment of dividends or anything else.*[4]

**statement of retained
earnings**
A statement reporting that
portion of earnings not paid out
in dividends. The figure that
appears on the balance sheet is
the sum of retained earnings for
each year of the company's
history.

The Statement of Changes in Financial Position

The graphic analysis given in Figure 6-1 is coverted to numerical form
and reported in annual reports as the **statement of changes in financial
position**, often called the *sources and uses of funds statement*. This statement is designed to show how funds were obtained and how they
were used. It helps answer questions such as these: Was the expansion
program financed by sale of debt or equity? How much of its required
capital has the firm been able to generate internally? Has the firm been

**statement of changes in
financial position.**
A statement reporting the firm's
sources of financing and the
uses of those funds over an
accounting period.

---

[4]Recall that the amount recorded in the retained earnings account is *not* an indication of
the amount of cash the firm has. That amount (as of the balance sheet date) is found in
the cash account—an asset account. A positive number in the retained earnings account
indicates only that, in the past, according to generally accepted accounting principles,
the firm has earned an income and its dividends have been less than that reported income.

Table 6-4
Carter Chemical Company: Cash Flows for 1984 (Millions of Dollars)

	Income Statement (1)	Cash Flows (2)
Sales	$3,000	$3,000
Costs and Expenses		
All costs except depreciation	2,634	2,634
Depreciation (D)	100	—
Earnings before interest and taxes (EBIT)	$ 266	$ 366
Interest expense	66	66
Earnings before taxes	$ 200	$ 300
Taxes	80	80
Net income (NI)	$ 120	
Cash flow: CF = NI + D = $120 + $100 =	$ 220	$ 220

building up its liquid assets, or is it becoming less liquid? Because information such as this is useful both for investment analysis and for corporate planning, the statement of changes in financial position is an important part of the annual report.

The Role of Depreciation

Before we discuss the statement of changes in financial position in detail, we should pause to consider one of its most important elements—**depreciation**. First, what is depreciation? In effect, it is an annual charge against income which reflects a rough estimate of the dollar cost of the capital equipment used in the production process. For example, suppose a machine with an expected useful life of 10 years and a zero expected salvage value was purchased in 1983 for $1 billion. This cost must be charged against production over the machine's 10-year life; otherwise profits will be overstated. If the machine is depreciated by the straight line method, the annual charge is $100 million. This amount is deducted from sales revenues, along with such other costs as labor and raw materials, to determine income. However, depreciation is not a cash outlay; funds were expended back in 1983, so the depreciation charged against the income in years 1984 through 1993 is not a cash outlay, as are labor or raw materials charges. *Depreciation is a noncash charge.*

This point is illustrated with data for Carter Chemical Company in Table 6-4. Here Column 1 shows an abbreviated version of Carter's income statement, while Column 2 shows the statement on a cash flow basis. Assume for the moment that (1) all sales are for cash, (2) all costs

depreciation
An annual noncash charge against income that reflects a rough estimate of the dollar cost of equipment used in the production process.

except depreciation were paid during 1984, and (3) no buildups occurred in inventories or other assets. How much cash would have been
generated from operations? From Column 2 we see that the answer is
$220 million. The sales are all for cash, so the firm took in $3 billion in
cash money. Its costs other than depreciation were $2,634 million, and
these were paid in cash, leaving $366 million. Depreciation is *not* a cash
charge—the firm does not pay out the $100 million of depreciation ex-
penses—so $366 million of cash money is still left after depreciation.
Taxes and interest, however, are paid in cash, so $66 million for inter-
est and $80 million for taxes must be deducted from the $366 million
EBIT cash flow, leaving a net cash flow from operations of $220 million.
As shown in Column 1, this $220 million is, of course, exactly equal to
profit after tax plus depreciation: $120 million plus $100 million equals
$220 million. Thus, since depreciation is a noncash charge and is added
back to net income to approximate cash flows from operations, it is
included as a source of funds in the statement of financial position.
Current methods of depreciation for tax purposes are detailed at the
end of this chapter in Appendix 6A.

Before leaving the subject of depreciation, we should sound a word
of caution. Depreciation does not *really* provide funds; it is simply a
noncash charge. Hence it is added back to net income to obtain an
estimate of the cash flow from operations. However, if the firm made
no sales, then depreciation would certainly not provide cash flows. To
see this point more clearly, consider the situation of Communications
Satellite Corporation (Comsat), which derives its income principally
from two satellites, one positioned over the Atlantic and one over the
Pacific. Comsat's cash flows are approximately equal to its net income
plus its depreciation charges. Yet, if its satellites stopped working,
sales would vanish, and although accountants might still calculate depreciation, this depreciation would provide no cash flows (except possibly some tax loss carry-backs).

Preparing the Statement of Changes in Financial Position

The statement of changes in financial position is designed to answer at
a glance these three questions: (1) Where did the firm get its funds
during the year? (2) What did it do with its available funds? (3) Did
operations during the year tend to increase or decrease the firm's liquidity as measured by the change in net working capital? (**Net working capital** is defined as current assets minus current liabilities. In general, the firm's financial position is stronger if net working capital
increases, weaker if it decreases.)

The starting point in preparing a statement of changes in financial
position is to determine the change in each balance sheet item, and
then to record it as either a source or a use of funds in accordance with
the following rules:

net working capital
Current assets minus current
liabilities.

Table 6-5
Carter Chemical Company: Changes in Balance Sheet Accounts during 1984
(Millions of Dollars)

	Dec. 31, 1984	Dec. 31 1983	Change	
			Source	Use
Cash	$ 50	$ 55	$ 5	$
Marketable securities	0	25	25	
Accounts receivable	350	315		35
Inventories	300	215		85
Gross plant and equipment	1,800	1,470		330
Accumulated depreciation[a]	500	400	100	
Accounts payable	60	30	30	
Notes payable	100	60	40	
Accrued wages	10	10		
Accrued taxes	130	120	10	
Mortgage bonds	500	520		20
Debentures	300	60	240	
Common stock	50	50		
Paid-in capital	100	100		
Retained earnings	750	730	20	
Totals			$470	$470

[a]Depreciation is a "contra-asset," not an asset. Hence an increase in depreciation is a source of funds.

Sources: (1) *Increase* in a claim, that is, in a liability or capital account
        (2) *Decrease* in an asset account

Uses: (1) *Decrease* in a claim against assets
        (2) *Increase* in an asset account

Thus sources of funds include bank loans and retained earnings, as well as money generated by selling assets, collecting receivables, and even drawing down the cash account. Uses include acquiring fixed assets, building up inventories, and paying off debts.

Table 6-5 shows the changes in Carter Chemical Company's balance sheet accounts during the calendar year 1984, with each change designated as a source or a use. Sources and uses each total $470 million.

The data contained in Table 6-5 are next used to prepare the formal statement of changes in financial position, or sources and uses of funds statement; the one contained in Carter's annual report is shown in Table 6-6. Notice that the statement provides answers to the three questions asked above: (1) the top section reports Carter's major sources of funds; (2) the middle section shows how Carter used funds; and (3) the lower section, which deals with current assets and liabilities, shows

Table 6-6
Carter Chemical Company: Statement of Changes in Financial Position
(Millions of Dollars)

Sources of Funds

Net income after taxes	$120
Depreciation	100
Funds from operations	$220
Proceeds from sale of debentures	240
Total sources	$460

Uses of Funds

Repayment of mortgage bonds	$ 20
Increase in net fixed assets	330
Dividend payments to common stockholders	100
Net increase in working capital (see detail below)	10
Total uses	$460

Analysis of Changes in Working Capital[a]

Increase (decrease) in current assets:	
Cash	($ 5)[b]
Marketable securities	(25)
Accounts receivable	35
Inventories	85
Net increase in current assets	$90
Increase (decrease) in current liabilities:	
Accounts payable	$30
Notes payable	40
Accrued taxes	10
Net increase in current liabilities	$80
Net increase (decrease) in working capital	$10

[a]*Net working capital* is defined as current assets minus current liabilities.
[b]Parentheses denote negative numbers here and throughout the book.

how the company's liquidity position changed during the year. We see that Carter's major sources of funds were net income, depreciation, and the sale of debentures (a type of long-term debt which is described in Chapter 17). These funds were used to reduce the mortgage debt, to increase fixed assets, and to pay dividends on common stock. Also, $10 million was used to increase net working capital.

As shown in the bottom section, Carter decreased its cash and marketable securities but increased accounts receivable and inventories, for a net increase in current assets of $90 million. Current liabilities increased by $80 million, so there was an increase of $10 million in net working capital (current assets minus current liabilities). This net increase in working capital is reported as a use in the middle section.

Notice also that every item in the "change" columns of Table 6-5 is carried over to Table 6-6 *except retained earnings*. The statement of changes in financial position reports net income as a source and dividends as a use, rather than netting these items out and just reporting the increase in retained earnings.

Carter Chemical Company is a strong, well-managed company, and its sources and uses statement shows nothing unusual or alarming. One does, however, occasionally see situations where huge increases in fixed assets are financed primarily by short-term debt, which must be repaid within a few months if the lender demands repayment. This would show up in the lower third of the table as a decrease in net working capital, and it is, as we shall see in detail later in the book, a dangerous situation.

Summary

In order to analyze any firm properly, managers and investors must be able to understand the company's financial data. The most obvious source of data for a publicly traded company is its annual report. This report contains four basic statements: the *income statement*, the *balance sheet*, the *statement of retained earnings*, and the *statement of changes in financial position*.

The income statement provides a detailed view of the flow of funds, both revenues and expenses, over the most recent accounting period. The focus of the income statement is the residual earnings available to stockholders after all financing and operating costs have been deducted and the claims of government (uninvited) partners have been satisfied. The income statement indicates the amount of current earnings that is paid to owners in the form of dividends or reinvested to finance future operations.

The income statement provides a view of the firm over a period of time, whereas the balance sheet indicates the status of the firm at a point in time. The balance sheet describes the assets controlled by the firm and how those assets were financed. The financing of the firm is divided between contributions of owners and those of the firm's creditors.

Changes in the equity accounts between balance sheet dates are reported in the statement of retained earnings. Since many firms generate the majority of equity funds internally, through undistributed profits, this statement is an important source of information on continuing equity financing.

The statement of changes in financial position restates information from the income statement and balance sheet. This statement answers the simple but critical questions, "Where did the money come from?" and "Where did the money go?" Thus it provides information about the sources of financing and the uses of those funds over the reporting period.

In the next chapter we explore methods that are available to further analyze the firm's financial data.

Resolution to Decision in Finance

Letters from Chairman Buffett

Of all the documents that large companies publish, none receives so much attention as the annual report to shareholders. At some companies—such as General Electric—top executives begin work on the report as much as six months before its publication. And most hire professional designers and writers to insure that the final product will look sharp and read well.

Obviously, so much fuss would hardly be necessary if the only goal of an annual report were to inform shareholders about financial results. But, in fact, most big companies have turned their annual report into flashy management showcases. In slick magazine format, using four-color photos, feature stories, and elaborate graphics, each firm tells the story its chairman would like to see told. And to get the desired results, most annual reports are now produced by the director of public relations instead of the chief financial officer.

Due to their puffery, annual reports have lost credibility with serious seekers of financial information. Instead, Wall Street analysts and other sophisticated investors prefer more straightforward financial disclosure documents, such as 10-K's, proxies, 8-K's, and 13-D's, all of which contain more detailed and unadorned information and must by law be filed with the Securities and Exchange Commission.

Of course, a company's philosophy and personality do count, and few other documents can offer better insight into these intangibles than can an annual report. But most financial experts believe that companies owe it to their investors to distinguish between the fanfare and the facts. They want to see more annual reports that realistically examine management conduct of business affairs and factually discuss projects that will improve corporate welfare in the future. They'd like to see annual reports become the equivalent of management report cards, detailing strengths and weaknesses and plans for improvement. Given such information, they claim, shareholders would be better equipped to make intelligent investment decisions.

Chairman Warren Buffett's letters, although probably a bit too subjective for financial reporting purists, represent a giant step in the desired direction. In fact, Berkshire Hathaway's annual reports contain no photographs, colored ink, bar charts, or graphs, freeing readers to focus on the company's financial statements and Buffett's interpretation of them. Some CEOs might contend that such a bare-bones approach is too dull for the average stockholder and, further, that some readers may actually be intimidated by the information overload. But

Buffett would no doubt counter that, whatever its shortcomings, his approach shows much greater respect for shareholders' intelligence and capacity to understand than does the average annual report.

A. A. Sommer, Jr., who chaired an SEC panel formed in 1976 to study disclosure practices, says that his group agreed that letters like Buffett's were important. But, he says, "Warren's letters are unique. Few CEOs are as smart in as many ways as Warren. It would be awfully hard to require that kind of discussion from all CEOs." In other words, it takes a chairman with interesting ideas to write an interesting chairman's letter.

Sources: "Letters from Chairman Buffett," *Fortune*, Aug. 22, 1983, 137–141; "Annual Reports Get an Editor in Washington," *Fortune*, May 7, 1979, 210–222; "Annual Reports: The Rites of Spring," *Wall Street Journal*, Mar. 12, 1984, 26.

Key Terms You should be able to define each of the following terms:

Annual report; income statement; balance sheet
Assets; liabilities
Equity; net worth
Par value
Paid-in capital

Cash flow
Statement of retained earnings
Statement of changes in financial position
Depreciation
Rapid depreciation methods
Net working capital

Questions

6-1 What four statements are contained in most annual reports?

6-2 Is it true that if a "typical" firm reports $20 million of retained earnings on its balance sheet, that firm's directors could declare a $20 million cash dividend without any qualms whatsoever?

6-3 What is the relationship between each rectangle in Figure 6-1 and each individual source and use in a sources and uses of funds statement?

Problems

6-1 Arrange these income statement items in their proper order:

Labor and material expense
Depreciation
Earnings before interest and taxes
Selling and administrative expense
Earnings before taxes

Net income
Lease payments on buildings
Sales
Federal tax
Interest payments

* 6-2 Ashley's Card Shop, Inc. sold 30,000 cards at 75 cents each this month. The cards cost 55 cents wholesale. Ashley's newspaper and radio advertising expenses are $800 monthly. Mr. and Mrs. Ashley work in the shop

---

*Refer to Appendix E for check answers to problems with asterisks.

and pay themselves a combined monthly salary of $2,800. The monthly rent payment for the shop is $1,800 and the depreciation on the store fixtures is $500 per month. The tax rate is 40 percent. What is the store's profit or loss for the month?

6-3 Balance sheet items may be categorized as:

Current assets (CA)   Long-term debt (LTD)
Fixed assets (FA)   Common stock equity (CSE)
Current liabilities (CL)

Categorize each of the following accounts:

____Debt maturing in less   ____Cash
    than one year   ____Common stock
____Accounts receivable   ____Short-term
____Debt maturing in more   notes payable
    than one year   ____Retained earnings
____Paid-in capital   ____Accruals
____Mortgage bond   ____Plant and equipment
____Inventory   ____Marketable securities
____Accounts payable

* **6-4** Oklahoma Gas and Electric has the following net worth section reported on its balance sheet:

Common stock ($1 par)	$10,000,000
Paid-in capital	12,000,000
Retained earnings	53,000,000
Total shareholders' equity	$75,000,000

The company is planning to sell an issue of $8,500,000 in equity at $8.50 per share. Fill in the following net worth section to reflect the sale of the new equity:

Common stock ($1 par)	$ _____
Paid-in capital	_____
Retained earnings	_____
Total shareholders' equity	$ _____

6-5 Shortly after the sale of the stock, Oklahoma Gas and Electric (from Problem 6-4) reported that net income for the year was $38,500,000. The company announced it would pay dividends totaling $25,000,000.
a. What was the firm's earnings per share?
b. What was the firm's dividends per share?
c. Complete the following net worth section to reflect the stock sales and the effect of the firm's earnings and dividend payment:

Common stock ($1 par)	$ _____
Paid-in capital	_____
Retained earnings	_____
Total shareholders' equity	$ _____

⁎ **6-6** Wilson's, Inc. had $8,750,000 in retained earnings on December 31, 1983. The firm paid $700,000 in dividends during 1984 and reported retained earnings on December 31, 1984 to be $9,362,500. What was Wilson's reported net income for 1984?

6-7 What effect would each of the following events have on a firm's balance sheet?
  ⁎ **a.** Purchase of a new asset for $2 million cash.
  ⁎ **b.** Purchase of a new asset for $2 million financed with 35 percent debt and 65 percent cash.
  c. Sale of $100,000 in merchandise for cash.
  d. Sale of $100,000 in merchandise for credit.
  e. Inventory write-off of $200,000 due to obsolescence.
  f. Payment of $50,000 to trade creditors.

6-8 Refer to Tables 6-1 and 6-2 to answer the following questions:
  a. What would Carter Chemical Company's balance sheet item "retained earnings" for 1984 have been if the firm paid $40,000 in dividends for the year?
  b. What would Carter's 1984 EPS have been had net income for that year been $150 million rather than $120 million?
  c. Suppose that you knew that Carter's EPS was $2.40 and that net income was $120 million. Could you use this information to determine the number of shares outstanding?
  d. If Carter sold inventories carried at $200 million for only $50 million, what effects would this have on the firm's balance sheet? (Disregard tax effects.)
  e. Carter's accountants find that ACRS depreciation (see Appendix 6A) shortens the tax life of assets. This would increase the firm's depreciation expense. How will this action affect the company's cash flows? No calculations are necessary.

6-9 Determine the increase or decrease in net working capital for Missouri Steel last year, given the information below. (Assume no other changes have occurred over the past year.)

Decrease in cash	$60
Decrease in marketable securities	50
Increase in accounts receivable	100
Decrease in accounts payable	40
Increase in accrued wages and taxes	30
Increase in inventories	70
Increase in notes payable	60

6-10 The consolidated balance sheets for the Oregon Lumber Company at the beginning and end of 1984 follow. The company bought $75 million worth of fixed assets. The charge for depreciation in 1984 was $15 million. Earnings after taxes were $38 million, and the company paid out $10 million in dividends.
  a. Fill in the amount of source or use in the appropriate column.
  b. Prepare a statement of changes in financial position.
  c. Briefly summarize your findings.

**Oregon Lumber Company: Balance Sheet, Beginning and End of 1984
(Millions of Dollars)**

	Jan. 1	Dec. 31	Change Source	Change Use
Cash	$ 15	$ 7	_____	_____
Marketable securities	11	0	_____	_____
Net receivables	22	30	_____	_____
Inventories	53	75	_____	_____
Total current assets	$101	$112	_____	_____
Gross fixed assets	$ 75	$150	_____	_____
Less: Depreciation	(26)	(41)	_____	_____
Net fixed assets	$ 49	$109	_____	_____
Total assets	$150	$221	_____	_____
Accounts payable	$ 15	$ 18	_____	_____
Notes payable	15	3	_____	_____
Other current liabilities	7	15	_____	_____
Long-term debt	8	26	_____	_____
Common stock	38	64	_____	_____
Retained earnings	67	95	_____	_____
Total claims on assets	$150	$221	_____	_____

Selected References

Two accounting publications aimed especially at the beginning student or the nonaccountant are:

Merrill Lynch, *How to Read a Financial Report*, 4th ed. (New York: 1979).

Tracy, John A., *How to Read a Financial Report*, 2nd ed. (New York: Wiley, 1983).

A more complete discussion of financial statements may be found in any introductory accounting texts. Such texts include:

Berney, Paul R., William P. Lyons, and Stanley J. Garstka, *Financial Accounting and Reporting: Text and Cases* (Homewood, IL: Irwin, 1981).

Reynolds, Isaac N., Allen B. Sanders, and A. Douglas Hillman, *Principles of Accounting* (Hinsdale, IL: Dryden Press, 1984).

More specialized readings for the finance student include:

Harrington, Diana R., and Brent D. Wilson, *Corporate Financial Analysis* (Plano, TX: Business Publications, 1983).

Helfert, Erich A., *Techniques of Financial Analysis*, 5th ed. (Homewood, IL: Irwin, 1982).

Hunt, Pearson, "Funds Position: Keystone in Financial Planning," *Harvard Business Review*, May–June 1975, 106–115.

Norby, William C., "Accounting for Financial Analysis," *Financial Analysts Journal*, July–August 1982, 33–35.

The Effects of Depreciation and Inventory Valuation on Reported Income

Don't worry about

The income statement presented in Table 6-1 appears simple and unambiguous in its construction. In actuality, the financial manager has many options in reporting income. A review of accounting texts reveals a multiplicity of generally accepted accounting procedures which may be used to report income.

It is quite possible (and legal, we hasten to add) to report one level of income to the tax authorities and another level to the owners of the firm. The purpose for "keeping two sets of books" is, of course, to minimize taxable income. Two widely used methods to delay tax liabilities are rapid depreciation methodologies and alternative methods used to value inventory.[1]

Depreciation

Depreciation is a deductible expense. Several different depreciation methods are permitted for tax purposes, and the choice of the method used can have a profound effect on a firm's tax liabilities and cash flows. The principal methods of depreciation are straight line and three **rapid depreciation methods:** *sum-of-years'-digits* and *double declining balance* for assets acquired before 1981 and the *accelerated cost recovery system* (ACRS) for assets acquired in 1981 and after.

rapid depreciation methods
Depreciation methods that write off the cost of an asset at a faster rate than the write-off under the straight line method.

Depreciation Methods Prior to 1981

We shall begin by assuming that a machine is purchased for $2,500 and has an estimated useful life of 6 years. It will have a scrap value of $400 after 6 years of use. Table 6A-1 illustrates each of the three depreciation

---

[1]As we noted earlier in the chapter, inventory valuation and the calculation of depreciation are only *two of several* methods which can be used to significantly restate income for a particular accounting period.

Table 6A-1
Comparison of Depreciation Methods for a 6-Year,
$2,500 Asset with a $400 Salvage Value[a]

Year	Straight Line	Double Declining Balance (DDB)	Sum-of-Years'-Digits (SYD)
1	$ 350	$ 833	$ 600
2	350	556	500
3	350	370	400
4	350	247	300
5	350	94[b]	200
6	350	—	100
Total	$2,100	$2,100	$2,100

[a]It is assumed these assets were acquired before 1981.
[b]The maximum depreciation that can be taken is the value of the cost minus the salvage value, or $2,100 in this example.

methods for assets acquired before 1981 and compares the depreciation charges under each method. Figure 6A-1 graphs the depreciation charges under the straight line and double declining balance methods.[2]

Straight Line

With the straight line method, a uniform annual depreciation charge of $350 a year is allowed. This figure is arrived at by simply dividing the economic life into the total cost of the machine minus the estimated salvage value:

$$\frac{\$2,500 \text{ cost } - \$400 \text{ salvage value}}{6 \text{ years}} = \$350 \text{ a year depreciation charge.}$$

If the estimated salvage value had been less than 10 percent of the original cost, it could have been ignored.

Double Declining Balance

The double declining balance (DDB) method of depreciation requires the application of a constant rate of depreciation each year to the undepreciated value of the asset at the close of the previous year. To calculate DDB depreciation, we first find the fraction 1/N, where N is

---

[2]These methodologies are important to today's financial manager for at least two reasons. First, they give historical perspective to the currently used ACRS depreciation methodology. Secondly, firms must still use sum-of-years'-digits or double declining balance rather than the ACRS method for many state tax returns.

Figure 6A-1
Double Declining Balance versus Straight Line Depreciation
In this graph the double declining balance method is compared to the straight line method in depreciating a $2,500 machine over a 6-year period. The total amount of depreciation taken, and thus total cash flows, are equal under both methods. Under DDB, however, depreciation and cash flows are higher in earlier years. Since cash received earlier is more valuable than cash received later, the DDB method will have a beneficial effect on cash flows (see Table 6A-2).

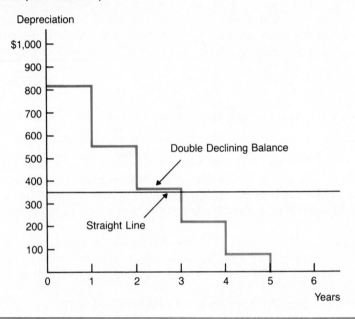

the life of the asset. In our example, 1/N = 1/6 = 0.1667. This fraction is then doubled, giving 0.3333 in this case, and it is called the "depreciation rate." This rate is applied to the full purchase price of the machine, not to the cost less the salvage value. Therefore depreciation under the DDB method during the first year is calculated as follows:

$$0.3333 \ (\$2,500) = \$833.$$

Depreciation during the second year is calculated by applying the 33.33 percent rate (or 0.3333) to the undepreciated balance as follows:

$$0.3333(\$2,500 - \$833) = 0.3333(\$1,667) = \$556.$$

The process is continued for other years until the total depreciation taken equals the cost of the asset less the estimated salvage value. Thus, in the illustrative case, the asset is fully depreciated during the fifth year.

The total amount of depreciation taken under the DDB method is equal to that under straight line, but under DDB the depreciation is taken faster, as it is under sum-of-years'-digits. Thus DDB and sum-of-years'-digits are called *accelerated depreciation methods.*[3]

Sum-of-Years'-Digits

Under the sum-of-years'-digits (SYD) method, the yearly depreciation allowance is determined as follows:

1. Calculate the SYDs. In our example there is a total of 21 digits: $1 + 2 + 3 + 4 + 5 + 6 = 21$. This figure can also be arrived at by means of the sum of an algebraic progression equation, where N is the life of the asset:

$$\text{Sum} = N \left(\frac{N + 1}{2} \right)$$

$$= 6 \left(\frac{6 + 1}{2} \right) = 21.$$

2. Divide the number of remaining years by the SYDs and multiply this fraction by the depreciable cost (total cost minus salvage value) of the asset:

$$\text{Year 1:} \quad \left(\frac{6}{21} \right) (\$2,100) = \$600 \text{ depreciation}$$

$$\text{Year 2:} \quad \left(\frac{5}{21} \right) (\$2,100) = \$500 \text{ depreciation}$$

$$\text{Year 6:} \quad \left(\frac{1}{21} \right) (\$2,100) = \$100 \text{ depreciation.}$$

Effect of Depreciation on Taxes Paid

The effect of the accelerated methods on a firm's income tax payment is easily demonstrated. In the first year, if the firm chooses to use the straight line method, only $350 may be deducted from its earnings to arrive at earnings before taxes (the amount of earnings to which the tax rate applies). However, using any one of the rapid depreciation methods, the firm would have a much greater deduction and therefore a lower tax liability.

---

[3]It should also be noted that a firm may switch from DDB (or SYD) to straight line whenever it becomes advantageous to do so. The undepreciated balance, less the estimated salvage value, is divided by the remaining life to get the annual depreciation. If this value is larger than the DDB depreciation, then the switch should be made. In our example it is not advantageous to switch. Had the salvage value been lower, then a switch would have been advantageous.

Table 6A-2
Cash Flow Effects: Straight Line versus DDB Depreciation

	Straight Line	DDB
Year 1		
Sales (all cash)	$2,000	$2,000
Costs other than depreciation (all cash)	1,000	1,000
Depreciation (not a cash charge)	350	833
Total deductible costs	$1,350	$1,833
Taxable income	650	167
Taxes (assume a 40% rate)	$ 260	$ 67
Cash flow = Sales − Other costs − Taxes	$ 740	$ 933
Year 6		
Sales (all cash)	$2,000	$2,000
Costs other than depreciation (all cash)	1,000	1,000
Depreciation (not a cash charge)	350	—
Total deductible costs	$1,350	$1,000
Taxable income	650	1,000
Taxes (assume a 40% rate)	$ 260	$ 400
Cash flow = Sales − Other costs − Taxes	$ 740	$ 600

This point is illustrated in Table 6A-2, which shows the cash flows a hypothetical firm will generate if it uses straight line versus double declining balance depreciation. In Year 1 taxes are lower under DDB depreciation, and hence cash flows are higher. However, the situation changes over time—in later years the depreciation tax shelter declines in the DDB case, causing taxes to rise and cash flows to decline.

Over the entire six-year period, total cash flows are the same for the two cases. However, since cash received sooner is more valuable than cash received later, a firm that uses accelerated depreciation and thus speeds up the cash flows from operations will have a higher value than a similar firm that uses straight line depreciation. Similarly, an asset that can be depreciated by an accelerated method will have a higher value than one that must be depreciated by straight line.[4]

---

[4]Firms may report profit to stockholders using straight line depreciation even though they use an accelerated depreciation method for tax purposes. The difference between taxes actually paid during the year (the actual tax bill) and the taxes that would have been paid had the firm used straight line for tax purposes is reported on the income statement as "deferred taxes," and the accumulated deferred taxes over the years is reported on the balance sheet as a liability item. This treatment, which is called "normalization" for timing differences in the reporting of depreciation for tax and book purposes, would keep our illustrative firm from having to report lower income just because it elected to use accelerated depreciation for tax purposes.

Depreciation Methods after 1981

The Economic Recovery Act of 1981 created the **accelerated cost recovery system (ACRS).** Congress enacted this legislation when it became convinced that the previous system of depreciation would not provide adequate stimulus for economic expansion. ACRS replaced the previous depreciation systems with a revised means of determining the tax life of an asset *and* of calculating depreciation for federal tax purposes. Technically, the new system refers to *cost recovery* rather than depreciation. However, since depreciation and cost recovery have the same effect, we retain the more familiar term *depreciation.*

In the past, depreciation charges for tax purposes had to be based on asset lives which more or less approximated expected economic lives. However, the 1981 tax law permits assets to be written off, for tax purposes, over periods which are generally much shorter than their operating lives. Under ACRS the cost of an asset is recovered over a 3-year, 5-year, 10-year, 15-year, or 18-year period, depending on the type of property. In general, the tax lives, called *recovery periods*, for various classes of property are:

3-year: Automobiles, light trucks, certain types of short-lived machinery and equipment.

5-year: Heavy trucks, aircraft, most types of production machinery and equipment, office furniture

10-year: Certain types of real estate with relatively short economic lives.

15-year: Most public utility assets

18-year: Most buildings

The accelerated cost recovery system allows a company to recover the entire cost of an asset, including any anticipated salvage value. For property acquired after 1981, ACRS utilizes a 150 percent declining balance method in the early years of the asset's life, and switches to straight line in the later years of the depreciation period. The method includes the use of a "half-year convention" which is built into the depreciation methodology. In other words, a 3-year class asset would be depreciated 1.5(⅓) = 50%, if the full depreciation were allowed in the first year. However, only one half of that amount may be used. Each of these factors is included in the recovery percentages for the ACRS method, which are presented in Table 6A-3.

How would the new ACRS method be used? Assume Columbia Printing Company is planning to buy a new production machine for

accelerated cost recovery system (ACRS)
A depreciation system that permits assets to be written off over periods much shorter than their operating lives.

Table 6A-3
Recovery (Depreciation) Percentages for Assets Placed in Service after 1981

| Year | Applicable Percentage for the Class of Property | | | |
	3-Year	5-Year	10-Year	15-Year
1	25	15	8	5
2	38	22	14	10
3	37	21	12	9
4		21	10	8
5		21	10	7
6			10	7
7			9	6
8			9	6
9			9	6
10			9	6
11				6
12				6
13				6
14				6
15				6

$100,000 and a delivery truck for $8,500. Both of these assets will be placed in service in 1985. The recovery percentages in Table 6A-3 are used to calculate the appropriate depreciation. Note that under the ACRS method the truck is a 3-year asset and the production machine is a 5-year asset.

Depreciation in 1985:
25% of $8,500 (truck) $ 2,125
15% of $100,000 (production machine)   15,000
                                                           $ 17,125

Depreciation in 1986:
38% of $8,500 (truck) $ 3,230
22% of $100,000 (production machine)   22,000
                                                           $ 25,230

Depreciation in 1987:
37% of $8,500 (truck) $ 3,145
21% of $100,000 (production machine)   21,000
                                                           $ 24,145

Depreciation in 1988:
21% of $100,000 (production machine) $ 21,000

Depreciation in 1989:
21% of $100,000 (production machine) $ 21,000
Total depreciation $108,500

Thus all that is required to implement the accelerated cost recovery system is to multiply the cost of the truck and production machine by the appropriate percentage in the 3-year and 5-year recovery tables. These tables have the half-year convention built in and automatically switch depreciation to straight line at the most appropriate time.

Would our annual depreciation charges change if the firm expected some residual (salvage) value for the assets after they were fully depreciated? *No.* Under ACRS the asset is depreciated fully even if residual value is expected. The market value of a fully depreciated asset is taxed as ordinary income to the extent that it represents a "recapture" of depreciation. In the event that the asset is sold for more than its original cost, the difference between the amount received and the original cost of the asset is taxed as a capital gain.

Straight Line Option

Although the prescribed class lives are normally used for tax purposes, ACRS does provide the option of figuring tax depreciation on a straight line basis using three alternative lives, as shown below:

  3-year: 3-, 5-, or 12-year optional recovery periods

  5-year: 5-, 12-, or 25-year optional recovery periods

 10-year: 10-, 25-, or 35-year optional recovery periods

 15-year: 15-, 35-, or 45-year optional recovery periods

The ACRS recovery allowances were set by Congress to always equal or exceed the straight line rates. Therefore a firm will always obtain a greater depreciation allowance from using ACRS than from using one of the optional straight line alternatives. Only companies which expect to lose money, and hence to have no tax liability for a period of years, would elect the straight line option. Use of the straight line method would give these firms more depreciation allowances in later years when, it is presumed, they will be earning profits and will need tax deductions.

If the straight line method is used, there are some important points to remember. First, the same method and recovery period must be used for all property in the same class placed into service in the same year. Second, the depreciation expense is based on the unadjusted cost; that is, salvage value is not considered. Third, the half-year convention is applicable—regardless of when the asset was placed into service, only one half of the straight line depreciation expense is allowed in the first year. However, when the straight line option is used, if the asset is held for the entire recovery period, the other half-year amount can be applied in the year following the end of the recovery period. *However, for ease of computation, this text will use straight line depreciation without the half-year convention. While we are technically incorrect in doing so, we feel that the inclusion of the half-year convention is cumbersome and adds little to the student's knowledge of finance.*

Caution

The information presented on depreciation represents the tax laws that were in effect at the time this text was written. However, as we reminded you in Chapter 2, tax laws are changed to some extent every year, and the tax laws are *extremely complex*. Consequently, it is vitally important to consult current regulations and, better yet, a qualified tax expert to determine the tax implications of any proposed action.

Inventory Valuation

Another means by which the financial manager can delay tax payments to the government is through the choice of inventory valuation methods.[5] If the most expensive materials are reportedly used in the production process, cost of goods sold (COGS) will be large, and the resulting taxable income will therefore be lower.

Consider the following example of raw materials purchases in the fourth quarter of the current year:

October: 10,000 units purchased at $5 each = $50,000

November: 10,000 units purchased at $7 each = $70,000

December: 10,000 units purchased at $9 each = $90,000

Further suppose that 24,000 units of final product are sold at a price of $10 each during this quarter. What is the resulting cost of goods sold for the period?

Although several alternatives exist in inventory valuation, we consider only two methods—**first-in, first-out (FIFO)** and **last-in, first-out (LIFO).** FIFO assumes that the available raw materials inventory will be used in the production process in the same order in which it was received. Conversely, the LIFO method assumes that the most recently received inventory will be the first used and sold. Table 6A-4 illustrates that, in a time of *rising prices*, the LIFO method minimizes both the

first-in, first-out (FIFO)
Inventory valuation method that assumes that production process inventory will be used in the same order in which it was received.

last-in, first-out (LIFO)
Inventory valuation method that assumes that the most recently received inventory will be the first used.

---

[5]It is important to note that rapid depreciation and various inventory valuation methods only defer, and do not enable the firm to avoid, tax liabilities. However, until the deferred tax payments are due, the firm may profitably utilize these funds.

Table 6A-4
Effects of Inventory Methodologies on Cost of Goods Sold, Ending Inventory, and Taxes

FIFO			LIFO		
Order of Use	Per-Unit Price	Cost	Order of Use	Per-Unit Price	Cost
October 10,000	$5	$ 50,000	December 10,000	$9	$ 90,000
November 10,000	7	70,000	November 10,000	7	70,000
December 4,000	9	36,000	October 4,000	5	20,000
Units 24,000		Total $156,000	Units 24,000		Total $180,000

Value of Ending Inventory

Units 6,000		Value $ 54,000	Units 6,000		Value $ 30,000

Income Statements

Sales (24,000 @ $10)		$240,000	Sales (24,000 @ $10)	$240,000
Cost of goods sold		156,000	Cost of goods sold	180,000
Profit before taxes		84,000	Profit before taxes	60,000
Taxes (40%)		33,600	Taxes (40%)	24,000
Reported profits		$ 50,400	Reported profits	$ 36,000

taxable income for the period (and thus the amount of taxes paid) and the value of the inventory at the end of the period.[6]

Thus, in periods of rising prices, LIFO can be used by financial managers interested in minimizing their firms' tax liability over the near term. The *Wall Street Journal* reported that in the inflationary environment of recent years many firms have switched from FIFO to LIFO to avoid higher taxes.[7]

Of course, when the lower-priced inventory is depleted, the firm's tax bill will increase. Thus inventory valuation methods, like depreciation, merely delay tax payments; they do not allow the firm to avoid its tax obligations.

---

[6]Of course, in periods of declining prices the opposite result would occur if LIFO were used. In other words, the FIFO method reports profits which move in the same direction as price changes, and LIFO reports profits which move counter to price changes.

[7]The IRS will allow only one change in inventory valuation methods. It will not allow further changes in inventory methods for the sole purpose of reducing taxes—the tax authorities have read this book too.

Key Terms You should be able to define each of the following terms:

Straight line method of depreciation

Double declining balance method of depreciation

Sum-of-years'-digits method of depreciation

Accelerated cost recovery system (ACRS)

First-in, first-out (FIFO); last-in, first-out (LIFO)

Problems

6A-1 The president of Baker Brothers Construction, Charles Young, has equipment needs for the next few years. Since the central Florida construction picture is brightening after a prolonged slump, Mr. Young feels it is time to invest in new trucks and heavy construction equipment. He plans to buy two pickup trucks for $7,500 each and $500,000 in heavy equipment. The trucks are 3-year-class assets and the heavy equipment belongs to the 5-year class. If the investment tax credit (see Chapter 2) is temporarily ignored, calculate the annual depreciation expense over the assets' lives, utilizing ACRS.

6A-2 Rework the depreciation computation in Problem 6A-1 assuming the applicable investment tax credit is taken.
  a. What is the total investment tax credit?
  b. What is the depreciable basis of each asset when the investment tax credit is taken?
  c. What is the annual depreciation?

6A-3 The wrong political party was elected (you choose the villain) and inflation is rampant. Fisher Enterprises has seen its cost of materials increase each month. Fisher's first quarter purchases are noted below:

> January: 50,000 units purchased at $10 each = $500,000
>
> February: 50,000 units purchased at $11 each = $550,000
>
> March: 50,000 units purchased at $12 each = $600,000

Suppose the firm is able to sell 130,000 units at $14 each.
  a. What is the value of the ending inventory under (1) the LIFO method and (2) the FIFO method of inventory valuation? (Assume zero inventory before January's purchases.)
  b. What is the quarter's reported profit if the inventory cost is the only component of cost of goods sold and the tax rate is 40 percent?

Interpreting Financial Statements

7

Decision in Finance

ring legitimate expenses to a later period—all designed to boost sales and earnings.

As you read this chapter, consider how falsified sales and earnings reports would affect the analysis of a company's financial statements. Since actual stealing isn't involved in cooking the books, does anyone get hurt? If so, who? What action should PepsiCo have taken when it discovered the deception?

See end of chapter for resolution.

In Chapter 6 we examined the major sources of financial information—the income statement and the balance sheet. We also discussed evaluative techniques, such as the statement of changes in financial position, which aid in the interpretation of the available financial data. In this chapter we continue our discussion of the techniques of financial analysis, specifically ratio analysis, by which firms' relative riskiness, creditworthiness, profit potential, and general managerial competence can be appraised.

Importance of Financial Statements

Financial statements report both on a firm's position at a point in time and on its operations over some past period. However, their real usefulness lies in the fact that they can be used to help predict the firm's future earnings and dividends, as well as the riskiness of these cash flows. From an equity investor's viewpoint, *predicting the future is what financial statement analysis is all about*. Of course, debtholders and those considering lending to the firm are also concerned with the firm's future, although the firm's "debt investors" and its equity investors are usually concerned with different aspects of the firm's future. From management's viewpoint, *financial statement analysis is useful both as a way to anticipate future conditions and, more importantly, as a starting point for planning actions that will influence the future course of events for the firm*.

Ratio Analysis

Financial ratios are designed to show relationships among financial statement accounts. Ratios put numbers into perspective. For example, Firm A might have $5,248,760 of debt and annual interest charges of $419,900, while Firm B's debt totals $52,647,980 and its interest charges are $3,948,600. The true burden of these debts, and the companies' ability to repay them, can be ascertained only by comparing each firm's debt to its assets and its interest charges to the income available for payment of interest. Such comparisons are made by **ratio analysis.**

ratio analysis
Analysis of the relationships among financial statement accounts.

A single ratio is relatively useless in making relevant evaluations of a firm's health. To be effectively interpreted, a ratio must be systematically compared in one of the following ways: (1) compared to several ratios in a network such as the Du Pont system of analysis[1] or other logical groupings, (2) compared to the trends of the firm's own ratios, (3) compared to management's goals for key ratios, or (4) compared to selected ratios of other firms in the same industry. When comparing a firm's ratios to those of other companies, care must be taken to select similar firms of corresponding size and industry type to insure the appropriate comparison of financial data. For example, small firms must often rely on trade credit and other short-term liabilities to finance the firm's assets, whereas larger firms have access to the capital markets for financing. This fact may lead to significant differences in liquidity and debt ratios if these firms are compared. Similarly, cross-industry comparisons often lead to incorrect conclusions. Thus an acceptable inventory turnover ratio for a retail jeweler would lead to disaster if adopted by a meat packer.

Ratios may be categorized into five groups: (1) liquidity ratios, (2) asset management ratios, (3) debt management ratios, (4) profitability ratios, and (5) market value ratios. Some of the most valuable ratios in each category are discussed and illustrated next, using Carter Chemical Company's financial data that were presented in Tables 6-1 and 6-2.

Industry Practice

Light in Dark Corners

The text in corporate annual reports used to be little more than a redundant summary of the figures. "Stuff like advertising expenditures were up because we spent more," explains one CPA.

Over the last several years, largely unnoticed by investors, all that has changed. With a little prodding from the Securities & Exchange Commission, the section labeled "Management Discussion and Analysis," which typically follows the chairman's letter, has improved dramatically.

Unfortunately, no annual report comes with a map for getting through the MD&A. There is a lot of complex numerical information packed into a few pages, and it takes some experience to appreciate it. Here's how to find a few useful nuggets:

1. Sales breakdowns. Naturally, the income statement will show you if

---

[1]Discussed later in this chapter.

revenues are going up, but in the MD&A you can learn if that change is caused by rising prices or an increase in the number of units sold. The distinction is important.

2. Extraordinary items that contributed to earnings. Windfalls like tax credits and sales of property by firms (whose business is not the sale of property) should be described in detail.

3. A breakdown of working capital. Remember when W. T. Grant filed for Chapter 11 back in 1975? Its working capital figures looked just fine—despite an unmentioned but considerable absence of cash. The MD&A should now show you how working capital is allocated among cash, receivables, and inventory, and how long it takes to convert current assets into cash. Those are all crucial factors in evaluating the strength of a company's real cash flow.

4. Significant financial ratios. "What you want to be looking for are the more difficult ratios, the ones that are not easily extracted from the financials," says Roger Cason, national director of accounting and auditing practices with accounting firm Main Hurdman. For example, cash to expenses, cash to total liabilities, inventory as a percentage of working capital. Cason thinks that if a company doesn't disclose any of these and just provides the ever-popular current ratio (current assets to current liabilities), you are being shortchanged.

5. Projections. The SEC has been encouraging companies to use the MD&A to present some "forward-looking information" of future operations; it even provides a safe harbor clause to protect a company just in case some projection should not come true. Items to keep an eye out for: upcoming union negotiations, new environmental negotiations, major capital expenditures and their possible impact on debt, and possible plant closings.

6. Broader problems. Finally, investors should find out if there are any industrywide issues that could possibly affect their company. For example, an electronics firm might have some commentary about foreign competition or an oil company about the recent slump in oil prices.

One more caution: Read the MD&A with an appreciation for what is not mentioned, too. Despite close SEC scrutiny of this portion of annual reports, corporations haven't suddenly become blabbermouths, eager to bare every secret. "Suppose you were looking at a publicly held thrift a year ago," says Cason, "and there was no talk of the impact of interest rates. You'd know you weren't getting the whole story."

The simple truth is that no company is going to do your work for you. As much as managements are constrained by the SEC to tell you the truth, everyone sees the truth in a different way. And corporate accountants are paid to be optimistic. So when you peruse the MD&A, wear your best glasses—and make sure they're not rose-colored.

Source: Excerpted from "Light in Dark Corners" by Christopher Power, *Forbes*, August 1, 1983. Reprinted by permission.

Liquidity Ratios

One of the first concerns of the financial analyst is liquidity: Will the firm be able to meet its maturing obligations? Carter Chemical Company has debts totaling $300 million that must be paid off within the coming year. Can those obligations be satisfied? A full liquidity analysis requires the use of cash budgets (described in Chapter 11); however, by relating the amount of cash and other current assets to the current obligations, ratio analysis provides a quick and easy-to-use measure of liquidity. Two commonly used **liquidity ratios** are presented below.

liquidity ratio
The relationship of a firm's cash and other current assets to its current obligations.

Current Ratio. The **current ratio** is computed by dividing current assets by current liabilities. Current assets normally include cash, marketable securities, accounts receivable, and inventories; current liabilities consist of accounts payable, short-term notes payable, current maturities of long-term debt, accrued income taxes, and other accrued expenses (principally wages).

current ratio
The ratio computed by dividing current assets by current liabilities.

If a company is getting into financial difficulty, it begins paying its bills (accounts payable) slowly, building up bank loans, and so on. If these current liabilities are rising faster than current assets, the current ratio will fall, and this could spell trouble. Accordingly, the current ratio is the most commonly used measure of short-term solvency, since it provides an indicator of the extent to which the claims of short-term creditors are covered by assets that are expected to be converted to cash in a period roughly corresponding to the maturity of the claims.

The calculation of the current ratio for Carter at year-end 1984 is shown below. (All dollar amounts in this section are in millions.)

$$\text{Current ratio} = \frac{\text{Current assets}}{\text{Current liabilities}} = \frac{\$700}{\$300} = 2.3 \text{ times.}$$

$$\text{Industry average} = 2.5 \text{ times.}$$

Carter's current ratio is slightly below the average for the industry, 2.5, but not low enough to cause concern. It appears that Carter is about in line with most other chemical firms. Since current assets are scheduled to be converted to cash in the near future, it is highly probable that they could be liquidated at close to their stated value. With a current ratio of 2.3, Carter could liquidate current assets at only 43 percent of book value and still pay off current creditors in full.[2]

---

[2] $(1/2.3) = 0.43$, or 43 percent. Note that $(0.43)(\$700) \approx \$300$, the amount of current liabilities.

Although industry average figures are discussed later in some detail, it should be stated at this point that an industry average is not a magic number that all firms should strive to maintain. In fact, some very well-managed firms will be above it, and other good firms will be below it. However, if a firm's ratios are very far removed from the average for its industry, the analyst must be concerned about why this variance occurs. Thus a deviation from the industry average should signal the analyst to check further.

Note also that Carter's current ratio declined to 2.3 in 1984 from 2.8 in 1983. Thus the *trend* is poor, and this could indicate potential future difficulties. More will be said about *trend analysis* later in the chapter.

quick (acid test) ratio
The ratio computed by deducting inventories from current assets and dividing the remainder by current liabilities.

Quick (Acid Test) Ratio. The **quick (acid test) ratio** is calculated by deducting inventories from current assets and dividing the remainder by current liabilities. Inventories are typically the least liquid of a firm's current assets and hence the assets on which losses are most likely to occur in the event of liquidation. Therefore this measure of the firm's ability to pay off short-term obligations without relying on the sale of inventories is important.

$$\text{Quick (acid test) ratio} = \frac{\text{Current assets} - \text{Inventory}}{\text{Current liabilities}} = \frac{\$400}{\$300}$$

$$= 1.3 \text{ times.}$$

$$\text{Industry average} = 1.0 \text{ times.}$$

The industry average quick ratio is 1.0, so Carter's 1.3 ratio compares favorably with other firms in the industry. If the accounts receivable can be collected, the company can pay off current liabilities even without selling any inventory. Again, however, it should be noted that the trend is downward: 1.3 in 1984 versus 1.8 in 1983.

Asset Management Ratios

asset management ratios
Set of several ratios, including inventory utilization, average collection period, and total asset utilization, which are designed to measure how effectively the firm's assets are being managed.

The second group of ratios is designed to measure how effectively the firm is managing its assets. In particular, the **asset management ratios** answer this question: Does the total amount of each type of asset as reported on the balance sheet seem "reasonable," too high, or too low in view of current and projected operating levels? Carter Chemical Company and other companies must borrow or obtain capital from other sources in order to acquire assets. If they have too many assets, then their interest expenses are too high, hence profits are too low. If assets are too low, then operations will not be as efficient as possible.

inventory utilization
The ratio of sales divided by inventories; also known as inventory turnover.

Inventory Utilization The **inventory utilization** ratio, sometimes called the *inventory turnover* ratio, is defined as sales divided by inventories.

$$\text{Inventory utilization (or turnover)} = \frac{\text{Sales}}{\text{Inventory}} = \frac{\$3,000}{\$300} = 10 \text{ times.}$$

$$\text{Industry average} = 9 \text{ times.}$$

Carter's ratio of 10 times compares favorably with an industry average of 9 times. This suggests that the company does not hold excessive stocks of inventory; excess stocks are, of course, unproductive and represent an investment with a low or zero rate of return. This high inventory utilization ratio also reinforces our faith in the current ratio. If the turnover were low—say, 3 or 4 times—we might wonder whether the firm was holding damaged or obsolete materials not actually worth their stated value.

Two problems arise in calculating and analyzing the inventory utilization ratio. First, sales are at market prices; if inventories are carried at cost, as they generally are, it would be more appropriate to use cost of goods sold in place of sales in the numerator of the formula. Established compilers of financial ratio statistics such as Dun & Bradstreet, however, use the ratio of sales to inventories carried at cost. To develop a figure that can be compared with those developed by Dun & Bradstreet, it is therefore necessary to measure inventory utilization with sales in the numerator, as we do here.

The second problem lies in the fact that sales occur over the entire year, whereas the inventory figure is for one point in time. This makes it better to use an average inventory.[3] If it is determined that the firm's business is highly seasonal, or if there has been a strong upward or downward sales trend during the year, it becomes essential to make some such adjustment. To maintain comparability with industry averages, we did not use the average inventory figure.

Average Collection Period. The average collection period, which is used to appraise the accounts receivable, is computed by dividing average daily sales into accounts receivable to find the number of days' sales tied up in receivables.[4] This is defined as the **average collection period (ACP),** because it represents the average length of time that the firm must wait after making a sale before receiving cash. The calculations for Carter show an average collection period of 42 days, slightly above the 36-day industry average.

average collection period (ACP)
The ratio computed by dividing average daily sales into accounts receivable to find the number of days' sales tied up in receivables.

---

[3]Preferably, the average inventory would be calculated by summing the monthly figures during the year and dividing by 12. If monthly data are not available, one can add the beginning and ending figures and divide by 2; this will adjust for secular trends but not for seasonal fluctuations.

[4]Because information on credit sales is generally unavailable, total sales must be used. Since all firms do not have the same percentage of credit sales, there is a good chance that the average collection period will be somewhat in error.

$$\text{Average collection period} = \frac{\text{Receivables}}{\text{Average sales per day}} = \frac{\text{Receivables}}{\text{Annual sales}/360}$$

$$= \frac{\$350}{\$3,000/360} = \frac{\$350}{\$8.333} = 42 \text{ days}.$$

$$\text{Industry average} = 36 \text{ days}.$$

This ratio can also be evaluated by comparison with the terms on which the firm sells its goods. For example, Carter's sales terms call for payment within 30 days, so the 42-day collection period indicates that customers, on the average, are not paying their bills on time. If the trend in the collection period over the past few years had been rising while the credit policy had not changed, this would be even stronger evidence that steps should be taken to expedite the collection of accounts receivable.

fixed assets utilization
The ratio of sales to fixed assets; also known as *fixed assets turnover*.

Fixed Assets Utilization. The **fixed assets utilization** ratio, often called the *fixed assets turnover* ratio, measures the utilization of plant and equipment:

$$\text{Fixed assets utilization} = \frac{\text{Sales}}{\text{Net fixed assets}} = \frac{\$3,000}{\$1,300} = 2.3 \text{ times}.$$

$$\text{Industry average} = 3.0 \text{ times}.$$

Carter's ratio of 2.3 times compares poorly with the industry average of 3 times, indicating that the firm is not using its fixed assets to as high a percentage of capacity as are the other firms in the industry. The financial manager should bear this fact in mind when production people request funds for new capital investments.

total assets utilization
The ratio that measures the turnover of all of a firm's assets, computed by dividing sales by total assets.

Total Assets Utilization. The **total assets utilization** ratio measures the utilization or turnover of all the firm's assets—it is calculated by dividing sales by total assets.

$$\text{Total assets utilization} = \frac{\text{Sales}}{\text{Total assets}} = \frac{\$3,000}{\$2,000} = 1.5 \text{ times}.$$

$$\text{Industry average} = 1.8 \text{ times}$$

Carter's ratio is somewhat below the industry average. The company is not generating a sufficient volume of business for the size of its asset investment. Sales should be increased, or some assets should be disposed of, or both steps should be taken.

Debt Management Ratios

The extent to which a firm uses debt financing, or **financial leverage**, has a number of implications. First, creditors look to the equity, or owner-supplied funds, to provide a margin of safety. Second, if owners have provided only a small proportion of total financing, the risks of the enterprise are borne mainly by the creditors. Third, by raising funds through debt, the owners gain the benefits of maintaining control of the firm with a limited investment. And fourth, if the firm earns more on the borrowed funds than it pays in interest, then the return on the owners' capital is magnified.

financial leverage
The extent to which a firm uses debt financing.

To illustrate the last point, we must introduce two ratios—the ratio of operating profits to assets and the rate of return on equity. The ratio of operating profits to assets is called the *basic earning power* ratio and is calculated by dividing earnings before interest and taxes by total assets. The *rate of return on equity* is calculated by dividing net income (the income available to stockholders) by the firm's common equity (the investment made by the firm's owners).

Suppose a firm has $200 in assets and a basic earning power ratio of 15 percent. The firm's tax rate is 40 percent. If the firm were totally financed with equity, there would be no interest expense, and the firm's return on equity (ROE) would equal:

$$\text{ROE} = \frac{(\text{Operating income} - \text{Interest})\,(1 - \text{Tax rate})}{\text{Common equity}}$$

$$= \frac{[(0.15)\,(\$200) - \$0]\,(1 - .4)}{\$200}$$

$$= \frac{\$18}{\$200}$$

$$= 9\%.$$

However, if the firm's assets were financed with $150 in 8 percent debt and only $50 equity financing, its ROE would be:

$$\text{ROE} = \frac{[(0.15)\,(\$200) - (0.08)\,(\$150)]\,(1 - .4)}{\$50}$$

$$= \frac{\$10.80}{\$50}$$

$$= 21.6\%.$$

Financial leverage raises the rate of return to stockholders for two reasons. (1) Since interest is deductible, the use of debt financing lowers the tax bill and leaves more of the firm's operating income available to its investors. (2) If the pre-tax rate of return on assets (the *basic earning power ratio*, EBIT/Total assets) exceeds the interest rate on debt, as it does in this example, then a company can use debt to finance assets, pay interest on the debt, and have something left over as a "bonus" for its stockholders.

However, financial leverage cuts both ways: if the return on assets declines, the leveraged firm's return on equity will fall further and faster. In our example, if the firm's pre-tax rate of return on assets, EBIT/Total Assets, falls to 7 percent, the return on equity would fall whether the firm employs debt or not. For the all-equity firm,

$$ROE = \frac{[(0.07)\ (\$200) - \$0]\ (1 - .4)}{\$200}$$

$$= 4.2\%,$$

but for the leveraged firm return on equity will decline to a greater extent:

$$ROE = \frac{[(0.07)\ (\$200) - (0.08)\ (\$150)]\ (1 - .4)}{\$50}$$

$$= 2.4\%.$$

Furthermore, if the firm's pre-tax rate of return on assets falls significantly below the interest rate on debt, the firm will be earning less than its interest payments. This inability to meet interest payments will eventually force the firm into bankruptcy, resulting in losses for the firm's owners.

We see, then, that firms with small amounts of debt have less risk of loss when the economy is in a recession, but they also have lower expected returns when the economy booms. Conversely, firms with high leverage ratios run the risk of large losses, but they also have a chance of gaining high profits. The prospect of high returns is desirable, but investors are averse to risk. Decisions about the use of leverage, then, must balance higher expected returns against increased risk.

Determining the optimal amount of debt for a given firm is a complicated process, and we defer a discussion of this topic until Chapter 19, when we shall be better prepared to deal with it. For now we shall simply look at the two ways analysts examine the firm's use of debt in a financial statement analysis: (1) they check balance sheet ratios to determine the extent to which borrowed funds have been used to finance the firm, and (2) they review income statement ratios to determine the number of times fixed charges are covered by operating profits. These two sets of ratios are complementary, and most analysts examine a firm's debt position with both types of leverage ratios.

Total Debt to Total Assets. The ratio of total debt to total assets, generally called the **debt ratio,** measures the percentage of total funds provided by creditors. Debt includes current liabilities and all bonds. Creditors prefer low debt ratios, since the lower the ratio, the greater the cushion against creditors' losses in the event of liquidation. The owners, on the other hand, may seek high leverage either (1) to magnify earnings or (2) because selling new stock means giving up some degree of control.

debt ratio
The ratio of total debt to total assets.

$$\text{Debt ratio} = \frac{\text{Total debt}}{\text{Total assets}} = \frac{\$1,100}{\$2,000} = 55\%.$$

$$\text{Industry average} = 40\%.$$

Carter's debt ratio is 55 percent; this means that creditors have supplied more than half the firm's total financing. Since the average debt ratio for this industry—and for manufacturing generally—is about 40 percent, Carter would find it difficult to borrow additional funds without first raising more equity capital. Creditors would be reluctant to lend the firm more money, and management would probably be subjecting the firm to the risk of bankruptcy if it sought to increase the debt ratio still more by borrowing.

Times Interest Earned. The **times-interest-earned (TIE)** ratio is determined by dividing earnings before interest and taxes (EBIT) by the interest charges. The TIE ratio measures the extent to which earnings can decline without resultant financial embarrassment to the firm because of an inability to meet annual interest costs. Failure to meet this obligation can bring legal action by the creditors, possibly resulting in bankruptcy. Note that the before-tax profit figure is used in the numerator. Because income taxes are computed after interest expense is deducted, the ability to pay current interest is not affected by income taxes.

times interest earned (TIE)
The ratio of earnings before interest and taxes to interest charges; measures the ability of a firm to meet its annual interest payments.

$$\text{TIE} = \frac{\text{EBIT}}{\text{Interest charges}} = \frac{\$266}{\$66} = 4 \text{ times.}$$

$$\text{Industry average} = 6 \text{ times.}$$

Carter's interest is covered 4 times. Since the industry average is 6 times, the company is covering its interest charges by a minimum margin of safety and deserves only a fair rating. This ratio reinforces the conclusion based on the debt ratio that the company might face some difficulties if it attempts to borrow additional funds.

Profitability Ratios

Profitability is the net result of a large number of policies and decisions. The ratios examined thus far reveal some interesting things about the way the firm is operating, but the **profitability ratios** show the combined effects of liquidity, asset management, and debt management on operating results.

profitability ratios
The ratios that show the combined effects of liquidity, asset management, and debt management on operating results.

profit margin on sales
Profit per dollar of sales, computed by dividing net income after taxes by sales.

Profit Margin on Sales. The **profit margin on sales,** computed by dividing net income after taxes by sales, gives the profit per dollar of sales.

$$\text{Profit margin} = \frac{\text{Net profit after taxes}}{\text{Sales}} = \frac{\$120}{\$3,000} = 4\%.$$

$$\text{Industry average} = 5\%.$$

Carter's profit margin is somewhat below the industry average of 5 percent, indicating that the firm's sales prices are relatively low or that its costs are relatively high, or both.

basic earning power ratio
The ratio of operating profits to assets; indicates the power of a firm's assets to generate operating income.

Basic Earning Power Ratio. The **basic earning power ratio,** which was discussed earlier in connection with financial leverage, is calculated by dividing the earnings before interest and taxes (EBIT) by total assets.

$$\text{Basic earning power ratio} = \frac{\text{EBIT}}{\text{Total assets}} = \frac{\$266}{\$2,000} = 13.3\%.$$

$$\text{Industry average} = 17.2\%.$$

This ratio is useful for comparing firms in different tax situations and with different degrees of financial leverage. Carter is not getting as much operating income out of its assets as is the average chemical company. This occurs because of its low turnover ratios and also because of its low profit margin on sales.

return on total assets (ROA)
The ratio of net income after taxes to total assets.

Return on Total Assets. The ratio of net profit to total assets measures the **return on total assets (ROA).**

$$\text{Return on total assets (ROA)} = \frac{\text{Net profit after taxes}}{\text{Total assets}} = \frac{\$120}{\$2,000} = 6\%.$$

$$\text{Industry average} = 9\%.$$

Carter's 6 percent return is well below the 9 percent average for the industry. This low rate results from three primary factors: (1) the low profit margin on sales, (2) the low utilization of total assets, and (3) Carter's above-average use of debt, which causes its interest payments to be high and its profits to be reduced.

Return on Common Equity. The ratio of net profit after taxes to common equity measures the **return on common equity (ROE).**

$$\text{Return on common equity (ROE)} = \frac{\overset{\text{NET INCOME}}{\text{Net profit after taxes}}}{\text{Common equity}} = \frac{\$120}{\$900} = 13.3\%.$$

$$\text{Industry average} = 15.0\%.$$

Carter's 13.3 percent return is below the 15.0 percent industry average, but not as far below as the return on total assets. This results from Carter's greater use of debt, a point analyzed in detail later in the chapter.[5]

Market Value Ratios

Market value ratios relate the firm's stock price to its earnings and book value per share. They give management an indication of what investors think of the company's past performance and future prospects. If the firm's liquidity, asset management, debt management, and profitability ratios are all good, then its market value ratios will be high, and the stock price will probably be as high as can be expected.

Price/Earnings Ratio. The **price/earnings (P/E) ratio** shows how much investors are willing to pay per dollar of reported profits. Carter's stock sells for $28.50, so with an EPS of $2.40, its P/E ratio is 11.9.

$$\text{Price/earnings ratio} = \frac{\text{Price per share}}{\text{Earnings per share}} = \frac{\$28.50}{\$2.40} = 11.9 \text{ times.}$$

$$\text{Industry average} = 12.5 \text{ times.}$$

Generally, P/E ratios are higher for firms with high growth prospects but lower for riskier firms. Carter's P/E ratio is slightly below those of other large chemical producers, which suggests that the company is regarded as being somewhat riskier than most, as having poorer growth prospects, or both.

Market/Book Ratios. The ratio of a stock's market price to its book value gives another indication of how investors regard the company. Companies with high rates of return on equity generally sell at higher

---

return on common equity (ROE)
The ratio of net profit after taxes to common equity; measures the rate of return on stockholders' investment.

market value ratios
The ratios that relate a firm's stock price to its earnings and book value per share.

price/earnings (P/E) ratio
The ratio of price to earnings; shows how much investors are willing to pay per dollar of profits.

---

[5]The fact that Carter's basic earning power and ROE are both 13.3 percent is a coincidence; normally, they differ. Actually, if more decimal places had been shown, the two ratios would have been different from each other.

multiples of book value than those with low returns. Carter's book value per share is $18.00:

$$\text{Book value per share} = \frac{\text{Stockholders' equity}}{\text{Shares outstanding}} = \frac{\$900}{50} = \$18.00.$$

market/book ratio
The ratio of a stock's market price to its book value.

Dividing this value into the market price per share gives a **market/book ratio** of 1.6 times:

$$\text{Market/book ratio} = \frac{\$28.50}{\$18.00} = 1.6 \text{ times.}$$

$$\text{Industry average} = 1.8 \text{ times.}$$

Investors are willing to pay slightly less for Carter's book value than for that of an average chemical company.

The typical railroad, which has a very low rate of return on assets, has a market value/book value ratio of less than 0.5. Very successful firms such as IBM achieve high rates of return on their assets and have market values that are four or five times their book values.

 Trend Analysis

trend analysis
The analysis of a firm's financial ratios over time to determine the improvement or deterioration of a financial situation.

It is important to analyze trends in ratios as well as their absolute levels, for the trends give clues as to whether the financial situation is improving or deteriorating. To do a **trend analysis,** one simply graphs a ratio against years, as shown in Figure 7-1. This graph shows that Carter's rate of return on common equity has been declining since 1981, even though the industry average has been relatively stable. Other ratios could be analyzed similarly.

 Summary of Ratio Analysis: The Du Pont System

Table 7-1 summarizes Carter Chemical Company's ratios, and Figure 7-2, which is called a *Du Pont chart* because that company's managers developed the general approach, shows the relationships among debt, asset utilization, and profitability ratios. The left-hand side of the chart develops the *profit margin on sales*. The various expense items are listed, then summed to obtain Carter's total costs. Subtracting costs from sales yields the company's net income, which, when divided by sales, indicates that 4 percent of each sales dollar is left over for stockholders.

The right-hand side of the chart lists the various categories of assets, which are summed and then divided into sales to find the number of times Carter "turns its assets over" each year. Carter's total asset utilization, or "turnover," ratio is 1.5 times.

Figure 7-1
Rate of Return on Common Equity, 1980–1984
In addition to comparing ratios to industry averages, it is important to analyze what trends various ratios are taking. By simply plotting Carter's rate of return on common equity for each year, one can determine the trend that ratio has taken from 1980 to 1984. A potential investor can quickly see that Carter's rate has declined since 1981, while the industry rate as a whole has been comparatively steady.

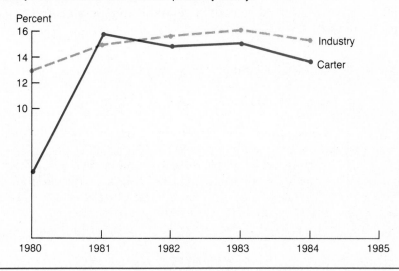

The profit margin times the total asset turnover ratio is defined as the *Du Pont equation*, which gives the rate of return on assets (ROA):

$$\text{ROA} = \frac{\text{Rate of return}}{\text{on assets}} = \text{Profit margin} \times \text{Total assets turnover}$$

$$= \frac{\text{Net profit after taxes}}{\text{Sales}} \times \frac{\text{Sales}}{\text{Total assets}}$$

$$= 4\% \times 1.5 = 6\%.$$

Carter makes 4 percent, or 4 cents, on each dollar of sales. Assets were "turned over" 1.5 times during the year, so Carter earned a return of 6 percent on its assets.

If Carter used only equity, the 6 percent rate of return on assets would equal the rate of return on equity. However, 55 percent of the firm's capital is supplied by creditors. Since the 6 percent return on *total* assets all goes to stockholders, who put up only 45 percent of the capital, the return on equity is higher than 6 percent. Specifically, the rate of return on assets (ROA) must be multiplied by the *equity multi-*

Table 7–1
Summary of Carter Chemical Company's Ratios (Millions of Dollars)

Ratio	Formula for Calculation	Calculation	Ratio	Industry Average	Evaluation
Liquidity					
Current	$\dfrac{\text{Current assets}}{\text{Current liabilities}}$	$\dfrac{\$\ 700}{\$\ 300}$	= 2.3 times	2.5 times	Good
Quick, or acid test	$\dfrac{\text{Current assets } - \text{ Inventory}}{\text{Current liabilities}}$	$\dfrac{\$\ 400}{\$\ 300}$	= 1.3 times	1 time	Good
Asset Management					
Inventory utilization	$\dfrac{\text{Sales}}{\text{Inventory}}$	$\dfrac{\$3,000}{\$\ 300}$	= 10 times	9 times	Good
Average collection period (ACP)	$\dfrac{\text{Receivables}}{\text{Sales}/360}$	$\dfrac{\$\ 350}{\$8.333}$	= 42 days	36 days	Bad
Fixed assets utilization	$\dfrac{\text{Sales}}{\text{Fixed assets}}$	$\dfrac{\$3,000}{\$1,300}$	= 2.3 times	3 times	Bad
Total assets utilization	$\dfrac{\text{Sales}}{\text{Total assets}}$	$\dfrac{\$3,000}{\$2,000}$	= 1.5 times	1.8 times	Bad

Debt Management

Ratio	Formula				
Debt to total assets	$\dfrac{\text{Total debt}}{\text{Total assets}}$	$= \dfrac{\$1,100}{\$2,000}$	= 55 percent	40 percent	Bad
Times interest earned (TIE)	$\dfrac{\text{Earnings before interest and taxes}}{\text{Interest charges}}$	$= \dfrac{\$\ 266}{\$\ 66}$	= 4 times	6 times	Bad

Profitability

Ratio	Formula				
Profit margin on sales	$\dfrac{\text{Net profit after taxes}}{\text{Sales}}$	$= \dfrac{\$\ 120}{\$3,000}$	= 4 percent	5 percent	Bad
Basic earning power	$\dfrac{\text{Earnings before interest and taxes}}{\text{Total assets}}$	$= \dfrac{\$\ 266}{\$2,000}$	= 13.3 percent	17.2 percent	Bad
Return on total assets (ROA)	$\dfrac{\text{Net profit after taxes}}{\text{Total assets}}$	$= \dfrac{\$\ 120}{\$2,000}$	= 6 percent	9 percent	Bad
Return on common equity (ROE)	$\dfrac{\text{Net profit after taxes}}{\text{Common equity}}$	$= \dfrac{\$\ 120}{\$\ 900}$	= 13.3 percent	15 percent	Bad

Market Value

Ratio	Formula				
Price/earnings (P/E)	$\dfrac{\text{Price per share}}{\text{Earnings per share}}$	$= \dfrac{\$28.50}{\$\ 2.40}$	= 11.9 times	12.5 times	Bad
Market/book	$\dfrac{\text{Market price per share}}{\text{Book value per share}}$	$= \dfrac{\$28.50}{\$18.00}$	= 1.6 times	1.8 times	Bad

Figure 7-2
Modified Du Pont Chart Applied to Carter Chemical Company (Millions of Dollars)

The Du Pont chart was created to illustrate the relationships between key financial ratios. The left side of the chart develops a firm's profit margin; the right side develops its total assets utilization ratio. The profit margin is then multiplied by the assets utilization ratio to arrive at the rate of return on assets (ROA). The matter of debt is brought into the chart by multiplying the ROA by the equity multiplier to arrive at the rate of return on equity (ROE). The ROE could be calculated more simply, but the Du Pont chart is useful for illustrating how debt, asset utilization, and profitability ratios interact to determine the ROE.

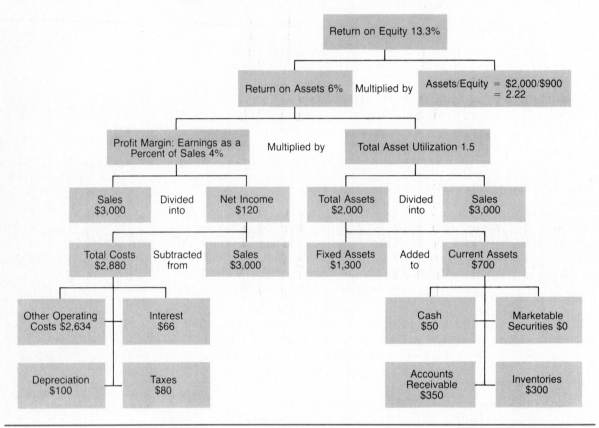

plier, which is the ratio of assets to common equity, to obtain the rate of return on equity (ROE):

$$ROE = ROA \times \text{Equity multiplier}$$

$$= \frac{\text{Net income}}{\text{Assets}} \times \frac{\text{Assets}}{\text{Common equity}}$$

$$= 6\% \times (\$2,000/\$900)$$

$$= 6\% \times 2.22 = 13.3\%.$$

This 13.3 percent rate of return could, of course, be calculated directly: net income after taxes/common equity = $120/$900 = 13.3 percent. However, the Du Pont equation shows how the rate of return on assets and the use of debt interact to determine the return on equity.

Management can use the **Du Pont system** to analyze ways of improving the firm's performance. On the left, or "profit margin," side of the chart, marketing people can study the effects of raising sales prices (or lowering them to get greater volume), of moving into new products or markets with higher margins, and so on. Cost accountants can study the expense items and, working with engineers, purchasing agents, and other operating personnel, seek ways of holding costs down. On the "turnover" or asset utilization side, financial analysts, working with both production and marketing people, can investigate ways of reducing the investment in various types of assets. At the same time, the treasurer can analyze the effects of alternative financing strategies, seeking to hold down interest expenses and the risks of debt while still using debt to increase the rate of return on equity.

Du Pont system
A system of analysis designed to show the relationships among return on investment, asset turnover, and profit margin.

Sources of Comparative Ratios

The preceding analysis of Carter Chemical Company pointed out the usefulness of **comparative ratio analysis** among firms in the same industry. Comparative ratios are available from a number of sources. One useful set of comparative data is compiled by Dun & Bradstreet, Inc. D&B provides 14 ratios calculated for a large number of industries. Useful ratios can also be found in the *Annual Statement Studies* published by Robert Morris Associates, the national association of bank loan officers. The Federal Trade Commission's *Quarterly Financial Report*, which is found in most libraries, gives a set of ratios for manufacturing firms by industry group and size of firm. Trade associations and individual firms' credit departments also compile industry average financial ratios. Finally, financial statement data are available on magnetic tapes for thousands of corporations, and since most of the larger brokerage houses, banks, and other financial institutions have access to these data, security analysts can and do generate comparative ratios tailored to their own individual needs.

comparative ratio analysis
The analysis based on a comparison of a firm's ratios with those of other firms in the same industry.

Each of these organizations uses a somewhat different set of ratios, designed for the organization's own purposes. For example, D&B deals mainly with small firms, many of which are proprietorships, and they are concerned largely with the creditors' viewpoint. Accordingly, their ratios emphasize current assets and liabilities, and D&B is completely unconcerned with market value ratios. Therefore, when you select your comparative data source, you should either be sure that your emphasis is similar to that of the agency or recognize the limitations of its ratios for your purposes.

MANUFACTURING

Line of Business (and number of concerns reporting)	Quick Ratio	Current Ratio	Current liabilities to net worth	Current liabilities to inventory	Total liabilities to net worth	Fixed assets to net worth	Collection period	Net sales to inventory	Total assets to net sales	Net sales to net working capital	Accounts payable to net sales	Return on net sales	Return on total assets	Return on net worth
	Times	Times	Percent	Percent	Percent	Percent	Days	Times	Percent	Times	Percent	Percent	Percent	Percent
2011-2017 Meat Products (113)	2.1	4.2	20.4	89.2	33.3	31.9	12.7	44.2	14.0	31.0	0.9	2.9	11.6	25.7
	1.3	2.2	47.0	144.8	71.8	57.9	17.8	29.0	19.2	15.3	1.8	1.5	6.5	13.9
	0.8	1.6	118.0	221.5	177.2	82.6	24.8	16.3	28.9	11.0	3.2	0.6	2.4	4.8
2021-2026 Dairy Products (125)	1.2	2.0	52.0	133.7	64.3	43.7	18.9	55.0	18.6	41.3	3.7	2.8	9.5	23.1
	1.0	1.4	84.6	228.8	114.7	68.2	26.4	26.9	23.1	19.1	5.6	1.2	5.2	11.1
	0.7	1.2	149.4	434.2	205.0	92.4	32.8	13.9	33.2	12.5	7.7	0.5	1.1	3.1
2051-2052 Bakery Products (113)	2.0	3.3	16.9	116.4	24.1	58.9	17.0	41.5	27.3	32.5	2.5	5.5	12.7	21.8
	1.1	1.9	36.2	216.8	49.1	85.6	24.4	29.8	37.0	15.0	4.3	2.4	6.9	13.8
	0.8	1.3	66.1	362.6	112.0	133.5	31.7	17.4	48.2	7.1	6.2	1.2	2.7	6.7
2082-2087 Beverages (140)	1.5	3.3	20.3	61.8	34.0	41.4	16.7	20.1	33.4	17.6	2.9	7.3	14.6	27.3
	0.9	2.0	38.7	118.1	68.2	72.1	24.9	13.2	44.8	9.6	4.8	4.1	8.3	15.6
	0.5	1.3	70.4	188.1	136.7	100.7	37.2	5.1	68.1	5.2	7.4	1.8	3.6	8.5
2321-2329 Men's & Boy's Apparel (114)	1.6	3.5	39.9	63.5	43.4	5.5	23.3	10.8	27.8	8.3	3.3	5.5	10.2	23.3
	1.0	2.4	80.9	99.8	97.2	11.8	43.8	6.3	42.1	5.2	6.4	3.0	5.1	11.4
	0.6	1.7	146.2	144.5	180.9	35.6	66.0	4.2	56.1	3.7	10.1	1.6	2.4	6.2
2331-2339 Women's, Misses' & Juniors' Outerwear (107)	1.5	2.7	35.4	112.0	59.7	3.3	23.7	16.4	25.1	14.8	4.3	3.2	10.4	31.4
	1.0	1.7	104.3	159.0	131.6	7.7	43.0	10.7	32.5	9.4	7.4	2.0	6.2	16.3
	0.7	1.4	207.3	237.6	235.9	18.6	62.6	7.3	43.5	5.6	10.5	0.5	1.2	3.8
2421 Sawmills & Planing Mills, General (128)	2.1	4.7	11.9	58.3	22.9	31.7	14.2	13.2	40.3	12.8	1.6	6.4	10.6	17.9
	0.9	2.4	30.2	94.9	63.2	67.9	20.4	8.0	57.9	6.4	2.6	4.3	7.1	10.7
	0.3	1.3	84.6	173.2	150.0	108.9	29.5	5.0	84.2	3.4	4.8	1.6	3.3	6.2
2511-2519 Household Furniture (116)	2.0	3.9	27.6	55.6	31.3	19.7	18.2	13.2	29.0	10.9	2.5	6.1	13.5	25.9
	1.1	2.5	46.9	83.6	71.3	35.9	34.1	9.4	42.2	6.9	3.7	3.0	7.0	13.3
	0.7	1.8	97.2	130.2	148.4	70.3	47.4	5.2	51.8	4.2	6.5	0.9	2.6	4.2
2651-2655 Paperboard Containers & Boxes (115)	2.1	3.3	28.1	81.1	39.6	32.6	30.2	21.9	31.5	14.0	3.1	5.0	9.7	18.7
	1.3	2.1	56.3	146.8	99.6	58.3	41.5	13.1	43.8	8.8	4.8	3.4	7.0	12.5
	0.9	1.5	110.0	248.0	197.4	107.7	46.3	7.6	55.8	4.8	7.6	0.9	2.6	4.6
2731-2732 Books (101)	1.9	4.2	20.4	57.1	30.0	5.6	32.1	14.1	45.0	6.8	2.6	12.6	14.8	20.7
	1.2	2.7	42.2	98.0	69.4	20.1	48.5	7.3	62.7	3.7	6.0	6.7	9.3	13.5
	0.7	1.8	90.0	167.8	150.5	45.4	81.3	3.6	97.7	2.4	10.6	2.8	5.4	7.6

Financial managers interested in comparing their company ratios with those of other industry firms can find this information in several sources, such as the *Key Business Ratios* compiled by Dun & Bradstreet. This excerpt from the D&B data provides 14 ratios for several manufacturing industries.

Source: Reprinted by permission of Dun & Bradstreet Credit Services, a company of The Dun & Bradstreet Corporation.

Limitations of Ratio Analysis

Although ratio analysis is useful in finance, it does have limitations, some of which are listed below.

1. Many large firms actually operate a number of different divisions in quite different industries, making it difficult to develop a meaningful set of industry averages for comparative purposes. This tends to make ratio analysis more useful for small than for large firms.

2. Most firms want to be better than average (although about half will be above and half below), so merely attaining average performance is not necessarily good. As a target for high-level performance, it is preferable to look at industry leaders' ratios.

3. The ratios can be distorted. For example, the inventory utilization ratio for a food processor will be radically different if the balance sheet figure used for inventory is the one just before versus just after the close of the canning season. This problem can be minimized by using average inventory figures.

Also, firms can employ **window dressing** techniques to make their financial statements look better to credit analysts. Recently, a firm sold its corporate aircraft for cash just prior to issuing a quarterly statement. This substantially improved its cash balance in time for the quarterly report.

window dressing
Use of certain techniques to make a financial statement look better to credit analysts.

4. Different operating and accounting practices distort comparisons. For example, if one firm leases a substantial amount of its productive equipment (and some airlines lease about half of their planes whereas others own virtually all equipment), then its assets may be low relative to sales because leased assets may not appear on the balance sheet. This improves utilization ratios. The accounting profession has recently taken steps which reduce but do not eliminate this problem.

5. It is difficult to generalize about whether a particular ratio is "good" or "bad." For example, a high current ratio may show a strong liquidity position, which is good, or excessive cash, which is bad because excess cash in the bank is a nonearning asset. Similarly, high asset utilization ratios may denote either a firm that uses assets efficiently or an under-capitalized firm that simply cannot afford to buy enough assets.

6. A firm may have some ratios which look "good" and others which look "bad," making it difficult to tell whether the firm is, on balance, in a strong or a weak position. A procedure called *discriminant analysis* can be used to analyze the net effects of a set of ratios, but a discussion of this topic goes beyond the scope of this book.[6]

Ratio analysis is useful in spite of these problems, but analysts should be aware of them and make adjustments as necessary. Ratio analysis conducted in a mechanical, unthinking manner is dangerous, but, used intelligently and with good judgment, ratios can provide useful insights into a firm's operations. Your judgment in interpreting a set of ratios is probably weak at this point, but it will be greatly enhanced as we go through the remainder of the book.

Summary

The primary purpose of this chapter has been to discuss the techniques used by investors, creditors, and managers to analyze the financial statements of businesses. Financial analysis is designed to determine the relative strengths and weaknesses of a company—whether the firm

---

[6]For a discussion of discriminant analysis as applied to financial ratios, see Eugene F. Brigham, *Financial Management: Theory and Practice*, 3rd ed. (Hinsdale, IL: Dryden Press, 1982), Appendix 6A.

is financially sound and profitable relative to other firms in its industry and whether its position is improving or deteriorating over time. Investors need such information in order to estimate both future cash flows from the firm and the riskiness of these flows. Managers need to be aware of their firms' financial positions in order to detect and strengthen weaknesses in a continuous quest for improvement.

Our study of financial analysis concentrated on a set of ratios designed to highlight the key aspects of a firm's operations. These ratios were broken down into five categories: (1) liquidity ratios, (2) asset management ratios, (3) debt management ratios, (4) profitability ratios, and (5) market value ratios. The ratios for a given firm are calculated, then compared with those of other firms in the same industry to judge the relative strength of the firm in question. Trends in the ratios are also analyzed, and the Du Pont system is used to pinpoint the cause of any weakness that is uncovered. Ratio analysis has limitations, but used with care and judgment, it can be most helpful.

Small Business $ $ $ $ $ $ $ $ $

Financial Analysis in the Small Firm

Financial ratio analysis is a tool that is useful in small businesses as well as in big ones. In fact, readily available sources of key financial ratios provide comparative data by size class, with the class size varying down to some very small firms. For example, Robert Morris Associates provides comparative ratios for a number of small-firm classes, including the size range of zero to $250,000 in annual sales. Nevertheless, the financial analysis of small firms presents some unique problems that are related to the risk of the small firm and to the depth and quality of management in the particular firm. Let's examine some of those problems from the standpoint of the bank credit officer.

The Banker Evaluates a Small Firm: Problems

One of the most common uses of financial ratios is credit analysis by commercial banks. In examining the small-business credit prospect, the banker is essentially making a prediction about the ability of the company to repay its debt if the bank extends credit to the firm. In making this prediction, the banker will be especially concerned about indicators of liquidity and about continuing prospects for profitability. The banker will elect to do business with a new customer if the banker believes that loans will be paid off on a timely basis and that the company will remain in business and therefore a customer of the bank for some years to come. Short-run viability and long-run viability are both of interest to the banker. On the other hand, the banker's perceptions of the business are important to the owner-manager because the bank may become a vital source of funds as the firm's needs increase in the future.

The first problem the banker is likely to encounter is that, unlike the bank's bigger customers, the small firm may not have audited financial statements. Furthermore, the statements that are available may have been produced on an irregular basis (for example, in some months or quarters but not in others). If the firm is young, it may have historical financial statements for only one year, or perhaps it may have none at all. The banker will probably require that periodic income statements and balance sheets be produced and that they be handled by a reputable accounting firm rather than by the owner's brother-in-law.

The quality of financial data may therefore be a problem for the small business in its attempt to establish a banking relationship. If it is a serious problem, the firm may fail to get credit even though it is in reality on solid financial ground. It is in the owner's interest to make sure that the firm's financial data are credible even if it is a little more expensive to do so. Furthermore, if the banker is uncomfortable with the data, then the firm's management should also be uncomfortable. Many of the business decisions to be made by the firm will depend on the numbers in the firm's accounting statements; those numbers should be as accurate as possible.

Given a set of financial ratios, the firm may be more or less risky depending on its size. Often small firms either are single-product firms or rely heavily on a relationship with a single customer. For example, back in the 1960s a company called Yard Man, Inc. manufactured and sold lawn equipment. Most of Yard Man's sales were to Sears, Roebuck, and so most of Yard Man's revenues and profits were due to its Sears, Roebuck account. When Sears, Roebuck decided to drop Yard Man as a supplier, the company was left without its most important customer. Losing the Sears, Roebuck account could have been a devastating blow to Yard Man, but the company was able to weather the storm and return to profitability. Because large firms typically have a broad customer base, they are not as susceptible to sudden loss of a large portion of their business.

A similar danger applies to the single-product company. Just as the loss of a key customer can be disastrous for a small business, so can a shift in the tides of consumer interest in a particular fad. For example, Coleco manufactured and sold the extremely popular Cabbage Patch dolls in the Christmas season of 1983. The phenomenal popularity of the dolls was a great boom for Coleco. But the public is fickle. One can almost never predict when such a fad will suddenly die out, leaving the company with a great deal of capacity to build a product that no one will buy and with a lot of inventory (valued, incidentally, at high dollar amount on the corporate books but in reality worth nearly nothing to the hapless banker who wins the inventory in bankruptcy).

Coleco is a sizable company that is sufficiently diversified to withstand the loss of such a fad item. But if the Cabbage Patch doll were manufactured instead by a small company with no other products, such a shift in fads could destroy the company. No matter how good the financial ratios *look* at the moment, the creditor of a small, single-product company has to be ever-mindful of the added risks.

The extension of credit to a small company, and especially a small owner-managed company, often involves one other risk that is quite different from those discussed above. Such a company is often highly dependent on the management or leadership of a single key individual. The unexpected death of that person could cause the company to be lost. Alternatively, if the company is family owned and managed, there is typically one key decision maker but perhaps several other family members are also involved in helping to manage the company. In this case the loss of the top person does not wipe out the management, although it may create the equally serious problem of no clear management succession. The loss of a key family member is a highly emotional event, and it is not at all unusual for it to be followed by an ugly and prolonged struggle for control of the business. It is in the family's interest, and certainly of concern to prospective creditors, to see that a plan of succession of management is clearly specified before trouble arises. If all of the standard financial ratios look good but there is a significant risk of loss of management, then an otherwise creditworthy firm may fail to get needed financing.

We have identified three concerns that must be added to standard financial analysis of the small firm. Two of them are concerns that the firm should be able to handle if it addresses them seriously. These are (1) the concern over the quality of the financial data made available by the firm and (2) the concern over succession of management. The third concern raised is that because of the lack of diversity of the product line or customer base, the firm may be susceptible to sudden loss of revenue. This is a risk the firm may elect not to eliminate, at least not early in its life. Entrepreneurs start businesses in hopes of earning very large returns. Very large returns ordinarily entail very large risks. Diversifying a business is a way of reducing risk, but it may also reduce returns. The entrepreneur may therefore be unwilling to use diversification as a part of his or her business strategy.

In determining the creditworthiness of a small firm, the financial analyst or credit analyst must be willing to look beyond the basic financial ratios and analyze the viability of the firm's product, customers, and market. It is not an easy task, but it must be done. Simple ratio analysis is only the starting point.

Resolution to Decision in Finance

Cooking the Books

When important income and asset figures are misreported, as they were at PepsiCo, the results can be far reaching. Because such numbers are key components of many liquidity, asset management, debt management, profitability, and market value ratios, a financial analysis based on them can become badly distorted. As a result, managers, creditors, shareholders, stock analysts, and the general public may draw false conclusions and make wrong decisions.

In a highly publicized case like that of PepsiCo, the company itself pays dearly because its reputation is publicly tarnished. Such negative publicity raises questions about managerial competence and the effectiveness of corporate financial countrols. Top management, whether it is a victim or an accomplice, usually gets blamed for middle-management fraud. Particularly when a number of employees were involved and when the situation continued undiscovered for a number of years, suspicions mount that management was either negligent or responsible.

Management is victimized in other ways too. It may set goals based on false information, allocate investments or take out loans based on phony numbers, and pay bonuses to dishonest employees. Honest managers may actually get punished—they may lose bonuses and promotions while their dishonest counterparts move quickly ahead.

Fraud affects shareholders as well, because they may buy or sell stock in response to erroneous information. For example, people may have bought PepsiCo's stock because they liked its healthy earnings per share and strong growth overseas. Shareholders' wealth may be further affected when the fraud comes to light. Stock prices can be expected to fall in response to such bad news, and their recovery depends on the size of the misstatement, the way that management handles the situation, and the company's overall reputation. It can take a long time for the market to regain confidence in a company that has suffered financial fraud.

In response to the falsified reports from its Mexican and Philippine operations, PepsiCo fired at least four employees, including a vice president at its corporate headquarters. At least eight other employees were replaced, although not all were fired.

In December 1982 two separate shareholder suits were filed charging PepsiCo and its directors with filing false financial statements. But the law on middle-management fraud is fuzzy. Some attorneys believe that it's hard to prove damages and management responsibility. Without proof, they contend, shareholders cannot determine either the amount of their losses or who should pay for them.

Source: Adapted from "Cooking the Books" by Arlene Hershman with Henriette Sender. Reprinted with the permission of *Dun's Business Month* (formerly *Dun's Review*), January 1983. Copyright 1983, Dun & Bradstreet Publications Corporation.

Key Terms You should be able to define each of the following terms:

Ratio analysis; comparative ratio
  analysis; trend analysis
Liquidity ratio; current ratio; quick
  (acid test) ratio
Asset management ratio; inventory
  utilization; fixed assets utilization;
  total assets utilization
Average collection period (ACP)
Financial leverage; debt ratio; times
  interest earned (TIE)

Profitability ratios; profit margin on
  sales; basic earning power ratio;
  return on total assets (ROA);
  return on common equity (ROE)
Market value ratios; price/earnings
  (P/E) ratio; market/book ratio
Du Pont system
Window dressing

Questions

7-1 How does inflation distort ratio analysis comparisons, both for one company over time (trend analysis) and when different companies are compared? Are only balance sheet items, or both balance sheet and income statement items, affected?

7-2 If a firm's ROE is low and management wants to improve it, explain how using more debt might provide a solution.

7-3 Suppose a firm used debt to leverage up its ROE, and in the process EPS was also boosted. Would this necessarily lead to an increase in the price of the firm's stock?

7-4 How might **(a)** seasonal factors and **(b)** different growth rates over time or across companies distort a comparative ratio analysis? Give some examples. How might these problems be alleviated?

7-5 Seasonal factors and differing growth rates are two problems that distort ratio analysis comparisons. What are some of the other factors that limit the effectiveness of ratio analysis?

Self-Test Problems

ST-1 H. Lanser & Co. had earnings per share of $2 last year, and it paid a $1 dividend. Book value per share at year end was $20, while total retained earnings increased by $6 million during the year. Lanser has no preferred stock, and no new common stock was issued during the year. If Lanser's year-end debt (which equals its total liabilities) was $60 million, what was the company's year-end debt/assets ratio?

ST-2 The following data apply to Horrigan & Company (dollar amounts in millions):

Cash and marketable securities	$100.00
Fixed assets	$283.50
Sales	$1,000.00
Net income	$50.00
Quick ratio	2.0 ×
Current ratio	3.0 ×
ACP	40 days
ROE	0.12 or 12%

Horrigan has no preferred stock—only common equity, current liabilities, and long-term debt. Find Horrigan's (a) accounts receivable (A/R), (b) current liabilities, (c) current assets, (d) total assets, (e) ROA, (f) common equity, and (g) long-term debt.

ST-3 In the preceding problem you should have found Horrigan's accounts receivable (A/R) = $111.1 million. If Horrigan could reduce its ACP from 40 days to 30 days while holding other things constant, how much cash would it generate? If this cash were used to buy back common stock (at book value) and thus to reduce the amount of common equity, how would this affect (a) the ROE, (b) the ROA, and (c) the total debt/total assets ratio?

Problems

* 7-1 Graphics Supply House, Inc. has sales of $7,200,000. Its accounts receivable balance is $860,000. If all sales are on credit, what is the company's average collection period?

* 7-2 Southern Appliance Stores, Inc. had sales of $10,800,000 last year. If the firm maintains $2,700,000 of inventory, what is its inventory utilization (turnover)? What is its inventory utilization (turnover) period?

* 7-3 Everybody's Department Store had sales of $9,000,000 this year. Thirty percent of those sales were for cash. If the firm maintains an accounts receivable balance of $700,000, what is its average collection period?

* 7-4 Minnesota Farm Equipment, Inc. has a net profit margin of 5 percent, its total assets utilization (turnover) is 2.0 times, and its assets/equity ratio is 1.49 times. What is its rate of return on equity? (Hint: Use the Du Pont ratio system.)

7-5 Massachusetts Manufacturing is 100 percent equity financed. Given the following information, calculate the firm's return on equity:

> Earnings before taxes = $4 million,
> Sales = $20 million,
> Dividend payout ratio = 60%,
> Total assets utilization (turnover) = 2.0 times,
> Tax rate = 40%.

* 7-6 Air Idaho, an emerging regional airline, earns 7 percent on total assets but has a return on equity of 17.5 percent. What percentage of the airline's assets is financed with debt?

* 7-7 Chuck Harper, president of Engineering Associates, has been reviewing his firm's financial statements. He knows the firm's return on equity is 18 percent, the debt/total assets ratio is .32, and the total asset turnover is 5 times. He is sure his accountant told him the net profit margin before she went home. Since he can't remember, would you determine the firm's net profit margin for him?

* 7-8 Boulder Clothiers, Inc. finds itself with more debt than it would like to have. Currently the firm has $18 million in sales, an average collection period of 40 days, and an inventory turnover of 6 times. Doc Kolb, the store manager, is certain he can lower the average collection period to 30

days and increase the inventory utilization (turnover) to 8 times without lowering sales. How much would be available to reduce debt if Doc succeeds in his proposed reduction of current assets?

7-9 Complete the balance sheet below by using the following financial information:

Total assets utilization (turnover) = 2.0 times,
Current ratio = 2.0 times,
Average collection period = 36 days,
Inventory utilization (turnover) = 4.5 times,
Debt/total assets = 40%,
Fixed assets turnover = 6 times,
Sales = $900,000.

Cash	$ 10,000	Current liabilities	$
Accounts receivable		Long-term debt	
Inventory	_____	Total debt	
Current assets		Common stock	100,000
Fixed assets	_____	Retained earnings	_____
Total assets	$_____	Total claims	$_____

7-10 Data for the Core Computer Company and its industry averages are given below.

   a. Calculate the indicated ratios for Core Computer.

   b. Outline Core Computer's strengths and weaknesses as revealed by your analysis. Can you detect any positive or negative trends developing?

   c. Suppose Core Computer had doubled its sales and also its inventories, accounts receivable, and common equity during 1983 and 1984. How would that information affect the validity of your ratio analysis? No calculations are necessary.

Core Computer Company: Balance Sheets, December 31, 1983 and 1984

	1984	1983		1984	1983
Cash	$ 220,000	$ 220,000	Accounts payable	$ 150,000	$ 165,000
Accounts receivable	300,000	275,000	Notes payable	240,000	220,000
Inventory	990,000	825,000	Other current liabilities	140,000	110,000
Total current assets	$1,510,000	$1,320,000	Total current liabilities	$ 530,000	$ 495,000
Net fixed assets	$ 810,000	$ 605,000	Long-term debt	$ 300,000	$ 220,000
			Common equity	1,490,000	1,210,000
Total assets	$2,320,000	$1,925,000	Total claims on assets	$2,320,000	$1,925,000

Core Computer Company: Income Statements for Years Ended December 31, 1983 and 1984

	1984	1983
Sales	$3,015,000	$2,750,000
Cost of goods sold:		
Materials	1,200,000	1,045,000
Labor	705,000	660,000
Heat, light, and power	109,000	99,000
Indirect labor	170,000	165,000
Depreciation	64,000	60,500
Gross profit	$ 767,000	$ 720,500
Selling expenses	285,000	275,000
General and administrative expenses	340,500	316,800
Earnings before interest and taxes	$ 141,500	$ 128,700
Less: Interest expense	19,400	13,200
Net profit before taxes	$ 122,100	$ 115,500
Less: Federal income taxes (50%)	61,050	57,750
Net profit	$ 61,050	$ 57,750

Ratios

Ratio	Industry Averages	Core 1984	1983
Current assets/current liabilities	2.4×	_____	_____
Average collection period	43 days	_____	_____
Sales/inventory	9.8×	_____	_____
Sales/total assets	2×	_____	_____
Net profit/sales	3.3%	_____	_____
Net profit/total assets	6.6%	_____	_____
Net profit/net worth	18.1%	_____	_____
Total debt/total assets	63.5%	_____	_____

7-11 The Williamsburg Furniture Company, a manufacturer and wholesaler of high-quality home furnishings, has been experiencing low profitability in recent years. As a result the board of directors has replaced the president of the firm with a new president, John Sharpe, who asks you to make an analysis of the firm's financial position using the Du Pont system. The last two years' financial statements are reproduced below.

  a. Calculate ratios to compare Williamsburg Furniture Company with the industry-average ratios.

  b. Do the balance sheet accounts or the income statement figures seem to be primarily responsible for the low profits?

  c. Which specific accounts seem to be most out of line in relation to other firms in the industry?

d. If Williamsburg had a pronounced seasonal sales pattern, or if it had grown rapidly during the two years, how might this affect the validity of your ratio analysis? How might you correct for such potential problems?

Industry Average Ratios

Current ratio	2×	Sales/fixed assets	6×
Total debt/total assets	30%	Sales/total assets	3×
Times interest earned	7×	Net profit on sales	3%
Sales/inventory	10×	Return on total assets	9%
Average collection period	24 days	Return on common equity	12.8%

Williamsburg Furniture Company: Balance Sheets, December 31, 1983 and 1984 (Millions of Dollars)

	1984	1983		1984	1983
Cash	$ 33	$ 30	Accounts payable	$ 42	$ 30
Marketable securities	26	22	Notes payable	30	30
Accounts receivable	40	44	Other current liabilities	18	14
Inventories	125	106	Total current liabilities	$ 90	$ 74
Total current assets	$224	$202	Long-term debt	22	16
			Total liabilities	$112	$ 90
Gross fixed assets	$185	$150			
Less: Depreciation	61	52	Common stock	$ 76	$ 76
Net fixed assets	$124	$ 98	Retained earnings	160	134
			Total stockholders' equity	$236	$210
Total assets	$348	$300	Total claims on assets	$348	$300

Williamsburg Furniture Company: Income Statements for Years Ended December 31, 1983 and 1984 (Millions of Dollars)

	1984	1983
Net sales	$560	$530
Cost of goods sold	465	440
Gross profit	$ 95	$ 90
Operating expenses	51	49
Depreciation expense	13	8
Interest expense	5	3
Total expenses	$ 69	$ 60
Net income before tax	$ 26	$ 30
Taxes (50%)	13	15
Net income	$ 13	$ 15

7-12 Indicate the effects of the transactions listed on pages 183 and 184 on each of the following: total current assets, net working capital, current ratio, and net profit. Use (+) to indicate an increase, (−) to indicate a decrease,

and (0) to indicate no effect or indeterminate effect. State necessary assumptions and assume an initial current ratio of more than 1 to 1. (Note:
As an introductory finance student, you are not expected to be familiar
with all the transactions listed. The purpose of this question is to stimulate thought about the effects of these transactions.)

	Total Current Assets	Net Working Capital[a]	Current Ratio	Effect on Net Profit
1. Cash is acquired through issuance of additional common stock.	+	+	+	0
2. Merchandise is sold for cash.	+	+	+	+
3. Federal income tax due for the previous year is paid.	−	0	+	0
4. A fixed asset is sold for less than book value.	+	+	+	−
5. A fixed asset is sold for more than book value.	+	+	+	+
6. Merchandise is sold on credit.	+	+	+	+
7. Payment is made to trade creditors for previous purchases.	−	0	+	0
8. A cash dividend is declared and paid.	−	−	−	0
9. Cash is obtained through short-term bank loans.	+	0	0	0
10. Short-term notes receivable are sold at a (discount.)	−	−	−	−
11. A profitable firm increases its rate of depreciation on fixed assets.	0	0	0	−
12. Marketable securities are sold below cost.	−	−	−	−
13. Advances are made to employees.	0	0	0	0
14. Obsolete inventory is written off.	−	−	−	−
15. Short-term promissory notes are issued to trade creditors for prior purchases.	0	0	0	0
16. Ten-year notes are issued to pay off accounts payable.	0	+	+	0

[a]Net working capital is defined as current assets minus current liabilities.

(handwritten column headings: total assets | working capital | Ratio | profit)

	total assets	working capital	Ratio	profit
17. A fully depreciated asset is retired.	0	0	0	0
18. Accounts receivable are collected.	0	0	0	0
19. A stock dividend is declared and paid.	0	0	0	0
20. Equipment is purchased with short-term notes.	0	—	—	0
21. Merchandise is purchased on credit.	+	0	0n–	0
22. The estimated taxes payable are increased.	0	—	—	—
23. Previously issued stock rights are exercised by company stockholders.	+	+	+	0
24. Uncollectible accounts are written off against the bad debt reserve.	0	0	0	0
25. A *cash* sinking fund for the retirement of bonds is created; a reserve for a bond sinking fund is also created.	—	—	—	0
26. Bonds are retired by use of the cash sinking fund.	0	0	0	0
27. The allowance for doubtful accounts is increased.	—	—	—	—

7-13 Kose Company has a quick ratio of 1.0, a current ratio of 3.0 times, an inventory turnover of 6 times, and current assets of $600,000. What are Kose's annual sales and, if cash and marketable securities are negligible, its ACP?

7-14 The following data pertain to Brennan Products, Inc. (BPI):

1. BPI has outstanding debt in the form of accounts payable, 6-month notes payable, and long-term bonds. The notes carry a 14 percent interest rate, and the bonds carry a 12 percent rate. Both the notes and bonds were outstanding for the entire year.
2. Retained earnings at the beginning of the year was $14,000.
3. The dividend payout ratio is 33.3 percent.
4. The debt to assets ratio is 60 percent.
5. The profit margin is 6 percent.
6. The return on equity (ROE) is 5 percent.
7. The inventory utilization ratio is 5 times.
8. The average collection period (ACP) is 122.4 days.

a. Given this information, complete BPI's balance sheet and income statement that follow.
b. The industry average inventory utilization ratio is 6 times, and the industry average ACP is 72 days. Assume that BPI, at the beginning of the year, had been able to adjust its inventory utilization and ACP to the industry averages, and that this (1) freed up capital and (2) re-

duced storage costs and bad debt losses. Assume that the reduction of storage costs and bad debts raised the profit margin to 10 percent. Assume further that the freed-up capital was used at the start of the year to pay an extra, one-time dividend which reduced the beginning retained earnings figure. What would have been the effect on BPI's ROE for 1984? (Hint: Construct a new balance sheet which will show lower inventories and accounts receivable, and a different value for December 31, 1984 retained earnings. The balance sheet will not balance; force it into balance by reducing accounts payable. Then calculate your new ROE. You can get your new net profit figures directly.)

Brennan Products, Inc.: Balance Sheet at December 31, 1984

Cash	$ 7,500	Accounts payable	
Inventories		Notes payable	$10,000
Accounts receivable			
Total current assets	_____	Total current liabilities	
Net fixed assets	54,000	Bonds payable	30,000
		Total debt	
		Common stock	
		Retained earnings	_____
		Total common equity	_____
Total assets	_____	Total claims	_____
	══════		══════

Brennan Products, Inc.:
Income Statement for Year Ended December 31, 1984

Sales	$25,000
Cost of goods sold	
Gross profit	
Selling expenses	2,700
General and administrative expenses	1,900
EBIT	
Interest expense	_____
Net profit before taxes	
Taxes	1,200
Net profit	══════

Answers to Self-Test Problems

ST-1 Lanser paid $1 and retained $1 per share. Since total retained earnings rose by $6 million, there must be 6 million shares outstanding. With a book value of $20 per share, total common equity must be $20(6 million) = $120 million. Thus the debt ratio must be 33.3 percent:

$$\frac{\text{Debt}}{\text{Assets}} = \frac{\text{Debt}}{\text{Debt} + \text{Equity}} = \frac{\$60 \text{ million}}{\$60 \text{ million} + \$120 \text{ million}}$$
$$= 0.333 = 33.3\%.$$

ST-2 a.
$$ACP = \frac{\text{Accounts receivable}}{\text{Sales/360}}$$

$$40 = \frac{A/R}{\$1,000/360}$$

$$A/R = 40(\$2.778) = \$111.1 \text{ million.}$$

b.
$$\text{Quick ratio} = \frac{\text{Current assets} - \text{Inventories}}{\text{Current liabilities}} = 2.0$$

$$= \frac{\text{Cash and marketable securities} + A/R}{\text{Current liabilities}} = 2.0.$$

$$\text{Current liabilities} = (\$100 + \$111.1)/2 = \$105.5 \text{ million.}$$

c.
$$\text{Current ratio} = \frac{\text{Current assets}}{\text{Current liabilities}} = 3.0.$$

$$\text{Current assets} = 3.0(\$105.5) = \$316.5 \text{ million.}$$

d.
$$\text{Total assets} = \text{Current assets} + \text{Fixed assets}$$
$$= \$316.5 + \$283.5 = \$600 \text{ million.}$$

e.
$$\text{ROA} = \text{Profit margin} \times \text{Total assets utilization}$$
$$= \frac{\text{Net income}}{\text{Sales}} \times \frac{\text{Sales}}{\text{Total assets}}$$
$$= \frac{\$50}{\$1,000} \times \frac{\$1,000}{\$600}$$
$$= 0.05 \times 1.667 = 0.0833 = 8.33\%.$$

f.
$$\text{ROE} = \text{ROA} \times \frac{\text{Assets}}{\text{Equity}}$$
$$12.0\% = 8.33\% \times \frac{\$600}{\text{Equity}}$$
$$\text{Equity} = \frac{(8.33\%)(\$600)}{12.0\%}$$
$$= \$416.5 \text{ million.}$$

g.
$$\text{Total assets} = \text{Total claims} = \$600$$
$$\text{Current liabilities} + \text{Long-term debt} + \text{Equity} = \$600$$
$$\$105.5 + \text{Long-term debt} + \$416.5 = \$600$$
$$\text{Long-term debt} = \$600 - \$105.5 - \$416.5 = \$78 \text{ million.}$$

Note: We could have found equity as follows:

$$\text{ROE} = \frac{\text{Net income}}{\text{Equity}}$$

$$0.12 = \frac{\$50}{\text{Equity}}$$

$$\text{Equity} = \$50/0.12$$
$$= \$416.67 \text{ million (rounding error difference).}$$

Then we could have gone on to find current liabilities and long-term debt.

ST-3 Horrigan's average sales per day were $1,000/360 = $2.777777 million. Its ACP was 40, so A/R = 40($2,777,777) = $111,111,111. Its new ACP of 30 would cause A/R = 30($2,777,777) = $83,333,333. The reduction in A/R = $111,111,111 − $83,333,333 = $27,777,777, which would equal the amount of new cash generated.

a.
$$\text{New equity} = \text{Old equity} - \text{Stock bought back}$$
$$= \$416,500,000 - \$27,777,777$$
$$= \$388,722,223.$$

Thus

$$\text{New ROE} = \frac{\text{Net income}}{\text{New equity}}$$
$$= \frac{\$50,000,000}{\$388,722,223}$$
$$= 12.86\% \text{ (versus old ROE of 12.00\%).}$$

b.
$$\text{New ROA} = \frac{\text{Net income}}{\text{Total assets} - \text{Reduction in A/R}}$$
$$= \frac{\$50,000,000}{\$600,000,000 - \$27,777,777}$$
$$= 8.74\% \text{ (versus old ROA of 8.33\%).}$$

c. The old debt is the same as the new debt:

$$\text{New debt} = \text{Total claims} - \text{Equity}$$
$$= \$600 - \$416.5 = \$183.5 \text{ million.}$$
$$\text{Old total assets} = \$600 \text{ million.}$$

$$\text{New total assets} = \text{Old total assets} - \text{Reduction in A/R}$$
$$= \$600 - \$27.78$$
$$= \$572.22 \text{ million.}$$

Therefore

$$\frac{\text{Old debt}}{\text{Old total assets}} = \frac{\$183.5}{\$600} = 30.6\%,$$

while

$$\frac{\text{New debt}}{\text{New total assets}} = \frac{\$183.5}{\$572.22} = 32.1\%.$$

Selected References

The effects of alternative accounting policies on both financial statements and ratios based on these statements are discussed in the many excellent texts on financial accounting. For example, see:

Kieso, Donald E., and Jerry J. Weygandt, *Intermediate Accounting* (New York: Wiley, 1980).

Smith, Jay M., and Fred K. Skousen, *Intermediate Accounting* (Cincinnati: Southwestern Publishing, 1981).

For additional insights into the use of ratio analysis in financial management, see:

Altman, Edward I., "Financial Ratios, Discriminant Analysis, and the Prediction of Corporate Bankruptcy," *Journal of Finance*, September 1968, 589–609.

Altman, Edward I., R. G. Haldeman, and P. Narayanan, "Zeta Analysis: A New Model to Identify Bankruptcy Risk of Corporations," *Journal of Banking and Finance*, June 1977, 29–54.

Beaver, William H., "Financial Ratios as Predictors of Failure," *Empirical Research in Accounting: Selected Studies* (Chicago: University of Chicago Press, 1966), 71–127.

Chen, Kung H., and Thomas A. Shimerda, "An Empirical Analysis of Useful Financial Ratios," *Financial Management*, Spring 1981, 51–60.

Gonedes, N. J., "Evidence on the Information Content of Accounting Numbers: Accounting-Based and Market-Based Estimates of Systematic Risk," *Journal of Financial and Quantitative Analysis*, June 1973, 407–443.

Horrigan, James C., "A Short History of Financial Ratio Analysis," *Accounting Review*, April 1968, 284–294.

Regarding earnings and dividend growth rate prediction, see:

Brown, Lawrence D., and Michael S. Rozeff, "The Superiority of Analyst Forecasts as a Measure of Expectations: Evidence from Earnings," *Journal of Finance*, March 1978, 1–15.

For sources of ratios, see the following:

Dun & Bradstreet, *Key Business Ratios* (99 Church Street, New York, NY: updated annually).

Financial Research Associates, *Financial Studies of the Small Business* (Arlington, VA: updated annually).

Robert Morris Associates, *Annual Statement Studies* (Philadelphia, PA: updated annually).

Troy, Leo, *Almanac of Business and Industrial Financial Ratios* (Englewood Cliffs, NJ: Prentice-Hall, 1980).

Determining Future Financial Needs

Decision in Finance

AT&T Conquers the Fear of Forecasting

In November 1983 AT&T took what many on Wall Street viewed as a brave step. It issued a 267-page prospectus detailing the plans for its breakup into eight separate companies and dared to include forecasted profits and dividends for the following year. Among the predictions: the eight companies combined would have 1984 earnings of $8.70 per share and would pay dividends of $1.36 per share for the first quarter.

Wall Street watchers were surprised by the move because companies traditionally have been reluctant to publish forecasts. But what was even rarer was that three big-name accounting firms—Coopers & Lybrand, Arthur Anderson, and Arthur Young—all gave their stamp of approval to the figures.

Actually, some might contend that AT&T had little choice. The breakup into a "new" AT&T plus seven regional operating companies was mandated by a federal court with the intention of promoting competition in the telephone industry. The results of the split, which would take effect on January 1, 1984, would definitely be far reaching. And by November 1983 speculation about increased telephone rates and the stock values of the new companies had reached fever pitch.

A classic "widows' and orphans' stock," AT&T had always been considered an especially safe investment. But after the divestiture stockholders would be left owning eight untested companies instead of the bluest of the blue chips they had held before. Faced with 3.2 million investors, all wondering about the fate of their 950 million shares in the company, AT&T no doubt felt the need to do something reassuring.

As you read this chapter, consider the pros and cons of AT&T's decision to publish forecasts about its future profits and dividends. If you were an AT&T stockholder, would you be reassured by the predictions? Why or why not?

See end of chapter for resolution.

As noted in Chapter 7, both managers and investors are vitally concerned with *future* financial statements. Also, managers regularly construct *pro forma*, or projected, statements and consider alternative courses of action in terms of the actions' effects on these projections. In this chapter we discuss briefly how pro forma statements are constructed and how they are used to help estimate the need for capital.

Sales Forecasts

sales (demand) forecast
Forecast of unit and dollar sales for some future period. Generally, sales forecasts are based on recent trends in sales plus forecasts of the economic prospects for the nation, region, industry, and so forth.

The most important element in financial planning is a **sales (or demand) forecast.** Because such forecasts are critical for production scheduling, for plant design, for financial planning, and so on, the entire management team participates in their preparation. In fact, most of the larger firms have a *planning group* or *planning committee*, with its own staff of economists, which coordinates the corporation's sales forecast. Since sales forecasting is a rather specialized subject, we do not consider the mechanics of the forecasting process in this chapter. Rather, we simply take the sales forecast as given and then use it to illustrate various types of financial decisions.

Forecasting Financial Requirements: The Percentage of Sales Method

percentage of sales method
A method of forecasting financial requirements by expressing various balance sheet items as a percentage of sales and then multiplying these percentages by expected future sales to construct pro forma balance sheets.

To use this simple but often practical method of forecasting financial requirements, we first express the various balance sheet items as a **percentage of sales,** then use these percentages, together with expected future sales, to construct **pro forma balance sheets**. To illustrate, consider the Arinson Products Company, whose December 31, 1984 balance sheet is given in Table 8-1. Arinson is operating at full capacity. Its 1984 sales were $400,000; its profit margin on sales was 10 percent;

pro forma statement
A financial statement that shows how an actual statement will look if certain specified assumptions are realized; used to forecast financial requirements.

Table 8-1
Arinson Products Company: Balance Sheet, December 31, 1984
(Thousands of Dollars)

Cash	$ 10	Accounts payable	$ 40
Accounts receivable	90	Notes payable	10
Inventories	200	Accrued wages and taxes	50
Total current assets	$300	Total current liabilities	$100
Net fixed assets	300	Mortgage bonds	150
		Common stock	50
		Retained earnings	300
Total assets	$600	Total claims	$600

Current ratio = 300/100 = 3:1; industry average = 2.6:1.
Total debt/total assets = 250/600 = 42%; industry average = 45%.

Unaudited Pro Forma
Condensed Balance Sheet
American Telephone and Telegraph Company

The following Unaudited Consolidated Historical Balance Sheet as of June 30, 1983 is derived from the unaudited financial statements of the Company and its consolidated subsidiaries included in its Quarterly Report filed with the Securities and Exchange Commission on Form 10-Q.

The following Unaudited Pro Forma Condensed Balance Sheet gives effect to the divestiture of the telephone subsidiaries by the Company as if it had occurred on June 30, 1983, in accordance with the Plan and reflects concurrent divestiture-related extraordinary charge for the discontinued application of accounting principles

appropriate only for a rate-regulated enterprise. The pro forma balance sheet is presented as of June 30, 1983 as a result of agreements reached with the Securities and Exchange Commission for the November 16, 1983 Form 8-K filing. Even though divestiture occurred on January 1, 1984, final data is not readily available for all of the divested companies and actual balances and adjustments will vary from those presented in the pro forma balance sheet below. The Unaudited Pro Forma Condensed Balance Sheet should be read in conjunction with the audited consolidated financial statements and notes for the years ended December 31, 1983, 1982 and 1981.

DOLLARS IN MILLIONS	Consolidated Historical June 30, 1983	Divestiture Pro Forma Adjustments	Divestiture-Related Extraordinary Charge	Pro Forma Consolidated June 30, 1983
		See Note (1)	See Note (2)	
ASSETS				
TELEPHONE PLANT–Net of Accumulated Depreciation	$130,056.5	$(121,087.1)(a) 15,431.3 (b) 377.0 (d) 3,993.3 (e)	$(8,857.0)	$19,914.0
INVESTMENTS	5,960.0	57,692.2 (a) (9,213.7)(b) (46,668.0)(c) (5,017.1)(e) (2,128.4)(f)	—	625.0
CURRENT ASSETS	14,887.3	(9,030.9)(a) 374.4 (b) 5,234.8 (e) 90.4 (f)	—	11,556.0
OTHER ASSETS AND DEFERRED CHARGES	2,614.6	(2,099.3)(a) 44.3 (b) 7.0 (e) 57.9 (f)	—	624.5
TOTAL ASSETS	$153,518.4	$(111,941.9)	$(8,857.0)	$32,719.5

See accompanying Notes to Unaudited Pro Forma Condensed Balance Sheet.

26

DOLLARS IN MILLIONS	Consolidated Historical June 30, 1983	Divestiture Pro Forma Adjustments	Divestiture-Related Extraordinary Charge	Pro Forma Consolidated June 30, 1983
		See Note (1)	See Note (2)	
INVESTED CAPITAL, LIABILITIES, AND DEFERRED CREDITS				
COMMON SHAREOWNERS' EQUITY:				
Common Shares–par value $1 per share	$ 936.7	$ —	$ —	$ 936.7
Proceeds in Excess of Par Value	34,629.6	(25,233.7)(c)	—	9,395.9
Reinvested Earnings	29,580.7	(21,495.4)(c)	(5,497.9)	2,587.4
CONVERTIBLE PREFERRED SHARES SUBJECT TO REDEMPTION	277.9	—	—	277.9
PREFERRED SHARES SUBJECT TO MANDATORY REDEMPTION	1,537.2	—	—	1,537.2
OWNERSHIP INTEREST OF OTHERS IN CONSOLIDATED SUBSIDIARIES	535.8	(535.8)(a)	—	—
LONG AND INTERMEDIATE TERM DEBT	45,319.5	(37,554.3)(a) 845.9 (b) 1,085.8 (e) (228.0)(f)	—	9,468.9
DEBT MATURING WITHIN ONE YEAR	1,617.4	(1,719.6)(a) 1,252.8 (b) 333.6 (e) (1,117.8)(f)	—	366.4
OTHER CURRENT LIABILITIES	11,277.0	(8,852.7)(a) 218.7 (b) 1,642.6 (e) (634.3)(f)	400.1	4,051.4
DEFERRED TAXES AND OTHER DEFERRED CREDITS	27,806.6	(25,862.7)(a) 4,318.9 (b) 61.1 (c) 377.0 (d) 1,156.0 (e)	(3,759.2)	4,097.7
TOTAL INVESTED CAPITAL, LIABILITIES, AND DEFERRED CREDITS	$153,518.4	$(111,941.9)	$(8,857.0)	$32,719.5

27

Notes to Unaudited Pro Forma Condensed Balance Sheet

Dollars in Millions (except per share amounts)

(1) Divestiture Pro Forma Adjustments

(A) This adjustment reflects the deconsolidation of the BOCs and the reversal of consolidating intercompany eliminations.

(B) This adjustment transfers assets and liabilities to and from the BOCs at net book value. The transfers are tax-free under the Internal Revenue Code. Accumulated deferred income tax reserves and unamortized investment credits are transferred along with the associated assets.

This adjustment also reflects the removal of debt by the Company from the BOCs as required by the provisions of the Plan. The amount expected to be removed at divestiture under terms of Reorganization and Divestiture Agreements between the Company and each RHC is approximately $2.6 billion. The Company's debt ratio (debt as a percent of total debt and equity) at the time of divestiture was approximately 40%.

(C) This adjustment reflects the divestiture of the investment in the BOCs.

(D) Under this adjustment, pursuant to a 1967 closing agreement with the IRS, telephone plant transferred to AT&T Information Systems is increased at original cost and the depreciation reserve is increased to what it would have been had the telephone plant been depreciated on the basis of the original cost. The closing agreement requires that when property ceases to be public utility property, the liability for deferred taxes associated with Western Electric profits reverts back to Western Electric. See Accounting Policies section of Historical Financial Statements, "Purchases From Western Electric," and "Telephone Plant."

(E) This adjustment effects the consolidation of Western Electric and Bell Laboratories.

(F) This adjustment eliminates significant intercompany accounts receivable and payable.

See Note (A) to Historical Financial Statements. These amounts differ from the amounts announced initially because of regulatory events and other adjustments.

See Note (Q) to Historical Financial Statements.

(2) Divestiture-Related Extraordinary Charge

(3) Contingent Liabilities

28

This Unaudited Pro Forma Consolidated Balance Sheet published by AT&T in its 1983 Annual Report was considered to be a bold move in the financial community. Most firms are reluctant to make public their financial forecasts. But AT&T, whose stock has traditionally been considered a safe, secure investment, decided to publish its forecast of future company profits and dividends to reassure stockholders of a promising future for AT&T after its divestiture.
Source: AT&T 1983 Annual Report.

and Arinson distributed 60 percent of its after-tax profits to stockholders as dividends. If Arinson expects sales to increase to $600,000 in 1985, what will be its pro forma December 31, 1985 balance sheet, and how much additional financing will the company require?

Our first step is to isolate those balance sheet items that vary directly with sales. Since Arinson is operating at full capacity, each asset item must increase if the higher level of sales is to be attained. More cash will be needed for transactions; receivables will be higher; additional inventory must be stocked; and new plant must be added.

If assets are to increase, liabilities and net worth must likewise rise—the balance sheet must balance, and increases in assets must be financed in some manner. Some of these funds will result spontaneously from routine business transactions, while other funds must be raised through formal means. **Spontaneously generated funds** come from sources such as accounts payable and accruals, which will increase spontaneously with sales: as sales increase, so will purchases, and larger purchases will result in higher levels of accounts payable. Thus, if sales double, accounts payable will also double. Similarly, a higher level of operations will require more labor, so accrued wages will increase, and assuming profit margins are maintained, an increase in profits will pull up accrued taxes. Retained earnings will also increase, but not in direct proportion to the increase in sales. Other sources of financing require formal action by the firm's financial manager. For example, neither notes payable, mortgage bonds, nor common stock increase automatically with sales. Management must obtain these funds from financial intermediaries or from investors.

We can use this information to construct a pro forma balance sheet for December 31, 1985, proceeding as outlined below.

Step 1 In Table 8-2, Column 1, we express those balance sheet items that vary directly with sales as a percentage of sales. An item such as notes payable that does not vary directly with sales is designated n.a., or "not applicable."

Step 2 Next we multiply these percentages by the $600,000 projected 1985 sales to obtain the projected amounts as of December 31, 1985; these are shown in Column 2 of the table.

Step 3 We simply insert figures for notes payable, mortgage bonds, and common stock from the December 31, 1984 balance sheet. At least one of these accounts may have to be changed later in the analysis.

Step 4 We next add the addition to retained earnings estimated for 1985 to the figure shown on the December 31, 1984 balance sheet to obtain the December 31, 1985 projected retained earnings. Recall that Arinson expects to earn 10 percent on sales of

spontaneously generated funds
Funds that arise automatically from routine business transactions.

Table 8-2
Arinson Products Company: December 31, 1984 Balance Sheet Expressed as
a Percentage of Sales and December 31, 1985 Pro Forma Balance Sheet
(Thousands of Dollars)

	Balance Sheet Items on Dec. 31, 1984 (as a % of the $400 1984 Sales) (1)	Pro Forma Balance Sheet on Dec. 31, 1985 (= Projected Sales of $600 Times Column 1) (2)
Cash	2.5% X 600 ≃	$ 15
Accounts receivable	22.5	135
Inventories	50.0	300
Total current assets	75.0%	$450
Net fixed assets	75.0	450
Total assets	150.0%	$900
Accounts payable	10.0%	$ 60
Notes payable	n.a.[a]	10[b]
Accrued wages and taxes	12.5	75
Total current liabilities	22.5%	$145
Mortgage bonds	n.a.	150[b] * } from balance sheet
Common stock	n.a.	50[b] *
Retained earnings	n.a.	324[c] *
	22.5%	Funds available $669
		Additional funds needed[d] 231
		$900

[a]n.a. = not applicable.
[b]1985 projections picked up from December 31, 1984 balance sheet.
[c]December 31, 1984 balance in retained earnings plus 1985 addition to retained earnings.
[d]"Additional funds needed" is a balancing figure: $900 − $669 = $231.

$600,000, or $60,000, and to pay 60 percent of this out in dividends to stockholders. (The **dividend payout ratio** is 60 percent.) Thus retained earnings for the year are projected to be $60,000 − 0.6($60,000) = $24,000. Adding the $24,000 addition to retained earnings to the $300,000 beginning balance gives the $324,000 projected retained earnings shown in Column 2.

dividend payout ratio
The percentage of earnings paid out in dividends.

Step 5 Next we sum the asset accounts, obtaining a total projected assets figure of $900,000, and also add the projected liabilities and net worth items to obtain $669,000, the estimate of available funds. Since liabilities and net worth must total $900,000, but only $669,000 is projected, we have a shortfall of $231,000 "additional funds needed," which will presumably be raised by selling securities. For simplicity, we disregard depreciation by assuming that cash flows from depreciation are reinvested in fixed assets.

Industry Practice

What Does the Future Hold?

"If you took all the economists in the land and laid them end to end. . . .

"It would be a good thing."

That joke was one of many circulating in Washington, DC, in the spring of 1982, after economic forecasters gazed into their computer models and made some of the biggest bloopers in years. They overestimated inflation, underestimated unemployment, and predicted that the Federal Reserve Board would relax its tight money policy much sooner than it did. Then there was the recovery—or more accurately, there wasn't the recovery. Month after month, quarter after quarter, these cheery oracles persisted in seeing an upturn in the economy just around the corner. When the recovery finally did arrive, it was a year late and came in like a lion, not like a lamb as predicted.

It is no surprise, therefore, that the economists who made these pronouncements found themselves the butt of jokes, but that seems to be as far as their suffering went. For although the 1982 forecasts were among the wackiest of the decade— and the worst since 1974–1975, when most economists predicted a major boom on the eve of a major bust—the business of forecasting remained bullish. American companies pay millions every year, some say as much as $125 million, to econometrics firms for advice. The largest chunk of this wealth goes to the three superstars of forecasting: Data Resources, Inc. (DRI), Chase Econometrics, and Wharton Econometric Forecasting Associates. Their prognostications are used by federal agencies, giant corporations, banks—even governments (Israel is one of DRI's clients). When Thomas Naylor, professor of economics at Duke University, polled 234 corporate economists in 1980, some 90 percent said they used one of the top three firms, and a whopping 68.3 percent reported using DRI. Needless to say, these firms wield awesome power. The data they generate affect decisions on everything from department store inventories to Social Security tax increases. "We forecast something like 15,000 numbers," says Elizabeth Allison, senior economist at DRI, "from very big numbers like the GNP to medium-sized numbers like profits in the advertising industry to very, very detailed numbers such as the landed price of a barrel of Nigerian crude in Rotterdam."

These numbers are generated in econometric models that simulate with mathematical formulas relationships between certain events in the real world; for example, the effect sagging interest rates will have on the sales of homes and cars or the effect a tax cut might have on consumer spending. These formulas, in turn, are grouped together to form a model, which reflects the interaction of all the variables. From the model, economists can determine relationships among the tax cut *and* sagging interest rates *and* consumer spending.

Over the years, DRI, Chase, and Wharton have developed such a huge mass of data that a subscription to their services is practically a must for anyone doing business. Although most large corporations depend on their own staff economists for inhouse predictions, nearly every company, large and small, subscribes to one of the firms and many Fortune 500 companies subscribe to more than one—they want to be sure they have access to the same information their competitors are getting. In-house economists comb the numbers in search of trends that might affect future sales, mergers, or acquisitions, and, sometimes, to make their own forecasts.

Allison contends that the data supplied by econometrics firms should be used as a tool to develop in-house strategies in light of projected economic trends. But she will admit that what customers really want is straightforward, simple answers: how much a one-cent increase in the price of donuts would affect sales, for example. And DRI, like its competitors, endeavors to produce those answers. Each firm has experts on everything from steel to farming to female participation in the work force, and these experts are responsible for tracking the very latest theories in their specialties and pumping them into the formulas.

While economists take great pleasure in describing the scientific merits of their work, it is still human judgment that shapes their predictions. The models sit silently in the computers until someone plugs in assumptions about future economic conditions and tells the computer to solve the equations based on those assumptions. Each forecaster must guess, for example, about the fate of important bills in Congress, future monetary policy, and whether consumers will save or spend their share of a tax cut. "The real fun begins when you take the model and try to coax an answer out of it that you can believe," says Stephen McNees, an economist with the Federal Reserve Bank in Boston. McNees has monitored the accuracy of economic forecasts for twelve years. "The answers you get depend almost entirely on the guesses you make," he says. If a single, specific number—e.g., projected housing starts—is extracted from the model without taking the underlying assumptions into consideration—e.g., the economist's estimate of interest rates over the same period—the number will be inaccurate if the assumption is inaccurate.

The sages' guesses about the future are often rooted in their past experiences, but current economic conditions are without historic precedent. "It's hard to guess what's going to happen at 22 percent interest rates if the only interest rates you've seen have fallen between 2.5 and 4 percent," says Allison. It isn't just interest rates that have taken a new direction and confounded the best efforts of forecasters. People didn't spend their tax cut dollars in 1982 as consumers of previous decades had; they socked the money into savings instead. Federal Reserve Chairman Paul Volcker defied historical trends by keeping a tight rein on the money supply. "We didn't believe he would stay the course," says Allison, ruefully. Previous chairmen had eased up in the face of a recession. And when inflation took an uncharacteristically dramatic plunge as well, all of the econometric models sprang leaks.

Thus, while economists like to think of their business as a science, many admit it is not. "We can't set up a test-tube experiment and say, 'Let's give everybody a tax cut, keep everything else constant, and see what happens,' " laments Allen Gutheim, formerly a senior economist at Wharton and now with First National Bank of Boston. "All we can do is look to the past and hope the future is not too different."

Source: "What Does the Future Hold?" *Savvy*, October 1983. © 1983 *Savvy* Co., New York, NY. Reprinted with permission.

Step 6 Arinson could use short-term notes, mortgage bonds, common stock, or a combination of these securities to make up the short-fall. Ordinarily, it would make this choice on the basis of the relative costs of these different types of securities. However, in this case the company has a contractual agreement with its bondholders to keep total debt at or below 50 percent of total assets, and also to keep the current ratio at a level of 3.0 or greater. These provisions restrict the financing choices as follows:

1. Restriction on additional debt

Maximum debt permitted   = 0.5 × Total assets
                         = 0.5 × \$900,000 = \$450,000
Less debt already projected for December 31, 1985:
          Current liabilities   \$145,000
          Mortgage bonds   150,000 =   295,000
Maximum additional debt   \$155,000

2. Restriction on additional current liabilities

Maximum current liabilities = ⅓ of current assets
                           =   \$450,000 ÷ 3 = \$150,000
Current liabilities already projected   145,000
Maximum additional current liabilities   \$ 5,000

3. Common equity requirements

Total external funds required (from Table 8-2)   \$231,000
Maximum additional debt permitted   155,000
Common equity funds required   \$ 76,000

We see, then, that Arinson needs a total of \$231,000 from external sources. Its existing debt contract limits new debt to \$155,000, and of that amount only \$5,000 can be short-term debt. Thus Arinson must plan to sell common stock in the amount of \$76,000, in addition to some debt financing, to cover its financial requirements.

Projected Financial Statements and Ratios

Arinson's financial manager can now construct a set of projected, or pro forma, financial statements and then analyze the ratios that are implied by these statements. Table 8-3 gives abbreviated versions of the final projected balance sheet, income statement, statement of changes in financial position, and a few key ratios. These statements,

---

Table 8-3
**Arinson Products Company: Projected Financial Statements for 1985
(Thousands of Dollars)**

I. Projected Balance Sheet, Dec. 31, 1985

Cash	$ 15	Accounts payable	$ 60
Accounts receivable	135	Notes payable[a]	15
Inventories	300	Accruals	75
Total current assets	$450	Total current liabilities	$150
Net fixed assets	$450	Long-term debt[b]	$300
		Common stock[c]	126
		Retained earnings	324
		Total equity	$450
Total assets	$900	Total claims	$900

II. Projected Income Statement, 1985

Sales	$600
Total costs	500
Taxable income	$100
Taxes (40%)	40
Net income after taxes	$ 60
Dividends	36
Addition to retained earnings	$ 24

III. Projected Statement of Changes in Financial Position, 1985

Sources of funds:		Uses of funds:	
Net income	$ 60	Increase in net fixed assets	$150
Funds from operations[d]	60	Dividend payments	36
Proceeds from sale of bonds	150	Increase in net working capital	100
Proceeds from sale of		(See detail below.)	
common stock	76		
Total sources	$286	Total uses	$286

[a]Assumes $5,000 additional is borrowed from bank. This is the maximum permissible increase in short-term debt.
[b]Assumes $150,000 additional long-term debt is sold. This is the maximum permissible increase in long-term debt, given the $5,000 increase in notes payable.
[c]Assumes $76,000 additional common stock is sold.
[d]*Funds from operations* normally includes depreciation. Here we have assumed that depreciation is reinvested in fixed assets; that is, depreciation is netted out against fixed asset additions.

(continued)

in turn, can be used by the financial manager to show the other executives the implications of the planned sales increase. For example, the projected rate of return on equity is 13.3 percent. Is this a reasonable target, or can it be improved? Also, the preliminary forecast calls for the sale of some common stock—but does top management really want

Table 8-3
Arinson Products Company: Projected Financial Statements for 1985
(Thousands of Dollars) *(continued)*

Analysis of Changes in Working Capital

Increase (decrease) in current assets:

Cash	$ 5
Accounts receivable	45
Inventories	100
Net increase (decrease) in current assets	$150

Increase (decrease) in current liabilities:

Accounts payable	$ 20
Notes payable	5
Accruals	25
Net increase (decrease) in current liabilities	$ 50
Increase (decrease) in net working capital	$100

IV. Key Ratios Projected for December 31, 1985

1. Current ratio	3.0×
2. Total debt/total assets	50%
3. Rate of return on equity	13.3%

(Other ratios could be calculated and analyzed by the Du Pont system.)

---

to sell any new stock? Suppose Arinson Products Company is owned entirely by John Arinson, who does not want to sell any stock and thereby lose his exclusive control of the company. How then can the needed funds be raised, or what adjustments should be made? In the remainder of the chapter, we look at approaches to answering questions such as these.

The Relationship between Growth in Sales and Capital Requirements[1]

Although the forecast of capital requirements can be made by constructing pro forma balance sheets as described above, it is often easier to use a simple forecasting formula. In addition, the formula that follows can be used to make clear the relationship between sales growth and financial requirements.

---

[1]At the instructor's option, this section may be omitted without loss of continuity. In any case, the reader should be careful in applying Equation 8-1 in practice. Several restrictive assumptions, implicit in the equation, may make the direct application of this model ineffectual. The model is most effective in highlighting factors that determine the magnitude of the demand for external funds.

$$\begin{matrix} \text{External} \\ \text{funds} \\ \text{needed} \end{matrix} = \begin{bmatrix} \text{Required} \\ \text{increase} \\ \text{in assets} \end{bmatrix} - \begin{bmatrix} \text{Spontaneous} \\ \text{increase in} \\ \text{liabilities} \end{bmatrix} - \begin{bmatrix} \text{Increase in} \\ \text{retained} \\ \text{earnings} \end{bmatrix}$$

$$EFN = \frac{A}{S}(\Delta S) - \frac{L}{S}(\Delta S) - MS_1(1 - d). \quad \textbf{(8-1)}$$

Here,

EFN = external funds needed.

$\frac{A}{S}$ = assets that increase spontaneously with sales as a percent of sales, or required dollar increase in assets per \$1 increase in sales. A/S = 600/400 = 150%, or 1.5, for Arinson.

$\frac{L}{S}$ = liabilities that increase spontaneously with sales as a percent of sales, or spontaneously generated financing per \$1 increase in sales. L/S = 90/400 = 22.5% for Arinson.

S_1 = total sales projected for next year. Note that S_0 = last year's sales. S_1 = \$600,000 for Arinson.

ΔS = change in sales = $S_1 - S_0$ = \$600,000 − \$400,000 = \$200,000 for Arinson.

M = profit margin, or rate of profit per \$1 of sales. M = 10%, or 0.10, for Arinson.

d = percentage of earnings paid out in dividends, or the dividend payout ratio; d = 60%. Notice that 1 − d = 1.0 − 0.6 = 0.4, or 40%. This is the percentage of earnings that Arinson retains, often called the **retention rate** or *retention ratio*.

retention rate
The percentage of earnings retained after payment of dividends.

Inserting values for Arinson into Equation 8-1, we find the external funds needed as follows:

$$\begin{aligned} EFN &= 1.5\,(\Delta S) - 0.225(\Delta S) - 0.1(S_1)\,(1 - 0.6) \\ &= 1.5(\$200{,}000) - 0.225(\$200{,}000) - 0.1(\$600{,}000)\,(0.4) \\ &= \$300{,}000 - \$45{,}000 - \$24{,}000 \\ &= \$231{,}000. \end{aligned}$$

To increase sales by \$200,000, Arinson must increase assets by \$300,000. The \$300,000 of new assets must be financed in some man-

external funds needed
Funds that must be acquired by a firm through borrowing or by selling new stock.

ner. Of the total, $45,000 will come from a spontaneous increase in liabilities, while another $24,000 will be raised from retained earnings. The **external funds needed** to finance this projected growth amount to $231,000, which must be raised over and above the internally and spontaneously generated funds. This value must, of course, agree with the figure developed in Table 8-2.

Graph of the Relationship between Growth and Funds Requirements

The faster Arinson's growth rate in sales, the greater its need for external financing; we can use Equation 8-1 to indicate this relationship. Consider Table 8-4, which shows Arinson's external financial require-

Table 8-4
Relationship between Growth in Sales and Financial Requirements,
Assuming $S_0 = \$400,000$

Growth Rate in Sales (%) (1)	Dollar Increase (Decrease) in Sales (ΔS in Thousands) (2)	New Sales (S_1 in Thousands) (3)	External Funds Requirements (Surplus in Thousands) (4)
100%	$400	$800	$478.0
50	200	600	231.0
25	100	500	107.5
10	40	440	33.4
3.239	12.956	412.956	0.0
0	0	400	(16.0)
−10	(40)	360	(65.4)
−25	(100)	300	(139.5)

Explanation of columns:

Col. 1: Growth rate in sales, g.
Col. 2: Increase (decrease) in sales, $\Delta S = g(S_0)$.
Col. 3: New sales, $S_1 = S_0 + g(S_0) = S_0(1 + g)$.
Col. 4: External funds required $= 1.5(\Delta S) - 0.225(\Delta S) - 0.04(S_1)$
$\qquad = 1.275(\Delta S) - 0.04(S_1)$
$\qquad = 1.275(g)(S_0) - 0.04(S_0)(1 + g)$
$\qquad = 510g - 16 - 16g$
$\qquad = -16 + 494g$
$\qquad =$ equation plotted in Figure 8-1.

Example: If $g = 10\%$, or 0.10, then
External funds required $\quad = -16 + 494g$
$\qquad\qquad = -16 + 494(0.10)$
$\qquad\qquad = 33.4$ or $33,400.

The maximum growth rate that can be financed without external funds is found by setting the equation equal to zero:

External funds required $\quad = 0 = -16 + 494g$
$\qquad\qquad 494g = 16$
$\qquad g = 16/494 = 0.03239$ or 3.239%.

Figure 8-1
Relationship between Arinson's Growth in Sales and Financial Requirements

This figure shows Arinson's external financial requirements at various growth rates. The data plotted were arrived at through Equation 8-1 and are also shown in Table 8-4. The faster Arinson's sales grow, the more external funds will be required. Beyond a growth rate of 3.239 percent, external capital must be raised.

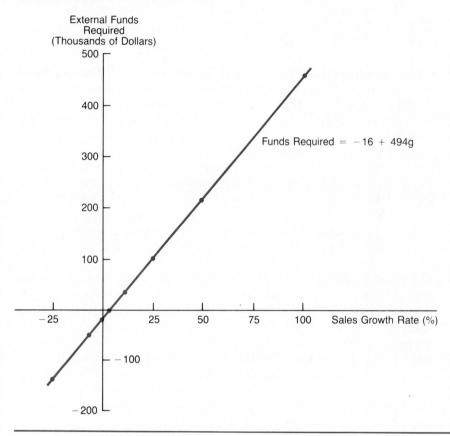

ments at various growth rates. These data also are plotted in Figure 8-1. Several points are apparent from the exhibits; they are discussed below.

Financial Planning. At low growth rates Arinson needs no external financing. However, if the company grows faster than 3.239 percent, it must raise capital from outside sources. If for any reason management foresees difficulties in raising this capital—perhaps because Arinson's owners do not want to sell additional stock—then the company might need to reconsider the feasibility of its expansion plans.

The Effect of Dividend Policy on Financing Needs. Dividend policy also affects external capital requirements, so if Arinson foresees difficulties in raising capital, it might want to consider a reduction in the dividend payout ratio. This would lower, or shift to the right, the line in Figure 8-1, indicating lower external capital requirements at all growth rates. However, before making this decision, management should consider the effects of changes in dividends on stock prices. These effects are described in Chapter 21.

Notice that the line in Figure 8-1 does *not* pass through the origin; thus at low growth rates surplus funds (negative external requirements) will be produced, because new retained earnings plus spontaneous funds will exceed the required asset increases. Only if the dividend payout ratio is 100 percent, meaning that the firm does not retain any of its earnings, will the "funds required" line pass through the origin.

capital intensity ratio
The amount of assets required per dollar of sales (A/S).

Capital Intensity. The amount of assets required per dollar of sales, A/S in Equation 8-1, is often called the **capital intensity ratio.** This factor has a major effect on capital requirements per unit of sales growth. If the capital intensity ratio is low, then sales can grow rapidly without much outside capital. However, if the firm is capital intensive, even a small growth in output will require a great deal of outside capital.

The Profit Margin and the Need for External Funds. The profit margin, M, is also an important determinant of the funds-required equation—the higher the margin, the lower the funds requirements, other things held constant. Arinson's profit margin was 10 percent. Now suppose M increased to 15 percent. This new value could be inserted into the funds-required formula, and the following relationship between external funds needed and growth would result: EFN = −24 + 486g. Thus we see that an increase in the profit margin lowers both the intercept term and the slope coefficient, so for all positive growth rates there is a reduction in external funds needed. Because of the relationship between profit margins and external capital requirements, some very rapidly growing firms do not need much external capital. Thus, for example, Xerox grew very rapidly with very little borrowing or stock sales. However, as the company lost patent protection, and as competition intensified in the copier industry, Xerox's profit margin declined, its needs for external capital rose, and it began to borrow heavily from banks and other sources.

excess capacity
Capacity that exists when an asset is not being fully utilized; in the context of this chapter, excess capacity exists when the firm's fixed assets are operated at less than full capacity.

Excess Capacity. We assumed that Arinson was initially operating at full capacity. Therefore any increase in sales required an increase in assets. However, had **excess capacity** existed initially, some level of sales expansion could have occurred with no increase in fixed assets. Thus the ratio of assets to sales, A/S in Equation 8-1, should include only those assets which vary directly with sales. Fixed assets would not be included in the ratio until excess capacity is reduced and more fixed assets are required to support expanding sales.

Changing Ratios. If the ratios of either assets or liabilities to sales are changing over time, then Equation 8-1 cannot be used to forecast financial requirements. The consequences of changing ratios are investigated in the next section.

Forecasting Financial Requirements When the Balance Sheet Ratios Are Subject to Change

To this point we have been assuming that the balance sheet ratios (A/S and L/S) are constant at all levels of sales. For the ratios to remain constant, each asset and liability item must increase at the same rate as sales. In graph form this assumption suggests the existence of the type of relationship indicated in Figure 8-2: a relationship that is linear and passes through the origin. The assumption of a constant ratio may or may not be appropriate, and certainly this is one of the things that should be discussed during the planning process.

Suppose, for example, that a ratio comparison showed that other firms in the industry had inventory-to-sales ratios of only 25 percent

---

Figure 8-2
Relationship between Assets and Sales If the Assets/Sales Ratio Is Constant for All Levels of Sales

Financial forecasting through the use of Equation 8-1 assumes that the assets/sales and liability/sales ratios will remain constant at all levels of sales. In such cases each relationship will appear as a straight line on a graph, as shown in this figure. For many companies, however, assumption of constant ratios is unrealistic; assets are added and/or liabilities are incurred at irregular or infrequent intervals. For such companies Equation 8-1 cannot be used to forecast financial requirements.

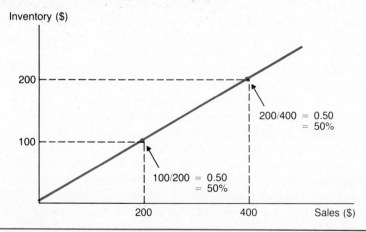

versus Arinson's 50 percent. If Arinson could reduce inventories to the industry average, its December 31, 1985 inventory forecast would be $150,000 rather than $300,000. This would reduce financial requirements by $150,000. (See Table 8-2.) Furthermore, if the assets side of the balance sheet were reduced by $150,000, the claims side would be reduced by the same amount. This would mean less equity or less debt (hence lower interest charges), which would result in a higher rate of return on equity in either case.

In many firms it is completely unrealistic to think that fixed assets will ever be a stable percentage of sales. For example, if the production process is such that fixed assets are added in "lumpy" increments at infrequent intervals, then the fixed assets/sales ratio will be low just *before* new capacity is added and high just *after* a new plant is put on line. Also, since sales tend to fluctuate over the business cycle, at the start of some years a firm will have excess manufacturing capacity and thus be able to expand sales greatly with little or no additions to fixed assets. On the other hand, if the firm is operating close to capacity and if fixed assets are **"lumpy,"** then even a small increase in sales may require a large increase in fixed assets.

"lumpy" assets
Those assets that cannot be acquired smoothly but require large, discrete additions.

Computerized Financial Planning Models

Although the type of financial forecasting described in this chapter can be done by hand, most well-managed firms with sales greater than a few million dollars employ some type of computerized financial planning model. Such models can be programmed to show the effects of different sales levels, different ratios of sales to operating assets, and even different assumptions about sales prices and input costs (labor, materials, and so forth). Plans are then made regarding how financial requirements are to be met—through bank loans, thus increasing short-term notes payable; by selling long-term bonds; or by selling new common stock. Pro forma balance sheets and income statements are generated under the different financing plans, and earnings per share are projected, along with such risk measures as the current ratio, the debt/assets ratio, and the times-interest-earned ratio.

Depending on how these projections look, management may modify its initial plans. For example, the firm may conclude that its sales forecast must be cut because the requirements for external capital exceed the firm's ability to raise money. Or management may decide to reduce dividends and thus generate more funds internally. Alternatively, the company may decide to investigate production processes that require fewer fixed assets, or to consider the possibility of buying rather than manufacturing certain components, thus eliminating raw materials and work-in process inventories, as well as certain manufacturing facilities.

In subsequent chapters we examine in detail ways of analyzing policy changes such as those mentioned above. In all such considerations the basic issue is the effect that a specific action will have on future earnings, on the riskiness of these earnings, and hence on the price of the firm's stock. Since computerized models help management assess these effects, such planning models are playing an ever-increasing role in corporate management.[2]

Summary

This chapter has described in broad outline how firms go about projecting their financial statements and determining their overall financial requirements. In brief, management establishes a target balance sheet based on the type of ratio analysis discussed in Chapter 7. Assuming that each balance sheet ratio is at the desired level and that the optimal levels for these ratios are stable, the *percentage of sales method* can be used to forecast the external financial requirements associated with any given increase in sales. If the balance sheet ratios are subject to change, as they will be if excess capacity exists, then each item in the projected balance sheet must be forecasted separately.

The type of forecasting described here is important for several reasons. First, if the projected operating results look poor, management can "go back to the drawing board" and reformulate its plans for the coming year. Second, it is possible that the funds required to meet the sales forecast simply cannot be obtained. If so, it is obviously better to know this in advance and to scale back the projected level of operations. And third, even if the required funds can be raised, it is desirable to plan for the acquisition of these funds well in advance. As we see in later chapters, raising capital takes time and is expensive, and both time and money can be saved by careful forward planning.

---

[2]Corporations can develop their own computerized models, but excellent and easy-to-use planning models are also available from a number of specialized computer software companies. One such model—Interactive Financial Planning System (IFPS)—is installed on the computer system of many universities and several hundred corporations, including 3M Corporation, Shell Oil, and Florida Power and Light.

Note that in this chapter we have concentrated on long-run, or strategic, financial planning. Within the framework of the long-run strategic plan, firms also develop short-run financial plans. For example, in Table 8-2 we saw that Arinson Products expects to need $231,000 by the end of 1985, and that it plans to raise this capital by using short-term debt, long-term debt, and common stock. However, we do not know when during the year the need for funds will occur, or when Arinson will obtain each of its different types of capital. To address these issues, the firm must develop a short-run financial plan, the centerpiece of which is the *cash budget*, which is a projection of cash inflows and outflows on a daily, weekly, or monthly basis during the coming year (or other budget period). Although considering the cash budget here would complete our examination of the basic types of analysis done in connection with financial planning, we nevertheless defer this discussion to Chapter 11, "Managing Cash and Marketable Securities," because cash budgets can best be understood after we have discussed the firm's target cash balance.

Resolution to Decision in Finance $$

AT&T Conquers the Fear of Forecasting

One of the greatest drawbacks of any financial forecast is the uncertainty of the information on which it is based. No one can be certain what the future holds, so, of necessity, forecasts are always subject to forces beyond a forecaster's control. For example, the AT&T predictions were based on many assumptions about the rates that the Federal Communications Commission, state regulators, and Congress would allow the new companies to charge. AT&T assumed that a monthly charge for access to telephone networks would pass Congress even though legislators were opposed to it, and that the rate increases pending in 30 states, many for enormous amounts, would be approved. AT&T also counted on quick approval of intrastate access charges from state regulators, most of whom disliked the notion as much as Congress did.

To avoid overoptimism, the prospectus quantified the uncertainty for the seven regionals. For example, it predicted revenues of $7,800,000,000 and profits of $870,000,000 for Southwestern Bell. But it stipulated that 44 percent of the revenues—$3,400,000,000—depended on the outcome of rate-increase applications that had to be approved by the states and the FCC. When such a huge sum is uncertain, even a small shortfall or overrun can have a magnified effect on actual profits.

Given the uncertainty that forecasting entails, it's no surprise that most companies hesitate to make their predictions public. Many fear that stockholders will bring lawsuits if results fall short of estimates. And they aren't reassured by the Securities and Exchange Commission's safe harbor provisions. Even though these provisions let a company that acts in good faith off the hook legally if its predictions don't come true, the standard corporate response is, "Why stick your neck out in the first place?"

Managers also feel that published forecasts place them in a do-or-die situation. They fear that their credibility will suffer if actual results fall short of the forecast. In such a case investors may conclude that management lacks control over the company's future and sell large quantities of stock.

On the other hand, some experts contend that issuing forecasts could give companies an advantage with investors. They believe that investors would appreciate management's willingness to share its special insights into their company's future. Then, when making investment decisions, investors could rely on the corporation's predictions and use securities analysts' research as supplementary—rather than primary—sources of data.

Most Wall Street watchers think that AT&T has set a precedent. Now that the biggest company on earth has paved the way for official public forecasts, other companies are sure to follow.

Sources: "AT&T Conquers the Fear of Forecasting," *Business Week*, Dec. 5, 1983, 72; "Rose-Colored View: AT&T's Upbeat Forecasts," *Fortune*, Dec. 12, 1983, 6; and "Ma Bell Forecasts a Modest '84 for Its Offspring," *Business Week*, Nov. 28, 1983, 38–39.

Key Terms

You should be able to define each of the following terms:

Sales (demand) forecast	Retention rate
Percentage of sales method	External funds needed
Pro forma statement	Capital intensity ratio
Spontaneously generated funds	Excess capacity
Dividend payout ratio	"Lumpy" assets

Questions

8-1 Certain liability and net worth items generally increase spontaneously with increases in sales. Put a check (✓) by those items that typically increase spontaneously:

Accounts payable   _____
Notes payable to banks   _____
Accrued wages   _____
Accrued taxes   _____
Mortgage bonds   _____
Common stock   _____
Retained earnings   _____
Marketable securities   _____

8-2 The following equation can, under certain assumptions, be used to forecast financial requirements:

$$\text{External funds needed} = \frac{A}{S}(\Delta S) - \frac{L}{S}(\Delta S) - MS_1(1 - d).$$

Under what conditions does the equation give satisfactory predictions, and when should it not be used?

8-3 Assume that an average firm in the office supply business has a 6 percent after-tax profit margin, a 40 percent debt/assets ratio, a turnover of 2 times, and a dividend payout ratio of 40 percent. Is it true that if such a firm is to have *any* sales growth ($g > 0$), it will be forced to sell either bonds or common stock (that is, it will need some nonspontaneous external capital, and this will be true even if g is very small)?

8-4 Is it true that computerized corporate planning models were a fad during the 1970s, but, because of a need for flexibility in corporate planning, they have been dropped by most firms?

8-5 Suppose a firm makes the following policy changes. If the change means that external, nonspontaneous financial requirements for any rate of growth will increase, indicate this by a ($+$); indicate decreases by a ($-$); and indicate indeterminant and/or no effect by a (0). Think in terms of the immediate, short-run effect on funds requirements.

a. The dividend payout ratio is increased.   _____

b. The firm contracts to buy rather than make certain components used in its products.   _____

c. The firm decides to pay all suppliers on delivery, rather than after a 30-day delay, in order to take advantage of discounts for rapid payment.   _____

d. The firm begins to sell on credit; previously all sales had been on a cash basis.   _____

e. The firm's profit margin is eroded by increased competition.   _____

f. Advertising expenditures are stepped up.   _____

g. A decision is made to substitute long-term mortgage bonds for short-term bank loans.   _____

h. The firm begins to pay employees on a weekly basis; previously it paid them at the end of each month.   _____

Self-Test Problems

ST-1 J. Bildersee, Inc. has these ratios: A/S = 1.6; L/S = 0.4; profit margin = 0.10; and dividend payout ratio = 0.45, or 45 percent. Sales last year were $100 million. Assuming that these ratios will remain constant and that all liabilities increase spontaneously with increases in sales, what is the maximum growth rate Bildersee can achieve without having to employ nonspontaneous external funds?

ST-2 Suppose Bildersee's financial consultants report (1) that the inventory utilization ratio is sales/inventory = 3 times versus an industry average of 4 times, and (2) that Bildersee could raise its utilization to 4 without affecting sales, the profit margin, or the other asset utilization ratios. Under these conditions, what amount of external funds would Bildersee expect to require during each of the next 2 years if sales grow at a rate of 20 percent per year?

Problems

8-1 A group of investors is planning to set up a new company to manufacture and distribute a novel type of running shoe. To help plan the new operation's financial requirements, you have been asked to construct a pro forma balance sheet for December 31, 1985, the end of the first year of operations. Sales for 1985 are projected at $20 million, and the following are industry average ratios for athletic shoe companies:

Sales to common equity	5×
Current debt to equity	50%

Total debt to equity	80%
Current ratio	2.2×
Net sales to inventory	9×
Accounts receivable to sales	10%
Fixed assets to equity	70%
Profit margin	3%
Dividend payout ratio	30%

Pro Forma Balance Sheet, December 31, 1985 (Millions of Dollars)

Cash	$_____	Current debt	$_____
Accounts receivable	_____	Long-term debt	_____
Inventories	_____	Total debt	_____
Total current assets	_____	Equity	_____
Fixed assets	_____		
Total assets	$_____	Total claims	$_____

a. Complete the pro forma balance sheet just above, assuming that 1985 sales are $20 million.

b. If our group supplies all the new firm's equity, how much capital will it be required to put up by December 31, 1985?

* **8-2** Rakes Restaurant Supply has been growing at a rapid rate lately. As a result Mr. Rakes has been unable to devote proper attention to the management of the firm's assets. Expected sales for next year are $1,800,000 with a net profit margin of 2.5 percent. Retained earnings at the beginning of the year were $255,000. Current liabilities were $200,000 at the beginning of the year. Long-term debt and common stock have remained constant for some time. Rakes computed the following financial ratios:

Average collection period = 40 days,
Inventory utilization = 6 times,
Fixed asset utilization = 4 times.

Rakes anticipates no dividend payout this year. Complete the following pro forma balance sheet. Short-term debt is the appropriate balancing item. According to your projections:

a. How much will Rakes have to raise to support the expected sales?
b. How much of the total will be raised internally (equity); externally (debt)?
c. What is Rakes's debt ratio?
d. What is Rakes's current ratio?
e. What is the firm's return on assets?

---

*Refer to Appendix E for check answers to problems with asterisks.

Rakes Restaurant Supply: Pro Forma Balance Sheet

Cash	$ 50,000	Short-term debt	$_____
Accounts receivable	_____	Long-term debt	275,000
Inventory	_____	Total debt	
Current assets	_____	Common stock	100,000
Fixed assets	_____	Retained earnings	_____
Total assets	$_____	Total claims	$_____

* **8-3** After making the projections in Problem 8-2, Rakes is determined to streamline his balance sheet. He is certain that the average collection period can be reduced to 30 days and that the inventory utilization can be increased to 8 times. He feels that cash and fixed assets will remain at their current level, however. Make another projection regarding Rakes's financial needs. Specifically:

    a. How much will Rakes have to raise to support sales under these new conditions?

    b. How much of the total will be raised internally (equity); externally (debt)?

    c. What is Rakes's debt ratio?

    d. What is Rakes's current ratio?

    e. What is the firm's return on assets?

* **8-4** Uncle Pettit's, Inc. has these ratios:

$$A/S = 1.8$$
$$L/S = .5$$
$$\text{Net profit margin, M} = 8\%$$
$$\text{Dividend payout ratio, d} = 35\%$$

Sales last year were $200 million. Assuming that these ratios remain constant and all liabilities increase spontaneously with increases in sales, what is the maximum growth rate Uncle Pettit's can achieve without having to employ nonspontaneous external funds?

* **8-5** The 1984 balance sheet for Joseph Black and Associates is shown below (in millions of dollars):

Cash	$ 6.0	Accounts payable	$ 4.0
Accounts receivable	6.0	Notes payable	3.0
Inventory	10.0	Long-term debt	6.0
Current assets	$22.0	Total debt	$13.0
Fixed assets	6.0	Common equity	15.0
Total assets	$28.0	Total claims	$28.0

Management believes that sales will increase in the next year by 20 percent over the current level of $120 million. The profit margin is expected to be 5 percent and the dividend payout will remain at 40 percent. If the firm has no excess capacity, what additional funding is required for 1985?

* 8-6 Refer to Problem 8-5. Assume that all relationships hold *except* for the capacity constraint. *Now* assume that the firm has excess capacity and that no increase in fixed assets will be required. Under this new condition, how much additional funding will be required for 1985?

8-7 Dandy Computers makes bulk purchases of small computers, stocks them in conveniently located warehouses, and then ships them to its chain of retail stores. Dandy's balance sheet as of December 31, 1984 is shown here (in millions of dollars):

Cash	$ 2.0	Accounts payable	$ 5.0
Accounts receivable	15.0	Notes payable	10.0
Inventories	33.0	Accruals	5.0
Total current assets	$50.0	Total current liabilities	$20.0
Net fixed assets	20.2	Mortgage loan	3.4
		Common stock	8.4
		Retained earnings	38.4
Total assets	$70.2	Total liabilities and net worth	$70.2

Sales for 1984 were $200 million, while net income after taxes for the year was $5,670,000. Dandy paid dividends of $2,268,000 to common stockholders. The firm is operating at full capacity.

* a. If sales are projected to increase by $50 million, or by 25 percent, during 1985, what are Dandy's projected external capital requirements?

b. Construct Dandy's pro forma balance sheet for December 31, 1985. Assume that all external capital requirements are met by bank loans and are reflected in notes payable.

c. Now calculate the following ratios, based on your projected December 31, 1985 balance sheet. Dandy's 1984 ratios and industry average ratios are shown here for comparison.

	Dandy Computers Dec. 31, 1985	Dandy Computers Dec. 31, 1984	Industry Average Dec. 31, 1984
Current ratio	_____	2.5×	3×
Debt/total assets	_____	33.3%	30%
Rate of return on net worth	_____	12.1%	12%

d. Now assume that Dandy grows by the same $50 million but that the growth is spread over 5 years; that is, sales grow by $10 million each year.

* 1. Calculate total external financial requirements over the 5-year period.

2. Construct a pro forma balance sheet as of December 31, 1989, using notes payable as the balancing item.

3. Calculate the current ratio, debt/assets ratio, and rate of return on net worth as of December 31, 1989. [Hint: Be sure to use *total sales*, which amount to $1,150,000, to calculate retained earnings, but 1989 profits to calculate the rate of return on net worth, that is, (1989 profits)/(December 31, 1989 net worth).]

e. Do the plans outlined in Parts c and d seem feasible to you? That is, do you think Dandy could borrow the required capital, and would the company be raising the odds on its bankruptcy to an excessive level in the event of some temporary misfortune?

8-8 The McCollough-Crum Company's 1984 sales were $24 million. The percentage of sales of each balance sheet item that varies directly with sales is given below:

Cash	3%
Accounts receivable	20
Inventories	25
Net fixed assets	40
Accounts payable	15
Accruals	10
Profit rate (after taxes) on sales	5

The dividend payout ratio is 40 percent; the December 31, 1983 balance sheet account for retained earnings was $8,200,000; and both common stock and mortgage bonds are constant and equal to the amounts shown on the balance sheet below.

a. Complete the following balance sheet.

**McCollough-Crum Company: Balance Sheet, December 31, 1984
(Thousands of Dollars)**

Cash	$____	Accounts payable	$____
Accounts receivable	____	Notes payable	2,200
Inventories	____	Accruals	____
Total current assets	____	Total current liabilities	____
Net fixed assets	____	Mortgage bonds	2,000
		Common stock	2,000
		Retained earnings	____
Total assets	$____	Total liabilities and net worth	$____

✱ b. Now suppose that 1985 sales increase by 10 percent over 1984 sales. How much additional external capital will be required? The company was operating at full capacity in 1984. Use Equation 8-1 to answer this question.

c. Develop a pro forma balance sheet for December 31, 1985. Assume that any required financing is borrowed as notes payable.

d. What would happen to external funds requirements under each of the following conditions? Answer in words, without calculations.

1. The profit margin went (i) from 5 to 6 percent, (ii) from 5 to 3 percent.
2. The dividend payout ratio (i) was raised from 40 to 90 percent, (ii) was lowered from 40 to 20 percent.

3. Credit terms on sales were relaxed substantially, giving customers longer to pay.

4. The company had excess manufacturing capacity at December 31, 1984.

8-9 Alabama Textile's 1984 sales were $72 million. The percentage of sales of each balance sheet item except notes payable, mortgage bonds, and common stock is given here:

Cash	4%
Accounts receivable	25
Inventories	30
Net fixed assets	50
Accounts payable	15
Accruals	5
Profit margin (after taxes) on sales	5

The dividend payout ratio is 60 percent; the December 31, 1983 balance sheet account for retained earnings was $41,800,000; and both common stock and mortgage bonds are constant and equal to the amounts shown on the balance sheet below.

a. Complete the following balance sheet.

Alabama Textile: Balance Sheet, December 31, 1984 (Thousands of Dollars)

Cash	$_____	Accounts payable	$_____
Accounts receivable	_____	Notes payable	6,840
Inventories	_____	Accruals	_____
Total current assets	_____	Total current liabilities	_____
Net fixed assets	_____	Mortgage bonds	10,000
		Common stock	4,000
		Retained earnings	_____
Total assets	$_____	Total liabilities and net worth	$_____

* b. Assume that the company was operating at full capacity in 1984 with regard to all items *except* fixed assets; had the fixed assets been used to full capacity, the fixed assets/sales ratio would have been 40 percent in 1984. By what percentage could 1985 sales increase over 1984 sales without the need for an increase in fixed assets?

* c. Now suppose that 1985 sales increase by 20 percent over 1984 sales. How much additional external capital will be required? Assume that Alabama Textile cannot sell any fixed assets. (Hint: Equation 8-1 can no longer be used. You must develop a pro forma balance sheet as in Table 8-2.) Assume that any required financing is borrowed as notes payable.

d. Suppose the industry averages for receivables and inventories are 20 percent and 25 percent, respectively, and that Alabama Textile matches these figures in 1985 and then uses the funds released to reduce equity. (It could pay a special dividend out of retained earnings.) What would this do to the rate of return on year-end 1985 equity?

Answers to Self-Test Problems

ST-1 To solve this problem, we will use the following three equations:

$$\Delta S = S_0(g).$$
$$S_1 = S_0(1 + g).$$
$$EFN = (A/S)\Delta S - (L/S)\Delta S - M(1 - d)S_1.$$

Set EFN = 0, substitute in known values for A/S, L/S, M, d, and S_0, and then solve for g:

$$
\begin{aligned}
0 &= 1.6(\$100g) - 0.4(\$100g) - 0.1(0.55)[\$100(1 + g)] \\
&= \$160g - \$40g - 0.055(\$100 + \$100g) \\
&= \$160g - \$40g - \$5.5 - \$5.5g \\
\$114.5g &= \$5.5
\end{aligned}
$$

$$g = \$5.5/\$114.5 = 0.048 = 4.8\% = \begin{array}{l}\text{Maximum growth rate} \\ \text{without external financing.}\end{array}$$

ST-2 Note that assets consist of cash, marketable securities, receivables, inventories, and fixed assets. Therefore we can break the A/S ratio into its components, cash/sales, inventories/sales, and so forth. Then

$$\frac{A}{S} = \frac{A - \text{Inventories}}{S} + \frac{\text{Inventories}}{S} = 1.6.$$

We know that the inventory utilization ratio is sales/inventories = 3 times, so inventories/sales = ⅓ = 0.3333. Furthermore, if the inventory utilization ratio could be increased to 4 times, then the inventory/sales ratio would fall to ¼ = 0.25, a difference of 0.3333 − 0.2500 = 0.0833. This in turn would cause the A/S ratio to fall from A/S = 1.6 to A/S = 1.6 − 0.0833 = 1.5167.

   This change would have two effects: (1) it would change the EFN equation, and (2) it would mean that Bildersee currently has excessive inventories, so there could be some sales growth without any additional inventories. Therefore we could set up the revised EFN equation, estimate the funds needed next year, and then subtract out the excess inventories currently on hand:

Present conditions:

$$\frac{\text{Sales}}{\text{Inventories}} = \frac{\$100}{\text{Inventories}} = 3,$$

so

$$\text{Current level of inventories} = \$100/3 = \$33.3 \text{ million.}$$

New conditions:

$$\frac{\text{Sales}}{\text{Inventories}} = \frac{\$100}{\text{Inventories}} = 4,$$

so

New level of inventories = \$100/4 = \$25 million.

Therefore

Excess inventories = \$33.3 − \$25 = \$8.3 million.

Forecast of funds needed, first year:

ΔS in first year = 0.2(\$100 million) = \$20 million.

EFN = 1.5167(\$20) − 0.4(\$20) − 0.1(0.55)(\$120) − \$8.3
      = \$30.3 − \$8 − \$6.6 − \$8.3
      = \$7.4 million.

Forecast of funds needed, second year:

ΔS in second year = 0.2(\$120 million) = \$24 million.

EFN = 1.5167(\$24) − 0.4(\$24) − 0.1(0.55)(\$144)
      = \$36.4 − \$9.6 − \$7.9
      = \$18.9 million.

Selected References

The heart of successful financial planning is the sales forecast. On this key subject, see:

Pan, Judy, Donald R. Nichols, and O. Maurice Joy, "Sales Forecasting Practices of Large U.S. Industrial Firms," *Financial Management*, Fall 1977, 72–77.

Pappas, James L., Eugene F. Brigham, and Mark Hirschey, *Managerial Economics*, 4th ed. (Hinsdale, IL: Dryden Press, 1983).

Computer modeling is becoming increasingly important. For general references see:

Carleton, W. T., C. L. Dick, Jr., and D. H. Downes, "Financial Policy Models: Theory and Practice," *Journal of Finance*, December 1973, 691–709.

Francis, Jack Clark, and Dexter R. Rowell, "A Simultaneous Equation Model of the Firm for Financial Analysis and Planning," *Financial Management*, Spring 1978, 29–44.

Grinyer, P. H., and J. Wooller, *Corporate Models Today—A New Tool for Financial Management* (London: Institute of Chartered Accountants, 1978).

Pappas, James L., and George P. Huber, "Probabilistic Short-Term Financial Planning," *Financial Management*, Autumn 1973, 36–44.

Traenkle, J. W., E. B. Cox, and J. A. Bullard, *The Use of Financial Models in Business* (New York: Financial Executives' Research Foundation, 1975).

For a detailed description of how one commercially available and widely used planning system operates, see:

Interactive Financial Planning System: Users' Manual, Execucom Systems Corporation, 3409 Executive Center Drive, Austin, TX 78731.

Analyzing Operations

9

Decision in Finance

Menpower versus Penpower

The Parker Pen Company was heading for financial disaster when James Peterson took over as chief executive officer in January 1982. Parker is the world's most widely known pen company. Ever since 1888, when George S. Parker introduced the first Parker pen, the company has easily sold its pricey pens abroad, especially in countries where a pen is a badge of literacy.

But the company hasn't done so well in its home country since the invention of the ballpoint pen in the 1940s. Parker doesn't even make a disposable pen, which is the fastest-growing segment of the $5 billion world pen market. And A. T. Cross now controls 50 percent of the over-$20 pen market in the United States, leaving Parker with less than 15 percent.

When Peterson took over, Parker, indifferent to economies of scale, produced 500 styles of pens and pencils in 18 separate plants. It also maintained 12 distribution centers in Europe. With a breakeven point of $192 million, in 1982 the writing group lost $8 million on sales of $155 million.

Peterson decided that Parker had been writing with red ink for long enough. The solution to the problem, he believed, lay in drastically reducing the writing group's breakeven point. And within three weeks of his arrival as CEO, he began making changes.

As you read this chapter, look for ways in which CEO Peterson could lower Parker Pen's breakeven point. Which methods do you think he finally chose?

See end of chapter for resolution.

In the preceding chapters we concentrated on analytical tools which aid the financial manager's evaluation of existing operations and the forecasting of future financial events. In this chapter we continue to concentrate on the means by which a financial manager can evaluate ongoing operations and forecast future opportunities.

This chapter emphasizes cost-volume-profit relationships in business planning and the factors which are most important in operations analysis. The major topics covered in this chapter are:

1. Breakeven analysis—a methodology for profit planning and operations analysis.

2. Business risk—the risk arising from a firm's operations.

3. Operating leverage—the sensitivity of a firm's operating income to changes in the level of sales.

Breakeven Analysis

Breakeven analysis is a well-known tool for profit planning. Its major benefit comes from the identification of critical cost-volume-profit relationships for present and future operations.

breakeven point
Level of operations wherein neither profits nor losses are incurred.

variable costs
Costs that vary with the level of output.

fixed costs
Costs that do not vary with the level of output.

The **breakeven point** is that level of operations where neither profits nor losses are incurred. Above this point each unit sold will provide a contribution to profits, and if sales fall below this point, losses will be incurred. Thus the breakeven point is that level of operations where all operating costs are exactly met. If a firm had all **variable costs** in its operations, the problem of a breakeven point would not arise since each sale would include a direct contribution to profit. However, few if any "real world" firms (that is, firms found outside textbooks) exist without some **fixed costs** arising from operations. Table 9-1 provides a breakdown of representative fixed and variable expenses. Of course,

Table 9-1
Examples of Fixed and Variable Costs

Fixed Costs	Variable Costs
Lease or rental expenses	Sales commissions
Depreciation	Manufacturing costs, including direct labor and
Executive salaries	material inputs
Interest	Advertising
	Variable overhead such as heat, air-conditioning,
	and lighting

Figure 9-1
Breakeven Chart: Industrial Technology, Inc.
Breakeven analysis emphasizes the relationship between cost, volume, and profits. This chart indicates that at a sales volume of 50,000 units, total costs and sales revenue will both equal $100,000. Only beyond this point will the company earn a profit; below it, losses would be incurred. Note that if there were no fixed costs, the company would begin to earn a profit on the first unit sold, and there would be no question of a breakeven point.

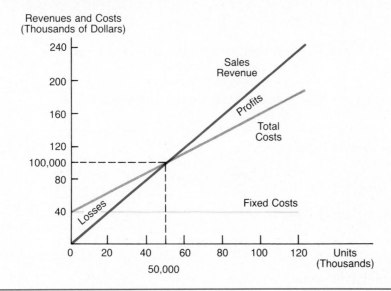

one must remember that no cost is always fixed or always variable. As a pundit once noted, all costs are fixed in the very short run and all are variable in the very long run. Thus, although the salary of a vice president in charge of stockholder relations may be fixed at least over the short term, his position (and hence his previously "fixed expense" salary) may be expendable after a prolonged profit squeeze.

The concept of breakeven may best be illustrated through the use of a hypothetical business firm, Industrial Technology, Inc., or IT. IT's single product sells for $2.00. Fixed costs—which by definition will be the same regardless of the number of units produced or sold—are $40,000. Finally, the variable costs on a per-unit basis are $1.20. With the price of $2.00 and the variable costs of $1.20, the difference, 80 cents, is the **contribution margin,** which contributes to covering fixed costs below the breakeven point and to profits above it. Figure 9-1 illustrates that below the breakeven point of 50,000 units or $100,000 in sales, revenues are below costs, resulting in losses. Above that point profits are incurred at the rate of 80 cents per extra unit of the firm's product that is sold.

contribution margin
The difference between sales price per unit and variable costs per unit.

The breakeven point can also be found algebraically. The breakeven point is the level of sales that just covers all costs, both fixed and variable. Therefore

$$\text{Total revenues} = \text{Total costs}$$
$$QP = QV + F,$$

where

$$Q = \text{number of units produced and sold,}$$
$$P = \text{selling price per unit,}$$
$$QP = \text{level of sales in dollars,}$$
$$V = \text{variable cost per unit produced,}$$
$$F = \text{fixed cost.}$$

If we combine terms,

$$QP - QV = F.$$

Factoring out Q leads to

$$Q(P - V) = F.$$

Dividing both sides of the equation by $(P-V)$, we have

$$Q = \frac{F}{(P - V)}. \qquad (9\text{-}1)$$

Equation 9-1 is the breakeven point, stated in terms of units of the company's product that must be sold in order to reach the threshold of profits. Using our previously determined figures and substituting into Equation 9-1, we have

$$Q = \frac{F}{(P - V)}$$
$$= \frac{\$40,000}{(\$2.00 - \$1.20)}$$
$$= 50,000 \text{ units.}$$

Translating the breakeven point into dollar sales simply requires multiplying the number of units required at the breakeven point by the price of each unit:

$$QP = 50,000 \times \$2.00$$
$$= \$100,000.$$

Industry Practice

Detroit Gets Lean and Mean

Faced with strong foreign competition, America's smokestack industries have been forced to figure out ways of fighting back. And though little noticed amid the gloom of recession, it is Detroit that has led the way in becoming lean and mean over the past few years. The automakers' massive overhaul of their operations is already getting results and promises to yield much greater gains.

The winds of change blowing through the industry are evident in everything from a streamlining of the white-collar work force—the automakers have laid off more than 50,000 salaried employees, most of them permanently—to major improvements in the production process: technological advances, dramatic reductions in inventories, an increased commonality of car parts, more efficient purchasing methods, and more.

As a result, the Big Three have already lowered their breakeven point—the number of cars they must sell to turn a profit—and industry analysts believe that auto profits will therefore soar. For all three the breakeven point dropped from 12,200,000 cars and trucks in 1979 to 8,900,000 in 1983. Chrysler has made the most progress, slashing its breakeven point from 2,400,000 to 1,200,000 in two years. "The U.S. industry is in an up cycle in terms of learning how to lower the breakeven point," says business professor Eugene Jennings of Michigan State University.

Admittedly, the industry's recognition of its deficiencies was somewhat belated. For years, U.S. auto executives complained that the main reason Japan could build cheaper cars was because of the lower wages paid Japanese workers. But studies have shown that higher union wages in the United States were a relatively small part of the problem.

The major Japanese advantages were more advanced technology and superior management, and Detroit's leaders finally accepted the fact that they must improve both. This was an about-face for top managers who had preferred to concentrate on the more glamorous area of strategic planning rather than face manufacturing problems. "We ignored these problems because we didn't think they were important," admits Alex Mair, a GM group vice president.

Since then, the auto companies have pared their management ranks severely, cutting out many layers of the stifling bureaucracies they had built up. And these days auto executives are paying more attention to the nuts-and-bolts planning of the factory and concentrating on ways to reduce the number of man-hours it takes to build a car. The U.S. industry's current average of 120 man-hours is twice the Japanese level.

In technology, Detroit has achieved a virtual revolution over the last three years. Up and down the production line, auto plants are utilizing more sophisticated and sensitive equipment, designed to improve both factory efficiency and the quality of the final product. Technology in the design and manufacturing functions is also being coordinated more closely, with design engineers required to consider not only the cost of the materials that go into a car but the cost of the machines needed to bend, fold, or cut those materials. GM recently merged its advanced technology design and production departments to that end.

In reducing their inventories of parts and components, the auto companies are switching to the Japanese inventory control system called *kanban*, under which supplies are not delivered until they are needed for production. Such a system requires more vigilance on the part of management; but it saves big bucks. GM has reduced its inventories by 10 percent, and cash-strapped Chrysler has saved $900,000 by slashing inventories 37.5 percent in three years.

Another aid to reducing inventories is the automakers' development of common parts to use in various car models. Chrysler, for example, has cut its number of parts by 30 percent and now puts its 2.2-liter engine in most of its small and big cars. The company's switch to front wheel drive, which it plans to use in all its cars, is also reducing its number of parts.

Geographic Change

In the 1970s the auto companies expanded their operations on the East and West Coasts in an effort to compete with the foreign imports arriving at these points. But as demand slowed, they found they were shipping parts and cars from one end of the country to another because no one geographic market could absorb the cars being made in that section.

Forced to close a number of East and West Coast facilities, they moved production back to their Midwest plants. And such consolidation in one central region, industry analysts believe, will reduce shipping costs considerably over the long run.

All these improvements will give the U.S. automakers the one talent they have always lacked: the ability to respond quickly to changes in consumer demand. Such flexibility is essential because of the volatility and unpredictability of fuel costs and interest rates—the two most important factors that determine the level of auto sales. Professor Jennings estimates that about 25 percent of GM's capacity now can be switched to produce either small or large cars. And according to Mair, "That is one of the things that will increase drastically in the next ten years."

As a result of the changes in the way they do business, capital spending by the auto companies will also change. In the past the industry has spent billions of dollars to retool. Future capital spending will be concentrated in the manufacturing area—automated materials-handling equipment and the like—and in the research and development of more technologically advanced cars.

Auto analysts figure it will take perhaps three to four years for auto sales to move from their trough to their peak. But they expect sales to remain at peak levels longer—perhaps up to three years instead of the traditional seven to eight quarters. With the industry's structural and operating changes now in place, they believe Detroit will be solidly positioned to do battle with the Japanese and make some hefty profits.

Source: Adapted from "Detroit Gets Lean and Mean" by Lynn Adkins. Reprinted with the permission of *Dun's Business Month* (formerly *Dun's Review*), January 1983. Copyright 1983, Dun & Bradstreet Publications Corporation.

Problems and Practical Uses of Breakeven Analysis

Breakeven analysis is often less easily applied in practice than in our simplistic illustration. For example, the model assumes the firm has only a single product, whereas in practice most business firms have multiple products. Another, potentially more important assumption implicit in the model is that of stability in costs and prices as production and sales increase. Problems with the direct application occur because, in order to promote new sales, prices must often be reduced to generate more demand for the product. Similarly, given economies of scale, the cost of each unit of output is reduced as production increases. At some point in expanding production, however, costs will rise as more shifts, training of new personnel, or increases in production facilities and overhead are required. As profit margins are eroded, the firm may reach a second breakeven point.

The result of these deviations from assumed linearity in price and costs is illustrated in Figure 9-2. The point of maximum profit occurs at 60,000 units or $150,000 in sales. Beyond this point, however, profits

Figure 9-2
Nonlinear Breakeven Chart
Breakeven analysis does not usually proceed in the linear fashion shown in Figure 9-1.
Deviations due to changes in costs and prices may result in a second breakeven point,
beyond which losses occur. This chart illustrates a maximum profit level at 60,000 units,
or $150,000 in sales, and shows that a firm cannot assume an infinite increase in
profitability beyond the breakeven point.

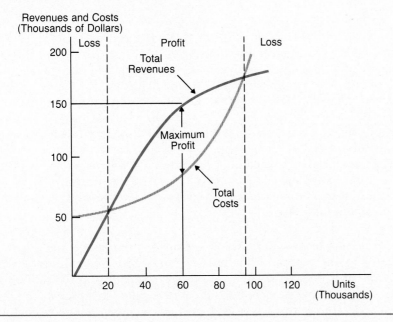

fall. Thus, rather than a model which encourages unlimited production above the breakeven point, there may be a finite zone of profitability for the company's product.

In spite of any deviations from real world considerations, breakeven analysis provides a needed framework to study the relationships between cost, volume, and profit. A dramatic example of the use of this analytical framework is provided by the restructuring of Chrysler Corporation. The third largest auto manufacturer was near bankruptcy after losing $1,100,000,000 in 1979 and $1,700,000,000 in 1980. The aid provided by the government almost surely kept the firm solvent during this period—yet major changes were required.

Among other actions, Chrysler's top management determined that the firm had to reduce its breakeven point in order to meet this challenge to the firm. The following cost-cutting procedures were instituted in an attempt to lower the breakeven point from its 1980 level of 2,400,000 units:

Reduction of salaried staff by 50 percent to 22,000.

Grants of $1,068,000,000 in concessions from unions from 1979 through mid-1982.

Reduction of inventories.

Closing of unprofitable plants.

More reliance on computers and robotics.

Institution of tougher cost control committees to scrutinize expenditures.

The result of these often difficult decisions proved gratifying. The firm's breakeven point fell by 50 percent to an approximate 1,200,000 units by mid-1982. These actions would allow the firm to cover all costs at a much lower volume of sales, thereby providing the company with much needed financial flexibility. Although this restructuring did not guarantee a secure future for Chrysler, the changes in both variable and previously fixed costs certainly positioned the firm in a much more competitive situation for success.

Thus appropriately used, the breakeven technique is an excellent means of evaluating new products or general expansion (or, as we have just seen, contraction) and measuring the responsiveness of profits to changes in sales:

1. Evaluation of new products or expansion. Breakeven analysis contributes to the evaluation of new ventures in two significant ways. First, it helps determine the level of sales required to reach the breakeven point. Management must then determine the probability that sales will actually reach this goal. Second, a more general benefit accrues from breakeven analysis in that the relationships between costs, level of production or sales, and profits are emphasized.

2. Measurement of the responsiveness of profits to changes in sales. Where fixed costs are present, a change in sales will lead to a greater than proportional change in profits. The effect of changes in sales or the effect of substituting fixed for variable costs can be analyzed using breakeven analysis.

Business Risk

The uncertainty associated with forecasting and realizing future **operating income**—earnings before interest and taxes (EBIT)—has been termed **business risk.** The element of uncertainty associated with business risk includes both the chance of not reaching a breakeven point and the problems associated with fluctuating returns. Year-to-year fluctuations can be caused by many factors—booms or recessions in the national economy, successful new products introduced either by the firm or by its competitors, labor strikes, price controls, changes in the prices of raw materials, or disasters such as fires, floods, and the like.

Business risk varies not only from industry to industry but also among firms within a given industry. Furthermore, business risk can change over time. For example, a business considered at one time to be fairly safe was the railroad industry before the advent of truck and airline competition for freight and passengers. More recently, electric utilities, regarded for years as having very little business risk, were affected by a combination of events in the 1960s and 1970s that drastically altered their situation, producing sharp declines in their operating income, and greatly increasing the industry's business risk. Today food processors and grocery retailers are frequently given as examples of an industry with low business risk, while cyclical manufacturing industries such as steel are regarded as having especially high business risks. Also, factors other than industry affiliation play a role in determining business risk. For example, smaller companies or companies dependent on a single product or customer are often regarded as having a high degree of business risk.

Business risk, then, depends on a number of factors, the more important of which are the following:

1. Demand variability. The more stable the demand for a firm's products, other things held constant, the lower its business risk.

2. Output price variability. Firms whose products are sold in highly volatile markets are exposed to more business risk than similar firms whose output prices are more stable.

operating income
Earnings before interest and taxes (EBIT).

business risk
The risk associated with future operating income.

3. Input price variability. Firms whose input prices are highly uncertain are exposed to a high degree of business risk.

4. Ability to adjust output prices for changes in input prices. Some firms are better able to raise their own output prices when input costs rise than are others. The greater the ability to adjust output prices, the lower the degree of business risk, other things held constant. This factor has become increasingly important in the past decade because of inflation.

5. The extent to which costs are fixed: operating leverage. If a high percentage of a firm's costs are fixed, hence do not decline when demand falls off, then it is exposed to a relatively high degree of business risk. This point is discussed at length in the next section.

Each of these factors is determined partly by the firm's industry characteristics, but each of them is also controllable to some extent. For example, most firms can, through their marketing policies, take actions to stabilize both unit sales and sales prices. However, this stabilization may require firms to spend a great deal on advertising and/or price concessions in order to get their customers to commit to purchasing fixed quantities at fixed prices in the future. Similarly, firms may reduce the volatility of future input costs by negotiating long-term labor and materials supply contracts, but they may have to agree to pay prices above the current spot price level to obtain these contracts.

Operating Leverage

As noted above, business risk depends in part on the extent to which a firm builds fixed costs into its operations. If fixed costs are high, even a small decline in sales can lead to a large decline in EBIT, so, other things held constant, the higher a firm's fixed costs, the greater its business risk. Higher fixed costs are generally associated with more highly automated, capital intensive firms and industries. Also, businesses that employ highly skilled workers who must be retained and paid even during business recessions have relatively high fixed costs.

operating leverage
The extent to which fixed costs are used in a firm's operation.

If a high percentage of a firm's total costs are fixed costs, then the firm is said to have a high degree of **operating leverage.** In physics, leverage implies the use of a lever to raise a heavy object with a small force. In politics, if individuals have leverage, their smallest word or action can accomplish a lot. *In business terminology, a high degree of operating leverage, other things held constant, implies that a relatively small change in sales will result in a large change in operating income.* The common element in all of these examples is that a small initiating change is met by a *greater than proportional effect.*

Figure 9-3 illustrates the concept of operating leverage by comparing the results that Industrial Technology, Inc. can expect if it changes the degree of operating leverage by altering its proportion of fixed to variable costs. Plan A reduces the fixed charges from their earlier level detailed in Figure 9-1. This might be accomplished by reducing its automated equipment so the firm's depreciation costs, maintenance expenses, property taxes, and so on would be low. Note, however, that under Plan A the total cost line has a relatively steep slope, indicating that variable costs per unit are higher than they would be if the firm used more operating leverage. Therefore the firm is not simply adding to its variable costs, but rather, in order to decrease its fixed costs from $40,000 to $20,000, it is increasing its variable costs on a per-unit basis from the original $1.20 to $1.50. Plan B calls for a higher level of fixed costs. Here the firm uses more automated equipment, thereby requiring fewer workers to produce its product. Automation allows one operator to turn out a few or many units at the same labor cost. Therefore, by raising its fixed costs, IT can reduce its variable costs on a per-unit basis. One result of this change is that the breakeven point is higher under Plan B: breakeven occurs at 40,000 units under Plan A versus 60,000 units under Plan B.

We have seen that changing the level of fixed and variable costs changes the breakeven point. But how does operating leverage affect business risk? Other things held constant, *the higher a firm's operating leverage, the higher its business risk.* Since Plan B requires a higher proportion of fixed to total costs, we can conclude that IT will have higher business risk if it adopts that plan. This point is demonstrated numerically in the lower part of Figure 9-3 and graphically in Figure 9-4.

The top section of Figure 9-4 gives the **probability distribution** of sales. This distribution depends on how demand for the product varies, not on whether the product is manufactured under Plan A or Plan B. Therefore the same sales probability distribution applies to both production plans, and expected sales for the next period are $220,000, with a range from zero to a bit above $450,000, under either plan.

If we had actually specified the sales probability distribution, then we could use this information, together with the operating profit (EBIT) at each sales level as shown in the lower part of Figure 9-3, to develop probability distributions for EBIT under Plans A and B. Typical EBIT distributions are shown in the lower part of Figure 9-4. At the expected sales level of $220,000, Plan B's operating profits are higher than those for Plan A. Unfortunately, chances for losses are also greater for Plan B than for Plan A. As we explain in Chapter 16, the greater the range of possible outcomes, the greater the risk.

We can, however, describe the risk associated with operating leverage in a different fashion, utilizing the sales and operating profit levels from Figure 9-3. But first note that if Industrial Technology had no

probability distribution
A listing of all possible outcomes or events, with a probability (the chance of the event's occurrence) assigned to each outcome.

Figure 9-3
Effect of Operating Leverage on Industrial Technology, Inc.

This figure demonstrates that higher operating leverage (i.e., higher fixed costs) will create higher business risk and greater potential for large swings in profits. Both plans project sales of 110,000 units at $2.00 each, but Plan A has one-third the fixed costs of Plan B. As a result Plan B has a higher breakeven point. As both graphs and tables show, the further sales move on either side of the breakeven point, the faster profits or losses under Plan B outstrip those under Plan A.

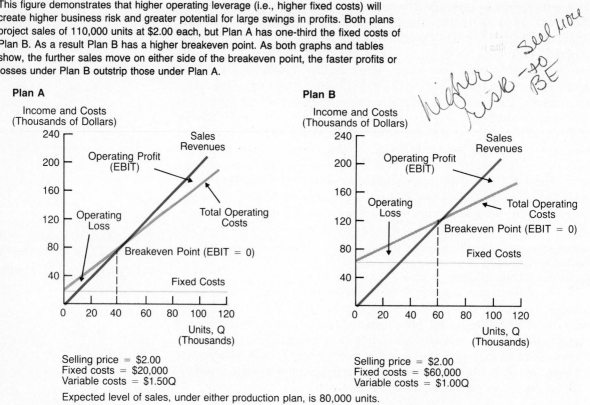

Selling price = $2.00   Selling price = $2.00
Fixed costs = $20,000   Fixed costs = $60,000
Variable costs = $1.50Q   Variable costs = $1.00Q

Expected level of sales, under either production plan, is 80,000 units.

Units Sold, Q	Sales	Operating Costs	Operating Profit (EBIT)	Units Sold, Q	Sales	Operating Costs	Operating Profit (EBIT)
0	$ 0	$ 20,000	$ −20,000	0	$ 0	$ 60,000	$ −60,000
40,000	80,000	80,000	0	40,000	80,000	100,000	−20,000
60,000	120,000	110,000	10,000	60,000	120,000	120,000	0
80,000	160,000	140,000	20,000	80,000	160,000	140,000	20,000
100,000	200,000	170,000	30,000	100,000	200,000	160,000	40,000
110,000	220,000	185,000	35,000	110,000	220,000	170,000	50,000
160,000	320,000	260,000	60,000	160,000	320,000	220,000	100,000
180,000	360,000	290,000	70,000	180,000	360,000	240,000	120,000
220,000	440,000	350,000	90,000	220,000	440,000	280,000	160,000

Figure 9-4
Analysis of Business Risk

Under both Plan A and Plan B, expected sales are 110,000 units, as shown in the top probability curve. Taking the information from such a curve together with the profit amounts at each level from the lower part of Figure 9-3, it is possible to create probability distributions for profits under Plans A and B, as shown in the lower curve of this figure. Again the greater volatility of Plan B is evident.

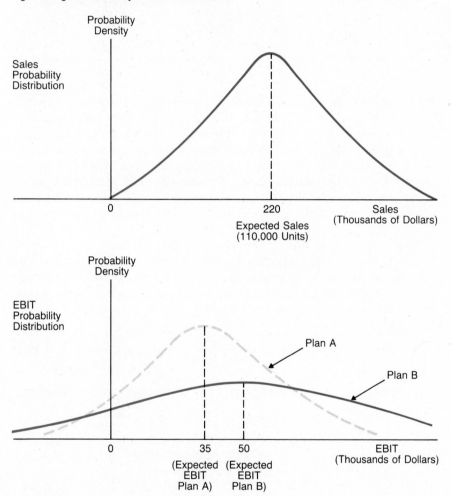

fixed costs, an increase of 25 percent in sales would lead to a proportional 25 percent increase in operating profits. However, with fixed operating costs, there will be a larger than proportional change in profits, given a change in sales. For example, if current sales were $160,000 and increased by 25 percent to $200,000, profits under Plan A would increase by 50 percent from $20,000 to $30,000. On the other hand,

Table 9-2
Degree of Operating Leverage at $160,000 in Sales

$$DOL_A = \frac{Q(P - V)}{Q(P - V) - F}$$

$$= \frac{80,000(\$2.00 - \$1.50)}{80,000(\$2.00 - \$1.50) - \$20,000}$$

$$= \frac{\$40,000}{\$20,000}$$

$$= 2.$$

$$DOL_B = \frac{Q(P - V)}{Q(P - V) - F}$$

$$= \frac{80,000(\$2.00 - \$1.00)}{80,000(\$2.00 - \$1.00) - \$60,000}$$

$$= \frac{\$80,000}{\$20,000}$$

$$= 4.$$

degree of operating leverage (DOL)

The ratio of the percentage change in operating income to the percentage change in sales.

under the larger operating leverage inherent in Plan B, the same 25 percent increase in sales would result in a 100 percent increase in operating profits. A problem with operating leverage arises when sales decline, however. Just as profits increased at a greater rate when sales were increasing, losses when sales decline are also magnified by the existence of fixed operating costs. For example, a 25 percent decline in sales from a level of 80,000 units will result in a 50 percent decline in operating profits under Plan A but in a much larger loss of 100 percent under Plan B!

The degree of operating leverage provides a more general way to measure the reaction of profits to changes in the volume of sales. The **degree of operating leverage (DOL)** is the ratio of the percentage change in operating income to the percentage change in sales. Equation 9-2 can be used to calculate the degree of operating leverage:

$$DOL = \frac{Q(P - V)}{Q(P - V) - F}. \qquad (9\text{-}2)$$

The symbols are the same as those developed earlier in this chapter:

$$Q = \text{units of output}$$
$$P = \text{sales price}$$
$$V = \text{variable cost per unit}$$
$$F = \text{fixed operating cost}$$

Utilizing Equation 9-2, we determine in Table 9-2 the degree of operating leverage for Plan A (DOL_A) and Plan B (DOL_B) at a particular level of sales—in this case $160,000 in sales.[1] A DOL of 2 means that

---

[1]A word of caution: the degree of operating leverage changes as the level of sales changes. For example, in Table 9-2 we found that at sales of $160,000 the $DOL_A = 2$ and the $DOL_B = 4$. However, at the expected sales level of $220,000 the $DOL_A = 1.57$ and the $DOL_B = 2.2$.

with a percentage change in sales, a doubled percentage change in EBIT will result under the operating leverage provided by Plan A. Thus a 10 percent increase in sales will result in a twice as large—20 percent—increase in operating profits. As we have already seen for Plan A, a 25 percent change in sales was doubled to a 50 percent change in operating profits. For Plan B the DOL of 4 means that a percentage change in sales will result in a quadrupled change in operating profits. Thus a 5 percent decline in sales will result in a four times larger—20 percent—decline in operating profits. Thus, before adopting Plan B, the financial planners at Industrial Technology will wish to consider the probability of future sales fluctuations.

To what extent can firms control their operating leverage? For the most part, operating leverage is determined by technology. Electric utilities, telephone companies, airlines, steel mills, and chemical companies simply *must* have heavy investments in fixed assets; this results in high fixed costs and operating leverage. Grocery stores, on the other hand, generally have significantly lower fixed costs, hence lower operating leverage. Still, all firms have some control over their operating leverage. For example, an electric utility can expand its generating capacity by building either a nuclear reactor or a coal-fired plant. The nuclear generator would require a larger investment in fixed assets, which would involve higher fixed costs, but its variable operating costs would be relatively low. The coal plant, on the other hand, would require a smaller investment in fixed assets and would have lower fixed costs, but the variable costs (for coal) would be high. Thus by its capital budgeting decisions a utility (or any other company) can influence its operating leverage, hence its basic business risk.

The concept of operating leverage was, in fact, originally developed for use in making capital budgeting decisions. Alternative methods for producing a given product often have different degrees of operating leverage, hence different breakeven points and different degrees of risk. Companies regularly undertake some type of breakeven analysis as part of their evaluation of proposed new projects. Thus, once established, the degree of operating leverage influences many other financial decisions. In Chapter 19 we investigate the interrelationships between operating leverage and financial leverage.

Summary

In this chapter the concepts of breakeven analysis, business risk, and operating leverage have been discussed. Breakeven analysis is an excellent tool for financial planning, as long as its assumptions and limitations are not ignored. The technique provides insights into the relationships between costs, volume, and profit.

Business risk is the uncertainty associated with future operating profit (EBIT). Unexpected variations in product demand or input costs are the major factors which contribute to business risk. Such fluctuations are disconcerting in that they may cause the firm's profits to fall below the breakeven point or at least fall short of the expected returns.

Another factor affecting the volatility of operating profits is operating leverage. Operating leverage is present whenever there are fixed costs in the firm's operations. The presence of operating leverage magnifies changes in sales into proportionally larger changes in operating profits. Thus the more operating leverage the firm has, the greater the potential for large swings in the company's operating profits.

In Chapter 19 we find that the amount of business risk inherent in the firm's operations will affect the amount of financial risk that the firm's managers are willing to accept.

Resolution to Decision in Finance

Menpower versus Penpower

CEO James Peterson began his attack on the Parker Pen writing group's breakeven point by cutting its work force from 4,200 to 2,800. He then committed $9.5 million to reequipping the Janesville plant, which will now manufacture only preordered products. He also consolidated the 12 European distribution units into a single center at Parker's British factory. As a result the writing group's breakeven point fell from $192 million to $134 million in 17 months.

Peterson slashed the swollen product line from 500 items to 100. Attacking at opposite ends of the market, he introduced a line of luxury pens and pencils, priced at $95 to $2,500, to showcase Parker quality. And he rolled out the RB-1, a $3.49 roller-ball pen that uses liquid ink instead of the usual ink paste, to help crack the U. S. market. It has been the company's most successful new product ever.

Thanks to Peterson's belt tightening, Parker showed a profit of 30 cents per share for the first half of fiscal 1983, compared to a loss of 23 cents in 1982. That's a far cry from the $1.25-per-share average of the late 1970s, but it's clearly a start. "I grew up in a time when every graduating senior got a Parker 51," Peterson says. "We can have that kind of profitability again if we just get the machine running the way we think it can run."

Source: "Menpower versus Penpower," *Forbes*, Dec. 19, 1983, 198, 202.

Key Terms You should be able to define each of the following terms:

Breakeven point

Variable costs; fixed costs

Contribution margin

Operating income

Business risk

Operating leverage; degree of
operating leverage (DOL)

Probability distribution

Questions

9-1 The uncertainty inherent in projections of future operating income is called what?

9-2 Firms with relatively high nonfinancial fixed costs are said to have a high degree of what?

9-3 What does breakeven analysis show the financial manager?

9-4 As the level of sales moves away from the breakeven point, what happens to the DOL? Why?

Self-Test Problem

ST-1 Gentry Motors, Inc. produces turbine generators which sell for $P = \$100,000$. Gentry's fixed costs are $2 million; 50 generators are produced and sold each year; profits total $500,000; and Gentry's assets (all equity financed) are $5 million. Gentry estimates that it can change its production process, adding $4 million to investment and $500,000 to fixed operating costs. This change will (1) reduce variable costs per unit by $10,000 and (2) increase output by 20 units, but (3) the sales price on all units will have to be lowered to $95,000 to permit sales of the additional output. Gentry has tax loss carry-forwards that cause its tax rate to be zero, and its cost of capital is 15 percent. Gentry uses no debt.

a. Should Gentry make the change?

b. Would Gentry's operating leverage increase or decrease if it made the change? What about its breakeven point?

c. Would the new situation have more or less business risk than the old one?

Problems

9-1 a. Given the graphs on the next page, calculate the fixed costs, variable costs per unit, and sales price for Firm A. Firm B's fixed costs are $120,000, its variable costs per unit are $4, and its sales price is $8 per unit.

* **b.** Which firm has the higher degree of operating leverage? Explain.

* **c.** At what *sales level* do both firms earn the same profit?

9-2 Tennessee Manufacturing, Inc. has a single product which sells at a price $BE = 40,000 \text{ units}$ of $15 and has a variable cost of $10 per unit. Fixed costs are $200,000.

* **a.** What is the firm's breakeven point in units?

* **b.** What is the firm's breakeven point expressed in sales dollars?

* **c.** What is the firm's DOL if sales are 10,000 units above breakeven?

d. The company's president wants you to explain what the firm's DOL means. Can you tell her?

---

*Refer to Appendix E for check answers to problems with asterisks.

Breakeven Charts for Firm A and Firm B

Firm A

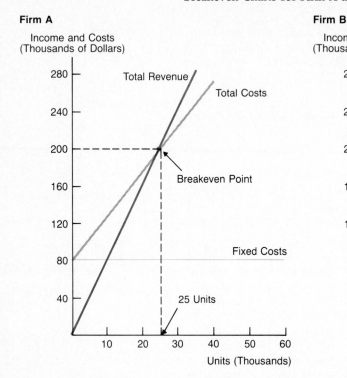

Firm B

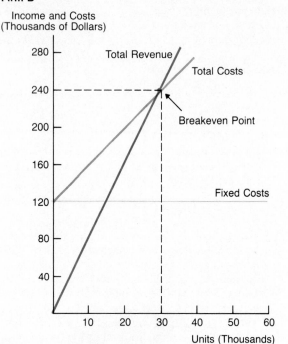

9-3 Now assume Tennessee Manufacturing (Problem 9-2) has begun an impressive modernization program. In order to reduce per-unit variable costs to $6, the company's fixed costs have been allowed to rise to $540,000 annually. Under these new conditions:

* **a.** What is the firm's breakeven point expressed in units?

* **b.** What is the firm's breakeven point expressed in sales dollars?

* **c.** What is the firm's DOL if sales are 10,000 units above breakeven?

   d. What is the implication of the new DOL as compared with the DOL before modernization?

9-4 Gulf States Industries is selling 2 million units of its only product at $25 per unit. Variable costs are $15 per unit, while annual fixed costs are $17,500,000.

* **a.** What is the firm's operating profit?

* **b.** What is the firm's DOL?

* **c.** If sales increase by 10 percent, what is the resulting operating profit? Use the DOL to answer this question.

   d. Confirm your answer in Part c by preparing an income statement showing the dollar level of sales, variable and fixed costs, and the operating profit.

   e. What would happen to operating profits if sales were to decline by 10 percent? Confirm your answer.

* 9-5 The Potter's Wheel Company will produce 100,000 large clay flower pots this year. Variable costs will be 40 percent of sales, and fixed costs are $230,000. What selling price is required for the firm to obtain an EBIT of $100,000 if all 100,000 pots are sold?

9-6 a. Refer to Figure 9-3. Calculate the degree of operating leverage for Plans A and B at sales of $40,000, $120,000, and $240,000. The degree of operating leverage for other levels of sales are:

Sales	DOL_A	DOL_B
$ 80,000	Undefined (or ∞)	−2.0
160,000	2.0	4.0
220,000	1.57	2.2

b. Is it true that the DOL is approximately equal to infinity just above the breakeven point, implying that a very small increase in sales will produce a huge percentage increase in EBIT, but that the DOL declines when calculated at higher levels of sales?

c. Is it true for all sales levels where DOL > 0 for both plans that $DOL_B <$ DOL_A? Explain.

Answer to Self-Test Problem

ST-1 a. 1. Determine the variable cost per unit at present, V, using the following definitions and equation:

$$Q = \text{units of output (sales)},$$
$$P = \text{average sales price per unit of output},$$
$$F = \text{fixed operating costs}.$$

$$\text{Profit} = P(Q) - F - V(Q)$$
$$\$500,000 = (\$100,000)(50) - \$2,000,000 - V(50)$$
$$50V = \$2,500,000$$
$$V = \$50,000.$$

2. Determine the new profit level if the change is made:

$$\text{New profit} = P_2(Q_2) - F_2 - V_2(Q_2)$$
$$= \$95,000(70) - \$2,500,000 - (\$50,000 - \$10,000)(70)$$
$$= \$1,350,000.$$

3. Determine the incremental profit:

$$\Delta\text{Profit} = \$1,350,000 - \$500,000 = \$850,000.$$

4. Estimate the approximate rate of return on the new investment:

$$\text{ROI} = \frac{\Delta\text{Profit}}{\Delta\text{Investment}} = \frac{\$850,000}{\$4,000,000} = 21.25\%.$$

Since the ROI exceeds the 15 percent cost of capital, this analysis suggests that Gentry should go ahead with the change.

b. If we measure operating leverage by the ratio of fixed costs to total costs at the expected output, then the change would increase operating leverage:[2]

$$\text{Old:}\quad \frac{F}{F + V(Q)} = \frac{\$2,000,000}{\$2,000,000 + \$2,500,000} = 44.44\%.$$

$$\text{New:}\quad \frac{F}{F + V(Q)} = \frac{\$2,500,000}{\$2,500,000 + \$2,800,000} = 47.17\%.$$

The change would also increase the breakeven point:

$$\text{Breakeven, old: } P(Q) = F + V(Q)$$

$$Q_{BE} = \frac{F}{P - V} = \frac{\$2,000,000}{\$100,000 - \$50,000} = 40 \text{ units.}$$

$$\text{Breakeven, new: } Q_{BE} = \frac{\$2,500,000}{\$95,000 - \$40,000} = 45.45 \text{ units.}$$

c. It is impossible to state unequivocally whether the new situation would have more or less business risk than the old one. We would need information on both the sales probability distribution and the uncertainty about variable input costs in order to make this determination. However, since a higher breakeven point, other things held constant, is more risky, the change in breakeven points—and also the higher percentage of fixed costs—suggests that the new situation is more risky.

Selected References

See the references at the end of Chapter 19, "The Capital Target Structure."

---

[2]The "old" degree of operating leverage is

$$\text{DOL} = \frac{Q(P - V)}{Q(P - V) - F} = \frac{50(\$50,000)}{50(\$50,000) - \$2,000,000} = 5.0.$$

The new DOL, at the expected sales level of 70, is

$$\text{DOL} = \frac{70(\$95,000 - \$40,000)}{70(\$55,000) - \$2,500,000} = 2.85.$$

The problem here is that we have changed both output and the sales price, so the DOLs are not really comparable.

Working Capital

IV

If a poll were taken, financial managers would reveal that the greater part of their workday is taken up with managing and financing the firm's short-term assets. Thus this section devotes four chapters to the important topic of working capital management and policy.

Chapter 10 demonstrates that the level of current assets and how those assets are financed contribute significantly to the firm's profitability and risk exposure. In the next two chapters we turn to the management of four current asset accounts. Chapter 11 considers cash and marketable securities, while Chapter 12 analyzes the management of accounts receivable and inventories. Chapter 13 discusses the various types of short-term credit that can be used to finance current assets. This chapter also evaluates the cost of these sources of short-term funds.

Working Capital Policy and Management

Decision in Finance

Not a Minute Too Soon

Wedtech Corp. Chairman John Mariotta was rightly proud of the company he'd founded. Sales had zoomed from $300,000 in 1976 to $20.4 million in 1982, with a healthy profit of $3.1 million. Housed in the Bronx, Wedtech was one of a select list of ghetto manufacturers operating at a profit.

The future looked even more promising. In 1981 Wedtech had landed the biggest contract in its history—a $30.7 million job to produce engines for the Defense Department. In addition, it was already working on two other defense jobs worth $20 million and financing work on a new coating process.

Landing the contracts and working to satisfy them was costing little Wedtech millions, however. By July 1983 the company was left with only $100,000 of cash on hand. That was enough to meet the payroll, but there would be nothing left over to buy needed parts.

Wedtech already owed $12 million to banks, individuals, and the U.S. government. And for the past four months the company had been unable to pay a cent on any of its debts. John Mariotta had badly underprojected Wedtech's cash outflows, and as a result the company was seriously undercapitalized. If Mariotta couldn't find some new sources of working capital, his firm would go bankrupt.

As you read this chapter, consider the financing alternatives available to Wedtech's chairman. Which do you think he finally chose?

See end of chapter for resolution.

In Part III we saw (1) that a firm's investment in assets is closely related to actual and projected sales, (2) that the various liability and equity accounts must be analyzed in terms of their relationships to assets, and (3) that risk, profitability, and consequently stock prices are all dependent on decisions relating to the acquisition and financing of assets. However, this discussion was very general, and we looked more at industry averages than at specific economic determinants of the different types of assets. Now, in Part IV, we examine the effect of the levels of current assets and current liabilities. We find that (1) the level of current assets and (2) how they are financed contribute significantly to both the firm's profitability and its risk exposure.

Defining Working Capital

The term *working capital* originated in the days of the old Yankee peddler who would load up his wagon with goods and then go off on his route to sell his wares. The merchandise was defined as his "working capital" because it was actually sold or "turned over" to produce profits.

The days of the Yankee peddler have long since passed, but the importance of working capital remains. Financial managers probably spend more of their time and energy on working capital matters than on any other single topic covered in this text. In contrast, the choice of business projects and the associated fixed asset commitment occurs, for most firms, perhaps once or twice a year. As we shall see, whether the decision concerns fixed or current assets, it will affect the firm's level of risk and return.

Before taking up the topics of primary interest in this chapter, it is useful to take an overview of the concepts of working capital and working capital management. We begin by defining the following terms:

working capital
A firm's investment in short-term assets—cash, marketable securities, inventory, and accounts receivable.

net working capital
Current assets less current liabilities.

working capital policy
Basic policy decisions regarding target levels for each category of current assets and for the financing of these assets.

working capital management
The administration, within policy guidelines, of current assets and current liabilities.

1. Working capital, sometimes termed *gross working capital*, simply refers to the firm's current assets (often called *short-term assets*)—commonly cash, marketable securities, inventory, and accounts receivable.

2. Net working capital is defined as current assets less current liabilities. As we discuss later in this chapter, net working capital would therefore be financed by long-term sources of funds. We shall find that the financing factor is most important in determining the firm's risk and return levels.

3. Working capital policy refers to basic policy decisions regarding target levels for each category of current assets and to the financing of these assets.

4. Working capital management involves the administration, within policy guidelines, of current assets and current liabilities.

Whereas working capital policy relates to setting long-run targets, working capital management deals with the implementation of policy. Both are critically important because working capital is used to make adjustments in operations to account for changing economic conditions. If demand begins to rise or fall, the immediate response is in the working capital accounts, and the appropriateness of the response can spell success or failure for the firm. For example, when its sales began to decline in the late 1970s, Chrysler decided that the decline was only a temporary dip, so production levels were maintained. By the time it became clear that the "dip" was really a major recession, Chrysler had built up huge inventories of new cars. The company had borrowed heavily to finance this inventory buildup, and these loans had to be repaid. The only choice was to slash prices below costs in order to move the cars. This poor management of working capital resulted in hundreds of millions of dollars in losses for Chrysler. However, as a result of the many difficult decisions described in Chapter 9, the company appears to have regained a healthy status in the automobile industry.

The types of credit available to finance current assets are discussed in detail in Chapter 13. At this point it is necessary only to know (1) that a major element of working capital policy and management relates to the financing of current assets and (2) that lining up sources of short-term credit, minimizing the cost of this credit, and making sure that it can be repaid on schedule are important aspects of working capital operations.

Impact of Current Assets on Risk and Return

As the preceding Chrysler example demonstrates, unplanned changes in working capital can affect a firm in adverse ways. Therefore financial managers must plan for levels of working capital which balance the amount of risk required to reach an acceptable level of return.

In general, we can say that the greater the proportion of current assets to fixed assets at a given level of output, the less risky the firm's working capital policy. How does this conservative working capital policy reduce risk?[1] In essence, all risk of shortages is removed. With high levels of working capital there will be ample inventory so that no stock outages will *ever* occur, sufficient cash or near-cash marketable securities will be available to prevent any conceivable liquidity problem, and accounts receivable will be expanded to prevent any loss in sales due to a too stringent credit policy. Of course, there is a price to

---

[1] It is important to distinguish between planned and unplanned increases in current assets. Unplanned increases in inventory that cannot be sold or accounts receivable that cannot be collected are *not* examples of a conservative, risk-reducing working capital policy. Of course, such a buildup in current assets is risky and even life threatening to the firm, as the Chrysler example indicates. The planned conservative policy that we are considering here concentrates on keeping more cash, inventory, or other current assets on hand to insure that no shortages will occur.

Table 10-1
Effect of Working Capital Policies on Rates of Return (Millions of Dollars)

	Conservative	Moderate	Aggressive
Sales	$40	$40	$40
EBIT	3	3	3
Current assets	$15	$10	$ 5
Fixed assets	10	10	10
Total assets	$25	$20	$15
Return on assets (EBIT/TA)	12%	15%	20%

pay for all this safety. That price, as we illustrate in Table 10-1, comes in the form of reduced return on investment.

The lower return associated with the conservative working capital position stems from the fact that the firm has acquired many more assets than are required to support sales. Obviously any level of sales requires the supporting assets of inventory, accounts receivable, and cash balances for business transactions. An overabundance of these assets, however, directs resources away from more productive assets. Therefore the rate of return is lower as the level of current assets increases. Remember, the fixed assets for a manufacturing firm are the productive assets that transform raw materials into finished products. The current assets merely support this process. As such, the returns from productive assets should exceed returns from nonproductive, or supporting, assets. To put it another way, if the return from an investment in current assets, such as marketable securities, exceeds the return provided by the firm's business projects, then the firm should sell its fixed assets and invest in the higher-yielding current assets. Since there has been little discernible rush to liquidate firms in order to make such investments, we are confident that, as a general rule, fixed assets help to generate a rate of return that is above that of current assets. We can conclude, therefore, that an overly conservative working capital policy misallocates resources to lower-returning assets, which in turn lowers the overall earning power of the firm.

From this discussion an unwary reader might conclude that the best working capital policy would be one which aggressively slashes current assets to the bare minimum. As seen in Table 10-1, the rate of return rises from 12 percent under the conservative policy to 20 percent under the aggressive policy. However, just as lower returns were the price for the safety of a conservative working capital policy, there is a price associated with the higher *potential*[2] returns in the aggressive policy—higher risk.

---

[2]If returns were *always* higher under the more risky working capital policy, there wouldn't be any risk, would there?

The probability that a given level of sales cannot be maintained is one of the risks associated with an aggressive working capital policy. For example, the high rate of return resulting from the aggressive policy in Table 10-1 explicitly assumes no change in sales as levels of current assets are manipulated. But how could an aggressive working capital policy affect sales? First, with lower levels of inventory, sales could decline as a result of stock outages. Second, other revenues might be lost due to a stringent credit policy which is designed to reduce accounts receivable rather than support sales. Of course, a decline in sales could result in lower returns.

Reduced sales is not the only risk associated with an aggressive working capital policy, however. Since current assets provide liquidity, their reduction may lead to difficulties in paying bills or other obligations as they come due. Slow payment could lead to poor credit ratings or even a reduction in suppliers' willingness to extend trade credit.

Therefore an overly aggressive working capital policy can lead to exactly the opposite result than intended. As is often the case in finance, the preferred working capital policy lies somewhere between the extreme levels of aggressive and conservative policies. Even so, it is difficult to prescribe an optimal level of working capital for each firm. However, a general guideline to working capital policy decisions does exist. *The level of current assets should be reduced as long as the marginal return from such an action is greater than the potential for resulting losses.* Thus inventory should be reduced to a point where there is only an acceptably low probability of lost sales due to stock outages. Similarly, the savings resulting from lower levels of accounts receivable must be compared to the potential losses from the more stringent credit policy. Finally, the return from minimizing cash holdings, in either demand deposits or marketable securities, must be compared to the potential losses if cash were in short supply.

Alternative Strategies for Financing Working Capital

The concept of financing working capital originated at a time when most industries were closely related to agriculture. Farmers would borrow to buy seed in the spring and, when the crops were harvested in the fall, repay the loan with the proceeds of the crop's sale. Similarly, processors would buy crops in the fall, process them, sell the finished product, and end up just before the next harvest with relatively low inventories. Bank loans with maximum maturities of one year were used to finance both the purchase and the processing costs, and these loans were retired with the proceeds from the sale of the finished products. Thus the loans were, in essence, self-liquidating.

This situation is depicted in Figure 10-1, where fixed assets are shown to be growing steadily over time, while current assets jump at harvest season, decline during the year, and end at zero just before the next crop is harvested. Short-term credit is used to finance current as-

Figure 10-1
Fixed and Current Assets and Their Financing
This figure shows an idealized model of the financing of current and fixed assets. Each season current assets rise sharply, then gradually fall to zero. Short-term loans, used to finance these current assets, are repaid and renewed with each season. Fixed assets, on the other hand, are financed with long-term debt and owners' equity.

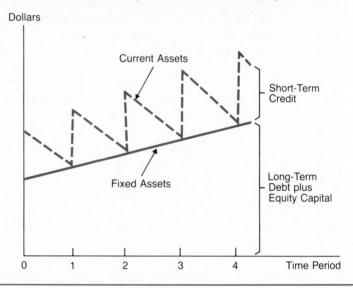

sets, and fixed assets are financed with long-term funds. Thus the top segment of the graph deals with working capital.

The figure represents an idealized situation—actually, current assets build up gradually as crops are purchased and processed; inventories are drawn down less regularly; and ending inventory balances do not decline to zero. Nevertheless, the example does illustrate the general nature of the production and financing process, and working capital management consists of decisions relating to the top section of the graph—managing current assets and arranging the short-term credit used to finance them.

As the economy became less oriented toward agriculture, the production and financing cycles of "typical" businesses changed. Although seasonal patterns still existed and business cycles also caused asset requirements to fluctuate, it became apparent that current assets rarely drop to zero. This realization led to the development of the idea of "permanent current assets," diagramed in Figure 10-2. As the figure is drawn, it maintains the traditional notion that permanent assets should be financed with long-term capital, while temporary assets should be financed with short-term credit.

The matching of asset and liability maturities as shown in Figures 10-1 and 10-2 was considered to be desirable because it minimizes the

Figure 10-2
Fluctuating versus Permanent Assets: Exactly Matching Maturities
Since in the modern business world current assets rarely drop to zero, the idea of
permanent current assets was developed. This figure shows these assets being financed,
along with fixed assets, by long-term debt and equity capital. Those current assets that
are still seasonal continue to be financed by short-term credit. Figures 10-1 and 10-2
illustrate the traditional approach of matching asset and liability maturities.

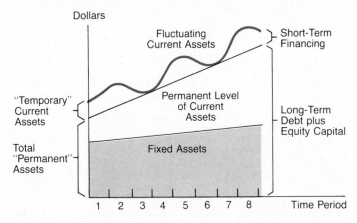

risk that the firm may be unable to pay off its maturing obligations. To
illustrate, suppose a firm borrows on a one-year basis and uses the
funds obtained to build and equip a plant. Cash flows from the plant
(profits plus depreciation) would almost never be sufficient to pay off
the loan at the end of only one year, so the loan must be renewed.
If for some reason the lender refuses to renew the loan, then the
firm has problems. Had the plant been financed with long-term debt,
however, cash flows over a longer time frame would have been sufficient
to retire the loan, and the problem of renewal would not have
arisen.

At the limit, a firm could attempt to match the maturity structure of
its assets and liabilities exactly. Inventory expected to be sold in a few
weeks could be financed with a short-term bank loan; a machine expected to last for 5 years could be financed by a 5-year loan; a 20-year
building could be financed by a 20-year mortgage bond; receivables
expected to be collected in 20 days could be financed by a 20-day bank
loan; and so forth. Actually, of course, uncertainty about the lives of
assets prevents this exact maturity matching. For example, a firm may
finance inventories with a 30-day loan, expecting to sell the inventories
and use the cash generated to retire the loan. But if sales are slow, the
cash will not be forthcoming, and the use of short-term credit may
cause a problem.

Figure 10-2 shows the situation for a firm that attempts to match
asset and liability maturities. Such a policy could be followed, but firms

Figure 10-3
Fluctuating versus Permanent Assets: Aggressive Position
In order to take better advantage of cheaper, short-term credit, a firm may finance a portion of its permanent current assets from short-term sources. The remainder of its permanent current assets, along with fixed and fluctuating (seasonal) current assets, are financed in the traditional way shown in the prior two figures. A firm taking this approach sacrifices a measure of safety to lower its finance costs, in hopes of thereby increasing profits.

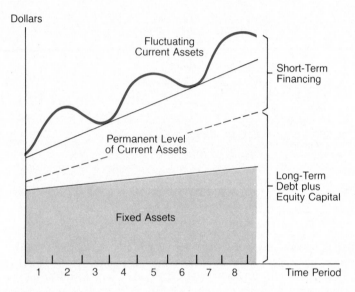

may also follow other maturity-matching policies. Figure 10-3, for example, illustrates the situation for a firm that finances all of its fixed assets with long-term capital but part of its permanent current assets with short-term credit.

Why would a firm wish to finance more of its assets with short-term credit? Basically, short-term credit is desirable because it is generally cheaper than long-term credit. Consider the two sources of short-term debt. Some sources of short-term financing are spontaneous, that is, they increase as the level of the firm's operations increases. Accounts payable and accruals are excellent examples of spontaneous financing. As we show in Chapter 13, when sales increase, a company obtains more raw materials from suppliers, and the increased trade credit offered by the suppliers finances the buildup in assets. Similarly, as operations increase, there is a resulting increase in accrued wages and taxes which helps to finance the buildup in operations. Used within limits, these sources constitute "free" capital. In addition, firms use contractual debt, such as short-term bank loans. As we noted in Chap-

Figure 10-4
Fluctuating versus Permanent Assets: Conservative Position
A very conservative approach to financing working capital is illustrated in this figure. Part of the short-term financing requirement is met by using long-term capital to "store up" marketable securities during the off season. During peak seasons these securities provide needed liquidity and are augmented by short-term borrowing.

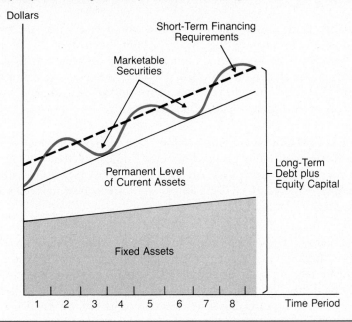

ter 5, the yield curve is generally upward sloping, indicating that short-term funds are cheaper than long-term financing.

The reliance on short-term credit could expand to financing all current assets and even a portion of the fixed assets. This highly aggressive, nonconservative position would subject the firm to fluctuating interest rates and the even more critical danger of loan renewal problems. Even so, since short-term debt is often cheaper than long-term debt, some firms may be willing to sacrifice safety for possibly higher profits.

Alternatively, as in Figure 10-4, the dashed line could be drawn *above* the line designating permanent current assets, indicating that permanent capital is being used to meet seasonal demands. In this case the firm uses a small amount of short-term credit to meet its peak requirements, but it also meets a part of its seasonal needs by "storing liquidity" in the form of marketable securities during the off-season. The humps above the dashed line represent short-term financing; the troughs below the dashed line represent short-term security holdings. This would represent a very safe, conservative position.

Advantages and Disadvantages of Short-Term Credit

Although using short-term debt is generally more risky than using long-term debt, short-term credit does have some offsetting advantages. The pros and cons of financing with short-term debt are considered in this section.

Flexibility. If its needs for funds are seasonal or cyclical, a firm may not want to commit itself to long-term debt. Such debt can be repaid early, provided the loan agreement includes a prepayment provision, but, even so, prepayment penalties can be expensive. Accordingly, if a firm thinks its need for funds will diminish in the near future, it should choose short-term debt for the flexibility it provides.

Cost of Long-Term versus Short-Term Debt. In Chapter 5 we saw that the yield curve is often upward sloping, indicating that interest rates are lower on short-term than on long-term debt. When this situation exists, interest expense will be lower if the firm borrows on a short-term rather than a long-term basis.

Risk of Long-Term versus Short-Term Debt. Even though short-term debt is generally less expensive than long-term debt, financing with short-term debt subjects the firm to more risk than does financing with long-term debt. This risk effect occurs for two reasons: (1) If a firm borrows on a long-term basis, its interest costs will be fixed (or if the interest rate is "floating," the cost will still be relatively stable over time), but if it borrows short-term, its interest expense will fluctuate widely, at times going quite high. For example, from 1977 to 1980 the short-term rate for large corporations more than *tripled*, going from 6.25 percent to 21 percent. (2) If a firm borrows on a short-term basis, naturally there will be less time in the borrowing period to generate cash to pay the debt's principal and interest as they come due. If the firm finds itself in a weak financial position on the loan's maturity date, it is possible that the lender will not extend the loan, thereby forcing the firm into bankruptcy. Braniff Airlines is an example.

Another good example of the riskiness of short-term debt is provided by Transamerica Corporation, a major financial services company. Transamerica's chairman described how his company was moving aggressively to reduce its dependency on short-term loans whose costs vary with short-term interest rates. He said Transamerica had reduced its variable-rate loans by about $450 million over the previous two years. "We aren't going to go through the enormous increase in debt expense again that had such a serious impact [on earnings]," he said. The company's earnings fell sharply because money rates had risen to record levels. "We were almost entirely in variable-rate debt," he said, but at that time out of total debt of slightly more than $1 billion, "about

65% is fixed rate and 35% variable. We've come a long way and we'll keep plugging away at it," he added. Transamerica's earnings had been depressed by the increase in short-term rates, but other companies were even less fortunate—they simply could not pay the interest charges, and this forced them into bankruptcy.

Combining Current Asset and Liability Decisions

From the preceding discussion it is obvious that a potentially profitable yet risky strategy would be to minimize investment in current assets while financing a large proportion of total assets with short-term debt. Alternatively, risk could be minimized, at the expense of profits, by increasing current assets and financing a large proportion of total assets with long-term debt.

In Table 10-2 we illustrate the results of each of these strategies along with a less extreme "moderate" plan for working capital and debt maturity policies. For these strategies the current ratio is our measure of risk, and return on equity evaluates the profitability of each plan.

The conservative policy of building current assets and financing with more expensive long-term debt has reduced the firm's return, as expected. However, the firm's level of risk is quite low. A high current

Table 10-2
Combined Effects of Asset and Debt Maturity Mix on Risk and Return
(Thousands of Dollars)

	Conservative	Moderate	Aggressive
Current assets	$15,000	$10,000	$ 5,000
Fixed assets	10,000	10,000	10,000
Total assets	$25,000	$20,000	$15,000
Short-term debt (10%)	$ 3,750	$ 5,000	$ 6,000
Long-term debt (14%)	8,750	5,000	1,500
Shareholders' equity	12,500	10,000	7,500
Total liabilities and equity	$25,000	$20,000	$15,000
Sales	$40,000	$40,000	$40,000
EBIT	3,000	3,000	3,000
Less: Interest	1,600	1,200	810
EBT	$ 1,400	$ 1,800	$ 2,190
Less: Taxes (40%)	560	720	876
Net income	$ 840	$ 1,080	$ 1,314
Current ratio (assets/liabilities)	4	2	.83
Return on equity (net income/shareholders' equity)	6.7%	10.8%	17.5%
Net working capital	$11,250	$5,000	($1,000)

ratio indicates that the firm has sufficient liquidity to meet almost any emergency. In contrast, the aggressive policy of minimizing current asset investment and utilizing less costly short-term debt has led to a much higher return. There are dangers associated with this higher return, however. First, at this low level of current assets, it is quite possible that the firm will be unable to maintain the proposed level of sales. Second, a potentially more critical problem is indicated by the firm's low level of liquidity as measured by the current ratio.[3] With this low current ratio, the firm may find future financing more difficult to obtain. Certainly it will be more expensive, due to the higher liquidity risk, if it can be obtained at all. The low current ratio also indicates that the firm may have significant problems meeting bills and interest and principal payments as they come due. Thus, although an aggressive working capital policy may lead to higher profits for the firm, it may also increase the potential for bankruptcy. Therefore a more moderate approach which represents a balancing of risk and return may be preferred by many financial managers.

The means by which financial managers evaluate their investment in each of the current asset and liability accounts is considered in the remaining chapters of Part IV.

Summary

Working capital represents a firm's investment in current assets. *Net working capital* (current assets minus current liabilities) indicates the proportion of current assets which are financed from long-term sources. *Working capital policy* is concerned not only with the management of current assets, but with the maturity structure of the firm's debt as well.

The firm's expected risk and return are affected by the amount and composition of its assets and liabilities. Current assets provide the firm with the liquidity necessary for the ongoing functions of the business. Too much liquidity reduces profitability, whereas too little jeopardizes the ability of the firm to function efficiently. Similarly, short-term credit generally offers the advantages of lower cost and greater flexibility over long-term debt. However, an overreliance on short-term debt can lead to less predictable interest costs, refinancing problems, and even bankruptcy. Thus the financial manager must formulate a working capital policy which balances risk and return to the ultimate benefit of the shareholders.

---

[3]Note that net working capital mirrors the liquidity risk factors that are identified by the current ratio.

Small Business $ $ $ $ $ $ $ $ $

Growth and Working Capital Needs

Working capital is one of the requirements in a new firm that is most often underestimated by the entrepreneur seeking funds to finance the business. The entrepreneur makes provisions for research and development and for the plant and equipment required to produce the products that are created. But working capital is frequently a surprise to the entrepreneur. He or she expects to come up with a product that the market will immediately accept and for which the market will pay a very substantial premium. This premium price will lead to very high profit margins, which will then "finance" all of the firm's other needs. As naive as this point of view appears to be, it nevertheless is common among less experienced founders of new businesses.

Mike was one of the founders of a new microcomputer software company that began seeking venture capital to support its products in the latter part of 1980. In speaking with a venture capitalist who was concerned about the low level of funding being sought, Mike explained that the company's products had such a high profit margin that the company would be essentially self-financing after marketing was well under way. In fact, Mike explained, there would even be funds available from internal sources to support continued new product development. The venture capitalist—we'll call him John—was a little disconcerted. He asked which firm was currently most successful in the microcomputer software business in which Mike was competing. Mike instantly responded, "Personal Software" (the company is now known as Visicorp). John asked, "Why, then, do you suppose that Personal Software has just completed raising an additional $2,500,000 in new venture capital? Isn't it as profitable as you expect it to be?" Mike fumbled around for a while with no answer; to his credit, he got the point.

Rapid growth consumes cash; it does not generate cash. Rapid growth does often generate profits, but profits do not pay the bills—cash does. Consider what a firm must do to sustain a very high growth rate. If it is a manufacturing firm, the components of the firm's assets include raw materials inventory, work-in-process inventory, finished goods inventory, and accounts receivable, as well as fixed assets. With the exception of fixed assets, these items are all components of gross working capital. When the firm produces a product, it makes an investment in each of these working capital items before any cash is received from collection of receivables, assuming all sales are credit sales.

Now imagine a small firm that has limited access to external financing or that chooses to finance itself internally from its retained earnings. It secures enough funding to acquire its fixed assets and to get started producing product. When receivables are collected, the company will have a little more money than it used to generate the products that generated the collections. Excluding any noncash expenses, suppose that for each dollar of sales generated, the company spends about 95 cents. That leaves a nickel in profit. Of course, the firm's silent partner (Uncle Sam) takes a cut, and suppose the firm pays out a little to stockholders. The bottom line is that the firm has 3 cents left in cash from its dollar in sales. Since the firm puts in 97 cents for each dollar that it has left at the end of a single "manufacture and sales cycle," the firm now has about 3 percent more to put into manufacturing and selling the next round of product. In other words, after one sales cycle, the firm can afford another sales cycle with about a 3 percent increase in sales without external financing.

Now recall the financial analysis of Chapter 7. Suppose the firm has an average of 120 days of sales in inventory and an average of 60 days of sales tied up in accounts receivable. If the firm pays cash for all of its materials and labor, then the firm essentially "turns" cash about twice a year (360/180). In other words, from the time new investment is made in inventory and receivables, it is 180 days, on average, before the invested cash is returned. The firm then has two complete cash cycles per year. In each cycle the firm ends up with a 3 percent growth in available funds. Therefore the firm can grow at about a 6 percent annual rate from its internal sources. If the firm is actually growing at, say, 20 percent, then it is generating a constant need for new funds. These must come from new equity or new debt; retained earnings will not be adequate.

The analysis above is only a crude approximation to the firm's internally fundable annual growth rate, but it gives a clear indication of how working capital requirements constrain growth. The small firm planning for supernormal growth must therefore also make provisions for capital to support its growth. The manager has some alternatives to growth at such a rate, and these should at least be considered. For example, the firm can vary its working capital policy in such a way as to limit or control growth. Tightening its credit policies, for example, may cost the firm some sales but will reduce the average collection period, thereby increasing the number of cash cycles per year. Reducing inventory investment will probably cost the firm some lost sales in the event of stock-outs, but it will again reduce the cash cycle and increase the number of cycles per year. Both of these measures tend to reduce sales growth and to increase the rate at which sales growth can be financed internally. For the firm with constraints on available financing, these discretionary policies may help the firm bring its rate of growth into balance with its ability to finance that growth.[1]

[1]Limits on growth and the concept of "sustainable growth" are explored in Chapter 6 of Robert C. Higgins, *Analysis for Financial Management* (Homewood, IL: Irwin, 1984).

Resolution to Decision in Finance

Not a Minute Too Soon

John Mariotta had recognized as early as April 1983 that Wedtech might have to sell shares to the public in order to raise the cash it needed. But he had hesitated to do so because of the company's complicated debt structure. Wedtech owed a substantial amount of money to the federal government, which would slow down the restructuring process and make it more difficult.

Despite the complications, New York's Bank Leumi agreed to lend Wedtech $5,400,000 to repay some of its debt, including a $2,100,000 government-guaranteed loan. In addition, the bank would advance $500,000 in working capital, all on the condition that it receive first lien on Wedtech's assets. Unfortunately, however, the government already had first claim on the company's real estate and equipment—a right it was reluctant to relinquish.

While negotiations with the government proceeded at a snail's pace, the hot market for new stock began to cool down. If Wedtech didn't issue its stock soon, the opportunity might evaporate.

Finally, at the end of July, the government yielded its claim on Wedtech's assets to Bank Leumi, freeing the company to issue its stock. Wedtech's investment bankers pushed the deal through SEC red tape in record time, and at the end of August Wedtech sold 1,900,000 shares at $16. After underwriting, discounts, and commissions, Wedtech was left with $22,200,000. Of that, $12,000,000 went immediately to creditors.

If any one of its deals with the government, the bank, and the SEC had fallen through, Wedtech's whole restructuring plan would have collapsed, taking the company with it. In the process Wedtech's executives learned an important lesson—that to run a successful business it is more important to have cash on hand than to show an accounting profit.

Source: "Not a Minute Too Soon," *Forbes,* Dec. 5, 1983, 162.

Key Terms You should be able to define each of the following terms:

Working capital; net working capital   Working capital policy; working
                                         capital management

Questions

10-1 What are the differences between permanent and temporary current assets?

10-2 What is the trade-off between risk and return in the management of the firm's working capital?

10-3 What is the relative earning power of current assets as opposed to that of fixed assets?

10-4 How would a period of rapidly increasing inflation affect the firm's working capital?

10-5 During a tight-money period, would you expect a business firm to hold higher or lower cash balances (demand deposits) than during an easy-money period? Assume the firm's volume of business remains constant over both economic periods.

10-6 How would management's ability to predict sales trends and patterns affect working capital policy?

10-7 Why is the use of short-term debt more risky than long-term debt in financing permanent current assets?

Problems

10-1 Consider the following balance sheet:

Lantern Industries: Balance Sheet, December 31, 1984

Assets	
Cash	$ 25,000
Marketable securities	10,000
Accounts receivable	165,000
Inventory	200,000
Plant and equipment (net)	500,000
Total assets	$900,000
Liabilities and Shareholders' Equity	
Accounts payable	$ 40,000
Notes payable	60,000
Accrued wages	10,000
Accrued taxes	35,000
Mortgage bonds	200,000
Debentures	105,000
Common stock	50,000
Paid-in capital	100,000
Retained earnings	300,000
Total liabilities and shareholders' equity	$900,000

[handwritten: current liab (short term) — brace around Accounts payable, Notes payable, Accrued wages, Accrued taxes]

[handwritten: long term — brace around Mortgage bonds, Debentures]

* **a.** Determine Lantern Industries' investment in working capital.
* **b.** Determine Lantern Industries' net working capital investment.
  c. Does the firm's financing mix (long-term versus short-term) appear to be conservative or aggressive?

10-2 Sharon James has been evaluating her firm's financing mix of short-term and long-term debt. She has projected the following two condensed balance sheets:

	Plan 1	Plan 2
Current assets	$1,250,000	$1,250,000
Fixed assets (net)	1,250,000	1,250,000
Total assets	$2,500,000	$2,500,000
Current liabilities	$ 250,000	$1,000,000
Long-term debt	1,000,000	250,000
Common stock equity	1,250,000	1,250,000
Total claims	$2,500,000	$2,500,000

Earnings before interest and taxes is $375,000 and the tax rate is 40 percent under either plan.

a. If current liabilities have a 10 percent interest rate and long-term debt has a 13 percent interest rate, what is the rate of return on equity under each plan?

b. Assume the yield curve is inverted and the short-term rate is 17 percent and the long-term rate is 13 percent. What is the rate of return on equity for the two plans?

c. Assume both long-term and short-term rates are 13 percent. What is the rate of return on equity?

d. Using your answers to Parts a, b, and c, graph the relationship between short-term interest rates and the rates of return on equity under Plans 1 and 2. Comment on the relative riskiness of the two plans.

10-3 Jim Harrison, financial manager for Cowtown Motors, has a problem. The firm's board of directors has complained about the firm's low liquidity. Jim has been ordered to raise the current ratio to at least 2.0 within a reasonable time period. One of his plans is to sell $2,500,000 in equity and invest the proceeds in Treasury bills which yield 10 percent before taxes. The firm has a 40 percent tax rate and, if no Treasury bills are purchased, net income after taxes is expected to be $2,200,000.

Cowtown Motors: Balance Sheet, December 31, 1984

Current assets	$10,000,000	Current liabilities	$ 6,250,000
Fixed assets	15,000,000	Long-term debt	3,750,000
		Common stock equity	15,000,000
Total assets	$25,000,000	Total claims	$25,000,000

---

*Refer to Appendix E for check answers to problems with asterisks.

   * **a.** Using the financial information in the accompanying table (which does not include the proposed purchase of Treasury bills), calculate the firm's current ratio, net working capital, and return on equity.

   * **b.** If Jim follows his plan and sells $2,500,000 in equity in order to purchase the 10 percent Treasury bills, what are the firm's resulting current ratio, net working capital, and return on equity?

   c. What result would the plan have on the firm's liquidity?

   d. Would you suggest acceptance of this plan?

10-4 Mission Manufacturing's management is concerned about the way in which their new firm will be financed. The three alternative plans that have been proposed are shown below:

	Plan 1	Plan 2	Plan 3
Current assets	$4,500,000	$4,500,000	$4,500,000
Fixed assets	8,000,000	8,000,000	8,000,000
Current liabilities (8.5%)	4,500,000	1,500,000	3,000,000
Long-term debt (12%)	1,500,000	4,500,000	0
Common stock equity	6,500,000	6,500,000	9,500,000

Whichever plan is chosen, sales are expected to be $20 million and operating profits (EBIT) will be $2 million. The marginal tax rate is 40 percent.

   a. For each plan, calculate the following: (1) current ratio, (2) net working capital, (3) debt/total assets ratio, and (4) return on equity.

   b. Compare the risk and return associated with each plan. Which plan would you accept?

 * **10-5** Block Printing Company's balance sheet appears below.

Cash	$ 50,000	Debt	$224,000
Accounts receivable	175,000		
Inventory	135,000	Equity	336,000
Fixed assets (net)	200,000		
Total assets	$560,000	Total claims	$560,000

The company's sales are $900,000 annually and the net margin is 5 percent. Compute the firm's: **(a)** inventory utilization (based on sales), **(b)** inventory utilization period, **(c)** average collection period, and **(d)** return on assets.

 * **10-6** Refer to the data in Problem 10-5. The company's owner, Bob Block, is too busy in the printing shop to oversee all the financial aspects of the business. He decides to hire Mr. Jefferies to reduce current assets. After some study Jefferies concludes he can reduce the firm's inventory utilization period by 14 days and the average collection period by 20 days without reducing sales or net margin. Under these new conditions:

   a. What is the new level of inventory?

   b. What is the new level of accounts receivable?

   c. If all savings are used to reduce debt, what is the firm's return on assets? (Assume the net margin remains constant.)

10-7 Providence Carpet Company is attempting to determine the optimal level of current assets for the coming year. Management expects sales to increase to $18,000,000 as a result of asset expansion currently underway. Fixed assets equal $7,500,000, and the firm wishes to maintain a 40 percent debt ratio. The firm's interest rate is 10 percent on both long- and short-term debt. There are three alternatives for determining the current asset level of the firm: (1) an aggressive policy requiring current assets of only 45 percent of projected sales, (2) a moderate policy of 50 percent of sales in current assets, and (3) a conservative policy requiring current assets of 60 percent of sales. The firm expects to maintain an operating margin of 15 percent (EBIT/Sales = 15%).

    a. What is the expected return on equity under each of the alternatives? Assume a 50 percent tax rate.

    b. What are the risks incurred in each policy alternative?

10-8 Refer to the data in the previous problem. Assume that long-term interest rates have now risen to 14 percent but short-term rates remain at 10 percent. Under the aggressive policy all debt financing will be short-term; under the moderate policy the firm will split debt equally between long- and short-term financing; and all debt will be financed with long-term sources under the conservative policy.

    a. What is the expected return under each policy?

    b. What new risks have been introduced?

Selected References

There are a number of books which deal with all aspects of working capital management and policy. Three are:

Metha, D. R., *Working Capital Management* (Englewood Cliffs, NJ: Prentice-Hall, 1974).

Smith, Keith V., *Guide to Working Capital Management* (New York: McGraw-Hill, 1979).

Smith Keith V., *Readings on the Management of Working Capital* (St. Paul: West, 1980).

Several articles emphasize the risk and return trade-off in working capital policy. See:

Cossaboom, R. A., "Let's Reassess the Profitability-Liquidity Tradeoff," *Financial Executive*, May 1971, 46–51.

Knight, W. D., "Working Capital Management—Satisficing versus Optimization," *Financial Management*, Spring 1972, 33–40.

Walker, Ernest W., "Towards a Theory of Working Capital," *Engineering Economist*, January–February 1964, 21–35.

Welter, Paul, "How to Calculate Savings Possible Through Reduction of Working Capital," *Financial Executive*, October 1970, 50–58.

Managing Cash and Marketable Securities

Decision in Finance

The Race Is to the Slow Payer

The goal of corporate cash managers is to squeeze the pennies out of every dollar under their control. From their point of view, idle cash is the worst possible nightmare. One of their pet peeves is noninterest-bearing checking accounts. Of course, companies must maintain checking accounts in order to pay their bills. And the larger a company is, the more money it needs to have tied up in checking accounts. So cash managers, and their bankers, have spent much time and ingenuity in finding ways to make the check-processing system work to their advantage.

In 1980 Herbert W. Eames, Jr., became chief financial officer of J. Walter Thompson, the gigantic, New York-based advertising agency. In assessing the company's financial policies and procedures, Eames discovered that JWT issued checks drawn on a New York bank. When paying the television networks for advertising time, JWT delivered its checks by hand. And if the networks and certain vendors wanted to be paid faster, they could send messengers to JWT's eighth-floor cashier's office to pick up their checks and then proceed to deposit them in the bank as soon as possible.

An experienced and savvy cash manager, Eames knew that this quick-pay policy was expensive for JWT. To help his company optimize the use of its cash, he opened a checking account at the Waukesha branch of the First Wisconsin National Bank for use in paying creditors. As a result JWT can now hold onto its cash longer, even though some checks are still picked up by hand.

As you read this chapter, look for the methods cash managers can employ to optimize their companies' use of cash. What probably prompted Herbert Eames's decision to open a checking account in Waukesha, Wisconsin? Do you agree with his decision? Why or why not?

See end of chapter for resolution.

Chapter 10 emphasized the risk and return implications of working capital policy. With this background we are now in a position to consider management decisions relating to specific types of current assets and sources of short-term credit available to finance these assets. We begin this discussion with an evaluation of the factors which determine the appropriate level of cash and marketable securities.

Cash Management

cash
The total of bank demand deposits plus currency.

Approximately 1.5 percent of the average industrial firm's assets are held in the form of **cash,** which is defined as the total of bank demand deposits plus currency. However, cash balances vary widely not only among industries but also among the firms within a given industry, depending on the individual firm's specific conditions and on their owners' and managers' aversion to risk. In this section we analyze the factors that determine firms' cash balances. These same factors, incidentally, apply to the cash holdings of individuals and nonprofit organizations, including government agencies.

Reasons for Holding Cash

Firms hold cash for four primary reasons:

transactions balances
Cash balances associated with payments and collections; balances necessary to conduct day-to-day business.

1. Transactions. Cash balances are necessary to conduct business. Payments must be made, and receipts are deposited in the cash account. Cash balances associated with payments and collections are known as **transactions balances.**

precautionary balances
Cash balances held in reserve for random, unforeseen fluctuations in inflows and outflows.

2. Precaution. Cash inflows and outflows are somewhat unpredictable, with the degree of predictability varying among firms and industries. Cash balances held in reserve for random, unforeseen fluctuations in inflows and outflows are defined as **precautionary balances.** The less predictable the firm's cash flows, the larger the necessary cash balances. However, if the firm has easy access to borrowed funds— that is, if the firm can borrow on short notice—then it need not hold much, if any, cash for precautionary purposes. Also, as is noted later in this chapter, firms that do need precautionary balances tend to hold them as highly liquid marketable securities: such holdings accomplish the same purposes as cash balances while providing income in the form of interest received.

speculative balances
Cash balances that are held to enable a firm to take advantage of any bargain purchases that might arise.

3. Speculation. Some cash balances may be held to enable the firm to take advantage of any bargain purchases that might arise; these are defined as **speculative balances.** However, as with precautionary balances, firms today are more likely to rely on reserve borrowing power and on marketable securities portfolios than on actual cash holdings for speculative purposes.

4. Compensation to banks for providing loans and services. This type of balance, defined as a compensating balance, is discussed in detail later in this chapter.

Although the actual cash balance can be thought of as consisting of transactions balances, speculative balances, precautionary balances, and compensating balances, we cannot calculate the amount needed for each type, add them together, and produce a total desired cash balance, because the same money serves all four purposes. Firms do, however, consider these four factors when establishing their target cash positions.

While there are good reasons for holding *adequate* cash balances, there is a strong reason for not holding *excessive* balances—cash is a low-earning asset, so excessive cash balances simply lower the total asset turnover, thereby reducing both the rate of return on net worth and the value of the stock. Thus firms are very much interested in establishing procedures for increasing the efficiency of their cash management; if they can make their cash work harder, they can reduce cash balances.

The Cash Budget

The most important tool in cash management is the **cash budget,** a statement showing the firm's projected cash inflows and outflows over some specified period of time. Cash budgets can be constructed on a monthly, a weekly, or even a daily basis. Table 11-1 shows a monthly cash budget covering the last six months of 1984 for the Dayton Printing Company, a leading producer of greeting cards.

cash budget
A schedule showing cash flows (receipts, disbursements, and net cash) for a firm over a specified period.

Dayton's birthday and get-well cards are sold year-round, but the bulk of the company's sales occurs during September, when retailers are stocking up for Christmas. All sales are made on terms that allow a cash discount for payments made within 20 days; if the discount is not taken, the full amount must be paid in 40 days. However, like most other companies, Dayton finds that some of its customers delay payment up to 90 days. Experience shows that on 20 percent of the sales, payment is made during the month in which the sale is made; on 70 percent of the sales, payment is made during the second month after the sale; and on 10 percent of the sales, payment is made during the third month.

Rather than produce at a uniform rate throughout the year, Dayton prints cards immediately before they are required for delivery. Paper, ink, and other materials amount to 70 percent of sales and are bought the month before the company expects to sell the finished product. Its own purchase terms permit Dayton to delay payment on its purchases for one month. Accordingly, if July sales are forecast at $10 million, then purchases during June will amount to $7 million, and this amount will actually be paid in July.

Table 11-1
Dayton Printing Company: Worksheet and Cash Budget
(Thousands of Dollars)

	May	June	July	Aug.	Sept.	Oct.	Nov.	Dec.	Jan.
Worksheet									
Sales (net of cash discounts)	$5,000	$5,000	$10,000	$15,000	$20,000	$10,000	$10,000	$5,000	$5,000
Collections									
During month of sale (20%)	1,000	1,000	2,000	3,000	4,000	2,000	2,000	1,000	
During first month after sale (70%)		3,500	3,500	7,000	10,500	14,000	7,000	7,000	
During second month after sale (10%)			500	500	1,000	1,500	2,000	1,000	
Total collections	$1,000	$4,500	$6,000	$10,500	$15,500	$17,500	$11,000	$9,000	
Purchases (70% of next month's sales)	$3,500	$7,000	$10,500	$14,000	$7,000	$7,000	$3,500	$3,500	
Payments (one-month lag)		$3,500	$7,000	$10,500	$14,000	$7,000	$7,000	$3,500	
Cash Budget									
(1) Collections			$ 6,000	$10,500	$15,500	$17,500	$11,000	$9,000	
(2) Payments									
(3) Purchases			$ 7,000	$10,500	$14,000	$ 7,000	$ 7,000	$3,500	
(4) Wages and salaries			750	1,000	1,250	750	750	500	
(5) Rent			250	250	250	250	250	250	
(6) Other expenses			100	150	200	100	100	50	
(7) Taxes					2,000			2,000	
(8) Payment for plant construction						5,000			
(9) Total payments			$ 8,100	$11,900	$17,700	$13,100	$ 8,100	$6,300	
(10) Net cash gain (loss) during month (Line 1 − Line 9)			($ 2,100)	($ 1,400)	($ 2,200)	$ 4,400	$ 2,900	$2,700	
(11) Cash at start of month if no borrowing is done			3,000	900	($ 500)	(2,700)	1,700	4,600	
(12) Cumulative cash (= cash at start plus gains or minus losses) (Line 10 + Line 11)			$ 900	($ 500)	($ 2,700)	$ 1,700	$ 4,600	$7,300	
(13) Deduct target level of cash			2,500	2,500	2,500	2,500	2,500	2,500	
(14) Total loans outstanding to maintain $2,500 cash balance			$ 1,600	$ 3,000	$ 5,200	$ 800			
(15) Surplus cash							$ 2,100	$4,800	

Notes
1. The amount shown on Line 11 for the first month, the $3,000 balance on July 1, is given. The values shown for each of the following months on Line 11 represent the "cumulative cash" as shown on Line 12 for the preceding month.
2. When the target cash balance of $2,500 (Line 13) is deducted from the cumulative cash balance (Line 12), if a negative figure results, it is shown on Line 14 as a required loan, whereas if a positive figure results, it is shown on Line 15 as surplus cash.

Such other cash expenditures as wages and rent are given in the lower part of Table 11-1. The company must also make tax payments of $2 million on September 15 and on December 15, while payment for a new plant must be made in October. Assuming the company needs to keep a minimum cash balance of $2.5 million at all times, and that it has $3 million on July 1, what are Dayton's financial requirements for the period July through December?

The monthly cash requirements are worked out in Table 11-1. The top half of the table provides a worksheet for calculating collections on sales and payments on purchases. The first line in the worksheet gives the sales forecast for the period May through January; May and June sales are necessary to determine collections for July and August. Next, cash collections are given. The first line of this section shows that 20 percent of the sales during any given month are collected that month. The second line shows the collections on the prior month's sales: 70 percent of sales in the preceding month. The third line gives collections from sales 2 months earlier: 10 percent of sales in that month. The collections are summed to find the total cash receipts from sales during each month under consideration.

With the worksheet completed, the cash budget itself can be constructed. Receipts from collections are given on the top line. Next, payments during each month are summarized. The difference between cash receipts and cash payments is the net cash gain or loss during the month; for July there is a net cash loss of $2.1 million. The initial cash on hand at the beginning of the month is added to the net cash gain or loss during the month to obtain the cumulative cash that would be on hand if no financing were done; at the end of July Dayton would have cumulative cash totaling $900,000.

The cumulative cash is next subtracted from the target cash balance, $2.5 million, to determine the firm's borrowing requirements or surplus cash, whichever the case may be. In July, as shown on Line 12, Dayton expects to have cumulative cash of $900,000. It has a target cash balance of $2.5 million. Thus, to maintain the target cash balance, it must borrow $1.6 million by the end of July. Assuming that this amount is indeed borrowed, loans outstanding will total $1.6 million at the end of July.

This same procedure is used in the following months. Sales will expand seasonally in August. With the increased sales will come increased payments for purchases, wages, and other items. Receipts from sales will go up too, but the firm will still be left with a $1.4 million cash outflow during the month. The total financial requirements at the end of August will be $3 million, the cumulative cash plus the target cash balance. The $3 million is also equal to the $1.6 million needed at the end of July plus the $1.4 million cash deficit for August. Thus, loans outstanding will total $3 million at the end of August.

Industry Practice

The Perils of Cash Management

Ever since interest rates began going through the roof back in the early 1970s, the watchword in corporate finance has been "cash management." Everybody has been getting into the act. These days, you can hardly open a magazine without running across a half-dozen ads for cash management services offered by banks, brokerage firms, mutual fund organizations, accountants, and what have you. Meanwhile, the whole idea of corporate cash management has been evolving and changing at a breathtaking pace.

Lately, however, a few voices have been raised to suggest that all this may have gone too far. The target of their criticism is the increasingly popular notion that the cash-management operation should be viewed as a potential profit center for the company—and that the cash manager should be evaluated in the same light as the firm's line managers.

"I find this trend very alarming," say Paul J. Beehler, director of treasury consulting services for Arthur Young & Co. in San Francisco and the author of *Contemporary Cash Management* (2nd ed., John Wiley & Sons, 1983). "Companies are in business to make money. The primary way they do this is to assume risks in the business areas in which they are involved. To view cash management as a profit center . . . means that additional risks will be taken in an area unrelated to the company's principal business. That can be very dangerous."

To illustrate his point, he cites the case of a medium-size company whose cash manager tried to improve dramatically the company's portfolio yield. As a result of the risks undertaken, the company was forced to record more than $15 million in losses in one year—losses representing about one-third of its total annual revenues. "This isn't going to happen to every company, but it happened in that case, and it could happen to others."

In many ways, the controversy reflects the immaturity of cash management as a discipline. Indeed, it scarcely existed 10 years ago. With the explosion in interest rates, however, companies suddenly discovered that—properly adjusted—their idle cash could serve as a source of capital.

Then came the credit crunch and the recession. "Capital wasn't available at any cost to a lot of companies, so they had to look inwardly and see what methods they could employ to improve cash flow," notes Sy Jones, a partner in the New York office of accountants Coopers & Lybrand. "It became an issue of survival more than . . . investing idle funds. Cash management became a critical need in order to survive the recession."

Most observers agree that cash management is now a permanent feature of the corporate landscape. Nevertheless, a host of questions remain to be answered. How do you invest idle funds in a low-interest-rate environment? How much risk is acceptable? What standards should apply? Should cash management play a largely supportive role? Or can it be expected to add to a company's bottom line?

Beehler, for one, strongly believes

that cash management should be strictly supportive. "I feel that way," he says, "because cash management essentially deals with the working capital base of the company. Mistakes can result in reducing levels of working capital or putting the company in an illiquid position—that is, not having funds available to pay debts or to cover expansion. . . . Would you consider your tax department a profit center?"

Of course, not everyone shares Beehler's concern about the "profit center" trend. "People who lose a lot of money are going to be distraught, but cash management is like anything else," says Jay Goldinger, an investment broker with the Beverly Hills firm of Cantor, Fitzgerald & Co. "You've got to earn as much as you can with as much safety as you can."

Others doubt that many companies have lost money through cash management. "I think it's a fiction," says Jones of Coopers & Lybrand. "What I've seen is the other way around. . . ."

Nevertheless, Jones agrees that there are risks involved. "You've got to remember what the game is," he says. "The primary game is simply the investment of temporarily idle funds. It's not to become the end game unto itself. . . . You can get into trouble if you start having ideas about how you're going to take this money and outsmart the stock market or [get into] commodities. That's not cash management. That's making a conscious decision that you're going to do something other than your normal business."

Beehler's concern is that the "profit center" orientation may, in fact, encourage cash managers to take precisely such risks. He admits, however, that he may be bucking the tide.

In any case, there is no denying that a lot of questions about cash management remain to be answered. For that reason, if no other, the debate is likely to heat up before it cools down.

Source: "The Perils of Cash Management" by Donna Sammons. Reprinted with permission, INC. magazine, June 1983. Copyright © 1983 by INC. Publishing Company, 38 Commercial Wharf, Boston, MA 02110.

Sales peak in September, and the cash deficit during this month will amount to another $2.2 million. The total borrowing requirements through September will increase to $5.2 million. Sales, purchases, and payments for past purchases will fall markedly in October; collections will be the highest of any month because they reflect the high September sales. As a result Dayton will enjoy a healthy $4.4 million cash surplus during October. This surplus can be used to pay off borrowings, so loans outstanding will decline by $4.4 million, to $800,000.

Dayton will have another cash surplus in November, which will permit it to eliminate completely the need for borrowing. In fact, the company is expected to have $2.1 million in surplus cash by the month's end, while another cash surplus in December will swell the extra cash to $4.8 million. With such a large amount of unneeded funds, Dayton's treasurer will doubtless want to invest in interest-bearing securities or put the funds to use in some other way.

Before concluding our discussion of the cash budget, we should make five additional points: (1) Our cash budget does not reflect interest on loans or income from the investment of surplus cash. This refinement could be added quite easily. (2) More importantly, if cash inflows and outflows are not uniform during the month, we could be seriously understating or overstating our financing requirements. For example, if all payments must be made on the fifth of each month, but collections come in uniformly throughout the month, then Dayton would need to borrow much larger amounts than those shown in Table 11-1. In such a case, the company would need to prepare cash budgets on a daily basis. (3) Since depreciation is a noncash charge, depreciation does not appear on the cash budget. (4) The cash budget represents a forecast, so all the values in the table are *expected* values. If actual sales, purchases, and so on are different from the forecasted levels, then our forecasted cash deficits and surpluses will also be incorrect. (5) Finally, we should note that the target cash balance would probably be adjusted over time, rising and falling with seasonal patterns and with longer-term changes in the scale of the firm's operations. Factors that influence the target cash balance are discussed in the next section.

Other Procedures for Increasing the Efficiency of Cash Management

Although a carefully prepared cash budget is a necessary starting point, there are other elements in a good cash management program. For example, the $2.5 million minimum cash balance in the preceding example could probably be reduced if Dayton could predict its inflows and outflows more precisely. Most firms do not know exactly when bills will come in or when payments will be received, and transactions balances must be sufficient to allow for a random increase in bills requiring payment at a time when receipts lag below expectations. Although we do not consider them in this book, statistical procedures are available to help improve cash flow forecasts, and the better the cash flow forecast, the lower the minimum cash balance.

synchronized cash flows
Cash flows that permit inflows to coincide with the timing of outflows, thereby holding transactions balances to a minimum.

Synchronizing Cash Inflows and Outflows. If you, as an individual, were to receive income on a daily basis instead of once a month, you could operate with a lower average checking account balance. If you could arrange to pay rent, tuition, and other charges on a daily basis, this would further reduce your required average cash balance. Exactly the same situation holds for business firms—by arranging things so that their cash receipts coincide with the timing of their cash outflows, firms can hold their transactions balances to a minimum. Recognizing this point, utility companies, oil companies, and other firms arrange to bill customers and to pay their own bills on a regular schedule throughout the month. In our cash budgeting example, if Dayton Printing Company could arrange a better synchronization of its cash inflows and outflows, it might be able to reduce somewhat its minimum cash balance and therefore its required bank loans.

Speeding Collections of Checks Received and Slowing Collections of Checks Written. Another important aspect of cash management deals with processing the checks a company writes and receives. It is obviously inefficient to put checks received in a drawer and deposit them every week or so; no well-run business would follow such a practice. Similarly, cash balances are drawn down unnecessarily if bills are paid earlier than required. In fact, efficient firms go to great lengths to speed up the processing of incoming checks, thus putting the funds to work faster, and they try to stretch out their own payments as long as possible.

When a customer writes and mails a check, this does *not* mean that the funds are immediately available to the receiving firm. Most of us have deposited a check in our account and then been told that we cannot write our own checks against this deposit until the **check-clearing** process is completed. Our bank must (1) make sure that the check we deposited is good and (2) receive funds itself before releasing funds for us to spend.

As shown on the left side of Figure 11-1, quite a bit of time may be required for a firm to process incoming checks and obtain the use of the money. A check must first be delivered through the mails and then cleared through the banking system before the money can be put to use. Checks received from customers in distant cities are especially subject to delays. First, possible mail delays can obviously cause problems. Second, clearing checks can also delay the effective use of funds received. Assume, for example, that we receive a check and deposit it in our bank. Our bank must present the check to the bank on which it was drawn. Only when this latter bank transfers funds to our bank are they available for us to use. Checks are generally cleared through the Federal Reserve System or through a clearinghouse set up by the banks in a particular city. Of course, if the check is drawn on the bank of deposit, that bank merely transfers funds by bookkeeping entries from one of its depositors to another. The length of time required for other checks to clear is a function of the distance between the payer's and the payee's banks; in the case of private clearinghouses, it can range from one to three days. The maximum time required for checks to clear through the Federal Reserve System is two days.

The right side of Figure 11-1 shows how the process can be speeded up. First, to reduce mail and clearing delays, a **lockbox plan** can be used. Suppose a New York firm makes sales to customers all across the country. It can arrange to have its customers send payments to post office boxes (lockboxes) in their own local areas. A local bank will

check clearing
Process of converting a check, after it is written and mailed, into cash in the payee's account. Firms try to speed up the clearing process for checks received and to slow down the process for checks disbursed.

lockbox plan
A procedure used to speed up collections and to reduce float through the use of post office boxes in payers' local areas.

Figure 11-1
Diagram of the Check-Clearing Process

This figure illustrates how a lockbox plan can accelerate a company's collection of receivables by three to five working days. With the regular check-cashing process, a company must wait six to eight working days for a customer's payment to pass through the mail and clear through the banks and the Federal Reserve System. When a company uses a mailing address and bank in a customer's hometown, however, the check-clearing process is expedited and the company gains quicker access to its funds. It is possible for a company to free up several million dollars in cash by using lockboxes.

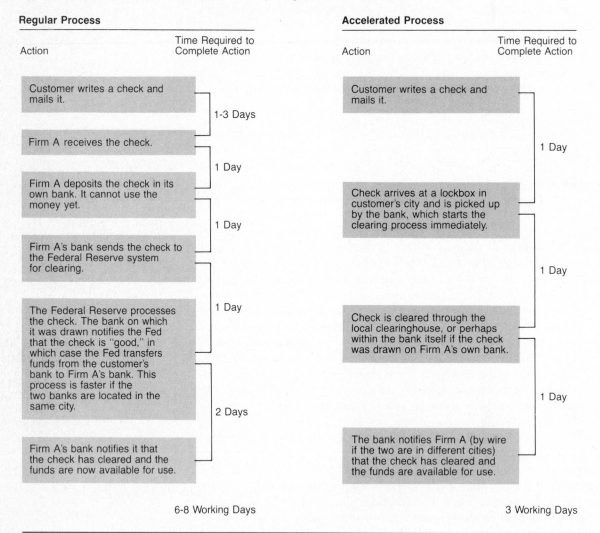

Regular Process

Action | Time Required to Complete Action

Customer writes a check and mails it.

1-3 Days

Firm A receives the check.

1 Day

Firm A deposits the check in its own bank. It cannot use the money yet.

1 Day

Firm A's bank sends the check to the Federal Reserve system for clearing.

1 Day

The Federal Reserve processes the check. The bank on which it was drawn notifies the Fed that the check is "good," in which case the Fed transfers funds from the customer's bank to Firm A's bank. This process is faster if the two banks are located in the same city.

2 Days

Firm A's bank notifies it that the check has cleared and the funds are now available for use.

6-8 Working Days

Accelerated Process

Action | Time Required to Complete Action

Customer writes a check and mails it.

1 Day

Check arrives at a lockbox in customer's city and is picked up by the bank, which starts the clearing process immediately.

1 Day

Check is cleared through the local clearinghouse, or perhaps within the bank itself if the check was drawn on Firm A's own bank.

1 Day

The bank notifies Firm A (by wire if the two are in different cities) that the check has cleared and the funds are available for use.

3 Working Days

pick up the checks, have them cleared in the local area, and then transfer the funds by wire to the company's New York bank. In this way collection time can be reduced by one to five days. Examples of freeing funds in the amount of $5 million or more by this method are not uncommon.

Just as expediting the collection process conserves cash, slowing down disbursements accomplishes the same thing by keeping cash on hand for longer periods. One obviously could simply delay payments, but this involves equally obvious difficulties. Firms have, in the past, devised rather ingenious methods for "legitimately" lengthening the collection period on their own checks, ranging from maintaining deposits in distant banks to using slow, awkward payment procedures. Since such practices are usually recognized for what they are, there are severe limits to their use.

The most widely publicized of these procedures in recent years is the use of drafts. While a check is payable on demand, a draft must be transmitted to the issuer, who approves it and deposits funds to cover it, after which it can be collected. AT&T has used drafts. In handling its payrolls, for instance, AT&T can pay an employee by draft on Friday. The employee cashes the draft at a local bank, which sends it on to AT&T's New York bank. It may be Wednesday or Thursday before the draft arrives. The bank then sends it to the company's accounting department, which has until 3 P.M. that day to inspect and approve it. Not until then does AT&T deposit funds in its bank to pay the draft. Many insurance companies also use drafts to pay claims.

Using Float. **Float** is defined as the difference between the balance shown in a firm's (or an individual's) checkbook and the balance on the bank's books. Suppose a firm writes checks in the amount of $5,000, on the average, each day. It takes about six days for these checks to clear and to be deducted from the firm's bank account. Thus the firm's own checking account records show a balance $30,000 smaller than the bank's records. If the firm receives checks in the amount of $5,000 daily but loses only four days while these checks are being deposited and cleared, its own books have a balance that is, because of this factor, $20,000 larger than the bank's balance. Thus the firm's net float—the difference between the $30,000 and the $20,000— is $10,000.

If a firm's own collection and clearing process is more efficient than that of the recipients of its checks—and this is generally true of larger, more efficient firms—then the firm could show a *negative* balance on its own records and a *positive* balance on the books of its bank. Some firms indicate that they *never* have true positive cash balances. One large manufacturer of construction equipment stated that, while its account according to its bank's records shows an average cash balance of about $2 million, its *actual* balance is *minus* $2 million; it has $4 million of net

float
The amount of funds tied up in checks that have been written but are still in process and have not yet been collected.

float. Obviously, the firm must be able to forecast its positive and negative clearings accurately in order to make such heavy use of float.

Matching the Costs and Benefits Associated with Cash Management

Although a number of procedures may be used to hold down cash balance requirements, implementing these procedures is not a costless operation. How far should a firm go in making its cash operations more efficient? As a general rule, the firm should incur these expenses so long as marginal returns exceed marginal expenses.

For example, suppose that by establishing a lockbox system and increasing the accuracy of cash inflow and outflow forecasts, a firm can reduce its investment in cash by $1 million without increasing the risk of running short of cash. Furthermore, suppose the firm borrows at a cost of 12 percent. The steps taken have released $1 million, which can be used to reduce bank loans and thus save $120,000 per year. If the costs of the procedures necessary to release the $1 million are less than $120,000, the move is a good one; if the costs exceed $120,000, the greater efficiency is not worth the cost. It is clear that larger firms, with larger cash balances, can better afford to hire the personnel necessary to maintain tight control over their cash positions. Cash management is one element of business operations in which economies of scale are present.

Very clearly, the value of careful cash management depends on the costs of funds invested in cash, which in turn depend on the current rate of interest. Although interest rates have receded from their historic highs of the early 1980s, business firms continue to devote more care than ever to cash management.

Compensating Balances

compensating balances
The required minimum checking account balances that firms must maintain with commercial banks, typically equal to 15 percent of the amount of loans outstanding.

Earlier in the chapter we listed **compensating balance** requirements as one of the major determinants of cash balances. Banks provide services to firms—they clear checks, operate lockbox plans, supply credit information, and the like. These services cost the banks money, so the banks must be compensated for rendering them.

Banks earn most of their income by lending money at interest, and most of the funds they lend are obtained in the form of deposits. If a firm maintains a deposit account with an average balance of $100,000, and if the bank can lend these funds at a net return of $8,000, then the account is, in a sense, worth $8,000 to the bank. Thus it is to the bank's advantage to provide services worth up to $8,000 to attract and hold the account.

Banks determine first the costs of the services rendered to their larger customers and then the average account balances necessary to provide enough income to compensate for these costs. Firms often maintain these compensating balances in order to avoid paying cash service charges to the bank.[1]

Compensating balances are also required by some bank loan agreements. During periods when the supply of credit is restricted and interest rates are high, banks frequently insist that borrowers maintain accounts that average some percentage of the loan amount as a condition for granting the loan; 15 percent is a typical figure. If the balance is larger than the firm would otherwise maintain, then the effective cost of the loan is increased; the excess balance presumably "compensates" the bank for making a loan at a rate below what it could earn on the funds if they were invested elsewhere.[2]

Compensating balances can be established (1) as an *absolute minimum,* say, $100,000, below which the actual balance must never fall, or (2) as a *minimum average balance,* perhaps $100,000, over some period, generally a month. The absolute minimum is a much more restrictive requirement, because the total amount of cash held during the month must be above $100,000 by the amount of the transactions balances. The $100,000 in this case is "dead money" from the firm's standpoint. The minimum average balance, however, could fall to zero one day provided it was $200,000 some other day, with the average working out to $100,000. Thus the $100,000 in this case is available for transactions.

Statistics on compensating balance requirements are not available, but average balances are typical and absolute minimums rare for business accounts. Discussions with bankers, however, indicate that absolute balance requirements are less rare during times of extremely tight money such as during the period 1979 through mid-1982.

Overdraft Systems

Most countries other than the United States use **overdraft systems.** In such systems depositors write checks in excess of their actual balances, and the bank automatically extends loans to cover the shortages. The maximum amount of such loans must, of course, be established beforehand. Although statistics are not available on the usage of overdrafts in the United States, a number of firms have worked out informal, and in some cases formal, overdraft arrangements. (Also, both banks and credit card companies regularly establish "cash reserve" systems for individuals.) Thus the use of overdrafts has been increasing in recent

overdraft systems
Systems wherein depositors may write checks in excess of their balances, with the banks automatically extending loans to cover the shortages.

---

[1]Compensating balance arrangements apply to individuals as well as to business firms. Thus you might get "free" checking services if you maintain a minimum balance of $200, but be charged 10 cents per check if your balance falls below $200 during the month.
[2]The interest rate effect of compensating balances is discussed further in Chapter 13.

years, and if this trend continues, we can anticipate a further reduction of cash balances.

Establishing the Target Cash Balance

target cash balances
The minimum cash balances that firms must maintain to conduct business.

The firm's **target cash balance** is set as the larger of (1) its transactions balances plus precautionary balances or (2) its required compensating balances. Both the transactions balances and the precautionary balances depend on the volume of business the firm does, the degree of uncertainty inherent in its forecasts of cash inflows and outflows, and its ability to borrow on short notice to meet cash shortfalls. Consider again the cash budget shown for Dayton Printing Company in Table 11-1. The target cash balance (or desired cash balance) is shown on Line 13 of the table. Other things held constant, the target cash balance would increase if Dayton expanded or decrease if Dayton contracted. Similarly, Dayton could afford to operate with a smaller target balance if it were more certain that inflows would come in as scheduled and that no unanticipated outflows such as those resulting from uninsured fire losses, lawsuits, and the like would occur. The higher the cash balance, the smaller the probability that reduced inflows or unexpected outflows will cause the firm to actually run out of cash.

Statistics are not available on whether transactions and precautionary balances or compensating balances actually control most firms' target cash balances, but compensating balance requirements do often dominate, especially during periods of high interest rates and tight money.

Cash Management in the Multidivisional Firm

The concepts, techniques, and procedures described thus far in the chapter must be extended when applied to large, national firms. Such corporations have plants and sales offices all across the nation (or the world), and they deal with banks in all of their operating territories. These companies must maintain the required compensating balances in each of their banks, and they must be sure that no bank account becomes overdrawn. Cash inflows and outflows are subject to random fluctuations, so, in the absence of close control and coordination, there would be a tendency for some accounts to have shortages while excess balances existed in others. Thus sound cash management programs for such multibank corporations necessarily include provisions for keeping strict account of the level of funds in each account and for shifting funds between accounts so as to minimize the total corporate cash balance. Mathematical models and electronic connections between a central computer and each branch location have been developed to help with such situations, but a discussion of these topics would go beyond the scope of this book.

THE FINANCIAL SOURCE:

Now it's launching INTERPLEX™ to give you total control of your corporate finances automatically and earlier than ever before.

Manufacturers Hanover establishes the new standard in treasury management systems.

It's early morning as you enter your office and your financial position is waiting for you. In complete detail. Account data from all of your banks has been automatically consolidated within the integrated data base and put into a single standardized format. You're ready to perform transaction verification and account reconciliation. You know hours earlier what investment or bor-

rowing decisions to make. And you quickly realize why INTERPLEX, a fully automated treasury management system, is the industry's new standard.

INTERPLEX from Manufacturers Hanover is the microcomputer-based, multi-user, multi-task treasury management system that gives you more control. Including the ability to automatically collect data from all of your banks. Store it. Process it. Merge it. Use it. Faster.

INTERPLEX lets you conduct target balance analyses, project end of day cash posi-

tion, make cash forecasts, transfer funds, and perform many other treasury functions. Sophisticated yet simple, this system is just the beginning of a family of fully integrated financial management products from Manufacturers Hanover.

State-of-the-art leadership. Backed by a longstanding commitment to innovation. Once again, The Financial Source delivers.

Learn how you can enter the new age of INTERPLEX and gain total control. Automatically. Just contact George Chelius, Vice President, at 1-800-MHT-PLEX.

MH Financial Management Systems, Inc.

⊞ MANUFACTURERS HANOVER
The Financial Source™ Worldwide.

Cash management software systems for computers, such as Interplex from Manufacturers Hanover, are available to financial managers to help them increase the efficiency of cash management.

Source: Courtesy of MH Financial Management Systems, Inc., New York.

Marketable Securities

Sizable holdings of such short-term **marketable securities** as U.S. Treasury bills (T-bills) or bank certificates of deposit (CDs) are often reported on financial statements. The reasons for such holdings, as well as the factors that influence the choice of securities held, are discussed in this section.

Reasons for Holding Marketable Securities

Marketable securities typically provide much lower yields than firms' operating assets; for example, International Business Machines (IBM) recently held a multibillion-dollar portfolio of marketable securities that yielded about 8 percent, while its operating assets provided a return of about 18 percent. Why would a company such as IBM have such large holdings of low-yielding assets? There are two basic reasons for these holdings: first, they serve as a substitute for cash balances, and second, they are used as a temporary investment. These points are considered below.

Marketable Securities as a Substitute for Cash. Some firms hold portfolios of marketable securities in lieu of larger cash balances, liquidating part of the portfolio to increase the cash account when cash outflows exceed inflows. In such situations the marketable securities could be a substitute for transactions balances, precautionary balances, speculative balances, or all three. In most cases the securities are held primarily for precautionary purposes—most firms prefer to rely on bank credit to meet temporary transactions or speculative needs, but to hold some liquid assets to guard against a possible shortage of bank credit.

During the late 1970s IBM had approximately $6 billion in marketable securities. This large liquid balance had been built up as a reserve for possible damage payments resulting from pending antitrust suits. When it became clear that IBM would win most of the suits, the liquidity need declined, and the company spent some of the funds on other assets, including repurchases of its own stock. This is a prime example of a firm's building up its precautionary balances to handle possible emergencies.

Marketable Securities Held as a Temporary Investment. Whenever a firm has over 1 or 2 percent of its total assets invested in marketable securities, chances are good that these funds represent a strictly temporary investment. Such temporary investments generally occur in one of the three situations described below:

1. When the firm must finance seasonal or cyclical operations. Firms engaged in seasonal operations frequently have surplus cash flows during part of the year and deficit cash flows during other months. Such firms may purchase marketable securities during their surplus periods and then liquidate them when cash deficits occur. Other firms, particularly in capital goods industries where fluctuations are violent, attempt to accumulate cash or near-cash securities during downturns in order to be ready to finance increases in assets when business returns to normal.

2. When the firm must meet some known financial requirements. If a major plant construction program is planned for the near future, or if a bond issue is about to mature, a firm may build up its marketable securities portfolio to provide the required funds. Furthermore, marketable securities holdings are frequently large immediately preceding quarterly corporate tax payment dates.

3. When the firm has just sold long-term securities. An expanding firm has to sell long-term securities (stocks or bonds) periodically. The funds from such sales can be invested in marketable securities, which can, in turn, be sold to provide funds as they are needed for permanent investments in operating assets.

Strategies Regarding Marketable Securities Holdings

Actually, each of the needs listed above can be met either by short-term loans or by holding marketable securities. Consider a firm such as Dayton Printing Company, which we discussed above, whose sales are growing over time but are fluctuating on a seasonal basis. As we saw from Dayton's cash budget (Table 11-1), the firm plans to borrow to meet seasonal needs. As an alternative financial strategy, Dayton could hold a portfolio of marketable securities and then liquidate these securities to meet its peak cash needs.

Figure 11-2 illustrates three alternative strategies for a firm such as Dayton. Under Plan A, Dayton would hold no marketable securities, relying completely on bank loans to meet seasonal peaks. Under Plan B, Dayton would stockpile marketable securities during slack periods and then sell these securities to raise funds for peak needs. Plan C is a compromise; under this alternative, the company would hold some securities but not enough to meet all of its peak needs. Dayton actually follows Plan C.

There are advantages and disadvantages to each of these strategies. Plan A is clearly the most risky—the firm's current ratio is always lower than under the other plans, indicating that it might encounter difficulties either in borrowing the funds needed or in repaying the loan. On the other hand, Plan A requires no holdings of low-yielding marketable securities, and this will probably lead to a relatively high expected rate of return on both total assets and net worth.

Figure 11-2
Alternative Strategies for Meeting Seasonal Cash Needs

This figure shows the effects of three different approaches to the use of marketable securities to finance short-term needs for cash. Under Plan A a company holds no marketable securities and relies entirely on bank loans for its short-term cash. Although it may create problems in borrowing funds or repaying loans, Plan A should provide a higher return on total assets and net worth because no funds are locked into low-yielding marketable securities. Under Plan B a company accumulates a large amount of marketable securities that it then sells off to raise cash. This plan avoids borrowing but lowers the company's return on total assets and net worth. The disadvantages of Plans A and B are moderated under Plan C, which uses a combination of marketable securities and short-term loans to finance seasonal cash needs.

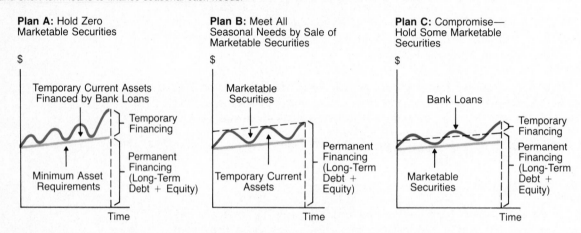

Factors Influencing the Choice of Securities

A wide variety of securities, differing in terms of default risk, interest risk, liquidity risk, and expected rate of return, are available. In this section we first consider the characteristics of different securities, and then we show how the financial manager selects the specific instruments held in the marketable securities portfolio. These same characteristics are, incidentally, as important for individuals' investment decisions as for businesses' decisions.

default risk
The risk that a borrower will not pay the interest or principal on a loan.

Default Risk. The risk that an issuer will be unable to make interest payments, or to repay the principal amount on schedule, is known as *default risk*. If the issuer is the U.S. Treasury, the default risk is negligible; thus Treasury securities are regarded as being default-free. (Treasury securities are not completely free of risk, since U.S. Government bonds are subject to risk due to interest rate fluctuations, and they are also subject to loss of purchasing power due to inflation.) Corporate securities and bonds issued by state and local governments are subject to some degree of default risk. Several organizations (for example, Moody's Investment Service and Standard & Poor's Corporation) "rate" bonds. They classify them on a scale from very high quality to highly speculative with a definite chance of going into default. Ratings change from time to time. Thus Penn Central's securities were given high ratings at one time, but the ratings were lowered as the company's financial position deteriorated.

Interest Rate Risk. We see in Chapter 17 that bond prices vary with changes in interest rates. Furthermore, the prices of long-term bonds are much more sensitive to shifts in interest rates than are prices of short-term securities. Thus, if Dayton's treasurer purchased at par $1 million of 25-year U.S. Government bonds paying 9 percent interest, and if interest rates rose to 13.5 percent, the market value of the bonds would fall from $1 million to approximately $680,000—a loss of over 30 percent.[3] Had 90-day Treasury bills been held, the capital loss resulting from the change in interest rates would have been negligible.

interest rate risk
The risk to which investors are exposed due to changing interest rates.

Purchasing Power Risk. Another type of risk is **purchasing power risk,** or the risk that inflation will reduce the purchasing power of a given sum of money. Purchasing power risk, which is important both to firms and to individual investors during times of inflation, is generally regarded to be lower on assets whose returns can be expected to rise during inflation than on assets whose returns are fixed. Thus real estate and common stocks are thought of as being better "hedges against inflation" than are bonds and other fixed-income securities.

purchasing power risk
The risk that inflation will reduce the purchasing power of a given sum of money.

Liquidity (or Marketability) Risk. An asset that can be sold on short notice for close to its quoted market price is defined as being highly liquid. If Dayton purchases $1 million of infrequently traded bonds of a relatively obscure company such as Bigham Pork Products, it will probably have to accept a price reduction to sell the bonds on short notice. On the other hand, if Dayton buys $1 million worth of U.S. Treasury bonds, or bonds issued by AT&T, General Motors, or Exxon, it will be able to dispose of them almost instantaneously at close to the quoted market price. These latter bonds are said to have very little **liquidity (or marketability) risk.**

liquidity (or marketability) risk
The risk that securities cannot be sold at a reasonable price on short notice.

Returns on Securities. As we know from our earlier study of the security markets, the higher a security's risk, the higher the required return on the security. Thus corporate treasurers, like other investors, must make a trade-off between risk and return when choosing investments for their marketable securities portfolios. Since the liquidity portfolio is generally held for a specific known need or for use in emergencies, the firm might be financially embarrassed should the portfolio

---

[3]These computations are explained in detail in Chapters 14 and 17.

decline in value. Furthermore, most nonfinancial corporations do not have investment departments specializing in appraising securities and determining the probability of their going into default. Accordingly, the marketable securities portfolio is generally confined to highly liquid, short-term securities issued by either the U.S. government or the very strongest corporations. Given the purpose of the securities portfolio, treasurers are unwilling to sacrifice safety for higher rates of return.

Types of Marketable Securities

Any investor wishes to minimize needless risks, but a manager investing temporary excess cash must be especially aware of liquidity risk. The manager has a wide variety of available securities to hold as near cash. These alternatives, both government and nongovernment securities, are discussed next with special emphasis given to liquidity risk. Additionally, Table 11-2 provides a listing of several investment sources, an indication of their suitability as a short-term investment, and an indication of their return.

Table 11-2
Securities Available for Investment of Surplus Cash

Type of Security	Typical Maturity at Time of Issue	Approximate Yield		Appropriate as a Near-Cash Reserve
		June 10, 1977	April 20, 1984	
U.S. Treasury bills	91 days	4.8%	10.13%	Yes
U.S. Treasury bills	1 year	—	10.94	Yes
U.S. Treasury notes	3 to 5 years	6.8	12.12	Questionable
U.S. Treasury bonds	Up to 30 years	7.6	12.62	No
Commercial paper	Varies; up to 270 days	5.5	10.56	Yes
Negotiable certificates of deposit	90 days	6.0	10.34	Yes
Money market mutual funds[a]	Instant liquidity	5.1	9.33	Yes
Eurodollar bank time deposits	Varies; up to 6 months	6.1	10.86	Questionable
Bonds of other corporations[b]	Varies; up to 40 years	8.2	12.79	No
State and local government bonds[c]	Varies; up to 30 years	5.7	9.89	No
Stocks of other corporations	Unlimited	Variable	Variable	No
Stock of the firm in question (Treasury stock)	Unlimited	Variable	Variable	No

[a]Representative yield; actual yields vary from fund to fund.
[b]The rate shown here is for AAA bonds; yields are higher on more risky corporate bonds.
[c]The yield shown here is for AAA long-term municipal bonds. Interest on these bonds is exempt from federal income taxes; thus the 1984 pre-tax equivalent yield on a taxable bond for a taxpayer in the 40 percent tax bracket was 16.48 percent. (Pre-tax equivalent yield = Tax-free rate ÷ (1 − Tax rate) = 9.89% ÷ (1 − .4) = 16.48%.)

Government Securities. The U.S. Treasury and other federal agencies issue a wide variety of securities with various maturities. Treasury bills are an extremely popular outlet for excess funds, in part because Treasury bills have a large and active secondary market to insure liquidity. Additionally, these securities are, as a practical matter, default-free.

Treasury bills are sold at weekly auctions with 13-week (91-day), 26-week (182-day), and 1-year maturities. Alternatively, they can be bought or sold in the secondary market with as little as one day remaining to maturity. Thus the investor has a wide choice of available maturities.

Other government securities with longer maturities are available. Treasury notes are government obligations with maturities of 3 to 5 years. Additionally, Treasury bonds are issued with maturities of up to 30 years. However, due to their long maturities and potentially unstable near-term prices,[4] these longer-term securities may be poor choices as investments for **near-cash reserves.** In addition, U.S. federal agencies, such as the Federal Home Loan Bank and the Federal National Mortgage Association, also issue notes and bonds. These securities are more risky than Treasury issues, since they are not directly backed by the U.S. Treasury. Therefore they yield a slightly higher return than Treasury issues. For example, on April 20, 1984 federal agency bonds yielded 12.92 percent versus 12.63 percent for 10-year Treasury bonds.

near-cash reserves
Reserves that are quickly and easily converted to cash.

Nongovernment Securities

Commercial Paper. Commerical paper is a short-term unsecured promissory note of large, financially stable corporations. Such firms as General Motors Acceptance Corporation, Ford Motor Credit Corporation, and C.I.T. Financial Corporation issue commercial paper regularly.

Maturities on commercial paper range from a few days to 270 days. Few corporations issue commercial paper for more than 270 days since issues with longer maturities must be registered with the Securities and Exchange Commission.

Because only the most creditworthy corporations sell commercial paper, default risk is low. However, there is some liquidity risk since no active secondary market exists for these marketable securities. Therefore most purchasers of commercial paper plan to hold them to maturity. The absence of liquidity thus causes commercial paper usually to sell at a yield above that of comparable Treasury bills.

commercial paper
Unsecured, short-term promissory notes of large firms, usually issued in denominations of $100,000 or more.

---

[4]We describe in Chapter 17 how, as interest rates rise, bond prices fall and, conversely, as interest rates fall, prices rise. Furthermore, the longer the term to maturity, the greater the price change for a given change in interest rates. These factors work against the use of bonds as a temporary store of value, since temporary excess cash should be invested in securities with stable and predictable returns.

Negotiable Certificates of Deposit. Major money-center commercial banks will issue certificates of deposit (CDs) as marketable receipts for large time deposits. These deposits are generally over $100,000 and mature from 1 to 18 months after issuance. The interest paid on these instruments is negotiated and is paid at maturity.

A secondary market for CDs exists, but it is not as well developed as that for Treasury bills. Therefore their yield is generally above Treasury bills but slightly below that of the often less liquid commercial paper.

These securities should not be mistaken for CDs typically purchased by individual small investors. The latter CDs are different from the marketable securities in that their interest is established by the financial institution, rather than negotiated, and these smaller CDs are not marketable.

Money Market Mutual Funds. Money market funds are a popular source of liquidity for both businesses and individuals. These mutual funds hold only short-term securities such as Treasury bills, CDs, and commercial paper. Shares in these funds are easily obtained—often without commissions. Since the required initial investment is small and the liquidity is comparable to lower-yielding checking and savings accounts, the money market funds are a popular temporary investment alternative, especially for smaller firms.

Eurodollar bank time deposits
Interest-bearing time deposits, denominated in U.S. dollars, placed in banks outside the United States.

Eurodollar Bank Time Deposits. Eurodollars are interest-bearing time deposits, denominated in U.S. dollars and placed in banks outside the United States. The term "Eurodollars" may be misleading since banks in Canada, Japan, and the Caribbean are important links in the market.

In many respects the Eurodollar is an international counterpart to the negotiable certificate of deposit. Interest and maturities are negotiated; however, interest on these invested dollars is generally above the CD rate to attract investment. Also, like CDs, there is a secondary market for Eurodollars, but it is still in the developmental stage and not a source of certain liquidity. Default risk is a function of the issuing bank.

Summary

The first topic covered in this chapter was *cash management*. We saw that the key element in any cash management system is the *cash budget*, which is a forecast of cash inflows and outflows during a given planning period. The cash budget shows whether the firm can expect a cash deficit, in which case plans must be made to obtain external capital, or a cash surplus, in which case plans should be made to invest the available funds. We also discussed ways of speeding up cash flows by the use of *lockboxes*, what *float* is and how it can be used to hold down bank loans, and *compensating balances*.

Our study of marketable securities began with a discussion of why securities are held. Primarily, they are held (1) as a reserve for future contingencies, (2) to meet seasonal needs, with holdings being built up during the slack season and then liquidated when cash requirements are high, (3) to meet known future cash requirements such as construction progress payments or taxes, and (4) immediately after the sale of long-term securities. Given the motives for holding them, treasurers generally do not want to gamble by holding risky securities—safety is the watchword, and rarely will a treasurer sacrifice safety for the higher yields offered on risky securities.

Resolution to Decision in Finance

The Race Is to the Slow Payer

Herbert Eames opened a controlled disbursement checking account in Wisconsin in order to slow payments to J. Walter Thompson's creditors. As a result of his decision, JWT gained an average of 1.5 days of additional float—that is, 1.5 days' additional use of its own money.

Large companies find that exploiting float can be extremely lucrative. For example, according to their own reports, National Distillers earns $3,000,000 a year on float, American Brands earns $5,000,000, and Foremost McKesson earns $5,500,000. At 10 percent interest, 1 day's float will gain $200,000, and so on.

To take full advantage of float, many companies open controlled disbursement checking accounts like the one Herbert Eames set up for JWT. This service is now offered by over 130 banks, including most of the big banks in the East. A controlled disbursement account may also be called a "zero-balance account" because it contains no cash at the end of the day, after all checks have been paid.

Each morning the bank tallies the checks presented against a company's controlled disbursement account and notifies the account holder of its total. The company then deposits exactly the amount needed to pay off that day's checks. Because no excess funds remain in the account, the company is free to employ its cash more productively elsewhere.

Although big-city banks may offer controlled disbursement accounts, they usually locate such accounts at a branch in a smaller city. Big-city banks receive too many check deliveries during the day to make the all-important phone call notifying the customer of the needed funds. But banks in small or remote cities usually receive only one delivery of checks per day and can thus perform the required tallying and phoning. Thus Chase Manhattan Bank keeps its controlled disbursement accounts in Syracuse, 240 miles from New York City, and Morgan Guaranty Trust uses a branch in Wilmington, Delaware.

The geographic remoteness of the small banks also adds to the float. A recent study showed that a check drawn on a New York City bank and deposited in a New York City bank took only 1.14 days to clear. But when a similar check was drawn on a Syracuse bank, it had an average clearance time of 1.92 days. The champion remote-pay banks were located in Helena, Montana; Midland, Texas; and Grand Junction, Colorado. Checks drawn on these banks took an average of 3.5 days to clear.

Source: "The Race Is to the Slow Payer," *Fortune*, Apr. 18, 1983, 75–80.

Key Terms   You should be able to define each of the following terms:

Cash

Transactions balances; precautionary
   balances; speculative balances;
   target cash balances; compensating
   balances

Cash budget

Synchronized cash flows

Check clearing

Lockbox plan; float

Overdraft systems

Marketable securities

Default risk

Interest rate risk

Purchasing power risk; liquidity (or
   marketability) risk

Near-cash reserves

Commercial paper; Eurodollar bank
   time deposits

Questions

11-1 What are the two principal reasons for holding cash? Can a firm estimate its target cash balance by summing the cash held to satisfy each of the two reasons?

11-2 Explain how each of the following factors would probably affect a firm's target cash balance if all other factors are held constant.

   a. The firm institutes a new billing procedure which better synchronizes its cash inflows and outflows.

   b. The firm develops a new sales forecasting technique which improves its forecasts.

   c. The firm reduces its portfolio of U.S. Treasury bills.

   d. The firm arranges to use an overdraft system for its checking account.

   e. The firm borrows a large amount of money from its bank, and it also begins to write far more checks than it did in the past.

   f. Interest rates on Treasury bills rise from 5 percent to 10 percent.

11-3 In the cash budget shown in Table 11-1, is the projected maximum funds requirement of $5,200,000 in September known with certainty, or should it be regarded as the expected value of a probability distribution? Consider how this peak would probably be affected by each of the following:
   a. A lengthening of the average collection period.
   b. An unanticipated decline in sales that occurred when sales were supposed to peak.
   c. A sharp drop in sales prices required to meet competition.
   d. A sharp increase in interest rates for a firm with a large amount of short-term debt outstanding.

11-4 Would a lockbox plan make more sense for a firm that makes sales all over the United States or for a firm with the same volume of business but concentrated in one city?

11-5 Would a corporate treasurer be more tempted to invest the firm's liquidity portfolio in long-term as opposed to short-term securities when the yield curve was upward sloping or downward sloping?

11-6 What does the term *liquidity* mean? Which would be more important to a firm that held a portfolio of marketable securities as precautionary balances against the possibility of losing a major lawsuit—liquidity or rate of return? Explain.

11-7 Firm A's management is very conservative, while Firm B's managers are more aggressive. Is it true that, other things the same, Firm B would probably have larger holdings of marketable securities? Explain.

11-8 Is it true that *interest rate risk* refers to the risk that a firm will be unable to pay the interest on its bonds? Explain.

11-9 The curve describing the relationship between interest rates and term to maturity is known as the _____ curve. Other things held constant, how would each of the following factors affect the slope and the general position of this curve? Indicate by a (+) if it would lead to an upward shift in the curve, a (−) if it would cause the curve to shift downward, or a (0) if it would have no effect or an indeterminant effect on the slope or position of the curve.

	Effect on the Yield Curve	
	Slope	Position
a. Investors perceive the risk of default to increase on securities with longer maturities; that is, they become increasingly uncertain about the more distant future.	_____	_____
b. Future interest rates are expected to fall.	_____	_____
c. The Federal Reserve pumps a large amount of money into the banking system.	_____	_____
d. Business firms begin a massive inventory buildup.	_____	_____
e. An inexpensive method of harnessing solar power is developed; this development leads to a decline in the expected rate of inflation.	_____	_____

11-10 Corporate treasurers, when selecting securities for portfolio investments, must make a trade-off between higher risk and higher returns. Is it true that most treasurers are willing to assume a fairly high exposure to risk to gain higher expected returns?

11-11 Assume that the yield curve is horizontal. Now you and other investors receive information that suggests the economy is headed into a recession. You and most other investors think that the Fed will soon relax credit and that this will lead to a decline in short-term interest rates. Over the long run (the next 5, 10, or 15 years) people expect a fairly high rate of inflation, and they expect that this will keep long-term rates fairly high. Explain what all of this will probably do to the yield curve. Use a graph to illustrate your answer.

Problems

11-1 The McShane-Blarney Company is setting up a new bank account with the First National Bank. McShane-Blarney plans to issue checks in the amount of $2,000,000 each day and to deduct them from its own records at the close of business on the day they are written. On average, the bank will receive and clear (that is, deduct from the firm's bank balance) the checks at 5 P.M. the fourth day after they are written. For example, a check written on Monday will be cleared on Friday afternoon. The firm's agreement with the bank requires it to maintain a $1,500,000 average compensating balance; this is $500,000 greater than the cash balance the firm would otherwise have on deposit—that is, without the compensating balance, it would carry an average deposit of $1,000,000.

    a. Assuming that the firm makes deposits at 4 P.M. each day (and the bank includes the deposit in that day's transactions), how much must the firm deposit each day to maintain a sufficient balance on the day it opens the account, during the first 4 days after it opens the account, and once it reaches a "steady state"? (Ignore weekends.)

   * b. What ending daily balance should the firm try to maintain (1) on the bank's records and (2) on its own records?

    c. Explain how net float can help increase the value of the firm's common stock.

11-2 Old Virginia Antique Store had sales of $40,000 in May, and it has forecasted sales for its peak tourist trade season as follows:

Actual:	April	$30,000
	May	40,000
Forecast	June	65,000
	July	90,000
	August	75,000

---

*Refer to Appendix E for check answers to problems with asterisks.

From experience, Old Virginia estimates that 25 percent of sales are for cash, 65 percent of sales are paid after 30 days, 8 percent of sales are paid after 60 days, and 2 percent of sales are uncollectible. Prepare a schedule of cash receipts for the firm's peak season (June through August).

11-3 Strackin, Inc. is scheduling the production of snowmobiles to be sold next season. Orders for the next 5 months are: July, 40,000 units; August, 50,000 units; September, 65,000 units; October, 40,000 units; and November, 20,000 units. Manufacturing costs for materials are $650 per unit, paid 1 month before manufacture. Direct labor costs equal $300 per unit, paid in the month of production. Shipping costs are $120 per unit, paid the month after manufacture. Depreciation expense is allocated on a units-of-production basis of $50 per unit in the month of production. Advertising expense is zero for July and August but will be $200,000 in September and $500,000 in October. Fixed overhead is $300,000 monthly. Taxes of $8 million will be paid at the end of September.

Prepare a schedule of cash disbursements for August through October.

11-4 Rick and Marlo Petteway recently leased space in the Southside Mall and opened a new business, Petteway's Coin Shop. Business has been good, but the Petteways have frequently run out of cash. This has necessitated late payment on certain orders, and this, in turn, is beginning to cause a problem with suppliers. The Petteways plan to borrow from the bank to have cash ready as needed, but first they need a forecast of just how much they must borrow. Accordingly, they have asked you to prepare a cash budget for a critical period around Christmas, when needs will be especially high.

Sales are made on a *cash basis only*. Petteway's purchases must be paid for the following month. The Petteways pay themselves a salary of $4,800 per month, and the rent is $2,000 per month. In addition, the Petteways must make a tax payment of $12,000 in December. The current cash on hand (on December 1) is $400, but the Petteways have agreed to maintain an average bank balance of $6,000—this is their target cash balance. (Disregard till cash, which is insignificant because the Petteways keep only a small amount on hand in order to lessen the chances of robbery.)

The estimated sales and purchases for December, January, and February are shown below. Purchases during November amounted to $140,000.

	Sales	Purchases
December	$160,000	$40,000
January	40,000	40,000
February	60,000	40,000

a. Prepare a cash budget for December, January, and February.
* b. Now suppose the Petteways were to start selling on a credit basis on December 1, giving customers 30 days to pay. All customers accept these terms, and all other facts in the problem are unchanged. What would the company's loan requirements be at the end of December in this case? (Hint: The calculations required to answer this question are minimal.)

11-5 The Taussig Company is planning to request a line of credit from its bank.[5] The following sales forecasts have been made for 1985 and 1986:

May 1985	$ 750,000
June	750,000
July	1,500,000
August	2,250,000
September	3,000,000
October	1,500,000
November	1,500,000
December	375,000
January 1986	750,000

Collection estimates were obtained from the credit and collection department as follows: collected within the month of sale, 5 percent; collected the month following the month of the sale, 80 percent; collected the second month following the month of the sale, 15 percent. Payments for labor and raw materials are typically made during the month following the month in which these costs are incurred. Total labor and raw materials costs are estimated for each month as follows (payments are made the following month):

May 1985	$ 375,000
June	375,000
July	525,000
August	3,675,000
September	1,275,000
October	975,000
November	675,000
December	375,000

General and administrative salaries will amount to approximately $112,500 a month; lease payments under long-term lease contracts will be $37,500 a month; depreciation charges will be $150,000 a month; miscellaneous expenses will be $11,500 a month; income tax payments of $262,500 will be due in both September and December; and a progress payment of $750,000 on a new research laboratory must be paid in October. Cash on hand on July 1 will amount to $550,000, and a minimum cash balance of $375,000 should be maintained throughout the cash budget period.

a. Prepare a monthly cash budget for the last 6 months of 1985.

b. Prepare an estimate of required financing (or excess funds) for each month during the same period, that is, the amount of money that the

---

[5]A line of credit is an agreement that the bank will lend a specified sum of money to the company during a stated time period. Lines of credit are discussed extensively in Chapter 13. Also, note that this problem is adapted from Eugene F. Brigham and Roy L. Crum, *Cases in Managerial Finance*, 5th ed. (Hinsdale, IL: Dryden Press, 1983), Case 5.

Taussig Company will need to borrow (or will have available to invest) each month.

c. Suppose receipts from sales come in uniformly during the month—that is, cash payments come in 1/30th each day—but all outflows are paid on the fifth of the month. Would this have an effect on the cash budget—that is, would the cash budget you have prepared be valid under these assumptions? If not, what could be done to make a valid estimation of financing requirements?

d. Taussig produces on a seasonal basis, just ahead of sales. Without making any calculations, discuss how the company's current ratio and debt ratio would vary during the year, assuming all financial requirements are met by short-term bank loans. Could changes in these ratios affect the firm's ability to obtain bank credit?

e. Now suppose a recession occurs, and sales fall below the forecasted, or budgeted, levels. However, the firm continues production according to the indicated plans. Also, because of the recession, customers delay payments, so the lag between sales and collections lengthens. What would all this do to the realized cash surpluses and deficits and to the external funds requirements?

f. If you prepared the cash budget in Part a correctly, you show a surplus of $426,000 at the end of July. Suggest some alternative investments for this money. Be sure to consider long-term bonds versus short-term debt instruments, and the appropriateness of investing in common stock.

g. Would your choice of securities in Part f be affected if the cash budget showed continuous cash surpluses versus alternating surpluses and deficits?

＊ 11-6 Suppose the interest rate on 1-year Treasury bills purchased today (January 1, 1985) is 12 percent. You and other investors anticipate that a recession is on the horizon and that the T-bill rate will fall to 10 percent next year (January 1, 1986) and to 8 percent the following year (January 1, 1987). Your best guess as to T-bill rates from January 1, 1988 on is 9 percent, which is based on an expected long-term inflation rate of 7 percent and a 2 percent real risk-free interest rate. Assuming that the expectations theory holds exactly, what is the approximate equilibrium interest rate for **(a)** 5-year Treasury bonds and **(b)** 10-year Treasury bonds?

Selected References

Some key references on cash management include the following:

Baumol, William J., "The Transactions Demand for Cash: An Inventory Theoretic Approach," *Quarterly Journal of Economics*, November 1952, 545–556.

Daellenbach, Hans G., "Are Cash Management Optimization Models Worthwhile?" *Journal of Financial and Quantitative Analysis*, September 1974, 607–626.

Emery, Gary W., "Some Empirical Evidence on the Properties of Daily Cash Flow," *Financial Management*, Spring 1981, 21–28.

Gitman, Lawrence J., D. Keith Forrester, and John R. Forrester, Jr., "Maximizing Cash Disbursement Float," *Financial Management*, Summer 1976, 15–24.

Gitman, Lawrence J., E. A. Moses, and I. T. White, "An Assessment of Corporate Cash Management Practices," *Financial Management*, Spring 1979, 32–41.

Maier, Steven F., David W. Robinson, and James H. Vander Weide, "A Short-Term Disbursement Forecasting Model," *Financial Management*, Spring 1981, 9–20.

Maier, Steven F., and James H. Vander Weide, "A Practical Approach to Short-Run Financial Planning," *Financial Management*, Winter 1978, 10–16.

Miller, Merton H., and Daniel Orr, "A Model of the Demand for Money by Firms," *Quarterly Journal of Economics*, August 1966, 413–435.

Mullins, David Wiley, Jr., and Richard B. Homonoff, "Applications of Inventory Cash Management Models," in *Modern Developments in Financial Management*, ed. Stewart C. Myers (New York: Praeger, 1976).

Stone, Bernell K., and Robert A. Wood, "Daily Cash Forecasting: A Simple Method for Implementing the Distribution Approach," *Financial Management*, Fall 1977, 40–50.

For more on the term structure of interest rates, see Chapter 5 and:

Van Horne, James C., *Financial Markets and Flows*, 2nd ed. (Englewood Cliffs, NJ: Prentice-Hall, 1984).

Accounts Receivable and Inventories

12

Decision in Finance

The King of Scrap Mountain

In the course of his 43-year career, John W. Bowman has bought over 21 million tons of ferrous scrap. As executive vice president of Northwestern Steel & Wire, Bowman's job is to get the scrap that feeds the company's electric furnaces, the largest in the world.

Despite his many years in the business, Bowman's eyes still light up when he talks about scrap. Due to the extraordinary volatility of the scrap market, Bowman sees his job as a constant challenge. Once, for example, the price for No. 1 heavy melting scrap rose by 74 percent over only 7 months' time. At other times prices have dropped by as much as 50 percent in 1 year.

Many factors affect the price of scrap. The most important is demand. A strong demand for steel translates directly into a strong demand for scrap and sends prices zooming. Sometimes one steel producer, worried about running out of raw materials, will begin buying huge quantities of scrap, thus single-handedly bidding the price up. At other times foreign buyers increase the demand, causing fears among domestic buyers that the United States may one day suffer a permanent shortage.

In the midst of all this uncertainty, Bowman enjoys a strategic advantage stemming from a decision that Northwestern made in the 1950s. Back then the company decided to maintain a high level of raw materials inventory at all times. As a result Bowman can always negotiate from a position of strength.

As you read this chapter, look for reasons that support Northwestern's decision to stockpile inventory. What are the advantages and disadvantages of this policy? Should other scrap consumers follow Northwestern's lead?

See end of chapter for resolution.

289

In the last chapter we examined the firm's investment in cash and marketable securities. To complete our analysis of current assets, we now turn to accounts receivable and inventories. The typical manufacturing firm has approximately 20 percent of its total financing invested in receivables and another 20 percent invested in inventory. With such a large percentage of its funds tied up in these two accounts, the effectiveness with which they are managed is obviously important to a firm's profitability and risk, and thus to its stock price.

Accounts Receivable

account receivable
A balance due from a debtor on a current account.

Most firms sell on credit. When goods are shipped, inventories are reduced, and an **account receivable** is created in the seller's accounting ledger.[1] Eventually, the customer will pay the account, at which time receivables will decline and cash will increase.

The total amount of accounts receivable outstanding at any given time is determined by two factors: (1) the volume of credit sales and (2) the average length of time between sales and collection. In other words, the level of accounts receivable is equal to the credit sales per day multiplied by the number of days in the collection period. Both of these factors are influenced by a set of controllable factors which comprise the firm's *credit policy*.

Credit Policy

credit policy
Basic decisions that determine a firm's credit period, credit standards, collection procedures, and discounts.

The success or failure of a business depends to a large extent on its level of sales. As a rule, the higher the sales volume, the greater the profits and the healthier the firm. Sales, in turn, depend on a number of factors, some of which are controllable by the firm. The major controllable variables which affect sales are sales price, product quality, advertising, and **credit policy**.

The credit manager has the responsibility for administering the firm's credit policy. However, because of the pervasive importance of credit, the credit policy itself is established by the executive committee, which usually consists of the president and the vice presidents in charge of finance, marketing, and production. If the credit policy is *eased* by lengthening the credit period, by relaxing credit standards, by following a less tough collection policy, or by offering cash discounts, then sales should increase: *easing the credit policy stimulates sales*. However, if the credit policy is eased and sales do rise, then costs will also rise because more labor, more materials, and so on will be required to

---

[1]Actually two accounts are created by a credit sale—an asset item entitled *account receivable* appears on the books of the seller, and a liability item called *account payable* appears on the books of the purchaser. In Chapter 13 we consider payables relative to other sources of funds.

produce more goods. Thus the basic question that credit policy makers must answer is this: will sales revenues rise more than costs, causing net income to increase, or will the increase in sales revenues be more than offset by higher costs?

The basic point of credit policy analysis is to provide an answer to the preceding question, and the basic approach employed is called **incremental analysis**. In incremental analysis we attempt to determine the increase or decrease in both sales and costs associated with a given easing or tightening of the credit policy. The difference between incremental sales and incremental costs is defined as **incremental profit.** If the expected incremental profit is positive, then the proposed credit policy change is a good one.

Incremental analysis is not a difficult concept, but care must be taken to insure that all the relevant costs and benefits of a proposed change are considered. Generally, a credit policy change will affect these variables: (1) sales, (2) production costs associated with a higher or lower sales volume, (3) bad debt losses, (4) discount expenses, (5) level of accounts receivable, hence the cost of the capital tied up in receivables, (6) costs of administering the credit department, and (7) collection expenses. It is far from easy to estimate these factors. For example, to estimate the effect on sales of a given credit policy change requires a knowledge not only of how customers will respond but also of how the firm's competitors will react. Similarly, to estimate the effects on production costs involves a consideration of both variable costs per unit of output and the firm's capacity situation—incremental production costs will be far different if the firm is currently operating at full capacity than if excess capacity exists.

A firm's credit policy consists of four elements:
1. The *credit period*, which is the length of time for which credit is granted.
2. The *credit standards*, which refers to the minimum financial strength of acceptable credit customers.
3. The firm's *collection policy*, which is measured by its toughness or laxity in following up on slow-paying accounts.
4. Any *discounts* given for early payment.

Credit Period

Lengthening the **credit period** stimulates sales, but there is a cost to tying up funds in receivables. For example, if a firm changes its terms from net 30 to net 60, the average receivables for the year might rise from $100,000 to $300,000, with the $200,000 increase caused partly by the longer credit terms and partly by the larger volume of sales. If the cost of capital needed to finance the investment in receivables is 8 percent, then the marginal cost of lengthening the credit period is $200,000

incremental analysis
An analysis to determine the increase or decrease in both sales and costs associated with a given easing or tightening of a credit policy.

incremental profit
The difference between incremental sales and incremental costs.

credit period
The length of time for which credit is granted.

Industry Practice

How to Spot a Professional Debtor

In the 12 months ending June 30, 1983, more than 95,000 American businesses declared bankruptcy, according to the bankruptcy division of the Administrative Office of the U.S. Courts. Most of those companies were simply unable to pay their debts. But some were in business for the sole purpose of going out of business.

In such bankruptcy operations, a company orders great amounts of merchandise, sells it at enormous discounts before paying for it, and then files for bankruptcy. The bankruptcy operator thus obtains merchandise free, and when it is sold, every cent is profit. Such professional debtors cost businesses millions of dollars nationally. No legitimate company, however large or small, is immune, but there are precautions that business people can take.

The first: Be wary of strangers. Background checks are easy to make when a company places an order, and such an investigation can save a firm a lot of money if it reveals that the company asking for credit is run by people with shady pasts.

However, good performance on a credit check is not always indicative of a solid company. Before they strike, bankruptcy operators establish accounts with many companies and pay their bills promptly. Sometimes they pay their bills for more than a year. As their credit improves with each payment, they increase the size of their orders. This gradually sets up their creditors for big, juicy orders—for which the operators will never pay.

Something else to watch for: A big rush order from a company you are unfamiliar with. Often the purchasing agent will act as though he is worried that you are not big enough or responsible enough to handle the order. This plants the idea that you are dealing with an important outfit, potentially a major account. It also makes you eager to prove that you are a first-rate company by shipping the order to the customer fast (before you take time to check the credit rating).

A bulk purchase of a single item by a small firm is another warning sign. Retailers who plan to stay around a long time usually buy a variety of items in order to attract repeat customers. But bankruptcy operators want a few very popular items that will move fast when sold at a hefty discount. They prefer color television sets to staplers, CB radios to car radios.

Even when such bulk orders come from old customers with blue-ribbon credit ratings, that means nothing if the old customer is a company under new ownership. One of the favorite tactics of bankruptcy operators is to buy an old, respected company, then use it to rip off established suppliers. The good record of such a company provides a cover so the swindlers can operate their scam longer than would otherwise be possible.

Another tip-off: If the purchaser sounds strangely reassuring that you will be paid promptly, it is often an indication that you are not going to be paid at all. Any mention of the purchaser's bank account by the purchaser is a similar reason to be wary. After all, how often does your average customer happen to mention the size, condition, or location of his account?

If you happen to drop by a customer's store and see that prices are abnormally low, that is another signal. For example, if merchandise is being sold below the wholesale price you charged for it, the store's owner is a crook or a poor business person or has discovered some new tax angle that you definitely should inquire about.

Beware of the friendly stall. Operators who write polite letters informing you that they are unable to pay their bills on time due to unforeseen circumstances and who ask for your understanding can often extend their scam for months longer. While you are waiting patiently for your financially troubled but apparently honest customer to pay his bill (maybe he even makes a few token payments), he may be ordering more and more merchandise on credit from other suppliers.

Watch out for high living by your customer. If the customer's company is growing fast enough to place even larger orders, the firm should be strapped for cash. So if its owner is driving around in a new Cadillac and telling time by an Omega wristwatch, something may be wrong. (A truly professional operator seldom makes this mistake.)

Be wary if you learn that a customer is transferring the assets but not the liabilities of Company A to Company B, planning to declare Company A bankrupt while retaining ownership (through Company B) of the goods for which the debts were originally incurred. This is perhaps the most popular ripoff with operators who plan to continue doing business in the same location for a long time. It is, fortunately, an easier form of fraud to prove than many others.

Be suspicious if a debtor you believe is an operator tells you that he has declared his company bankrupt. An operator can buy time by informing creditors that he has already declared bankruptcy when in fact he has not. Check with the nearest federal bankruptcy court.

Professional debtors generally run their scams to the very end, selling goods at enormous discounts even while their creditors are screaming to the police and the district attorney. When the end comes, it is usually in the form of an involuntary bankruptcy pressed by creditors to force them out of business.

If you suspect that you are being ripped off by a bankruptcy operator, be careful about the steps you take next. The presumed operator may be nothing more than an honest man or woman with poor business ability. There are many more of them around than there are con artists. But if you have actually stumbled onto a real pro, you must handle the situation with great care. Professional debtors know every trick, every legal loophole, every tactic and advantage that might help them. Or they hire lawyers who do.

Never threaten a debtor. Even though you are in the right, an operator may turn those threats against you, suing you for libel, slander, or even extortion. If you feel a debtor is crooked, do not speak to him, speak to your lawyer.

But your best protection against operators is prevention. Being wary—and taking time to investigate before granting credit—is simple and may save you a lot of money.

Source: From "How to Spot a Bankruptcy Swindle" by David Braly. Reprinted by permission from Nation's Business, October 1983. Copyright 1983, Chamber of Commerce of the United States.

× 8% = \$16,000. If the incremental profit—sales price minus all direct production, selling, and credit costs associated with the additional sales—exceeds \$16,000, then the change in credit policy is profitable. Determining the optimal credit period involves locating that period where marginal profits on increased sales are exactly offset by the costs of carrying the higher amount of accounts receivable.

Credit Standards

If a firm makes credit sales only to the strongest of customers, it will never have bad debt losses, nor will it incur much in the way of expenses for its credit department. On the other hand, it will probably be losing sales, and the profit forgone on these lost sales could be far larger than the costs it has avoided. Determining the optimal **credit standards** involves equating the marginal costs of credit to the marginal profits on the increased sales.

credit standards
Standards that stipulate the minimum financial strength of acceptable credit customers.

Marginal costs include production and selling costs, but we may abstract from these at this point and consider only those costs associated with the "quality" of the marginal accounts, or *credit quality costs*. These costs include (1) default, or bad debt losses, (2) higher investigation and collection costs, and (3) higher costs of capital tied up in receivables whenever selling to less creditworthy customers, who pay their accounts more slowly, causes the average collection period to lengthen. In the next section we first discuss the components of an optimal credit standard and then show, in Appendix 12A, how a company might construct such a standard.

Measuring Credit Quality. A key element in setting credit standards relates to the factors that determine the likelihood that a given customer will pay slowly or even end up as a bad debt loss. This is called *measuring credit quality.* To begin the analysis, we need to define *credit quality.* Perhaps the best way is in terms of the probability of default. These probability estimates are, for the most part, subjective estimates, but credit evaluation is a well-established practice, and a good credit manager can make reasonably accurate judgments of the probability of default by different classes of customers. To evaluate credit risk, credit managers consider the **five C's of credit:** character, capacity, capital, collateral, and conditions:

five C's of credit
Factors used to evaluate credit risk: character, capacity, capital, collateral, and conditions.

1. *Character* refers to the probability that customers will *try* to honor their obligations. This factor is of considerable importance, because every credit transaction implies a *promise* to pay. Will debtors make an honest effort to pay their debts, or are they likely to try to get away with something? Experienced credit managers frequently insist that the moral factor is the most important issue in a credit evaluation.
2. *Capacity* is a subjective judgment of customers' ability to pay. It is gauged by their past records, supplemented by physical observation of customers' plants or stores, and by their business methods.

3. *Capital* is measured by the general financial position of firms as indicated by a financial ratio analysis, with special emphasis on the risk
ratios—the debt/assets ratio, the current ratio, and the times-interest-
earned ratio.

4. *Collateral* is represented by assets that customers may offer as security to obtain credit.

5. *Conditions* refers to the impact of general economic trends or to special developments in certain geographic regions or sectors of the economy that may affect customers' ability to meet their obligations.

The five C's of credit represent the factors by which the credit risks
are judged. Information on these items is obtained from the firm's previous experience with customers, supplemented by a well-developed
system of information-gathering groups. Two major sources of external
information are available. The first is the work of the *credit associations*,
local groups which meet frequently and correspond with one another
to exchange information on credit customers. These local groups have
also banded together to create Credit Interchange, a system developed
by the National Association of Credit Management for assembling and
distributing information about debtors' past performances. The interchange reports show the paying records of different debtors, the industries from which they are buying, and the trading areas in which
purchases are being made.

The second source of external information is the work of the credit-
reporting agencies, which collect credit information and sell it for a fee;
the best known of these agencies are Dun & Bradstreet (D&B) and
TRW, Inc. D&B, TRW, and other agencies provide factual data that can
be used in credit analysis; they also provide ratings similar to those
available on corporate bonds.

Modern credit managers practice "management by exception". Under such a system, customers are first classified into five or six categories according to degree of risk, and then the credit manager concentrates time and attention on the weakest customers. For example, the
following classes might be established:

Risk Class	Percentage of Uncollectible Credit Sales	Percentage of Customers in This Class
1	0–1/2%	60%
2	1/2–2	20
3	2–5	10
4	5–10	5
5	Over 10	5

Firms in Class 1 might be extended credit automatically, and their
credit status reviewed only once a year. Those in Class 2 might also
receive credit (up to specified limits) automatically, but a ratio analysis
of these firms' financial condition would be conducted more frequently

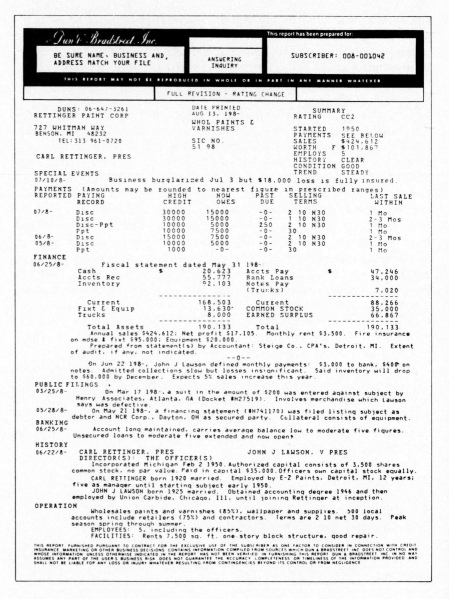

Credit reporting agencies (such as Dun & Bradstreet) compile and sell reports on specific companies; in this example, on Rettinger Paint Corporation. These reports provide a credit rating (in top right corner) as well as factual information on the company's current financial status, public record of legal activities, banking, company history, and a brief description of the business.

Source: Reprinted by permission of Dun & Bradstreet Credit Services, a company of Dun & Bradstreet Corporation.

(perhaps quarterly), and they would be moved down to Class 3 if their position deteriorated. Specific approvals might be required for credit sales to Classes 3 and 4, while sales to Class 5 might be on a COD (cash on delivery) basis only.

Managing such a system requires fast, accurate, up-to-date information, and to help get such information, the National Association of Credit Management (a group with 43,000 member firms) persuaded TRW to develop a computer-based, fully automated data retrieval system. Such a system is now in operation, and teletype credit reports are available within minutes. While Dun & Bradstreet's reports are more complete, they come in more slowly, through the U.S. mail. A typical credit report would include the following pieces of information:

1. A summary balance sheet and income statement.

2. A number of key ratios, with trend information.

3. Information obtained from the firm's suppliers telling whether the firm has been paying promptly or slowly or has failed to make payments.

4. A verbal description of the physical condition of the firm's operations.

5. A verbal description of the backgrounds of the firm's owners, including any previous bankruptcies, lawsuits, and the like.

6. A summary rating, going from A+ for the best credits down to F for those who are most likely to default.

Although a great deal of credit information is available, it must still be processed in a judgmental manner. The data and information systems can assist in making better credit decisions, but, in the final analysis, credit decisions are really exercises in informed judgment.

Collection Policy

Collection policy refers to the procedures the firm follows to collect past-due accounts. For example, a letter may be sent to such accounts when the bill is 10 days past due; a more severe letter, followed by a telephone call, may be used if payment is not received within 30 days; and the account may be turned over to a collection agency after 90 days.

collection policy
Procedures that a firm follows to collect past-due accounts.

The collection process can be expensive in terms of both out-of-pocket expenditures and lost goodwill, but at least some firmness is needed to prevent an undue lengthening in the collection period and to minimize outright losses. Again, a balance must be struck between the costs and benefits of different collection policies.

Cash Discounts

Cash discounts are often proposed as a means to encourage early payments. For example, Judy-Rose Fashions might decide to change its credit terms from 30 days (net 30) to allow a 2 percent discount if payment is received within 10 days (stated "2/10, net 30"). This change should produce two benefits: (1) it would attract new customers who consider discounts a type of price reduction, and (2) the discounts would cause a reduction in the average collection period, since some old customers would pay more promptly in order to take advantage of the discount. Offsetting these benefits is the dollar cost of the dis-

cash discount
A reduction in price given for early payment.

counts taken. The optimal discount is established at the point where the costs and benefits are exactly offsetting.

seasonal dating
Procedure which creates an invoice date during the purchaser's selling season, regardless of when the merchandise was shipped, to induce customers to buy early.

If sales are seasonal, a firm may use **seasonal dating** on discounts. For example, Jenson, Inc. is a swimsuit manufacturer which sells on terms of 2/10, net 30, May 1 dating. This means that the effective invoice date is May 1, so the discount may be taken until May 10, or the full amount must be paid on May 30, regardless of when the sale was made. If Jenson produces throughout the year but retail sales of bathing suits are concentrated in the spring and early summer, then offering seasonal datings may induce some customers to stock up early, saving Jenson storage costs and also "nailing down sales."

Profit Potential in Carrying Accounts Receivable

Thus far we have emphasized the costs of carrying receivables. *However, if it is possible to sell on credit and also to assess a carrying charge on the receivables that are outstanding, then credit sales can actually be more profitable than cash sales.* This is especially true for consumer durables (automobiles, appliances, clothing, and so on), but it is also true for certain types of industrial equipment. Thus the General Motors Acceptance Corporation (GMAC) unit, which finances automobiles, is highly profitable, as is Sears, Roebuck's credit subsidiary. Some encyclopedia companies are even reported to lose money on cash sales but to more than make up these losses from carrying charges on their credit sales; obviously, such companies would rather sell on credit than for cash!

The carrying charges on outstanding credit are generally about 18 percent on an annual interest rate basis ($1\frac{1}{2}\%$ per month, so $1.5\% \times 12 = 18\%$). Until the early 1980s, when short-term interest rates rose to unprecedented levels, having receivables outstanding that earned 18 percent was highly profitable.

How Effective Is the Firm's Credit Policy?

It is apparent from the preceding sections that the optimal credit policy, hence the optimal level of accounts receivable, depends on the firm's own unique operating conditions. Thus a firm with excess capacity and low variable production costs should extend credit more liberally and carry a higher level of accounts receivable than a firm operating at full capacity. However, in spite of the individualized nature of the credit management process, it is still useful to analyze the effectiveness of the firm's credit policy in an overall, aggregate sense.

As we saw in connection with the Du Pont analysis, an excessive investment in any asset account will lead to a low rate of return on net worth. For comparative purposes, we can examine the firm's accounts receivable turnover ratio (sales/receivables) both over time and against the industry average turnover, or we can focus on the average collection period as discussed in Chapter 7.

In Chapter 7 we saw that Carter Chemical Company's average collection period was 42 days, compared to an industry average of 36 days. If Carter lowered its average collection period by 6 days to 36 days, this would mean a reduction of $8,333,333 × 6 = $49,999,998 in the amount of capital tied up in receivables. If the cost of funds tied up in receivables is 10 percent, this would mean a savings of $5 million per year, other things held constant.

The average collection period can also be compared to Carter's credit terms. Carter typically sells on terms of 1/10, net 30, so its customers, on average, are not paying their bills on time: the 42-day average collection period is greater than the 30-day credit period. Note, however, that some of the customers could be paying within 10 days to take advantage of the discount, while others could be taking much longer than 42 days to pay. To check against this possibility, we use the **aging schedule,** which breaks down accounts receivable according to how long they have been outstanding. Carter's aging schedule is shown below:

aging schedule
A report showing how long accounts receivable have been outstanding; it gives the percentage of receivables now past due and the percentage past due in specific past periods.

Age of Account (Days)	Percent of Total Value of Accounts Receivable
0–10	52%
11–30	20
31–45	13
46–60	4
Over 60	11
Total	100%

Most of the accounts pay on schedule or after only a slight delay, but a significant number are over a month past due. This indicates that even though the average collection period is close to the 30-day credit period, Carter has quite a bit of capital tied up in slow-paying accounts, some of which may eventually result in losses.

Management analyzes the firm's average collection period and its aging schedule in comparison with industry averages, recent trends, and the firm's credit terms to see how effectively the credit department is operating. If the average collection period is much longer than the terms of the sale, and if the aging schedule shows a significant percentage of past-due accounts, then the credit standards may be too low, the credit manager may not be enforcing the standards closely enough, or the collection policy may be too lax. In any event, these tools are useful for reviewing the credit manager's performance.

Investors—both stockholders and bank loan officers—should pay close attention to accounts receivable management; otherwise they could be misled by the current financial statements and later suffer serious losses on their investments. When a sale is made, the following events occur: (1) inventories are reduced by the cost of goods sold, (2) accounts receivable are increased by the sales price, and (3) the difference is recorded as a profit. If the sale is for cash, the profit is definitely earned, but if the sale is on credit, the profit is not actually earned unless and until the account is collected. Firms have been known to encourage "sales" to very weak customers in order to inflate reported profits. This could boost the stock price, at least until credit losses begin to lower earnings, at which time the stock price falls. An analysis along the lines suggested above would detect any such questionable practice, as well as any unconscious deterioration in the quality of accounts receivable. Such early detection could help both investors and bankers avoid losses.

Inventory Management

Inventories, which may be classified as (1) *raw materials*, (2) *work-in-process*, and (3) *finished goods*, are an essential part of most business operations. Like accounts receivable, inventory levels depend heavily on sales. However, whereas receivables build up *after* sales have been made, inventories must be acquired *ahead* of sales. This is a critical difference, and the necessity of forecasting sales before establishing target inventory levels makes **inventory management** a difficult task.

inventory management
The balancing of a set of costs that increase with larger inventory holdings with a set of costs that decrease with larger order size.

In part, inventory policy is determined by the economics of the firm's industry; thus retailers have large stocks of finished goods, but little, if any, raw materials or work-in-process. Moreover, the inventory policies of firms in a given industry can vary widely—inventory policy is very much subject to discretionary decisions.

No single executive establishes inventory policy. Rather, the firm's inventory policy is set by its executive committee, since production, marketing, and financial people all have a stake in inventory management. The production manager is concerned with raw materials inventory to insure continuous production; he or she has direct control over the length of the production process, which influences work-in-process inventories, and is vitally concerned with whether the firm produces on a smooth, continuous basis throughout the year, stockpiling finished goods inventories for seasonal sales, or produces irregularly in response to orders. The marketing manager wants the firm to hold large stocks of inventories to insure rapid deliveries—this will make it easier to close sales. The financial manager is concerned with the level of inventories because of the effects excessive inventories have on profitability: (1) inventories reduce the total assets utilization ratio, and (2) there are substantial costs of carrying inventories, so excessive inventories erode the profit margin.

Through the accounting staff the financial manager maintains all records relating to inventories, and in this capacity he or she is responsible for establishing information systems to monitor inventory usage and to replenish stocks as necessary. This information system is not complex in a single-product, single-plant firm, but in most modern corporations the inventory control process is as complex as it is important. Visualize an automobile or an appliance manufacturer, with thousands of dealers stocking hundreds of styles and colors of various automobiles, stoves, or refrigerators, and also thousands of spare parts, all across the country. Production must be geared both to stocks on hand and to sales levels, and any mistake can result either in excessive stocks (which will lose value when the new models appear) or in lost sales. Grocery stores, department stores, plumbing manufacturers, textbook publishers, and most other firms are faced with similar problems.

In recent years computer technology, high-speed data transmission techniques, and operations research methods have all been used to improve the efficiency of inventory control. Although the techniques are far too diverse and complicated for a complete treatment in this book, the financial manager should be prepared to make use of the contributions of specialists who have developed effective procedures for minimizing the investment in inventory.

Illustrative of the techniques at the practical level is Allied Electronics' system, which works as follows. Tabulator cards are inserted in each package of five electronic tubes leaving Allied's warehouse. As the merchandise is sold, the distributor collects the cards and files the replacement order without doing paper work. He or she simply sends in the cards, which are identified by account number, type of merchandise, and price of the units ordered. Western Union Telegraph Company equipment accepts the punched cards and transmits information on them to the warehouse, where it is duplicated on other punched cards. A typical order of 5,000 tubes of varying types can be received in about 17 minutes, assembled in about 90 minutes, and delivered to Boston's Logan Airport in an additional 45 minutes. Orders from 3,000 miles away can be delivered within 24 hours, a saving of 13 days in some cases.

Information on the order also goes into a computer which keeps on file stock-on-hand data for each item. When an order draws the stock down below the *order point,* this triggers action in the production department—additional units of the item are then manufactured for stock. In the next section we examine both the optimal order point and the number of units that should be manufactured, which is called the *economic ordering quantity* (EOQ).

Inventory Models

Inventories are obviously necessary, but it is equally obvious that a firm will suffer if it has too much or too little inventory. How can one determine the *optimal* inventory level? One commonly used approach to determining optimal levels is the *Economic Ordering Quantity (EOQ) Model,* which is described in this section.

We begin the EOQ analysis by noting that the inventory of any item consists of a *working stock* and a *safety stock*. The working stock depends on the pattern of inflows and outflows, while the safety stock is designed to guard against unexpectedly high demand, delays in receiving shipments, or both. In this section we first analyze optimal working balances, then go on to look at safety stocks.

Figure 12-1 illustrates the basic premise on which inventory theory is built. First, we should recognize that the average investment in inventories depends on how frequently orders are placed and the size of each order—if we order every day, average inventories will be much smaller than if we order once a year. Furthermore, as Figure 12-1 shows, some of the firm's costs rise with larger orders: included here are warehousing costs, interest on funds tied up in inventory, insurance, and obsolescence. Other costs decline with larger orders and in-

Figure 12-1
Determination of the Optimal Order Quantity
To avoid the problems that may arise from carrying too much or too little inventory, a business must determine the optimal quantity of a product to purchase each time an order is placed. As this figure shows, carrying costs rise steadily as order size increases; ordering costs, on the other hand, decline with larger order sizes. The sum of these two curves is the total cost curve, and the lowest point on that curve is the optimal order size, or economic ordering quantity.

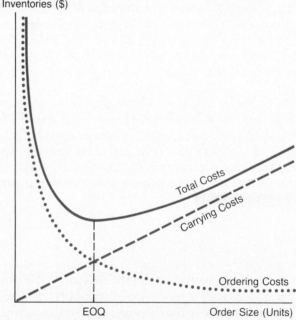

ventories: for example, lost profits on sales not made because of short-ages and the cost of production interruptions caused by inadequate inventories. If these two curves are added, the sum represents the total cost of ordering and holding inventories. The point where the total cost curve is minimized represents the **economic ordering quantity (EOQ),** which is the optimal order quantity.

It can be shown that, under certain reasonable assumptions, the or-der quantity that minimizes the total cost curve in Figure 12-1, or the EOQ, can be found by the use of this formula:[2]

$$EOQ = \sqrt{\frac{2FS}{CP}} . \qquad \text{(12-1)}$$

Here

> EOQ = the economic ordering quantity, or the optimal
> quantity to be ordered each time an order is placed,
> F = fixed costs of placing and receiving an order,
> S = annual sales in units,
> C = carrying cost expressed as a percentage of inventory value,
> P = purchase price per unit of inventory.

The assumptions of the **economic ordering quantity (EOQ) model,** which will be relaxed shortly, include the following: (1) sales can be forecast perfectly, (2) sales are evenly distributed throughout the year, and (3) orders are received with no delays whatever.

To illustrate the EOQ model, consider the following data, supplied by Romantic Books, Inc., publisher of the classic novel *Madame Boudoir:*

> S = sales = 26,000 copies per year,
> C = carrying cost = 20 percent of inventory value,[3]
> P = purchase price per book to Romantic Books from a printing
> company = $6.1538 per copy (the sales price is $9, but this is
> irrelevant for our purposes),
> F = fixed cost per order = $1,000 (the bulk of this cost is the labor
> cost for setting the plates on the presses, as well as for setting
> up the binding equipment for the production run; the printer
> bills this cost separately from the $6.1538 cost per copy).

economic ordering quantity (EOQ)
The optimal (least-cost) quantity of inventory that should be ordered.

economic ordering quantity (EOQ) model
Formula for determining the order quantity that minimizes the total inventory cost: EOQ = $\sqrt{2FS/CP}$.

---

[2]The EOQ model is derived in Eugene F. Brigham, *Financial Management: Theory and Practice,* 3rd ed. (Hinsdale, IL: Dryden Press, 1982), Appendix 8A.

[3]In an unpublished study the U.S. Department of Commerce estimated that, on the av-erage, manufacturing firms have an annual cost of carrying inventories that equals 25 percent of original inventory cost. This percentage is broken down as follows: obsoles-cence, 8 percent; physical depreciation, 4 percent; interest, 9 percent; handling, 2.50 percent; property taxes, 0.50 percent; insurance, 0.25 percent; storage, 0.75 percent.

Substituting these data into Equation 12-1, we obtain

$$EOQ = \sqrt{\frac{2FS}{CP}}$$

$$= \sqrt{\frac{(2)(1,000)(26,000)}{(0.2)(6.1538)}}$$

$$= \sqrt{42,250,316}$$

$$= 6,500 \text{ copies.}$$

Average inventory holdings depend directly on the EOQ; this relationship is illustrated graphically in Figure 12-2. Immediately after an order is received, 6,500 copies are in stock. The usage rate, or sales rate, is 500 copies per week (26,000/52 weeks), so inventories are drawn down by this amount each week. Thus the actual number of units held in inventory will vary from 6,500 books just after an order is received to zero just before an order arrives. On average, the number of units held will be 6,500/2 = 3,250 books. At a cost of $6.1538 per book, the average investment in inventories will be 3,250 × $6.1538 = $19,999.85 ≈ $20,000. If inventories are financed by bank loans, the loan will vary from a high of $40,000 to a low of $0.0, but the average amount outstanding over the course of a year will be $20,000.

Because a 2-week lead time is required for production and shipping, orders are placed when the stock falls to 1,000 copies, which is defined as the **order point**. Some procedure, perhaps computerized, should trigger an order when the stock hits this level. With a 6,500 beginning balance, a zero ending balance, and a uniform sales rate, inventories will average one half of the EOQ, or 3,250 copies, during the year.

order point
Point at which stock on hand must be replenished.

Safety Stocks

If Romantic Books knew for certain that both the sales rate and the order lead time would never vary, it could operate exactly as shown in Figure 12-2. However, sales rates do change, and production and/or shipping delays are frequently encountered; to guard against these events, the company will carry additional inventories, or **safety stocks**.

The concept of a safety stock is illustrated in Figure 12-3. First, note that the slope of the sales line measures the expected rate of sales. The company *expects* sales of 500 copies per week, but let us assume a maximum likely sales rate of twice this amount, or 1,000 copies per week. It initially orders 7,500, the EOQ plus a safety stock of 1,000 copies. Subsequently, it reorders the EOQ, 6,500 copies, whenever the inventory level falls to 2,000 copies, the safety stock of 1,000 copies plus the 1,000 copies expected to be used while awaiting delivery of the order.

safety stocks
Additional inventories carried to guard against changes in sales rates or production/shipping delays.

Figure 12-2
Inventory Position without Safety Stock
This figure shows Romantic Books' average inventory position between orders. The EOQ of 6,500 copies represents the maximum inventory and determines the average inventory (6,500/2 = 3,250). The expected sales rate of 500 copies per week determines the order frequency (every 13 weeks). Since a 2-week lead time is required on orders, the order point is reached when inventories reach 1,000 copies. Note that this model assumes that both the sales rate and the required lead time on orders will never change.

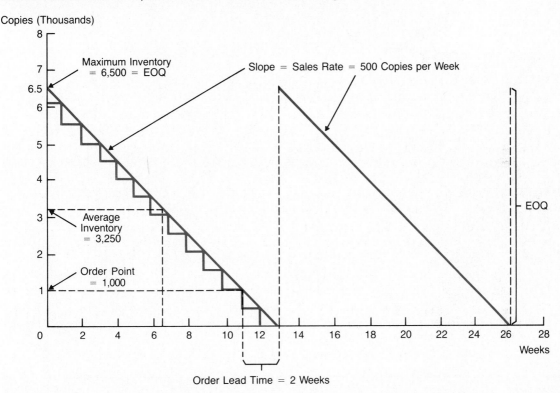

Notice that the company could, over the 2-week delivery period, sell 1,000 copies a week, or double its normal expected sales. This maximum rate of sales is shown by the steeper dashed line in Figure 12-3. The condition that makes possible this higher maximum sales rate is the introduction of a safety stock of 1,000 copies.

The safety stock is also useful to guard against delays in receiving orders. The expected delivery time is 2 weeks; however, with a 1,000-copy safety stock, the company could maintain sales at the expected rate of 500 copies per week for an additional 2 weeks if production or shipping delays held up an order.

The optimal safety stock varies from situation to situation, but in general it *increases* with (1) the uncertainty of demand forecasts, (2) the

Figure 12-3
Inventory Position with Safety Stock Included
Because sales rates and required lead times do vary, a business must carry safety stocks. In this example 1,000 copies of safety stock are ordered in addition to the EOQ of 6,500 copies. The order point now becomes 2,000 copies. Carrying safety stock allows the firm to cover a sales increase to 1,000 copies per week during the 2-week reorder lead time, should that occur. If delays are encountered in receiving orders, the company could continue its average sales rate for 2 weeks beyond the usual 2-week delivery time.

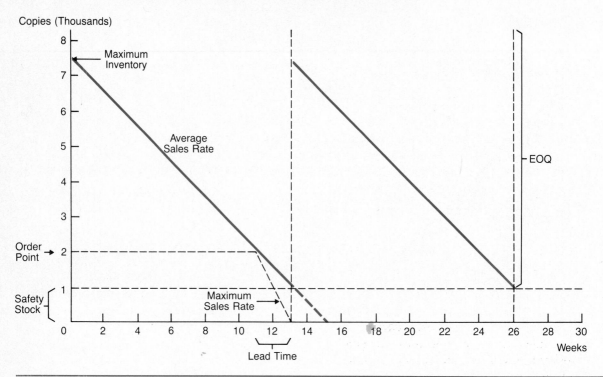

costs (in terms of lost sales and lost goodwill) that result from inventory shortages, and (3) the probability of delays in receiving shipments. The optimum safety stock *decreases* with the cost of carrying the extra inventory.

Inventory Control Systems

The EOQ model, plus safety stocks, helps establish proper inventory levels, but inventory management also involves the *inventory ordering and control system*. One simple control procedure is the **red-line method**—here inventory items are stocked in a bin, and a red line is drawn around the inside of the bin at the level of the order point. When the red line shows, the inventory clerk places an order. The **two-bin method** has inventory items stocked in two bins. When the working bin is empty, an order is placed and inventory is drawn from the second bin.

Larger companies employ **computerized inventory control systems**. The computer starts with an inventory count in memory. As withdrawals are made, they are recorded in the computer, and the inventory balance is revised. When the order point is reached, the computer automatically places an order, and when the order is received, the recorded balance is increased. Retail stores have carried this system quite far—each item has a magnetic code and as an item is checked out, it passes over a reader which adjusts the computer's inventory balance at the same time the price is fed into the cash register tape. When the balance drops to the order point, an order is placed.

A good inventory control system is dynamic, not static. A company such as IBM or General Motors stocks thousands of different types of items. The sales (or use) of these various items can rise or fall quite separately from rising or falling overall corporate sales. As the usage rate for an individual item begins to fall, the inventory manager must adjust its balance to avoid ending up with obsolete items—either finished goods or parts and materials for use in finished goods.

The EOQ model is useful for establishing order sizes and average inventory levels *given a correctly forecasted sales or usage rate*. However, usage rates change over time, and a good inventory management system must respond promptly to these changes in sales. One system that is used to monitor inventory usage rates, and then to modify EOQs and inventory levels, is the **ABC system**. Here the firm analyzes each inventory item on the basis of its cost, frequency of usage, seriousness of a stock-out, order lead time, and other criteria related to the importance of the item. Items which are expensive, are frequently used, and have long order lead times are put in the A category; somewhat less important items are put in the B category; and relatively unimportant items are designated C. Management reviews the A items' recent usage rates, stock position, and delivery time situation quite frequently, say monthly, and adjusts the EOQ as necessary. Category B items are reviewed and adjusted less frequently, say every quarter, and C items are reviewed, perhaps, annually. Thus the inventory control group's resources are concentrated where they will do the most good.

Good inventory management will result in a relatively high inventory utilization ratio, low write-offs of obsolete or deteriorated inventories, and few instances of work stoppages or lost sales due to stock-outs. All this, in turn, contributes to a high profit margin, a high total assets utilization, a high rate of return on investment, and a strong stock price.

two-bin method
An inventory control procedure wherein the order point is reached when one of two inventory-stocked bins is empty.

computerized inventory control system
Inventory control through the use of computers to indicate order points and to adjust inventory balances.

ABC system
A system used to categorize inventory items to ensure the most critical inventory items are reviewed most often.

Effects of Inflation on Inventory Management

Moderate inflation—say, 3 percent per year—can largely be ignored for purposes of inventory management, but the higher the rate of inflation, the more important it is to consider this factor. If the rate of inflation in the types of goods the firm stocks tends to be relatively constant, it can be dealt with quite easily—simply deduct the expected annual rate of inflation from the carrying cost percentage, C, in Equation 12-1, and use this modified version of the EOQ model to establish the working stock.

The reason for making this deduction is that inflation causes the value of the inventory to rise, thus offsetting somewhat the effects of depreciation and other carrying cost factors. Since C will now be smaller, the calculated EOQ, hence the average inventory, will increase. However, the higher the rate of inflation, the higher are interest rates, and this factor will increase C, thus lowering the EOQ and average inventories. On balance, there is no evidence that inflation either raises or lowers the optimal inventories of firms in the aggregate. Inflation should still be explicitly considered, however, for it will raise the individual firm's optimal holdings if the rate of inflation for its own inventories is above average (and is greater than the effects of inflation on interest rates), and vice versa.

Summary

The typical manufacturing firm has about 40 percent of its assets invested in inventories and receivables, so the management of these assets is obviously important. The investment in receivables is dependent on the firm's *credit policy*, and the four credit policy variables are these: (1) the *credit standards*, or the financial strength customers must exhibit in order to be granted credit, (2) the *credit period*, or length of time for which credit is extended, (3) *cash discounts* designed to encourage rapid payment, and (4) *collection policy*, which helps determine how long accounts remain outstanding. Credit policy has an important impact on the volume of sales, and the optimal credit policy involves a trade-off between the costs inherent in various credit policies and the profits generated by higher sales. From a practical standpoint, it is impossible to determine the optimal credit policy in a mathematical sense—good credit management involves a blending of quantitative analysis and business judgment.

Inventory management centers around the balancing of a set of costs that increase with larger inventory holdings (storage costs, cost of capital, physical deterioration) and a set of costs that decline with larger holdings (ordering costs, lost sales, disruptions of production schedules). Inventory management has been quantified to a greater extent than most aspects of business. The EOQ model is one important part of most inventory systems. This model can be used to determine optimal order quantity, which, when combined with a specified safety stock, determines the average inventory level.

Resolution to Decision in Finance

The King of Scrap Mountain

The mountains of ferrous scrap stored in Northwestern Steel & Wire's yards are its strongest defense against sudden rises in scrap prices. The huge inventory gives John Bowman the flexibility to buy less when prices are high and to turn down any deal that he doesn't like. As a result Bowman can use the scrap market's volatility to his own advantage: he can let inventory run off when prices are high and replenish when prices are low, secure in the knowledge that he has plenty of safety stock.

Although maintaining a large stockpile may seem to be an obvious way of coping with the volatile scrap market, not every company can adopt such a practice. For example, producers that use a variety of raw materials must allocate their capital to insure adequate amounts of all supplies. For them, overinvestment in one raw material may preclude the purchase of others that are equally important. Other companies don't want to tie up their cash in inventories because they believe that they can earn higher returns from other investments. But the most common reason that other companies don't stockpile scrap is that they can't afford to.

Northwestern has no qualms about its inventory policy. Says Bowman: "We consider a good inventory is worth more than money in the bank. When scrap doubles in price, you count your tons on the ground, and see that you've made some real money. You can carry an inventory a long time for that money."

Source: "The King of Scrap Mountain," *Fortune,* May 7, 1979, 236–250.

Key Terms You should be able to define each of the following terms:

Account receivable
Credit policy
Incremental analysis; incremental
　profit
Credit period
Credit standards
Five C's of credit
Collection policy
Cash discount

Seasonal dating
Aging schedule
Inventory management
Economic ordering quantity (EOQ)
Economic ordering quantity (EOQ)
　model; order point; safety stocks
Red-line method; two-bin method;
　computerized inventory control
　system; ABC system

Questions

12-1 Is it true that when one firm sells to another on credit, the seller records the transaction as an account receivable while the buyer records it as an account payable, and that, disregarding discounts, the receivable typically exceeds the payable by the amount of profit on the sale?

12-2 What are the four elements in a firm's credit policy? To what extent can firms set their own credit policies as opposed to having to accept credit policies dictated by "the competition"?

12-3 Suppose a firm makes a purchase and receives the shipment on February 1. The credit terms as stated on the invoice read, "2/10, net 40, May 1 dating." What is the latest date on which payment can be made and the discount still be taken? What is the date on which payment must be made if the discount is not taken?

12-4 a. What is the average collection period for a firm whose sales are $2,880,000 per year and whose accounts receivable are $312,000? (Use 360 days per year.)

　　　b. Is it true that if this firm sells on terms of 3/10, net 40, its customers probably all pay on time?

12-5 Is it true that if a firm calculates its average collection period, it has no need for an aging schedule?

12-6 Firm A had no credit losses last year, but 1 percent of Firm B's accounts receivable proved to be uncollectible and resulted in losses. Should Firm B fire its credit manager and hire A's?

12-7 Indicate by a (+), (−), or (0) whether each of the following events would probably cause accounts receivable (A/R), sales, and profits to increase, decrease, or be affected in an indeterminant manner:

	A/R	Sales	Profits
a. The firm tightens its credit standards.	____	____	____
b. The credit terms are changed from 2/10, net 30, to 3/10, net 30.	____	____	____
c. The terms are changed from 2/10, net 30, to 3/10, net 40.	____	____	____
d. The credit manager gets tough with past-due accounts.	____	____	____

12-8 If a firm calculates its optimal inventory of widgets to be 1,000 units when the general rate of inflation is 2 percent, is it true that the optimal inventory (in units) will almost certainly rise if the general rate of inflation climbs to 10 percent?

12-9 Indicate by a (+), (−), or (0) whether each of the following events would probably cause average annual inventories (the sum of the inventories held at the end of each month of the year divided by 12) to rise, fall, or be affected in an indeterminant manner:

   a. Our suppliers switch from delivering by train to air freight.   _____

   b. We change from producing to meet seasonal sales to steady year-round production. Sales peak at Christmas.   _____

   c. Competition in the markets in which we sell increases.   _____

   d. The rate of general inflation increases.   _____

   e. Interest rates rise; other things are constant   _____

Self-Test Problem

ST-1 The Moudry Company expects to have sales of $20 million this year under current operating policies. Currently Moudry's credit policy is net 25 (no discount for early payment). However, its average collection period (ACP) is 30 days, and its bad debt loss percentage is 3 percent.

   The credit manager is considering a change in credit policy from net 25 to net 40. She anticipates that such a move would increase credit sales by $2 million and would cause the firm's ACP to rise to 45 days. Bad debt losses are projected at 6 percent on new sales, but no change in the rate is anticipated for current sales. Find **(a)** the expected incremental change in investment in accounts receivable and **(b)** the incremental change in profits, taking into consideration the anticipated changes in carrying costs for accounts receivable, the probable bad debt losses, and the discounts likely to be taken. Moudry's cost of capital is 16 percent and its pre-tax profit margin is 20 percent.

Problems

* **12-1** Glen-Una, Inc. sells on terms of 2/10, net 30. Total sales for the year are $600,000. Forty percent of its customers pay on the tenth day and take discounts; the other 60 percent pay, on average, 40 days after their purchases.

   a. What is the average collection period (ACP)?

   b. What is the average investment in accounts receivable?

* **12-2** Refer to Problem 12-1. What would happen to the average investment in accounts receivable if Glen-Una toughened up on its collection policy, with the result that all nondiscount customers paid on the thirtieth day?

* **12-3** Curtis Cook, the new credit manager for Burk International, is studying the company's credit accounts. The company sells all its products on 2/10, net 30 credit terms. His predecessor told him the company's ACP is 36 days and that 60 percent of the customers take the discount. What is the ACP for customers who do not take the discount?

---

*Refer to Appendix E for check answers to problems with asterisks.

✱ **12-4** The Oh Drilling Company is considering changing its credit terms from 2/15, net 30, to 3/10, net 45. All of its sales are credit sales, but 70 percent of its customers presently take the 2 percent cash discount; under the new terms this percentage is expected to decline to 65 percent. The average collection period is also expected to change under the new policy, from 17 days at present to 20 days under the new plan. (Note: These averages are heavily weighted with customers who pay on the fifteenth and tenth day, respectively.)

Expected sales, before discounts are deducted, are $1,200,000 with the present terms, but they will rise to $1,350,000 if the new terms are used. Assume that Oh Drilling presently earns a 12 percent gross profit margin on sales, and that this margin will also apply after the change in credit policy. However, profits will be reduced somewhat if the new credit policy is put into effect because of additional credit-associated costs. Oh Drilling has a 12 percent cost of capital for any additional funds tied up in accounts receivable. Calculate the following items:

a. The increase in gross profits before credit costs.

b. The cost of increasing the cash discount.

c. The increased cost of carrying accounts receivable. (Hint: See the Self-Test Problem in this chapter.)

d. The net change in pre-tax profits.

✱ **12-5** Tampa Builders' Supply expects to sell 5,000 pounds of nails this year. Ordering costs are $50 per order, and carrying costs are $2 per pound.

a. What is the economic ordering quantity (EOQ)?

b. How many orders will be placed this year?

c. What is the average inventory under this plan, expressed in pounds?

12-6 The following relationships among inventory costs have been established for the Mehta Service Corporation: (1) orders must be placed in multiples of 200 units; (2) annual sales are 600,000 units; (3) purchase price per unit is $6; (4) carrying cost is 25 percent of the purchase price of goods; (5) cost per order placed is $40; (6) desired safety stock is 20,000 units—this amount is on hand initially; (7) three days are required for delivery.

a. What is the EOQ?

b. How many orders should Mehta place each year?

c. At what inventory level should a reorder be made?

d. Calculate the total cost of ordering and carrying inventories if the order quantity is (1) 4,000 units, (2) 5,600 units, or (3) 7,000 units. Keep separate the cost of carrying the active inventory versus the safety stock.

e. Construct a graph similar to Figure 12-1 based on your answer to Part d above.

12-7 King Keg, Inc. distributes keg beer to bars and restaurants in the Springfield area. Rob Moore, the owner-manager, is thinking of changing his credit terms from 2/15, net 30, to 3/15, net 45, in an effort to boost sales. Moore's main concern is the effect the change will have on his profits and financing needs. He asks you to help him analyze the effects of the change.

Moore's records are in terrible shape; he does not know exactly how many of his customers take the discount or when the others pay. He tells you, however, to assume that 60 percent of his accounts pay in 15 days and take the discount, while the other 40 percent pay in 30 days.

a. Do Moore's assumptions about his collections seem realistic to you?

* **b.** Assuming Moore's collection assumptions are correct, what is his average collection period? (Hint: Calculate a weighted average.)

* **c.** Sales last year were 10,000 kegs at a price of $50 per keg. How much does Moore have in outstanding receivables, assuming his collections data are correct? Use 360 days per year and disregard discounts.

* **d.** Moore estimates that the change in credit policy will increase annual sales by 4,000 kegs, that 60 percent of his customers will continue to take discounts, and that the other customers will pay on time. Under these assumptions, what will happen to his average collection period, and what will be the change in his investment in accounts receivable? (Hint: See the Self-Test Problem in this Chapter.)

* **e.** Moore estimates that his inventory carrying costs are 20 percent and that his ordering costs are $200 per order. Moore buys kegs of beer for $35 per keg. *Before* he changes his credit policy, what are (1) Moore's EOQ, (2) the number of orders he should place each year, and (3) his average inventory balance assuming a zero safety stock?

  f. Assume Moore changes his credit policy, and sales increase according to his forecast. Calculate his new EOQ, his new number of orders, his new average inventory balance (in dollars), and the change in average inventory balance.

  g. Assume Moore's general, administrative, and sales expenses (GA&S) amount to 20 percent of sales; that his income tax rate is 20 percent; and that he must borrow at a 10 percent interest rate the funds needed to carry his *added* receivables and inventory. (He currently has no debt outstanding.) Use $35 as the unit cost of goods sold. Calculate his net income under the two credit policies. Use the following income statement format:

	Old	New
Gross sales		
Less: Discounts	_____	_____
Net sales		
Cost of goods sold	_____	_____
Gross profit		
GA&S		
Interest	_____	_____
Net profit before taxes		
Taxes at 20%	_____	_____
Net income after taxes	==============	==============

  h. Should Moore change his credit policy? In answering this question, consider the reliability of the numerical answers you have developed and ways of improving the reliability factor.

Answer to Self-Test Problem[4]

ST-1 a. Change in Investment in Accounts Receivable = Expansion of the Accounts Receivable for Old Sales + Increase in Accounts Receivable Resulting from New Sales

$$\Delta I = (ACP_N - ACP_O)(S_O/360) + (ACP_N)(\Delta S/360)$$
$$= (45 - 30)(\$20,000,000/360) + (45)(\$2,000,000/360)$$
$$= \$833,333 + \$250,000$$
$$= \$1,083,333.$$

b. Incremental Profits = Change in Operating Profits − Bad Debts − Cost of Carrying Additional Accounts Receivable

$$\Delta P = \Delta S(\text{operating margin}) - (\% \text{ of bad debt})(\Delta S) - k(\Delta I)$$
$$= (\$2,000,000)(.2) - (.06)(\$2,000,000) - (.16)(\$1,083,333)$$
$$= \$400,000 - \$120,000 - \$173,333$$
$$= \$106,667.$$

Therefore the change appears to be a good one if the assumptions are correct. Note: In the incremental profit equation we do not bring in bad debts on old sales, because they are assumed to be unchanged. Had the lengthened credit period been assumed to lead to greater losses on old sales, the ΔP equation would have had to show Δ bad debts = $B_O S_O - B_N(S_O + \Delta S)$, where B_N is the bad debt loss percentage for new sales and B_O is the bad debt loss percentage on old sales.

Selected References

Three general references on credit policy at the applied level are:

Beckman, T. N., and R. S. Foster, *Credits and Collections: Management and Theory* (New York: McGraw-Hill, 1969).

Christie, George N., and Albert E. Bracuti, *Credit Management* (Lake Success, NY: Credit Research Foundation, 1981).

Cole, R. H., *Consumer and Commercial Credit Management* (Homewood, IL: Irwin, 1972).

More analytical books which deal with both credit policy and inventory management include the following:

Mehta, Dileep R., *Working Capital Management* (Englewood Cliffs, NJ: Prentice-Hall, 1974).

Smith, Keith V., *Management of Working Capital* (St. Paul: West, 1974).

---

[4]Many refinements are available for this basic model. The interested student should see Eugene F. Brigham, *Fundamentals of Financial Management*, 3rd ed. (Hinsdale, IL: Dryden Press, 1983), Chapter 17 and Appendix 17A.

Some recent articles which address credit policy and receivables management include the following:

Atkins, Joseph C., and Yong H. Kim, "Comment and Correction: Opportunity Cost in the Evaluation of Investment in Accounts Receivable," *Financial Management*, Winter 1977, 71–74.

Dyl, Edward A., "Another Look at the Evaluation of Investment in Accounts Receivable," *Financial Management*, Winter 1977, 67–70.

Hill, Ned C., and K. D. Riener, "Determining the Cash Discount in the Firm's Credit Policy," *Financial Management*, Spring 1979, 68–73.

Kim, Yong H., and Joseph C. Atkins, "Evaluating Investments in Accounts Receivable: A Wealth Maximizing Framework," *Journal of Finance*, May 1978, 403–412.

Lewellen, Wilbur G., and Robert W. Johnson, "A Better Way to Monitor Accounts Receivable," *Harvard Business Review*, May–June 1972, 101–109.

Oh, John S., "Opportunity Cost in the Evaluation of Investment in Accounts Receivable," *Financial Management*, Summer 1976, 32–36.

Roberts, Gordon S., and Jerry A. Viscione, "Captive Finance Subsidiaries: The Manager's View," *Financial Management*, Spring 1981, 36–42.

Stone, Bernell K., "The Payments-Pattern Approach to the Forecasting and Control of Accounts Receivable," *Financial Management*, Autumn 1976, 65–82.

Walia, Tirlochan S., "Explicit and Implicit Cost of Changes in the Level of Accounts Receivable and the Credit Policy Decision of the Firm," *Financial Management*, Winter 1977, 75–78.

Weston, J. Fred, and Pham D. Tuan, "Comment on Analysis of Credit Policy Changes," *Financial Management*, Winter 1980, 59–63.

12A Establishing a Credit Policy: An Illustration

Rexford Drug and Chemical Company manufactures and distributes drugs and related items to retail drugstores throughout the United States and Canada.[1] At a recent board meeting, several directors voiced concern over the firm's rising bad debt losses and increasing investment in accounts receivable. This group suggested to the financial vice president that she instruct her credit manager to tighten up the credit policy. Several other directors, including the marketing vice president, took exception to this suggestion, stating that a tougher credit policy would cause Rexford to lose profitable sales. This group emphasized that the gross profit margin on sales is 50 percent, and stated that, if anything, credit terms should be relaxed. After a heated discussion, the meeting broke up; but before adjournment the board instructed Nan Nantell, the financial vice president, to conduct a study of the firm's credit policy. Nantell aked her credit manager, Bob Carleton, to study the firm's policy and to report on the desirability of instituting changes.

Carleton decided to draw up two new credit policies as alternatives to the one currently in use. One could be described as an easy credit policy, the other as a tough credit policy. The current policy is an "average" policy in the sense that it closely corresponds to the practices of other drug supply firms.

The new plans require changes in all four credit policy variables. The easy credit policy involves (1) extending credit to a more risky class of customers; (2) extending the allowable payment period; (3) raising the cash discount allowed for prompt payments; and (4) reducing the "pressure" of the collection procedure on overdue accounts. The

---

[1] In part of this example we employ statistical concepts which may be unfamiliar to the reader. However, the "words" are more important than the "numbers," so if the statistics are confusing, just concentrate on the verbal sections.

new terms will be 3/15, net 45, instead of the current 2/10, net 30. These changes are expected to increase sales, but they will also increase the losses on bad debts and the investment in accounts receivable.

The tough credit policy involves (1) tightening credit standards; (2) reducing credit terms to 1/10, net 20; and (3) increasing the collection efforts on overdue accounts. It will result in lower sales but also in lower bad debt losses and a smaller investment in accounts receivable. Working with the sales manager, Carleton developed probability estimates of the *changes* in sales and in costs that could result from the two new policies. This information is presented in Table 12A-1, where the expected change in profits under each plan is also computed.

Columns 1, 2, and 3 give alternative sales levels, profit margins, and profits. Column 4 gives the estimated probability of each gross profit outcome. Column 5 gives an estimate of the incremental costs, including production, general and administrative, and credit costs, associated with each sales change. Notice that these cost estimates are themselves subject to probability distributions. For example, if sales increase by $100 million, costs may increase by $50, $60, or $70 million. The conditional probability estimate of each cost outcome is given in Column 6.

Depending on which sales and cost increases actually occur, net profit will increase or decrease by the amount given in Column 7. The joint probabilities, which represent the products of the probabilities in Columns 4 and 6, give the probability of each net profit increase, and these joint probabilities are used to derive the expected profits under each proposed credit policy change. Since the easier credit policy produces positive incremental profits, this policy is superior to the present policy and much superior to that of tightening credit.

Two points should be noted. First, this kind of analysis requires that some very difficult judgments be made—estimating the changes in sales and costs associated with changes in credit policies is, to say the least, a highly uncertain business. Second, even if the sales and cost estimates are reasonably accurate, there is no assurance that some other credit policy would not be even better. For instance, an easy credit policy that involved a different mix of the four policy variables might be superior to the one examined in Table 12A-1.

For both these reasons firms usually "iterate" slowly toward optimal credit policies. One or two credit variables are changed slightly, the effect of the changes is observed, and a decision is made to change these variables even more or to retract the changes. Furthermore, different credit policies are appropriate at different times, depending on economic conditions. We see, then, that credit policy is not a static, once-for-all-time decision. Rather, it should be fluid, dynamic, and ever changing in an effort to hit a continually moving optimal target.

Table 12A-1
Incremental Profits from Credit Policy Changes (Millions of Dollars)

Increase in Sales (1)	Profit Margin (2)	Increase in Gross Profit (3) = (1) × (2)	Probability of Sales Change (4)	Increase (or Decrease) in Cost (5)	Conditional Probability (6)	Increase (or Decrease) in Net Profit (7) = (3) − (5)	Joint Probability (8) = (4) × (6)	Product (9) = (7) × (8)
Easy Credit Policy								
$ 100	0.50	$ 50	0.20	$ 50	0.30	—	0.06	—
				60	0.40	$(10)	0.08	$(0.80)
				70	0.30	(20)	0.06	(1.20)
200	0.50	100	0.60	80	0.30	20	0.18	3.60
				90	0.40	10	0.24	2.40
				100	0.30	—	0.18	—
300	0.50	150	0.20	120	0.30	30	0.06	1.80
				130	0.40	20	0.08	1.60
				140	0.30	10	0.06	0.60
			1.00				1.00	
						Expected increase in profit =		$ 8.00
Tough Credit Policy								
$(50)	0.50	$(25)	0.25	$(20)	0.20	$(5)	0.05	$(0.25)
				(30)	0.60	5	0.15	0.75
				(40)	0.20	15	0.05	0.75
(150)	0.50	(75)	0.50	$(50)	0.20	(25)	0.10	(2.50)
				(60)	0.60	(15)	0.30	(4.50)
				(70)	0.20	(5)	0.10	(0.50)
(250)	0.50	(125)	0.25	(90)	0.20	(35)	0.05	(1.75)
				(100)	0.60	(25)	0.15	(3.75)
				(110)	0.20	(15)	0.05	(0.75)
			1.00				1.00	
						Expected increase in profit =		$(12.50)

Financing Current Assets: Short-Term Credit

13

Decision in Finance

A Bank That Looks at More than Numbers

In the mid-1970s the Northwestern National Bank of St. Paul, Minnesota, decided on a new commercial lending policy: it would lend to promising companies early, hoping thereby to develop loyal customers. Of course, even the most conservative banks want to attract new customers with great potential. But Northwestern was determined to go most banks one better: it would aggressively pursue new business, and when it found a company it believed in, it would bend traditional banking rules to sign up the company and keep it happy.

"Once a company becomes profitable and all the financial ratios are in place, then every bank in the country wants them," says Dennis McChesney, Northwestern's senior vice president. "We try to distinguish ourselves by being aggressive and getting them early." As a result of its willingness to work with smaller and younger companies, Northwestern has gained a reputation among financial professionals as a maverick lender, willing to take risks that other banks would find unacceptable.

As you read this chapter, look for steps that Northwestern could take to attract and hold business from promising young companies. Do you agree with the bank's decision to pursue such business? Why don't more banks follow such a policy?

See end of chapter for resolution.

319

As we noted in Chapter 10, working capital management involves decisions relating to current assets, including decisions about how these assets are to be financed. Any statement regarding the flexibility, cost, and riskiness of short-term versus long-term credit depends to a large extent on the nature of the short-term credit that is actually used. Thus the choice of the short-term credit instrument will affect both the firm's riskiness and its expected rate of return, hence the market value of its stock. Therefore the primary purpose of this chapter is to examine the sources and characteristics of the major types of short-term credit available to the firm. Additionally, special attention is given to the financial institution which specializes in short-term business loans—the commercial bank.

Accrued Wages and Taxes

Because firms generally pay employees on a weekly, biweekly, or monthly basis, the balance sheet will typically show some accrued wages. Similarly, because the firm's own estimated income taxes, social security and income taxes withheld from employee payrolls , and sales taxes collected by the firm are generally paid on a weekly, monthly, or quarterly basis, the balance sheet will typically show some accrued taxes.

accruals
Continually recurring short-term liabilities, such as accrued wages, accrued taxes, and accrued interest.

As we saw in Chapter 8, **accruals** increase spontaneously as a firm's operations expand. Furthermore, this type of debt is "free" in the sense that no interest must be paid on funds raised through accruals. However, a firm cannot ordinarily control its accruals—payrolls and the timing of wage payments are set by economic forces and by industry custom, while tax payment dates are established by law. Thus firms use all the accruals they can, but they have little control over the level of these accounts.

Accounts Payable, or Trade Credit

trade credit
Interfirm debt arising through credit sales and recorded as an account receivable by the seller and as an account payable by the buyer.

Firms generally make purchases from other firms on credit, recording the debt as an *account payable*. Accounts payable, or **trade credit,** as it is commonly called, is the largest single category of short-term debt, representing about 40 percent of the current liabilities of nonfinancial corporations. This percentage is somewhat larger for smaller firms— because small companies often do not qualify for financing from other sources, they rely rather heavily on trade credit.[1]

---

[1]In a credit sale the seller records the transaction as an *account receivable,* the buyer as an *account payable.* We examined accounts receivable as an asset investment in Chapter 12. Our focus in this chapter is on accounts payable, a liability item. We might also note that if a firm's accounts payable exceed its accounts receivable, it is said to be *receiving net trade credit,* while if its accounts receivable exceed its accounts payable, it is *extending net trade credit.* Smaller firms frequently receive net credit; larger firms extend it.

Trade credit, like accruals, is a "spontaneous" source of financing in that it arises from ordinary business transactions. For example, suppose a firm makes average purchases of $2,000 a day on terms of net 30. On average it will owe 30 times $2,000, or $60,000, to its suppliers. If its sales, and consequently its purchases, were to double, then its accounts payable would also double, to $120,000. The firm would have spontaneously generated an additional $60,000 of financing. Similarly, if the terms of credit were extended from 30 to 40 days, accounts payable would expand from $60,000 to $80,000. Thus lengthening the credit period, as well as expanding sales and purchases, generates additional financing.

The Cost of Trade Credit

As we saw in Chapter 12 in connection with accounts receivable management, firms that sell on credit have a *credit policy* that includes setting the *terms of credit*. For example, Carter Chemical Company's Textile Products division sells on terms of 2/10, net 30, meaning that a 2 percent discount is given if payment is made within 10 days of the invoice date and that the full invoice amount is due and payable within 30 days if the discount is not taken.

Suppose Fall Mills, Inc. buys an average of $12 million of materials from Carter each year, less a 2 percent discount, or net purchases of $11,760,000/360 = $32,666.67 per day. For simplicity, suppose Carter is Fall Mills's only supplier. If Fall Mills takes the discount, paying at the end of the tenth day, its payables will average (10)($32,666.67) = $326,667; Fall Mills will, on average, be receiving $326,667 of credit from its only supplier, Carter Chemical Company.

Now suppose Fall Mills decides *not* to take the discount; what will happen? First, Fall Mills will begin paying invoices after 30 days, so its accounts payable will increase to (30)($32,666.67) = $980,000. Carter will now be supplying Fall Mills with an *additional* $653,333 of credit. Fall Mills could use this additional credit to pay off bank loans, to expand inventories, to add fixed assets, to build up its cash account, or even to increase its own accounts receivable.

Fall Mills's new credit from Carter Chemical Company has a cost— Fall Mills is forgoing a 2 percent discount on its $12 million of purchases, so its costs will rise by $240,000 per year. Dividing this $240,000 by the additional credit, we find the implicit percentage cost of the added trade credit as follows:

$$\text{Percentage cost} = \frac{\$240,000}{\$653,333} = 36.7\%.$$

Assuming that Fall Mills can borrow from its bank (or from other sources) at an interest rate of less than 36.7 percent, it should not expand its payables by forgoing discounts.

The following equation may be used to calculate the approximate percentage cost, on an annual basis, of not taking discounts:

$$\begin{matrix}\text{Percentage} \\ \text{cost}\end{matrix} = \frac{\text{Discount percent}}{100 - \begin{pmatrix}\text{Discount} \\ \text{percent}\end{pmatrix}} \times \frac{360}{\begin{pmatrix}\text{Days credit} \\ \text{is} \\ \text{outstanding}\end{pmatrix} - \begin{pmatrix}\text{Discount} \\ \text{period}\end{pmatrix}}.\qquad \textbf{(13-1)}$$

The numerator of the first term, discount percent, is the cost per dollar of credit, while the denominator in this term (100 − discount percent) represents the funds made available by not taking the discount. The second term shows how many times each year this cost is incurred. To illustrate the equation, the cost of not taking a discount when the terms are 2/10, net 30, is computed as follows:[2]

$$\text{Cost} = \frac{2}{98} \times \frac{360}{20} = 0.0204 \times 18 = 0.367 = 36.7\%.$$

Notice also that the calculated cost can be reduced by paying late. Thus, if Fall Mills pays in 60 days rather than in the specified 30, the credit period becomes 60 − 10 = 50, and the calculated cost becomes

$$\text{Cost} = \frac{2}{98} \times \frac{360}{50} = 0.0204 \times 7.2 = 0.147 = 14.7\%.$$

In periods of excess capacity, firms may be able to get away with late payments, but they may also suffer a variety of problems associated with being a "slow payer" account. These problems are discussed later in the chapter.

_____

[2]Equation 13-1 may be adequately (for most purposes) approximated as follows:

1. Divide the number of days in the year (360) by the difference in days between the end of the discount period and the date of payment.
2. Multiply this quotient by the forgone discount percentage.

Using our illustration above, the cost of a forgone discount of 2/10, net 30, paid on the thirtieth day, can be approximated by 360/(30 − 10) = 18, or alternatively stated, there are eighteen 20-day periods in a year. Therefore (18)(0.02) = 36 percent is the approximate cost of forgoing the discount. However, if the payment date is delayed until the sixtieth day, 60 − 10 = 50 days, which is the difference between the discount period and the payment date. Then 360/50 = 7.2, and (7.2)(0.02) = 14.4 percent—a close approximation of the 14.7 percent determined in Equation 13-1.

Of course, both of these methods used to determine the cost of not taking advantage of a discount are approximations of the "true" or compound interest rate to be discussed in Chapter 14. As such, Equation 13-1 and its approximation, detailed in this note, may understate the cost of trade credit in a compound interest sense.

The cost of additional trade credit resulting from not taking discounts can be worked out for other purchase terms. Some illustrative costs are shown below:

Credit Terms	Cost of Additional Credit If Cash Discount Not Taken
1/10, net 20	36%
1/10, net 30	18
2/10, net 20	73
3/15, net 45	37

As these figures show, the cost of not taking discounts can be substantial. Incidentally, throughout the chapter we assume that payments are made either on the *last day* for taking discounts or on the last day of the credit period unless otherwise noted. It would be foolish to pay, say, on the fifth or twentieth day if the credit terms were 2/10, net 30.

Effects of Trade Credit on the Financial Statements

A firm's policy with regard to taking or not taking discounts can have a significant effect on its financial statements. To illustrate, let us assume that Fall Mills is just beginning its operations. On the first day, it makes net purchases of $32,666.67. This amount is recorded on the balance sheet under accounts payable. The second day it buys another $32,666.67. The first day's purchases are not yet paid for, so at the end of the second day accounts payable total $65,333.34. Accounts payable increase by another $32,666.67 the third day, to a total of $98,000, and after 10 days accounts payable are up to $326,667.

If Fall Mills takes discounts, then on the eleventh day it will have to pay for the $32,666.67 of purchases made on the first day, which will reduce accounts payable. However, it will buy another $32,666.67, which will increase payables. Thus, after the tenth day of operations, Fall Mills's balance sheet will level off, showing a balance of $326,667 in accounts payable, assuming the company pays on the tenth day in order to take discounts.

Now suppose Fall Mills decides not to take discounts. In this case on the eleventh day it will add another $32,666.67 to payables, but it will not pay for the purchases made on the first day. Thus the balance sheet figure for accounts payable will rise to 11 × $32,666.67 = $359,333.37. This buildup will continue through the thirtieth day, at which point payables will total 30 × $32,666.67 = $980,000. On the thirty-first day, it will buy another $32,667 of goods, which will increase accounts payable; but it will pay for the purchases made the first day, which will reduce payables. Thus the balance sheet item "ac-

---

Table 13-1
Fall Mills's Balance Sheet with Different Trade Credit Policies

A. Do Not Take Discounts; Use Maximum Trade Credit

Cash	$ 500,000	Accounts payable	$ 980,000
Accounts receivable	1,000,000	Notes payable	0
Inventories	2,000,000	Accruals	500,000
Fixed assets	2,980,000	Common equity	5,000,000
	$6,480,000		$6,480,000

B. Take Discounts; Borrow from Bank

Cash	$ 500,000	Accounts payable	$ 326,667
Accounts receivable	1,000,000	Notes payable (10%)	653,333
Inventories	2,000,000	Accruals	500,000
Fixed assets	2,980,000	Common equity	5,000,000
	$6,480,000		$6,480,000

---

counts payable'' will stabilize at $980,000 after 30 days, assuming Fall
Mills does not take discounts.

Table 13-1 shows Fall Mills's balance sheet, after it reaches a steady
state, under the two trade credit policies. The assets are unchanged by
this policy decision, and we also assume that accruals and common
equity are unchanged. The differences show up in accounts payable
and notes payable; when Fall Mills elects to take discounts and thus
gives up some of the trade credit it otherwise could have obtained, it
will have to raise $653,333 from some other source. It could have sold
more common stock, or it could have used long-term bonds, but it
chose to use bank credit, which has a 10 percent cost and is reflected
in notes payable.

Table 13-2
Fall Mills's Income Statement with Different Trade Credit Policies

	Do Not Take Discounts	Take Discounts
Sales	$15,000,000	$15,000,000
Purchases	11,760,000	11,760,000
Labor and other costs	2,000,000	2,000,000
Interest	0	65,333
Discounts lost	240,000	0
Total costs	$14,000,000	$13,825,333
Net income before tax	1,000,000	1,174,667
Tax (40%)	400,000	469,867
Net income after tax	$ 600,000	$ 704,800

Table 13-2 shows Fall Mills's income statement under the two policies. If the company does not take discounts, then its interest expense is zero, but it will have a $240,000 expense for "discounts lost." On the other hand, if it does take discounts, it incurs an interest expense of $65,333, but it also avoids the cost of discounts lost. Since discounts lost exceed the interest expense, the take-discounts policy results in the higher net income and thus in a higher value of the stock.

Components of Trade Credit: Free versus Costly

Based on the preceding discussion, trade credit can be divided into two components:

1. Free trade credit, which involves credit received during the discount period. For Fall Mills, this amounts to ten days of net purchases, or $326,667.[3]

2. Costly trade credit, which involves credit in excess of the free credit. This credit has an implicit cost equal to the forgone discounts. Fall Mills could obtain $653,333, or 20 days' net purchases, of such credit at a cost of approximately 37 percent.

Financial managers should always use the free component, but they should use the costly component only after analyzing the cost of this capital and determining that it is less than the cost of funds obtained from other sources. Under the terms of trade found in most industries, the costly component involves a relatively high percentage cost, so stronger firms avoid using it.

Another point which may be made about trade credit is that firms sometimes can and do deviate from the stated credit terms, thus altering the percentage cost figures cited above. To illustrate, a California manufacturing firm that buys on terms of 2/10, net 30, makes a practice of paying in 15 days (rather than 10) and still taking discounts. Its treasurer simply waits until 15 days after receipt of the goods to pay, then writes a check for the invoiced amount less the 2 percent discount. The company's suppliers want its business, so they tolerate this practice. Similarly, a Wisconsin firm that also buys on terms of 2/10, net 30, does not take discounts, but it pays in 60 rather than in 30 days. As shown above, both practices reduce the cost of trade credit. Neither of these firms is "loved" by its suppliers, and neither could continue these practices in times when suppliers were operating at full capacity and had order backlogs, but these practices can and do reduce the costs of trade credit during times when suppliers have excess capacity.

free trade credit
Credit received during the discount period.

costly trade credit
Credit taken in excess of the free trade credit period, thereby forfeiting the discount offered.

---

[3]There is some question as to whether any credit is really "free," because the supplier will have a cost of carrying receivables which must be passed on to the customer in the form of higher prices. Still, where suppliers sell on standard terms such as 2/10, net 30, and where the base price cannot be negotiated downward for early payment, then for all intents and purposes the 10 days of trade credit is indeed "free."

Short-Term Bank Loans

Commercial banks, whose loans appear on firms' balance sheets as notes payable, are second in importance to trade credit as a source of short-term financing. The banks' influence is actually greater than appears from the dollar amounts they lend, because banks provide *nonspontaneous* funds. As a firm's financing needs increase, it requests its bank to provide the additional funds. If the request is denied, often the firm is forced to slow down its rate of growth. In this section we discuss factors which influence the choice of a bank, how to approach a bank for a business loan, and some features of bank loans.

Choosing a Bank

Individuals whose only contact with their bank is through the use of its checking services generally choose a bank for the convenience of its location and the competitive cost of its checking service. However, a business that borrows from banks must look at other criteria, and a potential borrower seeking banking relations should recognize that important differences exist among banks. Some of these differences are considered below.

1. Banks have different basic policies toward risk. Some banks are inclined to follow relatively conservative lending practices; others engage in what are properly termed "creative banking practices." These policies reflect partly the personalities of officers of the bank and partly the characteristics of the bank's deposit liabilities. Thus a bank with fluctuating deposit liabilities in a static community will tend to be a conservative lender, while a bank whose deposits are growing with little interruption may follow liberal credit policies. A large bank with broad diversification over geographic regions or among industries served can obtain the benefit of combining and averaging risks. Thus marginal credit risks that might be unacceptable to a small bank or to a specialized unit bank can be pooled by a branch banking system to reduce the overall risks of a group of marginal accounts.

2. Some bank loan officers are active in providing counsel and in stimulating development loans with firms in their early and formative years. Certain banks have specialized departments to make loans to firms expected to grow and thus become more important customers. The personnel of these departments can provide much counseling to customers.

3. Banks differ in the extent to which they will support the activities of the borrower in bad times. This characteristic is referred to as the degree of *loyalty* of the banks. Some banks may put great pressure on a business to liquidate its loans when the firm's outlook becomes clouded, whereas others will stand by the firm and work diligently to help it get back on its feet. An especially dramatic illustration of this point was Bank of America's bailout of Memorex Corporation. The bank could have forced Memorex into bankruptcy, but instead it loaned the company additional capital and helped it survive a bad period. Memorex's stock price subsequently rose on the New York Stock Exchange from $1.50 to $68, so Bank of America's help was indeed substantial.

4. Banks differ greatly in their degrees of loan specialization. Larger banks have separate departments specializing in different kinds of loans, for example, real estate loans, installment loans, and commercial loans. Within these broad categories there may be a specialization by line of business, such as steel, machinery, or textiles. The strengths of banks are also likely to reflect the nature of the business and the economic environment in which they operate. For example, Texas banks have become specialists in lending to oil companies, while many midwestern banks are agricultural specialists. A firm can obtain more creative cooperation and more active support by going to the bank that has the greatest experience and familiarity with its particular type of business. The financial manager should therefore choose a bank with care. A bank that is excellent for one firm may be unsatisfactory for another.

5. The size of a bank can be an important factor. Since the maximum loan a bank can make to any one customer is generally limited to 10 percent of capital accounts (capital stock plus retained earnings), it will generally not be appropriate for large firms to develop borrowing relationships with small banks.

Applying for a Bank Loan

All firms, both large and small, often find a temporary need for short-term funds above current resources. At those times most business firms seek interim financing from a commercial bank.

Requests for loans take many forms. A request from a major corporation may be supported by professionally prepared and audited financial statements, complete credit analysis reports from agencies such as Dun & Bradstreet, and documentation from the company's legal counsel. On the other hand, a small firm may have only an unaudited financial statement to support the loan request.

Whatever the degree of sophistication of the data presented to support the loan request, bankers use the financial statements, both historical and pro forma, to answer questions regarding the term and adequacy of the loan, sources of repayment, and the certainty of those sources. The borrower therefore should anticipate the banker's questions and attempt to answer them in the loan application package. A successful application package would probably contain (1) a cover letter; (2) historical financial data; (3) projected, or pro forma, financial statements; and (4) a brief history of the firm and a resumé of its major officers.

The cover letter would indicate only the most relevant factors regarding the loan. The purpose of the loan, the amount requested, and the loan period should be indicated here. Balance sheets, income statements, and perhaps even tax records for the past three years of operation would be an integral part of the loan application package. These data will be used by bankers to learn more about the business, and they are especially helpful in determining management's business and financial acumen. Another important factor in a banker's evaluation is the firm's capitalization. Many small businesses are undercapitalized; that is, their long-term or permanent financing is insufficient to support a larger volume of business. A bank is not the proper source for permanent capital. Additionally, bankers demand that the owner's equity investment in the business be sufficient to give the owner a significant stake in the success or failure of the firm.

Of course, the pro forma financial statements receive a great deal of attention from the bank's loan officer. First, the officer will determine whether the requested loan amount is sufficient for its intended purpose. Bankers note that one of the most prevalent mistakes that novice borrowers make is to underestimate the amount needed for a loan. Second, the banker will review the projected financial statements and even the firm's purchase orders for an indication of the sources of repayment from operations and the relative certainty of those sources. If the loan is to cover only seasonal working capital requirements, a monthly or even a weekly cash budget, such as the one developed in Chapter 11, is an excellent addition to the loan documentation package. Finally, if the bank's credit officers are unfamiliar with the applicants or their business, a summary of the educational and managerial backgrounds of the firm's principals and a brief history of the firm, including a review of recent company and industry trends, should be provided.

Banks and bankers are in business to lend money. The loan documentation package should therefore provide the banker with enough data to support a positive response to the loan request. Additionally, the loan request should indicate the type of security or **collateral** that is offered to support the loan. Unpleasant as the prospect is, collateral is important since it indicates a source of funds available to the bank if unforeseen events cause default. Collateral therefore reduces the lending risk to the bank and may thus reduce the cost of the loan or may even be the determining factor in the decision to accept or reject the loan request. The topic of collateral is discussed in more detail later in this chapter.

collateral
Assets that are used to secure a loan.

Some Features of Bank Loans

Maturity. Although banks do make longer-term loans, *the bulk of their lending is on a short-term basis*—about two thirds of all bank loans mature in a year or less. Bank loans to businesses are frequently written as 90-day notes, so the loan must be repaid or renewed at the end of 90 days. Of course, if a borrower's financial position has deteriorated, the bank may well refuse to renew the loan. This can mean serious trouble for the borrower.

Promissory Note. When a bank loan is taken out, the agreement is executed by the signing of a **promissory note.** The note specifies (1) the amount borrowed; (2) the percentage interest rate; (3) the repayment schedule, which can involve either a lump sum or a series of installments; (4) any collateral that might be put up as security for the loan; and (5) any other terms and conditions to which the bank and the borrower may have agreed. When the note is signed, the bank credits the borrower's demand deposit with the amount of the loan. On the borrower's balance sheet both cash and notes payable increase.

promissory note
A document specifying the amount, percentage interest rate, repayment schedule, and other terms and conditions of a loan.

Compensating Balances. In Chapter 11 compensating balances were discussed in connection with the firm's cash account. As noted there, banks typically require that a regular borrower maintain an average checking account balance of 10 to 20 percent of the face amount of the loan. These compensating balances raise the effective interest rate. For example, if a firm needs $80,000 to pay off outstanding obligations, but it must maintain a 20 percent compensating balance, then it must borrow $100,000 to obtain a usable $80,000. If the stated interest rate is 8 percent, the effective cost is actually 10 percent: $8,000 divided by $80,000 equals 10 percent.[4]

Line of Credit. A **line of credit** is a formal or an informal understanding between the bank and the borrower indicating the maximum size loan the bank will allow the borrower. For example, on December 31 a bank loan officer may indicate to a financial manager that the bank regards the firm as being "good" for up to $80,000 for the forthcoming year. On January 10 the manager signs a promissory note for $15,000 for 90 days—this is called "taking down" $15,000 of the total line of credit. This amount is credited to the firm's checking account at the bank. Before repayment of the $15,000, the firm may borrow additional amounts up to a total outstanding at any one time of $80,000.

line of credit
An arrangement whereby a financial institution commits itself to lend up to a specified maximum amount of funds during a specified period.

Revolving Credit Agreement. A **revolving credit agreement** is a more formal line of credit arrangement often used by large firms. To illustrate, Carter Chemical Company negotiated a revolving credit agreement for $100 million with a group of banks. The banks were formally committed for 4 years to lend Carter up to $100 million if the funds

revolving credit agreement
A formal line of credit extended to a firm by a bank.

---

[4]Note, however, that the compensating balance may be set as a minimum monthly *average;* if the firm would maintain this average anyway, the compensating balance requirement does not entail higher effective rates.

were needed. Carter, in turn, paid a commitment fee of one quarter of 1 percent on the unused balance of the commitment to compensate the banks for making the funds available. Thus, if Carter did not take down any of the $100 million commitment during a year, it would still be required to pay a $250,000 fee. If it borrowed $50 million, the unused portion of the line of credit would fall to $50 million, and the fee would fall to $125,000. Of course, interest also had to be paid on the amount of money Carter actually borrowed. As a general rule, the rate of interest on "revolvers" is pegged to the prime rate (see next section), so the cost of the loan varies over time as interest rates vary. Carter's rate was set at prime plus ½ percent.

The Cost of Bank Loans

The cost of bank loans varies for different types of borrowers at a given point in time, and for all borrowers over time. Interest rates are higher for more risky borrowers. Rates are also higher on smaller loans because of the fixed costs of making and servicing loans. If a firm can qualify as a "prime risk" because of its size and financial strength, it can borrow at the **prime rate,** the lowest rate banks charge. Rates on other loans are scaled up from the prime rate.[5]

prime rate
A published rate of interest that commercial banks charge very large, strong corporations.

Bank rates vary widely over time depending on economic conditions and Federal Reserve policy. When the economy is weak, then loan demand is usually slack, and the Fed also makes plenty of money available to the system. As a result rates on all types of loans are relatively low. Conversely, when the economy is booming, loan demand is typically strong, and the Fed generally restricts the money supply. The result is high interest rates. As an indication of the kinds of fluctuations that can occur, the prime rate in 1974 varied from a low of 8½ percent to a high of 12 percent, and it rose to 21 percent in 1980. Interest rates on other bank loans vary more or less with the prime rate.

Interest rates on bank loans are calculated in three ways: as *simple* interest, as *discount* interest, and as *add-on* interest. These three methods are explained next.

simple interest
Interest calculated on funds received and paid on maturity of a loan.

Regular, or Simple, Interest. Exactly the type of interest rate we shall discuss in Chapter 14 is involved in **simple interest.** On the typical

[5]Each bank sets its own prime rate, but, because of competitive forces, most banks' prime rates are identical. Furthermore, most banks follow the rate set by the large New York City banks, and they, in turn, generally follow the rate set by Citibank, New York City's largest. Citibank sets the prime rate each week at 1¼ to 1½ percentage points above the average rate on large certificates of deposit (CDs) during the three weeks immediately preceding. CD rates represent the "price" of money in the open market, and they rise and fall with the supply of and demand for money, so CD rates are "market-clearing" rates. By tying the prime rate to CD rates, the banking system insures that the prime rate will also be a market-clearing rate.

loan for $10,000 for 1 year at 9 percent, the borrower receives $10,000 now and repays $10,900 at the end of the year:

$$\text{Effective rate of interest} = \frac{\text{Interest}}{\begin{array}{c}\text{Borrowed}\\\text{amount}\end{array}} = \frac{\$900}{\$10,000} = 9\%. \quad \textbf{(13-2)}$$

Discounted Interest. If the bank deducts the interest in advance (**discounts** the loan), the effective rate of interest is increased. On the $10,000 loan at 9 percent, the discount is $900, and the borrower obtains the use of only $9,100. The effective rate of interest is 9.9 percent versus 9 percent on a simple interest loan:

discounted interest
Interest calculated on the face amount of a loan and deducted in advance.

$$\begin{array}{c}\text{Effective rate}\\\text{of interest}\end{array} = \frac{\text{Interest}}{\text{Amount borrowed} - \text{Interest}}$$

$$= \frac{\$900}{\$9,100} = 9.9\%. \quad \textbf{(13-3)}$$

Installment Loans: Add-On Interest. Banks (and other lenders) typically charge **add-on interest** on automobile and other types of installment loans of under about $10,000. The term *add-on* means that interest is calculated and added on to the funds received to determine the face amount of the note. To illustrate, suppose our $10,000 loan is to be repaid in 12 monthly installments. At a 9 percent add-on rate, the borrower pays a total interest charge of $900. Thus the note signed is for $10,900. However, since the loan is paid off in installments, the borrower has the full $10,000 only during the first month, and by the last month eleven twelfths of the loan will have been repaid. The borrower must pay $900 for the use of only about half the amount received, as the *average* amount of the original loan outstanding during the year is only about $5,000. Therefore the effective rate on the loan is *approximately* 18 percent, calculated as follows:

add-on interest
Interest calculated and added to funds received to determine the face amount of an installment loan.

$$\begin{array}{c}\text{Approximate interest rate}\\\text{on installment loan}\end{array} = \frac{\text{Interest paid}}{\text{Loan amount} \div 2}$$

$$= \frac{\$900}{\$5,000} = 18\%. \quad \textbf{(13-4)}$$

The main point to note here is that interest is paid on the *original* amount of the loan, not on the amount actually outstanding (the declining balance), which causes the effective interest rate to be almost double the stated rate.[6]

---

[6]Equation 13-4 is an approximation of the true interest rate, which is determined by utilizing the compound interest techniques described in Chapter 14.

Consumer Revolving Credit Interest. Credit card companies, department stores, and banks grant consumers lines of credit up to specified limits. Interest is calculated each month on the outstanding balance, and this interest is added to the previous balance. Frequently the rate is set at 1½ percent per month, and the annual percentage rate (APR) is stated to be $12 \times 1\frac{1}{2} = 18\%$.

Effective Interest Rates When Compensating Balances Apply. Compensating balances tend to raise the effective interest rate on bank loans. To illustrate this, suppose a firm needs $10,000 to pay for some equipment that it recently purchased. A bank offers to lend the company money at a 9 percent simple interest rate, but the company must maintain a compensating balance equal to 20 percent of the amount of the loan. If it did not take the loan, the firm would keep no deposits with the bank. What is the most effective interest rate on the loan?

First, note that although the firm needs only $10,000, it must borrow $12,500, calculated as follows:

$$\text{Amount of loan} = \frac{\text{Funds needed}}{1.0 - \text{Compensating balance percentage}}.$$

$$= \frac{\$10,000}{0.8} = \$12,500. \tag{13-5}$$

The interest paid will be $(0.09)(\$12,500) = \$1,125$, but the firm will get the use of only $10,000. Therefore the effective interest rate is

$$\frac{\text{Effective}}{\text{interest rate}} = \frac{\text{Interest paid}}{\text{Funds actually used}} = \frac{\$1,125}{\$10,000} = 0.1125 = 11.25\%.$$

In general, we can use this formula to find the effective interest rate when compensating balances apply:

$$\frac{\text{Effective}}{\text{interest rate}} = \frac{\text{Stated interest rate}}{1.0 - \text{Compensating balance percentage}}. \tag{13-6}$$

In our example

$$\frac{\text{Effective}}{\text{interest rate}} = \frac{9\%}{1 - 0.2} = \frac{9\%}{0.8} = 11.25\%.$$

The analysis can be extended to the case where compensating balances are required and the loan is based on discounted interest:

$$\text{Effective interest rate} = \frac{\text{Stated interest rate}}{(1.0) - \left(\begin{array}{c}\text{Compensating balance}\\ \text{percentage}\end{array}\right) - \left(\begin{array}{c}\text{Stated interest}\\ \text{rate}\end{array}\right)}.$$

For example, if we needed $10,000 and were offered a loan with a stated interest rate of 9 percent, discounted interest, with a 20 percent compensating balance, the effective interest rate would be

$$\text{Effective interest rate} = \frac{9\%}{1.0 - 0.2 - 0.09} = \frac{9\%}{0.71} = 12.68\%.$$

The amount that we would need to borrow would be

$$\text{Amount borrowed} = \frac{\$10,000}{1.0 - 0.2 - 0.09} = \$14,084.51.$$

We would use this $14,084.51 as follows:

To make required payment	$10,000.00
Compensating balance (20% of $14,084.51)	2,816.90
Prepaid interest (9% of $14,084.51)	1,267.61
	$14,084.51

In our example compensating balances and discounted interest combined to push the effective rate of interest up from 9 percent to 12.68 percent. Note, however, that our analysis assumed that the compensating balance requirements forced the firm to increase its bank deposits. Had the company had transactions balances which could be used to supply all or part of the compensating balances, the effective interest rate would have been less than 12.68 percent.

Commercial Paper

In Chapter 11 we discussed the use of commercial paper as an investment medium for temporary excess cash. The present chapter would be incomplete if we did not include a discussion of commercial paper as a source of short-term financing available to the most financially secure firms. Commercial paper consists of unsecured promissory notes of large, strong firms and is sold primarily to other business firms, to insurance companies, to pension funds, and to banks. Although the amounts of commercial paper outstanding are smaller than bank loans outstanding, this form of financing has grown rapidly in recent years. For example, the amount of commercial paper outstand-

An increasingly popular form of short-term financing among large, secure firms, *commercial paper* looks a lot like a bank check, except that it is issued by a large corporation instead of a bank. Commercial paper is really just a promise to pay the bearer. It is used primarily by firms that are excellent credit risks.
Source: Courtesy of General Telephone Company of Florida.

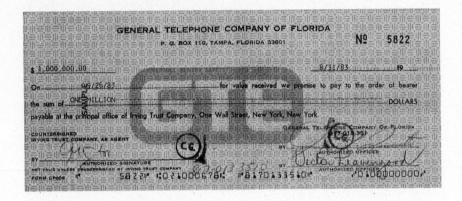

ing doubled from $83 billion in December 1978 to $166 billion in December 1981. Although the growth in commercial paper has slowed recently, in early 1984 there was still an impressive $191 billion in commercial paper outstanding.

Maturity and Cost

Maturities of commercial paper generally vary from two to six months from the time of issue, with an average of about five months. The rates on commercial paper fluctuate with supply and demand conditions—they are determined in the marketplace and vary daily as conditions change. Typically, commercial paper rates range from 1¼ to 1½ percentage points below rates on prime business loans. Also, since compensating balances are not required for commercial paper, the *effective* cost differential is still wider.

Use

The use of commercial paper is restricted to a comparatively small number of concerns that are exceptionally good credit risks. Dealers prefer to handle the paper of concerns whose net worth is $10 million or more and whose annual borrowing exceeds $1 million.

Other Factors

One potential problem with commercial paper is that a debtor who is in temporary financial difficulty may receive little help, because commercial paper dealings are generally less personal than are bank relationships. Thus banks are generally more able and willing to help a good customer weather a temporary storm than is a commercial paper dealer. On the other hand, using commercial paper permits a corporation to tap a wide range of credit sources, including banks outside its own area and industrial corporations across the country.

Use of Security in Short-Term Financing

Given a choice, it is ordinarily better to borrow on an unsecured basis, as the bookkeeping costs of **secured loans** are often high. However, small or weak firms may find (1) that they can borrow only if they put up some type of security to protect the lender or (2) that by using some security they can borrow at a much lower rate.

secured loan
A loan backed by collateral.

Several different kinds of collateral can be employed—marketable stocks or bonds, land or buildings, equipment, inventory, and accounts receivable. Marketable securities make excellent collateral, but few firms hold portfolios of stocks and bonds. Similarly, real property (land and buildings) and equipment are good forms of collateral, but they are generally used as security for long-term loans. However, a great deal of secured short-term business borrowing involves the use of accounts receivable and inventories.

To understand the use of security, consider the case of a Gainesville hardware dealer who wanted to modernize and expand his store. He requested a $200,000 bank loan. After examining his business's financial statements, the bank indicated (1) that it would lend him a maximum of $100,000 and (2) that the interest rate would be 20 percent discount, or an effective rate of 25 percent. The owner had a substantial personal portfolio of stocks, so he offered to put up $300,000 of high-quality stocks to support the $200,000 loan. The bank then granted the full $200,000 loan, and at a rate of 18 percent simple interest. The store owner might also have used his inventories or receivables as security for the loan.

In the past, state laws varied greatly with regard to the use of security in financing. Today, however, all states except Louisiana operate under the **Uniform Commercial Code,** which standardizes and simplifies the procedure for establishing loan security. The heart of the Uniform Commercial Code is the **Security Agreement,** a standardized document, or form, on which the specific assets that are pledged are stated. The assets can be items of equipment, accounts receivable, or inventories. Procedures for financing under the Uniform Commercial Code are described in Appendix 13A.

Uniform Commercial Code
A system of standards that simplifies the procedure for establishing loan security.

Security Agreement
A standardized document that includes a description of the specific assets pledged for the purpose of securing a loan.

Summary

This section of the text began in Chapter 10 with a discussion of short-term or long-term debt to finance current assets. We saw that because short-term credit offers advantages of lower cost and greater flexibility, most firms use at least some current debt, in spite of the fact that short-term debt increases the firm's risk.

The chapter also examined the four major types of short-term credit available to a firm: (1) *accruals*, (2) *accounts payable*, or *trade credit*, (3) *bank loans*, and (4) *commercial paper*. Companies use accruals on a regular basis, but this usage is not subject to discretionary actions. The other types of credit are controllable, at least within limits.

Accounts payable may be divided into two components, *free trade credit* and *costly trade credit*. The cost of the latter is based on discounts lost, and it can be quite high. The financial manager should use all the free trade credit that is available, but costly trade credit should be used only if other credit is not available on better terms.

The third major source of short-term credit is the *commercial banking system*. Bank loans may be obtained as the need arises, or they may be obtained on a regular basis under a *line of credit*. There are three different kinds of interest charges on bank loans: (1) *simple interest,* (2) *discounted interest,* and (3) *add-on interest* for installment loans. Banks often require borrowers to maintain compensating balances; if the required balance exceeds the balance the firm would otherwise maintain, compensating balances raise the effective cost of bank loans.

Commercial paper constitutes another important source of short-term credit, but it is available only to large, financially strong firms. Interest rates on commercial paper are generally below the prime bank rate, and the relative cost of paper is even lower when compensating balances on bank loans are considered. However, commercial paper does have disadvantages—if a firm that depends heavily on commercial paper experiences problems, its source of funds will immediately dry up. Commercial bankers are much more likely to help their customers ride out bad times.

Small Business $ $ $ $ $ $ $ $ $

Financing Receivables Directly

The growing small firm that offers its customers credit will often find that its accounts receivable account grows rapidly. As discussed in Chapter 10, growth usually entails a growing need to finance the firm's working capital. Accounts receivable are a major portion of working capital. Growth in accounts receivable places a strain on the firm's financing ability, but it may also offer the firm special opportunities to obtain financing.

Accounts receivable comprise an important asset account within the firm, an asset that may be particularly liquid and thus attractive to a lender as collateral. There are two common strategies for financing receivables that make use of these desirable features of receivables: (1) pledging of receivables as collateral for debt and (2) factoring of receivables.

In the case of pledged receivables, the firm needing capital merely borrows funds and offers its receivables as collateral for the loan. For example, suppose that Main Street Builders'

Supply sells materials wholesale to builders. In order to increase its sales, Main Street offers trade credit terms of 2/10, net 60. Most of its customers elect to delay payment. As Main Street grows, it realizes that its cash reserves are being badly strained, making it difficult to finance inventory requirements. Approaching the Last Gasp National Bank, the firm arranges to pledge its receivables to the bank. The bank in turns agrees to review Main Street's major receivable accounts and select the acceptable risks to serve as collateral. The bank lends Main Street about 70 percent of the face value of the acceptable accounts, reducing some of the financial pressure the firm had felt.

Pledging of receivables may be sensible for the small firm that has customers with better credit histories than the firm itself. It allows the firm to take some advantage of the strength of its customer base. However, the firm must ultimately bear the risk of nonpayment on the part of its customers, and it gets only a relatively small portion of the funds due from its customers. An alternative some firms have found preferable is to factor their receivables.

Factoring is quite different from pledging receivables because it involves the sale of receivables to a third party, called the "factor," and usually without recourse. The factor, then, accepts the credit risk for the firm. Furthermore, it is up to the factor to check the customers' creditworthiness and to actually collect the receivable accounts.

The small firm employing a factor therefore gets more than just credit. If Main Street Builders' Supply employed a factor, the factor would take over Main Street's collection function almost entirely. It would be up to the factor to decide which of Main Street's customers merited credit.

Also, if one of Main Street's Customers, such as Reliable Homes, became unable to pay its debts, the factor would absorb the loss rather than Main Street. Of course, if Main Street wanted to sell to a customer that the factor found unacceptable, then Main Street would have to bear the credit risk itself.

The small firm employing a factor may find that it no longer needs a credit department either for checking credit or for collecting receivables. Such a deal! But of course, the factor is also in business to make money, so it stands to reason that Main Street will pay dearly for the services of the factor. Main Street's problem, then, is to decide whether the comparatively high cost of the factor is warranted in view of the full set of services that Main Street receives, including short-term funds, credit services, and collection services.

There is a good reason why many small firms find that factors are indeed an economical alternative. The reason is that the small firm has its own special expertise—in Main Street's case, buying and selling building materials—while the factors have their own—credit services. Because managerial talent is often especially limited in small firms, it may turn out that the factor's services are a bargain by comparison to the cost of the firm's maintaining its own credit services and exposing itself to credit risks.

The fees charged by the factor normally include an interest charge for lending the funds in advance of payment, a credit fee for evaluating customers' credit, and perhaps an amount to reflect the credit risk of the customers. Also, usually the factor does not advance all of the net proceeds, making an allowance for possible returns due to disputes between the buyer and seller. For example, suppose Main Street agrees to deliver $25,000 in building supplies to Reliable Homes on terms of net 30. Main Street approaches Factor, Inc., a wholly owned subsidiary of the major local bank holding company, and Factor accepts the account. Factor charges Main Street interest at the rate of 18 percent, 3 points over prime, resulting in an interest charge of $\frac{1}{12} \times 18\% \times \$25,000 = \$375$ on the $25,000 invoice amount. Factor charges an additional 2 percent as a credit fee, for another $500. Finally, Factor advances only $21,625 rather than $24,125, holding a 10 percent (or $2,500) allowance in the event that Reliable disputes the order or finds some problem with the merchandise.

At the end of the month Reliable pays $24,000 directly to Factor after deducting $1,000 for defective sinks it had to return to Main Street. At that point Factor pays Main Street the remaining $1,500 due the firm on its net $24,000 sale of materials to Reliable Homes.

Considering the $875 total fee paid by Main Street to Factor for 30 days' use of $24,000, the factor seems an expensive source of financing. Main Street must bear in mind, however, that Factor bore the cost of credit verification as well as the risk of nonpayment or delayed payment by Reliable. In deciding on the use of a factor, Main Street must consider not only the financial cost of other forms of financing, but also the cost of duplicating the additional services provided by the factor.

In small firms with limited managerial resources and perhaps limited experience in monitoring and collecting credit accounts, factors may be economical sources of financing and credit services. The firm's comparative advantage is delivering a product; the factor's advantage is in providing financial and credit services. It may be advantageous to both to work out an arrangement by which the firm does what it does best and the factor provides financing and credit services. The desirability to the firm of such an arrangement will depend both on the costs of alternative means of financing and on the costs of providing its own credit and collection services.

Resolution to Decision in Finance

A Bank That Looks at More than Numbers

The Northwestern National Bank of St. Paul uses a number of tactics to attract and hold business from promising young companies. The basis of its approach is its willingness to lend money to companies that other, more conservative banks would turn down. In fact, rather than putting the burden of proof on the customer, Northwestern often works hard on its own to justify making a loan. Even when a conventional credit analysis indicates that a company could be a poor risk, the bank might still lend it money if the company shows compensating strengths, such as strong management talent or solid production performance.

In support of its commitment to young businesses, in 1981 Northwestern established a special division to help identify and analyze unusual lending opportunities. The division's three lending officers concentrate primarily on companies involved in high technology and other specialized areas, such as plastics and chemicals. But Northwestern's interests aren't limited to those areas alone. And its readiness to override traditional financial criteria with good judgment dates back further than the founding of the special lending division.

In fact, the bank approved its most extraordinary loan application in early 1976. At the time, the applying company had yet to generate its first dollar of revenue. And its product, a highly sophisticated supercomputer, was still in development. Based on the company's financial statements, Northwestern couldn't justify giving it a loan. So the bank decided to look instead at the product and the people. After talking to some of the company's competitors and potential customers, the bank was convinced that it could make the company a sizable loan without great risk. So, even though a much larger bank turned the company down, Northwestern agreed to give it a $1 million line of credit.

Ironically, the company, Cray Research, Inc., never used its new credit line. Shortly after the loan approval, the company went public, and today it is a proven performer, with annual sales in excess of $100 million.

Northwestern also believes in helping its customers survive tough financial times. For example, Detector Electronics Corporation ran into a cash crunch that threatened its ability to maintain its rapid growth. Northwestern had already given the company a fairly standard asset-based line of credit: it could borrow as needed up to 80 percent against its accounts receivable and 25 percent of the value of its inventory. But this formula wouldn't make cash available fast enough for Detector to fill all of its incoming orders.

Based on his company's assets and heavily leveraged balance sheet, Ted Larsen, Detector's president and chief executive officer, assumed that any bank would turn down his request for a larger credit line. But he hadn't taken into account Northwestern's willingness to turn aside conventional lending criteria. Because the bank believed in Detector's ability to turn its orders into sales and its sales into profits, it agreed to provide more financing for working capital by advancing cash based on a share of confirmed orders as well as on receivables and inventory. As a result, Detector was able to avert the impending financial crisis.

Of course, like any other bank, Northwestern usually charges higher rates for its more risky loans. But higher rates alone do not explain the bank's willingness to break with traditional lending policies. The real motivator, according to senior vice president Dennis McChesney, is the opportunity to establish ground-level relationships with newer businesses that will stay with the bank as they grow. "We think the best payoff is a loyal customer," McChesney says.

Source: Adapted from "A Bank That Looks at More than Numbers," *Inc.*, March 1983, 117–118.

Key Terms   You should be able to define each of the following terms:

Accruals

Trade credit; free trade credit; costly trade credit

Collateral

Promissory note; line of credit; revolving credit agreement

Prime rate

Simple interest; discounted interest; add-on interest; consumer revolving credit interest

Secured loan

Uniform Commercial Code; Security Agreement

Questions

13-1 "Firms can control their accruals within fairly wide limits; depending on the cost of accruals, financing from this source will be increased or decreased." Discuss.

13-2 Is it true that both trade credit and accruals represent a spontaneous source of capital to finance growth? Explain.

13-3 Is it true that most firms are able to obtain some "free" trade credit, and that additional trade credit is often available but at a cost? Explain.

13-4 What kinds of firms use commercial paper? Could Mamma and Pappa Gus's Corner Grocery borrow using commercial paper?

13-5 From the standpoint of the borrower, is long-term or short-term credit more risky? Explain.

13-6 If long-term credit exposes a borrower to less risk, why would people or firms borrow on a short-term basis?

13-7 Suppose that a firm can borrow at the prime rate and it can also sell commercial paper.

   a. If the prime rate is 12 percent, what is a reasonable estimate for the cost of commercial paper?

   b. If a substantial cost differential exists, why might a firm such as this one actually borrow from both markets?

13-8 What is meant by the term *"stretching" accounts payable?*

13-9 The chapter indicated that required compensating balances usually increase the cost of a bank loan. What would be a situation in which a compensating balance does not increase the cost of a bank loan?

Problems

* 13-1 Calculate the implicit cost of nonfree trade credit under the following terms, using Equation 13-1: **(a)** 2/15, net 40; **(b)** 3/10, net 20; and **(c)** 1/10, net 60.

13-2 **a.** If a firm buys under terms of 2/10, net 40, but actually pays after 15 days and still takes the discount, what is the cost of its nonfree trade credit?

  b. Does it receive more or less trade credit than it would if it paid within 10 days?

13-3 Suppose a firm makes purchases of $1.2 million per year under terms of 2/10, net 30. It takes discounts.

  a. What is the average amount of its accounts payable, net of discounts? (Assume the $1.2 million purchases are net of discounts; that is, gross purchases are $1,224,490, discounts are $24,490, and net purchases are $1.2 million. Also, use 360 days in a year.)

  b. Is there a cost of the trade credit it uses?

  c. If it did not take discounts, what would its average payables be, and what would be the cost of this nonfree trade credit?

13-4 You plan to borrow $5,000 from the bank. The bank offers to lend you the money at an 8 percent interest rate on a 1-year loan. What is the true, or effective, rate of interest for **(a)** simple interest, **(b)** discounted interest, and **(c)** add-on interest, if the loan is a 12-month installment loan?

*13-5 Zock's Lumberama is negotiating a $200,000 1-year working capital loan with four area banks. The banks have provided the loan alternatives listed below. What is the effective interest rate being offered by each bank?

  a. First National Bank offered a 14.5 percent loan with principal and interest due at the end of 1 year. No compensating balance is required.

  b. Second National Bank would lend at 12 percent stated interest if Mr. Zock kept a 20 percent compensating balance. Mr. Zock had not planned to keep any borrowed funds in the bank.

  c. Third National Bank suggested it would approve a loan at 11 percent if Mr. Zock kept a 10 percent compensating balance and discounted the loan.

  d. Fourth National Bank would lend to the company at 9 percent if the principal and interest were paid in 12 equal monthly installments.

13-6 Hadaway's Discount Marts needs to purchase $250,000 in inventory. The local bank agrees to the loan with a stated interest rate of 11 percent and a compensating balance of 15 percent. The loan will mature in 1 year.

  a. What is the loan's effective interest rate?

  b. How much interest will Mr. Hadaway pay if he agrees to the loan as stated? (Hint: Remember he needs the loan proceeds to be $250,000.)

*13-7 Von Horne's Music Supply is borrowing $35,000 from the local bank. Terms of the loan require a 10 percent compensating balance in order to qualify for a 13 percent stated interest rate. If Mr. Horne always keeps his bank cash balance as close to zero as possible, what is the

---

*Refer to Appendix E for check answers to problems with asterisks.

effective cost of the loan? Interest and principal are due at the end of the year.

13-8 Refer to Problem 13-7. Assume that, rather than a zero balance, Mr. Horne, as a matter of company policy, always keeps $2,000 in the company's checking account as a cushion over expected needs. These precautionary balances may be used as part of the compensating balance. What is the effective cost of the loan under these conditions?

13-9 Jim Buck of Pirate's Plumbing Warehouse is worried. Cash flow problems have prevented him from taking a 3/5, net 30, discount from his trade creditors. In fact, he has stretched payment to 55 days after purchase and his suppliers are threatening a cutoff of credit. East Carolina National Bank has agreed to lend enough money to alleviate the firm's cash flow problems and to allow Jim to take all discounts offered. The loan provides a 14 percent stated interest rate and requires a 20 percent compensating balance.

a. What is the firm's effective cost of trade credit at the present time?

b. What is the effective cost of the bank loan offered?

c. What should Jim do?

13-10 Fetzer Manufacturing has opened a revolving credit agreement with Great Lakes National Bank. Terms of the agreement allow the firm to borrow up to $50 million as the funds are needed. The firm will pay ¼ percent for the unused balance and prime plus 2 percent for the funds that are actually borrowed. The prime rate is expected to remain at 11 percent over the period covered by the loan. Determine the effective annual percentage cost of each of the following amounts borrowed under the revolving credit agreement: **(a)** no funds are used; **(b)** $15 million; **(c)** $25 million; **(d)** $40 million; **(e)** $50 million.

13-11 Engineering Associates, Inc. (EA) projects an increase in sales from $1 million to $1.5 million, but the company needs an additional $300,000 of assets to support this expansion. The money can be obtained from the bank at an interest rate of 9 percent discounted interest. Alternatively, EA can finance the expansion by no longer taking discounts, thus increasing accounts payable. EA purchases under terms of 2/10, net 30, but it can delay payment for an additional 30 days, paying in 60 days and thus becoming 30 days past due, without penalty at this time.

a. Based strictly on an interest rate comparison, how should EA finance its expansion? Show your work.

b. What additional qualitative factors should EA consider in reaching a decision?

13-12 The Adcock Corporation had sales of $1.95 million last year and earned a 3 percent return, after taxes, on sales. Although its terms of purchase are net 30 days, its accounts payable represent 60 days' purchases. The president of the company is seeking to increase the company's bank borrowings in order to become current (that is, have 30 days' payables outstanding) in meeting its trade obligations. The company's balance sheet is shown on the next page.

a. How much bank financing is needed to eliminate past-due accounts payable?

b. Would you as a bank loan officer make the loan? Why?

Adcock Corporation: Balance Sheet

Cash	$ 25,000	Accounts payable	$ 300,000
Accounts receivable	125,000	Bank loans	250,000
Inventory	650,000	Accruals	125,000
Current assets	$ 800,000	Current liabilities	$ 675,000
Land and buildings	250,000	Mortgage on real estate	250,000
Equipment	250,000	Common stock, par 10 cents	125,000
		Retained earnings	250,000
Total assets	$1,300,000	Total liabilities and net worth	$1,300,000

* 13-13 Parelli & Sons sells on terms of 2/10, net 40. Annual sales last year were
$4.6 million. Half of Parelli's customers pay on the tenth day and take
discounts.
   a. If accounts receivable averaged $447,230, what is Parelli's average col-
   lection period *on nondiscount sales?*
   b. What rate of return is Parelli earning on its nondiscount receivables,
   where this rate of return is defined to be equal to the cost of this trade
   credit to the nondiscount customers?

13-14 Swink & Daughter, Inc. has the following balance sheet:

Swink & Daughter: Balance Sheet

Cash	$ 50,000	Accounts payable[a]	$ 500,000
Accounts receivable	450,000	Notes payable	50,000
Inventories	750,000	Accruals	50,000
Total current assets	$1,250,000	Total current liabilities	$ 600,000
		Long-term debt	150,000
Fixed assets	750,000	Common equity	1,250,000
Total assets	$2,000,000	Total liabilities and equity	$2,000,000

[a]Stated net of discounts, even though discounts may not be taken.

Swink buys on terms of 1/10, net 30, but it has not been taking discounts
and has actually been paying in 70 days rather than 30 days. Now
Swink's suppliers are threatening to stop shipments unless the company
begins making prompt payments (that is, pays in 30 days or less). Swink
can borrow on a 1-year note (call this a current liability) from its bank at
a rate of 9 percent, discounted interest, with a 20 percent compensating
balance required (All of the cash now on hand is needed for transactions; it cannot be used as part of the compensating balance.)
   * a. Determine what action Swink should take by (1) calculating the cost
   of nonfree trade credit and (2) calculating the cost of the bank loan.
   b. Based on your decision in Part a, construct a pro forma balance sheet.
   (Hint: You will need to include an account entitled "prepaid interest"
   under current assets.)

Selected References

For a further discussion of trade credit, see the credit policy texts referenced in Chapter 12. In addition, see:

Moskowitz, L. A., *Modern Factoring and Commercial Finance* (New York: Crowell, 1977).

For more on bank lending and commercial credit in general, see:

Hayes, Douglas A., *Bank Lending Policies, Domestic and International* (Ann Arbor, MI: Bureau of Business Research, University of Michigan, 1971).

Jessup, Paul F., *Modern Bank Management* (St. Paul: West, 1980).

Reed, Edward W., Richard V. Cotter, Edward K. Gill, and Richard K. Smith, *Commercial Banking* (Englewood Cliffs, NJ: Prentice-Hall, 1976).

Rose, Peter, and Donald R. Fraser, *Financial Institutions* (Dallas: Business Publications, 1980).

Stigum, M., *The Money Market: Myth, Reality, and Practice* (Homewood, IL: Irwin, 1978).

For a good discussion of the effective interest rate on installment loans, especially when they are paid off ahead of schedule, see:

Bonker, Dick, "The Rule of 78," *Journal of Finance*, June 1976, 877–888.

The Use of Security in Short-Term Financing

13A

Procedures under the Uniform Commercial Code for using accounts receivable and inventories as security for short-term credit are described in this appendix. As noted in this chapter, secured short-term loans involve quite a bit of paperwork and other administrative costs; hence they are relatively expensive. However, this is often the only type of financing available to weaker firms.

Financing Accounts Receivable

Accounts receivable financing involves either the pledging of receivables or the selling of receivables (factoring). The **pledging of accounts receivable** is characterized by the fact that the lender not only has a claim against the receivables but also has recourse to the borrower (seller); if the person or the firm that bought the goods does not pay, the selling firm must take the loss. In other words, the risk of default on the accounts receivable pledged remains with the borrower. Also, the buyer of the goods is not ordinarily notified about the pledging of the receivables. The financial institution that lends on the security of accounts receivable is generally either a commercial bank or one of the large industrial finance companies.

Factoring, or *selling accounts receivable*, involves the purchase of accounts receivable by the lender without recourse to the borrower (seller). With factoring, the buyer of the goods is typically notified of the transfer and makes payment directly to the lender. Since the factoring firm assumes the risk of default on bad accounts, it must do the credit checking. Accordingly, factors provide not only money but also a credit department for the borrower. Incidentally, the same financial institutions that make loans against pledged receivables also serve as factors. Thus, depending on the circumstances and the wishes of the borrower, a financial institution will provide either form of receivables financing.

pledging of accounts receivable
Short-term borrowing from financial institutions where the loan is secured by accounts receivable; also called *discounting of accounts receivable*.

factoring
A method of financing accounts receivable under which a firm sells its accounts receivable to a financial institution.

345

Procedure for Pledging Accounts Receivable

The financing of accounts receivable is initiated by a legally binding agreement between the seller of the goods and the financing institution. The agreement sets forth in detail the procedures to be followed and the legal obligations of both parties. Once the working relationship has been established, the seller periodically takes a batch of invoices to the financing institution. The lender reviews the invoices and makes credit appraisals of the buyers. Invoices of companies that do not meet the lender's credit standards are not accepted for pledging.

The financial institution seeks to protect itself at every phase of the operation. Selection of sound invoices is the essential first step in safeguarding the financial institution. If the buyer of the goods does not pay the invoice, the lender still has recourse against the seller of the goods. However, if many buyers default, the seller firm may be unable to meet its obligation to the financial institution. Additional protection is afforded the lender in that the loan will generally be for less than 100 percent of the pledged receivables; for example, the lender may advance the selling firm only 75 percent of the amount of the pledged receivables.

Procedure for Factoring Accounts Receivable

The procedure for factoring is somewhat different from that for pledging. Again, an agreement between the seller and the factor is made to specify legal obligations and procedural arrangements. When the seller receives an order from a buyer, a credit approval slip is written and immediately sent to the factoring company for a credit check. If the factor does not approve the sale, the seller generally refuses to fill the order. This procedure informs the seller, prior to the sale, about the buyer's creditworthiness and acceptability to the factor. If the sale is approved, shipment is made and the invoice is stamped to notify the buyer to make payment directly to the factoring company.

The factor performs three functions in carrying out the normal procedure as outlined above: (1) credit checking, (2) lending, and (3) risk bearing. The seller can select various combinations of these functions by changing provisions in the factoring agreement. For example, a small or a medium-sized firm can avoid establishing a credit department. The factor's service might well be less costly than a department that may have excess capacity for the firm's credit volume. At the same time, if the firm uses part of the time of a noncredit specialist to perform credit checking, then lack of education, training, and experience may result in excessive losses.

The seller may utilize the factor to perform the credit-checking and risk-taking functions but not the lending function. The following procedure is carried out on receipt of a $10,000 order. The factor checks and approves the invoices. The goods are shipped on terms of net 30. Payment is made to the factor, who remits to the seller. But assume that the factor has received only $5,000 by the end of the credit period. The $10,000 must still be remitted to the seller (less a fee, of course). If the remaining $5,000 is never paid, the factor sustains a $5,000 loss.

Now consider the more typical situation in which the factor performs a lending function by making payment in advance of collection. The goods are shipped and, even though payment is not due for 30 days, the factor immediately makes funds available to the seller. Suppose $10,000 of goods is shipped. The factoring commission for credit checking is 2.5 percent of the invoice price, or $250, and the interest expense is computed at a 9 percent annual rate on the invoice balance, or $75.[1] The seller's accounting entry is as follows:

Cash	$ 9,175
Interest expense	75
Factoring commission	250
Reserve due from factor on collection of account	500
Accounts receivable	$10,000

The $500 due from the factor on collection of account is a reserve established by the factor to cover disputes between sellers and buyers on damaged goods, goods returned by the buyers to the seller, and failure to make outright sale of goods. The reserve is paid to the selling firm when the factor collects on the account.

Factoring is normally a continuous process instead of the single cycle described above. The firm selling the goods receives orders; it transmits the purchase orders to the factor for approval; on approval, the goods are shipped; the factor advances the money to the seller; the buyers pay the factor when payment is due; and the factor periodically remits any excess reserve to the seller of the goods. Once a routine is established, a continuous circular flow of goods and funds takes place between the seller, the buyers of the goods, and the factor. Thus, once the factoring agreement is in force, funds from this source are *spontaneous*.

---

[1]Since the interest is only for 1 month, we take one twelfth of the stated rate, 9 percent, and multiply this by the $10,000 invoice price:

$$\frac{1}{12} \times 0.09 \times \$10,000 = \$75.$$

Note that the effective rate of interest is really above 9 percent, because a discounting procedure is used and the borrower does not get the full $10,000. In many instances, however, the factoring contract calls for interest to be computed on the invoice price *less* the factoring commission and the reserve account.

Cost of Receivables Financing

Accounts receivable pledging and factoring services are convenient and advantageous, but they can be costly. The credit-checking commission is 1 to 3 percent of the dollar amount of invoices accepted by the factor. The cost of money is reflected in the interest rate (usually two to three percentage points over the prime rate) charged on the unpaid balance of the funds advanced by the factor. When risk to the factoring firm is excessive, it purchases the invoices (with or without recourse) at discounts from face value.

Evaluation of Receivables Financing

It cannot be said categorically that accounts receivable financing is always either a good or a poor method of raising funds for an individual business. Among the advantages is, first, the flexibility of this source of financing. As the firm's sales expand and more financing is needed, a larger volume of invoices is generated automatically. Because the dollar amounts of invoices vary directly with sales, the amount of readily available financing increases. Second, receivables or invoices provide security for a loan that a firm might otherwise be unable to obtain. Third, factoring provides the services of a credit department that might otherwise be available to the firm only under much more expensive conditions.

Accounts receivable financing also has disadvantages. First, when invoices are numerous and relatively small in dollar amount, the administrative costs involved may render this method of financing inconvenient and expensive. Second, the firm is using a highly liquid asset as security. For a long time accounts receivable financing was frowned upon by most trade creditors. In fact, such financing was regarded as a confession of a firm's unsound financial position. It is no longer regarded in this light, and many sound firms engage in receivables pledging or factoring. However, the traditional attitude causes some trade creditors to refuse to sell on credit to a firm that is factoring or pledging its receivables, on the grounds that this practice removes one of the most liquid of the firm's assets and accordingly weakens the position of other creditors.

Future Use of Receivables Financing

We might make a prediction at this point: in the future, accounts receivable financing will increase in relative importance. Computer technology is rapidly advancing toward the point where credit records of individuals and firms can be kept in computer memory units. Systems have been devised so that a retailer can have a unit on hand that, when an individual's magnetic credit card is inserted into a box, gives a signal that the credit is "good" and that a bank is willing to "buy" the receivable created when the store completes the sale. The cost of handling invoices will be greatly reduced over present-day costs because the new systems will be so highly automated. This will make it possible to use accounts receivable financing for very small sales, and it will reduce the cost of all receivables financing. The net result will be a marked expansion of accounts receivable financing.

Inventory Financing

A rather large volume of credit is secured by business inventories. If a firm is a relatively good credit risk, the mere existence of the inventory may be a sufficient basis for receiving an unsecured loan. If the firm is a relatively poor risk, the lending institution may insist upon security, which often takes the form of a *blanket lien* against the inventory. Alternatively, *trust receipts* or *field warehouse receipts* can be used to secure the loan. These methods of using inventories as security are discussed below.

Blanket Inventory Lien

The **blanket inventory lien** gives the lending institution a lien against all inventories of the borrower. However, the borrower is free to sell inventories; thus the value of the collateral can be reduced.

blanket inventory lien
A claim on all inventories of a borrower.

Trust Receipts

Because of the weakness of the blanket lien for inventory financing, another kind of security is used—the **trust receipt.** A trust receipt is an instrument acknowledging that the borrower holds the goods in trust for the lender. When trust receipts are used, the borrowing firm, on receiving funds from the lender, conveys a trust receipt for the goods. The goods can be stored in a public warehouse or held on the premises of the borrower. The trust receipt states that the goods are held in trust for the lender or are segregated on the borrower's premises on behalf of the lender, and proceeds from the sale of goods held under trust receipts are transmitted to the lender at the end of each day. Automobile dealer financing is the best example of trust receipt financing.

   One defect of trust receipt financing is the requirement that a trust receipt must be issued for specific goods. For example, if the security is bags of coffee beans, the trust receipts must indicate the bags by number. In order to validate its trust receipts, the lending institution would have to send someone to the premises of the borrower to see that the bag numbers are correctly listed. Furthermore, complex legal requirements of trust receipts require the attention of a bank officer.

trust receipt
An instrument acknowledging that the borrower holds certain goods in trust for the lender.

Problems are compounded if borrowers are widely separated geographically from the lender. To offset these inconveniences, *warehousing* has come into wide use as a method of securing loans with inventory.

Warehouse Financing

Like trust receipts, **warehouse financing** uses inventory as security. A *public warehouse* represents an independent third party engaged in the business of storing goods. Items which must age, such as tobacco and liquor, are often financed and stored in public warehouses. Sometimes a public warehouse is not practical because of the bulkiness of goods and the expense of transporting them to and from the borrower's premises. *Field warehouse* financing represents an economical method of inventory financing in which the warehouse is established at the place of the borrower. To provide inventory supervision, the lending institution employs a third party in the arrangement—the field warehousing company. This company acts as the control (or supervisory) agent for the lending institution.

Field warehousing is illustrated by a simple example. Suppose a potential borrower firm has stacked iron in an open yard on its premises. A field warehouse can be established if a field warehousing concern places a temporary fence around the iron and erects a sign stating: "This is a field warehouse supervised and conducted by the Smith Field Warehousing Corporation." These are minimal conditions, of course.

The example illustrates the two elements in the establishment of a warehouse: (1) public notification of the field warehousing arrangement and (2) supervision of the field warehouse by a custodian of the field warehousing concern. When the field warehousing operation is relatively small, the second condition is sometimes violated by hiring an employee of the borrower to supervise the inventory. This practice is viewed as undesirable by the lending institution, because there is no control over the collateral by a person independent of the borrowing concern.[2]

The field warehouse financing operation is described best by a specific illustration. Assume that a tomato cannery is interested in financ-

---

[2]This absence of independent control was the main cause of the breakdown that resulted in the huge losses connected with the loans to the Allied Crude Vegetable Oil Company. American Express Field Warehousing Company hired men from Allied's staff as custodians. Their dishonesty was not discovered because of another breakdown—the fact that the American Express touring inspector did not actually take a physical inventory of the warehouses. As a consequence, the swindle was not discovered until losses running into the hundreds of millions of dollars had been suffered. See N. C. Miller, *The Great Salad Oil Swindle* (Baltimore, MD: Penguin Books, 1965), 72–77.

ing its operations by bank borrowing. The cannery has sufficient funds to finance 15 to 20 percent of its operations during the canning season. These funds are adequate to purchase and process an initial batch of tomatoes. As the cans are put into boxes and rolled into the store-rooms, the cannery needs additional funds for both raw materials and labor. Because of the cannery's poor credit rating, the bank decides that a field warehousing operation is necessary to secure its loans.

The field warehouse is established, and the custodian notifies the lending institution of the description, by number, of the boxes of canned tomatoes in storage and under warehouse control. Thereupon the lending institution establishes for the cannery a deposit on which it can draw. From this point on, the bank finances the operations. The cannery needs only enough cash to initiate the cycle. The farmers bring more tomatoes; the cannery processes them; the cans are boxed and the boxes are put into the field warehouse; field warehouse receipts are drawn up and sent to the bank; the bank establishes further depos-its for the cannery on the basis of the receipts; and the cannery can draw on the deposits to continue the cycle.

Of course, the cannery's ultimate objective is to sell the canned to-matoes. As the cannery receives purchase orders, it transmits them to the bank, and the bank directs the custodian to release the inventories. It is agreed that, as remittances are received by the cannery, they will be turned over to the bank. These remittances by the cannery pay off the loans made by the bank.

Typically, a seasonal pattern exists. At the beginning of the tomato harvesting and canning season, the cannery's cash needs and loan re-quirements begin to rise and reach a maximum at the end of the can-ning season. It is hoped that well before the new canning season be-gins the cannery will have sold a sufficient volume to have paid off the loan completely. If for some reason the cannery has had a bad year, the bank may carry it over another year to enable it to work off its inventory.

Acceptable Products. In addition to canned foods, which account for about 17 percent of all field warehousing loans, many other product inventories provide a basis for field warehouse financing. Some of these are miscellaneous groceries, which represent about 13 percent; lumber products, about 10 percent; and coal and coke, about 6 percent. These products are relatively nonperishable and are sold in well-devel-oped, organized markets. Nonperishability protects the lender if it should have to take over the security. For this reason a bank would not make a field warehousing loan on perishables such as fresh fish. However, frozen fish, which can be stored for a long time, can be field warehoused. An organized market aids the lender in disposing of an inventory that it takes over. Banks are not interested in going into the canning or the fish business. They want to be able to dispose of an inventory with the expenditure of a minimum of time.

Cost of Financing. The fixed costs of a field warehousing arrangement are relatively high; such financing is therefore not suitable for a very small firm. If a field warehousing company sets up the field warehouse itself, it will typically set a minimum charge of about $350 to $600 a year, plus about 1 to 2 percent of the amount of credit extended to the borrower. Furthermore, the financing institution will charge an interest rate of two to three percentage points over the prime rate. An efficient field warehousing operation requires a minimum inventory of about $500,000.

Appraisal. The use of field warehouse financing as a source of funds for business firms has many advantages. First, the amount of funds available is flexible because the financing is tied to the growth of inventories, which in turn is related directly to financing needs. Second, the field warehousing arrangement increases the acceptability of inventories as loan collateral. Some inventories would not be accepted by a bank as security without a field warehousing arrangement. Third, the necessity for inventory control, safekeeping, and the use of specialists in warehousing has resulted in improved warehousing practices. The services of the field warehousing companies have often saved money for firms in spite of the costs of financing mentioned above. The field warehousing company may suggest inventory practices which reduce the labor that the firm has to employ, and reduce inventory damage and loss as well. The major disadvantage of a field warehousing operation is the fixed cost element, which reduces the feasibility of this form of financing for small firms.

Key Terms You should be able to define each of the following terms:

Pledging of accounts receivable	Trust receipt
Factoring	Warehouse financing
Blanket inventory lien	

Capital Budgeting: Investment in Fixed Assets

V

The previous section dealt with investment decisions concerning assets with short-term lives. In this section we present techniques that evaluate investment opportunities in long-term assets.

Since financial management often deals with future cash returns for present cash expenditures, we must develop techniques that correctly evaluate cash flows from differing time periods. This important concept, the time value of money, is presented in Chapter 14. This concept is first applied in Chapter 15, which covers the basic methods in capital budgeting analysis. Chapter 16 extends the basic capital budgeting analysis and also introduces the concept of risk, describes ways of measuring risk, and discusses how risk may be reduced.

Time Value of Money

14

Decision in Finance

Reenlisting with the Generals

Quarterback Steve Young is one of the latest young stars to be lured by a multimillion-dollar deal to the fledgling U.S. Football League; his contract with the Los Angeles Express is estimated to be worth $40 million over 43 years, an impressive deal even in the big-money world of pro sports. Yet running back Herschel Walker, who recently extended his own contract with another football team, the New Jersey Generals, for an estimated $6 million over 4 years, doesn't feel the least bit deferential to Young.

Because no deferred payments are involved, Walker thinks his contract extension with the Generals will win the money race with Young in the long run. All involved with Walker's contract agree that the running back may have gotten the better deal.

"It's better now," Walker said. "Eventually it will be a whole lot better." That depends on the decisions made by his financial advisers, the International Management Group, who will invest the money for him. "If you have good people around you, you don't have to defer money," Walker said.

As you read this chapter consider the pros and cons of Herschel Walker's contract. How is it possible that Walker's $6 million deal could be worth more than Young's $40 million contract? If you could choose, which contract would you accept—Walker's or Young's? Why?

See end of chapter for resolution.

In the first chapter of this text we said that the goal of the firm is to maximize the wealth of the shareholder by maximizing the market value of the firm's common stock. One of the variables critical to meeting that goal is the timing of the returns investors expect to receive. In this chapter we learn why earlier cash flows are better than later ones. This concept is quantified in this chapter and extended in later chapters.

We hesitate to claim that one chapter in this text is more important than another. Such a claim tends to start arguments, but, more importantly, a reader might be encouraged to think that the other chapters are not important. Although the other chapters are important in building a unified whole of the theories and methodologies of financial management, we must emphasize that a firm grasp of the concepts presented in this chapter is critical for a thorough understanding of many of the later topics we cover. A thorough understanding of the material in this chapter is essential before continuing.

Future Value (or Compound Value)

The first law of finance, simply stated, is: *A dollar today is worth more than a dollar tomorrow.* Why? Because today's dollar can be invested today so that tomorrow the dollar will have earned interest.[1] Before we begin, let us define terms that we will use throughout this chapter:

rate of return (k)
The rate of interest offered by or required of an investment.

future value (FV)
The amount to which a payment or series of payments will grow by a given future date when compounded by a given interest rate.

PV = the *present value* of an amount of money
k = the **rate of return** offered by or required of an investment opportunity
FV = the **future value** of an investment some number of periods, n, from now; sometimes referred to as *terminal value*
n = the *number of periods* covered by an investment.

To illustrate, suppose you have $100 which you wish to invest for 1 year at a rate of 8 percent compounded annually. How much would you have at the end of 1 year? Using our general terminology, we have

$$FV = PV(1 + k)^n. \tag{14-1}$$

---

[1]What about inflation? Doesn't that lower the value of tomorrow's dollar? Although we address this question in detail in later chapters, it is important to at least mention the answer now. The simple answer is that the rate of return must indemnify the investor for all the risks faced in the investment. Therefore, since the loss of purchasing power is one of today's largest risks, the investor must believe an investment will provide a rate of return which will be larger than the inflation rate. Otherwise the investor would not make that investment.

Substituting numbers for the general terms, we have

$$
\begin{aligned}
FV &= \$100(1 + .08)^1 \\
&= \$100(1) + \$100(.08)^1 \\
&= \$100 + \$8 \\
&= \$108.
\end{aligned}
$$

If we decided to invest both the principal and interest for another year, we would have

$$
\begin{aligned}
FV &= \$100(1.08)^1 + \$8(1.08)^1 \\
&= \$108 + \$8.64 \\
&= \$116.64.
\end{aligned}
$$

Note that the value of the investment at the end of 2 years is larger than the value of the interest in the first year ($8) paid twice. This is because the second year's interest was computed on the principal plus the accumulated interest from the first year. Thus interest was paid on interest; in other words, the interest was **compounded.** Therefore another way to express this relationship is

compounding
The arithmetic process of determining the final value of a payment or series of payments when compound interest is applied.

$$
\begin{aligned}
FV &= \$100(1 + .08)^2 \\
&= \$116.64.
\end{aligned}
$$

Now suppose you wish to leave your funds invested for 5 years; how much will you have at the end of the fifth year? The answer is computed in Table 14-1. However, we can arrive at the same conclusion with a great savings in effort by utilizing Equation 14-1:

$$
\begin{aligned}
FV &= PV(1 + k)^n \\
&= \$100 (1 + .08)^5 \\
&= \$146.93.
\end{aligned}
$$

Table 14-1
Compound Interest Calculations

Year	Beginning Amount (PV)	×	(1 + k)	=	Ending Amount (FV)
1	$100.00		(1 + .08)		$108.00
2	108.00		(1 + .08)		116.64
3	116.64		(1 + .08)		125.97
4	125.97		(1 + .08)		136.05
5	136.05		(1 + .08)		146.93

This is, of course, the same value which we found (after a great deal more work) in Table 14-1.

If an electronic calculator is available, it is easy enough to calculate the interest factor, $(1 + k)^n$, directly. But as the number of periods, n, becomes large, the calculations of the interest factor, even with a calculator, become cumbersome. Therefore tables have been constructed for values of $(1 + k)^n$ for wide ranges of k and n. Table 14-2 is illustrative. A much more detailed table (Appendix A) is included at the end of this text.

We set the term *future value interest factor*, IF, equal to $(1 + k)^n$. Thus Equation 14-1, $FV = PV(1 + k)^n$, can be further rewritten to

$$FV = PV(IF). \tag{14-1a}$$

Therefore it will only be necessary to go to the appropriate table to find the proper interest factor. In our previous example the correct interest factor for the 5-year, 8 percent illustration can be found in Table 14-2. We look down the Period column to 5, then across this row to the 8 percent column to find the interest factor, 1.4693. Then, using this interest factor, we find the value of $100 after 5 years:

$$
\begin{aligned}
FV &= PV\ (IF) \\
&= \$100(1.4693) \\
&= \$146.93,
\end{aligned}
$$

Table 14-2
Future Value of $1 at the End of n Periods: IF = $(1 + k)^n$

Period (n)	1%	2%	3%	4%	5%	6%	7%	8%	9%	10%
0	1.0000	1.0000	1.0000	1.0000	1.0000	1.0000	1.0000	1.0000	1.0000	1.0000
1	1.0100	1.0200	1.0300	1.0400	1.0500	1.0600	1.0700	1.0800	1.0900	1.1000
2	1.0201	1.0404	1.0609	1.0816	1.1025	1.1236	1.1449	1.1664	1.1881	1.2100
3	1.0303	1.0612	1.0927	1.1249	1.1576	1.1910	1.2250	1.2597	1.2950	1.3310
4	1.0406	1.0824	1.1255	1.1699	1.2155	1.2625	1.3108	1.3605	1.4116	1.4641
5	1.0510	1.1041	1.1593	1.2167	1.2763	1.3382	1.4026	1.4693	1.5386	1.6105
6	1.0615	1.1262	1.1941	1.2653	1.3401	1.4185	1.5007	1.5869	1.6771	1.7716
7	1.0721	1.1487	1.2299	1.3159	1.4071	1.5036	1.6058	1.7138	1.8280	1.9487
8	1.0829	1.1717	1.2668	1.3686	1.4775	1.5938	1.7182	1.8509	1.9926	2.1436
9	1.0937	1.1951	1.3048	1.4233	1.5513	1.6895	1.8385	1.9990	2.1719	2.3579
10	1.1046	1.2190	1.3439	1.4802	1.6289	1.7908	1.9672	2.1589	2.3674	2.5937
11	1.1157	1.2434	1.3842	1.5395	1.7103	1.8983	2.1049	2.3316	2.5804	2.8531
12	1.1268	1.2682	1.4258	1.6010	1.7959	2.0122	2.2522	2.5182	2.8127	3.1384
13	1.1381	1.2936	1.4685	1.6651	1.8856	2.1329	2.4098	2.7196	3.0658	3.4523
14	1.1495	1.3195	1.5126	1.7317	1.9799	2.2609	2.5785	2.9372	3.3417	3.7975
15	1.1610	1.3459	1.5580	1.8009	2.0789	2.3966	2.7590	3.1722	3.6425	4.1772

Figure 14-1
Relationship between Future Value Interest Factors, Interest Rates, and Time

This figure shows the future value of $1.00 for various rates of interest over various periods of time. Due to compounding, the higher the interest rate, the faster the growth in future value. Thus $1.00 invested at 10 percent will grow more than twice as fast as $1.00 invested at 5 percent. Note, for example, that for a 10-year period the future value of $1.00 at 5 percent is only $1.63, but its future value at 10 percent is $2.59.

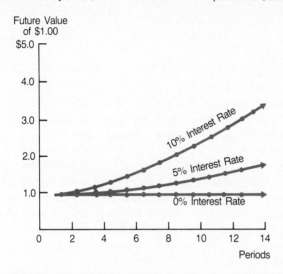

which is identical to the values obtained by the long method in Table 14-1 and the direct utilization of Equation 14-1.

Graphic View of the Compounding Process: Growth

Figure 14-1 shows how $1 (or any other sum) grows over time at various rates of interest. The points plotted on the 5 percent and 10 percent curves are taken from the appropriate columns of Table 14-2. Notice that the higher the rate of interest, the faster the rate of growth.[2] The interest rate is, in fact, a growth rate. Thus, if a sum is invested at a rate of 5 percent, then the investment fund will grow at a rate of 5 percent per period.

---

[2]We should emphasize that this relationship is curvilinear and not linear. This means that funds invested at 10 percent will grow at a rate that is *more* than twice as fast as funds invested at 5 percent. This is, of course, due to compounding one fund at a faster rate than the other. The difference between the funds will grow as either time or the rate of interest increases.

Present Value

Suppose you are offered the alternatives of receiving $146.93 in 5 years or some amount today. Let's assume that there is no question that the $146.93 will be paid exactly 5 years from today. We further assume you have no current need for the money (a highly theoretical yet necessary assumption) and will therefore invest it at 8 percent. (Eight percent is defined as your "opportunity cost," which is the rate you could earn on alternative investments of equal risk.) What amount of money today would make you indifferent to receiving $146.93 in 5 years or that X amount today?

Table 14-1 shows that an initial investment of $100 growing at 8 percent a year yields $146.93 at the end of 5 years. Therefore, in a strictly financial sense, you would be indifferent in your choice between $100 today and $146.93 at the end of 5 years. The $100 is defined as the **present value,** PV, of the future $146.93, due in 5 years, when the applicable return rate is 8 percent. Therefore, if the unknown present amount is any sum less than $100, you would prefer the future promised amount, $146.93. Conversely, if the amount X is greater than $100, you would accept that present offering since, when invested at 8 percent, its value 5 years hence would be greater than $146.93.

present value (PV)
The value today of a future payment or series of payments, discounted at the appropriate discount rate.

discounting
The process of finding the present value of a payment or a series of future cash flows; discounting is the reverse of compounding.

Finding the present value of some future amount (or **discounting** that future value, as the process is often called) is simply the reverse of compounding. We can use Equation 14-1 to illustrate this point:

$$FV = PV(1 + k)^n. \qquad \textbf{(14-1)}$$

To solve for the present value, PV, divide both sides of the equation by the interest factor, $(1 + k)^n$:

$$PV = \frac{FV}{(1 + k)^n}.$$

Since dividing by a number and multiplying by its reciprocal give equivalent results,[3] we can rewrite our equation to

$$PV = FV\left[\frac{1}{(1 + k)^n}\right]. \qquad \textbf{(14-2)}$$

The term in the brackets is called a *discount factor (DF)* and is equal to the reciprocal of the interest factor, 1/IF. Just as with the interest factor, a table has been constructed for various values of k and n in the dis-

---

[3]For example, dividing by 2 is the same as multiplying by ½, or dividing by 4 is equivalent to multiplying by ¼.

count factor, DF, as illustrated by Table 14-3. (For a more complete table of discount factors, see Appendix B at the end of this text.) Therefore, rather than directly utilizing Equation 14-2, we can use a modified version of that equation, which utilizes the discount factors in Table 14-3:

$$PV = FV(DF). \qquad \text{(14-2a)}$$

Using the table values of k and n makes direct computation of these variables in Equation 14-2 unnecessary.

Reverting to our original problem and using Equation 14-2a, we can find the discount factor, DF, by looking down the 8 percent column in Table 14-3 to the row for the fifth period, n. The figure shown there, .6806, is the discount factor, DF, used to determine the present value of $146.93 to be received in 5 years, discounted at 8 percent:

$$
\begin{aligned}
PV &= FV(DF) \\
&= \$146.93(.6806) \\
&= \$100.00.
\end{aligned}
$$

Graphic View of the Discounting Process

Figure 14-2 graphically depicts how the discount factors decrease as the discounting period increases. These curves, plotted with the data presented in Table 14-3, show that the present value of a sum to be received at some future time decreases as either (1) the payment date is extended further into the future or (2) the discount rate increases. To illustrate, the present value of $1 due in 10 years is about 61 cents if

Table 14-3
Present Value of $1 Due at the End of n Periods: $DF = 1/(1 + k)^n = [1/(1 + k)]^n$

Period (n)	1%	2%	3%	4%	5%	6%	7%	8%	9%	10%	12%	14%	15%
1	.9901	.9804	.9709	.9615	.9524	.9434	.9346	.9259	.9174	.9091	.8929	.8772	.8696
2	.9803	.9612	.9426	.9246	.9070	.8900	.8734	.8573	.8417	.8264	.7972	.7695	.7561
3	.9706	.9423	.9151	.8890	.8638	.8396	.8163	.7938	.7722	.7513	.7118	.6750	.6575
4	.9610	.9238	.8885	.8548	.8227	.7921	.7629	.7350	.7084	.6830	.6355	.5921	.5718
5	.9515	.9057	.8626	.8219	.7835	.7473	.7130	.6806	.6499	.6209	.5674	.5194	.4972
6	.9420	.8880	.8375	.7903	.7462	.7050	.6663	.6302	.5963	.5645	.5066	.4556	.4323
7	.9327	.8706	.8131	.7599	.7107	.6651	.6227	.5835	.5470	.5132	.4523	.3996	.3759
8	.9235	.8535	.7894	.7307	.6768	.6274	.5820	.5403	.5019	.4665	.4039	.3506	.3269
9	.9143	.8368	.7664	.7026	.6446	.5919	.5439	.5002	.4604	.4241	.3606	.3075	.2843
10	.9053	.8203	.7441	.6756	.6139	.5584	.5083	.4632	.4224	.3855	.3220	.2697	.2472

Figure 14-2
Relationship between Present Value Interest Factors,
Interest Rates, and Time

This graph shows the discounting process at various interest rates. The longer the time until payment or the higher the interest rate, the less invested funds will be worth in today's dollars. For example, if the interest rate is 10 percent, the present value of $1.00 due in 4 years is $.68, but the value drops to about $.39 if due in 10 years. If we vary the interest rate, we see that $1.00 invested at 5 percent for 10 years has a present value of about $.61, while if invested at 15 percent for 10 years, its present value is about $.25.

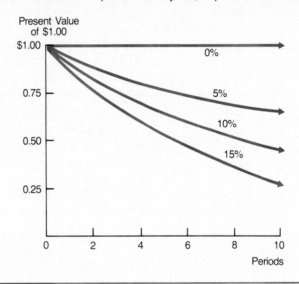

the discount rate is 5 percent, but is worth only 25 cents today if the discount rate is 15 percent. Thus, since you are investing in a project with a higher rate of return, a smaller initial payment is required to earn $1 in the future. The length of time until money is paid or received is also important. For example, $1 due in 5 years at 10 percent is worth 62 cents today, but at the same discount rate $1 due in 10 years is worth only about 39 cents today.

Thus present values are dependent on two factors, the discount rate and time. If relatively high discount rates apply, funds due in the future are worth comparatively very little today. Even at relatively low discount rates, the present values of funds due in the distant future are quite small. Notice that where no investment opportunity exists or where no investment is made, the discount rate (interest rate) is zero, which means the present and future values of a dollar are the same.

Present Value versus Future Value

By now you have noticed that Equations 14-1 and 14-2 (and their equivalent versions, Equations 14-1a and 14-2a, which have the table values computed for them) are really two ways of looking at the same process. People in everyday life must decide, just as financial managers do, how much to invest in order to receive future returns. The problem is that present and future amounts cannot be directly compared. We must either compound present amounts into the future or discount future dollars back to the present by using the appropriate formulas.

To illustrate this point, let's use the following farfetched example. Conrad Dunn is a college student who is going to sell his car for $2,500 and invest the money in a project that promises a 12 percent return. An uncle suggests that he would like to have the car, but he cannot pay cash for it. He is, however, willing to include Conrad in his willl for a tax-free inheritance of $10,000—four times the car's value, he notes. If his uncle lives another 15 years (the warranty period on his pacemaker), should Conrad give him the car rather than sell it for cash?

Even though the value of the inheritance money is four times the value of the car, we cannot compare the amounts since one is a future value and the other is a present sum. In order to make the values comparable, we must discount the future payment back to the present or we must compound the present amount into the future. Even though we shall arrive at the same decision (to accept or reject the uncle's offer), we shall use both methods.

If we wish to discount the future amount back to the present, we can use Equation 14-2a, utilizing a discount factor from Appendix B for 12 percent, 15 years:

$$
\begin{aligned}
PV &= FV(DF) \\
&= \$10,000(.1827) \\
&= \$1,827.
\end{aligned}
$$

Obviously, the offer made by Conrad's uncle is not financially attractive to him since the present value of $10,000 discounted at 12 percent for 15 years is less than the amount Conrad could receive if he sold the car today.

We come to the same conclusion if the cash value of the car if sold, $2,500, is compounded 15 years into the future. We use the interest factors from Appendix A for 12 percent, 15 years, in Equation 14-1a:

$$
\begin{aligned}
FV &= PV(IF) \\
&= \$2,500(5.4736) \\
&= \$13,684.
\end{aligned}
$$

As we expected, the value of $2,500 invested at a 12 percent rate of interest for 15 years exceeds the $10,000 Conrad's uncle promised for the car.

Figure 14-3 serves to illustrate our point that present and future values cannot be directly compared. A present amount can be com-

Figure 14-3
Discounting and Compounding Compared
To compare a present value to a future value, we must either compound the present sum into the future or discount the future amount back to the present. Whichever method is used, the result gives us the only firm basis on which to compare the two values. In this figure the future values are shown on the right ($13,684 was arrived at by compounding $2,500 over 15 periods), and the present values are shown on the left ($1,827 was reached by discounting $10,000 over 15 periods).

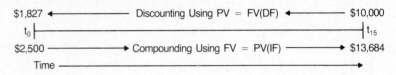

pounded into the future and thus compared with a promised future amount. Conversely, a future sum may be discounted back to the present and compared with the present value of the uncle's offer. Thus we can compare $2,500 with $1,827 or $13,684 with $10,000, but we cannot compare $2,500 with $10,000. Conrad may wish to give his uncle the car for a promise of $10,000 in the future, but it will not be for financial reasons.

Future Value of an Annuity

So far we have been dealing with situations characterized by a single payment or receipt in the present and a single amount in the future. We now turn to a discussion of a special case of equal annual payments or receipts, called *annuities*. An **annuity** is defined as *a series of equal payments or receipts for a specified number of periods.* If the payments are made or received at the beginning of each period, then we have an **annuity due.** Since **regular** (or **deferred**) **annuities** are far more common in finance, when the word *annuity* is used in this book, you may assume that payments are received at the end of each period unless otherwise indicated.

A promise to pay $1,000 a year for 3 years is a 3-year annuity. If you were to receive such an annuity and deposited each annual payment in a savings account paying 7 percent interest, how much would you have at the end of 3 years? The process may be shown graphically as a *time line* in Figure 14-4. The first payment is made at the end of Year 1, the second at the end of Year 2, and the third at the end of Year 3. The last payment is not compounded at all; the second year's payment is compounded for 1 year; and the first is compounded for 2 years. When the future values of each of the $1,000 payments are added, their total is the sum of an annuity, which in this case is equal to $3,214.90.

annuity
A series of equal payments or receipts for a specified number of periods.

annuity due
A series of payments of a fixed amount for a specified number of periods where the payments occur at the beginning of the period.

regular annuity
A series of payments of a fixed amount for a specified number of periods where the payments occur at the end of the period; also called a *deferred annuity.*

Figure 14-4
Time Line for an Annuity: Future Value with k = 7%
This figure shows how the future value of an annuity is calculated. In this case there was a promise to pay $1,000 per year for 3 years, so a $1,000 payment is received at the end of each of three periods. Upon receipt, each payment is invested at 7 percent interest. The first payment is compounded for 2 years, the second for 1 year, and the third is not compounded at all. The sum of the three future values is the total value of the annuity.

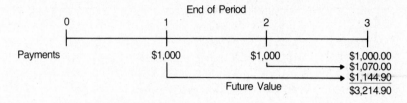

Of course, you could go through the effort of calculating the interest factors yourself,[4] but the interest factor for an annuity (IFa) has already been calculated for various combinations of interest rates, k, and time periods, n, in Appendix C. An illustrative set of these annuity factors is given in Table 14-4. In order to answer the question posed above, we would utilize Equation 14-3:

$$FVa = Pmt(IFa), \qquad (14\text{-}3)$$

where

FVa = the future compound value of an annuity
Pmt = the annuity payment or receipt
IFa = the future value interest factor for an annuity.

To find the future value of the 3-year, $1,000 annuity problem posed earlier, first find the interest factor for an annuity, IFa, by simply referring to Table 14-4. Look down the 7 percent column to the third-period row, and multiply the factor 3.2149 by the $1,000:

$$
\begin{aligned}
FVa &= Pmt(IFa) \\
&= \$1,000(3.2149) \\
&= \$3,214.90.
\end{aligned}
$$

---

[4]Expressed algebraically, the future value of an annuity, FVa, can be computed by multiplying the annuity, Pmt, by the interest factor for an annuity, IFa:

$$
\begin{aligned}
FVa &= Pmt(1 + k)^{n-1} + Pmt(1 + k)^{n-2} + \cdots + Pmt(1 + k)^{1} + Pmt(1 + k)^{0} \\
&= Pmt[(1 + k)^{n-1} + (1 + k)^{n-2} + \cdots + (1 + k)^{1} + (1 + k)^{0}] \\
&= Pmt \sum_{t=1}^{n} (1 + k)^{n-t} \\
&= Pmt(IFa).
\end{aligned}
$$

Table 14-4
Sum of an Annuity of $1 per Period for n Periods:

$$IFa = \sum_{t=1}^{n} (1 + k)^{n-t} = \frac{(1 + k)^n - 1}{k}$$

Period (n)	1%	2%	3%	4%	5%	6%	7%	8%
1	1.0000	1.0000	1.0000	1.0000	1.0000	1.0000	1.0000	1.0000
2	2.0100	2.0200	2.0300	2.0400	2.0500	2.0600	2.0700	2.0800
3	3.0301	3.0604	3.0909	3.1216	3.1525	3.1836	3.2149	3.2464
4	4.0604	4.1216	4.1836	4.2465	4.3101	4.3746	4.4399	4.5061
5	5.1010	5.2040	5.3091	5.4163	5.5256	5.6371	5.7507	5.8666
6	6.1520	6.3081	6.4684	6.6330	6.8019	6.9753	7.1533	7.3359
7	7.2135	7.4343	7.6625	7.8983	8.1420	8.3938	8.6540	8.9228
8	8.2857	8.5830	8.8923	9.2142	9.5491	9.8975	10.2598	10.6366
9	9.3685	9.7546	10.1591	10.5828	11.0266	11.4913	11.9780	12.4876
10	10.4622	10.9497	11.4639	12.0061	12.5779	13.1808	13.8164	14.4866

Thus the future value of an annuity of $1,000 a year, received at the end of each year and invested at 7 percent annually, is $3,214.90.[5]

Present Value of an Annuity

In the preceding section we learned techniques which allow us to determine the value in some future period of a stream of equal annual payments or receipts. You may also wish to determine the present value of an annuity. Suppose you were offered the following alternatives: a 4-year annuity of $1,000 a year or a lump-sum payment today. Let's assume that you have no immediate need for the money during the next 4 years (remember that we said finance was sometimes a theoretical subject), so if you accept the annuity, you would simply deposit the annual payments in an investment venture that pays 9 percent interest. How large must today's lump-sum payment be to make

---

[5]Had the annuity been an *annuity due*, then the three payments would have occurred at the beginning rather than the end of the period, or at $t = 0$, $t = 1$, $t = 2$. To find the future value of an annuity due, (1) look up the IFa for $n + 1$ years, then subtract 1.0 from the amount to get the IFa for the annuity due. In our previous example the annuity due interest factor is $4.4399 - 1.0 = 3.4399$. The same results can be obtained if we remember that an annuity due has one more compounding period than a regular annuity. Therefore we need to "compound" the IFa for one more period by multiplying it by $(1 + k)$; thus $3.2149(1.07) = 3.4399$. Therefore a 3-year annuity of $1,000 annually with its first payment made today and invested in a 7 percent account will equal $1,000(3.4399) = $3,439.90$ at the end of 3 years. Because payments on an annuity due come earlier, it is a little more valuable than a regular (deferred) annuity.

Figure 14-5
Time Line for an Annuity: Present Value with k = 9%
This figure shows how to derive the present value of a 4-year annuity of $1,000 per year at an interest rate of 9 percent. The present value is calculated by multiplying each year's receipt by the appropriate discount factor from Table 14-3 and adding the resulting amounts. One can then compare this present value with any other present value in order to determine the wisdom of accepting this annuity.

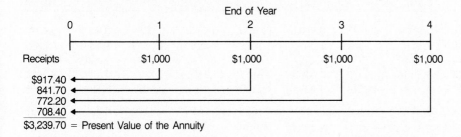

it equivalent to the annuity? The time line in Figure 14-5 will help explain the problem.

Rather than multiplying each year's receipt by factors from Table 14-3 and summing the results as suggested by Figure 14-5, a table has been constructed to facilitate the computation of the present value of an annuity. Table 14-5 is illustrative of the more complete set of discount factors for an annuity, DFa[6], that is presented in Appendix D. Utilizing Equation 14-4 and the appropriate DFa contained in Table 14-5, we can solve our problem in a direct fashion:

$$
\begin{aligned}
PVa &= Pmt(DFa) \qquad\qquad \textbf{(14-4)} \\
&= \$1,000(3.2397) \\
&= \$3,239.70.
\end{aligned}
$$

Thus the present value of an annuity, PVa, equals the annuity multiplied by the appropriate discount factor for an annuity, DFa. In our

---

[6]The discount factor for an annuity, DFa, is computed by summing the discount factors for each year's receipt. Therefore the present value of the first receipt is a $[1/(1 + k)]$, the second is a $[1/(1 + k)^2]$, and so on. Thus:

$$
\begin{aligned}
PVa &= Pmt\left(\frac{1}{1 + k}\right)^1 + Pmt\left(\frac{1}{1 + k}\right)^2 + \cdots + Pmt\left(\frac{1}{1 + k}\right)^n \\
&= Pmt\left[\frac{1}{(1 + k)^2} + \frac{1}{(1 + k)^2} + \cdots + \frac{1}{(1 + k)^n}\right] \\
&= Pmt\sum_{t=1}^{n}\left(\frac{1}{1 + k}\right)^t \\
&= Pmt(DFa). \qquad\qquad \textbf{(14-4)}
\end{aligned}
$$

Table 14-5
Present Value of an Annuity of $1 per Period for n Periods:

$$DFa = \sum_{t=1}^{n} \frac{1}{(1 + k)^t} = \frac{1 - [1/(1 + k)^n]}{k}$$

Number of Periods (n)	1%	2%	3%	4%	5%	6%	7%	8%	9%	10%
1	0.9901	0.9804	0.9709	0.9615	0.9524	0.9434	0.9346	0.9259	0.9174	0.9091
2	1.9704	1.9416	1.9135	1.8861	1.8594	1.8334	1.8080	1.7833	1.7591	1.7355
3	2.9410	2.8839	2.8286	2.7751	2.7232	2.6730	2.6243	2.5771	2.5313	2.4869
4	3.9020	3.8077	3.7171	3.6299	3.5460	3.4651	3.3872	3.3121	3.2397	3.1699
5	4.8534	4.7135	4.5797	4.4518	4.3295	4.2124	4.1002	3.9927	3.8897	3.7908
6	5.7955	5.6014	5.4172	5.2421	5.0757	4.9173	4.7665	4.6229	4.4859	4.3553
7	6.7282	6.4720	6.2303	6.0021	5.7864	5.5824	5.3893	5.2064	5.0330	4.8684
8	7.6517	7.3255	7.0197	6.7327	6.4632	6.2098	5.9713	5.7466	5.5348	5.3349
9	8.5660	8.1622	7.7861	7.4353	7.1078	6.8017	6.5152	6.2469	5.9952	5.7590
10	9.4713	8.9826	8.5302	8.1109	7.7217	7.3601	7.0236	6.7101	6.4177	6.1446

present problem the DFa for a 4-year, 9 percent annuity from Table 14-5 is found to be 3.2397. Multiplying this factor by the $1,000 annual receipt gives $3,239.70, the present value of the annuity. This figure is, of course, identical to the long method suggested by Figure 14-5.

Notice that the entry for each period n in Table 14-5 is equal to the sum of the entries in Table 14-3 up to and including Period n. For example, the DFa for 9 percent, 4 periods in Table 14-5 could have been calculated by summing the DF from Table 14-3:

$$0.9174 + 0.8417 + 0.7722 + 0.7084 = 3.2397.$$

Present Value of an Uneven Series of Receipts

The definition of an annuity includes the concept of a fixed amount—in other words, annuities involve situations where cash flows are *identical* in every year. Although many financial decisions do involve constant cash flows, some important decisions are concerned with uneven flows of cash. In particular, common stock investments ordinarily involve uneven, hopefully increasing, dividend payments over time. Consequently, it is necessary to expand our analysis to deal with varying payment streams.

The present value of an uneven stream of future income is equal to the sum of the PVs of the individual components of the stream. For example, suppose we are trying to find the PV of the stream of receipts shown in Table 14-6, discounted at 6 percent. As shown in the table, we multiply each receipt by the appropriate DF, then sum these prod-

Table 14-6
Present Value of an Uneven Stream of Receipts

Year	Stream of Receipts	×	DF (6%)	=	PV of Individual Receipts
1	$ 100		.9434		$ 94.34
2	200		.8900		178.00
3	200		.8396		167.92
4	200		.7921		158.42
5	200		.7473		149.46
6	0		.7050		0
7	1,000		.6651		665.10
				PV = Sum =	$1,413.24

ucts to obtain the PV of the stream, $1,413.24. Figure 14-6 gives a graphic view of the cash flow stream.

The PV of the receipts shown in Table 14-6 and Figure 14-6 can also be found by using the annuity equation; the steps in this alternative solution process are outlined below:

Step 1 Find the PV of $100 due in Year 1:

$$\$100(0.9434) = \$94.34.$$

Step 2 Recognize that a $200 annuity will be received during Years 2 through 5. Thus we could determine the value of a 5-year an-

Figure 14-6
Time Line for an Uneven Cash Flow Stream with k = 6%
How to calculate the present value of an uneven stream of future payments is illustrated in this figure. Each amount to be received is multiplied by the appropriate discount factor from Table 14-3 to arrive at its individual present value. The resulting amounts are then totaled to arrive at the present value of the stream of receipts.

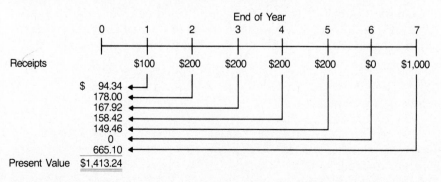

nuity, subtract from it the value of a 1-year annuity, and have remaining the value of a 4-year annuity whose first payment is due in 2 years. This result is achieved by subtracting the DFa for a 1-year, 6 percent annuity from the DFa for a 5-year annuity and then multiplying the difference by $200:

$$
\begin{aligned}
\text{PV of the annuity} &= \$200(\text{DFa} - 6\%, 5 \text{ years}) \\
&\quad - \$200(\text{DFa} - 6\%, 1 \text{ year}) \\
&= \$200[(\text{DFa} - 6\%, 5 \text{ years}) \\
&\quad - (\text{DFa} - 6\%, 1 \text{ year})] \\
&= \$200(4.2124 - 0.9434) \\
&= \$653.80.
\end{aligned}
$$

Thus the present value of the annuity component of the uneven stream is $653.80.

Step 3 Find the PV of the $1,000 due in Year 7:

$$\$1,000(0.6651) = \$665.10.$$

Step 4 Sum the components:

$$\$94.34 + \$653.80 + \$665.10 = \$1,413.24.$$

Either of the two methods can be used to solve problems of this type. However, the alternative (annuity) solution is easier if the annuity component runs for many years. For example, the alternative solution would be clearly superior for finding the PV of a stream consisting of $100 in Year 1, $200 in Years 2 through 29, and $1,000 in Year 30.

Determining Interest Rates

We can use the basic equations developed above to determine the interest rates implicit in financial contracts.

Example 1 A bank offers to lend you $1,000 if you sign a note to repay 1,610.50 at the end of 5 years. What rate of interest are you paying?
1. Recognize that $1,000 is the PV of $1,610.50 due in 5 years:

$$\text{PV} = \$1,000 = \$1,610.50(\text{DF}).$$

2. Solve for DF:

$$\text{DF} = \frac{\$1,000}{\$1,610.50} = 0.6209.$$

3. Now turn to Table 14-3 or Appendix B. Look across the row for Period 5 until you find the value .6209. It is in the 10 percent column,

so you would be paying a 10 percent rate of interest if you were to take out the loan.

Example 2 A bank offers to lend you $75,000 to buy a home. You must sign a mortgage calling for a payment of $7,635.48 at the end of each of the next 25 years. What interest rate is the bank charging you?
1. Recognize that $75,000 is the PV of a 25-year, $7,635.48 annuity:

$$PVa = \$75,000 = \sum_{t=1}^{25} \$7,635.48 \left[\frac{1}{(1 + k)^t}\right] = \$7,635.48 \, (DFa).$$

2. Solve for DFa:

$$DFa = \$75,000/\$7,635.48 = 9.8226.$$

3. Turn to Appendix D. Looking across the row for 25 periods, you will find 9.8226 under the column for 9 percent. Therefore the rate of interest on this mortgage loan is 9 percent.

Although the tables can be used to find the interest rate implicit in single payments and annuities, it is more difficult to find the interest rate implicit in an uneven series of payments. One can use a trial-and-error procedure, use more efficient but more complicated analytic procedures, or use a computer. We defer further discussion of this problem for now, but we take it up later in the capital budgeting chapters and again in our discussion of bond values.

Amortized Loans

One of the most important applications of compound interest concepts involves loans that are to be paid off in installments over time. Examples include automobile loans, home mortgage loans, and most business debt other than very short-term debt. If a loan is to be repaid in equal periodic amounts (monthly, quarterly, or annually), then it is said to be an **amortized loan.**

To illustrate, suppose a firm borrows $1,000 to be repaid in 3 equal payments at the end of each of the next 3 years. The lender is to receive 6 percent interest on funds outstanding. The first task is to determine the amount the firm must repay each year, or the annual payment. To find this amount, recognize that the $1,000 represents the present value of an annuity of Pmt dollars per year for 3 years, discounted at 6 percent:

amortized loan
A loan in which the principal amount is repaid in installments during the life of the loan.

$$\$1,000 = PV \text{ of annuity} = Pmt(DFa).$$

The DFa is 2.6730, so

$$\$1,000 = Pmt(2.6730).$$

Table 14-7
Loan Amortization Schedule

Year	Payment (1)	Interest[a] (2)	Repayment of Principal[b] (3)	Remaining Balance (4)
1	$ 374.11	$ 60.00	$ 314.11	$685.89
2	374.11	41.15	332.96	352.93
3	374.11	21.18	352.93	0
	$1,122.33	$122.33	$1,000.00	

[a]Interest is calculated by multiplying the loan balance at the beginning of the year by the interest rate. Therefore interest in Year 1 is $1,000(0.06) = $60; in Year 2 interest is $685.89(0.06) = $41.15; and in Year 3 interest is $352.93(0.06) = $21.18.
[b]Repayment of principal is equal to the payment of $374.11 minus the interest charge.

Solving for Pmt, we obtain

$$Pmt = \$1,000/2.6730 = \$374.11.$$

If the firm pays the lender $374.11 at the end of each of the next 3 years, the percentage cost to the borrower, and the return to the lender, will be 6 percent.

Each payment consists partly of interest and partly of a repayment of principal. This breakdown is given in the **amortization schedule** shown in Table 14-7. The interest component is largest in the first year, and it declines as the outstanding balance of the loan decreases. For tax purposes the borrower reports as a deductible cost each year the interest payments in Column 2, while the lender reports these same amounts as taxable income.

amortization schedule
A schedule that shows precisely how a loan will be repaid. It gives the payment required on each specific date and a breakdown of each payment showing how much of it constitutes interest and how much constitutes repayment of principal.

Review of Chapter Concepts

In light of the seemingly large number of formulas and the importance of this chapter, we believe a review of the concepts presented in this chapter is warranted.

Actually, all problems dealing with the time value of money (compounding or discounting) can be solved by utilizing one or a combination of the four formulas listed in Table 14-8.

Sample Problems

Problem: Compounding a Lump Sum to a Future Period. Your aunt has given you a $3,000 tax-free gift. If you invest it in a 5-year, 8 percent certificate of deposit, how much will you have when the certificate matures?

Table 14-8
Applications of the Time Value of Money

Formula	Equation Number	Interest or Discount Factor Table	Appendix
FV = PV(IF)	14-1a	14-2	A
PV = FV(DF)	14-2a	14-3	B
FVa = Pmt(IFa)	14-3	14-4	C
PVa = Pmt(DFa)	14-4	14-5	D

Discussion. The elements of this problem are a present amount, PV, of $3,000, a length of time for the investment, n, of 5 years, and an investment (interest) rate, k, of 8 percent. A future amount, FV—the value of $3,000 compounded at 8 percent for 5 years—is to be found. Since we are compounding a single, present amount, we use the IF found in either Table 14-2 or Appendix A.

Solution.

$$FV = PV(IF) \qquad\qquad\qquad \textbf{(14-1a)}$$
$$= \$3,000(1.4693)$$
$$= \$4,407.90.$$

Problem: Present Value of a Future Lump Sum. Your friend Howard has suggested that you invest, along with him, in a real estate deal. He predicts your portion of the property in question will be worth $40,000 in 8 years. If you can make an investment with equal risk at 10 percent, what is the maximum that you would wish to invest today in the venture?

Discussion. Here we are concerned with finding the present value, PV, of a future amount, FV, of $40,000 to be received in 8 years, n, with a discount rate, k, of 10 percent. With a lump-sum amount to be discounted back to the present, we use a discount factor, DF, found in Table 14-3 or in Appendix B.

Solution.

$$PV = FV(DF) \qquad\qquad\qquad \textbf{(14-2a)}$$
$$= \$40,000(.4665)$$
$$= \$18,660.$$

Problem: Future Value of a Regular Annuity. You are planning a great vacation trip to Europe in 15 years. You plan to save $500 annually, beginning next year after you graduate. How much will you have in your vacation fund in 15 years if you invest at 9 percent?

Discussion. In this situation we need to determine the future value, FVa, of an annuity of $500, Pmt, deposited annually for 15 years, n, at 9 percent, k. To do so we would use the interest factor for an annuity, IFa, where n = 15 and k = 9%, from Appendix C.

Solution.

$$FVa = Pmt(IFa) \qquad (14\text{-}3)$$
$$= \$500(29.360)$$
$$= \$14,680.$$

Alternative Problem. Let's keep the scenario that you are saving for your vacation trip to Europe, but change some of the elements of the problem. Now let's assume that you still want to save $500 each year for 15 years, but this time let's assume you know the trip will cost $14,680. What is the rate of return you must earn in order to reach your goal?

Discussion. In this situation we use the same formula, Equation 14-3, but this time we solve for the interest factor for an annuity, IFa. Once we have the IFa, we can determine the rate of return required to meet the goal.

Solution.

$$FVa = Pmt(IFa) \qquad (14\text{-}3)$$
$$\$14,680 = \$500(IFa)$$
$$IFa = \$14,680/\$500$$
$$IFa = 29.360.$$

Now go to Appendix C and find the 15-year row. Moving to the right along the 15-year row, we find the interest factor 29.360 in the 9 percent column. Thus 9 percent is the rate at which we must invest our annuity of $500 annually for 15 years in order to have a terminal value of $14,680.

Problem: Present Value of an Annuity. Lefty Holland, star center for Central State College, has been approached by the Buffalo Bouncers of the Professional Basketball League. The Bouncers have offered Lefty a generous contract which offers him a choice in the payment of his bonus. He may choose between (1) receiving a payment of $25,000 annually for 15 years or (2) receiving an equivalent amount today. If Lefty can invest at 8 percent, what would be the equivalent amount if the bonus were paid today? (Ignore tax consequences for the time being.)

Discussion. Under the conditions outlined, we want to find the present value of an annuity, PVa, of $25,000 annually, Pmt, for 15 years, n, which could be invested at 8 percent, k. The discount factor for an annuity, DFa, is found in Appendix D.

Solution.

$$\text{PVa} = \text{Pmt(DFa)} \qquad \qquad \textbf{(14-4)}$$
$$= \$25,000(8.5595)$$
$$= \$213,987.50.$$

Alternative Problem. In order to demonstrate how a single formula (Equation 14-4) can be used to determine unknowns other than PVa, let's change our basketball scenario. Now, assume Lefty is given the choice of (1) taking an immediate bonus of $213,987.50 or (2) taking an annuity for 15 years which he could invest at 8 percent annually. What is the annuity?

Discussion. We still utilize Equation 14-4, but now we solve for the annuity, Pmt. The discount factor for the annuity, 8.5595, comes, of course, from Appendix D.

Solution.

$$\text{PVa} = \text{Pmt(DFa)} \qquad \qquad \textbf{(14-4)}$$
$$\$213,987.50 = \text{Pmt}(8.5595)$$
$$\text{Pmt} = \$213,987.50/8.5595$$
$$\text{Pmt} = \$25,000.$$

Conclusions

With a bit of practice, perhaps gained by working the end-of-chapter problems, you will find that the problems associated with the time value of money are not as difficult as they may first appear. One trick to remember is that if you wish to know a future value, you use the formulas associated with Appendix A or C. You use Appendix A if there is only a single, present investment; however, if the investment is an annuity, you use Appendix C. On the other hand, if you wish to learn the present value of some future amount, you use Appendix B or D. You use Appendix B if the future amount to be discounted is a single, lump-sum amount. If the future receipt (or payment) is an annuity, you use Appendix D.

Summary

Financial decisions often involve determining the present value of a stream of future cash flows—this is true in stock, bond, and real estate valuation. Also, we often need to know the amount to which funds now on hand will grow during a specified time period. At other times we must calculate the interest rate built into a bond or loan contract. The basic concepts involved in these processes are called the "math of finance," which is the subject of this chapter.

The key procedures covered in the chapter are summarized below:

Future Value. $FV = PV (1 + k)^n$, where FV is the future value of an initial amount, PV, compounded at the percentage rate, k, for n periods. The term $(1 + k)^n$ is defined as IF, the *future value interest factor*.

Present Value. $PV = FV [1/(1 + k)]^n$. This equation is simply a transformation of the future value equation. The term $[1/(1 + k)]^n$ is defined as DF, the *discount factor*. The term k, when used to find present values, is often called the *discount rate*.

Future Value of an Annuity. An annuity is defined as a series of constant or equal payments of Pmt dollars per period. The sum, or future value as an annuity, is given the symbol FVa, and it is found as follows:

$$FVa = Pmt \sum_{t=1}^{n} (1 + k)^{n-t}.$$

The term

$$\sum_{t=1}^{n} (1 + k)^{n-t}$$

is defined as IFa, the *future value interest factor for an annuity*.

Present Value of an Annuity. The present value of an annuity is given the symbol PVa, and it is found as follows:

$$PVa = Pmt \sum_{t=1}^{n} \left(\frac{1}{1 + k}\right)^t.$$

The term

$$\sum_{t=1}^{n} \left(\frac{1}{1 + k}\right)^t = DFa$$

is defined as the *discount factor for an annuity*.

These four basic equations can be used to find the present or the future value of any lump sum or series of cash flows and also the interest rate built into any financial contract. These concepts will be used throughout the remainder of the book. In the next chapter the same basic concepts learned in this chapter are applied to business decisions involving expenditures on capital assets. In subsequent chapters the present value concepts will be used to determine the value of stocks and bonds, and also to analyze decisions involving the types of capital that should be used to pay for assets.

Resolution to Decision in Finance

Reenlisting with the Generals

Due to the time value of money, it's entirely possible that in the long run Herschel Walker's $6 million contract could be worth more than Steve Young's $40 million contract. Because Walker will receive his money over the next 4 years, he will be free to invest it as he chooses and thus increase its value. On the other hand, Young must wait for most of his money, with the last payment due in 2027. Because the payments extend so far into the future, their present value is greatly reduced.

From the players' point of view, Walker probably did get the better financial deal. Yet Young's contract appears to offer more security than Walker's does. Young is assured payments for the next 43 years, while Walker's financial future carries a degree of risk. Depending on the investment decisions of his advisers, Walker's income has greater potential, both upside and downside. But Young is also tied into the USFL for 43 years, and the future of the new league—financial and otherwise—may not be as stable as Young might wish.

Not surprisingly, sources say Generals owner Donald Trump will lay out more money for Walker's contract than Express owner J. William Oldenburg put up for former Brigham Young quarterback Young. Young actually receives only about $1 million in salary over the next 4 years; during the same time span Walker will receive his full $6 million from the Generals. But the bulk of Young's money reportedly is an annuity-like arrangement that will bring him about $30 million from 1990 to 2027. That's $810,810 a year, or $67,567 a month, if payments are made in equal amounts.

The Express won't say, of course, but several insurance firms used their annuity formulas—minus fees to financiers—to determine how much money the Express would have to set aside today to provide Young with $30 million. Assuming a guaranteed interest rate of 9 percent, the Express would need slightly less than $5.4 million. By 1990—when the payments to Young begin—that would have grown to more than $9 million. Still earning 9 percent, that $9 million would generate enough interest to pay the entire $30 million to Young through 2027 without ever having to make another payment to the original fund of $5.4 million.

Source: "Walker Prefers $6 Million Pact to Young's Deal," *San Jose Mercury News*, Mar. 9, 1984, 2E.

Key Terms   You should be able to define each of the following terms:

Future value (FV); present value (PV)   Annuity; annuity due; regular
Rate of return (k)   (deferred) annuity
Compounding; discounting   Amortized loan; amortization
                                                               schedule

Questions

14-1 Is it true that for all positive interest rates the following conditions hold: $IF_{k,n} \geq 1.0$; $DF_{k,n} \leq 1.0$; $FVa_{k,n} \geq$ number of periods the annuity lasts; $DFa_{k,n} \leq$ number of periods the annuity lasts?

14-2 An annuity is defined as a series of payments of a fixed amount for a specific number of periods. Thus $100 a year for 10 years is an annuity, but $100 in Year 1, $200 in Year 2, and $400 a year in Years 3 through 10 is *not* an annuity. However, the second series *contains* an annuity. Is this last statement true or false?

14-3 If a firm's earnings per share grew from $1 to $2 over a 10-year period, the *total growth* was 100 percent, but the *annual growth rate* was *less than* 10 percent. Why is this so?

14-4 To find the present value of an uneven series of payments, you must use the DF tables; the DFa tables can never be of use, even if some of the payments constitute an annuity (for example, $100 each year for Years 3, 4, 5, and 6), because the entire series is not an annuity. Is this statement true or false?

Self-Test Problems

ST-1 Assume it is now January 1, 1985. If you were to put $1,000 into a savings account on January 1, 1986 at an 8 percent interest rate, compounded annually, how much would you have in your account on January 1, 1989?

ST-2 Suppose instead that you deposited the $1,000 in 4 equal payments of $250 each on January 1 of 1986, 1987, 1988, and 1989. How much would you have in your account on January 1, 1989 if you deposited the $1,000 in this fashion?

ST-3 How large would each of your payments in Problem ST-2 have to be for you to obtain the same ending balance as you would have obtained by the single $1,000 deposit?

ST-4 If you need $1,000 as an ending balance in your account on January 1, 1989, how much would you have to deposit on January 1, 1986? Only one deposit will be made, and the compounding rate is 8 percent annually.

ST-5 If you want to make equal payments on January 1 of each year from 1986 through 1989 to accumulate the $1,000 you need, how large must each of the 4 payments be? The compounding rate is 8 percent annually.

ST-6 If your father were to offer either to make the payments given in Self-Test Problem ST-5 or to give you a lump sum of $750 on January 1, 1986, which would you choose?

ST-7 If you have only $750 on January 1, 1986, what interest rate, compounded annually, would you have to earn to have the necessary $1,000 on January 1, 1989?

ST-8 Suppose you could deposit only $186.29 on January 1 of each year from 1986 through 1989, but you still need $1,000 on January 1, 1989. What interest rate, with annual compounding, must you seek out to achieve your goal?

ST-9 Due to unfortunate circumstances, your brother must borrow $1,000 from you. He wants to repay the loan in 3 equal installments which include 9 percent interest. How much should he pay annually for the next 3 years? (The first payment is due one year from today.)

ST-10 Your Uncle Rodney promises that if you invest $1,500 today in his newest "get rich quick" scheme, he will pay you $530.30 each year for the next 3 years. What rate of return is his project offering?

Problems

14-1 Find the following values *without* using the tables, then work the problems *with* the tables to check your answers. Disregard rounding errors.

   a. An initial $1,000 compounded for 1 year at 5 percent.

   b. An initial $1,000 compounded for 2 years at 5 percent.

   c. The present value of $1,000 due in 1 year at a discount rate of 5 percent.

   d. The present value of $1,000 due in 2 years at a discount rate of 5 percent.

14-2 Use the tables to find the following values:

   ✱ **a.** An initial $1,000 compounded for 10 years at 5 percent.

   b. An initial $1,000 compounded for 10 years at 10 percent.

   ✱ **c.** The present value of $1,000 due in 10 years at a 5 percent discount rate.

   d. The present value of $2,594 due in 10 years at a 10 percent discount rate.

14-3 To the closest year, how long will it take $1,000 to double if it is deposited and earns the following rates?

   ✱ **a.** 10 percent.

*Refer to Appendix E for check answers to problems with asterisks.

  ∗ b. 15 percent.
  c. 100 percent.
14-4 Find the *future value* of the following annuities. The first payment in these annuities is made at the end of Year 1.
  a. $1,000 per year for 10 years at 10 percent.
  b. $2,000 per year for 5 years at 5 percent.
  c. $1,000 per year for 5 years at zero percent.
14-5 Find the *present value* of the following annuities:
  ∗ a. $1,000 per year for 10 years at 10 percent.
  b. $2,000 per year for 5 years at 5 percent.
  ∗ c. $1,000 per year for 5 years at zero percent.
14-6 a. Find the present value of the following cash flow streams when the discount rate is 8 percent:

Year	Cash Flow Stream A	Cash Flow Stream B
1	$1,000	$3,000
2	2,000	2,000
3	2,000	2,000
4	2,000	2,000
5	3,000	1,000

  b. What is the value of each cash flow stream at a zero percent discount rate?
∗ 14-7 Find the present value of the following cash flow stream, discounted at 5 percent: Year 1, $300; Year 2, $200; Years 3 to 20, $100.
14-8 Last year California Chemical's sales were $3 million. Sales were $1.5 million 5 years earlier.
  ∗ a. To the nearest percentage point, at what rate have sales been growing?
  b. Suppose someone calculated the sales growth in Part a as follows: "Sales doubled in 5 years. This represents a growth of 100 percent in 5 years; so dividing 100 percent by 5, we find the growth rate to be 20 percent per year." Explain what is wrong with this calculation.
14-9 a. You have decided to turn over a new leaf and begin to save money for a change. If you save $2,000 annually for the next 5 years in an 8 percent money market account, what will be the total at the end of the period? Assume that your investment will occur at the end of each year.
  b. Since the savings look so good in Part a, you want to get your savings started today. What is the value of the $2,000 annual investment if your first payment is made today and continues as before with 5 annual payments at an assumed rate of 8 percent?
14-10 Find the interest rates, or rates of return, on each of the following:
  a. You borrow $1,000 and promise to pay back $1,050 at the end of 1 year.
  b. You lend $1,000 and receive a promise of $1,050 at the end of 1 year.
  c. You borrow $10,000 and promise to pay back $16,289 at the end of 10 years.

    d. You borrow $10,000 and promise to make payments of $2,570.90 per year for 5 years.

* **14-11** The Dickenson Company buys a machine for $100,000 and expects a return of $23,852.10 per year for the next 10 years. What is the expected rate of return on the machine?

* **14-12** Washington Orchards invests $500,000 to clear a tract of land and set out some young apple trees. The trees will mature in 10 years, at which time the firm plans to sell the orchard at an expected price of $1.5 million. What is Washington Orchard's expected rate of return?

14-13 Your broker offers to sell you a note for $2,395.62 that will pay $600 per year for 5 years. If you buy the note, what rate of interest will you be earning?

14-14 Great Atlantic Mortgage Company offers to lend you $75,000; the loan calls for annual payments of $8,216.04 for 20 years. What interest rate is the company charging you?

14-15 To enable you to complete your last year in college and then go through law school, you need $7,500 per year for the next 4 years, starting next year (that is, you need the first payment of $7,500 one year from today). Your rich aunt has offered to provide you with a sum of money sufficient to put you through school. She plans to deposit this sum today in a bank account that is expected to yield 8 percent interest.

    * **a.** How large must the deposit be?

    b. How much will be in the account immediately after you make the first withdrawal? After the last withdrawal?

14-16 Set up an amortization schedule for a $100,000 loan to be repaid in equal installments at the end of each of the next three years. The interest rate is 10 percent.

Answers to Self-Test Problems

ST-1

1/1/85	1/1/86	1/1/87	1/1/88	1/1/89

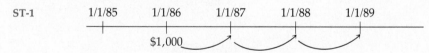

$1,000 is being compounded for 3 years:

$$FV = PV(1 + k)^n$$
$$= \$1,000(1 + 0.08)^3$$
$$= \$1,259.71.$$

ST-2

1/1/85	1/1/86	1/1/87	1/1/88	1/1/89
	$250	$250	$250	$250

Future value of an annuity:

$$FVa = Pmt(IFa) = \$250(4.5061)$$
$$= \$1,126.53.$$

ST-3
$$FVa = \$1,259.71$$
$$k = 8\%$$
$$n = 4.$$

$$Pmt(IFa) = FVa$$
$$Pmt(4.5061) = \$1,259.71$$
$$Pmt = \$1,259.71/4.5061$$
$$= \$279.56.$$

ST-4
$$FV = \$1,000$$
$$n = 3$$
$$k = 8\%.$$

$$FV(DF) = PV$$
$$\$1,000(0.7938) = \$793.80 \; (= \text{Initial deposit}$$
$$\text{necessary to accumulate } \$1,000).$$

ST-5
$$FVa = \$1,000$$
$$n = 4$$
$$k = 8\%.$$

$$Pmt(IFa) = FVa$$
$$Pmt = \frac{FVa}{(IFa_{8\%,4})}$$
$$= \frac{\$1,000}{4.5061}$$
$$= \$221.92.$$

ST-6
$$Pmt = \$221.92$$
$$k = 8\%$$
$$n = 4.$$

$$Pmt(DFa) = PVa$$
$$\$221.92(3.3121) = \$735.02.$$

This is less than the $750 lump-sum offer, so your initial reaction might be to accept the lump sum of $750. However, this would be a mistake. Note that if you were to deposit the $750 on January 1, 1986 at an 8 percent interest rate, to be withdrawn on January 1, 1989, interest would be compounded for only 3 years, from January 1, 1986 to December 31, 1988, and the future value would be only

$$PV(IF) = \$750(1.2597)$$
$$= \$944.78.$$

The problem is that when you found the $735.02 present value of the annuity, you were finding the value of the annuity *today*, on January 1, 1985. You were comparing $735.02 today with the lump sum $750 one year from now. This is, of course, invalid. What you should have done was take the $735.02 found in Step 1, recognize that this is the present value of an annuity as of January 1, 1985, multiply 735.02 times 1.08 to get $793.82, and compare $793.82 with the lump sum of $750. You would then take your father's offer to pay off the loan rather than the lump sum on January 1, 1986.

ST-7

$$PV = \$750$$
$$FV = \$1,000$$
$$n = 3$$
$$k = ?$$

$$PV(IF) = FV$$
$$IF = \frac{FV}{PV}$$
$$= \frac{\$1,000}{\$750}$$
$$= 1.3333.$$

Use the future value of $1 (Appendix A at the end of the book) for 3 periods to find the interest rate corresponding to an IF of 1.3333. Look across the third-period row of Appendix A until you come to 1.3333. The closest value is 1.3310 in the 10 percent column. Therefore you would require an interest rate of approximately 10 percent to achieve your $1,000 goal. The exact rate required, found with a financial calculator, is 10.0642 percent.

ST-8

$$FVa = \$1,000$$
$$Pmt = \$186.29$$
$$k = ?$$
$$n = 4.$$

$$Pmt(IFa) = FVa$$
$$\$186.29(IFa) = \$1,000$$
$$= \frac{\$1,000}{\$186.29}$$
$$= 5.3680.$$

Using the sum of an annuity table for 4 periods (Appendix C at the end of the book), we find that 5.3680 corresponds to a 20 percent interest rate. You might be able to find a borrower willing to offer you a 20 percent interest rate, but there would be some risk involved, and he or she might not actually pay you your $1,000!

ST-9

$$PVa = \$1,000$$
$$Pmt = ?$$
$$k = 9\%$$
$$n = 3.$$

$$PVa = Pmt(DFa)$$
$$\$1{,}000 = Pmt(2.5313)$$
$$Pmt = \frac{\$1{,}000}{2.5313}$$
$$= \$395.05.$$

ST-10

$$PVa = \$1{,}500$$
$$Pmt = \$530.30$$
$$k = ?$$
$$n = 3.$$

$$PVa = Pmt(DFa)$$
$$\$1{,}500 = \$530.30(DFa)$$
$$DFa = \frac{\$1{,}500}{\$530.30}$$
$$= 2.8286.$$

Using the present value of an annuity table for 3 periods (Appendix D at the end of the book), we find that 2.8286 corresponds to only a 3 percent rate of return. Therefore this would not appear to be a very profitable investment opportunity.

The Process
of Capital Budgeting

Decision in Finance

Jack Welch's New GE

When Jack Welch took over as chairman and chief executive officer of General Electric in 1981, he was faced with a confusing mass of separate businesses. GE had never intended to become a conglomerate, but through internal development it had become one anyway. The company makes refrigerators and jet engines, turbines and dishwashers; finances leveraged buyouts; owns a TV station; and, until recently, mined coal in Australia.

The trouble with such diversity is that it's impossible to be outstanding in so many fields. In fact, 16 main businesses account for 92 percent of GE's profit and 87 percent of its sales. These are GE's traditional businesses: major appliances, lighting, electric motors; the newer technologies such as jet engines, medical equipment, electronics; and services such as GE Credit. In all of these fields, GE is a leader.

But GE is also involved in 20 or so other businesses in which it is not a leader, and these drag down the corporation's overall profit margins and return on equity. These laggards, businesses such as large transformer and television set manufacturing, tie up capital and management talent without earning a commensurate return.

Jack Welch recognizes this overdiversification as one of GE's biggest problems. He knows it's important for GE to stop spending capital on businesses that don't pull their own weight. But it's by opening up GE's businesses, not by closing them down, that Welch wants to make his mark on the company.

As you read this chapter, consider the alternatives available to Jack Welch. How should he allocate funds to GE's many businesses? What should he do about the laggards?

See end of chapter for resolution.

In Part IV we analyzed decisions relating to current assets and current liabilities, or working capital management. Now we turn to investment decisions involving fixed assets, or the process of capital budgeting. The term *capital* refers to fixed assets used in production, while a *budget* is a plan detailing projected inflows and outflows during some future period. Thus, the *capital budget* outlines the planned expenditures on fixed assets, and **capital budgeting** is the whole process of analyzing projects and deciding whether they should be included in the capital budget.

capital budgeting
The process of analyzing projects and deciding whether an investment should be made.

Each year businesses invest hundreds of billions of dollars in fixed assets. The selection of business projects and the real assets associated with these projects not only involves large sums of capital for a firm, but also determines to a large extent its future productivity and cash flows. Thus by their very nature such investments critically affect a firm's future. A good decision can boost earnings sharply and increase dramatically the price of the firm's stock. A bad decision, on the other hand, can lead to bankruptcy.

Our treatment of capital budgeting is divided into two parts. First, this chapter gives an overview of the process and explains the basic analytical steps required in evaluating projects. Then, in the next chapter, we go on to consider the special case of replacement decisions as well as risk analysis in capital budgeting.

Steps in Capital Budgeting

Fixed assets are, by definition, expected to provide cash flows for some years into the future. Thus the discounting process, which is largely ignored in current asset analysis, is of critical importance in capital budgeting. This chapter emphasizes the following six steps involved in the capital investment evaluation process:

1. First, management estimates the expected cash flows from a given project, including the value of the asset at a specified terminal date.

2. Next, the riskiness of projected cash flows must be estimated.

cost of capital
The discount rate that should be used in the capital budgeting process.

3. The firm then chooses an appropriate discount rate, called the **cost of capital,** at which these cash flows are to be discounted.

4. The expected cash flows are then discounted and put on a present value basis to obtain an estimate of the asset's value to the firm.

5. This calculated value is next compared to the cost of the project; if the asset's present value exceeds its cost, the project should be accepted.

6. Finally, and very importantly, the effect of the capital budgeting process on the value of the firm is considered. If the firm identifies (or creates) investment opportunities with present values greater than their costs, the value of the firm will be increased. Thus there is a very direct link between the capital budgeting decision and the firm's value.

The more effective the firm's capital budgeting procedures, the greater the firm's growth, and hence the higher the value of the firm as reflected in the price of its common stock.

Ideas for Capital Projects

A firm's growth and development, even its ability to remain competitive and to survive, depend on a constant flow of new investment ideas. Accordingly, a well-managed firm will go to great lengths to develop good capital budgeting proposals. For example, the executive vice president of a major corporation indicated that his company takes the following steps to generate projects:

> Our R & D department is constantly searching for new products, or for ways to improve existing products. In addition, our Executive Committee, which consists of senior executives in marketing, production, and finance, identifies the products and markets in which our company will compete, and the Committee sets long-run targets for each division. These targets, which are formalized in the Corporation's strategic plan, provide a general guide to the operating executives who must meet them. These executives then seek new products, set expansion plans for existing products, and look for ways to reduce production and distribution costs. Since bonuses and promotions are based in large part on each unit's ability to meet or exceed its targets, these economic incentives encourage our operating executives to seek out profitable investment opportunities.
>
> While our senior executives are judged and rewarded on the basis of how well their units perform, people further down the line are given bonuses for specific suggestions, including ideas that lead to profitable investments. Additionally, a percentage of our corporate profit is set aside for distribution to nonexecutive employees. Our objective is to encourage lower level workers to keep on the lookout for good ideas, including those that lead to capital investments.

However, not all capital project ideas come from R & D or senior management. For example, a salesperson may report that customers are asking for a particular product that the company does not now produce. The sales manager then discusses the idea with people in the marketing research group to determine whether a sizable market exists for the proposed product. If it appears likely that a market does exist, cost accountants and engineers will be brought in to estimate production costs. If this type of investigation suggests that the product can be produced and sold to yield a sufficient profit, then the project will be undertaken.

If the firm has capable and imaginative executives and employees, and if its incentive system is working properly, many ideas for capital investment will be advanced. Since some ideas will be good ones while others will not, procedures must be established for screening projects. Steps in the screening process are discussed in the following sections.

Project Classification

Analyzing capital expenditure proposals is not a costless operation— benefits can be gained from a careful analysis, but such an investigation does have a cost. For certain types of projects a relatively refined analysis may be warranted; for others cost/benefit studies may suggest that a simpler procedure should be used. Accordingly, firms frequently classify projects into the following categories:

1. Replacement: maintenance of business. Expenditures necessary to replace worn-out or damaged equipment are in this group. These expenditures need not be "in kind," but they do not increase capacity or alter production processes.

2. Replacement: cost reduction. Expenditures to replace serviceable but obsolete equipment fall into this category. The purpose of these expenditures is to lower the cost of labor, materials, or other items such as electricity.

3. Expansion of existing products or markets. Expenditures to increase output of existing products, or to expand outlets or distribution facilities in markets now being served, are included here.

An example of a capital project where equipment replaces human labor is robot painting in the automobile industry. This photo from Chrysler shows robots painting car interiors. The enormous capital investment in this equipment was offset by savings incurred due to the decreased cost of using equipment instead of labor. *Source: Courtesy of Chrysler Corporation.*

4. Expansion into new products or markets. Expenditures necessary to produce a new product, or to expand into a geographic area not currently being served, are in this category.

5. Safety and/or environmental projects. Expenditures necessary to comply with government orders, labor agreements, or insurance policy terms are listed here. These expenditures are often called *mandatory investments,* or *non-revenue-producing projects.*

6. Other. This catch-all includes home office buildings, parking lots, and so on.

In general, relatively simple calculations and only a few supporting documents are required to support replacement decisions, especially maintenance-type investments in profitable plants. More detailed analysis is required for cost reduction replacements, for expansion of existing product lines, and for investments into new products or areas. Also, within each category, projects are broken down by their dollar costs: the larger the required investment, the more detailed the analysis and the higher the level of the officer who must authorize the expenditure. Thus, while a plant manager may be authorized to approve maintenance expenditures up to $10,000 on the basis of a relatively unsophisticated analysis, the full board of directors may have to approve decisions which involve either amounts over $1 million or expansions into new products or markets, and a very detailed, refined analysis will be required to support these decisions.

Estimating the Cash Flows

The most important, but also the most difficult, step in the analysis of a capital expenditure proposal is the estimation of the cash flows associated with the project—the outflows associated with building and equipping the new facility and the annual cash inflows the project will produce after it goes into operation. A great many variables are involved in the cash flow forecast, and many individuals and departments participate in developing them. For example, the Market Research Group projects sales via industry analysis and by test marketing potential products, the Marketing Department determines pricing policy, the Production and Engineering Departments combine to establish production and labor requirements, while the Industrial Relations Department must consider labor requirements and determine wage and benefit packages. Furthermore, the Accounting Department must evaluate overhead expenses attributable to the new project. Still other inputs to the preparation of the cash flow estimates must come from the Finance Department, which forecasts future economic developments that would affect the project, such as changes in inflation or GNP. Of course, in smaller firms, fewer managers will be available to participate in these forecasts. Still, no matter what the size of the firm, the better the forecast, the more likely it is that a poor project will be rejected and a good one accepted.

From these estimates a series of financial statements is developed which details the expected cash flows during the life of the proposed project. Often the financial statements are prepared under several different economic scenarios to determine their impact on profitability.

It is important to note that accounting-determined profitability is not the most important variable in evaluating a capital project. Rather, in evaluating the contributions of a project to the firm, management is generally more concerned with the project's **cash flow**. To better understand the importance of cash flow in the firm's capital investment decision, let's assume that Spartan Manufacturing Company has a new project, known around the firm as "Project X," which will require $100,000 in new equipment. This equipment will be depreciated on a straight line basis for the 5-year life of the project. The effect of the project on Spartan's reported earnings is seen in the first column of numbers in Table 15-1.

In the second column of numbers are listed the aggregate cash transactions associated with the project. Costs of goods sold, COGS, is the total of all of the expenditures for the production, labor, and materials of Project X. The selling and administrative expenses are those allocated or directly attributable to the project. The taxes are, of course, those which are paid as a direct result of the revenues generated by the new project.

Note that each of the expenditures in the second number column of

cash flow
The actual net cash, as opposed to accounting net income, that flows into (or out of) a firm during some specified period.

Table 15-1
Spartan Manufacturing Company: Project X

	Effect of Project X on:	
	Reported Earnings	Cash Transactions
Sales	$90,000	$90,000
Less: COGS (except depreciation)	40,000	40,000
Less: Depreciation	20,000	
Gross margin	30,000	
Less: Selling and administrative	15,000	15,000
Operating profit	15,000	
Less: Taxes (40%)	6,000	6,000
Earnings after taxes	9,000	
Plus: Depreciation	20,000	
Cash flow	$29,000	$29,000

Table 15-1 are actual *cash* receipts or payments. However, in the first number column one expense is only a "bookkeeping" entry—depreciation. As we discussed in our review of accounting, depreciation is a noncash allocation of the expense of a fixed asset over its useful (or IRS-determined) life. This allocation permits the company to reduce its tax burden each period but *involves no actual payment of cash.* Therefore we can add the *depreciation* back to the accounting-determined *after-tax earnings* attributable to the project, which in Table 15-1 equal the project's *cash flow* of $29,000.

An equivalent method of determining the cash flow is presented in Equation 15-1:

$$\text{Cash flow} = (\$R - \$E)(1 - t) + (D)(t), \qquad \textbf{(15-1)}$$

where

$\$R$ = cash revenues generated by the project
$\$E$ = cash expenses associated with the project
t = marginal tax rate
D = depreciation on the project's fixed assets.

When we utilize this formula and the data from Project X found in Table 15-1,

$$
\begin{aligned}
\text{Cash flow} &= (\$R - \$E)(1 - t) + (D)(t) \\
&= (\$90,000 - 55,000)(1 - .4) + (\$20,000)(.4) \\
&= (\$35,000)(.6) + (\$20,000)(.4) \\
&= \$21,000 + \$8,000 \\
&= \$29,000,
\end{aligned}
$$

we arrive at the same conclusion as we did when we found the *cash flow* by adding the accounting-determined *earnings after taxes* and *depreciation.*

Note that the cash flow *does not* contain any financing expenses such as interest or preferred or common stock dividends. As we learn in a subsequent chapter, the minimum acceptable rate of return for any project is the cost of capital. That is, the cost of capital is the weighted average of the required returns, or cost, of all sources of financing. Therefore, if financing charges were included in determining the project's cash flow, and the net cash flows were later discounted by the cost of capital, we would be double counting the financing costs. Thus it is convenient to compute the cash flow *as if* the project were financed entirely with common stock equity funding. In essence, this approach allows us to concentrate on selecting the best project available. Then, once the best project is identified, we proceed to find the optimal means by which it can be financed.

Methods Used to Evaluate Proposed Projects

A number of different methods are used to rank projects and to decide whether or not they should be accepted for inclusion in the capital budget. Three of the most commonly used are:

1. Payback (or payback period). This is the number of years required to return the original investment.

2. Net present value (NPV). This is the present value of future cash flows, discounted at the appropriate cost of capital, minus the cost of the investment. The NPV method is called a *discounted cash flow (DCF)* method.

3. Internal rate of return (IRR). This is the discount rate that equates the present value of future cash flows to the initial cost of the project. The IRR is also a discounted cash flow (DCF) method.

Future cash flows are, in all cases, defined as the net cash inflows from the investments. The nature and characteristics of these methods are illustrated and explained below, where we use the cash flow data shown in Table 15-2 for two projects which we call Project E and Project L. Note that the returns from Project E are much greater early in its life than those of Project L, whose returns are larger comparatively late in its life. We assume that the cash flows consist of both after-tax profits and depreciation, not just profits alone. Furthermore, the investment outlay includes all costs required to implement the project. Thus the **investment outlay** includes not only the cost of the fixed assets required for the project, but also any working capital outlays such as increases in inventories and accounts receivable which occur due to the project.[1]

investment outlay
Funds expended for fixed assets of a specified project plus working capital funds expended as a result of the project's adoption.

Payback Method

payback (or payback period)
The length of time required for the cash flows to return the cost of the investment.

The **payback period** is defined as the number of years it takes a firm to recover its original investment from net cash flows. In Table 15-2 each project costs $25,000, so the payback period for Project E is 2.375 years [$12,000 + $10,000 + ($3,000/$8,000)], and the payback period for Project L is 3.133 years [$5,400 + $8,000 + $10,000 + ($1,600/$12,000)]. Since Project E's largest cash flows occur early in its life, it is not surprising that it has the faster recovery of the initial investment. On the basis of payback, Project E is superior to Project L if the projects are of equal risk.

---

[1]Of course, only the investment in fixed assets is depreciable. When the project ends, the investment in working capital is often recovered through reductions in inventory and collection of accounts receivable outstanding. This recovery is not taxable since it represents a conversion of assets without economic gain.

Table 15-2
Cash Flows for Projects E and L
(Investment Outlay for Each Project Is $25,000)

| | Net Cash Flow (After-Tax Profits plus Depreciation) | |
| | Project E | Project L |
Year		
1	$12,000	$ 5,400
2	10,000	8,000
3	8,000	10,000
4	5,400	12,000
Total inflows	$35,400	$35,400

Of course, the payback method's principal strength is its ease of calculation and application. Prior to the 1960s payback was the most commonly used method for screening capital expenditure proposals. However, the payback technique has conceptual problems which make total reliance on this technique financially undesirable. Two of the major conceptual weaknesses of payback are:

1. It ignores returns beyond the payback period. One glaring weakness of the payback period is that it ignores any cash flow which occurs beyond the payback period. For example, if Project L had an additional return of $20,000 in Year 5, this fact would not influence the payback or payback ranking of Projects E and L. Ignoring returns in the distant future means that the payback method is biased against long-term projects.

2. It ignores the time value of money. The timing of cash flows is obviously important (as the last chapter emphasized), yet the payback method ignores the time value of money. By this method a dollar in Year 3 is given the same weight as a dollar in Year 1.

In spite of the conceptual drawbacks to the payback technique, this project-screening device has shown remarkable vitality over the years. Managers still use payback because it tells them something they want to know. In the 1970s and, it appears, in the 1980s managers face capital shortages. Therefore a project that returns its investment quickly will allow these funds to be reinvested quickly in other projects. Such a project would be especially valuable to a small or growing firm which is unable to raise capital quickly or in large amounts. By focusing on the speed of cash inflows, the payback method provides important information to the financial manager. However, in light of payback's weaknesses, the technique should be used in conjunction with other, more technically correct project-screening devices such as net present value and internal rate of return.

Net Present Value (NPV) Method

discounted cash flow (DCF) techniques
Methods of ranking investment proposals, including the internal rate of return method and net present value method.

net present value (NPV)
A method of ranking investment proposals. The NPV is equal to the present value of future returns, discounted at the marginal cost of capital, minus the present value of the cost of the investment.

As the flaws in the payback method were recognized, people began to search for methods of evaluating projects which would recognize that a dollar received immediately is preferable to a dollar received at some future date. This led to the development of **discounted cash flow (DCF) techniques** to take account of the time value of money. One such DCF technique is called the *net present value method. To implement this approach, find the present value of the expected net cash flows of an investment, discounted at an appropriate percentage rate, and subtract from it the initial cost outlay of the project.* If its net present value is positive, the project should be accepted; if negative, it should be rejected.

The equation for the **net present value (NPV) is**

$$NPV = \sum_{t=1}^{n} \frac{CF_t}{(1 + k)^t} - C$$

$$= \left[\frac{CF_1}{(1 + k)^1} + \frac{CF_2}{(1 + k)^2} + \cdots + \frac{CF_n}{(1 + k)^n} \right] - C$$

$$= CF_1(DF_1) + CF_2(DF_2) + \cdots + CF_n(DF_n) - C. \quad \textbf{(15-2)}$$

Here CF_1, CF_2, and so forth represent the annual cash flows from the project, discounted at the appropriate discount rate, k, represented by the discount factor, DF, in each period. For most projects the minimum acceptable rate of return, k, is the cost of capital. C is the investment outlay or initial cost of the project (if the costs are spread over several years, C may be expressed as the present value of all costs required to "put the project on line"); and n is the project's expected life. The cost of capital, k, depends on the riskiness of the project, the level of interest rates in the economy, and several other factors. In this chapter we take k as a given, but it is discussed in detail in Chapter 20.

Under the assumption that the two projects are equally risky, the net present values of Projects E and L are calculated in Table 15-3, using the discounting procedures developed in Chapter 14 and Equation 15-2. Assuming a required rate of return of 12 percent for both projects, Project E has an NPV of $2,813 and Project L's NPV is $944. On this basis both projects should be accepted if possible; however, if only one can be chosen, Project E is the better choice since it has the higher NPV.

The value of a firm is a composite of the values of its parts. Thus, when a firm takes on a project with a positive NPV, the value of the firm should increase by the amount of the NPV. A positive NPV means that the project covers all operating and financial costs and still has excess returns over these costs. In our example the value of the firm will increase by $2,813 if the firm chooses Project E, but by only $944 if it chooses Project L. Of course, the firm's value will increase by

Table 15-3
Calculating the Net Present Values (NPVs) of Projects E and L

Year	Project E Cash Flow	Project E DF (12%)	Project E PV of Cash Flow	Project L Cash Flow	Project L DF (12%)	Project L PV of Cash Flow
1	$12,000	.8929	$ 10,715	$ 5,400	.8929	$ 4,822
2	10,000	.7972	7,972	8,000	.7972	6,378
3	8,000	.7118	5,694	10,000	.7118	7,118
4	5,400	.6355	3,432	12,000	.6355	$ 7,626
		PV of inflows	$ 27,813		PV of inflows	$ 25,944
		Less cost	− 25,000		Less cost	− 25,000
		NPV	$ 2,813		NPV	$ 944

$3,757 if it is possible to accept both projects. *The increase in the value of the firm from its capital budget for the year is the sum of the NPVs of all accepted projects.* Thus, if Projects E and L are mutually exclusive, it is easy to see why Project E is preferable to Project L, but if they are independent, both are acceptable since each has a positive NPV.[2]

The Internal Rate of Return (IRR) Method

In the previous section on NPV we learned that if a project's NPV is positive, the project is acceptable, and if the NPV is negative, the project is unacceptable. When the NPV is neither positive nor negative, the rate used to discount future cash flows back to the present is the project's **internal rate of return (IRR).** More formally, *the internal rate of return is the discount rate that equates the present value of the expected future cash flows, or receipts, to the initial cost of the project.* The equation for calculating this rate is

internal rate of return (IRR)
The rate of return on an asset investment, calculated by finding the discount rate that equates the present value of future cash flows to the cost of the investment.

$$\sum_{t=1}^{n} \frac{CF_t}{(1 + r)^t} - C = 0$$

$$\frac{CF_1}{(1 + r)^1} + \frac{CF_2}{(1 + r)^2} + \cdots \frac{CF_n}{(1 + r)^n} - C = 0$$

$$CF_1(DF_1) + CF_2(DF_2) + \cdots + CF_n(DF_n) - C = 0. \qquad \textbf{(15-3)}$$

---

[2]*Mutually exclusive* projects are alternative investments; if one project is taken on, the other must be rejected. For example, the installation of a conveyor belt system in a warehouse and the purchase of a fleet of forklift trucks for the same warehouse would be mutually exclusive projects—accepting one implies rejection of the other. *Independent* projects are those whose costs and revenues are independent of one another. For example, the purchase of the company president's automobile and the purchase of a corporate jet would represent independent projects.

discount rate
The interest rate used in the discounting process.

Here we know the value of the investment outlay, C, and the cash flows, CF_1, CF_2, $\cdot \cdot \cdot$, CF_n as well, but we do not know the value of the **discount rate,** r, that equates the future cash flows and the present value of the investment outlays. *Some value of r will cause the sum of the discounted cash receipts to equal the initial cost of the project, making the equation equal zero: this value of r is defined as the internal rate of return.* In other words, the solution value for r is the IRR.

A simple example may make this concept easier to understand. If we invest $10,000 for 6 years at 14 percent, using Equation 14-1a, we can determine the terminal value of the investment:

$$FV = PV(IF) \qquad\qquad\qquad \textbf{(14-1a)}$$
$$= \$10,000(2.1950)$$
$$= \$21,950.$$

Now let's assume that we know that if we invest $10,000 today, our investment will return $21,950 in 6 years. What is the rate of return on this investment? Of course, we need to find the discount rate that equates the value of our investment today, $10,000, with the future value of $21,950 to be received 6 years hence. This is the same as finding the discount rate that causes the NPV of the investment to equal zero. Therefore, as Equation 15-3 suggests, we solve for the discount factor to determine the discount rate:

$$PV = FV(DF)$$
$$DF = \frac{PV}{FV}$$
$$= \frac{\$10,000}{\$21,950}$$
$$= .455581 = .4556.$$

We can find the discount factor .4556 in Appendix B, by looking across the sixth-year row to the 14 percent column. Thus the rate that equates the present cost and future return is the internal rate of return—14 percent.

Notice that the internal rate of return formula, Equation 15-3, is simply the NPV formula, Equation 15-2, solved for the particular discount rate that causes the NPV to equal zero. Thus the same basic equation is used for both methods, but in the NPV method the discount rate, k, is specified and the NPV is found, while in the IRR method the NPV is specified to equal zero and the value of r that forces the NPV to equal zero is found.

The internal rate of return may be found in a number of ways. Several methods are discussed below.

Procedure 1: IRR with Constant Cash Inflows. If the cash flows from a project are constant, or equal in each year, then the project's internal rate of return can be found by a relatively simple process. In essence, such a project is an annuity: the firm makes an outlay, C, and receives a stream of cash flow benefits, Pmt, for a given number of years. The IRR for the project is found by applying Equation 14-4, discussed in Chapter 14.

To illustrate, suppose a project has a cost of $10,000 and is expected to produce cash flows of $1,627.45 a year for 10 years. The cost of the project, $10,000, is the present value of an annuity of $1,627.45 a year for 10 years. Applying Equation 14-4, we obtain

$$\frac{\text{Cost}}{\text{Pmt}} = \frac{\$10,000}{\$1,627.45} = 6.1446 = \text{DFa.}$$

Looking up DFa in Appendix D (at the end of the text) across the row for Year 10, we find it located under the 10 percent column. Accordingly, 10 percent is the project's IRR. In other words, 10 percent is the value or r that would force Equation 15-3 to zero when Pmt is constant at $1,627.45 for 10 years and C is $10,000. This procedure works only if the project has constant annual cash flows; if it does not, the IRR must be found by one of the other methods discussed next.

Procedure 2: Trial and Error. In the trial-and-error method we first compute the present value of cash flows from an investment, using a somewhat arbitrarily selected discount rate. Since the cost of capital for most firms is in the range of 12 to 18 percent, it is hoped that projects will promise a return of at least 12 percent. Therefore 12 percent is a good starting point for most problems. Then we compare the present value thus obtained with the investment's cost. Suppose the present value of the inflows is larger than the project's cost. What do we do now? We must *lower* the present value, and to do this we must *raise* the discount rate and go through the process again. Conversely, if the present value is lower than the cost, we lower the discount rate and repeat the process. We continue until the present value of the flows from the investment is approximately equal to the project's cost. *The discount rate that brings about this equality is defined as the internal rate of return.*

This calculation process is illustrated next for the same Projects E and L that we analyzed earlier. In Table 15-4 we review the steps required to find the IRR for Project L. First, the 12 percent interest factors are obtained from Appendix B at the end of the text. These factors are then multiplied by the cash flows for the corresponding years, and the present values of the cash flows are placed in the appropriate columns. Next, the present values of the yearly cash flows are summed to obtain the investment's total present value. Subtracting the cost of the project from this figure gives the net present value of the project's cash flow. Since the NPV of Project L's cash flow is positive, we know the internal rate of return of this investment opportunity is greater than 12 percent.

Table 15-4
Finding the Internal Rate of Return of Project L

		12%		14%	
Year	Cash Flow	DF	PV	DF	PV
1	$ 5,400	.8929	$ 4,844	.8772	$ 4,737
2	8,000	.7972	6,378	.7695	6,156
3	10,000	.7118	7,118	.6750	6,750
4	12,000	.6355	7,626	.5921	7,105
		PV of inflows	$ 25,944		$ 24,748
		Less cost	− 25,000		− 25,000
		NPV	$ 944		$ (252)

However, the NPV is rather small, indicating the IRR is close to 12 percent. Thus we increase the discount rate slightly to 14 percent. At 14 percent the NPV of Project L is a negative $252. Therefore, since the internal rate of return (IRR) causes the NPV to equal zero, we know the internal rate of return for Project L is between 12 and 14 percent.

If we wish to be more accurate in our IRR, we can interpolate between these results. To do so, we bracket the discount rate that causes the project's NPV to equal zero:

$$PV = \$25,944 \text{ at } 12.\ 0\%$$
$$PV = \$25,000 \text{ at } 12.+\% \left. \right\} \$944 \left. \right\} \$1,196$$
$$PV = \$24,748 \text{ at } \underline{14.\ 0\%}$$
$$2.\ 0\%$$

Thus

$$IRR = 12.00\% + (\$944/\$1,196)(2.0\%)$$
$$= 12.00\% + .789(2.0\%)$$
$$= 13.58\%.$$

We see that the IRR lies 944/1196 percent of the way between 12 and 14 percent. Since there is a two-percentage-point difference between 12 and 14 percent, we multiply the fraction by 2 percent before adding the quantity to 12 percent for our IRR of 13.58 percent. For all practical purposes, an IRR that is accurate to within one-half percent is usually sufficient. The calculations may be carried out to several decimal places, but for most projects, when the assumptions associated with forecasting cash flows several years into the future are considered, this is spurious accuracy.

Just as we found the IRR of Project L, we now trace the steps in determining the IRR for Project E (see Table 15-5). Again, the 12 percent discount rate is employed as a starting point in our search for the

Table 15-5
Finding the Internal Rate of Return of Project E

Year	Cash Flow	12% DF	12% PV	16% DF	16% PV	18% DF	18% PV
1	$12,000	.8929	$ 10,715	.8621	$ 10,345	.8475	$ 10,170
2	10,000	.7972	7,972	.7432	7,432	.7182	7,182
3	8,000	.7118	5,694	.6407	5,126	.6086	4,869
4	5,400	.6355	3,432	.5523	2,982	.5158	2,785
		PV of inflows	$ 27,813		$ 25,885		$ 25,006
		Less cost	− 25,000		− 25,000		− 25,000
		NPV	$ 2,813		$ 885		$ 6

project's internal rate of return. The firm's cost of capital, or the return on the best alternative investment opportunity, is usually the first discount rate used in the trial-and-error process. Since the NPV at 12 percent is positive, we know the project's IRR is greater than 12 percent. Because the NPV is significantly greater than zero at 12 percent, we know the IRR is much greater than that rate. Multiplying the project's cash flows by a greater discount rate (the rate of 16 percent is chosen arbitrarily), we find that the NPV is still positive, though less than before. At 18 percent the NPV is barely larger than zero; thus for all practical purposes the IRR of Project E is 18 percent, since at that rate the project's NPV is essentially zero.

Procedure 3: Computer Solutions. Since the internal rates of return can be calculated by computers, many firms have computerized their capital budgeting processes and automatically generate IRRs, NPVs, and paybacks for all projects. Even some of the more powerful hand-held calculators are programmed to compute IRRs. Thus business firms have no difficulty with the mechanical side of capital budgeting. However, we believe students should become proficient in solving IRR problems before allowing a calculator or computer to do the work for them so that they really understand the computations performed by these labor-saving devices.

Whether computers, calculators, or the trial-and-error method is used to calculate the IRR for the projects, it is clear that the internal rate of return for Project E is greater than Project L's IRR. Additionally, since the NPV for Project E is greater than the NPV for Project L, Project E should be selected if the two projects are mutually exclusive. But which project should be chosen if the present value decision rules give mixed results? That is, if Project A has the larger NPV, but Project B has the higher IRR, which of the two decision rules (IRR or NPV) should prevail? We answer this question in Appendix 15A. (Hint: Don't bet against the NPV rule.)

An Expanded Case in Capital Budgeting

Jefferson Electronics Company is entering into the video game market. Although this is a very competitive industry, the company's president, Lee Davis, believes its product will be unique and quite competitive.

The new equipment required for the project will cost $130,000, with no additional installation charges (modification of the plant needed to accommodate new equipment is fully depreciable). Due to the high rate of technical obsolescence in electronic equipment and products, the project has an expected life of only 5 years. The equipment will be depreciated as a 3-year-class property using the accelerated cost recovery system (ACRS). The equipment is expected to have a market value of $15,000 at the end of the 5-year period. As 3-year-class property, the equipment is eligible for a 6 percent investment tax credit.

Table 15-6 contains Davis's forecast of sales along with operating cost projections. In addition to these annual costs, he believes the project will require a net additional investment of $50,000 in inventory and accounts receivable. This increase in working capital should be fully recoverable at the end of the project's life.

If Davis believes the minimum acceptable rate of return is 15 percent

Table 15-6
Jefferson Manufacturing Company:
Cash Flow Projections for Video Game Project

	Year 1	Year 2	Year 3	Year 4	Year 5
Sales	$120,000	$170,000	$250,000	$200,000	$120,000
Less: COGS (less Dpr.)	55,000	68,000	88,000	88,000	48,000
Less: Depreciation*	31,525	47,918	46,657	——	——
Gross profit	33,475	54,082	115,343	112,000	72,000
Less: S&A	30,000	34,000	38,000	32,000	26,000
Operating profit	3,475	20,082	77,343	80,000	46,000
Less: Taxes (40%)	1,390	8,033	30,937	32,000	18,400
Net income	2,085	12,049	46,406	48,000	27,600
Plus: Depreciation	31,525	47,918	46,657	——	——
Cash flow	$ 33,610	$ 59,967	$ 93,063	$ 48,000	$ 27,600

*Depreciation Schedule, ACRS Method

Year	ACRS	Depreciation Basis[a]	Depreciation
1	25%	$126,100	$31,525
2	38%	126,100	47,918
3	37%	126,100	46,657

[a]When the full 6 percent ITC is taken, the ACRS requires that the depreciable basis of the asset be reduced by one half of the ITC. In this case 6%($130,000) = $7,800 ITC. Therefore the depreciable basis is $130,000 − $7,800/2 = $126,100.

for a project entailing this amount of risk, what are the project's pay-back period, net present value, and internal rate of return?

In Table 15-6 we compute the cash flows of the project, utilizing Davis's revenue and operating cost projections.

The *investment outlay* for the project is equal to:

Cost of the asset	$130,000
Plus: Installation charges	0
Plus: Working capital requirements –DON'T 50,000 *include*	
Less: ITC – DON'T *include*	(7,800)
Investment outlay, C	$172,200

The *payback period* for the project is 2.8 years:

$33,610 + $59,967 + $78,623/$93,063 = 2.84 years to equal $172,200.

The *net present value* of the project is determined by discount-ing the cash flows using the 15 percent required-return discount fac-tors:

Year	15% DF	Cash Flows	Discounted Cash Flow
1	.8696	$33,610	$ 29,227
2	.7561	59,967	45,341
3	.6575	93,063	61,189
4	.5718	48,000	27,446
5	.4972	86,600[a]	43,058
		Present value	$ 206,261
		Investment outlay	– 172,200
		Net present value	$ 34,061

[a]The cash flow in the last year consists of Net income + Depreciation (if any) + Recapture of working capital (not taxable) + Salvage value of the asset (since ACRS allows full depreciation without regard to salvage value, the sale price of the asset represents a "recapture of depreciation" and is taxed as ordinary income); thus $27,600 + $0 + $50,000 + $15,000 (1 − .4) = $86,600.

Since the NPV is positive, the project is acceptable under the net present value rule.

The *internal rate of return* of the project is greater than the required rate of return, 15 percent, since the NPV is positive at that rate. The project's IRR is computed in Table 15-7. The internal rate of return is the discount rate that equates present cash outlays with the pres-ent value of future cash inflows, or to state it a different way, the IRR is the rate that causes the NPV to equal zero. We know that the NPV is equal to zero at a rate between 20 and 24 percent. By inter-

Table 15-7
Jefferson Manufacturing Company: Internal Rate of Return Computations for Video Game Project

Year	Cash Flow	20% DF	20% PV	24% DF	24% PV
1	$33,610	.8333	$ 28,007	.8065	$ 27,106
2	59,967	.6944	41,641	.6504	39,003
3	93,063	.5787	53,856	.5245	48,812
4	48,000	.4823	23,150	.4230	20,304
5	86,600	.4019	34,805	.3411	29,539
		PV of inflows	$181,459		$164,764
		Less: Cost	172,200		172,200
		NPV	$ 9,259		$ (7,436)

polation we can find that the internal rate of return of the video game project is 22.2 percent:

$$PV = \$181,459 \text{ at } 20.\ 0\%$$
$$PV = \$172,200 \text{ at } 20.+\% \left.\right\} \$9,259$$
$$PV = \$164,764 \text{ at } 24.\ 0\%. \left.\right\} \$16,695$$

Thus

$$IRR = 20.0\% + (\$9,259/\$16,695)(4.0\%)$$
$$= 20.0\% + (.555)(0.04)$$
$$= 20.0\% + 2.2\%$$
$$= 22.2\%.$$

The question still remains: Should Jefferson Electronics invest in the video game project? Assuming the forecasts of revenues and costs are reasonably correct: Yes, the firm should invest in the project; the NPV is positive at the company's required rate of return and the IRR is greater than the required rate of return.[3] However, the financial manager's responsibility for the project does not end with the acceptance of the investment opportunity. The project must be monitored closely by means of a *post-audit* to determine if it is living up to expectations.

---

[3]As we note later, if a single project has a positive NPV, the project's IRR will always be larger than the project's required rate of return. However, complications *may* arise when evaluating two or more investment opportunities. In that situation the NPV ranking of multiple projects *may* differ from the IRR ranking.

The Post-Audit

The final aspect of the capital budgeting process is the *post-completion audit*, or **post-audit**, which involves (1) a comparison of actual results to those predicted in the request for funds and (2) an explanation of observed differences. For example, firms often require that the operating divisions send a monthly report for the first six months after a project goes into operation and a quarterly report thereafter until the project's results are up to expectations. From then on reports on the operation are handled like those on other operations.

The post-audit has several purposes, including the following:

1. Improve forecasts. When decision makers systematically compare their projections to actual outcomes, there is a tendency for estimates to improve. Conscious or unconscious biases are observed and eliminated; new forecasting methods are sought as the need for them becomes apparent; and people simply tend to do everything better, including forecasting, if they know that their actions are being monitored.

2. Improve operations. Businesses are run by people, and people can perform at higher or lower levels of efficiency. When a divisional team has made a forecast about a new installation, its members are, in a sense, putting their reputations on the line. If costs are above predicted levels, sales below expectations, and so on, then executives in production, sales, and other areas will strive to improve operations and to bring results into line with forecasts.

The post-audit is not a simple process. First, we must recognize that each element of the cash flow forecast is subject to uncertainty, so a percentage of all projects undertaken by any reasonably venturesome firm will necessarily go awry. This fact must be considered when appraising the performances of the operating executives who submit capital expenditure requests. Second, projects sometimes fail to meet expectations for reasons beyond the control of the operating executives and for reasons that no one could realistically be expected to anticipate. For example, the imposition of price controls in the early 1970s adversely affected many projects for which price increases had been projected, and the quadrupling of oil prices in the mid-1970s hurt others. Third, it is often difficult to separate the operating results of one investment from those of a larger system. While projects must stand alone to permit ready identification of costs and revenues, the actual cost savings that result from a replacement project may be very hard to measure. Fourth, if the post-audit process is not used with care, executives may be reluctant to suggest potentially profitable but risky projects. And fifth, the executives who were actually responsible for a

post-audit
A comparison of the actual and expected results for a given capital project.

given decision may have moved on by the time the results of the decision are known.

Because of these difficulties, some firms tend to play down the importance of the post-audit. However, observations of both businesses and government units suggest that the best-run and most successful organizations are the ones that put the greatest stress on post-audits. Accordingly, the post-audit is one of the most important elements in a good capital budgeting system.

Summary

Capital budgeting requires that the financial manager estimate future cash flows, appraise risks and incorporate that evaluation into the required rate of return, and place the expected cash flows on a present value basis; if a project's *net present value* is positive, it is accepted.

The capital budgeting process centers around the steps outlined below:

1. Ideas for projects are developed.

2. Projects are classified by type of investment: replacement, expansion of existing product lines, expansion into new markets, and "other."

3. The expected future cash flows from a project are estimated. This involves (a) estimating the investment outlay required for the project and (b) estimating the cash inflows over the project's projected life.

4. The riskiness inherent in the project is appraised. This important subject is taken up in Chapter 16.

5. The next step is to rank projects by their NPVs or IRRs, accepting those with NPV > 0 or IRR > the cost of capital.

6. The final step in a good capital budgeting system is the *post-audit*, which involves comparing actual to predicted results. Post-audits help get the best results from every accepted project; they also lead to improvements in the forecasting process and hence to better future capital budgeting decisions.

While this chapter has presented the basic elements of the capital budgeting process, there are many other aspects of this important topic. Some of the more technical ones are discussed in the appendix to this chapter, and others are taken up in Chapter 16.

Resolution to Decision in Finance

Jack Welch's New GE

Under Jack Welch, General Electric's laggard businesses have been put on notice: Become a dominant player or be sold or closed. Welch's policy is simple and straightforward: Disinvest in tired businesses; reinvest in vigorous ones. For example, the sagging television division has been told to devise new products using microelectronics or it will be sold or closed. And the small household appliance business, in which GE felt it was impossible to become a leader, has already been sold to Black & Decker.

By getting rid of its laggards and misfits, GE frees up capital for reinvestment in fields where it can become a leader. Much money is spent on technical evolution. For example, the major appliance group is a main focus of attention these days. Not only is the appliance business booming, but Roger Shipke, vice president in charge, has drastically cut the division's breakeven. In the process ten vice presidents have been cut back to four and 10,000 employees have changed bosses. Since 1977 the hourly labor force has been almost halved, to 11,400, and breakeven is down 25 percent. Welch plans to invest $800 million in this group over the next four years, double the level of the past five, as a reward for such outstanding performance.

As a result of realigning its businesses, GE started 1984 with $3 billion in cash and planned to have well over $5 billion by year's end. With that much cash the company could afford to make some very flashy acquisitions. But Welch prefers a more conservative approach. Instead, GE has begun to acquire specialty businesses that fill in the gaps in its own lines. For example, it recently bought Calma, a West Coast maker of computer-aided design machines, which ties in well with its factory automation business. It also acquired a ceramics company that fits into its light bulb and jet engine efforts.

As long as interest rates remain high, Welch prefers to conserve his cash. And having it enables him to be generous with promising areas of business. He recently pumped $4 million into two projects that the medical systems division had been reluctant to ask for. Welch was willing to take the risk because he sensed the new products would give GE a tremendous competitive advantage.

GE's heaviest spending will be on new plant investment—which was $1.9 billion in 1983, 19 percent more than the year before—and on research and development—which was a record $2 billion in 1983, up 20 percent over the year before.

Right now, Jack Welch says he's accomplished only 15 percent of what he intends to do. But since he's only 48, he expects to have plenty of time to build GE into the company he envisions.

Source: "General Electric—Going with the Winners," *Forbes,* Mar. 26, 1984, 97–106.

Key Terms You should be able to define each of the following terms:

Capital budgeting
Cost of capital; discount rate
Cash flow
Investment outlay
Discounted cash flow (DCF)
  techniques

Payback (payback period); net
  present value (NPV); internal rate
  of return (IRR)
Post-audit

Questions

15-1 How is a project classification scheme (for example, replacement, expansion into new markets, and so forth) used in the capital budgeting process?

15-2 a. Why is the investment tax credit subtracted from expenditures on fixed assets?

   b. Why is working capital included in a capital budgeting analysis?

   c. Why are "payables and accruals" deducted from working capital?

   d. Would working capital be considered if the project were a replacement rather than an expansion project?

15-3 If a firm like Carter Chemical Company used straight line rather than a rapid depreciation methodology, how would this affect **(a)** the total amount of depreciation, net income, and net cash flows over the project's expected life; **(b)** the timing of depreciation, net income, and net cash flows; and **(c)** the project's payback and NPV?

15-4 Net cash flows rather than profits are listed in Table 15-1. What is the basis for this emphasis on cash as opposed to profits?

15-5 Why is the NPV of a relatively long-term project, defined as one with a high percentage of its cash flows expected in distant future years, more sensitive to changes in the cost of capital than is the NPV of a short-term project?

15-6 Explain why, if two mutually exclusive projects are being compared, the short-term project might have the higher ranking under the NPV criterion if the cost of capital is high, but the long-term project might be deemed better if the cost of capital is low. Would changes in the cost of capital ever cause a change in the IRR ranking of two such projects?

Self-Test Problems

ST-1 Moses Manufacturing is considering the purchase of a new machine which will dramatically increase the firm's manufacturing capacity. The machine, if purchased today, would cost $40,550,000 and provide annual cash flows after taxes (net income plus depreciation) of $13,425,000 per year for 6 years.

   a. Determine the project's payback.

   b. Determine the project's NPV if the required return is 15 percent.

   c. Determine the project's IRR.

ST-2 Mountain States Chemical Company (MSC) is considering an investment in a shale oil project. The investment involves acquiring land, developing a new plant, operating the plant during the shale oil project, and then disposing of the salvageable assets from the project. Here is a summary of the project's characteristics (dollars in millions):

1. A total of $50 has been spent thus far to investigate the feasibility of the process used in the shale oil project. These funds were expensed.
2. MSC will purchase the land immediately at a cost of $300.
3. A shale operations building will be put up at a cost of $400. This expenditure will occur at t = 1, that is, at the end of Year 1.
4. Equipment will be installed at a cost of $200. This outlay will occur at t = 2, the end of Year 2.
5. MSC will bring in net working capital with a cost of $100. This outlay will occur at the end of Year 3, t = 3, and the working capital will be recovered at the end of the project's life, t = 8, the end of Year 8.
6. The plant will commence operations at the beginning of Year 4. The operation will continue for 5 years, until the end of Year 8. After-tax cash flows from the project (net income plus depreciation) will equal $425 annually for the 5-year operating period.
7. Even though the operating assets will be fully depreciated, management believes the building and equipment will have a combined salvage value of $150 at the end of Year 8.
8. MSC's effective tax rate is 40 percent.
9. Assume that the project is not eligible for an investment tax credit.

If the required return for a high-risk project, such as the shale oil project at MSC, is 20 percent, should the firm invest in this project?

Problems

15-1 Verner Construction Company's Nino Project has a cost of $1 million, and its expected net cash inflows are $263,800 per year for 5 years.
   a. What is the payback for the Nino Project?
   b. The cost of capital is 8 percent. What is the project's NPV?
   c. What is the project's IRR? (Hint: Recognize that the project's cash flows are an annuity.)

15-2 Dodd Graham is evaluating an investment opportunity that costs $25,000 today but promises to return the following cash flows (net income plus depreciation) over the next 4 years:

Year	Cash Flow
1	$ 5,000
2	10,000
3	9,000
4	6,000

30,000

   a. What is the investment's payback?
   b. What is the NPV of the project if the required return is 10 percent?
   c. Is the IRR of the investment greater or less than the required return?

15-3 Overstreet Associates is investigating a project which costs $100,000 and is expected to produce cash flows of $33,438.10 per year for 5 years.

  a. What is the project's payback?
* **b.** If the cost of capital is 12 percent, what is the project's NPV?
* **c.** What is the project's IRR? (Hint: Recognize that the project's cash flows are an annuity.)

* **15-4** Fargo Enterprises is considering an investment in a new machine which will provide dramatic cost savings over the next 5 years. The cost of the machine is $72,107.10. Annual after-tax cash flows (net income plus depreciation) are projected as follows:

Year	Cash Flow
1	$18,000
2	25,000
3	22,000
4	20,000
5	20,000

  a. If the firm's required return for a project of this type is 12 percent, what is the investment's NPV?
  b. What is the project's IRR?

15-5 Snowfun Manufacturing Company is considering a new production line for its rapidly expanding ski equipment division. The line will have a cost of $480,000 and will be depreciated toward a zero salvage value over the next 3 years, using straight line depreciation. Other important factors are: (1) The new ski products will be responsible for new sales of $500,000 next year, $550,000 the following year, and $600,000 in the last year. (2) Cost of goods sold (excluding depreciation) is 40 percent of sales. (3) The increase in selling and administrative expenses caused by the new line is predicted to be $40,000 annually. (4) The company's cost of capital is 15 percent, and its tax rate is 40 percent.
  a. What are the project's annual cash flows?
  b. What is the project's NPV?

15-6 Two projects each involve an investment of $18,000. Cash flows (after-tax profits plus depreciation) are $12,000 a year for 2 years for Project S and $4,800 annually for 6 years for Project L.
  a. Compute the NPV for each project if the firm's cost of capital is zero percent and if it is 6 percent. NPVs for Project S at 10 and 20 percent, respectively, are $2,826 and $333.60, while NPVs for Project L at 10 and 20 percent are $2,905.44 and ($2,037.60).
  b. Graph the present value profiles of the two projects, putting NPV on the Y axis and the cost of capital on the X axis, and use the graph to estimate each project's IRR.
* **c.** Calculate the IRR for each project using a formula.
  d. If these projects were mutually exclusive, which one would you select, assuming a cost of capital of (1) 8 percent, (2) 10.3 percent, or (3) 12 percent? Explain. For this problem, assume that the operation will terminate at the end of the project's life, making an analysis based on equal lives unnecessary.

15-7 The net cash flows for Projects X and Y follow. Each project has a cost of $20,000, and the company uses a 10 percent cost of capital.

---

*Refer to Appendix E for check answers to problems with asterisks.

Net Cash Flows

Year	Project X	Project Y
1	$13,000	$7,000
2	6,000	7,000
3	6,000	7,000
4	2,000	7,000

   a. Calculate each project's payback.
* b. Calculate each project's NPV at the 10 percent cost of capital.
* c. Calculate each project's IRR. (Hints: Use the graphic approach for Project X, and notice that Project Y is an annuity.)
   d. Should X and/or Y be accepted if they are independent projects?
   e. Which of the two projects should be accepted if they are mutually exclusive?
   f. How might a change in the cost of capital produce a conflict between NPV and IRR? At what values of k would this conflict exist?

15-8 The director of capital budgeting for Hytec Electronics is analyzing a proposal to build a new plant in Arizona. The following data have been developed thus far:

Land acquisition, cost incurred at start of Year 1 (t = 0)	$ 300,000
Plant construction, cost incurred at start of Year 2 (t = 1)	$ 700,000
Equipment purchase, cost incurred at start of Year 3 (t = 2)	$1,000,000
Net working capital, investment made at start of Year 4 (t = 3)	$ 400,000

Operations will begin in Year 4 and will continue for 10 years, through Year 13. Sales revenues and operating costs are assumed to come at the end of each year. Since the plant will be in operation for 10 years, operating costs and revenues occur at the end of Years 4 through 13 (t = 4 to 13). The following additional assumptions are made: (1) The plant and equipment will be depreciated over a 10-year life, starting in Year 4. The buildings and equipment will be worthless after 10 years' use, but Hytec expects to sell the land for $300,000 when the plant is closed down. Hytec uses straight line depreciation. (2) Hytec uses a cost of capital of 14 percent to evaluate projects such as this one. (3) Annual sales = 10,000 units at $113.50 per unit; annual sales revenues = $1,135,000. (4) Annual fixed operating costs *excluding* depreciation are $130,000. (5) Annual variable operating costs are $200,385, assuming the plant operates at full capacity. (6) Hytec's marginal income tax rate is 40 percent. (7) Assume that the project is not eligible for an investment tax credit.
* a. Calculate the project's NPV. Should Hytec's management accept this project?
   b. Assuming constant sales prices and constant variable costs per unit, what will happen to the NPV if unit sales fall 10 percent below the forecasted level?

15-9 D. Harrington & Co. is considering the installation of a new production line for its rapidly expanding skate division. The line will have a cost of $100,000. The asset will be 5-year-class property for the purpose of ACRS depreciation. No salvage value is expected for the assets when the project ends in 5 years. Sales are expected to be $100,000 annually. Operating costs other than depreciation will be $70,000 annually. The company's required rate of return is 12 percent, and its tax rate is 40 percent.

a. Determine the project's cash flows, and then calculate the project's net present value. (Refer to Appendix 6A for the depreciation calculation.)

b. Suppose a 10 percent investment tax credit had been applicable. How would this have affected your decision? (Remember that under ACRS, the asset's basis for depreciation falls by one half of the ITC.)

Answers to Self-Test Problems

ST-1 a. The payback is defined as the length of time it takes to recover the investment in a project. For this proposed purchase, payback is determined in the following table:

Year	Cash Flow	Cumulative Cash Flow
1	$13,425,000	$13,425,000
2	13,425,000	26,850,000
3	13,425,000	40,275,000
4	13,425,000	

$40,550,000 - $40,275,000 = $275,000 unrecovered after 3 years.
$13,425,000/365 = $36,781 recovery per day.
$275,000/$36,781 = 7.5 days.

Therefore the payback period is 3 years and 1 week, which would be rounded to 3 years. (Note: Since this project's cash flows are level, we could have found the payback by $40,550,000/$13,425,000 = 3.02 years, which is, of course, 3 years and 1 week.)

b. The NPV is calculated thus:

$$
\begin{aligned}
NPV &= CF(DFa) - Cost \\
&= \$13,425,000(3.7845) - \$40,550,000 \\
&= \$50,806,912 - \$40,550,000 \\
&= \$10,256,912.
\end{aligned}
$$

c. Since the cash flows of this project take the form of an annuity, we can solve the equation below to determine the discount factor:

$$
PVa = Pmt(DFa)
$$
$$
DFa = \frac{PVa}{Pmt}
$$

or

$$
\$40,550,000 = \$13,425,000(DFa)
$$
$$
DFa = \frac{\$40,550,000}{\$13,425,000}
$$
$$
= 3.0205.
$$

For a 6-year annuity the discount factor of 3.0205 corresponds to a 24 percent rate of return.

ST-2 The costs associated with the shale oil project (in millions of dollars) are:

Time	Cost	Purpose
t = 0	$300	Land
t = 1	$400	Building
t = 2	$200	Equipment
t = 3	$100	Working capital

$$\text{Present value of costs} = -\$300 - \$400(0.8333)$$
$$- \$200(0.6944) - \$100(0.5787)$$
$$= -\$830.07 = -\$830,070,000.$$

The cash flows associated with the project (in millions of dollars) are:

Time	Cash Flow	Source
t = 4 − 8	$425	Cash flow from operations
t = 8	$100	Recapture of working capital
t = 8	$150	Sale of salvageable assets (taxed as ordinary income)

$$\text{Present value of cash flows} = \$425(1.7307)^* + \$100(0.2326)$$
$$+ \$150(1 - .4)(0.2326)$$
$$= \$779.7415 = \$779,741,500.$$

$$\text{Net present value} = \text{Discounted cash flows} - \text{Costs}$$
$$= \$779.7415 - \$830.07$$
$$= -\$50.3285 = \$-50,328,500.$$

$^*DFa_{20\%,8n} - DFa_{20\%,3n} = 3.8372 - 2.1065 = 1.7307.$

Since the project's NPV is negative, MSC should abandon the shale oil project. Of course, the same decision would have been reached if we had found the project's IRR. For single projects a negative NPV indicates the IRR of the project is less than the required return for the project. Whichever method is used, MSC should not invest in the shale oil project.

Selected References

For a more thorough treatment of capital budgeting techniques, see:
Bierman, Harold, Jr., and Seymour Smidt, *The Capital Budgeting Decision*, 4th ed. (New York: Macmillan, 1975).
Brigham, Eugene, and Louis C. Gapenski, *Intermediate Financial Management* (Hinsdale, IL: Dryden Press, 1985).

Grant, E. L., W. G. Ireson, and R. S. Leavenworth, *Principles of Engineering Economy*, 6th ed. (New York: Ronald, 1976).

Levy, Haim, and Marshall Sarnat, *Capital Investment and Financial Decisions* (Englewood Cliffs, NJ: Prentice-Hall, 1978).

Osteryoung, Jerome, *Capital Budgeting: Long-Term Asset Selection* (Columbus, Ohio: Grid, 1974).

For a discussion of strategic considerations in capital budgeting, see:

Crum, R., and F. D. J. Derkinderen, eds., *Readings in Strategies for Corporate Investments* (New York: Pitman, 1980).

Five articles related directly to the materials in this chapter are:

Bacon, Peter W., "The Evaluation of Mutually Exclusive Investments," *Financial Management*, Summer 1977, 55–58.

Durand, David, "Comprehensiveness in Capital Budgeting," *Financial Management*, Winter 1981, 7–13.

Gitman, L. J., and J. R. Forrester, "A Survey of Capital Budgeting Techniques Used by Major U.S. Firms," *Financial Management*, Fall 1977, 66–71.

Kim, Suk H., and Edward J. Farragher, "Current Capital Budgeting Practices," *Management Accounting*, June 1981, 26–30.

Lewellen, Wilbur G., Howard P. Lanser, and John J. McConnell, "Payback Substitutes for Discounted Cash Flow," *Financial Management*, Summer 1973, 17–23.

Other capital budgeting references are provided in Chapter 16.

Conflicts between NPV and IRR

15A

When evaluating projects, we have suggested two appropriate methodologies—the NPV and the IRR methods. For single project evaluation these two methodologies will *always* give consistent *accept* or *reject* signals. As noted in Table 15A-1, if the project's internal rate of return, r, is greater than the company's or project's required rate of return, k, the NPV will be positive, and we would thus deem the project acceptable. Under normal circumstances we would reject any project that provided a return less than the required return. In this situation the project's NPV will always be negative. Of course, where NPV = 0, the project's required and internal rates of return are equal, and the firm will be indifferent between this project and other alternatives of the same risk (remember that k is also an opportunity cost representing the return of the best other available investment opportunity).

However, when we consider ranking two or more investment projects, as in the following example, these decision rules may not apply. Assume that MBI Corporation has two competing, mutually exclusive projects, Projects A and B. Each project requires an initial investment outlay of $1,000,000. Further assume that the firm has a cost of capital of 5 percent (obviously your authors are very optimistic). The NPV of Project A is $180,410 and B's NPV is $206,480, as seen in Table 15A-2. We approximate the IRRs of both projects graphically in Figure 15A-1. Note that while the NPV_B is larger than NPV_A at 5 percent, the IRR_A

Table 15A-1
Comparison of NPV and IRR Project Evaluation Rules for Single Projects

Method	Accept	Reject	Indifferent
NPV	Positive	Negative	Zero
IRR	Greater than k	Less than k	k = r

Table 15A-2
Calculating the NPVs of Projects A and B where k = 5%

	Project A			Project B		
Year	Cash Flow	DF = 5%	Discounted Cash Flow	Cash Flow	DF = 5%	Discounted Cash Flow
1	$500,000	.9524	$ 476,200	$100,000	.9524	$ 95,240
2	400,000	.9070	362,800	300,000	.9070	272,100
3	300,000	.8638	259,140	400,000	.8638	345,520
4	100,000	.8227	82,270	600,000	.8227	493,620
		PV of inflows	$1,180,410			$1,206,480
		Less: Cost	1,000,000			1,000,000
		NPV	$ 180,410			$ 206,480

is greater than the IRR_B. Thus there is a conflict in the ranking methodologies of NPV and IRR. Which of the two methods will always give us an unambiguous, correct means of ranking mutually exclusive projects?

For several reasons, one should always select the project with the highest NPV. We consider only two of these reasons here, the problem of absolute versus relative returns and the reinvestment assumptions.[1]

Absolute versus Relative Returns

Suppose we are offered the choice between two competing one-year projects. Project Y's IRR is 10 percent, while Project Z's IRR is 20 percent. If we rank and select projects by the IRR criterion, we would choose the project with the larger IRR—Project Z. However, if we learned that Project Z's maximum available investment is $1,000, it would leave us with an NPV of $200; but we can invest up to $10,000 in Project Y, which gives us an NPV of $1,000. Which is the best project? We would agree that the project that provides the highest true return—dollars—is the best. Thus we would opt for the project that gives the highest *absolute* return, the one with the highest NPV.

Reinvestment Assumption

Those who use the NPV method to compare projects implicitly assume that the opportunity exists to reinvest the cash flows generated by a project at the cost of capital, whereas use of the IRR method implies

---

[1]For a much more detailed and complete discussion of these factors, see Eugene F. Brigham, *Financial Management: Theory and Practice*, 3rd ed. (Hinsdale, IL: Dryden Press, 1982), Chapter 11 and especially Appendix 11A.

Figure 15A-1
Net Present Value Profiles of Project A and B at Different Discount Rates
(Thousands of Dollars)
Conflicting results may arise when both net present value and internal rate of return are
used to rank mutually exclusive capital projects. In this example Project A has a NPV of
$180.41 and an IRR of 14.5 percent, while Project B has a NPV of $206.48 and an IRR
of 11.8 percent. Based on NPV, Project B would be preferred, but based on IRR, Project
A would seem more attractive. In such cases NPV provides the least ambiguous means
of ranking projects.

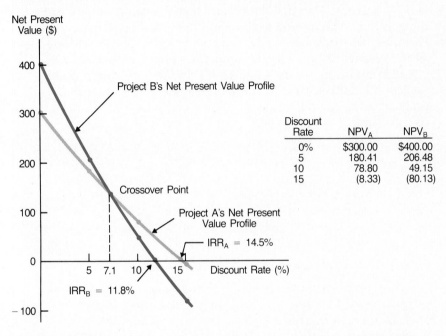

Discount Rate	NPV$_A$	NPV$_B$
0%	$300.00	$400.00
5	180.41	206.48
10	78.80	49.15
15	(8.33)	(80.13)

Note: Notice that the present value profiles are curved—they are *not* straight lines. We should also
note that under certain conditions the NPV profiles can cross the horizontal axis several times or
never cross it.

the opportunity to reinvest exists at the IRR rate. The cash flows may
actually be withdrawn and spent on beer and pizza, but the assumption of a reinvestment opportunity is still implicit in the calculations.
Consider our previous example of Projects A and B (Table 15A-2 and
Figure 15A-1). If we assume the firm's reinvestment rate is less than
7.1 percent, we will choose Project B. However, if the firm can reinvest
at a rate above 7.1 percent, we should choose Project A.

Since both the IRR and NPV methods use discount factors, we
should consider again how present value tables are constructed. *The
present value of any future sum is defined as the beginning amount which,
when compounded at a specified and constant rate, will grow to equal the
future amount over the stated time period.* From Table 14-1 we can see that

the present value of $146.93 due in 5 years, when discounted at 8 percent, is $100 because $100, when the amount earned is reinvested and compounded at 8 percent for 5 years, will grow to $146.93. Thus compounding and discounting are reciprocal relationships, and the *very construction of PV tables implies a reinvestment process.*

Thus if a project has a *computed* IRR of 40 percent, but the best alternative for reinvesting the intervening cash flows from the project is 8 percent, the true rate of return from the project will definitely be less than 40 percent. This does not mean that the project may not be acceptable, only that its true return, r, will be less than its computed IRR. However, when we use the NPV method, it is implicitly assumed that all reinvestment is made at the company's opportunity cost, k.

Naturally, the closer the project's IRR to the firm's opportunity cost, the less the reinvestment assumption matters. Yet there will *never* be a problem using the NPV rule in ranking competing or mutually exclusive investment opportunities.

Evaluating Risk in Capital Budgeting

16

Decision in Finance

Gambling on a State-of-the-Art Refinery

In the spring of 1980 Chairman William E. Greehey set an ambitious goal for Valero Energy Corp.: To diversify the $1 billion San Antonio firm into a full-fledged energy company. At the time Valero operated the nation's largest intrastate natural-gas pipeline, but that wasn't enough for Greehey. In short order he added gas storage facilities, signed up new gas sources in Texas and Mexico, and built new collection lines. And if all went according to plan, Valero would soon begin production of natural gas liquids and launch its own drilling projects.

Late in 1980 Greehey took a bold step toward his goal of making Valero into an integrated energy producer: he purchased 50 percent of Saber Energy, Inc., a small gasoline marketer. What especially caught Greehey's eye was Saber's tiny refinery in Corpus Christi, Texas. The way Greehey saw it, he could turn the refinery into a high-volume, state-of-the-art facility that would yield margins up to three times higher than the average for other refineries.

The cost of upgrading the old facility would be high—$617 million. But, according to Greehey, the economics were unbelievably promising. The new 50,000-barrel-per-day refinery would crack low-value heavy crude oil into gasoline. Because the raw material—called "resid"—could be bought from the Middle East for about $20 per barrel, Greehey projected Valero's profits at $16 per barrel. At that rate the Saber refinery could be expected to pay for itself in three years and would eventually generate more than half of Valero's profits.

As you read this chapter, look for the factors that Greehey should consider in deciding whether to replace the old refinery. Would you recommend that Valero build the new refinery? Why or why not?

See end of chapter for resolution.

Our discussion of capital budgeting in the last chapter was incomplete in two important respects. First, we did not discuss asset replacement decisions at length, and second, we did not consider the effects of risk on capital budgeting. These topics are covered in this chapter.

Replacement Decisions

replacement decision
The decision to replace an existing asset that is still productive with a new one—an example of mutually exclusive projects.

Jefferson Manufacturing Company's video game project was used in the last chapter to illustrate how expansion projects are analyzed. Not all project analysis is for new projects, however. Some investment opportunities are evaluated as part of replacement decisions. Accordingly, the analysis relating to a **replacement decision** is somewhat different from that for expansion projects. These differences are illustrated here with a capital asset (lathe) replacement analysis for Universal Technologies, Incorporated (UT).

UT has a lathe for trimming molded plastic pieces that was purchased 5 years ago at a cost of $7,500. The machine had an expected life of 15 years at the time it was purchased, and it was estimated then that its salvage value would be zero at the end of the 15 years. The machine is being depreciated on a straight line basis, so its annual depreciation charge is $500, and its present book value is $5,000.

The division manager reports that a new machine can be purchased for $12,000 (including installation), which, over its 10-year life, will reduce labor and raw materials usage sufficiently to cut operating costs from $7,000 to $4,000. This reduction in costs will cause before-tax profits to rise by $7,000 − $4,000 = $3,000 per year.

It is estimated that the new machine can be sold for $2,000 at the end of 10 years; this is its estimated salvage value. The old machine's actual current market value is $1,000, which is well below its book value. Taxes are at a 46 percent rate and are paid quarterly, and the appropriate discount rate is 12 percent. An investment tax credit (ITC) of 10 percent of the purchase price can be used if the new machine is acquired. As we discussed in Appendix 6A, taking the full 10 percent ITC requires that the asset's depreciable basis be reduced by 50 percent of the ITC—that is, the depreciable basis for this asset is $12,000 − $600 = $11,400. Under these conditions should UT buy the new machine?

Provided the annual cash flows are constant, as they are in this example, the worksheet presented in Table 16–1 can be used to analyze the project.[1] A description of the analysis items follows the table.

---

[1]Since the purpose of this example is to demonstrate the quantitative aspects of the replacement decision, straight line rather than ACRS depreciation is used. The straight line method allows the cash flows to be level over the depreciation period, thus simplifying the computation process. If cash flows are not level over the time period, then it would be necessary to calculate the cash flow for *each year*. These extra steps would be required if ACRS or other rapid-depreciation methodologies were used.

Table 16-1
Worksheet for Replacement Analysis

	Amount before Tax (1)	Amount after Tax (2)	Year Event Occurs (3)	PV Factor at 12% (4)	PV (5)
Net Outflows at the Time the Investment is Made:					
t = 0					
1. Cost of new equipment	$12,000	$12,000	0	1.0	$12,000
2. Market value of old equipment	(1,000)	(1,000)	0	1.0	(1,000)
3. Tax effect of sale of old equipment	(4,000)	(1,840)	0	1.0	(1,840)
4. Increased working capital (if necessary)	1,000	1,000	0	1.0	1,000
5. Investment tax credit	(1,200)	(1,200)	0	1.0	(1,200)
6. Total initial outflows (PV of costs)					$ 8,960
Net Inflows over the Project's Life: t = 1 to 10					
7. Decrease in costs	$ 3,000	$ 1,620	1-10	5.6502	$ 9,153
8. Depreciation on new machine	1,140	—	—	—	—
9. Depreciation on old machine	(500)	—	—	—	—
10. Net change in depreciation	640	294	1-10	5.6502	1,661
11. Estimated salvage value of new machine	2,000	1,080	10	0.3220	348
12. Return of working capital (if applicable)	1,000	1,000	10	0.3220	322
13. Total PV of cash inflows					$11,484
14. NPV = PV of inflows − PV of costs					
= $11,484 − $8,960 = $2,524					

Line 1 The top section of the table, Lines 1 through 6, relates to cash flows which occur at (approximately) t = 0, the time the investment is made. Line 1 shows the purchase price of the machine, including any installation charges. No discounting is required, so the present value factor is 1.0, indicating that the present value of a dollar today is a dollar.

Line 2 Here we show the price received for sale of old equipment. The parentheses denote that this amount is deducted when finding the net cash outflow at t = 0.

Line 3 Since the old equipment was sold at a loss, this reduces UT's taxable income, hence its next quarterly income tax payment. The tax savings is equal to (Loss × t) = ($4,000)(0.46) = $1,840. Here t is the tax rate. The tax code defines this loss as an operating loss, not a capital loss, because it reflects the fact that inadequate depreciation was taken on the old asset. If there had been a profit on the sale (that is, if the sales price had exceeded book value), Line 3 would have shown taxes *paid*, a cash outflow. In the actual case the equipment was sold at a loss, so no taxes were paid. In effect, UT receives a tax credit of $1,840.

Line 4 The investment in additional net working capital (current assets required less spontaneous accounts payable and accruals) is shown here. This investment will be recovered at the end of the project's life (Line 12). No taxes are involved.

Line 5 The ITC is equal to 10 percent of the purchase price.

Line 6 Here we show the net cash outflows at the time the replacement is made. UT writes a check for $12,000 to pay for the machine, and another $1,000 is invested in working capital, but these outlays are partially offset by the items on Lines 2, 3, and 5.

incremental future cash flow
The net cash flow attributable to an investment project.

Line 7 The lower section of the table shows the **incremental future cash flows,** or benefits, that will result if the replacement is made. The first of these benefits is the reduction in operating costs shown in Column 1. This amount is multiplied by $(1 - t)$ to obtain the after-tax benefits: thus $3,000(1 - 0.46) = \$3,000(0.54) = \$1,620$. These benefits occur in Years 1–10, so the PV of this annuity is equal to $\$1,620(5.6502) = \$9,153$, the amount shown in the last column. Also, note that had the replacement resulted in an increase in sales in addition to the reduction in costs (if the new machine had been both larger and more efficient), then this amount would also be reported on Line 7.

Lines 8, 9, and 10 Lines 8 and 9 show the depreciation on the new and old machines, while Line 10 shows both the net addition to depreciation and the tax savings from this additional depreciation. Depreciation is not in itself a cash inflow, but the increase in depreciation reduces UT's taxes. The amount of the taxes saved by the increased depreciation is $\$640(t) = \$640(0.46) = \$294$; this figure is shown in Column 2. The savings occur in Years 1–10, and the present value of this 10-year annuity is $\$294(5.6502) = \$1,661$, the amount shown in Line 10, Column 5.

Note that the relevant cash flow is the tax savings on the *net increase* in depreciation, not the depreciation on the new equipment. Replacement decisions are based on *incremental* cash flows. Since we lose $500 of depreciation if we replace the old machine, the incremental or additional depreciation is only $\$1,140 - \$500 = \$640$.

Line 11 The estimated salvage value on the new machine at the end of its 10-year life is $2,000. This is a recapture of depreciation, so it is taxed as ordinary income. The PV of the after-tax salvage value is $\$2,000(1 - .46)(0.3220) = \$348$.

Line 12 An investment of $1,000 was made in net working capital at $t = 0$. This investment, like the salvage value, will be recovered when the project is terminated at the end of Year 10. Accounts receivable will be collected, inventories will be drawn down and not replaced, and the cash required to operate the facility will no longer

Table 16-2
Replacement Decision Framework

New Asset Investment	Old Asset Disinvestment	Difference
− Investment outlay	+ Cash for asset	= Net cost
+ Cash flow	− Cash flow	= Incremental cash flow

be needed. The present value of the recovered working capital is $322.

Line 13 This line sums the PVs of the benefits.

Line 14 Here we calculate the net present value of the replacement project. The PV of the benefits exceeds the investment outlay, so the project has a positive NPV of $2,524. Therefore the old machine should be replaced. Of course, if the NPV were negative, Universal Technologies would reject the proposal for a new lathe and keep the original lathe.

In essence, the replacement decision is a combination of an investment decision and, to coin a phrase, a disinvestment decision. An investment decision involves an *investment outlay* of cash to purchase an asset which will produce a forecasted *cash inflow* consisting of after-tax earnings and depreciation. Disinvestment is just the reverse—if the old machine is sold, the firm receives an *inflow* of cash and/or a cash equivalent tax credit on any book loss created by the sale. Additionally, since the company no longer owns the asset, there is an opportunity loss of the asset's cash inflow. This process is presented in Table 16-2. Our concern is that the replacement should be considered only in terms of the net cost outlays for the asset (less all "trade-in" allowances) and the differential increase in cash flows. To do otherwise would double-count costs or benefits associated with the asset under evaluation.

Comparing Projects with Unequal Lives

To simplify matters, our example of replacement decisions assumed that the new machine had a life equal to the remaining life of the existing one. Suppose, however, that we must choose between two mutually exclusive replacement alternatives that have *different* lives. For example, Machine S has an expected life of 10 years, while L has a 15-year life. The most typical procedure for solving problems of this type is to set up a series of *replacement chains* extending out to the "common denominator" year, that is, the year in which both alternatives would require replacement. For Machines S and L this would be Year 30, so it would be necessary to compare a 3-chain cycle for S, the 10-year machine, with a 2-chain cycle for L, the 15-year project.

To illustrate both the replacement chain problem and its solution, suppose we are considering the replacement of a fully depreciated printing press with a new one. The plant in which the press is used is profitable and is expected to continue in operation for many years. The old press could continue to be used indefinitely, but it is as not as efficient as new presses. Two replacement machines are available. Press A has a cost of $36,100, will last for 5 years, and will produce after-tax incremental cash flows of $9,700 per year for 5 years. Press B has a cost of $57,500, will last for 10 years, and will produce net cash flows of $9,500 per year. Both the costs and performances of Presses A and B have been constant in recent years and are expected to remain constant in the future. The company's cost of capital is 10 percent.

Should the old press be replaced, and, if so, with A or with B? To answer these questions, we first calculate A's NPV as follows:

$$NPV_A = \$9,700(3.7908) - \$36,100 = \$36,771 - \$36,100 = \$671.$$

B's NPV is

$$NPV_B = \$9,500(6.1446) - \$57,500 = \$58,374 - \$57,500 = \$874.$$

These calculations suggest that the old press should indeed be replaced, and that Press B should be selected. However, the analysis is incomplete, and the decision to choose Press B is incorrect. If we choose Press A, we will have an opportunity to make another new investment after 5 years, and this second investment will also be profitable. However, if we choose Press B, we will not have this second investment opportunity. Therefore, to make a proper comparison of Presses A and B, we must find the present value of Press A over a 10-year period and compare it with Press B over the same 10 years.

The NPV for Press B as calculated above is correct as it stands. For Press A, however, we must take three additional steps: (1) determine the NPV of the second Press A 5 years hence, (2) bring this NPV back to the present, and (3) sum these two component NPVs:

1. NPV_{A2} 5 years in future $= \$9,700(3.7908) - \$36,100 = \$671.$
2. PV of $NPV_{A2} = \$671(DF_{10\%,5 \text{ years}}) = \$671(0.6209) = \$417.$
3. "True" $NPV_A = \$671 + \$417 = \$1,088.$

The "true" NPV of Press A, $1,088, can be compared with NPV_B. Since the value of the firm will increase more if the old press is replaced by Press A than if the firm goes with Press B, Press A should be selected.

Effects of Inflation on Capital Budgeting Analysis

Inflation is a fact of life in the United States and most other nations, and thus it must be considered in any sound capital budgeting analysis. Several procedures are available for dealing with inflation. The two most frequently used methods are to (1) explicitly adjust both the discount rate and the expected cash flows and (2) make no explicit adjustment in either the discount rate or the expected cash flows to compensate for inflation. Both methods are discussed in this section.

To see how inflation enters the picture, suppose an investor lends $100 for 1 year at a rate of 5 percent. At the end of the year the investor will have $100(1.05) = $105.

Now suppose prices rise by 6 percent during the year. This means that the ending $105 will have a purchasing power, in terms of beginning-of-year values, of only $105/1.06 = $99. Thus the investor will have lost $1, or 1 percent of the original purchasing power, in spite of having earned 5 percent interest: $105 at the end of the year will buy only as much in goods as $99 would have bought at the beginning of the year.

Investors recognize this problem, and, as we saw in earlier chapters, they incorporate expectations about inflation into the required rate of return. For example, suppose investors seek a *real rate of return* (k_r) of 8 percent on an investment with a given degree of risk. Suppose further that they anticipate an *annual rate of inflation (i)* of 6 percent. Then, in order to end up with the 8 percent real rate of return, the nominal rate of return (k_n) must be a value such that

$$1 + k_n = (1 + k_r)(1 + i),$$

or

$$
\begin{aligned}
k_n &= (1 + k_r)(1 + i) - 1 \\
&= 1 + k_r + i + k_r i - 1 \\
&= k_r + i + k_r i.
\end{aligned}
$$

In words, the nominal rate (k_n) must be set equal to the real rate (k_r) plus the expected inflation (i) plus a cross-product term $(k_r i)$. In our example,

$$
\begin{aligned}
k_n &= 0.08 + 0.06 + (0.08)(0.06) \\
&= 0.08 + 0.06 + 0.0048 \\
&= 0.1448 = 14.48\%.
\end{aligned}
$$

If the investor earns a nominal return of 14.48 percent on a $100 investment, the ending value, in real terms, will be

$$\$100(1.1448)/(1.06) = \$114.48/1.06 = \$108,$$

producing the required 8 percent real rate of return.

We can use these concepts to analyze capital budgeting under inflation. First, note that a project's NPV in the absence of inflation, where

$k_r = k_n$ and RCF_t = the *real* net cash flow in Year t, is calculated as follows:

$$NPV = \sum_{t=1}^{n} \frac{RCF_t}{(1 + k_r)^t} - Cost.$$

Now suppose the situation changes. We begin to expect inflation to occur, and we expect both sales prices and input costs to rise at the rate i, the same inflation rate that is built into the estimated cost of capital that we find in the capital markets. In this event the *nominal* cash flow (CF_t) will increase annually at the rate i percent, producing this situation:

$$CF_t = Actual\ cash\ flow_t = RCF_t(1 + i)^t.$$

For example, if we expected a net cash flow of $100 in Year 5 in the absence of inflation, then with a 5 percent rate of inflation, $CF_t = \$100(1.05)^5 = \$127.63$.

Now if net cash flows increase at the rate i percent per year, and if this same inflation factor is built into the cost of capital, then

$$NPV = \sum_{t=1}^{n} \frac{RCF_t(1 + i)^t}{(1 + k_r)^t(1 + i)^t} - Cost.$$

Since the $(1 + i)^t$ terms in the numerator and denominator cancel, we are left with

$$NPV = \sum_{t=1}^{n} \frac{RCF_t}{(1 + k_r)^t} - Cost = \begin{array}{l} \text{The same NPV as} \\ \text{we found earlier} \\ \text{in the absence of} \\ \text{inflation.} \end{array}$$

Thus, whenever sales prices and costs are both expected to rise at the rate i percent, and if this is the same inflation rate that investors have built into the cost of capital, then (1) the inflation-adjusted NPV is identical to the inflation-free NPV, and (2) we can find a project's NPV by taking its real cash flows, RCF_t, and discounting them at the *real* risk-adjusted rate, k_r.

Sometimes the procedure just set forth is not followed—people sometimes discount cash flows that have *not* been inflation adjusted by the *nominal* cost of capital, which *does* include an inflation premium. If this is done, *then the calculated NPV will be downward biased.* The denominator will reflect inflation, but the numerator will not, and this produces the bias. If sales prices and all costs are expected to rise at exactly the same rate, then the bias can be corrected by having current cash flows increase at the inflation rate, or by using the real rate as the cost of capital.

While it is often appropriate to assume that *variable costs* will rise at the same rate as sales prices, fixed costs, especially the depreciation associated with a project, generally increase at a lower rate. In this case, or in any situation where both revenues and all costs are not expected to rise at exactly the same rate of inflation as is built into the cost of capital, the best procedure is to build inflation into the basic cash flow component projections for each year. If significant rates of inflation are projected, and if expected inflation rates for sales prices and input costs differ materially, such an adjustment must be made.

Risk and the Capital Budgeting Decision

Up to this point in our discussion of capital budgeting project evaluations, we have assumed that future cash flows were known with virtual certainty. We now turn to a more realistic situation—the case where future events are not known with certainty. In the following sections we define the term *risk* as it applies to financial matters, discuss procedures for measuring it, and then determine how these characteristics may be incorporated into the capital budgeting decision process.

Defining and Measuring Risk

Risk is defined in *Webster's* as "a hazard; a peril; exposure to loss or injury." Thus risk refers to the chance that some unfavorable event will occur. If you engage in skydiving, you take a chance with your life—skydiving is risky. If you bet on the horses, you risk losing your money. If you invest in speculative stocks (or, really, *any* stock), you are taking a risk in the hope of making an appreciable capital gain.

risk
The probability that actual future returns will be below expected returns.

To illustrate the riskiness of financial assets, suppose an investor buys $100,000 of short-term government bonds with an interest rate of 8 percent. In this case the yield to maturity on the investment, 8 percent, can be estimated quite precisely, and the investment is defined as being risk-free. However, if the $100,000 is invested in the stock of a company just being organized to prospect for oil in the mid-Atlantic, then the investment's return cannot be estimated precisely. The rate of return could range from some extremely large positive figure to minus 100 percent, and because there is a significant danger of loss, the stock is described as being relatively risky.

Of course, no investment will be made unless the expected rate of return is high enough to compensate the investor for taking extra risks. In fact, we can generalize that the higher the perceived risk associated with an investment opportunity, the greater the expected return must be in order to persuade a manager to accept the project. In our investment example, it is clear that few if any investors would buy the oil company stock if its expected return were the same as that of the government bond. Naturally, the more risky investment may not realize the higher rate of return, since if the highest-risk projects always provided the highest returns, there would be no risk.

Investment risk, then, is associated with the probability of loss—the greater the chance of loss, the more risky the investment. In the following sections, therefore, we describe means by which we may evaluate more precisely the risk and return in capital budgeting.

Probability Distributions. An event's *probability* is defined as the chance that the event will occur. For example, a weather forecaster may state, "There is a 40 percent chance of rain today and a 60 percent chance that it will not rain." If all possible events, or outcomes, are listed, and if a probability is assigned to each event, then the listing is defined as a **probability distribution.** For our weather forecast, we could set up the following probability distribution:

probability distribution
A listing of all possible outcomes or events, with a probability (the chance of the event's occurrence) assigned to each outcome.

Outcome (1)	Probability (2)
Rain	0.4 = 40%
No rain	0.6 = 60%
	1.0 = 100%

The possible outcomes are listed in Column 1, and the probabilities of these outcomes, expressed both as decimals and as percentages, are given in Column 2. Notice that the probabilities must sum to 1.0, or 100 percent.

Eastern Communications, Inc., a manufacturer and retailer of business and consumer telephones, is considering the expected rate of return on two of its consumer lines of telephones. The two lines consist of its Standard Phone line and its new Designer Phone line. Most of the firm's marketing managers believe that the Designer line should have a return higher than the Standard equipment in "boom" and "normal" economic periods. In recessionary periods, when consumers typically have less to spend on luxury items, the Designer line is not expected to be profitable. Before money is invested to initiate the manufacture and sale of both lines, Eastern Communications wishes to determine the risk and return of these two product lines in a more direct manner. The state of the economy and the resulting rate of return on each product line are presented in Table 16-3. Here we see that there is a 30 percent chance of a boom, in which case both product lines will enjoy high rates of return; a 40 percent chance of a normal economy and moderate returns; and a 30 percent probability of a recession, which will mean low or even negative returns for both product lines.

Table 16-3
Projected Return on Each Phone Line Based on the State of the Economy

	Designer Phone Line	
State of the Economy	Probability of This State Occurring	Rate of Return under This State
Boom	0.3	100%
Normal	0.4	15
Recession	0.3	−70
	1.0	

	Standard Phone Line	
State of the Economy	Probability of This State Occurring	Rate of Return under This State
Boom	0.3	20%
Normal	0.4	15
Recession	0.3	10
	1.0	

Of course, the profits of the luxury Designer line are more sensitive to the economic environment than the profits of the Standard line. In fact, in recessionary periods the return on the Designer line can drop significantly, whereas the Standard line has little chance for loss.

Expected Rate of Return. If we multiply each possible outcome by its probability of occurrence and then sum these products, we have a *weighted average* of outcomes. This weighted average of outcomes can be expressed in equation form as the **expected rate of return, $\hat{k}$,** of a probability distribution:

expected rate of return, $\hat{k}$
The rate of return expected to be realized from an investment; the mean value of the probability distribution of possible returns.

$$\text{Expected rate of return} = \hat{k} = \sum_{i=1}^{n} P_i k_i. \qquad \textbf{(16-1)}$$

Here the expected rate of return, $\hat{k}$, is the weighted average of each possible outcome, k_i, weighted by the probability of its occurrence, P_i. Using the data for the Designer line, we obtain its expected rate of return as follows:

$$\begin{aligned}
\hat{k} &= P_1(k_1) + P_2(k_2) + P_3(k_3) \\
&= 0.3(100\%) + 0.4(15\%) + 0.3(-70\%) \\
&= 15\%.
\end{aligned}$$

Similarly, we can use Equation 16-1 to determine the expected rate of return for the Standard line:

$$\hat{k} = 0.3(20\%) + 0.4(15\%) + 0.3(10\%)$$
$$= 15\%.$$

We can graph the rates of return to obtain a picture of the variability of the possible outcomes; this is shown in the bar charts in Figure 16-1. The height of each bar signifies the probability that a given outcome will occur. The range of probable returns for the Designer line is from 100 percent to −70 percent, with an average or expected return of 15 percent. The expected return for the Standard line is also 15 percent, but with a much narrower range of return possibilities. The wider the range of possible events, the greater the probability that the outcome will differ from the expected outcome. Thus with greater uncer-

Figure 16-1
Probability Distributions of the Rates of Return for the Designer and Standard Telephone Projects: Eastern Communications, Inc.
The expected rate of return on a project is equal to the average of all possible outcomes, with each outcome weighted by the probability of its occurrence. These bar charts show the variability of three possible outcomes for each of two projects. For both an average (or expected) return of 15 percent is most probable, but the Designer line has a much wider range of return possibilities. Because this wider range means a greater probability that the return will differ from 15 percent, the Designer line is a more risky project.

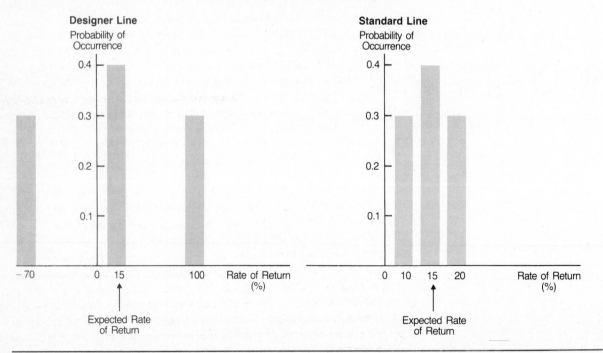

tainty involved in a capital budgeting opportunity, such as the Designer line of phones, comes greater risk.

Continuous Probability Distributions. Thus far we have assumed that only three states of the economy can exist: recession, normal, and boom. Actually, of course, the state of the economy could range from a deep depression to a fantastic boom, and there are an unlimited number of possibilities in between. Suppose we had the time and patience to assign a probability to each possible state of the economy (with the sum of the probabilities still equaling 1.0), and to assign a rate of return to each project for each state of the economy. We would have an equation similar to Equation 16-1 except that it would have many more entries. This equation could be used to calculate expected rates of return as shown above, and the probabilities and outcomes could be approximated by the continuous curves presented in Figure 16-2. Here we have changed the assumptions so that there is essentially a zero probability that the Designer line's return will be less than −70 percent or more than 100 percent, or that the Standard line will return less than 10 percent or more than 20 percent.

The tighter the probability distribution, the more likely it is that the actual outcome will be close to the expected value, and the less likely it is that the actual return will be far below the expected return. Thus the tighter the probability distribution, the lower the risk assigned to a project. Since the Standard line has a relatively tight probability distribution, its *actual return* is likely to be closer to the 15 percent expected return than is that of the Designer line.

Measuring Risk: The Standard Deviation. Risk is a difficult concept to grasp, and a great deal of controversy has surrounded attempts to define and measure it. However, a common definition, and one that is satisfactory for many purposes, is stated in terms of probability distributions such as those presented in Figure 16-2: *The tighter the probability distribution of expected future returns, the smaller the risk of a given investment.* According to this definition, the Standard line of telephones is less risky than the Designer line because the chances of a large loss on the Standard line are smaller than the chances of a similar loss on the Designer line.

To be most useful, any measure of risk should have a definite value—we need a measure of the tightness of the probability distribution. One such measure is the **standard deviation**, the symbol for which is σ, pronounced "sigma." The smaller the standard deviation, the tighter the probability distribution and, accordingly, the lower the riskiness of the project. The calculation of the standard deviation is outlined as follows:

1. Calculate the expected rate of return:

$$\text{Expected rate of return} = \hat{k} = \sum_{i=1}^{n} P_i k_i. \qquad \textbf{(16-1)}$$

measuring risk
The tighter the probability distribution of expected future returns, the smaller the risk of a given investment.

standard deviation, σ
A statistical measurement of the variability of a set of observations.

Figure 16-2
**Continuous Probability Distributions of the Designer and Standard Lines'
Rates of Return**

Figure 16-1 graphed the probabilities of three possible outcomes for each telephone project. In reality, both projects could have numerous rates of return, which could be best illustrated by the continuous probability curves shown here. These curves indicate that the most likely rate of return for both product lines is 15 percent. In addition, the relative flatness of the curves indicates the extent to which returns are likely to vary from 15 percent. The height of the curve for the Standard line indicates a tight probability distribution and reflects the fact that there is zero probability that the return will be below 10 percent or above 20 percent. The curve for the Designer line is much flatter, meaning that this project has a higher probability of returning either more or less than 15 percent and is thus a higher risk.

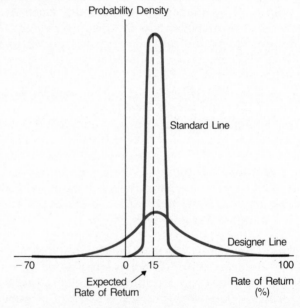

Note: The assumptions regarding the probabilities of various outcomes have been changed from those in Figure 16-1. The probability of obtaining exactly 15 percent was 40 percent in Figure 16-1; in Figure 16-2 it is much smaller because here there are many possible outcomes instead of just three. With continuous distributions such as in Figure 16-2, it is more appropriate to ask what the probability is of obtaining *at least* some specified rate of return than to ask what the probability is of obtaining exactly that rate of return. This cumulative probability is equal to the area under the probability distribution curve to the right of the point of interest or 1 minus the area under the curve up to the point of interest. This topic is covered in detail in statistics courses.

2. Subtract the expected rate of return from each possible outcome to obtain a set of deviations about the expected rate of return:

$$\text{Deviation}_i = k_i - \hat{k}.$$

3. Square each deviation, multiply the squared deviation by the probability of occurrence for its related outcome, and sum these products to obtain the *variance* of the probability distribution:

$$\text{Variance} = \sigma^2 = \sum_{i=1}^{n} (k_i - \hat{k})^2 P_i. \qquad \textbf{(16-2)}$$

4. Find the standard deviation by obtaining the square root of the variance:

$$\text{Standard deviation} = \sigma = \sqrt{\sum_{i=1}^{n} (k_i - \hat{k})^2 P_i}. \qquad \textbf{(16-3)}$$

5. We can illustrate these procedures by calculating the standard deviation for both the Designer and Standard lines:

a. Designer line:
  1. The expected rate of return, $\hat{k}$, was found, using Equation 16-1, to be 15 percent.
  2. We set up a table to work out the value for Equation 16-3:

$k_i - \hat{k}$	=	$(k_i - \hat{k})$	$(k_i - \hat{k})^2$	$(k_i - \hat{k})^2 P_i$	
100 − 15		85	7225	(7225) (0.3) =	2167.5
15 − 15		0	0	(0) (0.4) =	0.0
−70 − 15		−85	7225	(7225) (0.3) =	2167.5
				Variance = σ_k^2 =	4335.0

Standard deviation = $\sigma_k = \sqrt{\sigma_k^2} = \sqrt{4335.0} = 65.84\%$.

b. Standard line:
  1. The expected rate of return, $\hat{k}$, is 15 percent.
  2. We compute the project's risk measure, the standard deviation, by utilizing Equation 16-3:

$k_i - \hat{k}$	=	$(k_i - \hat{k})$	$(k_i - \hat{k})^2$	$(k_i - \hat{k})^2 P_i$	
20 − 15		5	25	(25) (0.3) =	7.5
15 − 15		0	0	(0) (0.4) =	0.0
10 − 15		−5	25	(25) (0.3) =	7.5
				Variance = σ_k^2 =	15.0

Standard deviation = $\sigma_k = \sqrt{\sigma_k^2} = \sqrt{15} = 3.87\%$.

If a probability distribution is normal, as pictured in Figure 16-3, the actual return will lie within ±1 standard deviation of the *expected* return about 68 percent of the time. Figure 16-3 illustrates this point and also shows the situation for ±2σ and ±3σ. For the Designer line $\hat{k}$ = 15 percent and σ = 65.84 percent. Thus there is a 68.26 percent probability that the actual return will be in the range of 15 percent ±65.84 percent, or from −50.84 percent to 80.84 percent. In a similar fashion, the expected return for the Standard line is 15 percent, but there is a

Figure 16-3
Probability Ranges for a Normal Distribution
This figure illustrates a normal probability curve. In a normal distribution the actual value will fall within ±1 standard deviation of the expected value about 68 percent of the time. Thus, in the Eastern Communications, Inc. example, 68 percent of the time the Standard line's actual return will be in the range of 15 percent ± 3.87 percent. Similarly, there is a 68 percent chance that the Designer line's return will fall in the range of 15 percent ± 65.84 percent. The normal curve again highlights the greater risk associated with the Designer line.

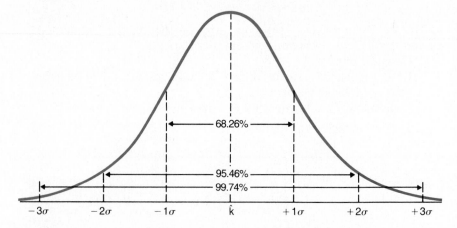

Notes:
1. The area under the normal curve equals 1.0, or 100%. *Thus the areas under any pair of normal curves drawn on the same scale, whether they are peaked or flat, must be equal.*
2. Half of the area under a normal curve is to the left of the mean, indicating that there is a 50% probability that the actual outcome will be less than the mean and a 50% probability that it will be greater than the mean, or to the right of it.
3. Of the area under the curve, 68.26% is within ±1σ of the mean, indicating that the probability is 68.26% that the actual outcome will be within the range $\hat{k} - 1\sigma$ to $\hat{k} + 1\sigma$.
4. Procedures are available for finding the probability of other earnings ranges. These procedures are covered in statistics courses.
5. For a normal distribution, the larger the value of σ, the greater the probability that the actual outcome will vary widely from, hence perhaps be far below, the expected, or most likely, outcome. *Since the probability of having the actual results turn out to be bad is our definition of risk, and since σ measures this probability, we can use σ as a measure of risk.* This definition may not be a good one, however, if we are dealing with an asset held in a diversified portfolio. This point is covered later in the chapter.

68 percent chance (68.26 percent, to be exact) that the return can range between 11.13 percent and 18.87 percent. With such a small standard deviation for the Standard line, we can conclude that there will be little chance of significant loss from investing in that product line.

portfolio theory
The theory that deals with the selection of optimal portfolios—those that provide the highest possible return for any specified degree of risk.

Portfolio Theory and the Capital Asset Pricing Model

In the preceding section we considered the description and measurement of risk and return for individual capital budgeting projects. Now we analyze the effect of combining two or more investments into a portfolio of either financial or real assets. As we shall see, investing in more than one project may actually reduce the overall risk of the firm. In order to investigate this phenomenon, we utilize a slightly different type of investment, common stock, as opposed to an investment in capital budgeting projects. We make this shift in our analysis since the risk reduction qualities of investment in multiple assets was first recognized in a stock market context. Even though the analysis in real and financial assets is quite similar on an analytical basis, we shall return to our capital budgeting framework later in the chapter. We know that portfolios are less risky than individual securities, and this fact has been incorporated into a generalized framework for analyzing the relationship between risk and return; this framework is called the **Capital Asset Pricing Model**, or **CAPM.** The CAPM framework is, as we shall see, an extremely important analytical tool in *both* financial management and investment analysis.

Capital Asset Pricing Model (CAPM)
A model based on the proposition that any stock's required rate of return is equal to the riskless rate of return plus its risk premium.

Portfolio Risk

Most financial assets are not held in isolation; rather, they are held as parts of portfolios. Banks, pension funds, insurance companies, mutual funds, and other financial institutions are required by law to hold diversified portfolios. Even individual investors—at least those individuals whose security holdings constitute a significant part of their total wealth—generally hold stock portfolios, not just the stock of one firm. This being the case, from an investor's standpoint the fact that a particular stock goes up or down is not very important; *what is important is the value of the portfolio and the portfolio's return.*

To illustrate this point, suppose you have $100,000 to invest. You are considering two stocks, Atlas Industries and Walker Products, whose total returns (dividend yield plus capital gains or minus capital losses) over the last four years are shown in Columns 2 and 3 below:

	Rate of Return		
Year (1)	Atlas (2)	Walker (3)	Portfolio (4)
1981	40%	−20%	10%
1982	−10	50	20
1983	35	−9	13
1984	−5	39	17
Average return	15%	15%	15%
Standard deviation	26%	35%	4%

If you invested your entire $100,000 in either Atlas or Walker, and if returns in the future varied as they have in the past, then your *expected return* on this one-stock portfolio would be $15,000, or 15 percent.

However, your *actual return* could easily be negative. On the other hand, if you put half of your money into each stock, your expected return would still be $15,000, or 15 percent, but this return would be much less risky. These results are graphed in Figure 16-4, where we see that the ups and downs in the portfolio's returns are not nearly so pronounced as are those on the individual stocks.

What conditions are necessary for diversification to cause the riskiness of a portfolio to be less than the riskiness of the individual assets contained in the portfolio? The only condition necessary is that the returns on the stocks in the portfolio do not move exactly together. If Atlas's and Walker's returns always moved in the same direction and by the same amount, then diversification into these two stocks would do no good. *In technical terms this means that for diversification to be effective, returns must not be perfectly positively correlated.* Since most stocks

Figure 16-4
Rates of Return on Atlas Industries, Walker Products, and Portfolio Consisting of 50 Percent in Each Stock

Diversification of stock holdings reduces an investor's portfolio risk. For example, both Atlas Industries and Walker Products had widely varying rates of return from 1981 through 1984, making each a risky investment by itself. Note, however, that the two stocks' rates of return rose and fell in opposition to each other. Thus, if the two were combined into a single portfolio, their ups and downs would tend to cancel each other out. Because the fluctuations in returns would then be less pronounced, the combined investment would be less risky.

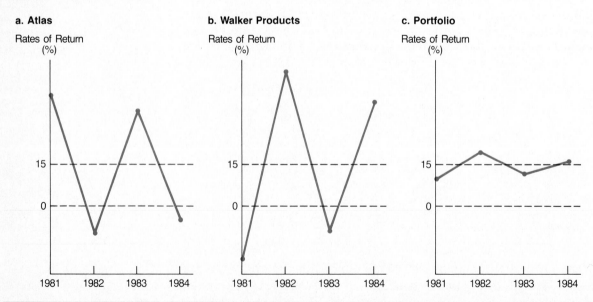

are not perfectly correlated, diversification generally reduces, but does not eliminate, portfolio risk.[2]

To see better how diversification affects portfolio risk, consider Figure 16-5, which shows that the riskiness of a portfolio declines as more and more stocks are added.[3] Here risk is measured by the standard deviation of annual returns on the portfolio, σ_p. With just one stock such as Stock S in the portfolio, σ_p equals the standard deviation of returns on Stock S, or 30 percent. Notice, however, that as more stocks are added, the portfolio's risk declines and approaches a limit, 15 percent in this example. (It is a coincidence that σ_p and k are both 15 percent.) Adding more and more stocks (diversification) can eliminate *some* of the riskiness of a portfolio, *but not all of it*. Thus risk consists of two parts: (1) *company specific, or diversifiable, risk*, which can be eliminated by adding enough securities to the portfolio, and (2) *market, or nondiversifiable*, risk, which is related to broad swings in the stock market and which cannot be eliminated by diversification.[4]

Company risk is caused by such things as lawsuits, strikes, successful and unsuccessful marketing programs, winning and losing major contracts, and other events that are *unique to a particular firm*. Since these events are essentially random, their effects on a portfolio can be eliminated by diversification—bad events in one firm will be offset by good events in another. **Market risk,** on the other hand, stems from such things as inflation, recessions, and high interest rates, factors which *affect all firms simultaneously*. However, not all firms are affected equally by market risk; for example, some firms are much more sensitive to changes in interest rates than others. Later in this chapter, we discuss a means by which we can measure a firm's sensitivity to market risk. Still, since all firms are affected simultaneously by these factors, market risk cannot be eliminated by diversification.

company risk
That part of a security's risk associated with random events; such risk can be eliminated by proper diversification.

market risk
That part of a security's risk that cannot be eliminated by diversification. It is measured by the beta coefficient.

---

[2]*Correlation* is defined as the tendency of two variables to move together. The *correlation coefficient, r*, measures this tendency and can range from +1.0, denoting that the two variables move up and down in perfect synchronization, to −1.0, denoting that the variables always move in exactly opposite directions. A correlation coefficient of zero suggests that the two variables are not related to each other, that is, changes in one variable are independent of changes in the other. If stocks were negatively correlated, or if there were zero correlation, then a properly constructed portfolio would have very little risk. However, stocks tend to be positively (but less than perfectly) correlated with one another, so all stock portfolios tend to be somewhat risky.

[3]The data used in this example are adapted from W. H. Wagner and S. C. Lau, "The Effect of Diversification on Risk," *Financial Analysts' Journal*, November–December 1971, 48–53. Wagner and Lau divided a sample of 200 New York Stock Exchange stocks into 6 subgroups based on quality ratings. Then they constructed portfolios from each of the subgroups, using from 1 to 20 randomly selected securities, and applied equal weights to each security.

[4]Market risk is sometimes called "systematic risk," while company risk is called "unsystematic risk."

Figure 16-5
Reduction of Portfolio Risk through Diversification

Increasing diversification decreases the risk in an investor's portfolio. When an investor owns only one stock, the risk equals the standard deviation of the returns on that stock, or, in this case, 30 percent. Risk declines as more stocks are added until the level of market risk (here, 15 percent) is reached. Market risk is related to broad swings in the stock market as a whole and cannot be eliminated through diversification.

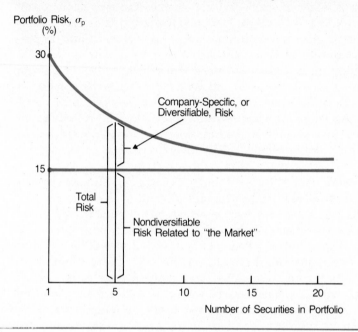

We know that investors demand a premium for bearing risk; that is, the higher the riskiness of a security, the higher its expected return must be in order to induce investors to buy (or to hold) it. But if investors are primarily concerned with *portfolio risk* rather than the risk of the individual securities in the portfolio, how should the riskiness of the individual stocks be measured? The answer is this: *The relevant riskiness of an individual stock is its contribution to the riskiness of a well-diversified portfolio.* In other words, the riskiness of Stock X to a doctor who has a portfolio of 30 stocks, or to a trust officer managing a 150-stock portfolio, is the contribution that Stock X makes to the portfolio's riskiness. The stock might be quite risky if held by itself, but if most of its risk can be eliminated by diversification, the stock's *relevant risk*, which is its contribution to the *portfolio's risk*, may be small.

A simple example will help make this point clear. Suppose you can flip a coin once. If a head comes up, you win $10,000, but you lose $9,500 if it comes up tails. Although this may be considered to be a good bet—the expected return is $250—it is a highly risky proposition.

Alternatively, suppose you can flip 100 coins and win $100 for each head but lose $95 for each tail. It is possible that you would hit all heads and win $10,000, and it is also possible that you would flip all tails and lose $9,500, but the chances are very high that you would actually flip about 50 heads and about 50 tails, winning a net $250. Although each individual flip is a risky bet, collectively you have a very low-risk proposition because you have diversified away most of the risk. This is the idea behind holding portfolios of stocks rather than just one stock, except that with stocks all of the risk cannot be eliminated by diversification—those risks related to broad changes in the stock market as reflected in the Dow Jones index and other stock market averages will remain.

Are all stocks equally risky in the sense that adding them to a well-diversified portfolio would have the same effect on the portfolio's riskiness? The answer is no—different stocks will affect the portfolio differently; hence different securities have different degrees of relevant risk.

How can the relevant risk of a stock be measured? As we saw above, all risk except that related to broad market movements can, and presumably will, be diversified away. After all, why accept risk that can easily be eliminated? *The risk that remains after diversifying is market risk, or risk that is inherent in the market, and this risk can be measured by the degree to which a given stock tends to move up and down with the market.*

The Concept of Beta

The tendency of a stock to move with the market is reflected in its **beta coefficient,** which is a measure of the stock's *volatility* relative to an average stock. Betas are discussed at an intuitive level in this section, then in more detail later in the chapter.

An *average-risk stock* is defined as one which tends to move up and down in step with the general market as measured by some index such as the Dow Jones or the New York Stock Exchange Index. Such a stock will have a beta (b) of 1.0, which indicates that, in general, if the market moves up by 10 percent, the stock will also move up by 10 percent, and that if the market falls by 10 percent, the stock will likewise fall by 10 percent. A portfolio of such b = 1.0 stocks will move up and down with the broad market averages and will be just as risky as the averages. If b = 0.5, the stock is only half as volatile as the market—it will rise and fall only half as much—and a portfolio of such stocks will be half as risky as a portfolio of b = 1.0 stocks. On the other hand, if b = 2.0, the stock is twice as volatile as an average stock, so a portfolio of such stocks will be twice as risky as an average portfolio.

Betas are calculated and published by Merrill Lynch, Value Line, and numerous other organizations. The beta coefficients of some well-known companies, as calculated by Merrill Lynch, are shown in Table

beta coefficient
A measurement of the extent to which the returns of a given stock move with the stock market.

Table 16-4
Illustrative List of Beta Coefficients

Stock	Beta
Campbell Soup Company	0.69
Caterpillar Tractor	1.13
Data 100 Corporation	2.02
Dean Foods Company	0.88
Eastman Kodak	1.24
General Electric	1.40
General Motors	0.76
Olympia Brewing Company	0.67
Oceanic Drilling & Exploration	1.96
Polaroid	2.17
Safeway Stores	0.70
St. Regis Paper	1.21

Source: Merrill Lynch, Pierce, Fenner & Smith, November 1980.

16-4. Most stocks have betas in the range of 0.75 to 1.50. The average for all stocks is 1.0 by definition.

If a high beta stock (one whose beta is greater than 1.0) is added to an average risk (b = 1.0) portfolio, both the beta and the riskiness of the portfolio will increase. Conversely, if a low beta stock (one whose beta is less than 1.0) is added to an average risk portfolio, the portfolio's beta and risk will decline. *Thus, since a stock's beta measures its contribution to the riskiness of any portfolio, beta is the appropriate measure of the stock's riskiness.*

We can summarize our analysis to this point as follows:

1. A stock's risk consists of two components, market and company risk.

2. The company risk can be eliminated by diversification, and most investors do indeed diversify. We are left, then, with market risk, which is caused by general movements in the stock market. This market risk is the only relevant risk to a rational, diversified investor.

3. The market risk of a stock is measured by its beta coefficient, which is an index of the stock's relative volatility. Some benchmark betas are given below:

b = 0.5: Stock is only half as volatile, or risky, as the average stock.
b = 1.0: Stock is of average risk.
b = 2.0: Stock is twice as risky as the average stock.

4. *Since a stock's beta coefficient determines how it affects the riskiness of a diversified portfolio, beta is the most relevant measure of a stock's risk. Henceforth, we shall rely heavily on beta coefficients to measure security risk.*

The Relationship between Risk and Rate of Return

Now that we have established beta as an appropriate measure of most stocks' risks, the next step in the Capital Asset Pricing Model (CAPM) framework is to specify the relationship between risk and return. This relationship is known as the **Security Market Line (SML),** and it is given by this equation:

$$k = R_F + b(k_M - R_F). \qquad \textbf{(16-4)}$$

Security Market Line (SML)
The line that shows the relationship between risk and rate of return for individual securities.

Here:

k = the required rate of return on the stock in question. If the expected future return, $\hat{k}$, is less than k, then you would not purchase this stock, or you would sell it if you owned it.

R_F = the risk-free rate of return, generally measured by the rate of return on short-term U.S. Treasury securities.

b = the beta coefficient of the stock in question.

k_M = the required rate of return on an average ($b = 1.0$) stock. k_M is also the required rate of return on a portfolio consisting of all stocks.

$(k_M - R_F)$ = the market risk premium, or the price of risk for an average stock. It is the additional return over the riskless rate required to compensate investors for assuming an "average" amount of risk.

$b(k_M - R_F)$ = the risk premium on the stock in question. The stock's risk premium is less than, equal to, or greater than the premium on an average stock depending on whether its beta is less than, equal to, or greater than 1.0.

In words, the SML equation shows that the required rate of return on a given stock, k, is equal to the return required in the marketplace for securities that have no risk, R_F, plus a risk premium equal to the risk premium demanded on an average stock, $k_M - R_F$, scaled up or down by the relative riskiness of the firm as measured by its beta coefficient, b. Thus, if $R_F = 8\%$, $b = 0.5$, and $k_M = 12\%$, then

$$
\begin{aligned}
k &= 8\% + 0.5(12\% - 8\%) \\
&= 8\% + 0.5(4\%) \\
&= 10\%.
\end{aligned}
$$

An average firm, with $b = 1.0$, would have

$$k = 8\% + 1.0(4\%) = 12\%,$$

while a riskier firm, with b = 2.0, would have

$$k = 8\% + 2.0(4\%) = 16\%.$$

Figure 16-6 shows a graph of the SML and the required rate of return for the three stocks described above when $R_F = 8\%$ and $k_M = 12\%$. Several features of the graph are worth noting:

1. Required rates of return are shown on the vertical axis, while risk as measured by beta is shown on the horizontal axis.

2. Riskless securities have b = 0; therefore R_F appears as the vertical axis intercept.

Figure 16-6
The Security Market Line (SML)

The Security Market Line reflects the relationship between a stock's riskiness and its rate of return. According to the SML equation, a stock's required rate of return equals the rate for riskless securities (U.S. Treasury bills) plus a risk premium. This premium is set according to whether a stock is considered of average risk (beta = 1.0), less than average risk (beta < 1.0), or greater than average risk (beta > 1.0). When the riskless rate is 8 percent, a stock with a beta of 0.5 will have a 2 percent risk premium, a stock with a beta of 1.0 will have a 4 percent risk premium, and a stock with a beta of 2.0 will have an 8 percent risk premium.

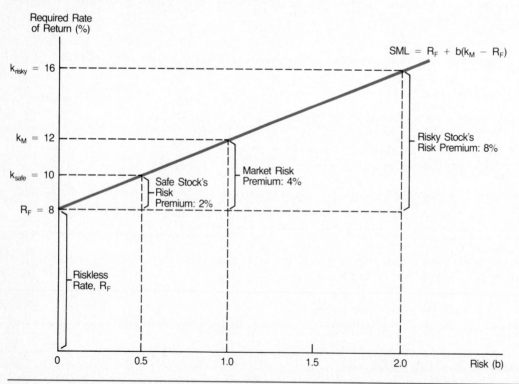

3. The slope of the SML reflects the degree of risk aversion in the economy—the greater the average investor's aversion to risk, then (1) the steeper the slope of the line, (2) the greater the risk premium for any risky asset, and (3) the higher the required rate of return on risky assets.[5]

4. The values for the low risk stock with b = .5, the average risk stock with b = 1.0, and the high risk stock with b = 2.0 are shown on the graph for k_{safe}, $k_M = k_{average}$, and k_{risky}.

Risk Analysis in Capital Budgeting

Risk analysis is important in all financial decisions. We have just analyzed the relationship between risk and return in portfolios of financial assets. The basic concept of this analysis is that the higher the risk associated with an investment, the higher the rate of return must be in order to compensate investors for assuming risk. The same principle holds for analysts evaluating a capital budgeting investment opportunity for a firm. Procedures for both measuring project risk and incorporating it into the accept-reject decision are covered in this section.

We also distinguish between two separate and distinct types of risk in capital budgeting: (1) *beta risk*, which measures risk only from the standpoint of an investor who holds a highly diversified portfolio, and (2) *total* or *corporate risk*, which looks at risk from other parties' viewpoints.

Beta Risk

As we have seen, the Capital Asset Pricing Model provides a framework for analyzing the relationship between risk and return. Basically, the model holds that there is a minimum return required, even if there were no risk, and a premium for all unavoidable risks associated with the investment. Therefore

> Required return = Risk-free rate + Risk premiums,

which translates into Equation 16-4,

$$k = R_F + b(k_M - R_F),$$

beta risk
The risk of a firm measured from the standpoint of an investor who holds a highly diversified portfolio.

---

[5]Students sometimes confuse beta with the slope of the SML. This is a mistake. The confusion arises partly because the SML equation is generally written, in this book and throughout the finance literature, as $k_i = R_F + b_i(k_M - R_F)$, and in this form b_i looks like the slope coefficient and $(k_M - R_F)$ the variable. It would perhaps be less confusing if the second term were written $(k_M - R_F)b_i$, but this is not generally done.

where the required return on an investment, k, is equal to the riskless rate, R_F, plus a risk premium that is equal to the stock's beta coefficient, b, times the market risk premium, $k_M - R_F$.[6] The greater the nondiversifiable risk from a stock or project, the greater the beta and hence the larger the risk premium.

For example, consider the case of Erie Steel Company, an integrated producer operating in the Great Lakes region. Erie Steel's beta is 1.1, so if $R_F = 8\%$ and $k_M = 12\%$, then

$$k = 8\% + 1.1(4\%) = 12.4\%.$$

Stockholders are willing to have Erie invest their money if the company can earn 12.4 percent on this money. *Therefore, as a first approximation, Erie should invest in capital projects if and only if these projects have an expected return of 12.4 percent or more.*[7] In other words, Erie should use 12.4 percent as its discount rate to determine projects' NPVs or as the "hurdle rate" if the IRR method is used.

Suppose, however, that taking on a particular project will change Erie's beta coefficient. For example, the company might be considering the construction of a fleet of barges to haul iron ore, and barge operations might have betas of about 1.5. Since the corporation itself may be regarded as a "portfolio of assets," and since the beta of any portfolio is a weighted average of the betas of the individual assets, taking on the barge investment will cause the overall corporate beta to rise and to end up somewhere between the original beta of 1.1 and the barge division's beta of 1.5. The exact position will depend on the relative size of the investment in basic steel versus that in barges. If 80 percent of the total corporate funds were in basic steel and 20 percent were in barges, then the new beta would be $0.8(1.1) + 0.2(1.5) = 1.18$.

An increase in the beta coefficient will cause the stock price to decline *unless the increased beta is offset by a higher expected rate of return.* Specifically, the overall corporate cost of capital will rise to 12.72 percent:

$$k_{(new)} = 8\% + 1.18(4\%) = 12.72\%.$$

Therefore, to keep the barge investment from lowering the value of the firm, Erie's expected overall rate of return must rise from 12.4 percent to 12.72 percent.

---

[6] Both the risk-free rate, R_F, and the return on a diversified portfolio of securities, k_M, are market determined and outside the control of the firm.

[7] To simplify things somewhat, we assume at this point that the firm uses only equity capital. If debt is used, then the cost of capital used must be a weighted average of the cost of debt and equity. This point is discussed at length in Chapter 20.

If investments in basic steel earn 12.4 percent, how much must the barge investment earn in order for the new overall rate of return to equal 12.72 percent? Let X be the required return on the barge investment, and then calculate the value of X as follows:

$$0.8(12.4\%) + 0.2(X) = 12.72\%$$
$$X = 14.0\%.$$

In summary, if Erie makes the barge investment, its beta will rise from 1.1 to 1.18; its overall required rate of return will rise from 12.4 percent to 12.72 percent; and it will achieve this new required rate if the barge investment earns 14 percent. If the barge investment has an expected return of more than 14 percent, taking it on will increase the value of Erie's stock. If the expected return is less than 14 percent, taking it on will decrease the stock's value. At an expected return of 14 percent, the barge project is a breakeven proposition in terms of its effect on the value of the stock.

This line of reasoning leads to the conclusion that, if the beta coefficient for each project could be determined, individual projects' costs of capital could be found as follows:

$$k_{(project)} = R_F + b_{(project)}(k_M - R_F).$$

Thus, for basic steel projects with $b = 1.1$, Erie should use 12.4 percent as the discount rate. The barge project should be evaluated at a 14 percent discount rate:

$$k_{(barge)} = 8\% + 1.5(4\%) = 8\% + 6\% = 14\%.$$

A low-risk project such as a new steel distribution center with a beta of only 0.5 would have a cost of capital of 10 percent:

$$k_{(center)} = 8\% + 0.5(4\%) = 10\%.$$

Figure 16-7 gives a graphic summary of these concepts as applied to Erie Steel. Note the following points:

1. The SML shows how investors are willing to make trade-offs between risk as measured by beta and expected returns. The higher the risk, the higher the rate of return needed to compensate investors for bearing this risk, and the SML specifies the nature of this relationship.

2. Erie Steel initially had a beta of 1.1, so its required rate of return on average-risk investments is 12.4 percent.

3. High-risk investments like the barge line require higher rates of return, while low-risk investments like the distribution center have lower required rates of return. Note also that if Erie makes relatively large investments in either high- or low-risk projects, as opposed to those

Figure 16-7
Using the Security Market Line Concept in Capital Budgeting
The Security Market Line can be used in the accept-reject decision for potential projects
in capital budgeting decisions. A project whose expected rate of return lies above the
SML should be accepted. A project whose return falls below the SML should be rejected
because its return will not be high enough to overcome its higher risk. In this case Project
M would be accepted, while Project N would be rejected.

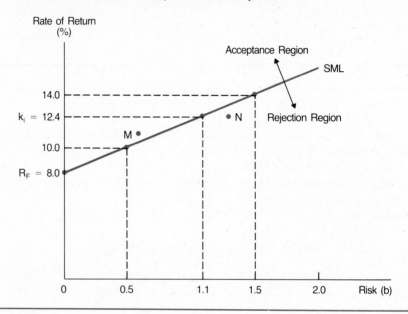

with average risks, both the corporate beta and the required rate of
return on the common stock (k_s) will change.

4. If the expected rate of return on a given capital project lies *above* the
SML, the expected rate of return on the project is more than enough
to compensate for its risk, so it should be accepted. Conversely, if the
project's rate of return lies *below* the SML, it should be rejected. Thus
Project M in Figure 16-7 is acceptable, while Project N should be rejected. Therefore, N has a higher expected return than M, but the differential is not enough to offset N's much higher risk.

Corporate Risk versus Beta Risk

corporate risk
The risk that relates to the
probability that a project will incur
losses that will destabilize profits
or, at worst, cause bankruptcy.
Sometimes referred to as total
risk.

A particular project might have highly uncertain returns, yet taking it
on might not affect the firm's beta coefficient at all. Recall that the beta
coefficient reflects only that part of an investor's risk which cannot be
eliminated by holding a large portfolio of stocks. Now suppose that
100 firms in the oil business each drill one wildcat well. Each company

has invested $1 million. If a firm strikes oil, then it will earn $1.4 million, whereas if it hits a dry hole, it will suffer a $1 million loss and go bankrupt. The probability of striking oil is 50 percent.

From the standpoint of the individual firms, this is a very risky business. Their expected rate of return is 20 percent, calculated as follows:

$$\frac{\text{Expected rate}}{\text{of return}} = \frac{\text{Expected profit}}{\text{Investment}} = \frac{0.5(-\$1 \text{ million}) + 0.5(+\$1.4 \text{ million})}{\$1 \text{ million}}$$

$$= \frac{-\$500,000 + \$700,000}{\$1,000,000} = 20\%.$$

Note, however, that even though the expected return is 20 percent, there is a 50 percent probability of each firm's being wiped out.

Although the riskiness of each individual firm is high, if a stockholder constructs a portfolio consisting of a few shares of each of the 100 companies, the riskiness of this portfolio will not be high at all. Some of the stocks will hit and do well, others will miss and go out of business, but the portfolio's return will be very close to the expected 20 percent. Therefore, since investors can diversify away the risks inherent in each of the individual companies, these risks are *not market-related*; that is, they do not affect the companies' beta coefficients.[8]

With this background, *we may define the corporate risk of a capital budgeting project as the probability that the project will incur losses which will, at a minimum, destabilize the corporation's earnings and, at the extreme, cause it to go bankrupt.* A project with a high degree of corporate risk will not necessarily affect the firm's beta to any great extent; our hypothetical example demonstrates this point. On the other hand, if the riskiness of a project is not diversifiable, then it may have a high degree of both corporate and beta risk. For example, suppose a firm decides to undertake a major expansion to build solar-powered automobiles. The firm is not sure if its technology will work on a mass production basis, so there are great risks in the venture. Management also estimates that the project will have a higher probability of success if the economy is strong, for then people will have the money to spend on buying the new automobiles. This means that the plant will tend to do well when other companies are also doing well, and to do badly when they do badly, so the plant's beta coefficient will be high. A project like this will have a high degree of both corporate risk and beta risk.

---

[8]Note also that if the 100 separate companies were merged, the combined company would not be very risky—it would drill lots of wells, losing on some and hitting on others, but it would earn a relatively steady profit.

Beta risk is obviously important because of beta's effect on the value of a firm's stock. At the same time, corporate risk is also important for two primary reasons:

1. Undiversified stockholders, including the owners of small businesses, are more concerned about corporate risk than about beta risk.
2. The firm's stability is important to its managers, workers, customers, suppliers, and creditors, and also to the community in which it operates. Firms that are in serious danger of bankruptcy, or even of suffering low profits and reduced output, have difficulty attracting and retaining good managers and workers. Also, both suppliers and customers will be reluctant to depend on the firm, and it will have difficulty borrowing money except at high interest rates. These factors will tend to reduce the firm's profitability, hence the price of its stock.

Summary

This chapter has dealt with several issues in capital budgeting, including equipment replacement decisions, inflation adjustments, and risk.

The key to making good replacement decisions is to develop accurate estimates of incremental cash flows—how large an investment will the replacement entail, and what net savings will it produce? If the present value of the net savings exceeds the cost of the equipment, then the replacement should be undertaken. However, as noted in the chapter, if the various replacement alternatives have different lives, it is necessary to adjust to a common life. This adjustment may be accomplished through the creation of replacement chains.

Inflation exists in the United States and most other economies, and it must be dealt with in capital budgeting analysis. If inflation is simply ignored, then (1) the cash flows in the numerator of the NPV equation are *not* adjusted for expected inflation, but (2) an adjustment is automatically (and generally unconsciously) made in the denominator, because market forces build inflation into the cost of capital. Thus the net result of ignoring inflation is to create a downward bias in evaluating projects (that is, to reject projects that should be accepted). The best way of correcting for the bias is to build price increases based on expected inflation rates directly into the cash flows.

Our analysis of risk first focused on the measurement of risk and return for a single capital budgeting project. However, we soon learned that rational investors hold portfolios of stocks, since a portion of the risk is eliminated thereby. We considered two issues: (1) the effect of a given project on the firm's beta coefficient *(beta risk)* and (2) the project's effect on the probability of bankruptcy *(corporate risk)*. Both types of risk are important. Beta risk directly affects the value of the firm's stock. Corporate risk affects the financial strength of the firm, and this in turn influences its ability to use debt, to maintain smooth operations over time, and to avoid crises that might consume the energy of the firm's managers and disrupt its employees, customers, suppliers, and community.

The major difficulty in determining the beta risk of a given project is in establishing the project's beta coefficient. It is not really meaningful to think about the beta of a particular asset like a truck or a machine, but it is meaningful to think of betas of divisions which are large enough to be operated as independent firms. Therefore, in practice, beta risk is estimated for large divisions of firms and used to establish divisional costs of capital, which are then scaled up or down in a somewhat ad hoc manner to reflect a given project's own risk.

Both measuring risk and incorporating it into capital budgeting decisions involve judgment. It is possible to use techniques such as simulation and sensitivity analysis, but the assessment of risk in capital budgeting nonetheless remains a judgmental process.

Small Business $ $ $ $ $ $ $ $ $

Capital Budgeting in the Small Firm

The allocation of capital in small firms is as important as it is in large firms. In fact, given their comparative lack of inexpensive access to the capital markets, it may be even more important in the small firm; a mistake in allocating capital to investment in a small firm could cost the firm its very existence. Normally, large firms with capital budgets of $100 million or more allocate capital to numerous projects. A mistake can get lost in the rounding error associated with annual earnings per share. In a small firm with relatively narrow markets, however, a mistake may cost the firm dearly. It follows that capital budgeting is very important to small businesses.

In spite of the importance of capital expenditures to small business, studies of the way firms make capital budgeting decisions frequently find that small firms use very unsophisticated analysis, or perhaps even no analysis at all, in making capital budgeting decisions. For example, in a study of small manufacturing firms in Iowa 20 years ago, Robert Soldofsky[1] found that more than 50 percent of the firms used payback or some similar criterion, and over 40 percent of them used no formal analysis at all. More recently, Runyon[2] studied 214 firms with net worths of from $500,000 to $1,000,000. He found that among these firms almost 70 percent used either payback or accounting rate of return criteria, and only 14 percent used a discounted cash flow analysis. About 9 percent of Runyon's sample indicated that they used no formal analysis at all. Studies of larger firms typically find that well over half of the firms support their capital budgeting decisions with discounted cash flow techniques.

We are left with a puzzle. Capital budgeting decisions are clearly of great importance to small firms, yet the firms neglect to use the tools that have been developed to aid their decision making. Why does this situation exist?

One of the arguments often presented is that managers of small firms are simply not well trained; they are unsophisticated. This argument suggests that the managers would use the more sophisticated techniques if they were aware of the techniques or understood them better.

An argument related to the claim that small business managers are unsophisticated is that managerial talent is a scarce resource in small firms. That is, even if the managers are exceptionally sophisticated, perhaps the demands on their time are such that they are unwilling to use elaborate techniques to analyze a problem. In other words, the managers are capable of doing a careful discounted cash flow analysis, but they are unwilling to allocate the time required for such an analysis.

The managerial time required to undertake an analysis is just one example of the cost of analysis. To some extent, the costs of doing an analysis of a capital expenditure decision are fixed; the costs are generally larger for bigger expenditures, but not necessarily. To the extent that the costs of analysis are fixed, it may not be economical to incur the costs of analysis when the project itself is relatively small. This argument suggests that small firms with projects that are comparatively small may in some cases be making the sensible decision that the cost of analysis is too great for projects when management feels confident that the project should definitely be undertaken. Small firms may do less analysis simply because it is often not economical to perform a full-blown analysis when the dollar value of the project is small. Thus one

decision to be made is how much to spend making decisions. In some cases a reasoned appraisal might suggest that the cost of analysis is greater than the value of the expected benefits.

As Soldofsky learned in his study of manufacturing firms, small firms tend to be cash oriented. They are very concerned with basic survival, so they tend to look at expenditures from the standpoint of their effects on cash, and in the very near term. This cash and survival orientation leads the firm to look only at relatively short time horizons, and it leads to an emphasis on the payback criterion as a decision tool. The limitations of payback were discussed in Chapter 15, but in spite of those limitations the technique is popular in small business (and in big business). Payback gives the firm a crude feel for the time required to recover the cash committed to an investment and make cash available for new opportunities. Small firms that are cash oriented and have scarce managerial time resources may find the technique an appealing compromise between the need for extensive analysis on the one hand and the high costs of analysis on the other.

Small firms often face very great uncertainty in the cash flows they might generate beyond the immediate future. Many business people are very uncomfortable making forecasts beyond a short horizon. Since discounted cash flow techniques require explicit estimates of cash flows through the life of the project, small business managers may feel that they cannot take seriously an analysis that hinges on very suspect numbers. This argument seems to appeal to many business people, but, of course, discounting techniques contain built-in mechanisms for handling the fact that some cash flow estimates may be more uncertain than others. For example, one can increase the discount rate in accordance with the greater perceived uncertainty.

The Value of the Firm and Capital Budgeting

The single most appealing argument for the use of net present value in capital expenditure decisions is that NPV gives an explicit measure of the effect of the investment on the value of the firm. If NPV is positive, in theory the investment will increase the value of the firm and make all owners of the firm simultaneously more wealthy. In small firms, however, it is often the case that the equity of the firm is not tradable in public markets; its value cannot be easily observed. And for reasons of control or because their size does not permit the making of a market in their stock, many small business owners and managers may be content not to let the ownership broaden into the public markets.

It is difficult to argue for value-based techniques when the value of the firm itself is unobservable. Furthermore, in a very closely held firm the objectives of the individual owner-manager may not be easily expressible in terms of the firm's value. For example, the manager may not hold a well-diversified investment portfolio but may instead have a heavy financial commitment to the firm. In that case the manager is sensitive to the total risk of the firm, not just to its systematic or undiversifiable component. A project then might be viewed as desirable because of its contribution to risk reduction in the firm as a whole. Similarly, a project with high unsystematic risk might be unacceptable even though in a CAPM framework it would be judged acceptable.

Another problem that nonmarketability causes the small firm is that the cost of equity capital is not easily determined. A cost of capital estimate is required for a NPV or IRR analysis, and such estimates are generally based on market data. The small firm in an industry of small firms may even find that it cannot identify a "surrogate" firm in the market with which to estimate its cost of capital.

Conclusions

Small firms make less extensive use of discounted cash flow techniques than do larger firms. The decision to use relatively informal procedures may arise from conflicts between the objectives of the firms and the objectives which motivate the use of DCF, and it may result in part from the determination that the cost of analysis exceeds the benefits. Small businesses must do all they can to compete effectively with big business. To the extent that small businesses fail to use DCF because the managers are unsophisticated or uninformed, the small firms may be putting themselves at a competitive disadvantage. Making poor capital investment decisions may cost the small firms their very existence. It follows that small firms should use every means at their disposal to insure that the projects to which they allocate scarce capital are good projects. Errors can be terribly costly.

[1]Robert M. Soldofsky, "Capital Budgeting Practices in Small Manufacturing Companies," in *Studies in the Factor Markets for Small Business Firms*, ed. Donald G. Luckett (Washington, DC: Small Business Administration, 1964).

[2]L. R. Runyon, "Capital Expenditure Decision Making in Small Firms," *Journal of Business Research*, September 1983, 389–397.

Resolution to Decision in Finance

$$

Gambling on a State-of-the-Art Refinery

Despite the expense and riskiness of the venture, Valero went ahead with its plans to upgrade the Saber refinery. In its actions it followed the lead of numerous other U.S. refiners, who planned to spend a combined total of $7 billion on converting their facilities to run on less expensive, low-grade crude oils. By the fall of 1983 all were taking a second look at their calculations, and few were happy with what they saw. It seems that no had anticipated the many changes that had hit the oil industry since the decision to upgrade had been made.

It took Valero three years to retool the Saber plant. And by the time it was ready to begin operations, economic circumstances had vastly changed. Most unexpected and damaging was the price of resid, which had risen from $20 per barrel to $26. With lighter crude selling at $29 per barrel, the heavy crude was no longer the attractive bargain it had been in 1980. In addition, the price of gasoline had not risen as expected.

With gasoline selling at under $36 per barrel, Valero was lucky to squeeze out a gross margin of $8 per barrel. That was still twice the industry average, but Valero also had higher-than-average expenses. It cost the company over $4 per barrel to service its $550 million debt. And the plant itself had high operating costs.

Although Valero claimed that the phasing in of its new operation was on schedule, industry sources contended that the company was having trouble getting its costly new plant to work. They speculated that one setback could have stemmed from the fact that constant processing of heavy crude can create refining problems. The usual solution would be to mix in lighter, more expensive crude, but that would have cut even further into Valero's margins. And, in another snag, the plant was having trouble meeting federal air pollution standards.

Not surprisingly, the price of Valero's stock reflected the difficulties the company was having with its refining operations. Analysts and investors had been extremely enthusiastic when Valero first announced its plans in late 1980, sending the stock up to 43⅞ per share. But by fall 1983, the price had fallen below 30.

Throughout, Chairman Greehey remained optimistic, arguing that Valero's troubles were only temporary. According to him, the quality of available crude oil would steadily drop, eventually restoring the greater price spread between heavy and light crudes. "We will be right

> back where we started," he insisted. "Take your potshots now, be-
> cause this thing will be profitable."
>
> Source: "Valero Energy: Gambling on a State-of-the-Art Refinery," *Business Week*, Oct.
> 24, 1983, 96; and "Heavy Crude Has Backfired on the Refiners," *Business Week*, Nov. 7,
> 1983, 126, 130.

Key Terms   You should be able to define each of the following terms:

Replacement decision
Incremental future cash flow
Risk
Probability distribution
Expected rate of return, $\hat{k}$, versus
   required rate of return, k, versus
   realized rate of return
Measuring risk

Standard deviation, σ
Capital Asset Pricing Model (CAPM)
Portfolio theory
Company risk; market risk; beta risk;
   corporate risk
Beta coefficient
Security Market Line (SML)

Questions

16-1   Look at Table 16-1 and answer the following questions:
  a. Why are the salvage values reduced for taxes on Line 11 but not on Line 2?
  b. Why is depreciation on the old machine deducted on Line 9?
  c. What would happen if the new machine permitted a *reduction* in working capital?
  d. Why are the cost savings on Line 7 reduced by multiplying the before-tax figure by $(1 - t)$, whereas the net depreciation figure in Line 10 is multiplied by t?
  e. Why is there no tax for the recapture of working capital on Line 12?

16-2   The probability distribution of a less risky expected return is more peaked than that of a risky return. What shape would the probability distribution have (**a**) for completely certain returns and (**b**) for completely uncertain returns?

16-3   Distinguish between the beta risk and the corporate risk of a project being considered for inclusion in the capital budget. Which type do you feel should be given the greater weight in capital budgeting decisions?

Self-Test Problem

ST-1   The Harrington-Wilson Corporation (HWC) currently uses an injection molding machine that was purchased several years ago. This old machine is being depreciated on a straight line basis. It has 5 years of remaining life with zero expected salvage value. Its current book value is $5,000, and it can be sold for $6,000 at this time.

   HWC is offered a replacement machine which has a cost of $16,000, a tax and useful life of 5 years, and an estimated salvage value of $2,000.

This machine is also depreciated on a straight line basis. A 10 percent tax credit is applicable. The replacement machine will permit an output expansion, so sales will rise by $2,000 annually; yet the new machine's much greater efficiency will cause operating expenses to decline by $3,000 per year. The new machine will cause inventories to increase by $4,000 and accounts payable to increase by $1,000.

HWC's effective tax rate is 40 percent, and its cost of capital is 15 percent. Should it replace the old machine?

Problems

* **16-1** Miller's Mills has an average cost of capital equaling 10 percent. The company is choosing between two mutually exclusive projects. Project B is of average risk, it has a cost of $50,000, and it has expected cash flows of $14,701.80 per year for 5 years. Project A is of above-average risk, and management estimates that its cost of capital would be 12 percent. Project A also costs $50,000, and it is expected to provide cash flows of $9,380.53 per year for 10 years. Each project will terminate at the end of its designated life. Calculate risk-adjusted NPVs for the two projects, and use these NPVs to choose between them.

16-2 Stocks A and B have the following probability distributions of expected future returns:

Probability	A	B
0.1	−10%	−30%
0.2	5	0
0.4	15	17
0.2	25	34
0.1	40	64

a. Calculate the expected rate of return, $\hat{k}$, for Stock B. $\hat{k}_A = 15\%$.

b. Calculate the standard deviation of expected returns for Stock A. That for Stock B is 23.6 percent. Is it possible that most investors might regard Stock B as being *less* risky than Stock A? Explain.

* **16-3** Tidewater Consulting has provided the following estimates for a proposed investment project:

Annual Cash Flows	
Probability	Amount
0.3	$40,000
0.5	50,000
0.2	65,000

An investment of $250,000 is required to make the project operational. The asset is not eligible for an investment tax credit, and it has an

---

*Refer to Appendix E for check answers to problems with asterisks.

expected salvage value of zero. The expected economic and tax life of the project is 10 years.

a. If the firm requires a 14 percent return, what is the project's NPV?

b. What is the project's IRR?

16-4 Landry Equipment Company is considering the purchase of a new machine to replace an obsolete one. The machine used in current operations has both a book value and a market value of zero. It is in good working order and will operate at an acceptable level for an additional 5 years. The proposed machine will perform operations so much more efficiently that Landry's engineers estimate that labor, materials, and other direct costs of the operation will be reduced by $28,000 annually if it is installed. The proposed machine costs $96,000 delivered and installed. The asset has a useful life of 5 years even though it is classified as 3-year-class property for tax purposes. The company plans to depreciate the asset over the optional 5-year period on a straight line basis. The expected salvage value of the asset is zero. The company expects to earn 10 percent on its investment after taxes (10 percent is the firm's cost of capital). The tax rate is 40 percent.

a. If the investment tax credit (ITC) does not apply, should Landry buy the new machine?

b. If the 6 percent ITC applies, what is the project's NPV?

＊ 16-5 Refer to Problem 16-4.

a. Compute the NPV of the project if Landry uses the ACRS method of depreciation (cost recovery). The project ends in 5 years.

b. Compute the NPV of the project if the firm uses ACRS *and* if the ITC is applied immediately. The project ends in 5 years.

16-6 Gainesville Publishing Company is contemplating the replacement of one of its bookbinding machines with a newer and more efficient one. The old machine has a book value of $200,000 and a remaining useful life of 5 years. The firm does not expect to realize any return from scrapping the old machine in 5 years, but if it is sold now to another publisher, Gainesville would receive $120,000 for it.

The new machine has a purchase price of $440,000, an estimated useful life of 5 years, and an estimated salvage value of $40,000. A 10 percent investment tax credit is in effect. The new machine is expected to economize on electric power usage, labor, and repair costs, and to reduce the number of defective bindings; in total, an annual saving of $100,000 will be realized if the new machine is installed. The company is in the 40 percent tax bracket, has a 10 percent cost of capital, and uses straight line depreciation.

a. Should Gainesville purchase the new machine? Why or why not?

b. In general, how would each of the following factors affect the investment decision, and how would each be treated? (Give verbal answers.)

1. The expected life of the old machine decreases.

2. Improvements in the equipment to be purchased are expected to occur each year, and the result will be to increase the returns or expected savings from new machines over the savings expected from this year's model for every year in the foreseeable future.

＊ 16-7 Great Eastern Corporation is evaluating three investment opportunities. Great Eastern's financial manager has forecasted the risk-free rate as R_F

= 10% and the market rate of return as $k_M = 14\%$. What is the appropriate rate of return for a project if:

a. The project beta is .5?

b. The project beta is 1.0?

c. The project beta is 2.0?

16-8 The risk-free rate, R_F, is 7 percent and the market rate of return, k_M, is 12 percent. The beta for the project under consideration is 1.8. The project's cash flows after taxes are expected to be $127,910 annually for 5 years. The investment outlay required for the project is $400,000.

a. What is the project's required rate of return?

b. Should the project be accepted?

   1. What is its NPV?

   2. What is its IRR?

16-9 Goodtread Rubber Company has two divisions: (1) the Tire Division, which manufactures tires for new automobiles, and (2) the Recap Division, which manufactures recapping materials that are sold to independent tire recapping shops throughout the United States. Since auto manufacturing moves up and down with the general economy, the Tire Division's earnings contribution to Goodtread's stock price is highly correlated with returns on most other stocks. If the Tire Division were operated as a separate company, its beta coefficient would be about 1.60. The sales and profits of the Recap Division, on the other hand, tend to be countercyclical, as recap sales boom when people cannot afford to buy new tires. Recap's beta is estimated to be 0.40. Approximately 75 percent of Goodtread's corporate assets are invested in the Tire Division and 25 percent are in the Recap Division.

Currently, the rate of interest in Treasury securities is 10 percent, and the expected rate of return on an average share of stock is 15 percent. Goodtread uses only common equity capital, and it has no debt outstanding.

＊ a. What is the required rate of return on Goodtread's stock?

b. What discount rate should be used to evaluate capital budgeting projects in each division? Explain your answer fully, and in the process illustrate your answer with a project which costs $100,000, has a 10-year life, and provides after-tax cash flows of $20,000 per year.

Answer to Self-Test Problem

ST-1 To solve the problem, set up a worksheet similar to Table 16-1 and as illustrated on the next page. You will find the old machine needs to be replaced.

	Amount before Tax	Amount after Tax	Year	Discount Factor at 15%	PV
Net Outflows at t = 0					
Purchase price	$16,000	$16,000	0	1.0	$16,000
ITC (10%)	(1,600)	(1,600)	0	1.0	(1,600)
Sale of old machine					
Return of capital	(5,000)	(5,000)	0	1.0	(5,000)
Recapture of depreciation	(1,000)	(600)	0	1.0	(600)
Working capital					
ΔInventory	4,000	—	—	—	—
ΔAccounts payable	(1,000)	—	—	—	—
ΔNet working capital	$ 3,000	3,000	0	1.0	3,000
Net investment outlay at t = 0					$11,800
Net Inflows over Project's Life:					
t = 1–5					
Increase in sales	$ 2,000	$ 1,200	1–5	3.3522	$ 4,023
Reduction in expenses	3,000	1,800	1–5	3.3522	6,034
Depreciation: New[a]	3,040				
Old[b]	1,000				
ΔDepreciation	$ 2,040	816	1–5	3.3522	2,735
Salvage value	2,000	1,200	5	.4972	597
Return of working capital	3,000	3,000	5	.4972	1,492
				PV of inflows	$14,881
				Less PV of outflows	11,800
				Net present value	$ 3,081

[a]Depreciation basis on asset is reduced by half of the ITC: $16,000 − [(.5)(1,600)] = $15,200; thus $15,200/5 = $3,040 annual depreciation.
[b]Book value is $5,000; thus, with 5 years' remaining depreciation, $5,000/5 = $1,000 annual depreciation.

Selected References

For further depth on replacement analysis, as well as for other aspects of capital budgeting, see the Bierman and Smidt, the Grant, Ireson, and Leavenworth, and the Levy and Sarnat texts referenced in Chapter 15.

The literature on risk analysis in capital budgeting is vast; here is a small but useful selection of papers that bear directly on the topics covered in this chapter:

Bower, Richard S., and J. M. Jenks, "Divisional Screening Rates," *Financial Management*, Autumn 1975, 42–49.

Fama, E. F., "Risk-Adjusted Discount Rates and Capital Budgeting under Uncertainty," *Journal of Financial Economics*, August 1977, 3–24.

Fuller, Russell J., and Halbert S. Kerr, "Estimating the Divisional Cost of Capital: An Analysis of Pure-Play Technique," *Journal of Finance*, December 1981, 997–1009.

Hertz, David B., "Risk Analysis in Capital Investment," *Harvard Business Review,* January–February 1964, 95–106.

Lessard, Donald R., and Richard S. Bower, "An Optional Approach to Risk Screening," *Journal of Finance,* May 1973, 321–338.

Myers, Stewart C., and Stuart M. Turnbull, "Capital Budgeting and the Capital Asset Pricing Model: Good News and Bad News," *Journal of Finance,* May 1977, 321–333.

Robichek, Alexander A., "Interpreting the Results of Risk Analysis," *Journal of Finance,* December 1975, 1384–1386.

Robichek, Alexander A., and James C. Van Horne, "Abandonment Value and Capital Budgeting," *Journal of Finance,* December 1967, 577–590.

Those who want to start at the beginning in studying the CAPM in depth should see:

Markowitz, Harry M., "Portfolio Selection," *Journal of Finance,* March 1952, 77–91.

Sharpe, William F., "Capital Asset Prices: A Theory of Market Equilibrium under Conditions of Risk," *Journal of Finance,* September 1964, 425–442.

Literally thousands of articles providing theoretical extensions and tests of the CAPM theory have appeared in the last 20 years. Some of the more important earlier papers appeared in a book compiled by Jensen:

Jensen, Michael C., ed., *Studies in the Theory of Capital Markets* (New York: Praeger, 1972).

However, the validity of the empirical tests has been questioned; see:

Roll, Richard, "A Critique of the Asset Pricing Theory's Tests," *Journal of Financial Economics,* March 1977, 129–176.

Wallace, Anise, "Is Beta Dead?" *Institutional Investor,* July 1980, 23–30.

The following articles provide some valuable general insights into the use of the CAPM in financial management:

Beaver, W. H., Paul Kettler, and Myron Scholes, "The Association between Market Determined and Accounting Determined Risk Measures," *Accounting Review,* October 1970, 654.

Blume, M. E., "Betas and Their Regression Tendencies," *Journal of Finance,* June 1975, 785–795.

Bowman, R. G., "The Theoretical Relationship between Systematic Risk and Financial (Accounting) Variables," *Journal of Finance,* June 1979, 617–630.

Rosenberg, Barr, and James Guy, "Beta and Investment Fundamentals," *Financial Analysts' Journal,* May–June 1976, 60–72.

Long-Term Financing   VI

In the previous section we discussed means by which a firm can identify and evaluate investment opportunities. This section identifies the primary types of long-term capital and the analysis firms employ when deciding which combination of securities to use. We begin in Chapters 17 and 18 by examining the characteristics of long-term debt, preferred stock, and common stock. Portions of these chapters are dedicated to the determination of stock and bond values. In Chapter 19 we consider the optimal mix of securities, the capital structure decision. All providers of financial support require a return on their invested capital. Chapter 20 shows how the costs of different sources of capital are combined to form the weighted average cost of capital. Finally, Chapter 21 shows how a firm's investment opportunities and cost of capital interact to determine its dividend policy.

Bonds and Preferred Stock   17

Decision in Finance

U.S. Steel

Until recently, well-established U.S. companies raised capital by selling either stocks or fixed-interest bonds. By time-honored tradition, they preferred "plain old vanilla" and looked down on companies that attached bells and whistles to their securities offerings.

Today that's no longer the case. Behind the sudden change in attitude toward creative financing were the stormy money markets of the late 1970s and early 1980s. Because interest rates were high and volatile, corporations found it prohibitively expensive to issue traditional forms of long-term, fixed-rate debt. And corporate treasurers feared the effect that high-cost, long-term bonds would have on their balance sheets if interest rates declined in the future. Companies needed simultaneously to reduce their borrowing costs and induce investors to lend them money. Whether they liked it or not, they had to find creative ways to attract capital.

United States Steel is one old-line company that has set the pace for raising capital in creative ways. In early 1980, when the debt markets were in serious disarray, the company decided to seek financing for a pollution-control program. William E. Lewellyn, U.S. Steel's vice president for financial services, wanted to develop an instrument that would protect bondholders from price fluctuations and keep down the company's costs at the same time. Because the capital would be used for pollution control, the bonds would be tax-exempt. But institutional investors, the usual buyers of tax-exempts, were resisting U.S. Steel's issues due to the company's huge debt load and lackluster profits.

Mr. Lewellyn eventually devised a bond package that was the first of its kind in the United States. The issue was so successful that it raised $124,200,000 for U.S. Steel, saved the company huge sums of money that otherwise would have been spent on interest, and created

459

so much demand among a new group of investors in tax-exempts that other companies quickly jumped on the bandwagon.

As you read this chapter, look for the innovative techniques that William Lewellyn might have considered as he put together U.S. Steel's 1980 pollution-control bond issue. Which kind of bond do you think he finally chose?

See end of chapter for resolution.

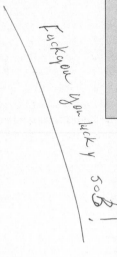

Most firms find it both necessary and desirable to use long-term debt financing, and some also use preferred stock. There are many types of fixed-income securities: secured and unsecured, marketable and non-marketable, convertible and nonconvertible, and so on. Different groups of investors favor different types of securities, and their tastes change over time. An astute financial manager knows how to "package" securities at a given point in time to make them most attractive to the most potential investors, thereby keeping the firm's cost of capital to a minimum. This chapter first discusses long-term securities in general, then analyzes the three most important types of *fixed-income securities*—term loans, bonds, and preferred stocks. Later chapters deal with other types of long-term capital, while the proper mix of securities is discussed in Chapter 19.

Funded Debt

funded debt
Long-term debt.

Funded debt is simply long-term debt. When a firm is said to be planning to "fund" its floating debt, it is planning to replace short-term debt with securities of longer maturity. Funding does not imply placing money with a trustee or other repository; it is simply part of the jargon of finance and means making debt long term. Tampa Electric Company provides a good example of funding. This company has a continuous construction program. Typically, it uses short-term debt to finance construction expenditures. However, once short-term debt has built up to about $75 million, the company sells a stock or bond issue, uses the proceeds to pay off its bank loans, and starts the cycle again. The high flotation cost on a small security issue, discussed in the next chapter, makes this process desirable.

Term Loans

term loan
A loan, generally obtained from a bank or insurance company, with a maturity greater than one year.

A **term loan** is a contract under which a borrower agrees to make payments of interest and principal, on specific dates, to a lender.[1] Term loans are usually negotiated directly between the borrowing firm and

---

[1]If the interest and maturity payments are not met on schedule, the issuing firm is said to have *defaulted* and can then be forced into *bankruptcy*. See Chapter 23 for a discussion of bankruptcy.

a financial institution—generally a bank, an insurance company, or a pension fund. Although the maturities of term loans vary from two to thirty years, most are for periods in the three- to fifteen-year range.

Advantages of Term Loans

Term loans have three major advantages over publicly issued securities—*speed*, *flexibility*, and *low issuance costs*. Because they are negotiated directly between the lender and the borrower, formal procedures are minimized. The key provisions of the loan can be worked out much more quickly, and with more flexibility, than can those for a public issue, and it is not necessary for a term loan to go through the Securities and Exchange Commission (SEC) registration process. A further advantage of term loans over publicly held debt securities has to do with future flexibility: if a bond issue is held by many different bondholders, it is difficult to obtain permission to alter the terms of the agreement, even though new economic conditions may make such changes desirable. With a term loan, the borrower generally can sit down with the lender and work out modifications in the contract.

Amortization

Most term loans are **amortized,** or paid off, in equal installments over the life of the loan. (At this point you should review the discussion of amortization in Chapter 14.) The purpose of amortization is to have the loan repaid gradually over its life rather than fall due all at once. Amortization forces the borrower to retire the loan slowly; this protects both the lender and the borrower against the possibility that the borrower will not make adequate provisions for its retirement during the life of the loan. Amortization is especially important whenever the loan is used to purchase a specific item of equipment; here the repayment schedule should be matched to the productive life of the equipment, with the payments being made from cash flows resulting from its use.

amortize
To liquidate on an installment basis; an amortized loan is one in which the principal amount of the loan is repaid in installments during the life of the loan.

Interest Rate

The interest rate on a term loan can be either fixed for the life of the loan or variable. If it is fixed, the rate used will be close to the rate on long-term bonds for companies of equivalent risk. If the rate is variable, it is usually set at a certain number of percentage points over the prime rate. Thus, when the prime rate goes up or down, so does the rate on the outstanding balance of the term loan.

Bonds

A **bond** is a long-term contract under which a borrower agrees to make payments of interest and principal, on specific dates, to the holder of the bond. Bonds are generally issued with maturities of between 20

bond
A long-term debt instrument.

and 30 years. Although bonds are similar to term loans, a bond issue is generally advertised, offered to all investors (the "public"), and actually sold to many different investors. Indeed, thousands of individual and institutional investors may purchase bonds when a firm sells a bond issue, while there is generally only one lender in the case of a term loan. With bonds the interest rate, or **coupon rate,** is almost always fixed. There are a number of different types of bonds, the more important of which are discussed in this chapter.

coupon rate
The stated rate of interest on a bond.

Indenture and Trustee

An **indenture** is a legal document that spells out the rights of both the bondholders and the issuing corporation, and a **trustee** is an official (usually of a bank) who represents the bondholders and makes sure the terms of the indenture are carried out. The indenture may be several hundred pages in length, and it will cover such points as the conditions under which the issuer can pay off the bonds prior to maturity, the times-interest-earned ratio the issuer must maintain if it is to sell additional bonds, restrictions against the payment of dividends unless earnings meet certain specifications, and the like. The trustee monitors the situation and takes action on behalf of the bondholders in the event that the issuer violates any provision in the indenture.

indenture
A formal contract between the issuer of a bond and the bondholders.

trustee
The representative of bondholders who acts in their interest and facilitates communication between them and the bond issuer.

The Securities and Exchange Commission (1) approves indentures and (2) makes sure that all indenture provisions are met before allowing a company to sell new securities to the public. Also, it should be noted that the indentures of most larger corporations were actually written back in the 1930s or 1940s, and that many issues of new bonds, all covered by this same indenture, have been sold down through the years. The interest rates on the bonds and perhaps their maturities will change from issue to issue, but bondholders' protections as spelled out in the indenture will be the same for all bonds in the class. Some of the more important provisions in most indentures are discussed in the following sections.

Bond Repayment Provisions

Sinking Fund. A **sinking fund** is a provision that facilitates the orderly retirement of a bond issue (or, in some cases, an issue of preferred stock). Typically, the sinking fund provision requires the firm to retire a portion of the bond issue each year. On rare occasions, the firm is required to deposit money with a trustee, who invests the money and then uses the accumulated sum to retire the bonds when they mature. Sometimes the stipulated sinking fund payment is tied to sales or earnings of the current year, but usually it is a mandatory fixed amount. If it is mandatory, a failure to meet the sinking fund requirement causes

sinking fund
A required annual payment designed to retire a bond or a preferred stock issue.

the bond issue to be thrown into default, which may force the company into bankruptcy. Obviously, then, a sinking fund can constitute a dangerous cash drain on the firm.

In most cases the firm is given the right to handle the sinking fund in either of two ways:

1. It may call in for redemption a certain percentage of the bonds at a stipulated price each year—for example, 2 percent of the total original amount of the issue at a price of $1,000. The bonds are numbered serially, and the ones called for redemption are determined by a lottery.

2. It may buy the required amount of bonds on the open market.

The firm will take whichever action results in the greatest reduction of outstanding bonds for a given expenditure. Therefore, if interest rates have risen and bond prices have fallen, the company will elect to use the option of buying bonds at a discount in the open market.

It must be recognized that the sinking fund may at times work to the detriment of bondholders. If, for example, the bond carries a 9 percent interest rate, and if yields on similar securities are 6 percent, then the bond will sell above par. A sinking fund call at par would thus greatly disadvantage some bondholders.

On balance, securities that provide for a sinking fund and continuing redemption are likely to be offered initially on a lower-yield basis than are securities without such a fund. Since sinking funds provide additional protection to investors, bond issues which have them are likely to sell initially at higher prices; hence they have a lower cost of capital to the issuer.

Call Provision. A **call provision** gives the issuing corporation the right to call the bond for redemption. If it is used, the call provision generally states that the company must pay an amount greater than the par value for the bond, with this additional sum being defined as the *call premium*. The call premium is typically set equal to one year's interest if the bond is called during the first year, with the premium declining at a constant rate each year thereafter. For example, the call premium on a $1,000 par value, 20-year, 8 percent bond would generally be $80 if it were called during the first year, $76 during the second year (calculated by reducing the $80, or 8 percent, premium by one twentieth), and so on.

The call privilege is valuable to the firm but potentially detrimental to the investor, especially if the bond is issued in a period when interest rates are cyclically high. Accordingly, the interest rate on a new issue of callable bonds will exceed that on a new issue of noncallable bonds. For example, on May 24, 1979 Great Falls Power Company sold an issue of A-rated bonds to yield 10.375 percent. These bonds were callable immediately. On the same day Midwest Electric sold an issue of A-rated bonds to yield 10.20 percent. Midwest's bonds were noncallable for ten years. (This is known as a *deferred call*.) Investors were

call provision
A provision in a bond contract that gives the issuer the right to redeem the bonds under specified terms prior to the normal maturity date.

apparently willing to accept a 0.175 percent lower interest rate on Midwest's bonds for the assurance that the relatively high (by historic standards) rate of interest would be earned for at least ten years. Great Falls, on the other hand, had to incur a 0.175 percent higher annual interest rate to obtain the option of calling the bonds in the event of a subsequent decline in interest rates.

Note that the call for refunding purposes is quite different from the call for sinking fund purposes. The call for sinking fund purposes generally has no call premium, but only a small percentage of the issue is callable each year.

Restrictive Covenants

restrictive covenant
A provision in a bond indenture or term loan agreement that requires the bond issuer to meet certain stated conditions.

A **restrictive covenant** is a provision in a bond indenture or term loan agreement that requires the issuer of the bond to meet certain stated conditions. Typical provisions include requirements that debt not exceed a specific percentage of total capital, that the current ratio be maintained above a specific level, that dividends not be paid on common stock unless earnings are maintained at a given level, and so on. Overall, these covenants are designed to insure, insofar as possible, that the firm does nothing to cause the bonds' quality to deteriorate after they are issued.

The trustee is responsible for making sure the covenants are not violated, or for taking appropriate action if a violation occurs. What constitutes "appropriate action" varies with the circumstances. It might be that to insist on immediate compliance would result in bankruptcy and possibly large losses on the bonds. In such a case the trustee may decide that the bondholders would be better served by giving the company a chance to work out its problems and thus avoid bankruptcy.[2]

Types of Bonds

Mortgage Bonds

mortgage bond
A pledge of certain of a firm's real assets as security for a bond.

Under a **mortgage bond** *the corporation pledges certain real assets as security for the bond.* To illustrate, suppose $10 million is required to purchase land and to build a plant. Bonds in the amount of $4 million, secured by a mortgage on the property, are issued. If the company defaults on the bonds (that is, if it does not pay interest or required payments on the principal on time), the bondholders can foreclose on the plant and sell it to satisfy their claims.

If our illustrative company chose to, it could issue *second mortgage bonds* secured by the same $10 million plant. In the event of liquidation the holders of these second mortgage bonds would have a claim

---

[2]Bankruptcy and its consequences are covered in detail in Chapter 23.

against the property only after the first mortgage bondholders had been paid off in full. Thus second mortgages are sometimes called *junior mortgages* because they are junior in priority to the claims of senior mortgages, or *first mortgage bonds*.

The first mortgage indentures of most major corporations were written 20, 30, 40, or more years ago. These indentures are generally "open-ended," meaning that new bonds may be issued from time to time under the existing indenture. However, the amount of new bonds that can be issued is virtually always limited by clauses in the indenture to a specified percentage of the firm's total "bondable property," which generally includes all plant and equipment. For example, Savannah Electric can issue first mortgage bonds in total up to 60 percent of its fixed assets. If fixed assets totaled $200 million, and if the company had $100 million of first mortgage bonds outstanding, then it could, by the property test, issue another $20 million of bonds (60% of $200 million = $120 million).

In 1979 Savannah Electric could not issue any new first mortgage bonds at all because of another indenture provision: its times-interest-earned ratio was below 2.5 times, the minimum coverage that must be attained prior to the sale of new bonds. Thus Savannah Electric passed the property test but failed the coverage test; hence it could not issue first mortgage bonds. Since first mortgage bonds carry lower rates of interest, this restriction is a costly one.

Debentures

A **debenture** is an unsecured bond and, as such, provides no lien on specific property as security for the obligation. Debenture holders are therefore general creditors whose claims are protected by property not otherwise pledged. In practice, the use of debentures depends on the nature of the firm's assets and its general credit strength. If its credit position is exceptionally strong, the firm can issue debentures—it simply does not need specific security. American Telephone & Telegraph finances mainly through debentures; AT&T is such a strong corporation that it does not have to put up property as security for its debt issues. Debentures are also issued by companies in industries where it would not be practical to provide security through a mortgage on fixed assets. Examples of such industries are the large mail-order houses and the finance companies, which characteristically hold most of their assets in the form of inventory or receivables, neither of which is satisfactory security for a mortgage bond.

debenture
A long-term debt instrument that is not secured by a mortgage on specific property.

Subordinated Debentures

The term *subordinate* means "below," or "inferior." Thus subordinated debt has claims on assets in the event of bankruptcy only after senior debt (usually mortgage bonds) has been paid off. Debentures may be subordinated to designated notes payable—usually bank loans—or to all other debt. In the event of liquidation or reorganization, holders of **subordinated debentures** cannot be paid until senior debt as named in the debentures' indenture has been paid.

subordinated debenture
A bond having a claim on assets only after the senior debt has been paid off in the event of liquidation.

convertible bond
A security that is convertible into shares of common stock.

income bond
A bond that pays interest to bondholders only if the interest is earned.

floating rate bond
A bond whose interest rate fluctuates with shifts in interest rates.

par value
The nominal value of a stock or bond.

zero coupon bond
A bond that pays no annual interest but sells at a discount below par and therefore provides compensation to investors in the form of capital appreciation.

Other Types of Bonds

Several other types of bonds are used sufficiently often to merit mention. **Convertible bonds** are securities that are convertible into shares of common stock, at a predetermined price, at the option of the bondholder. This class of bond is discussed in detail in Appendix 18A. **Income bonds** are bonds that pay interest only when the interest is earned. These bonds are often issued by companies in reorganization or by firms whose financial situation would not allow a fixed, inescapable interest charge common to all other classes of bonds. Thus these securities cannot bankrupt a company, but from an investor's perspective they are more risky than "regular" bonds, owing to the weakness of the issuing firm and the uncertainty of the timing of interest receipts.

Increasing interest rates over the past decade have caused bond market participants to turn to several new and innovative means of packaging long-term debt instruments. Some interesting examples of these new bonds include *floating rate bonds*, bonds that are *redeemable at par at the option of the holder*, and *zero coupon bonds*.

Ordinarily, a bond's coupon interest payment is fixed when it is issued and remains fixed for the life of the bond. **Floating rate bonds,** which have been used extensively by major banks, including Chase Manhattan and Citibank, have interest payments that move up or down (generally within limits) as interest rates in general shift. Thus the investor's interest income will vary (as will the borrower's interest expense), but the market value of the bond will not fluctuate much.

Bonds that are redeemable at the holder's option also protect the holder against a rise in interest rates. If rates rise, fixed-rate bonds' prices decline. Should these redeemable bonds' prices go down due to rising rates, the holders would simply turn them in, receive the **par value,** and invest in new, high-rate bonds. Examples of such bonds include Transamerica's $50 million issue of 25-year, 8½ percent bonds sold in June 1976. The bonds are not callable by the company, and holders can turn them in for redemption at par on or after July 1984. If interest rates rise, holders will turn in the bonds and reinvest the proceeds at a higher rate. This feature enabled Transamerica to sell the bonds with an 8½ percent coupon at a time when other similarly rated bonds had yields of 8¾ percent.

An interesting and quite recent development in the corporate bond market is the use of very low or **zero coupon bonds.** These bonds are unique in that, like many government bonds, they are sold at less than

In this convertible subordinated debenture (or bond) issued by Deere & Company, the borrower (Deere) agrees to make payments of interest (on March 15 and September 15) to the holder of the bond. Terms of the bond are 9 percent; it is due in the year 2008. The term "convertible" means that this bond gives the bondholder the option of converting it into shares of common stock; the term "subordinated" means that, in the event of liquidation or reorganization, the bondholder would not be paid until senior debt has been paid off.

Source: Courtesy of Deere & Company.

face value and mature at par, usually $1,000. Assume a firm wishes to sell a 12 percent, 10-year, zero coupon bond. Just as in Chapter 14, the present value of $1,000 to be received in 10 years and discounted at 12 percent would equal $322.00 today. Thus, by using Equation 14-2a,

$$PV = FV(DF)$$
$$= \$1,000(.322)$$
$$= \$322.00,$$

we can find the price an investor would pay for this zero coupon bond.

Now that we have illustrated the basic mechanics of a zero coupon bond, let's consider an actual case—Penney's $200 million par-value issue of bonds which (1) have no coupons and (2) pay no annual interest. These bonds mature in 1989, at which time holders will be paid $1,000. The bonds were sold in 1981 at a discount of 66.753 percent below par, or for $332.47 per $1,000 bond, so someone who bought a bond for $332.47 in 1981 and held it until it matured in 1989 would receive a return of 14.25 percent (on a semiannual basis). Penney received $66,494,000, less underwriting expenses, for the issue, but it will have to pay back $200,000,000 in 1989.

The advantages to Penney include the following: (1) no cash outlays are required for either interest or principal until the bond matures; (2) these bonds have a relatively low yield to maturity (Penney would have had to pay approximately 15 percent versus the actual 14.25 percent had it issued regular coupon bonds at par); and (3) Penney receives an annual tax deduction equal to the yearly amortization of the discount ($667.53/8 = $83.44), which means that the bonds provide a positive cash flow over their life. There are also two disadvantages to Penney: (1) the bond is, in effect, simply not callable, so Penney cannot refund it if interest rates should fall, and (2) Penney will have a very large nondeductible cash outlay coming up in 1989.

There are two principal advantages to the purchasers: (1) they have no danger whatever of a call, and (2) they are guaranteed a "true" yield of 14.25 percent irrespective of what happens to interest rates—the holders of these bonds do not have to worry about having to reinvest coupons received at low rates if interest rates should fall, which would result in a "true" yield to maturity of less than 14.25 percent. This second feature is extremely important to pension funds, life insurance companies, and other institutions which make actuarial contracts based on assumed reinvestment rates; for such investors the risk of declining interest rates, hence an inability to reinvest cash inflows at the assumed rates, is greater than the risk of an increase in rates and the accompanying fall in bond values.

Because of tax considerations (the difference between the purchase price and the maturity value is treated as ordinary income and not as a lower-taxed capital gain for individuals), these bonds are best suited for tax-exempt organizations, especially pension funds. However, since pension funds are by far the largest purchasers of corporate bonds, the potential market for zero coupon bonds is by no means small.

If interest rates remain high in the 1980s, businesses will continue to seek innovative devices to reduce interest charges. Additionally, high interest rates will cause issuing companies to reduce the maturities of bonds to avoid being locked in to high rates. During 1981 about half of the fixed rate bonds that were issued had intermediate maturities—maturities of 7 to 10 years as opposed to the usual range of 20 to 30 years.

Bond Ratings

Since the early 1900s bonds have been assigned quality ratings that reflect their probability of going into default. The two major rating agencies are Moody's Investors Service and Standard & Poor's Corporation (S&P). These agencies' rating designations are shown in Table 17-1.

The triple A bonds are extremely safe, while the double A and single A bonds are also strong enough to be held in conservative portfolios.[3] The triple Bs are strong enough to be called "investment grade," and

---

[3]In the discussion to follow, reference to the S&P code is intended to imply the Moody code as well. Thus, for example, *triple B bonds* means both BBB and Baa bonds, *double B bonds* both BB and Ba bonds.

Table 17-1
Comparison of Bond Ratings

	High Quality	Investment Grade	Substandard	Speculative
Moody's	Aaa Aa	A Baa	Ba B	Caa to D
S&P	AAA AA	A BBB	BB B	CCC to D

banks and other institutional investors are permitted by law to hold these bonds. Double B and lower bonds are considered speculative with a higher probability of default, and many financial institutions are prohibited from buying them.

Although the rating assignments are judgmental, they are based on both qualitative and quantitative factors, some of which are listed below:

Ratio analysis: The firm's leverage position, liquidity, and debt coverage are among the first factors considered by the bond-rating agencies. We discuss in a later section two of the more important coverage ratios—the times-interest-earned and the fixed charge ratios.

Security provisions: Whether the bond is backed by real assets (mortgage bond) or not (debenture), or by another firm (guaranteed bond), or whether funds are distributed to these bondholders after others receive theirs, are also important factors in the rating scheme.

Sinking fund: If the issue has a sinking fund to insure systematic repayment, it is a plus factor to the rating agencies.

Maturity: Other things being the same, a bond with a shorter maturity will be judged less risky than a longer-term bond, and this will be reflected in the rating.

Stability: As a general rule, the more stable the firm's sales and earnings, the stronger the rating.

Legal actions: Any major legal controversies such as antitrust suits could erode the ratings.

Pension liabilities: If the firm has unfunded pension liabilities that could cause a problem, that fact is reflected in its bond ratings.

Other: Many other factors enter into the bond-rating scheme used by agencies. A sample of other factors would include potential for labor problems, political unrest in host countries for multinational firms, and the regulatory climate for public utilities and other regulated industries.

Analysts at the rating agencies have consistently stated that no precise formula is used when setting a firm's rating—all the factors listed, plus others, are taken into account, but not in a mathematically precise manner. Statistical studies have borne out this contention; researchers who have tried to predict bond ratings on the basis of quantitative data have had only limited success, indicating that the agencies do indeed use a good deal of subjective judgment when establishing a firm's rating.[4]

Bond ratings are very important both to firms and to investors. First, a bond's rating is an indicator of its risk; hence the rating has a direct, measurable influence on the bond's interest rate and the firm's cost of debt capital. Second, most bonds are purchased by institutional investors, not by individuals, and these institutions are generally restricted to investment-grade securities. Thus, if a firm's bonds fall below BBB, it will have a difficult time selling new bonds, as most of the potential purchasers will not be allowed to buy them.

Ratings also have an effect on the availability of debt capital. If an institutional investor buys BBB bonds and these bonds are subsequently downgraded to BBB or lower, then (1) the institution's regulators will reprimand or perhaps impose restrictions on the institution if it continues to hold the bonds, but (2) since many other institutional investors cannot purchase the bonds, the institution that owns them will probably not be able to sell them except at a sizable loss. Because of this fear of downgrading, many institutions restrict their bond portfolios to at least A, or even AA, bonds. Some even confine purchases to AAA bonds. Thus the lower a firm's bond rating, the smaller the group of available purchasers for its new issues.

As a result of their higher risk and more restricted market, lower-grade bonds have much higher required rates of return, k_d, than do high-grade bonds. Figure 17-1 illustrates this point—throughout the 31 years shown on the graph, U.S. Government bonds always have had the lowest yields, AAA bonds have been next, and the BBB bonds have had the highest yields of the three types.

Figure 17-1 also shows that the gaps between yields on the three types of bonds vary over time; in other words, the cost differentials, or risk premiums, fluctuate from year to year. This point is highlighted in Table 17-2, which gives the yields on the three types of bonds, and the risk premiums for AAA and BBB bonds, in June of 1963, 1975, and 1983. All yields were higher in the more recent years, but risk premiums rose most dramatically from 1979 through 1981, causing an especially sharp increase in the rates on BBB bonds. Even though the rates fell significantly in the 1982–1983 period, they still remained high from an historical perspective.

The Table 17-2 data are plotted in Figure 17-2 to show approximately

---

[4]See G. E. Pinches and K. A. Mingo, "A Multivariate Analysis of Industrial Bond Ratings," *Journal of Finance*, March 1973, 1–18.

Figure 17-1

Yields on U.S. Government Bonds, AAA Corporates, and BBB Corporates, 1953–1983

A bond's rating is an indicator of its risk. Because a lower-grade bond entails greater risk, it must pay a higher interest rate to attract investors. During the 31 years shown here, U.S. Government long-term bonds, which are considered default-free, paid the lowest interest rates. Corporate AAA bonds paid somewhat higher interest rates, while corporate BBB bonds paid the highest rates. The spreads between the curves indicate the risk premiums that corporate bond issuers had to pay to raise capital.

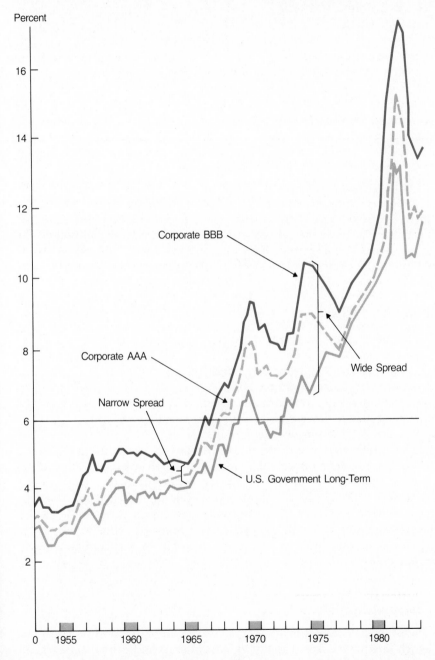

Sources: *Federal Reserve Board Historical Chart Book, 1979,* and *Federal Reserve Bulletin,* various issues.

Table 17-2
Risk Premiums in June 1963, 1975, and 1983

	Long-Term Government Bonds (Risk-Free) (1)	AAA Corporate Bonds (2)	BBB Corporate Bonds (3)	Risk Premiums	
				AAA (4) = (2) − (1)	BBB (5) = (3) − (1)
June 1963	4.00%	4.23%	4.84%	0.23%	0.84%
June 1975	6.86	8.77	10.40	1.91	3.54
June 1983	10.64	11.74	13.37	1.10	2.73

Source: *Federal Reserve Bulletin*, December 1963, December 1975, and July 1983.

what happened to risk premiums as measured in 1963, 1975, and 1983. Comparing 1963 and 1983, we find that the riskless rate, or vertical axis intercept, rose more than six and one-half percentage points—this reflected the increase in realized and anticipated inflation. Moreover, the slope of the line also rose, indicating increased investor risk aversion, although the slope was less steep in 1983 than in 1975.

Changes in Ratings

A change in a firm's bond rating will have a significant effect on its ability to borrow long-term capital and on the cost of that capital. Rating agencies review outstanding bonds on a periodic basis, occasionally upgrading or downgrading a bond as a result of its issuer's changed circumstances. Also, an announcement of a new issue of bonds will trigger agency reviews and possibly lead to rating changes.

If a firm's situation has deteriorated somewhat but its bonds have not been reviewed and downgraded, it may choose to use a term loan or short-term debt rather than finance through a public bond issue. This will perhaps postpone an agency review until the situation has improved. For example, a number of public utilities delayed bond issues in 1974 and 1975, financing with short-term debt until rate increases could be obtained to raise interest coverage ratios to acceptable levels. After rate increases were put into effect, the companies sold bonds and used the proceeds to retire the excess short-term debt.

coverage
The measure of a firm's ability to meet interest and principal payments; times interest earned is the most common coverage ratio.

Coverage Ratios

One of the key elements in the analysis of corporate bonds is **coverage,** which measures a firm's ability to meet interest and principal payments and thus avoid default. The most commonly used coverage ratio is the *times interest earned (TIE)*. This ratio is defined below and illustrated

Figure 17-2
Relationship Between Bond Ratings and Bond Yields, 1963, 1975, and 1983
This figure takes a closer look at the relationship between bond ratings and bond yields. Between 1963 and 1983 the default-free rate of interest rose from 4.0 percent to 10.64 percent to reflect both realized and anticipated inflation. Corporate borrowers, of course, had to pay a risk premium in addition. In 1963 corporate AAA bonds paid a risk premium of 0.23 percent, and corporate BBB bonds paid a risk premium of 0.84 percent. In 1975 the risk premium rose to 1.91 percent for AAA bonds and to 3.54 percent for BBB bonds. In 1983 the risk premium dropped to 1.10 percent for AAA bonds and to 2.73 percent for BBB bonds. The risk premiums fluctuated to reflect changes in investors' attitudes toward assuming risk.

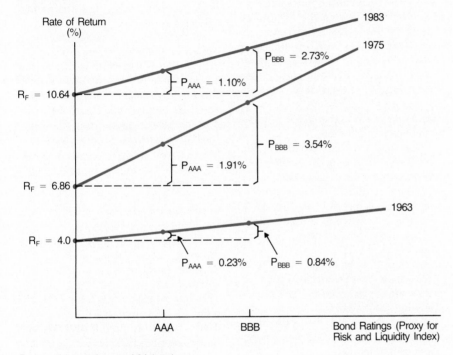

P_{AAA} = risk premium on AAA bonds.
P_{BBB} = risk premium on BBB bonds.

Source: Table 17-2

with data for Carter Chemical Company (see Chapters 6 and 7 for the basic data):

$$\text{Times interest earned} = \frac{\text{Earnings before interest and taxes (EBIT)}}{\text{Interest}} = \frac{\$266}{\$66}$$

$$= 4.03 \text{ for Carter.}$$

$$\text{Industry average} = 6 \text{ times.}$$

Industry Practice

Junk Collecting

Junk bonds, they're called, but more in jest than with malice. Savvy investors know that junk bonds—rated by Standard & Poor's in the BB to CCC range, below investment-grade issues—rarely wind up on the scrap heap. The issuing companies may not be blue chips, but with few exceptions they meet their debt payments as promised. Meantime, junk bonds yield more than higher-grade bonds—sometimes much more.

The gap can be especially eye-catching. For example, when AAA corporates are yielding around 11 percent and AAA Bell paper around 12 percent, it is possible to lock in 13 percent to 18 percent or higher yields on low-rated issues—often with only a moderate increase in risk. If interest rates fall, junk bond buyers could be looking at 30-percent-plus total returns for the year ahead. The accompanying table, which is not intended as a recommended list, provides a sampling of the BB-rated merchandise now on the market.

Bias Toward Bigness

"Junk bonds is a misnomer," says Richard E. Omohundro, Jr., manager of Merrill Lynch's high-yield bond group. "Many of these companies have bright or improving futures." Frequently, he explains, they get low ratings from Moody's and Standard & Poor's because they are emerging growth companies with little or no credit history, or they are established companies that have hit a cyclical downturn. Adds longtime junk enthusiast Jeffrey Hill, first vice president at Prudential-Bache: "Often the BB- or B-rated issues of growth companies offer more debt protection than A-rated issues, but the rating agencies are biased in favor of size."

As investors have recognized how deceptive the lower ratings frequently are, a flourishing mini-industry has grown up around junk bonds over the past five years. Today, there are some 20 mutual funds with $4.5 billion in assets specializing in what they prefer to call high-yield bonds. Major brokerage firms now have high-yield specialists in their bond departments—not only because customers' interest is high, but because junk bonds tend to behave differently from higher-rated issues.

While the top-rated bonds tend to move as a group in tandem with Treasury bonds, the high-yield issues sometimes behave more like equities. The prices and yields of individual bonds, for example, often make major moves based on the market's perception of changes in a company's credit-worthiness, long before the bond has been upgraded or downgraded by a rating agency. The current yield of Chrysler's 8s of '98 CCC bonds fell from 28.5 percent early last year to 13.6 percent now, while the price has jumped from 34 to 59—as market confidence in the automaker's survival increased.

The trick to successfully playing the high-yield bond market is to pick bonds as carefully, and with as much analytical work, as one would pick common stocks. High-yield analysts and mutual fund managers try to select "undervalued" industries and

Junk Bond Sampler

Rating	Issue	Description	Recent Price	1982 Price Range	Current Yield	Yield to Maturity	Interest Coverage Period	1981	1982
BB+	Allis-Chalmers Corp.	SF Deb 5.10s '90	45	50 -40	11.33	18.68	9mo Sep	1.61	(2.79)
BB+	Armour & Co.	Sub SF Inc Deb. 5s '84	95	95⅛-83⅞	5.26	7.87	6mo Jun	2.10	2.21
BB+	Baldwin-United Corp.	Sub SF Deb 10s '09	72½	75⅛-58¼	13.79	13.98	6mo Jun	1.41	1.38
BB+	Caesars World	Sr SF Deb 11¼s '97	76	79⅛-60⅜	14.80	15.65	9mo Apr	1.69	1.45
BB−	Charter Medical Corp.	SF Deb 16½s '98	102	102 -97¼	16.24	16.21	9mo Jun	1.86	2.20
BB−	Chemetron Corp.	SF Deb 9s '94	81	82 -63⅜	11.11	12.23	6mo Jun	2.87	1.32
BB	City Investing	SR Nts 14½s '92	102	102 -98	14.45	14.42	12mo Dec	1.48	N/A
BB−	Gelco Corp.	Sub SF Deb 14⅝s '99	96¼	99 -77	15.10	15.26	9mo Apr	1.14	1.11
BB+	Hudson's Bay Oil & Gas	SF Deb 14¾s '04	84	87 -68⅜	17.56	17.62	9mo Sep	1.49	0.78
BB	Illinois Cent. Gulf RR	1st 1 11¼s '99	84	85 -74½	13.39	13.77	9mo Sep	2.17	0.54
BB−	Martin Marietta Alum	SF Deb 9⅜s '96	70	75 -60¾	13.39	14.67	9mo Sep	2.01	0.68
BB−	MCI Communications	Sub SF Deb 15s '00	107½	108 -81	13.95	13.83	6mo Sep	2.01	3.15
BB	MGM Grand Hotels	SF CT 9s '92	72	72 -60⅜	12.50	14.83	9mo May	3.56	2.02
BB+	Montgomery Ward Co.	SF Deb 4⅞s '90	52⅛	53⅝-40¾	9.22	16.83	6mo Jun	0.72	0.67
BB−	New Jersey Pwr & Lt	1st 3⅛s '84	82⅜	82⅜-68¾	3.79	15.58	6mo Jun	1.47	1.27
BB	Outboard Marine Corp.	SF Deb 7¾s '96	62⅞	64 -58	12.33	14.00	6mo Jun	2.23	2.77
BB	Pennsylvania Electric	1st 9⅜s '00	64½	64½-49⅛	14.53	15.24	6mo Jun	1.82	2.06
BB	Republic Steel Corp.	SF Deb 8.90s '95	63½	68 -56	12.11	15.89	9mo Sep	6.81	(3.64)
BB+	Resorts Int'l	Sub SF Deb 10s '99	73½	75½-55⅝	13.61	14.18	9mo Sep	0.83	1.82
BB	Schlitz (Jos.) Brewing	SF Deb 9½s '99	67	70 -54½	14.18	15.06	3mo Jun	5.22	1.89
BB	Sherwin-Williams	SF Deb 9.45s '99	73	73 -54¼	12.95	13.54	9mo Sep	3.42	3.61
BB−	Singer Co.	SF Deb 8.5s '99	64⅛	66 -50½	12.48	13.52	6mo Jun	1.39	1.08
BB+	Sun Chemical	Sub SF Deb 11¼s '96	85⅛	85⅛-67	13.22	13.66	12mo Dec	2.32	N/A
BB+	Sunbeam Corp.	SF Deb 5½s '92	55	55½-47¾	10.00	14.17	6mo Jun	N/A	1.48
BB+	USAir	Sub Deb 5½s '87	84	84 -51	6.55	10.15	9mo Sep	3.70	2.77
BB−	Youngst'n Sheet & Tube	1st J10½s '00	67¾	73 -60⅜	15.50	16.15	12mo Sep	11.50	N/A

companies, just as stock analysts do, then wait until the rest of the market jumps on the bandwagon, pushing prices up and yields down. Experts cite the example of Metropolitan Edison and other subsidiaries of General Public Utilities, which owns the Three Mile Island nuclear power plant in Pennsylvania. In the wake of the 1979 "accident" at TMI, amid fears about GPU's survival, yields soared as high as 22 percent on some of the company's bond issues in early 1981. Since then, as the bankruptcy fears have subsided, the yields have come down to the 14.5 percent to 15 percent range.

Perhaps the greatest risk in the better junk bonds, even more than default, is marketability. There are always buyers around for the big AAA-rated issues, but selling less popular, low-rated bonds can be a problem. An order to sell can be greeted by the classic broker response: "To whom?" "Why sacrifice marketability and safety when we're in a recession with the possibility of a depression loom-

ing?" asks Gerald Guild of Lion Capital Associates. "I don't think the premium is enough to justify the risk."

Counters Merrill Lynch's Omohundro: "High-yield bonds are speculative, but they are a lot safer than options, futures, and some OTC stocks. It's always amazed me that people buy grossly speculative stocks, but keep away from BB bonds." He points out that high-yield bonds are generally less volatile than stocks, are senior to equity securities in the event of liquidation, and offer a current yield that dwarfs those of stocks and higher-rated bonds.

Buying junk bonds, of course, requires a special appetite. While defaults are rare, the high yields are more speculative and harder to sell than top-quality bonds. But for the stouthearted, opportunistic investor, there are times when junk bonds look especially inviting.

Source: Adapted with permission from "Junk Collecting," *Financial World*, Feb. 15, 1983, 23–25.

Delete

The times-interest-earned ratio (TIE) depends on the level of interest payments, which in turn depends on the percentage of total capital represented by debt. For example, if Carter had used twice as much debt (with a corresponding reduction in equity) and if the interest rate remained constant, then its interest charges would be $66 × 2 = $132. EBIT is not affected by changes in capital structure, so the increased use of debt would lower Carter's TIE to 2.02:

$$\text{TIE} = \frac{\$266}{\$132} = 2.02 \text{ times.}$$

As we see in Chapter 19, the times-interest-earned ratio is given careful consideration when a firm establishes its target capital structure. The pro forma, or projected, TIE that would result under different financing plans is calculated, and care is taken to insure that the use of debt does not lower the TIE to an unacceptable level.

Another ratio that is often used to measure a company's ability to service its debt is the *fixed charge coverage ratio*, defined as follows:

$$\text{Fixed charge coverage ratio} = \frac{\text{EBIT} + \text{Lease payments}}{\text{Interest} + \left(\begin{array}{c}\text{Lease} \\ \text{payments}\end{array}\right) + \left(\dfrac{\text{Sinking fund payment}}{1 - \text{Tax rate}}\right)}$$

$$= \frac{\$266 + \$28}{\$66 + \$28 + [\$20/(1 - 0.4)]}$$

$$= 2.3 \text{ times for Carter.}$$

Industry average = 2.5 times.

Delete

Sinking funds were discussed earlier in this chapter; in essence, a sinking fund payment goes toward the retirement of the bond. Since sinking fund payments are not tax deductible, and the interest and lease payments are deductible, the sinking fund payment is divided by (1 − Tax rate) to find the before-tax income required to pay taxes and have enough left to make the sinking fund payment.

Valuation of Bonds

In Chapter 15 we indicated that the value of a capital budgeting project is its discounted future cash flow. What is true for the valuation of real assets is true for financial asset valuation as well. That is, the value of a financial asset—a bond, a share of preferred stock, or a share of common stock—is equal to the cash returns (both the level and timing of these returns) provided by the security discounted back to the present.

A bond is a contractual debt instrument, calling for the payment of a specified amount of interest for a stated number of years, and for the repayment of the par value on the bond's maturity date.[5] Thus the bond's cash flow is represented by an annuity plus a lump sum, and its value is found as the present value of this cash stream.

The following equation is used to find a bond's value:

$$\text{Value} = V = \sum_{t=1}^{n} I \left(\frac{1}{1 + k_d}\right)^t + M \left(\frac{1}{1 + k_d}\right)^n$$

$$= I(DF_a) + M(DF), \qquad\qquad \textbf{(17-1)}$$

---

[5]Actually, most bonds pay interest semiannually rather than annually, which would make it necessary to modify our valuation formula, Equation 17-1, slightly. We will use annual compounding at this point to avoid unnecessary detail.

where

I = dollars of interest paid each year = coupon interest rate × par value.

M = the par value, or maturity value, which is typically $1,000.

k_d = the appropriate rate of interest on the bond.[6]

n = the number of years until the bond matures; n declines each year after the bond is issued.

We can use Equation 17-1 to find the value of Carter Chemical Company's bonds. Simply substitute $90 for I, $1,000 for M, and the values for DF_a (found in Appendix D) and for DF (found in Appendix B) at 9 percent, Period 15:

$$V = \$90(8.0607) + \$1,000(.2745)$$
$$= \$725.46 + \$274.50$$
$$= \$999.96 \cong \$1,000 \text{ when } k_d = 9\%.$$

Figure 17-3 gives a graphic view of the bond valuation process.

If k_d remained constant at 9 percent, what would the value of the bond be 1 year after it was issued? We can find this value using the same valuation formula, but now the term to maturity is only 14 years; that is, n = 14:

$$V = \$90(7.7862) + \$1,000(.2992)$$
$$= \$999.96 \cong \$1,000.$$

This same result will hold for every year so long as the appropriate interest rate for the bond remains constant at 9 percent.

Now suppose that interest rates in the economy rose immediately after Carter's 9 percent bonds were issued, and as a result k_d increased from 9 to 10 percent. Of course, the interest and principal payments on the bonds are set, yet new investors now require a higher rate of return on investments of this type. How would investors increase the effective yield on these bonds to an acceptable level—in this case 10 percent? In essence, investors would be unwilling to pay as much for Carter's promise to pay $90 a year for 15 years and $1,000 at the end of the fifteenth year. How much would they pay for the cash flow from Carter's 9 percent bond if a 10 percent return were demanded? To an-

---

[6]An appropriate interest rate is determined by a number of factors, most of which are reflected in the bond's rating but also include such factors as supply and demand in the capital markets.

Figure 17-3
Time Line for Carter Chemical Bonds
A bond's value is equal to the sum of its future interest payments and its final lump sum payment discounted to their present value. For example, the discounted cash flows from a 15-year 9 percent Carter Chemical bond purchased in 1979 totaled approximately $1,000 because the first interest payment of $90.00 was discounted for one year in the future to $82.57, the second interest payment of $90.00 was discounted for two years in the future to $75.75, and so on.

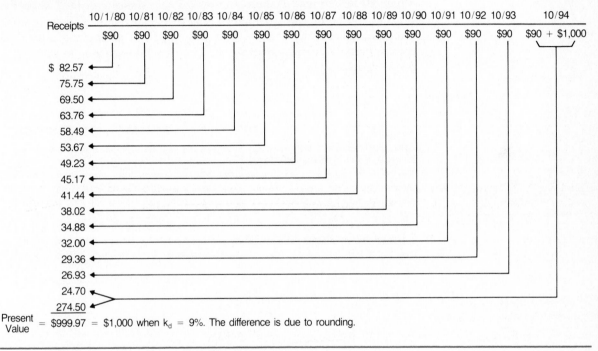

swer this question, we will again use Equation 17-1, substituting the 10 percent values at Period 15 in the equation for DF_a and DF:

$$V = \$90(7.6061) + \$1,000(.2394)$$
$$= \$684.55 + \$239.40$$
$$= \$923.95 \text{ when } k_d = 10\% \text{ and } n = 15.$$

Had interest rates fallen during the first year to 8 percent rather than risen, the value of Carter's bonds at the end of one year would have increased to $1,082.48:

$$V = \$90(8.2442) + \$1,000(.3405)$$
$$= \$741.98 + \$340.50$$
$$= \$1,082.48 \text{ when } k_d = 8\% \text{ and } n = 14.$$

In this case the bond would sell at a *premium* above its par value. Its total yield would again consist of a current interest yield and a capital gains yield, but the capital gains yield would be *negative* as the premium was amortized over time. The total yield would, of course, be 8 percent.

Figure 17-4 graphs the value of the bond over time, assuming that interest rates remain constant at 9 percent, rise to 10 percent, or fall to 8 percent. Of course, if interest rates do *not* remain constant, then the price of the bond will fluctuate. However, regardless of what interest rates do, the bond's price will approach $1,000 as the maturity date comes nearer (barring bankruptcy, in which case the bond's value might drop to zero).

Figure 17-4
Time Path of the Value of a 9% Coupon, $1,000 Par Value Bond When Interest Rates Are 8%, 9%, and 10%

The value of a bond fluctuates in response to changes in market interest rates. When a bond's coupon rate is equal to the market rate of interest, the bond sells at par. When the market rate falls below a bond's coupon rate, the bond sells above par. And when the market rate rises above a bond's coupon rate, the bond sells below par. This graph shows how the selling price of a 15-year 9 percent bond with a par value of $1,000 will change if market interest rates rise to 10 percent or fall to 8 percent. Note that as the bond's maturity date approaches, its value fluctuates less and less until it finally reaches par.

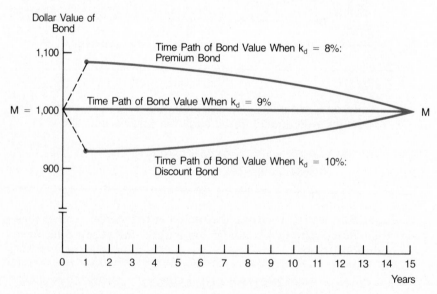

Note: The curves for 8% and 10% appear to be straight, but they actually have a slight bow.

Figure 17-4 illustrates the following key points:

1. Whenever the going rate of interest (k_d) is equal to the coupon rate, a bond will sell at its par value.

2. Whenever the going rate of interest is above the coupon rate, a bond will sell below its par value. Such a bond is called a **discount bond.**

3. Whenever the going rate of interest is below the coupon rate, a bond will sell above its par value. Such a bond is said to sell at a **premium.**

4. An increase in interest rates will cause the price of outstanding bonds to fall, while a decrease in rates will cause bond prices to rise.

5. The market value of a bond will approach its par value as its maturity date approaches.

These points are very important to investors, for they show that bondholders may suffer capital losses or make capital gains depending on whether interest rates rise or fall. And, as we saw earlier in the chapter, interest rates do indeed change over time.

discount bond
A bond that sells below its par value which occurs when the coupon rate is lower than the going rate of interest.

premium
The amount that a bond sells for above its par value which occurs when the coupon rate is higher than the going rate of interest.

Finding the Interest Rate on a Bond: Yield to Maturity

Suppose you were offered a 14-year, 9 percent coupon, $1,000 par value bond at a price of $1,082.48. What rate of interest would you earn if you bought the bond and held it to maturity? This rate is defined as the bond's **yield to maturity,** and it is the interest rate discussed by bond traders when they talk about rates of return. To find the yield to maturity, often called the **YTM,** you could solve the following equation for k_d:

yield to maturity (YTM)
The rate of return earned on a bond if it is held to maturity.

$$V = \$1,082.48$$

$$= \frac{\$90}{(1 + k_d)^1} + \frac{\$90}{(1 + k_d)^2} + \cdots + \frac{\$90}{(1 + k_d)^{14}} + \frac{\$1,000}{(1 + k_d)^{14}}$$

$$= \$90(DF_a) + \$1,000(DF).$$

Just as we did in finding the IRR for a project in Chapter 15, we can substitute values of DF_a and DF in the equation until we find a rate that *just equates* the present market price of the bond with its future cash flow of interest and principal. Thus

$$\$1082.48 = \$90(DF_a) + \$1,000(DF).$$

What would be a good interest rate to use as a starting point? First, referring to Point 3 in the preceding subsection, we know that since the bond is selling at a premium over its par value ($1,082.48 versus $1,000), the bond's yield is *below* the 9 percent coupon rate. Therefore

YTM

we might try a rate of 7 percent. Substituting in factors for 7 percent, we obtain

$$\$90(8.7455) + \$1,000(0.3878) = \$1,174.90 \neq \$1,082.48.$$

Our calculated bond value, $1,174.90, is *above* the actual market price, so the yield to maturity is *not* 7 percent. To lower the calculated value, we must *raise* the interest rate used in the process. Inserting factors for 8 percent, we obtain

$$\begin{aligned} V &= \$90(8.2442) + \$1,000(0.3405) \\ &= \$741.98 + \$340.50 \\ &= \$1,082.48. \end{aligned}$$

This calculated value is exactly equal to the market price of the bond; thus 8 percent is the bond's yield to maturity.[7]

Preferred Stock

preferred stock
A long-term equity security paying a fixed dividend.

Preferred stock is similar to bonds in some respects and similar to common stock in other ways. Preferred has a par value, usually either $25 or $100. The dividend is indicated either as a percentage of par, or in dollars, or sometimes both ways. For example, Mississippi Power Company recently sold 150,000 shares of $100 par value preferred stock for a total of $15 million. This preferred had a stated dividend of $12 per share, so the preferred dividend yield was $12/$100 = 0.12, or 12 percent, at the time of issue. The dividend was set when the stock was issued—it will not be changed in the future. Therefore, if the market price of the stock changes from $100 after the issue date—as it certainly will—then the yield will go up or down. For example, if the market price rises to $120, the current yield will fall to $12/$120 = 10 percent.

If the preferred dividend is not earned, the company does not have to pay it. However, most preferred issues are *cumulative*, meaning that the cumulative total of all unpaid preferred dividends must be paid

---

[7]There is also a formula that can be used to find the approximate yield to maturity on a bond:

$$k_d = YTM = \frac{I + (M - V)/n}{(M + V)/2}.$$

In the situation where I = $90, M = $1,000, V = $1,082.48, and n = 14,

$$k_d = \frac{\$90 + (\$1,000 - \$1,082.48)/14}{(\$1,000 + \$1,082.48)/2} = 0.0808 = 8.08\%.$$

This is close to the exact value, 8 percent. This formula can also be used to obtain a starting point for the trial-and-error method.

before dividends can be paid on common stock. Unpaid preferred dividends are called **arrearages.**

arrearage
An unpaid dividend on preferred stock.

Even though nonpayment of preferred dividends will not bankrupt a company, corporations issue preferred with every intention of paying the dividends. Failure to pay the preferred dividend precludes payment of common dividends and, in addition, makes it virtually impossible for a firm to raise capital by selling bonds, more preferred, or common stock. However, having preferred stock outstanding does give a firm that experiences temporary problems a chance to overcome its difficulties; had bonds been used instead of preferred stock, the company might have been forced into bankruptcy. Thus preferred stock is less risky than bonds from the viewpoint of the issuing corporation.

Investors, on the other hand, regard preferred stock as being more risky than bonds for two reasons: (1) preferred stockholders' claims are subordinated to bondholders' in the event of liquidation, and (2) bondholders are more likely to continue receiving income during hard times than are preferred stockholders. Accordingly, investors historically have required a higher rate of return on a given firm's preferred stock than on its bonds. However, the fact that preferred dividends are largely exempt from the corporate tax has made preferred stock attractive to corporate investors.[8] In recent years high-grade preferred stock, on average, has sold on a lower-yield basis than high-grade bonds. As an example, on March 27, 1973 AT&T sold a preferred issue that yielded 7.28 percent to an investor. On that same date AT&T's bonds yielded 7.55 percent, or 0.27 percentage points *more* than its preferred. The tax treatment accounted for this differential; the after-tax yield to corporate investors was greater on the preferred stock than on the bonds.[9]

About half of all preferred stock issued in recent years is convertible into common stock. For example, a firm might issue preferred stock whereby one share of preferred could be converted into three shares of common, at the option of the preferred stockholder. Convertibles are discussed at length in Appendix 18A.

Preferred stock generally has no maturity date. However, many preferred stocks do have a sinking fund provision; if the sinking fund called for the retirement of 1 percent of the issue each year, the issue would "mature" in a maximum of 100 years. Also, many preferred issues are callable by the issuing corporation; this feature, if exercised, will limit the life of the preferred stock.

---

[8] Recall from Chapter 2 that 85 percent of dividends received by one corporation from another corporation is exempt from corporate income taxes.

[9] The after-tax yield on a 7.5 percent bond to a corporate investor paying a 46 percent marginal tax rate is $7.5(1 - t) = 7.5(0.54) = 4.05\%$. The after-tax yield on a 7.5 percent preferred stock is $7.5(0.85) + 7.5(0.15)(0.54) = 6.9825\%$.

Advantages and Disadvantages of Bonds and Preferred Stock

There are pros and cons to holding bonds and preferred stocks as investments, and also to their use as a means of financing by corporations. Some of these factors are considered below:

Income and cost   Regardless of how profitable the company is or may become, bondholders and preferred stockholders receive only a fixed, limited income. This is an advantage from the firm's standpoint, as more of the operating income is available for the common stockholders, but it is a distinct disadvantage to the bondholders or preferred stockholders.

Control Typically, bondholders and preferred stockholders are not entitled to vote for directors—voting control lies in the hands of the common stockholders. Thus, when a firm is considering alternative means of financing, if the existing management group is concerned about losing voting control of the business, then selling bonds or preferred stock will have an advantage over financing with common stock. This point is covered in more detail in Chapter 18.

Taxes Bond interest is a deductible expense to the issuing firm, so for a firm in the 46 percent tax bracket, the federal government in effect pays 46 percent of the interest charges on debt. Thus bonds have an advantage over common and preferred stock to a corporation planning to raise new capital. (This point was covered in Chapter 2 and is examined again in Chapters 19 and 20.)

Risk To the corporation, bonds or term loans, especially those with sinking funds or amortization payments, entail significantly more risk than do preferred or common stocks. Furthermore, the shorter the maturity, the greater the risk. However, from the investor's viewpoint, bonds (or term loans) are safer.

Flexibility The indenture provisions (restrictive covenants) on a long-term bond are generally much more stringent than they are either in a short-term credit agreement or for common or preferred stock. Hence the firm may be subject to much more disturbing and crippling restrictions under a long-term debt arrangement than would be the case if it had borrowed on a short-term basis or had issued common or preferred stock.

Similarly, there is a limit on the extent to which funds can be raised through long-term debt. Generally accepted standards of financial policy dictate that the debt ratio must not exceed certain limits. When debt grows beyond these limits, its cost rises rapidly, or it may simply cease to be available.

Another significant point connected with flexibility relates to the ability to finance in times of economic stress. As a firm's fortunes deteriorate, it experiences greater difficulties in raising capital. More-over, in such times investors are increasingly concerned with the se-curity of their investments, and they may refuse to advance funds to the firm except on the basis of well-secured loans. A firm that fi-nances with debt during good times to the point where its debt/assets ratio is at the upper limits for its industry simply may not be able to finance at all during times of stress. Thus corporate trea-surers like to maintain some reserve borrowing capacity; this re-strains their use of debt financing.

These points are always considered by firms planning new security issues. However, we defer further consideration of the pros and cons of alternative securities until we have analyzed in the next chapter the other principal type of long-term capital—common stock.

Summary

This chapter described the characteristics, advantages, and disadvan-tages of the major types of long-term, fixed-income securities: *term loans, bonds*, and *preferred stocks*. The key difference between bonds and term loans is the fact that term loans are sold directly by a corpo-rate borrower to between one and twenty lenders, whereas bonds are generally sold to many public investors through investment bankers. Preferred stocks are similar to bonds in that they offer a fixed return. However, preferred stock is less risky than bonds from the corpora-tion's viewpoint because (1) the dividend does not have to be paid if it is not earned, and (2) nonpayment of preferred dividends will not bankrupt the firm. From the investors' standpoint, however, preferred stocks are more risky than bonds because (1) firms are more likely to omit preferred dividends than to fail to pay interest, and (2) bonds have priority over preferred stock in the event of bankruptcy.

Resolution to Decision in Finance

U.S. Steel

As the debt markets tightened up in the late 1970s and early 1980s, corporations found that the key to success in raising funds was to tailor innovative financing packages to appeal to the needs of specific groups of investors. Most securities buyers can be divided into two general categories: those who believe that interest rates will fluctuate and thus prefer investments that will keep their returns at prevailing market rates and those who believe that interest rates will fall and thus prefer to lock in current high rates. Within these two general categories are many subcategories—individuals, both speculative and conservative; institutions, both taxable and tax-exempt; foreign investors; and so forth. Thus a company has many factors to consider when planning to raise new capital, but its primary goal should be to create a financial package that will be so attractive to a specific group of investors that they will be willing to settle for an interest rate that is below the market.

William Lewellyn responded smartly to the demands of the changing debt markets when he masterminded U.S. Steel's unique new financing plan. Beginning in April 1980, the company sold three issues of tax-exempt, floating-rate pollution-control bonds. The new bonds were a great improvement over other floating-rate bonds of the time because they were tax-free and their interest rate was adjusted weekly. Their rate was pegged at either 67 percent of the 13-week Treasury bill rate or 75 percent of the current 30-year Treasury bond rate, whichever was higher.

The bonds were especially attractive to individual investors because the weekly adjustments in interest rates kept the bonds' market price stable. Thus U.S. Steel sidestepped institutional buyers, who were skeptical of the company's financial position, and attracted a new class of buyers to tax-exempts.

Source: *Dun's Review*, December 1980 and July 1981.

Key Terms You should be able to define each of the following terms:

Funded debt	Mortgage bond; convertible bond;
Term loan	income bond; floating rate bond;
Amortize	zero coupon bond; discount bond
Bond	Debenture; subordinated debenture
Coupon rate	Par value
Indenture; trustee	Coverage
Sinking fund	Premium
Call provision	Yield to maturity (YTM)
Restrictive covenant	Preferred stock
	Arrearage

Questions

17-1 What effect would each of the following items have on the interest rate a firm must pay on a new issue of long-term debt? Indicate by a plus (+), minus (−), or zero (0) whether the factor will tend to raise, lower, or have an indeterminate effect on the firm's interest rate.

	Effect on Interest Rate
a. The firm uses bonds rather than a term loan.	_____
b. The firm uses nonsubordinated debentures rather than first mortgage bonds.	_____
c. The firm makes its bonds convertible into common stock.	_____
d. The firm makes its debentures subordinated to its bank debt. What will the effect be:	
(1) On the debentures?	_____
(2) On the bank debt?	_____
(3) On the average total debt?	_____
e. The firm sells income bonds rather than debentures.	_____

f. The firm must raise $100 million, all of which will be used to construct a new plant, and is debating the sale of mortgage bonds or debentures. If it decides to issue $50 million of each type, as opposed to $75 million of mortgage bonds and $25 million of debentures, how will this affect:

(1) The debentures?	
(2) The mortgage bonds?	_____
(3) The average cost of the $100 million?	_____

g. The firm is planning to raise $25 million of long-term capital. Its outstanding bonds yield 9 percent. If it sells preferred stock, how will this affect the yield on the outstanding debt? _____

h. The firm puts a call provision on its new issue of bonds. _____

i. The firm includes a sinking fund on its new issue of bonds. _____

j. The firm's bonds are downgraded from A to BBB. _____

17-2 Rank the following securities from lowest (1) to highest (10) in terms of their riskiness for an investor. All securities (except the government bond) are for a given firm. If you think two or more securities are equally risky, so indicate.

	Rank (10 = Highest Risk)
a. Income bond	_____
b. Subordinated debentures—noncallable	_____
c. First mortgage bond—no sinking fund	_____
d. Preferred stock	_____
e. Common stock	_____
f. U.S. Treasury bond	_____
g. First mortgage bond—with sinking fund	_____
h. Subordinated debentures—callable	_____
i. Amortized term loan	_____
j. Nonamortized term loan	_____

17-3 A bond that pays interest forever and has no maturity date is a perpetual bond. In what respect is a perpetual bond similar to a no-growth stock and to a share of preferred stock?

17-4 "The values of outstanding bonds change whenever the going rate of interest changes. In general, short-term interest rates are more volatile than long-term interest rates. Therefore short-term bond prices are more sensitive to interest rate changes than are long-term bond prices." Is this statement true or false? Explain.

Self-Test Problem

ST-1 A firm issued a new series of bonds on January 2, 1970. The bonds were sold at par ($1,000), have an 8 percent coupon, and mature 30 years after the date of issue. Interest is paid annually on December 31.
   a. What was the yield to maturity (YTM) of the bond on January 2, 1970?
   b. What was the price of the bond on January 2, 1975, five years later, assuming the level of interest rates had risen to 10 percent?
   c. If, for this type of bond, interest rates had been 6 percent on January 2, 1975, what would investors have paid for the bond?
   d. Find the current yield and capital gains yield on the bond if interest rates as of January 2, 1975 were 6 percent as in Part c.
   e. On January 2, 1980 the bond sold for $525.70. What was the YTM on that date?
   f. What was the current yield and capital gains yield for the bond under the conditions described in Part e?
   g. It is now January 2, 1985. The going rate of interest is 14 percent. How large a check must you write to buy the bond?

Problems

17-1 Datamerge Corporation has a $100 par, $5 dividend preferred stock outstanding. Investors require a 14 percent return on investments of this type.
   * a. What is the current market price of Datamerge's preferred stock?
   b. Is the price you computed in Part a the same price that you would find if you discounted each future dividend back to the present using the 14 percent discount factors?
   c. If the investment community's required return fell for Datamerge's preferred stock, what would happen to the price?

* **17-2** Eureka Publications sold a 20-year, 10 percent coupon, $1,000 par bond 8 years ago. Today, with 12 years to maturity, the bond is selling for $773.63. What is the bond's:
   a. Nominal yield?
   b. Current yield?
   c. Yield to maturity?

* **17-3** Hytec sold a 15-year, 16 percent coupon bond at a par value of $1,000 in September 1980. In September 1985 the bond's yield to maturity is 12 percent. What is the current price of the bond?

17-4 a. Videomax Corporation's bonds pay $100 annual interest, mature in 10 years, and pay $1,000 on maturity. What will be the value of these

---

*Refer to Appendix E for check answers to problems with asterisks.

bonds when the going rate of interest is: **(a)** 8 percent, **(b)** 10 percent, and **(c)** 12 percent?

b. Now suppose that Videomax has some other bonds that pay $100 interest per year, $1,000 at maturity, and mature in 1 year. What is the price of these bonds if the going rate of interest is: **(a)** 8 percent, **(b)** 10 percent, and **(c)** 12 percent? Assume there is only one more interest payment to be made.

c. Why do the longer-term bond prices fluctuate more when interest rates change than do the shorter-term bond prices?

17-5 The Phillips Company's bonds have 3 years remaining to maturity. Interest is paid annually, the bonds have a $1,000 par value, and the coupon interest rate is 9 percent.

* **a.** What is the yield to maturity at a current market price of: **(1)** $928 and **(2)** $1,080? You may wish to use the approximation formula found in Footnote 7.

b. Would you pay $928 for the bond described in Part a if you thought that the appropriate rate of interest for these bonds is 10 percent? Explain your answer.

17-6 Suppose Olympic Industries sold an issue of bonds with a 10-year maturity, a $1,000 par value, and a 12 percent coupon rate paid annually.

* **a.** Suppose that 3 years after the issue, the going rate of interest had risen to 15 percent. At what price would the bonds sell?

b. Suppose the conditions in Part a continued (that is, interest rates remained at 15 percent throughout the bond's life). What would happen to the price of Olympic's bonds over time?

17-7 Suppose a firm is setting up an amortized term loan. What are the annual payments for a $2 million loan under the following terms:

a. 8 percent, 5 years?

b. 8 percent, 10 years?

c. 10 percent, 5 years?

d. 10 percent, 10 years?

17-8 Set up an amortization schedule for a $1 million, 3-year, 9 percent term loan.

17-9 A company borrows $1 million on a 3-year, 9 percent, partially amortized term loan.The annual payments are to be set so as to amortize $700,000 over the loan's 3-year life, and also pay interest on the $300,000 nonamortized portion of the loan.

a. How large must each annual payment be? (Hint: Think of the loan as consisting of two loans, one fully amortized for $700,000 and one on which interest only is paid each year until the end of the third year.)

b. Suppose the firm requested a $1 million, 9 percent, 3-year loan with payments of $250,000 per year (interest plus some principal repayment) for the first 2 years and the remainder to be paid off at the end of the third year. How large must the final payment be?

Answer to Self-Test Problem

ST-1 **a.** The bonds were sold at par. Therefore the YTM equals the coupon rate, which is 8 percent. The coupon rate is also referred to as the *nominal yield* or *stated yield*.

b. We must find the PV of the 25 remaining interest payments of $80 each and the $1,000 lump sum payment of principal to be paid when the bond matures in 25 years. Therefore

$$\text{Bond value} = \$80(DFa_{10\%, 25 \text{ years}}) + \$1,000(DF_{10\%, 25n})$$
$$= \$80(9.0770) + \$1,000(.0923)$$
$$= \$726.16 + \$92.30$$
$$= \$818.46.$$

c. Using the 6 percent discount factors, we find

$$\text{Bond value} = \$80(12.7834) + \$1,000(.2330)$$
$$= \$1,022.67 + \$233.00$$
$$= \$1,255.67.$$

d. If interest rates were 6 percent on January 1, 1975, the bond's price was $1,255.67, as found in Part c. Thus

$$\text{Current yield} = \frac{\text{Coupon payment}}{\text{Price}}$$
$$= \frac{\$80}{\$1,255.67}$$
$$= .0637 = 6.37\%.$$

$$\text{Capital gains yield} = \text{Total yield} - \text{Current yield}$$
$$= 6\% - 6.37\% = -.37\%.$$

e. Use the approximate YTM formula to get a starting point:

$$\text{Approximate YTM} = \frac{I + (M - V)/n}{(M + V)/2}$$
$$= \frac{\$80 + [(\$1,000 - \$525.70)/20]}{(\$1,000 + \$525.70)/2}$$
$$= \frac{\$103.715}{\$762.85}$$
$$= 13.6\%.$$

Because this approximation understates the true return, we will try a bit higher discount rate:

$$k_d = 16\%$$
$$V = I(DFa_{16\%, 20}) + M(DF_{16\%, 20})$$
$$= \$80(5.9288) + \$1,000(.0514)$$
$$= \$474.30 + \$51.40$$
$$= \$525.70.$$

Therefore the YTM at the beginning of January 1980 was 16 percent.

f.
$$\text{Current yield} = \$80/\$525.70$$
$$= 15.22\%.$$

$$\text{Capital gains yield} = 16\% - 15.22\%$$
$$= .78.$$

g. The bond has 15 years until it matures; at 14 percent the price would be

$$V = \$80(6.1422) + \$1,000(.1401)$$
$$= \$491.38 + \$140.10 = \$631.48.$$

Selected References

Many investment textbooks contain information on fixed-income securities such as bonds and preferred stock, as well as the markets in which they are traded. In addition, the following articles offer useful insights:

Backer, Morton, and Martin L. Gosman, "The Use of Financial Ratios in Credit Downgrade Decisions," *Financial Management*, Spring 1980, 53–56.

Clark, John J., with Brenton W. Harries, "Some Recent Trends in Municipal and Corporate Securities Markets: An Interview with Brenton W. Harries, President of Standard & Poor's Corporation," *Financial Management*, Spring 1976, 9–17.

Ferri, Michael G., "An Empirical Examination of the Determinants of Bond Yield Spreads," *Financial Management*, Autumn 1978, 40–46.

Neuberger, Brian, and C. T. Hammond, "A Study of Underwriters' Experience with Unseasoned New Issues," *Journal of Financial and Quantitative Analysis*, March 1974, 165–177.

Pinches, George E., J. Clay Singleton, and Ali Jahankhani, "Fixed Coverage as a Determinant of Electric Utility Bond Ratings," *Financial Management*, Summer 1978, 45–55.

Silvers, J. B., "Liquidity, Risk, and Duration Patterns in Corporate Financing," *Financial Management*, Autumn 1976, 54–64.

Smith, Clifford W., and J. B. Warner, "On Financial Contracting: An Analysis of Bond Covenants," *Journal of Financial Economics*, June 1979, 117–161.

Weinsten, Mark I., "The Seasoning Process of New Corporate Bond Issues," *Journal of Finance*, December 1978, 1343–1354.

Zwick, Burton, "Yields on Privately Placed Corporate Bonds," *Journal of Finance*, March 1980, 23–29.

Common Stock

18

Decision in Finance

Fred Adler's Big Giveaway

In 1983 Biotechnology General Corporation was like a lot of other small genetic engineering companies: it did research only and did not as yet have any products ready to market. During its three years of existence, BTG had lost $5.86 million, and it now badly needed a new infusion of capital.

BTG's chairman was Fred Adler, a venture capitalist with a reputation for backing hot new businesses. To raise the needed capital, Adler, who owned 60 percent of the company's stock, decided to sell shares to the public.

Adler's original plan was to sell 1 million shares of common stock at $15 to $17 per share. But due to unpredictable market conditions, however, he reduced the offering to 800,000 shares at $13 each. Adler could have chosen to delay the offering until the market for new issues improved, but he preferred to go ahead as the market had been generally good that year. From his point of view, his job as a venture capitalist was to fund his company, not try to figure out when the market would be ripe. "If the company does a good job, its stock price will eventually reflect that," Adler observed.

According to Robert Doolittle, corporate finance manager at BTG's lead underwriter, J. C. Bradford & Co., orders for the stock looked solid after the reduction. No one could have predicted what happened next.

Trouble began the first day the stock was issued. Because Adler's name was involved, a lot of people rushed to buy BTG stock. But when the price didn't rise rapidly, as had been expected, they began selling back to the syndicate. Under so much pressure, the syndicate was unable to maintain the stock's price, which fell from 13 to 10¼.

493

A week later, things got even worse. BTG conducted its research in Israel. When a currency crisis hit that country, nervous BTG investors sold off their stock, knocking the price down to 8¼. At that point Adler decided he should do something nice for his remaining shareholders.

As you read this chapter, consider the pros and cons of Adler's decision to issue BTG stock despite a highly volatile market. How were investors, the investment banking syndicate, and BTG each affected by the decision? What could Adler do to compensate his shareholders for their losses?

See end of chapter for resolution.

Common stock—or, for unincorporated businesses, the proprietors' or partners' capital—represents the ownership of a firm. In earlier chapters we discussed the legal and accounting aspects of common stock and the markets in which it is traded. Now we consider some of the rights and privileges of equity holders, the process by which investors establish the value of equity shares in the marketplace, and the procedures involved when firms raise new capital by issuing additional shares of stock.

Legal Rights and Privileges of the Common Stockholders

The common stockholders are the owners of the corporation, and as such they have certain rights and privileges. The most important of these are discussed in this section.

Control of the Firm

The stockholders have the right to elect the firm's directors, who in turn select the officers who manage the business. In a small firm the major stockholder typically assumes the positions of president and chairman of the board of directors. In a large, publicly owned firm the managers typically have some stock, but their personal holdings are insufficient to exercise voting control; thus the management of a publicly owned firm can be removed by the stockholders if the stockholder group decides the management is not effective.

Various state and federal laws stipulate how stockholder control is to be exercised. First, corporations must hold an election of directors periodically, usually once a year, with the vote taken at the annual meeting. Frequently, one third of the directors are elected each year for a three-year term. Each share of stock has one vote; thus the owner of 1,000 shares has 1,000 votes. Stockholders can appear at the annual meeting and vote in person, or they can transfer their right to vote to a second party by means of an instrument known as a **proxy.** Management always solicits stockholders' proxies and usually gets them. However, if earnings are poor and stockholders are dissatisfied, an outside group may solicit the proxies in an effort to overthrow management and take over control of the business. This is known as a **proxy fight.**

The question of control has become a central issue in finance in recent years. The frequency of proxy fights has increased, as have attempts by one corporation to take over another by purchasing a majority of the outstanding stock. This latter action, which is called a *takeover*, is discussed in detail in Chapter 22. Managers who do not have majority control of their firms' stocks (over 50 percent) are very much concerned about takeovers, and many of them are attempting to get stockholder approval for changes in their corporate charters that would make takeovers more difficult. For example, a number of companies tried recently to get their stockholders to agree (1) to elect only one third of the directors each year (rather than to elect all directors each year) and (2) to require 75 percent of the stockholders (rather than 50 percent) to approve a merger. Managements seeking such changes generally indicate a fear of the firm's being picked up at a bargain price, but some stockholders wonder whether concern about their jobs might not be an even more important consideration.

The Right to Purchase New Stock: The Preemptive Right

Common stockholders often have the right, called the **preemptive right,** to purchase, on a pro rata basis, any additional shares sold by the firm. In some states the preemptive right is made a part of every corporate charter; in others it is necessary to insert the preemptive right specifically into the charter.

The purpose of the preemptive right is twofold. First, it protects the power of control of present stockholders. If it were not for this safeguard, the management of a corporation under criticism from stockholders could prevent stockholders from removing it from office by issuing a large number of additional shares and purchasing these shares itself. Management would thereby secure control of the corporation to frustrate the will of the current stockholders.

The second, and by far the more important, protection that the preemptive right affords stockholders regards dilution of value. For example, assume that 1,000 shares of common stock, each with a price of $100, are outstanding, making the total market value of the firm $100,000. An additional 1,000 shares are sold at $50 a share, or for $50,000, thus raising the total market value of the firm to $150,000. When the total market value is divided by the new total shares outstanding, a value of $75 a share is obtained. Thus selling common stock at below-market value will dilute the price of the stock and will be

proxy
A document giving one person the authority or power to act for another; typically, the authority in question is the power to vote shares of common stock.

proxy fight
An attempt by a person, group, or company to gain control of a company by getting the stockholders to vote a new management into office.

preemptive right
A provision contained in the corporate charter and bylaws that gives holders of common stock the right to purchase on a pro rata basis new issues of common stock (or securities convertible into common stock).

Stock certificates, such as this sample from The Boeing Company, are issued to common stockholders as owners of the corporation. The certificate states the value of the stock (in this case $5 each) and the number of shares purchased, which would be noted in the boxed area in the upper right corner. Note the similarity of this certificate to that of the bond in Chapter 17. The intricate border designs of both are done to make counterfeiting difficult (as with U.S. dollar bills).

Source: Courtesy of The Boeing Company.

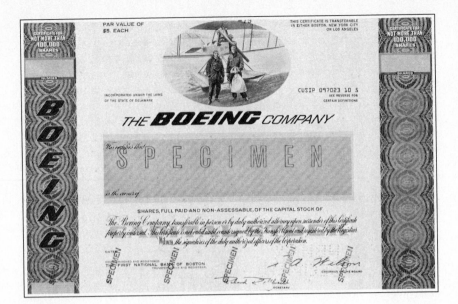

detrimental to present stockholders and beneficial to those who purchase the new shares. The preemptive right prevents such a loss of wealth for the original stockholders.[1]

Types of Common Stock

Although most firms have only one type of common stock, in some instances special classifications of stock are created to meet the special needs of the company. Generally, when different types of stock are used, one type is designated *Class A*, the second *Class B*, and so on. Small, new companies seeking to acquire funds from outside sources sometimes use different types of common stock. For example, stock designated Class A may be sold to the public, pay a dividend, and have full voting rights. Stock designated Class B, however, may be retained by the organizers of the company, and the legal terms may state that dividends will not be paid on it until the company has established its earning power by building up retained earnings to a designated level. By the use of classified stock, the public can take a position in a conservatively financed growth company without sacrificing income. In situations such as this, the Class B stock is often called **founders' shares** and given *sole* voting rights for a number of years. This

founders' shares
Classified stock that has sole voting rights and restricted dividends; it is owned by the firm's founders.

---

[1]The procedure for issuing stock to existing stockholders, called a *rights offering,* is discussed in detail in Eugene F. Brigham, *Financial Management: Theory and Practice,* 3rd ed. (Hinsdale, IL: Dryden Press, 1982), Appendix 14A.

permits the organizers of the firm to maintain complete control of the operations in the crucial early stages of the firm's development. At the same time other investors are protected against excessive withdrawals of funds by the original owners.

Savannah Electric provides an example of yet another type of classification. This company has Class A common that pays a $1.34 annual dividend versus $1.20 for the Class B common. If earnings increase and the dividend on the Class B stock is raised to a level above $1.34, the Class A stockholders can convert to Class B. Conversion from A to B occurred automatically in 1984, since voluntary conversion had not occurred earlier. The reason for selling the Class A was quite simple—while Savannah needed money badly in 1972, it could not sell debt because of indenture restrictions, it could not sell preferred stock because of other restrictions, and it could not sell "regular" common because the market would not absorb it without depressing the price very badly. The Class A common was the only feasible alternative.

Note that "Class A," "Class B," and so on have no standard meanings. First, most firms have no classified shares. Also, one firm may designate its Class B shares as founders' shares and its Class A shares as those sold to the public. Another firm can reverse these designations. Other firms, like Savannah Electric, can use the A and B designations for entirely different purposes.

Common Stock Valuation

A share of common stock represents participation in the ownership of a firm, but to the vast majority of shareholders it is more valued for the returns that can be gained from its purchase. These returns come from two main sources:

1. Cash dividends—which are usually expected to increase as long as the stock is held.

2. Capital gains—which are received if the stock is sold at a price above its original purchase price.

Of course, both of these returns are uncertain. The company must first earn and then declare dividends for them to be received. These dividends are uncertain in both their size and their payment schedule.[2] Naturally, being able to sell a share of common stock for more than its purchase price is even more uncertain. However, most persons, when they buy common stock, expect to receive capital gains; otherwise they would not be willing to purchase the shares.

---

[2]We note in Chapter 21 that although most companies will make extraordinary efforts to pay dividends regularly and not let the dollar amount of those dividends decline, this effort does not guarantee the firm's ability to maintain its dividends.

Definitions of Terms Used in the Stock Valuation Models

We shall develop some models to help determine the value of a share of stock under several different sets of conditions, but let us first define the following terms:

D_t = the dividend the stockholder expects to receive at the end of Year t. D_0 is the most recent dividend, which has already been paid; D_1 is the next dividend, which will be paid at the end of this year; D_2 is the dividend expected at the end of two years; and so on.

P_t = the price of the stock at the end of each year t. P_0 is the price of the stock today; P_1 is the price expected at the end of one year; and so on.

g = the expected rate of growth in the stock price. (In most of our models, g is also the expected rate of growth in earnings and dividends. In addition, we assume that g will be constant over time.)

required rate of return
The minimum rate of return on common stock that stockholders consider acceptable.

k_s = the minimum acceptable or **required rate of return** on the stock, considering both its riskiness and the returns available on other investments.

expected rate of return
The rate of return on common stock that an individual stockholder actually expects to receive.

$\hat{k}_s$ = (pronounced "k hat") the **expected rate of return** which the individual who buys the stock actually expects to receive. The caret, or "hat," is used to indicate that $\hat{k}_s$ is a predicted value. $\hat{k}_s$ could be above or below k_s, but one would buy the stock only if $\hat{k}_s$ were equal to or greater than k_s.

dividend yield
The ratio of the current dividend to the current price of a share of stock.

D_1/P_0 = the expected **dividend yield** on the stock during the coming year. If the stock is expected to pay a dividend of $1 during the next 12 months, and if its current price is $10, then the dividend yield is $1/$10 = 0.10 = 10%.

capital gains yield
The capital gain during any one year divided by the beginning price.

$\dfrac{P_1 - P_0}{P_0}$ = the expected **capital gains yield** on the stock during the coming year. If the stock sells for $10 today, and if it is expected to rise to $10.50 at the end of one year, then the expected capital gain is $P_1 - P_0$ = $10.50 - $10.00 = $0.50, and the expected capital gains yield is $0.50/$10 = 0.05 = 5%. If the stock price grows at a constant rate, then the growth rate, g, is equal to the capital gains yield.

Total return = Dividend yield + Capital gains yield = k_s = 10% + 5% = 15%.

Expected Dividends as the Basis for Stock Values

The value of any financial or real asset that we will study is the present value of its cash flows. For example, in our discussion of capital budgeting, the present value of a project was equal to the project's cash flow (consisting of the project-related net income and depreciation) discounted back to the present:

$$V = \sum_{t=1}^{n} \frac{CF_t}{(1 + k)^t}.$$

Similarly, in Chapter 17 we found the value of a bond to be the present value of its stream of payments, in this case the present value of the interest payments over the life of the bond plus the present value of the bond's maturity or par value:

$$V = \frac{I}{(1 + k_d)} + \frac{I}{(1 + k_d)^2} + \cdots + \frac{I}{(1 + k_d)^n} + \frac{M}{(1 + k_d)^n}.$$

Since all other assets are valued at the present value of their future expected cash returns, one should not expect the valuation model for common stock to be any different. Thus common stock values are determined by the present value of a stream of cash flows associated with owning the stock. But what is the stream of cash flows that a corporation provides its stockholders? As long as an individual owns stock, the only cash received is in the form of *dividends*. Therefore the value of a share of common stock is calculated as the present value of an infinite stream of dividends:

Value of stock $= P_0 =$ PV of expected future dividends

$$= \frac{D_1}{(1 + k_s)^1} + \frac{D_2}{1 + k_s)^2} + \cdots + \frac{D_\infty}{(1 + k_s)^\infty}. \quad \textbf{(18-1)}$$

What about a more reasonable case, one in which stock is purchased to be held for a shorter, finite period? Will the value of the stock change? In a word, *no*. Assume that you plan to hold a share of stock for only five years. The value of the stock would be equal to the present value of the dividends over the five-year period plus the present value of the stock's selling price in the fifth year:

$$P_0 = \sum_{t=1}^{5} \frac{D_t}{(1 + k_s)^t} + \frac{P_5}{(1 + k_s)^5}. \quad \textbf{(18-2)}$$

The next question is: What would a rational investor pay for the stock in that future year? The rational investor would only be willing to pay the present value of the future flows that are expected during the future ownership period. What are those flows? *Dividends*, of course! Therefore

$$P_5 = \sum_{t=6}^{\infty} \frac{D_t}{(1 + k_s)^t}. \quad \textbf{(18-3)}$$

If we substitute into Equation 18-2 the value of the stock in Year 5, found in Equation 18-3, it is obvious that even when the stock is sold at some future date *the value of the stock is still determined by the general model presented in Equation 18-1.* Thus a rational investor will pay an amount equal to the present value of the expected returns to be received from the purchase of an asset. Equation 18-1 is a generalized stock valuation model in the sense that the pattern of dividend payments can be anything: D_t can be rising, falling, or constant, or it can even be fluctuating randomly, and Equation 18-1 will still hold. Even so, it is often difficult, even for expert professionals, to estimate future dividend payments beyond a few periods. In the next section we develop a simplified stock valuation model based on the concepts of Equation 18-1, which makes only two simplifying assumptions: (1) that the growth in earnings and dividends for the firm will progress at a constant rate into the future, and (2) that $k_s > g$.

"Normal," or Constant, Growth

As firms stabilize in the maturity phase of their life cycle, the growth of their earnings and dividends tends to stabilize as well. This period of stability is not one of stagnation but rather one of moderate growth. In general, this growth is expected to continue into the foreseeable future, perhaps at the same rate as inflation, population growth, or the gross national product.

If we wish to determine next year's dividend, D_1, for a firm whose future growth is expected to be "normal," we need only multiply last year's dividend, D_0, by the expected growth rate. Thus, if Carter Chemical Company has just paid a dividend of $1.92 and investors expect a 4 percent growth for the company throughout the foreseeable future, next year's dividend, D_1, may be found in the following manner:

$$
\begin{aligned}
D_1 &= D_0(1 + g) \\
&= \$1.92(1.04) \\
&= \$2.00.
\end{aligned}
$$

Equation 18-1 describes the valuation of a share of common stock as the present value of all future cash flows (for common stock that flow is dividends). If those dividends are expected to grow *at a constant rate, g,* Equation 18-1 can be simplified as follows:[3]

---

[3]We spare the reader the mathematical proof of our assertion. For those who are interested, the derivation of Equation 18-4 is provided in Eugene F. Brigham, *Financial Management: Theory and Practice,* 3rd ed. (Hinsdale, IL: Dryden Press, 1982), Appendix 4A, 114–116.

$$P_0 = \frac{D_0(1+g)}{\frac{1}{R} - g}. \qquad (18\text{-}4)$$

If investors require a 9 percent return from an investment in Carter's common stock, k_s, the value of the firm's common stock can be determined by substituting into Equation 18-4 the values for next year's dividend, the required return on Carter's equity, and the firm's expected growth:

$$P_0 = \frac{D_1}{k_s - g}$$
$$= \frac{\$2.00}{.09 - .04}$$
$$= \frac{\$2.00}{.05} = \$40.00.$$

Recall that we can come to the same conclusion—the price of Carter's common stock is $40—by utilizing the more cumbersome Equation 18-1. The simplification provided by Equation 18-4 is often referred to as the *Gordon Model,* after Professor Myron J. Gordon, who did much to develop and popularize it.

The concept underlying the valuation process in Equation 18-4 is presented graphically in Figure 18-1. The top dashed curve represents the dollar value of Carter's dividends growing at a 4 percent rate. The bottom dashed line plots the present value of those dividends. The value of the firm's common stock may be obtained by adding the present value of each future year's dividend, as suggested by Equation 18-1, or, since the dividends are growing at a constant rate, the value may be found by utilizing Equation 18-4. In either case the result will be the same.

It should be clear that the constant-growth valuation model is intended to price the equity shares of a company that has normal or constantly growing earnings and dividends. However, for a firm that is in the early stages of its life cycle or in a highly variable economic environment, Equation 18-4 may not provide an effective means of equity valuation. Thus Equation 18-4 would be a poor choice to use in evaluating the share price of a new high-technology firm, but it would probably provide an excellent approximation of the economic value of a mature company. Therefore the more variable the growth rate in earnings and hence dividends, the less satisfactory job the model represented by Equation 18-4 will do in valuing a firm.

One caveat, other than the assumption of constant growth, must be observed in utilizing Equation 18-4. The growth rate, g, must be assumed to be always *less than* the required rate of return, k_s. While there are several excellent economic reasons to assert that k_s will never be

Figure 18-1
Growing Dividend Stream and Present Value of the Stream:
$D_0 = \$1.92$, $g = 4\%$, $k_e = 9\%$

This figure illustrates a stock valuation model. The value of a share of common stock equals the present value of all future dividends. This example assumes that these dividends will grow at a constant rate. The $2.00 dividend for the first year (D_1) has a present value (PV) of $1.83. At a growth rate (g) of 4 percent and an expected rate of return (k_s) of 9 percent, we can plot the growing dividend stream both in actual dollar amounts and in present values into infinity. Adding discounted future dividends yields the present value of the firm's stock.

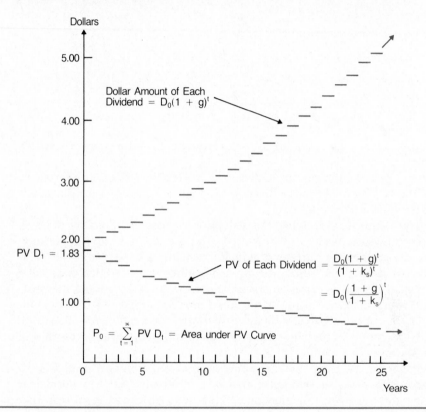

smaller than g, the model has no rational meaning if $g \geq k_s$. For example, if Carter's $k_s = 9\%$, $D_1 = \$2.00$, but $g = 13\%$, then

$$P_0 = \frac{\$2.00}{.09 - .13}$$

$$= \frac{\$2.00}{-.04}$$

$$= -\$50.$$

This result indicates that a present owner of Carter's equity would be willing to give you a share of the stock *and* $50 to induce you to take it. A highly unlikely scenario! Therefore the Gordon Model, Equation 18-4, always requires that $k_s > g$.

Issuing Common Stock

Suppose a firm has analyzed its investment opportunities, concluded that its profitable investments exceed its internally generated funds, and decided to float a stock issue to raise the needed capital. In this section we trace through the procedures for marketing the issue.

Choosing an Investment Banker

Most established firms will already have a working relationship with an investment banking firm. If not, or if the firm is not satisfied with the service it has been receiving, an underwriter must be selected.

Deciding Whether the Issue Should Be a Rights Offering

If the firm's stockholders have the preemptive right, then the stock must be offered to the existing stockholders. Otherwise the firm, in consultation with its bankers, must decide whether to offer the stock to existing stockholders or to the general public. The complex technical issues involved in a **rights offering** are discussed elsewhere.[4]

rights offering
A securities flotation offered to existing stockholders.

Registration with the SEC

A **registration statement** must be filed with the SEC. This statement will be completed by the firm and its investment banker, with the aid of lawyers and accountants who specialize in security offerings. The statutes set a 20-day waiting period (which in practice may be shortened or lengthened by the SEC) during which time the SEC staff analyzes the registration statement to determine whether there are any omissions or misrepresentations of fact. The SEC may file exceptions to the registration statement or may ask for additional information from the issuing company or the underwriters during the examination period. During this period the investment bankers are not permitted to offer the securities for sale, although they may print preliminary **prospectuses** with all the customary information except the offering price.

registration statement
A statement of facts filed with the SEC about a company planning to issue securities.

prospectus
A document issued for the purpose of describing a new security issue and the issuing company.

---

[4]See, for example, Eugene F. Brigham, *Financial Management: Theory and Practice*, 3rd ed. (Hinsdale, IL: Dryden Press, 1982), Appendix 14B.

Determining Flotation Costs

flotation cost
The cost of issuing new stocks or bonds.

The firm and its investment bankers must agree on the banker's compensation, or the **flotation cost** involved in issuing the stock. Table 18-1 gives an indication of the flotation costs associated with public issues of bonds, preferred stocks, and common stocks. As the table shows, costs as a percentage of the proceeds are higher for stocks than for bonds; and for all types of securities, costs are higher for small issues than for large issues. The relationship between cost and size of issue may be traced to the existence of fixed flotation costs. Since certain costs must be incurred regardless of the size of the issue, the percentage flotation cost is therefore quite high for small issues. In fact, the table indicates flotation charges range from 23.7 percent for the small equity issue to 3.5 percent for issues involving stock with a value of over $50 million. Since these figures are averages, the extremes may be even wider, especially on smaller issues.

Flotation costs to the firm consist of two elements: (1) direct compensation to the investment banker and (2) indirect, out-of-pocket expenses which must be paid by the firm for accounting, printing, legal, and other services required to issue the stock. The investment banker's compensation consists of the **spread** between the price the company is paid for the stock and the price at which the stock is sold to the public, called the **offering price.** Naturally, the company wants to receive the highest possible price for the stock, so it bargains with the banker over both the offering price and the spread. The higher the offering price and the lower the spread, the more the company receives per share of stock sold; and the more it receives per share, the fewer the number of shares required to raise a given amount of money.

spread
The difference between the price a security dealer offers to pay for securities (the "bid" price) and the price at which the dealer offers to sell them (the "asked" price).

offering price
The price at which common stock is sold to the public.

Setting the Offering Price

The offering price is generally not determined until the close of the registration period. There is no universally followed practice, but one common arrangement for a new issue of stock calls for the investment banker to buy the securities at a prescribed number of points below the closing price on the last day of registration. Suppose that in October 1985 the stock of Carter Chemical Company had a current price of $28.50 and that it had traded between $25 and $30 a share during the previous 3 months. Suppose further that Carter and its underwriter agreed that the investment banker would buy 10 million new shares at $1 below the closing price on the last day of registration. If the stock closed at $26 on the day the SEC released the issue, Carter would receive $25 a share. Typically, such agreements have an escape clause that provides for the contract to be voided if the price of the securities ends below some predetermined figure. In the illustrative case this "upset" price might be set at $25 a share. Thus, if the closing price of

Table 18-1
Costs of Flotation, 1971–1972 (Costs Expressed as Percentages of Gross Proceeds)

Size of Issue (Millions of Dollars)	Debt			Preferred Stock			Common Stock		
	Underwriting Commission	Other Expenses	Total Costs	Underwriting Commission	Other Expenses	Total Costs	Underwriting Commission	Other Expenses	Total Costs
Under 0.5	—	⎫	—	—	—	—	13.3	10.4	23.7
0.5–0.9	9.9	⎬ 3.4	13.3	—	—	—	12.6	8.3	20.9
1.0–1.9	—	⎭	—	8.3	3.5	11.8	11.0	5.9	16.9
2.0–4.9	4.0	2.2	6.2	1.9	0.7	2.6	8.6	3.8	12.4
5.0–9.9	2.4	0.8	3.2	1.4	0.4	1.8	6.3	1.9	8.1
10.0–19.9	1.2	0.7	1.9	1.4	0.3	1.7	5.1	0.9	5.9
20.0–49.9	1.0	0.4	1.4	1.4	0.2	1.6	4.1	0.5	4.6
50.0 and over	0.9	0.2	1.1				3.3	0.2	3.5

Source: Securities and Exchange Commission, *Cost of Flotation of Registered Equity Issues, 1971–1972* (Washington, DC: U.S. Government Printing Office, December 1974).
Note: Because of rounding errors, totals may not equal the sum of the parts. Preferred stocks were used infrequently, as were bond issues of under $2 million. Therefore (1) all bond issues of under $2 million were lumped together, and (2) blanks are shown for several preferred stock categories because no issues in those size ranges were reported.

the shares on the last day of registration had been $24.50, Carter would have had the option of withdrawing from the agreement.

Of course, the preceding example assumes that there is an existing market for the firm's common stock and that the issue is one which adds shares to the previously traded stock. If the firm is selling its shares on the market for the first time, the investment banker's job is made more difficult. The investment banker must depend on an analysis of similar security issues to determine a fair opening price. Since there is no market already existing, the company and its investment banker must negotiate a firm issuing price.

Formation of an Investment Banking Group

Stocks are generally offered to the public the day after the issue is cleared by the SEC. Investors are required to pay for the stock within ten days, and the investment bankers must pay the issuing firm within four days of the time the offering officially begins. Typically, the bankers sell the stock within a day or two after the offering begins, but on occasion the bankers miscalculate, set the offering price too high, and are unable to move the issue. At still other times the stock market declines during the offering period, forcing the bankers to reduce the price of the stock. In either instance the firm receives the price that was agreed upon, and the bankers must absorb any losses that may be incurred.

Because they are exposed to large potential losses, investment bankers typically do not handle the purchase and distribution of issues singlehandedly unless the issue is a very small one. If the sum of money involved is large and the risk of price fluctuation is substantial, investment bankers form **underwriting syndicates** in an effort to minimize the amount of risk each one carries.

underwriting syndicate
A syndicate of investment firms formed to spread the risk associated with the purchase and distribution of a new issue of securities.

In addition to the underwriting syndicate, on larger offerings still more investment bankers are included in the **selling group,** which handles the distribution of securities to individual investors. The selling group includes dealers who take relatively small participations, or shares of the total issue, from the members of the underwriting syndicate. Thus the underwriters act as wholesalers, while members of the selling group act as retailers. The number of houses in a selling group depends partly on the size of the issue; for example, the one for Communications Satellite Corporation consisted of 385 members.

selling group
A group of stock brokerage firms formed for the purpose of distributing a new issue of securities.

Maintenance of the Secondary Market

In the case of a large, established firm such as Carter Chemical Company, the investment banking firm's job is finished once it has disposed of the stock and turned the net proceeds over to the issuing firm. However, in the case of a company going public for the first time, the investment banker is under some obligation to maintain a market in the shares after the issue has been completed. Such stocks are typically traded in the over-the-counter market, and the principal underwriter generally agrees to "make a market" in the stock so as to keep it reasonably liquid. The company wants a good market to exist for its stock, as do the stockholders. Therefore, if the banking house wants to do business with the company in the future, keep its own brokerage customers happy, and have future referral business, it will hold an inventory and help to maintain an active secondary market in the stock.

Summary

Common stock represents ownership shares in the firm. The common stockholders are the owners of the firm and enjoy all rights and privileges associated with control of the firm.

However, most purchasers buy common stock for its investment qualities. Some buy stock to hold for the foreseeable future, depending on the dividend income for their major source of returns. Others are less interested in current dividend income, but rather are concerned with potential capital gains. This chapter has emphasized that while the goals of these two types of investors are different, each investor should evaluate a potential investment in the same manner. Despite all the folklore associated with pricing common stock (ranging from Uncle Bernie's "inside tips" to the "bigger fool theory"), this chapter has stressed that common stock valuation is no different from the valuation of any other financial or real asset. The value of any asset is the present value of the cash flows associated with the asset's acquisition. The only cash flow that is available to the common shareholder, as long as the asset is held, is dividends. Therefore the value of a share of common stock is the present value of all of its future dividends. Similarly, if the stock is subsequently sold, its value at that future date is the present value of future cash flows (dividends) which the buyer will receive from that point on.

The chapter concluded with a brief discussion of the process by which common stock is sold by the firm. The functions of the investment banker in this capital accumulation process were also evaluated.

Small Business $ $ $ $ $ $ $ $ $

Raising Equity Capital for the Small Firm

Small firms are generally disadvantaged in competing for funds in public equity markets. Nevertheless, the public markets are accessible, and the Securities and Exchange Commission also makes available some special opportunities for smaller firms to raise equity funds without incurring the expense of a public offering. *Venture Capital Journal* reports that in the year 1983, 477 small firms made public offerings of common stock, raising a stunning total of $3.67 billion, an average of $7.7 million per firm. These statistics are for firms whose per-offering net worths were all under $5 million. So, while it is true that smaller firms are at a disadvantage, the public equity markets are by no means the exclusive domain of giant companies.

Biotechnology General Corporation provides a good example of a firm with a new public offering in 1983. (See this chapter's Decision in Finance for more information on the peculiar circumstances of this offering.) For the full year of 1982 Biotechnology General (BTG) had total sales of $150,000. It lost $2.3 million, not unusual for a young firm in a heavily research-oriented industry. In the first half of 1982 BTG had revenues of $50,000 and losses of $2.77 per share. Yet, on September 29, 1983 BTG went public at an offering price of $13 per share, and, despite the difficulties recounted in the Decision in Finance, it quickly raised a total of over $10 million.

How could a firm with essentially no revenues go public and obtain $10 million? How could the public decide on a value for the shares? The an-swers to these questions can prove problematic. BTG illustrates several features of a public offering that can have a major effect on its success for a young, small firm. The features we highlight are market timing, interest in the nature of the business, and the company's success in developing a new product. Another point BTG illustrates is the great difficulty of valuing shares by traditional means under such circumstances.

Market timing is thought by many investment underwriters to be a critical element in the success of a new public offering. The year 1983 was phenomenally successful for the stock market. The Dow Jones Industrial Average reached its all-time historical high, and many investors told stories of great success with their equity investments. Pension funds and other large institutional investors shifted huge sums into the equity markets. As public interest in the equity markets grew, public interest in new equity offerings increased radically. The year 1983 was by far the most successful in history for new public offerings. New offerings are especially interesting to investors during bull market periods because new-issue prices tend to be highly volatile. Volatility is attractive to investors who are optimistic—it means a higher probability of unusually high returns. Of course, investors have to keep in mind that price volatility also means a higher probability of unusually large losses.

The bull market of 1983 soured quickly, turning into a bear market in 1984. As investor concerns about general economic conditions worsened, prices tumbled rapidly. Companies that had delayed their offerings during the bull market period suddenly found that the markets had reduced the values of new issues. Many firms planning to go public found either that they had to sell their issues at disappointingly low prices or that, as often occurred, they were advised to postpone their offerings indefinitely.

BTG made its offering in September 1983, just as the market was beginning to turn. At that time the market was still receptive to new issues, though subsequent events indicate how volatile the initial market reception can be. BTG had no difficulty selling its shares at the desired price. Despite substantial problems with the offering, the firm was able to successfully raise $10 million. Had BTG waited and come to market just three or four months later, however, the shares may not have sold at all.

A second factor is the firm's line of business. The market is very sensitive to this point since there tend to be general expectations about particular industries. For example, earlier in 1983 Osborne Computer Corporation had filed for bankruptcy. The market was at that time especially careful in evaluating new computer hardware firms. BTG, however, was a member of the exciting new breed of genetic engineering firms. Spurred on by the incredible success of Genentech, the market had a very strong interest in new issues of biological and genetic engineering companies.

A third factor is that BTG had completed the development of its first product, a promising new biological wonder that demonstrated the firm's expertise in biological engineering. The firm needed funds for continued product development and had just demonstrated its ability to deliver.

We are still left with the question of how BTG's underwriters came up with a market value for BTG. The answer is unclear. Although the firm was three years old at the time, it had never produced positive earnings, and it had certainly never paid a dividend. In fact, there could be no reasonable expectation of dividends for the foreseeable future. So clearly one could not apply the simple dividend models discussed earlier in this chapter. The growth rate of dividends wouldn't apply, and one certainly could not apply a constant-growth model. One could not even apply a price/earnings multiple to current earnings, since there were no current earnings. In essence, the underwriters had to do the best they could to set a price at which the issue would be appealing to the public in spite of the huge uncertainty about the future financial performance of the firm. As it was, the issue price was dropped from $15–$17 to $13 per share even before the offering was ever made public. Had the firm not been in biogenetics, or perhaps computer software, it is doubtful the issue would have been offered at all. BTG's decision to sell stock illustrates the value of being in the right place at the right time: in a hot industry, with a promising new product, and in a receptive market. The subsequent scenario that evolved after the stock offering (described in Decision in Finance) serves as a caution to over-eager investors and again points up the volatility that can beset the new issues market.

We can see, though, that there can be a market for the stock of very promising small and young firms. A number of factors figure in the success of a public offering of a small firm's equity, and not all of the factors are under the firm's control. But the firms do have some access to public markets if the firms have at least some promise of growing into more substantial enterprises. Managing those growth opportunities is something that *is* under the control of the firm and its managers.

Resolution to Decision in Finance

$$

Fred Adler's Big Giveaway

Because the market for Biotechnology General's stock deteriorated so rapidly, it was impossible for Fred Adler to cancel the offering before things got too far out of hand. As a result, stockholders, BTG's investment bankers, and Adler himself all lost money. Obviously, investors who bought at the original offering price of $13 and then panicked and sold at a lower price lost money in proportion to their original investments.

Investment bankers like to price an issue to maximize the money raised while simultaneously allowing room for about 15 to 20 percent market appreciation in the first day or two. Since an underwriting syndicate purchases a stock offering from the issuing company at a fixed price, it stands to benefit if the stock price rises. But it must also absorb any losses that occur if the stock sells below the expected price. BTG's underwriters had to buy back stock that investors didn't want, were forced to lower the stock's price, and then were left with unsold shares. Although underwriters never disclose their losses, it's a good bet that members of BTG's syndicate lost a substantial amount.

Fred Adler didn't like to see his public shareholders suffer, so he came up with an unorthodox plan to compensate them for their losses: he would give them five shares of BTG stock for every four shares they held. Such a generous act would only be possible for a company like BTG, where one person controls the majority of stock and needs the agreement of only a small group of insiders. And before Fred Adler no one had ever done such a thing.

Although Fred Adler's extraordinary giveaway didn't send BTG stock prices soaring, the stock has been steady since then, and it is doing as well as its major competitor. Adler is optimistic about the future because some of BTG's products could become commercially available very soon. Industry analysts remain cautious, however; with so many promising bio-tech companies working on similar products, it may take time for the winners to surface.

Source: "Fred Adler's One-Time-Only Stock Giveback," *Venture*, February 1984, 102.

Key Terms   You should be able to define each of the following terms:

Proxy; proxy fight	Rights offering
Preemptive right	Registration statement
Founders' shares	Prospectus

Required rate of return; expected rate   Flotation cost
  of return   Spread
Dividend yield; capital gains yield   Offering price
                                               Underwriting syndicate; selling
                                                 group

Questions

18-1 Two investors are investigating IBM's stock for possible purchase. They agree on the expected value of D_1 and also on the expected future dividend growth rate. However, one investor normally holds stock for 2 years, while the other holds stock for 10 years. Based on the analysis presented in this chapter, they should both be willing to pay the same price for IBM's stock. True or false? Explain.

18-2 If you buy a share of common stock, you typically expect to receive dividends plus capital gains. Would you expect the distribution between dividend yield and capital gains to be influenced by a firm's decision to pay more dividends rather than retain and reinvest more earnings?

18-3 The SEC attempts to protect investors who are purchasing newly issued securities by making sure that the information put out by a company and its investment bankers is correct and is not misleading. However, the SEC *does not* provide any information about the real value of the securities; hence an investor might pay too much for some new stock and consequently lose heavily. Do you think the SEC should, as a part of every new stock or bond offering, render an opinion to investors as to the proper value of the securities being offered? Explain.

18-4 Draw a Security Market Line graph. Put dots on the graph to show (approximately) where you think a particular company's **(a)** common stock and **(b)** bonds would lie. Now where would you add a dot to represent the common stock of a more risky company?

Self-Test Problems

ST-1 You are considering buying the stock of two very similar companies. Both companies are expected to earn $3 per share this year. However, Company A is expected to pay all of its earnings out as dividends, while Company B is expected to pay out only one third of its earnings, or $1. A's stock price is $20. Which of the following is most likely to be true?

  a. Company B will have a faster growth rate than Company A. Therefore B's stock price should be greater than $20.

  b. Although B's growth rate should exceed A's, A's current dividend exceeds that of B, and this should cause A's price to exceed B's.

  c. An investor in A will get his or her money back faster because A pays out more of its earnings as dividends. Thus, in a sense, A's stock is like a short-term bond, and B's is like a long-term bond. Therefore, if economic shifts cause k_d and k_s to increase, and if the expected streams of dividends from A and B remain constant, then A's and B's stock prices will both decline, but A's price should decline further.

  d. A's expected and required rate of return is $\hat{k}_s = k_s = 15$ percent. B's expected return will be higher because of its higher expected growth rate.

e. Based on the available information, the best estimate of B's growth rate is 10 percent.

ST-2 You can buy a share of the Karp Company's stock today for $24. Karp's last dividend was $1.60. In view of Karp's low risk, its required rate of return is only 12 percent. If dividends are expected to grow at a constant rate, g, in the future, and if k is expected to remain at 12 percent, what is Karp Company's expected stock price 5 years from now?

ST-3 Minuscule Computer Chips, Inc. is experiencing a period of rapid growth. Earnings and dividends are expected to grow at a rate of 18 percent during the next 2 years, 15 percent in the third year, and then at a constant rate of 6 percent thereafter. Minuscule's last dividend was $1.15, and the required rate of return on the stock is 12 percent.

a. Calculate the price of the stock today.

b. Calculate P_1 and P_2.

c. Calculate the dividend yield and capital gains yield for Years 1, 2, and 3.

Problems

* **18-1** Sarge's Chicken Shack Restaurant Corporation has enjoyed many years of rapid growth in both dividends and earnings. However, the firm's treasurer believes the company has entered a more mature, constant-growth phase of its existence. If next year's dividend, D_1, is $1.70, and dividends are expected to grow into the foreseeable future at 5 percent annually, what price should investors pay if they want a 13 percent return on their investment?

* **18-2** Emory Medical's dividend is $2.00 ($D_0$ = $2.00). Emory's growth rate is expected to remain at a constant 7 percent. If investors demand a 12 percent return, what is Emory's current market price?

* **18-3** What would you expect Emory Medical's (Problem 18-2 above) common stock price to be at the end of next year? That is, solve for P_1. Assume that growth projections and investor-required returns remain constant.

* **18-4** You can buy a share of Mori Electronics common stock today for $36. Next year's dividend (D_1) is expected to be $2.52. The market rate of return for stocks in this risk class is 13 percent. If investors expect Mori Electronics to grow at a constant rate in the future, what rate of growth, g, are they expecting?

18-5 Thornhill, Inc. paid a dividend of $2.50 last year. You expect the dividend to grow at 5 percent per year for the next 3 years, and you plan to hold the stock for 3 years and then sell it—if you do indeed decide to purchase the stock.

* a. What is the expected dividend for each of the next three years? That is, calculate D_1, D_2, and D_3. Note that D_0 = $2.50.

* b. If the appropriate discount rate is 10 percent, and the first of these dividend payments will occur one year from today, what is the present value of the dividend stream? That is, calculate the PV of D_1, D_2, and D_3, and sum these PVs.

*Refer to Appendix E for check answers to problems with asterisks.

c. You expect the price of the stock to be $60.78 three years from now; that is, you expect P_3 to equal $60.78. Discounted at a 10 percent rate, what is the present value of this future stock price? That is, calculate the PV of $60.78.

* d. If you plan to buy the stock, hold it for 3 years, and then sell it for $60.78, what is the most you should pay for it if your minimum required return is 10 percent?

e. Use Equation 18-4 to calculate the present value of this stock. Assume that the rate of growth is a constant 5 percent.

f. Is the value of this stock to you dependent on how long you plan to hold it? In other words, if your planned holding period were 2 years or 5 years rather than 3 years, would this affect the value of the stock today, P_0?

18-6 a. Investors require a 15 percent rate of return on Baker Company's stock (k_s = 15%). At what price will the stock sell if the previous dividend was D_0 = $2 and investors expect dividends to grow at a constant compound rate of (1) minus 5 percent, (2) 0 percent, (3) 5 percent, and (4) 14 percent? [Hint: Use D_1 = D_0 (1 + g), not D_0, in the formula.]

b. In Part a what is the "formula price" for Baker's stock if the required rate of return is 15 percent and the expected growth rate is (1) 15 percent or (2) 20 percent? Are these results reasonable? Explain.

GR > MRR doesn't work

* 18-7 Tulsa Oil Company's oil and gas reserves are being depleted, and its costs of recovering a declining amount of crude petroleum products are rising each year. As a result, the company's earnings and dividends are declining at the rate of 10 percent per year. If D_0 = $5 and k_s = 12%, what is the value of Tulsa Oil's stock?

18-8 Dave Upton, an analyst at McEnally Associates, is in the process of evaluating Carolina Furniture Company's common stock. Carolina's earnings and dividends have been growing at a constant 7 percent for the past few years. Earnings last year were $3.00 per share and the payout ratio is 70 percent. Upton believes the security should sell to yield a 12 percent return.

a. Assuming the past growth rate and payout ratios continue, what is the indicated value of Carolina's stock?

b. Suppose that upon further investigation Upton determines that the firm's earnings and dividends will grow at 9 percent annually into the foreseeable future. This growth will result from Carolina's decision to move into new market areas. If no change in the firm's risk is foreseen, what is the value of the firm's stock, considering the new growth projections?

c. After consultation with fellow analysts, Upton determines that Carolina's expansion may trigger heavy competition from firms in the proposed expansion areas. This would increase Carolina's business risk and reduce its growth expectations. After considerable evaluation, Upton concludes that the investors' required return would rise to 15 percent and their growth expectations would return to the original 7 percent. What price for Carolina's stock would be warranted under these conditions?

18-9 Mountain Mike's (MM), a chain of stores specializing in camping and backpacking equipment, has been growing at a rate of 25 percent per year in recent years. This same growth rate is expected to last another 2 years.

After that time MM's financial manager expects the firm's growth will slow to a constant 6 percent.

  * **a.** Assuming that $D_0 = \$1$ and that the firm's required return, k_s, is 14 percent, what is MM's stock worth today? (Note: While we have not directly discussed a firm's valuation under supernormal growth conditions, the problem should be approached in a manner similar to that in Self-Test Problem 3.)

  b. Now assume that MM's period of supernormal (25 percent) growth will last for 5 years rather than 2 years. Describe how this longer supernormal growth period will affect the stock's price, dividend yield, and capital gains yield.

  c. Of what interest to investors is the changing relationship between dividend yield and capital gains over time?

18-10 The Callaway Company is a small jewelry manufacturer. The company has been successful and has grown. Now Callaway is planning to sell an issue of common stock to the public for the first time, and it faces the problem of setting an appropriate price on its common stock. The company and its investment bankers feel that the proper procedure is to select firms similar to it with publicly traded common stock and to make relevant comparisons.

Several jewelry manufacturers are reasonably similar to Callaway with respect to product mix, size, asset composition, and debt/equity proportions. Of these, Sonnet and Mailers are most similar. Data are given below. When analyzing these data, assume that 1979 and 1984 were reasonably "normal" years for all three companies; that is, these years were neither especially good nor bad in terms of sales, earnings, and dividends. At the time of the analysis, R_F was 10 percent and k_M was 15 percent. Sonnet is listed on the American Exchange, and Mailers on the NYSE, while Callaway will be traded in the OTC market.

	Sonnet	Mailers	Callaway (Totals)
Earnings per share			
1984	$ 4.50	$ 7.50	$1,200,000
1979	3.00	5.50	816,000
Price per share			
1984	$36.00	$65.00	———
Dividends per share			
1984	$ 2.25	$ 3.75	$ 600,000
1979	1.50	2.75	420,000
Book value per share			
1984	$30.00	$55.00	$9,000,000
Market/book ratio			
1984	120%	118%	———
Total assets, 1984	$28 million	$ 82 million	$20 million
Total debt, 1984	$12 million	$ 30 million	$11 million
Sales, 1984	$41 million	$140 million	$37 million

a. Assume that Callaway has 100 shares of stock outstanding. Use this information to calculate earnings per share (EPS), dividends per share (DPS), and book value per share for Callaway. (Note: Since there are only 100 shares outstanding, your results may seem a bit large.)

b. Based on your answer to Part a, do you think Callaway's stock would sell at a price in the same "ballpark" as Sonnet's and Mailers's, that is, sell in the range of $25 to $100 per share?

c. Assuming that Callaway's management can split the stock so that the 100 shares could be changed to 1,000 shares, 100,000 shares, or any other number, would such an action make sense in this case? Why?

d. Now assume that Callaway did split its stock and has 400,000 shares. Calculate new values for EPS, DPS, and book value per share.

e. What can you say about the relative growth rates of the three companies?

f. What can you say about their dividend payout policies?

g. Return on equity (ROE) can be measured as EPS/book value per share, or as total earnings/total equity. Calculate ROEs for the three companies.

h. Calculate debt/total assets ratios for the three companies.

i. Calculate P/E ratios for Sonnet and Mailers. Are these P/Es consistent with the growth and ROE data? If not, what other factors could explain the relative P/E ratios?

j. Now determine a range of values for Callaway's stock, with 400,000 shares outstanding, by applying Sonnet's and Mailers' P/E ratios, price/dividends ratios, and price/book value ratios to your data for Callaway. For example, one possible price for Callaway's stock is (P/E Sonnet)(EPS Callaway) = (8)($3) = $24 per share. Similar calculations would produce a range of prices based on both Sonnet and Mailers data.

k. Using the equation $k = D_1/P_0 + g$, find approximate k values for Sonnet and Mailers. Then use these values in the constant growth stock price model to find a price for Callaway's stock.

l. At what price do you think Callaway's shares should be offered to the public? You will want to find the *equilibrium price,* i.e., a price that will be low enough to induce investors to buy the stock, but not so low that it will rise sharply immediately after it is issued. Think about relative growth rates, ROEs, dividend yields, and total returns ($k = D/P + g$). Also, as you think about the appropriate price, recognize that when Howard Hughes let the Hughes Tool Company go public, different investment bankers proposed prices that ranged from $20 to $30 per share. Hughes naturally accepted the $30 price, and the stock jumped to $40 almost immediately. Nobody's perfect!

m. Would your recommended price be different if the offering were by the Callaway family, selling some of their 400,000 shares, or if it were new stock authorized by the company? For example, another 100,000 shares could be authorized, which when issued would bring the outstanding shares up to 500,000, with 400,000 shares owned by the Callaways and 100,000 shares held by the public. If the Callaways sell their own shares, they receive the proceeds as their own personal funds. If the company sells newly issued shares, the company receives the funds and presumably uses the money to expand the business.

n. If the price you selected in Part l above were actually established as the price at which the stock would be offered to the public, approximately how much money, in total, would Callaway actually receive?

Answers to Self-Test Problems

ST-1　a. This is not necessarily true. Since Company B plows back two thirds of its earnings, its growth rate should exceed that of Company A, but A pays higher dividends ($3 versus $1). We cannot say which stock should have the higher price.

　　b. Again, we just do not know which price would be higher.

　　c. This is false. The changes in k_d and k_s would have a greater impact on B's stock—its price would decline more.

　　d. Once again, we just do not know which expected return would be higher. The total expected return for A is $k_A = D_1/P_0 + g = 15\% + 0\% = 15\%$. The total expected return for B will have D_1/P_0 less than 15 percent and g greater than 0 percent, but $\hat{k}_B$ could be either greater or less than A's total expected return, 15 percent.

　　e. We have eliminated a, b, c, and d, so e must be correct. Based on the available information, A's and B's stocks should sell at about the same price, $20. Thus $\hat{k}_s = \$3/\$20 = 15\%$ for both A and B. B's current dividend yield is $\$1/\$20 = 5\%$. Therefore $g = 15\% - 5\% = 10\%$.

ST-2 The first step is to solve for g, the unknown variable, in the constant growth equation. Since D_1 is unknown, substitute $D_0(1 + g)$ as follows:

$$P_0 = \frac{D_0(1 + g)}{k_s - g}$$

$$\$24 = \frac{\$1.60(1 + g)}{0.12 - g}.$$

Solving for g, we find the growth rate to be 5 percent. The next step is to use the growth rate to project the stock price 5 years hence:

$$P_5 = \frac{D_0(1 + g)^6}{k_s - g}$$

$$= \frac{\$1.60(1.05)^6}{0.12 - 0.05}$$

$$= \$30.63.$$

[Alternatively, $P_5 = \$24(1.05)^5 = \$30.63$.]

Therefore, Karp Company's expected stock price 5 years from now, P_5, is $30.63.

ST-3　a. *Step 1:* Calculate the PV of the dividends paid during the supernormal growth period:

$$D_1 = \$1.1500(1.18) = \$1.3570.$$
$$D_2 = \$1.3570(1.18) = \$1.6013.$$
$$D_3 = \$1.6013(1.15) = \$1.8415.$$

$$\text{PV D} = \$1.3570(0.8929) + \$1.6013(0.7972) + \$1.8415(0.7118)$$
$$= \$1.2117 + \$1.2766 + \$1.3108$$
$$= \$3.7991 \cong \$3.80.$$

Step 2: Find the PV of the stock's price at the end of Year 3:

$$P_3 = \frac{D_4}{k_s - g} = \frac{D_3(1 + g)}{k_s - g}$$

$$= \frac{\$1.8415(1.06)}{0.12 - 0.06}$$

$$= \$32.53.$$

$$\text{PV } P_3 = \$32.53(0.7118) = \$23.15.$$

Step 3: Sum the two components to find the price of the stock today:

$$P_0 = \$3.80 + \$23.15 = \$26.95.$$

b.
$$P_1 = \$1.6013(0.8929) + \$1.8415(0.7972) + \$32.53(0.7972)$$
$$= \$1.4298 + \$1.4680 + \$25.9329$$
$$= \$28.8307 \cong \$28.83.$$

$$P_2 = \$1.8415(0.8929) + \$32.53(0.8929)$$
$$= \$1.6443 + \$29.0460$$
$$= \$30.6903 \cong \$30.69.$$

c.

Year	Dividend Yield	Capital Gains Yield	Total Return
1	$\dfrac{\$1.3570}{\$26.95} = 5.04\%$	$\dfrac{\$28.83 - \$26.95}{\$26.95} = 6.98\%$	$\cong 12\%$
2	$\dfrac{\$1.6013}{\$28.83} = 5.55\%$	$\dfrac{\$30.69 - \$28.83}{\$28.83} = 6.45\%$	12
3	$\dfrac{\$1.8415}{\$30.69} = 6.00\%$	$\dfrac{\$32.53 - \$30.69}{\$30.69} = 6.00\%$	12

Selected References

For a wealth of facts and figures on a major segment of the stock market, see:
New York Stock Exchange, *Fact Book* (New York, published annually).

For both a description of the stock markets and some further facts and figures, see:
Reilly, Frank K., *Investment Analysis and Portfolio Management*, 2nd ed. (Hinsdale, IL: Dryden Press, 1985).

Sharpe, William F., *Investments,* 2nd ed. (Englewood Cliffs, NJ: Prentice-Hall, 1984).

For a discussion of the current state of investment banking and trends in the industry, see:

Hayes, S. L., "The Transformation of Investment Banking," *Harvard Business Review,* January–February 1979, 153–170.

Other good references on specific aspects of equity financing include the following:

Block, Stanley, and Marjorie Stanley, "The Financial Characteristics and Price Movement Patterns of Companies Approaching the Unseasoned Securities Market in the Late 1970s," *Financial Management,* Winter 1980, 30–36.

Bowyer, J. W., and J. B. Yawitz, "The Effect of New Equity Issues on Utility Stock Prices," *Public Utilities Fortnightly,* May 22, 1980, 25–28.

Fabozzi, Frank J., "Does Listing on the AMEX Increase the Value of Equity?" *Financial Management,* Spring 1981, 43–50.

Hansen, Robert S., and John M. Pinkerton, "Direct Equity Financing: A Resolution to a Paradox," *Journal of Finance,* June 1982, 651–665.

Logue, D. E., and R. A. Jarrow, "Negotiation versus Competitive Bidding in the Sale of Securities by Public Utilities," *Financial Management,* Autumn 1978, 31–39.

Warrants and Convertibles

18A

In Chapter 18 we discussed the sale of equity securities to investors. It happens at times that a company may wish to sell equity but its management determines that market conditions are not favorable for an immediate equity issue. In such a situation the company may decide to sell equity indirectly—through convertible securities or securities with warrants attached. Additionally, the use of warrants and convertibles can make a company's securities attractive to an even broader range of investors, thereby increasing the supply of capital and decreasing its cost. Reducing the cost of capital, as we learn in Chapter 20, helps to maximize the value of the firm's stock. Because warrants and convertibles are rapidly gaining popularity, a knowledge of these instruments is especially important today.

Warrants

A **warrant** is an **option** to buy a stated number of shares of stock at a specified price. Generally, warrants are distributed with debt, and they are used to induce investors to buy a firm's long-term debt at a lower interest rate than would otherwise be required. For example, when Trans Pacific Airlines (TPA) wanted to sell $50 million of 20-year bonds in 1976, the company's investment bankers informed the financial vice president that the bonds would be difficult to sell and that an interest rate of 14 percent would be required. As an alternative, the bankers suggested that investors might be willing to buy the bonds at a rate as low as 10⅜ percent if the company would offer 30 warrants with each $1,000 bond, each warrant entitling the holder to buy one share of common stock at a price of $22 per share. The stock was selling for $20 per share at the time. The warrants would expire in 1986 if not exercised previously.

Why would investors be willing to buy Trans Pacific's bonds at a yield of only 10⅜ percent just because warrants were also offered as

warrant
An option to buy a stated number of shares of common stock at a specified price.

option
A contract giving the holder the right to buy or sell an asset at some predetermined price within a specified period of time.

519

part of the package? To answer this question, we must first see how warrants are valued in the market.

Formula Value of a Warrant

Warrants have both a **formula,** or **exercise, value,** which is equal to the value of the warrant if it were exercised today, and an actual price that is determined in the marketplace. The formula value is found by use of the following equation:

$$\begin{matrix} \text{Formula,} \\ \text{of exercise,} \\ \text{value} \end{matrix} = \left(\begin{matrix} \text{Market price} \\ \text{of common} \\ \text{stock} \end{matrix} - \begin{matrix} \text{Option} \\ \text{price} \end{matrix} \right) \times \left(\begin{matrix} \text{Number of shares} \\ \text{each warrant entitles} \\ \text{owner to purchase} \end{matrix} \right).$$

For instance, a TPA warrant entitles the holder to purchase one share of common stock at $22 a share. If the market price of the common stock rose to $64.50, the formula value of the warrant would be

$$(\$64.50 - \$22) \times 1.0 = \$42.50.$$

The formula gives a negative value when the stock is selling for less than the option price. For example, if TPA stock is selling for $20, the formula value of the warrants is minus $2.

Actual Price of a Warrant

Generally, warrants actually sell at prices above their formula values. When TPA stock sold for $20, the warrants had a formula value of minus $2 but were selling at a price of $8. This represented a premium of $10 above the formula value.

Table 18A-1
**Formula and Actual Values of TPA Warrants at
Different Market Prices of Common Stock**

Price of Stock	Formula Value	Actual Warrant Price	Premium
$ 20.00	$−2.00	$ 8.00	$10.00
22.00	0.00	9.00	9.00
23.00	1.00	9.75	8.75
24.00	2.00	10.50	8.50
33.67	11.67	17.37	5.70
52.00	30.00	32.00	2.00
75.00	53.00	54.00	1.00
100.00	78.00	78.50	0.50
150.00	128.00	Not available	—

TPA stock rose substantially after the bonds with warrants were issued in 1976. A set of TPA stock prices, together with actual and formula warrant values, is given in Table 18A-1 and plotted in Figure
18A-1. At any stock price below $22, the formula value of the warrants
is negative; beyond $22, each $1 increase in the price of the stock
brings with it a $1 increase in the formula value of the warrants. The
actual market price of the warrants lies above the formula value at each
price of the common stock. Notice, however, that the premium of market price over formula value declines as the price of the common stock
increases. For example, when the common stock sold for $22 and the
warrants had a zero formula value, their actual price, and the premium, was $9. As the price of the stock rises, the *formula value* of the
warrants matches the increase dollar for dollar, but for a while the *market price* of the warrants climbs less rapidly and the premium declines.

Figure 18A-1
Formula and Actual Values of
TPA Warrants at Different Common Stock Prices
Warrants have both a formula value (value if exercised today) and an actual market
value, the operations of which are compared graphically in this figure. As the formula
warrant value increases dollar for dollar with the stock price, the premium of market
warrant price over formula value declines. At low formula values, premiums are high
because the investor has large gain and small loss potentials. As stock prices (and
formula values) rise, this leverage effect is diminished, causing the premium to decrease.

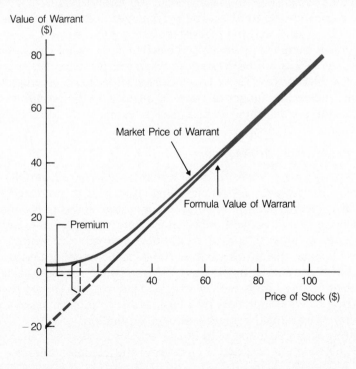

The premium is $9 when the stock sells for $22 a share, but it declines to $1 by the time the stock price has risen to $75 a share. Beyond this point the premium seems virtually to disappear.

Why does this pattern exist? Why should the warrant ever sell for more than its formula value, and why does the premium decline as the price of the stock increases? The answer lies in the speculative appeal of warrants—they enable a person to gain a high degree of personal leverage when buying securities. To illustrate, suppose TPA warrants sold for exactly their formula value. Now suppose you are thinking of investing in the company's common stock at a time when it is selling for $25 a share. If you buy a share and the price rises to $50 in a year, you have made a 100 percent capital gain. However, had you bought the warrants at their formula value ($3 when the stock sells for $25), your capital gain would have been $25 on a $3 investment, or 833 percent. At the same time, your total loss potential with the warrant is only $3, while the loss potential from the purchase of the stock is $25. The huge capital gains potential, combined with the loss limitation, is clearly worth something—the exact amount it is worth to investors is the amount of the premium.

But why does the premium decline as the price of the stock rises? The answer is that both the leverage effect and the loss protection feature decline at high stock prices. For example, if you are thinking of buying the stock at $75 a share, the formula value of the warrants is $53. If the stock price doubles to $150, the formula value of TPA warrants goes from $53 to $128. The percentage capital gain on the stock is still 100 percent, but the percentage gain on the warrant is now only 142 percent versus 833 percent in the earlier case. Moreover, notice that the loss potential on the warrant is much greater when the warrant is selling at high prices. These two factors, the declining leverage impact and the increasing danger of losses, explain why the premium diminishes as the price of the common stock rises.

Use of Warrants in Financing

In the past, warrants have generally been used by small, rapidly growing firms as "sweeteners" when selling either debt or preferred stocks. Such firms are frequently regarded by investors as being highly risky. Their bonds could be sold only if they were willing to pay extremely high rates of interest and to accept very restrictive indenture provisions. To avoid this, firms such as Trans Pacific often offered warrants along with the bonds. In the early 1970s, however, AT&T raised $1.57 billion by selling bonds with warrants. This was the largest financing of any type ever undertaken by a business firm, and it marked the first use ever of warrants by a large, strong corporation.

Getting warrants along with bonds enables investors to share in the company's growth, if it does in fact grow and prosper; therefore investors are willing to accept a lower bond interest rate and less restrictive indenture provisions. A bond with warrants has some characteristics of debt and some characteristics of equity. It is a hybrid security that provides the financial manager with an opportunity to expand the firm's mix of securities, appealing to a broader group of investors, and thus possibly lowering the firm's cost of capital.

Warrants can also bring in additional funds. The option price is generally set at from 10 to 20 percent above the market price of the stock at the time of the bond issue. If the firm does grow and prosper, and if its stock price rises above the option price at which shares may be purchased, warrant holders will surrender their warrants and buy stock at the stated price.

Convertible Securities

Convertible securities are bonds or preferred stocks that can be exchanged for common stock at the option of the holder and under specified terms and conditions. Unlike the exercise of warrants, which brings in additional funds to the firm, converting a bond does not bring in additional capital; debt on the balance sheet is simply replaced by common stock. Of course, this reduction of the debt ratio will make it easier to obtain additional debt capital, but this is a separate action.

One of the most important provisions of a convertible bond is the number of shares of stock a bondholder receives upon conversion, defined as the **conversion ratio, R.** Related to the conversion ratio is the **conversion price, P_c,** which is the effective price paid for the common stock when conversion occurs. The relationship between the conversion ratio and the conversion price is illustrated by the Adams Electric Company's convertible debentures, issued at their $1,000 par value in 1978. At any time prior to maturity on July 1, 1998, a debenture holder can turn in a bond and receive in its place 20 shares of common stock; therefore R = 20. The bond has a par value of $1,000, so the holder is giving up this amount upon conversion. Dividing the $1,000 par value by the 20 shares received gives a conversion price of $50 a share:

convertible securities
Bonds or preferred stocks that are exchangeable at the option of the holder for common stock of the issuing firm.

conversion ratio, R
The number of shares of common stock that may be obtained by converting a convertible bond or share of convertible preferred stock.

conversion price, P_c
The effective price paid for common stock when the stock is obtained by converting either convertible preferred stocks or convertible bonds.

$$\text{Conversion price} = P_c = \frac{\text{Par value of bond}}{\text{Shares received}},$$

or

$$P_c = \frac{\$1,000}{R} = \frac{\$1,000}{20} = \$50.$$

Therefore

$$R = \frac{\$1,000}{P_c} = \frac{\$1,000}{\$50} = 20 \text{ shares.}$$

Once R is set, this establishes the value of P_c, and vice versa.

Like warrant option prices, the conversion price is characteristically set at from 10 to 20 percent above the prevailing market price of the common stock at the time the convertible issue is sold. Exactly how the conversion price is established can best be understood after examining some of the reasons firms use convertibles.

Advantages of Convertibles

Convertibles offer advantages to corporations as well as to individual investors by functioning in the following two ways:

1. As a "sweetener" when selling debt. A company can sell debt with lower interest rates and less restrictive convenants by giving investors a chance to share in potential capital gains. Convertibles, like bonds with warrants, offer this possibility.

2. To sell common stock at prices higher than those currently prevailing. Many companies actually want to sell common stock, not debt, but feel that the price of their stock is temporarily depressed. Management may know, for example, that earnings are depressed because of a strike but think that they will snap back during the next year and pull the price of the stock up with them. To sell stock now would require giving up more shares to raise a given amount of money than management thinks is necessary. However, setting the conversion price 10 to 20 percent above the present market price of the stock will require giving up 10 to 20 percent fewer shares when the bonds are converted than would be required if stock were sold directly.

Notice, however, that management is counting on the stock's price rising above the conversion price to make the bonds attractive in conversion. If the stock price does not rise and conversion does not occur, then the company is saddled with debt.

How can the company be sure that conversion will occur when the price of the stock rises above the conversion price? Typically, convertibles contain a **call provision** that enables the issuing firm to force bondholders to convert. Suppose the conversion price is $50, the conversion ratio is 20, the market price of the common stock has risen to $60, and the call price on the convertible bond is $1,050. If the company calls the bond, bondholders can either convert into common stock with a market value of $1,200 or allow the company to redeem the bond for $1,050. Naturally, bondholders prefer $1,200 to $1,050, so conversion occurs. The call provision therefore gives the company a means of forcing conversion, provided the market price of the stock is greater than the conversion price.

call provision
A provision in a bond contract that gives the issuer the right to redeem the bonds under specified terms prior to the normal maturity date.

Disadvantages of Convertibles

From the standpoint of the issuer, convertibles have two important disadvantages: (1) Although the convertible bond does give the issuer the opportunity to sell common stock at a price 10 to 20 percent higher than the price at which it could otherwise be sold, if the common stock greatly increases in price, the issuing firm may find that it would have been better off if it had waited and simply sold the common stock. (2) If the company truly wants to raise equity capital, and if the price of the stock does not rise sufficiently after the bond is issued, then the company is stuck with debt. This debt will, however, have a low interest rate.

Decisions on the Use of Warrants and Convertibles

The Winchester Company, an electronic circuit and component manufacturer with assets of $60 million, illustrates a typical case in which convertibles proved useful. Winchester's profits had been depressed as a result of its heavy expenditures on research and development for a new product. This situation held down the growth rate of earnings and dividends; the price/earnings ratio was only 18 times, as compared with an industry average of 22. At the current $2 earnings per share and P/E of 18, the stock was selling for $36 a share. The Winchester family owned 70 percent of the 1,500,000 shares outstanding, or 1,050,000 shares. It wanted to retain majority control but could not buy more stock.

The heavy R&D expenditures had resulted in the development of a new type of printed circuit that management believed would be highly profitable. Twenty-five million dollars was needed to build and equip new production facilities, but profits were not expected to flow into the company for some 18 months after construction on the new plant was started. Winchester's debt amounted to $27 million, or 45 percent of assets, well above the 25 percent industry average. Its debt indenture provisions restricted the company from selling additional debt unless the new debt was subordinated to outstanding debt.

The company's investment bankers informed J. H. Winchester, Jr., the financial vice president, that subordinated debentures could not be sold at any reasonable interest rate unless they were convertible or had warrants attached. The investment bankers were willing to sell either convertibles or bonds with warrants at a 10 percent interest rate. They concluded that the convertible bonds would have a conversion price of $43.48. If bonds were sold with warrants attached, investors would be allowed to buy 20 new shares of Winchester's common stock at a special exercise price of $40 over the next 5 years. On the other hand, if the firm chose to sell common stock directly, it would net, after flota-

Table 18A-2
Financing Options Available to the Winchester Company Prior to Conversion or Exercise of Warrants (in Thousands of Dollars)

Original Position

	Current liabilities	$10,000
	Long-term debt	17,000
	Common stock ($2)	3,000
	Paid-in capital	10,000
	Retained earnings	20,000
Total assets $60,000	Total claims on assets	$60,000

Shares outstanding	= 1.50 million.
Family-controlled shares	= 1.05 million.
Family control (%)	= 70%.
Debt ratio (D/TA)	= 45%.

Equity Option

	Current liabilities	$10,000
	Long-term debt	17,000
	Common stock ($2)	4,515
	Paid-in capital	33,485
	Retained earnings	20,000
Total assets $85,000	Total claims on assets	$85,000

Shares outstanding	= 2.26 million.
Family-controlled shares	= 1.05 million.
Family control (%)	= 47%.
Debt ratio (D/TA)	= 32%.

Debt Option[a]

	Current liabilities	$10,000
	Long-term debt	42,000
	Common stock ($2)	3,000
	Paid-in capital	10,000
	Retained earnings	20,000
Total assets $85,000	Total claims on assets	$85,000

Shares outstanding	= 1.50 million.
Family-controlled shares	= 1.05 million.
Family control (%)	= 70%.
Debt ratio (D/TA)	= 61%.

[a]The balance sheet will not differ under either the convertible or debt-with-warrants option before exercise of the options.

tion costs, $33 a share. The effect of each of these three financing options is presented in Table 18A-2. Note that there is no difference on the balance sheet between the convertible debt and the debt with warrants attached as long as the options are unexercised.

Which of the alternatives should Winchester choose? First, note that if common stock were used, the company would have to sell 757,576 shares ($25 million divided by $33). Combined with the 450,000 shares already held outside the family, this amounts to 1,207,576 shares versus the family holdings of 1,050,000. Thus the family would lose majority control if common stock were sold.

However, if the 10 percent convertible bonds were sold, conversion would yield only 575,000 new shares. In this case the family would have 1,050,000 shares versus 1,025,000 for outsiders. If bonds with warrants were sold, the results would be much the same with respect to control. If all warrants were exercised, 500,000 new shares would be created, meaning the family would still control 52.5 percent of the common stock. Thus in either of the debt options the Winchester family could retain absolute control.

In addition to assuring family control, using the convertibles or warrants would also benefit earnings per share in the long run—the total number of shares would be smaller because fewer new shares would be issued to get the $25 million, so earnings per share would be greater. Before conversion or exercise, however, the firm would have a considerable amount of debt outstanding. Adding $25 million would raise the total debt to $52 million against new total assets of $85 million, so the debt ratio would be over 61 percent versus the 25 percent industry average. This could be dangerous. If delays were encountered in bringing the new plant into production, if demand failed to meet expectations, if the company experienced a strike, if the economy went into a recession—if any of these things occurred—the company would be extremely vulnerable because of its high debt ratio.

In the present case the decision was made to sell the 10 percent convertible debentures. Two years later earnings climbed to $3 a share, the P/E ratio to 20, and the price of the stock to $60. The bonds were called, and, of course, conversion occurred. After conversion, debt amounted to approximately $27.5 million against total assets of $87.5 million (some earnings had been retained), so the debt ratio was down to a more reasonable 31 percent. The effect of conversion on Winchester's balance sheet along with the effect of warrant exercise (if that option had been chosen) is presented in Table 18A-3.

Convertibles were chosen rather than bonds with warrants for the following reason. If a firm has a high debt ratio and its near-term prospects are favorable, it can anticipate a rise in the price of its stock and thus be able to call the bonds and force conversion. Warrants, on the other hand, have a stated life, and even though the price of the firm's stock rises, the warrants may not be exercised until near their expira-

Table 18A-3
The Winchester Company after Conversion of Debt or Exercise of Warrants (in Thousands of Dollars)

After Debt Conversion

	Current liabilities	$10,500
	Long-term debt	17,000
	Common stock ($2)	4,150
	Paid-in capital	33,850
	Retained earnings[a]	22,000
Total assets $87,500	Total claims on assets	$87,500

Shares outstanding   = 2.075 million.
Family-controlled shares = 1.050 million.
Family control (%)   = 50.6%.
Debt ratio (D/TA)   = 31%.

After Exercise of Warrants

	Current liabilities	$ 10,500
	Long-term debt	42,000
	Common stock ($2)	4,000
	Paid-in capital	29,000
	Retained earnings[b]	22,000
Total assets $107,500	Total claims on assets	$107,500

Shares outstanding   = 2.00 million.
Family-controlled shares = 1.05 million.
Family control (%)   = 52.5%
Debt ratio (D/TA)   = 48.8%.

[a]The change in retained earnings is due to prior years' profitability and is not the result of the conversion of debt into equity.
[b]Again, the change in retained earnings is due to operations and not to the exercise of warrants.

---

tion date. If, subsequent to the favorable period (during which convertibles could have been called), the firm finds itself in a less favorable position and the price of its stock falls, the warrants lose their value and may never be exercised. The heavy debt burden will then become aggravated. Therefore the use of convertibles gives the firm greater control over the timing of future capital structure changes. This factor is of particular importance to the firm if its debt ratio is already high in relation to the risks of its line of business.

Reporting Earnings if Warrants or Convertibles are Outstanding

If warrants or convertibles are outstanding, a firm could theoretically report earnings per share in three ways:
1. *Simple EPS,* where earnings available to common stockholders are

divided by the average number of shares actually outstanding during the period.

2. *Primary EPS,* where earnings available are divided by the average number of shares that would have been outstanding if warrants and convertibles "likely to be converted in the near future" had actually been exercised or converted. The accountants have a formula which basically compares the conversion or option price with the actual market value of the stock to determine the likelihood of conversion, and they also add interest on the convertible bonds back into earnings.

3. *Fully diluted EPS,* which is similar to primary EPS except that *all* warrants and convertibles are assumed to be exercised or converted, regardless of the likelihood of exercise or conversion.

Simple EPS is virtually never reported by firms which have warrants or convertibles likely to be exercised or converted—the SEC requires that primary and fully diluted earnings be shown. For firms with large amounts of option securities outstanding, there can be a substantial difference between the two EPS figures. The purpose of the provision is, of course, to give investors a more accurate picture of the firm's true profit position.

Summary

Both warrants and convertibles are forms of options used to finance business firms. The use of such long-term options is encouraged by an economic environment in which either recessions or booms can occur. The senior position of the securities protects against recessions, while the option feature offers the opportunity for participation in rising stock markets.

Both convertibles and warrants are used as "sweeteners." The option privileges they grant may make it possible for small companies to sell debt or preferred stock that otherwise could not be sold. For large companies the "sweeteners" result in lower costs of the securities sold.

The conversion of bonds by their holders does not provide additional funds to the company. The exercise of warrants does provide such funds. The conversion of securities results in reduced debt ratios. The exercise of warrants also strengthens the equity position, but it still leaves the debt or preferred stock on the balance sheet. A firm with a high debt ratio should probably choose to use convertibles rather than senior securities carrying warrants. A firm with a moderate or low debt ratio may choose to employ warrants.

In the past, larger and stronger firms tended to favor convertibles over bonds with warrants, so most warrants have been issued by smaller, weaker concerns. AT&T's use of warrants in its $1.57 billion financing has caused other large firms to reexamine their positions on warrants, and warrants have come into increasing use since that time.

Key Terms You should be able to define each of the following terms:

Warrant

Option

Formula, or exercise, value

Convertible securities

Conversion ratio, R

Conversion price, P_c

Call provision

Problem

18A-1 The Dirk Manufacturing Company has grown rapidly during the past 5 years. Recently its investment bankers urged the company to consider increasing its permanent financing. Its bank loan under a line of credit has risen to $250,000, carrying 8 percent interest. Dirk has been 30 to 60 days late in paying trade creditors.

Discussions with the investment bankers have resulted in the decision to raise $500,000 at this time. The investment bankers have assured Dirk that the following alternatives are feasible (flotation costs will be ignored):

1. Sell common stock at $8.

2. Sell convertible bonds at an 8 percent coupon, convertible into 100 shares of common stock for each $1,000 bond (that is, the conversion price is $10 per share).

3. Sell debentures at an 8 percent coupon, each $1,000 bond carrying 100 warrants to buy common stock at $10.

Tom O'Brien, the president, owns 80 percent of the common stock of Dirk Manufacturing Company and wishes to retain control of the company. One hundred thousand shares are outstanding. Additional information is given in the tables below.

a. Show the new balance sheet under each alternative. For Alternatives 2 and 3, show the balance sheet after conversion of the debentures or exercise of the warrants. Assume that one half of the funds raised will be used to reduce the bank loan and one half to increase total assets.

b. Show O'Brien's control position under each alternative, assuming that he does not purchase additional shares.

c. What is the effect on earnings per share of each alternative if it is assumed that profits before interest and taxes will be 20 percent of total assets?

d. What will be the debt ratio under each alternative?

e. Which of the three alternatives would you recommend to O'Brien, and why?

Dirk Manufacturing Company: Balance Sheet

		Current liabilities	$400,000
		Common stock, par $1	100,000
		Retained earnings	50,000
Total assests	$550,000	Total claims	$550,000

Dirk Manufacturing Company: Income Statement

Sales	$1,100,000
All costs except interest	990,000
Gross profit	$ 110,000
Interest	20,000
Profit before taxes	$ 90,000
Taxes at 50%	45,000
Profits after taxes	$ 45,000
Shares	100,000
Earnings per share	$0.45
Price/earnings ratio	19×
Market price of stock	$8.55

The Target Capital Structure   19

Decision in Finance

Is Cities Service Worth the Price?

From Armand Hammer's point of view, Cities Service was a perfect acquisition for Occidental Petroleum. Cities, rich in domestic oil and gas holdings, would offset one of Oxy's long-standing weaknesses: its heavy dependence on volatile foreign sources of crude.

Granted, Cities' $4 billion purchase price was a little steep, but Oxy was a huge company and its chairman, the 84-year-old Dr. Hammer, was a very resourceful fund-raiser. His plans called for Oxy to borrow $1.9 billion, issue $1.6 billion in preferred stock, and float $530 million in zero coupon notes with accrued interest at about 13 percent that would start coming due 3 years hence, in 1985.

As a result of its own borrowing and its assumption of Cities' obligations, Oxy's long-term debt would rise from $1 billion to almost $5 billion, doubling its long-term liabilities to 50 percent of total capitalization. In addition, issuing new shares would raise its preferred stock obligations from 12 percent to 21 percent of capitalization. Oxy's annual interest charges would increase to $277 million, and its preferred stock dividends would cost $327 million. To meet its preferred stock obligations alone, Oxy would need to earn $4 per share.

Chairman Hammer was optimistic about Oxy's ability to absorb Cities Service and the ensuing debt load, however. After all, Oxy's earnings had hit a record $7.55 per share in 1981. And Dr. Hammer's calculations showed that Oxy would be paying only $5 per barrel for Cities' 530 million barrels of oil in the ground, while the rest of the domestic oil industry was averaging a cost of $11 per barrel to find oil or its equivalent in gas.

As you read this chapter, consider the effects that the Cities Service acquisition might have on Occidental Petroleum's capital structure. If you were Armand Hammer, would you go through with the purchase? Why or why not?

See end of chapter for resolution.

This chapter considers the proper mix of securities: What proportions of short-term debt, long-term debt, and common equity should be used to finance a business? As we shall see, the firm analyzes a number of factors, then establishes a *target capital structure*. This target may change over time as conditions vary, but at any given moment the firm's management does have a specific capital structure in mind, and individual financing decisions should be consistent with this target. If the actual debt ratio is below the prescribed ratio, expansion capital will probably be raised by issuing debt, whereas stock will probably be sold if the debt ratio is above the target level.

capital structure
The percentage of each type of capital used by the firm—debt, preferred stock, and common equity.

Capital structure policy involves a choice between risk and expected returns. Using more debt raises the riskiness of the firm's earnings stream, but more debt generally means a higher expected rate of return. Higher risk tends to lower the stock's price, but a higher expected rate of return raises it. The **optimal capital structure** strikes a balance between these risks and returns and thus maximizes the price of the stock.

optimal capital structure
The capital structure that balances risks and returns to maximize stock price.

Types of Risk

Thus far in this text we have examined several types of risk that business firms face. For example, in Chapter 9 we examined *business risk,* the risk inherent in a firm's operations. In Chapter 16 we considered how capital budgeting affects the riskiness of the firm. In the same chapter we distinguished between *market risk,* which is measured by the firm's beta coefficient, and *total risk,* which includes both the beta risk *and* an element of risk which can be eliminated by diversification.

financial risk
The portion of total corporate risk over and above the basic business risk that results from using debt.

Now we introduce another dimension of the risk picture—**financial risk,** the additional risk borne by the investors as a result of the decision to use financing with a fixed financial charge, such as interest with debt financing.[1] Conceptually, the firm has a certain amount of risk inherent in its operations—this is its business risk. In the absence of debt in the capital structure, business risk equals total risk. When debt is used, total risk is apportioned, with most of it being allotted to one class of investors—the common stockholders. However, the common stockholders are compensated by a higher *expected* rate of return.

Financial Leverage

financial leverage
The extent to which fixed-income securities (debt and preferred stock) are used in a firm's capital structure.

Whereas operating leverage refers to the use of fixed operating costs, **financial leverage** refers to the use of fixed income securities—debt and preferred stock. In this section we show how financial leverage affects a firm's expected earnings per share, the riskiness of these earnings, and consequently the price of the firm's stock. As we shall see, the

---

[1]Preferred stock also adds to financial risk.

value of a firm that has no debt first rises as it substitutes debt for equity, then hits a peak, and finally declines as the use of debt becomes excessive. The objective of our analysis is to determine the point at which value is maximized; this point is then used as the **target capital structure.**

We can illustrate the effects of financial leverage with data for a firm, Santa Clara Industries (SCI). As shown in Table 19-1, the company now has no debt. Should it continue the policy of using no debt, or should it start using financial leverage? And if it does decide to substitute debt for equity, how far should it go? As in all such decisions, *the correct answer is that it should choose the capital structure that maximizes the price of its stock.*

Since the price of a share of stock is the present value of the stock's expected future dividends, if the use of financial leverage is to affect the stock's price, it must do so by changing either the expected dividend stream or the required rate of return on equity, k_s, or both. We first consider the effect of capital structure on earnings and dividends; then we examine its effect on k_s.

target capital structure
The point at which a firm's value is maximized.

Table 19-1
Data on Santa Clara Industries

I. Balance Sheet on 12/31/84

Current assets	$100,000	Debt	$	0
Net fixed assets	100,000	Common equity (10,000		
		shares outstanding)		200,000
Total assets	$200,000	Total claims		$200,000

II. Income Statement for 1984

Sales			$200,000
Fixed operating costs	$ 40,000		
Variable operating costs	120,000	160,000	
Earnings before interest and taxes (EBIT)		$ 40,000	
Interest		0	
Taxable income		$ 40,000	
Taxes (40%)		16,000	
Net income after taxes		$ 24,000	

III. Other Data
  1. Earnings per share = EPS = $24,000/10,000 shares = $2.40.
  2. Dividends per share = DPS = $24,000/10,000 shares = $2.40. (Thus SCI pays all of its earnings out as dividends. Alternatively stated, SCI has a 100 percent payout ratio.)
  3. Book value per share = $200,000/10,000 shares = $20.
  4. Market price per share = P_0 = $20. Thus the stock sells at its book value.
  5. Price/earnings ratio = P/E = $20/$2.40 = 8.33 times.

The Effect of Financial Leverage on Expected EPS

Changes in the use of debt will cause changes in earnings per share (EPS), and consequently in the stock price. To understand the relationship between financial leverage and EPS, consider first Table 19-2, which shows how SCI's cost of debt would vary if it used different percentages of debt in its capital structure. Naturally, the higher the percentage of debt, the more risky the debt, hence the higher the interest rate lenders will charge.

Table 19-3 shows how expected EPS varies with changes in financial leverage. The top third of the table shows EBIT at sales of $100,000, $200,000, and $300,000. EBIT is independent of financial leverage: EBIT does depend on operating leverage, but *EBIT does not depend on financial leverage.*

The middle third of Table 19-3 goes on to show the situation *if SCI continues to use no debt.* Net income after taxes is divided by the 10,000 shares outstanding to calculate EPS. If sales are as low as $100,000, EPS will be zero, but EPS will rise to $4.80 at sales of $300,000.

The EPS at each sales level is next multiplied by the probability of that sales level to calculate the expected EPS, which is $2.40 if SCI uses no debt. We also calculate the standard deviation of EPS to get an idea of the firm's risk at a zero debt ratio: $\sigma_{EPS} = \$1.52.$[2]

The lower third of the table shows the financial results that would occur *if the company financed with a debt/assets ratio of 50 percent.* In this situation $100,000 of the $200,000 total capital would be debt. The interest rate on the debt, 12 percent, is taken from Table 19-2. With $100,000 of 12 percent debt outstanding, the company's interest ex-

---

Table 19-2
Interest Rates for SCI with Different Debt/Assets Ratios

Amount Borrowed	Debt/Assets Ratio[a]	Interest Rate, k_d, on All Debt
$20,000	10%	8.0%
$40,000	20	8.3
$60,000	30	9.0
$80,000	40	10.0
$100,000	50	12.0
$120,000	60	15.0

[a]We assume that the firm must borrow in increments of $20,000. Also, we assume that SCI is unable to borrow more than $120,000, or 60 percent of assets, because of restrictions in its corporate charter.

---

[2]The procedure for calculating the standard deviation is explained in Chapter 16.

Table 19-3
SCI: EPS with Different Amounts of Financial Leverage
(Thousands of Dollars except Per Share Figures)

Probability of Indicated Sales	0.2	0.6	0.2
Sales	$100.0	$200.0	$300.0
Fixed costs	40.0	40.0	40.0
Variable costs (60% of sales)	60.0	120.0	180.0
Total costs (except interest)	$100.0	$160.0	$220.0
Earnings before interest and taxes (EBIT)	$ 0.0	$ 40.0	$ 80.0
Debt/Assets (D/A) = 0%			
Less: Interest	0.0	0.0	0.0
Earnings before taxes	0.0	40.0	80.0
Taxes (40%)	0.0	(16.0)	(32.0)
Net income after taxes	$ 0.0	$ 24.0	$ 48.0
Earnings per share on 10,000 shares (EPS)	$ 0.0	$ 2.40	$ 4.80
Expected EPS		$ 2.40	
Standard deviation of EPS		$ 1.52	
Debt/Assets (D/A) = 50%			
Less: Interest (0.12 × $100,000)	$ 12.0	$ 12.0	$ 12.0
Earnings before taxes	(12.0)	28.0	68.0
Taxes (40%)	4.8[a]	(11.2)	(27.2)
Net income after taxes	($ 7.2)	$ 16.8	$ 40.8
Earnings per share on 5,000 shares (EPS)	($ 1.44)	$ 3.36	$ 8.16
Expected EPS		$ 3.36	
Standard deviation of EPS		$ 3.04	

[a]Assumes tax credit on losses.

pense in Table 19-3 is $12,000 per year. This is a fixed cost, and it is deducted from EBIT as calculated in the top section. Next, taxes are taken out, to derive total net income. Then we calculate EPS = Net income after taxes ÷ Shares outstanding. With debt = 0, there are 10,000 shares outstanding. However, if half the equity is replaced by debt (debt = $100,000), then there will be only 5,000 shares outstanding, and we use this fact to determine the EPS figures that will result at each sales level. With a debt/assets ratio of 50 percent, EPS will be a negative $1.44 if sales are as low as $100,000; it will rise to $3.36 if sales are $200,000; and it will soar to $8.16 if sales are as high as $300,000.

The EPS distributions under the two financial structures are represented in Figure 19-1. Although expected EPS is much higher if financial leverage is employed, the graph makes it clear that the risk of low or even negative EPS is also higher if debt is used.

Figure 19-1
SCI: Probability Distribution of EPS with
Different Amounts of Financial Leverage

Financial leverage (debt via fixed-income securities) affects a firm's expected earnings per share and thus the price of its stock. With zero financial leverage, expected EPS is lower than expected EPS with 50 percent debt ($2.40 versus $3.36). Simultaneously, the probability of attaining $2.40 in EPS with zero debt is much higher than the probability of attaining $3.36 in EPS with 50 percent debt. In addition, with greater leverage, the probability of lower or even negative earnings is increased. Clearly, increased financial leverage carries with it both higher earnings and greater risk.

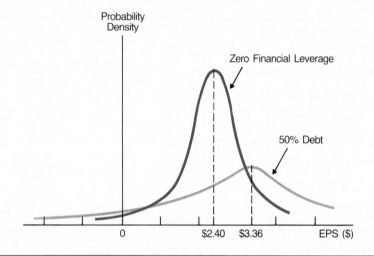

In their quarterly or annual reports, companies give stockholders an explanation of how earnings per share have been affected by an increase or decrease in debt financing. In this excerpt from the 1983 CBS Annual Report, under the Capital Structure section, CBS reports that reducing its current debt, increasing long-term debt, and issuing common stock have resulted in increased liquidity. Therefore, earnings per share increased from $3.95 in 1982 to $6.31 in 1983. (The EPS figures are not shown in this table but are reported in the company's Income Statement.)

Source: 1983 CBS Annual Report.

Capital Structure

In 1982 the Company strengthened its balance sheet. The maturity of total debt was significantly lengthened through the issuance of $150 million of AA rated ten-year 14½% notes in June 1982. The public sale of 1,650,000 shares of common stock in December 1982 added to the Company's capital base and enhanced debt capacity, providing greater flexibility for financial planning. In 1983, commercial paper and other current debt were substantially reduced. With the Company's ability to generate cash internally and a low level of total debt to capital, the Company believes its ample liquidity and capital resources position it well for the competitive environment of the 1980's.

	December 31				
	1983	1982	1981	1980	1979
	(Dollars in millions)				
Current Debt	$ 75.5	$ 123.1	$ 25.8	$ 22.8	$ 199.9
Long-Term Debt	232.5	238.0	222.6	217.2	104.3
Total Debt	308.0	361.1	248.4	240.0	304.2
Shareholders' Equity	1,440.5	1,336.3	1,245.2	1,183.6	1,071.1
Total Capital	**$1,748.5**	**$1,697.4**	**$1,493.6**	**$1,423.6**	**$1,375.3**
Debt as a Percentage of Capital	**17.6%**	**21.3%**	**16.6%**	**16.9%**	**22.1%**

Table 19-4
SCI: Expected EPS and Standard Deviation with Different Degrees of
Financial Leverage[a]

Debt/Assets Ratio	Expected EPS	Standard Deviation of EPS
0%	$2.40	$1.52
10	2.56	1.69
20	2.75	1.90
30	2.97	2.17
40	3.20	2.53
50	3.36	3.04
60	3.30	3.79

[a]Values for D/A = 0 and 50 percent are taken from Table 19-3. Values at other D/A ratios are calculated similarly.

These relationships among expected EPS, risk, and financial leverage are extended in Table 19-4 and Figure 19-2. Here we see that expected EPS rises for a while as the use of debt increases—interest charges rise, but a smaller number of shares outstanding as debt is substituted for equity still causes EPS to increase. However, EPS peaks at a debt ratio of 50 percent. Beyond this ratio interest rates rise so fast that EPS is depressed in spite of the falling number of shares outstanding. Risk, as measured by the standard deviation of EPS, rises continuously, and at an increasing rate, as debt is substituted for equity.

We see, then, that using leverage involves a risk/return trade-off; higher leverage increases expected earnings per share (at least for a while), but it also increases the firm's risk. Exactly how this trade-off should be resolved is discussed in the next section.

The Effect of Financial Leverage on Stock Prices

As we saw in the preceding section, Santa Clara Industries' EPS is maximized at a debt/assets ratio of 50 percent. Does this mean that SCI's optimal capital structure is 50 percent debt, 50 percent equity? Not necessarily. *The optimal capital structure is the one which maximizes the price of the firm's stock, and this may well call for a debt ratio different from the one which maximizes EPS.*

This statement is demonstrated in Table 19-5, which develops SCI's estimated stock price at different debt/assets ratios. The data in Columns 1, 2, and 3 are taken from Tables 19-2 and 19-4. The beta coefficients shown in Column 4 were estimated. Recall from Chapter 16 that beta measures a stock's relative volatility as compared to an average stock. It has been demonstrated both theoretically and empirically that

Figure 19-2
SCI: Relationship among Expected EPS, Risk, and Financial Leverage
As shown on the right side of this figure, financial risk rises at an increasing rate with
each addition of financial leverage. Earnings per share, on the other hand, rise only to a
certain point, as shown on the left. Beyond this peak, interest rates become prohibitive
and EPS begins to fall.

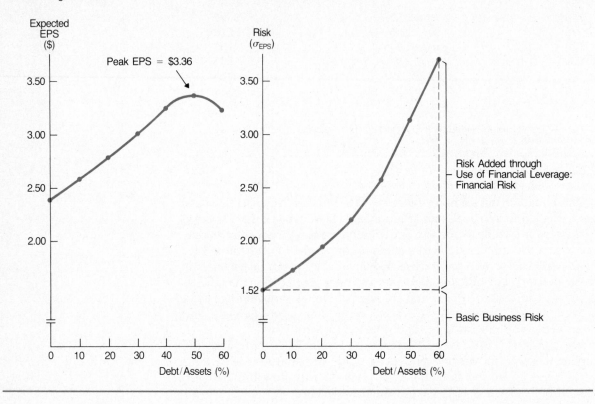

a firm's beta increases with its degree of financial leverage.[3] The exact
nature of this relationship for a given firm such as SCI is difficult to
estimate, but the values in Column 4 do show the approximate relationship.

Assuming that the riskless rate of return, R_F, is 6 percent and that
the required return on an average stock, k_M, is 10 percent, we use the
CAPM equation to develop the required rates of return for SCI as
shown in Column 5. Here we see that k_s is 12 percent if no financial
leverage is used, but that k_s rises to 16.8 percent if the company finances with 60 percent debt.

The "zero growth" stock valuation model developed in footnote c of
Table 19-5 is used, along with the Column 3 values of dividends and

---

[3]This point is discussed in detail in Eugene F. Brigham, *Financial Management: Theory and
Practice*, 3rd ed. (Hinsdale, IL: Dryden Press, 1982), Chapters 15 and 16.

See p. 537   541

Table 19-5
SCI: Stock Price Estimates with Different Debt/Assets Ratios

Debt/Assets (1)	k_d (2)	EPS (and DPS)[a] (3)	Estimated Beta (4)	$k_s = [R_F + b(k_M - R_F)]$[b] (5)	Implied Price[c] (6)	Resulting P/E Ratio (7)
0%	8.0%	$2.40	1.50	12.0%	$20.00	8.33
10	8.0	2.56	1.55	12.2	20.98	8.20
20	8.3	2.75	1.65	12.6	21.83	7.94
30	9.0	2.97	1.80	13.2	22.50	7.58
40	10.0	3.20	2.00	14.0	22.86	7.14
50	12.0	3.36 1.68	2.30	15.2	22.11	6.58
60	15.0	3.30	2.70	16.8	19.64	5.95

[a]We assume that SCI pays all of its earnings out as dividends, hence EPS = DPS.
[b]We assume that $R_F = 6\%$ and $k_M = 10\%$. Therefore, at debt/assets = 0, $k_s = 6\% + 1.5 (10\% - 6\%) = 6\% + 6\% = 12\%$. Other values of k_s are calculated similarly.
[c]In Chapter 18 we learned that under certain conditions the value of a share of stock is equal to $P = D_1/(k - g)$. We have already noted that SCI's payout is 100 percent; thus dividends and earnings are equivalent. Additionally, if all earnings are paid out as dividends, no retained earnings will be plowed back into the firm, and growth in earnings and dividends will be zero. Thus, in this special case, D = E and g = 0. Therefore at debt/assets = 0,

$$P_0 = \frac{E}{k_s}$$

$$P_0 = \frac{\$2.40}{0.12} = \$20.$$

$$\frac{1.68}{15.2}$$

Other prices are calculated similarly.

---

earnings per share and the Column 5 values of k_s, to develop the implied stock prices shown in Column 6. Here we see that the expected stock price first rises with financial leverage, hits a peak of $22.86 at a debt/assets ratio of 40 percent, and then begins to decline. *Thus SCI's optimal capital structure calls for 40 percent debt.*

The price/earnings ratios shown in Column 7 were calculated by dividing the implied price in Column 6 by the expected earnings given in Column 3. We use the pattern of P/E ratios as a check on the "reasonableness" of the other data. As a rule, P/E ratios do decline as the riskiness of a firm increases. Also, at the time the example was developed, the P/Es shown here were generally consistent with those of zero growth companies with varying amounts of financial leverage. Thus the data in Column 7 reinforce our confidence that the implied prices shown in Column 6 are reasonable.

The EPS and stock price data in Table 19-5 are plotted in Figure 19-3. As the graph shows, the debt/assets ratio that maximizes SCI's expected EPS is 50 percent, but the expected stock price is maximized with 40 percent debt. *Thus the optimal capital structure calls for 40 percent debt, 60 percent equity.* Management should set its target capital structure at these ratios, and if the present ratios are off target, move toward the target when new security offerings are made.

Figure 19-3
SCI: Relationship among Debt/Assets Ratio,
EPS, and Estimated Stock Prices

The amount of financial leverage that maximizes a firm's earnings per share is not necessarily the amount that will maximize its stock price. In this example, with data plotted from Table 19-5, the stock price is maximized at a debt/assets ratio of 40 percent, even though EPS would be higher at 50 percent. This firm will thus seek to target its capital structure at 40 percent debt, 60 percent equity.

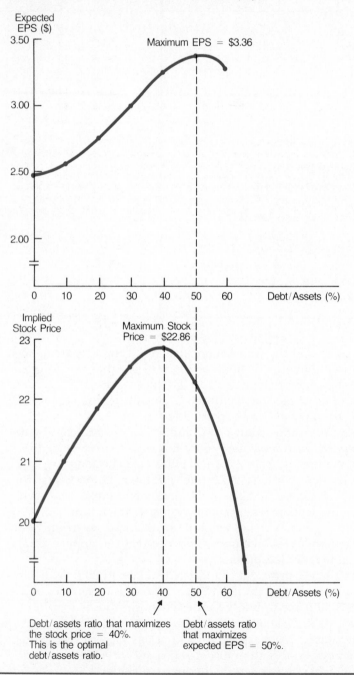

Degree of Financial Leverage

In Chapter 9 we investigated the effects of fixed operating charges on the firm's operating profits, EBIT. Changes in sales were magnified into greater than proportional changes in operating profits due to fixed operating charges.[4] As we have discussed in this chapter, the existence of fixed financial costs increases the variability (as measured by the standard deviation) of the firm's earnings. Another technique used to describe the firm's financial risk is its *degree of financial leverage (DFL)*.

Operating leverage affects earnings before interest and taxes (EBIT), while financial leverage affects earnings after interest and taxes, or the earnings available to common stockholders. In terms of Table 19-6, operating leverage affects the top section of the table, financial leverage the lower section. Thus, if SCI had more operating leverage, its fixed costs would be higher than $40,000, its variable cost ratio would be lower than 60 percent of sales, and earnings before interest and taxes would vary with sales to a greater extent. Financial leverage takes over where operating leverage leaves off, further magnifying the effect on earnings per share of a change in the level of sales. For this reason, operating leverage is sometimes referred to as *first-stage leverage* and financial leverage as *second-stage leverage*.

The **degree of financial leverage** is defined as the percentage change in earnings available to common shareholders that is associated with a given percentage change in earnings before interest and taxes (EBIT). Where fixed financial charges exist, a change in EBIT will result in a greater than proportional change in earnings per share for the firm. An equation has been developed as an aid in calculating the degree of financial leverage[5] for any given level of EBIT and financing charges, I:

degree of financial leverage The percentage change in earnings available to common shareholders that is associated with a given percentage change in earnings before interest and taxes.

---

[4]The degree of operating leverage, DOL, was computed in Equation 9-2 as

$$DOL = Q(P - V)/Q(P - V) - F.$$

For SCI,

$$DOL = (\$200{,}000 - 120{,}000)/(\$200{,}000 - 120{,}000 - 40{,}000)$$
$$= 2.0.$$

Therefore a change in sales will be magnified into a $2\times$ larger change in EBIT. Thus a 10 percent increase in sales will lead to a 20 percent increase in EBIT, but a sales decline of 7.5 percent will cause a 15 percent decline in EBIT.

[5]Utilizing the same symbols as those introduced in Chapter 9, we have

$$DFL = \frac{Q(P - V) - F}{Q(P - V) - F - I}.$$

However, since EBIT $\;\angle(P - V) - F$, Equation 19-1 represents a less cumbersome statement of DFL. While we have ignored preferred stock, its presence in the firm's financial structure will also increase the firm's financial leverage, and hence the DFL.

Table 19-6
Operating, Financial, and Total Leverage Effects for SCI with a 20 Percent Increase in Sales

Income Statement	Previous Status	Percentage Increase	Resulting Status
QP = Sales	$200,000	20%	$240,000
QV = Variable operating costs (60% of sales)	120,000		144,000
F = Fixed operating costs	40,000		40,000
EBIT = Operating profits	40,000	40	56,000
−I = Fixed financing charges[a]	12,000		12,000
EBT = Earnings before taxes	28,000		44,000
−T = Taxes (40%)	11,200		17,600
NI = Net income	$ 16,800	57[b]	$ 26,400
Common stock equity shares outstanding	5,000		5,000
Earnings per share	$3.36	57[c]	$5.28

(DOL brackets QP, QV, F, EBIT; DFL brackets EBIT through NI; DTL spans the combination.)

[a]Fixed financing charges include both interest and/or a tax-adjusted preferred dividend equivalent. Since preferred dividends are paid after taxes and interest is a pre-tax expense, preferred dividends must be modified for the tax effect. Thus:

Pre-tax equivalent preferred dividend = Preferred dividend/(1 − Tax rate).

In this case all financing costs result from interest charges.

[b]Note that EBT also increases by the same 57 percent. Since taxes are a variable cost, they do not affect the degree of leverage.

[c]Note that due to operating leverage (DOL = 2.0) a 20 percent increase in sales will result in a twice as large change in operating profits. Similarly, the effects of the combination of operating and financial leverage cause a change in sales to be magnified by 2.86. Recall that DOL = 2.0 and DFL = 1.43; therefore 2.0 × 1.43 = 2.86, and if sales increase by 20 percent, 0.20(2.86) = 57 percent increase in EBT, NI, and EPS. Unfortunately, a 20 percent decrease in sales will likewise be magnified into a 57 percent decline in EBT, NI, and EPS!

$$\text{Degree of financial leverage} = \frac{\text{EBIT}}{\text{EBIT} - \text{I}}. \qquad \textbf{(19-1)}$$

For SCI at sales of $200,000 and EBIT of $40,000, the degree of financial leverage with a 50 percent debt ratio is

$$\text{DFL at 50\% debt} = \frac{\$40,000}{\$40,000 - \$12,000}$$
$$= 1.43.$$

Therefore a 20 percent increase in EBIT would result in a 20%(1.43) = 28.6% increase in earnings per share. If no debt were used, I in Equation 19-1 would equal zero, and the DFL = 1.0. Thus, in the absence of fixed financial charges such as interest, a 20 percent increase in EBIT would produce a proportional 20 percent increase in EPS. Table 19-6 illustrates these statements.

Combining Operating and Financial Leverage

We have seen that operating leverage causes a change in sales volume to have a magnified effect on EBIT, and if financial leverage is super-imposed on operating leverage, changes in EBIT will have a magnified effect on earnings per share. Therefore, if a firm uses a considerable amount of both operating leverage and financial leverage, even small changes in the level of sales will produce wide fluctuations in EPS.

Equation 9-2 (for the degree of operating leverage) can be combined with Equation 19-1 (for financial leverage) to show the **total leveraging effect** of a given change in sales on earnings per share:[6]

total leveraging effect
The combination of operating leverage and financial leverage that results in a magnified effect on earnings per share from any change in sales.

$$\text{Degree of total leverage (DTL)} = \frac{Q(P - V)}{Q(P - V) - F - I}. \qquad \textbf{(19-2)}$$

For SCI, at sales of $200,000 the degree of total leverage, using 50 percent debt, is

$$\text{DTL} = \frac{\$200,000 - \$120,000}{\$200,000 - \$120,000 - \$40,000 - \$12,000}$$
$$= \frac{\$80,000}{\$28,000}$$
$$= 2.86.$$

---

[6]The degree of total leverage, DTL, is equal to the product of the DOL and DFL:

$$\text{DFL} = \frac{Q(P - V)}{Q(P - V) - F} \times \frac{Q(P - V) - F}{Q(P - V) - F - I} = \frac{Q(P - V)}{Q(P - V) - F - I},$$

and thus DTL = DOL × DFL.

Therefore a 40 percent increase in sales would lead to a 2.86× larger increase in earnings, or a 40%(2.86) = 114 percent increase in SCI's net income. Table 19-6 illustrates that a small increase in sales, 20 percent, leads to a much larger increase in SCI's earnings.

The usefulness of the degree of leverage concept lies in the facts (1) that it enables us to specify the precise effect of a change in sales volume on earnings available to common stock and (2) that it permits us to show the interrelationship between operating and financial leverage. For example, if SCI could *reduce* its degree of operating leverage, then it could probably *increase* its use of financial leverage. On the other hand, if the company decided to use more operating leverage, then its optimal capital structure would probably call for a lower debt ratio. Thus there is a trade-off between operating risk and financial risk.

Taxes, Bankruptcy Costs, and the Value of the Firm

Why does the expected stock price first rise as the firm begins to use financial leverage, then hit a peak, and finally decline when leverage becomes excessive? This pattern occurs primarily because of *corporate income taxes* and *bankruptcy costs*. Since interest on debt is tax deductible, the more debt a firm has, the greater the proportion of its operating income that flows through to investors, hence the higher the value of the firm. On the other hand, the larger the debt, the greater the risk of bankruptcy. At very high levels of debt, the odds are very great that bankruptcy will occur, and if this happens, lawyers may end up with almost as much of the firm's assets as will the investors.[7]

Figure 19-4 illustrates this concept. When SCI has zero debt, the value of its stock is $20 per share. As it begins to use debt, the stock price begins to rise because of the tax shelter benefits of debt. Prior to D_1, potential bankruptcy costs are insignificant. However, at D_1 investors begin to worry about the effects of debt, so potential bankruptcy costs begin to offset the debt's tax shelter benefits. At D_2 the marginal tax shelter benefits are equal to the marginal potential bankruptcy costs, and the value of the stock is maximized. Beyond D_2 potential bankruptcy costs more than offset the benefits of additional debt, so further increases in leverage reduce the price of the stock. Thus D_2 represents the optimal capital structure.[8]

---

[7]See Chapter 23 for a discussion of actual bankruptcy costs.

[8]This entire concept—including (1) why the tax shelter benefits cause a linear increase in value, (2) the specific elements that make up bankruptcy-related costs, and (3) the effects of personal income taxes on capital structure decisions—is discussed in Eugene F. Brigham, *Financial Management: Theory and Practice*, 3rd ed. (Hinsdale, IL: Dryden Press, 1982), Chapter 17.

Figure 19-4
SCI: Effects of Tax Deductions and Bankruptcy Costs on Stock Value

When a firm uses financial leverage, its expected stock price first rises and then falls. The initial rise occurs because the interest payments on corporate debt are tax-deductible. Thus, as a firm's debt load increases, more of its operating income escapes taxation and flows through to investors. As levels of debt increase, however, so does the risk of bankruptcy. Consequently, at point D_1, when investors begin to worry about the effects of debt, the potential risk of bankruptcy begins to offset the benefits of the tax-deductible interest. At point D_2 the balance between the benefits of leverage and the potential cost of bankruptcy is reached and the firm's capital structure is optimized. Beyond point D_2 the potential cost of bankruptcy overshadows the benefits of leverage and the stock's price falls.

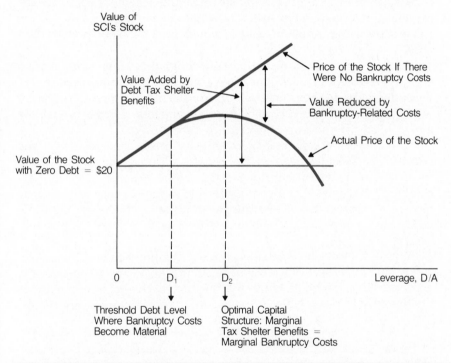

Liquidity and Cash Flow Analysis

There are some difficult problems with the type of analysis described above. Included are the following:

1. Because of the difficulties in determining exactly how P/E ratios and equity capitalization rates (k_s values) are affected by different degrees of financial leverage, management rarely, if ever, has sufficient confidence in this type of analysis to use it as the sole determinant of the target capital structure.

2. Many firms are not publicly owned. If the owners do not plan to ever have the firm go public, then potential market value data are irrelevant. However, an analysis based on implied market values for a privately owned firm is useful if the owner is interested in knowing how the market value of the firm would be affected by leverage should the decision be made to go public.

3. Even for publicly owned firms, the managers may be more or less conservative than the average stockholder, hence may set a somewhat different target capital structure than the one that would maximize the stock price. The managers of a publicly owned firm would never admit this, for unless they owned voting control, they would quickly be removed from office. However, in view of the uncertainties about what constitutes the value-maximizing structure, management could always say that the target capital structure employed is, in its judgment, the value-maximizing structure, and it would be difficult to prove otherwise.

4. Managers of large firms, especially those providing vital services such as electricity or telephones, have a responsibility to provide *continuous* service, so they must refrain from using leverage to the point where the firm's long-run viability is endangered. Long-run viability may conflict with short-run stock price maximization.

For all of these reasons managers are very much concerned with the effects of financial leverage on the risk of bankruptcy, so an analysis of this factor is an important input in the capital structure decision. Accordingly, managements give considerable weight to such ratios as the *times-interest-earned ratio (TIE)*. The lower this ratio, the higher the probability that a firm will default on its debt and be forced into bankruptcy.

Table 19-7 shows how SCI's expected TIE ratio declines as the debt/ assets ratio increases. When the debt/assets ratio is only 10 percent, the expected TIE is a high 25 times, but the interest coverage ratio declines rapidly as debt rises. Note, however, that these coverages are the ex-

Table 19-7
SCI: Expected Times-Interest-Earned Ratio at Different Debt/Assets Ratios

Debt/Assets	TIE[a]
0%	Undefined
10	25.0
20	12.1
30	7.4
40	5.0
50	3.3
60	2.2

[a]TIE = EBIT/Interest. For example, if debt/assets = 50%, then TIE = \$40,000/\$12,000 = 3.3. Data are from Tables 19-2 and 19-3.

Figure 19-5
SCI: Probability Distributions of Times-Interest-Earned Ratios with Different Capital Structures
The times-interest-earned ratio is an important indicator of bankruptcy risk. The lower the TIE, the greater the potential for bankruptcy. Management will be especially concerned with keeping the TIE above 1.0, the point below which a firm's earnings will not cover its required interest payments. This figure shows that a 60 percent capital structure not only creates an overall lower TIE than a 40 percent structure, but also results in a much higher probability of a TIE below 1.0.

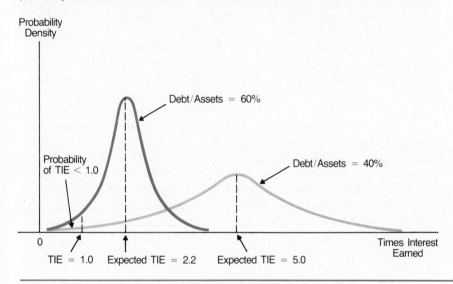

pected values—the actual TIE will be higher if sales exceed the expected $200,000 level, but lower if sales fall below $200,000. The variability of the TIE ratios is highlighted in Figure 19-5, which shows the probability distributions of the ratios at debt/assets ratios of 40 percent and 60 percent. The expected TIE is much higher if only 40 percent debt is used. Even more important, with less debt there is a much lower probability of a TIE of less than 1.0, the level at which the firm is not earning enough to meet its required interest payments and is thus seriously exposed to the threat of bankruptcy.

Capital Structure and Mergers

One of the most exciting developments in the financial world during the 1970s and continuing into the 1980s has been the high level of merger activity, especially takeovers. A *takeover* occurs when one firm buys out another over the opposition of the acquired firm's management. The acquired firm's stock is considered to be undervalued, so the acquiring firm is willing to pay a premium of perhaps 50 percent to gain control. Mergers are discussed at length in Chapter 22, but it is useful to make these points now: (1) very often the acquiring firm issues debt and uses it to buy the target firm's stock; (2) this action effectively changes the enterprise's capital structure; and (3) the value enhancement resulting from the use of debt is apparently sufficient to cover the premium offered for the stock and still leave a profit for the acquiring company.

Recognizing the validity of the type of analysis described in this chapter led to the creation of companies whose major function was to acquire other companies as described above. The managers of these acquiring companies (often called "conglomerates") frequently made huge personal fortunes. Even shrewd individual investors, including a few professors, selected stock portfolios heavily weighted with prime acquisition targets and did well in the market. Of course, the managements of firms with low leverage ratios who did not want to be taken over could be expected to react by attempting to find their optimal debt levels and then issuing debt and repurchasing stock. Thereby they would be raising the price of their stock and making their companies less attractive acquisition targets.

The game is far from over—indeed, it can never end, because economic shifts lead to continuing changes in optimal capital structures. This makes it especially important that the lessons to be learned from this chapter be thoroughly understood by everyone actively involved in financial management.

Checklist of Factors That Influence Capital Structure Decisions

The factors listed and briefly discussed below all have an important, though hard to measure, bearing on a firm's choice of a target capital structure.

1. Sales stability. If its sales are relatively stable, a firm can safely take on more debt and incur higher fixed charges than can a company with unstable sales. Utility companies, because of their stable demand, have thus been able to undertake more debt financing than the average industrial firm.

2. Asset structure. Firms whose assets are suitable as security for loans tend to use debt rather heavily. Thus real estate companies tend to be highly leveraged, while manufacturers with heavy investments in specialized machinery and work-in-process inventories employ less debt.

3. Operating leverage. Other things held constant, a firm with less operating leverage is better able to employ financial leverage. Earlier in this chapter we discussed how operating and financial leverage interact

to determine the overall impact of a decline in sales on operating income and earnings per share.

4. Growth rate. Other things held constant, faster-growing firms must
rely more heavily on external capital (see Chapter 8). Furthermore, the
flotation costs involved in selling common stock exceed those incurred
when selling debt. Thus, to minimize financing costs, rapidly growing
firms tend to use somewhat more debt than do slower-growing companies.

5. Profitability. One often observes that firms with very high rates of
return on investment use relatively little debt. Although there is no
theoretical justification for this fact, the practical reason seems to be
that very profitable firms such as IBM and 3M simply do not need to
do much debt financing—their high profit margins enable them to do
most of their financing with retained earnings.

6. Taxes. Interest is a deductible expense, while dividends are not deductible. Hence the higher a firm's corporate tax rate, the greater the
advantage of using debt. This point is also discussed in more detail in
Chapter 20.

7. Control. The effect that debt or stock financing might have on a
management's control position may influence its capital structure decision. If management has voting control (51 percent of the stock) but
is not in a position to buy any more stock, debt may be the choice for
new financings. On the other hand, a management group that is not
concerned about voting control may decide to use equity rather than
debt if the firm's financial situation is so weak that the use of debt
might subject the firm to risk of default: if the firm goes into default,
the managers will almost surely lose their jobs. However, if too little
debt is used, management runs the risk of a takeover attempt; here
some other company or management group tries to persuade stockholders to turn over control to the new group, which may plan to boost
earnings by using financial leverage. In general, control considerations
do not necessarily suggest the use of debt or equity, but if management
is at all insecure, the effects of capital structure on control will certainly
be taken into account.

8. Management attitudes. In the absence of proof that one capital
structure will lead to higher stock prices than another, management
can exercise its own judgment about a proper capital structure. Some
managements tend to be more (or less) conservative than others, and
thus use less (or more) debt than the average firm in their industry.

9. Lender and rating agency attitudes. Regardless of managers' own
analyses of the proper leverage factors for their firms, there is no ques-

tion that lenders' and rating agencies' attitudes are frequently important determinants of financial structures. In the majority of cases the corporation discusses its financial structure with lenders and rating agencies and gives much weight to their advice. But when management is so confident of the future that it seeks to use leverage beyond the norms for its industry, lenders may be unwilling to accept such debt increases or may do so only at a high price.

10. Market conditions. Conditions in the stock and bond markets undergo both long- and short-run changes, which can have an important bearing on a firm's optimal capital structure. For example, during the credit crunch in the winter of 1982, there was simply no market at any "reasonable" interest rate for new long-term bonds rated below A. Low-rated companies that needed capital were forced to go to the stock market or to the short-term debt market. Actions such as this could represent either changes in their target capital structures or temporary departures from these targets, but the important point is that stock and bond market conditions at a point in time do influence the type of securities used for a given financing.

11. The firm's internal conditions. A firm's own internal conditions also have a bearing on its target capital structure. For example, suppose a firm has just successfully completed an R&D program and projects higher earnings in the immediate future. However, these new earnings are not yet anticipated by investors, hence are not reflected in the price of the stock. This company would not want to issue stock—it would prefer to finance with debt until the higher earnings materialized and were reflected in the stock price, at which time it might want to sell an issue of common stock, retire the debt, and return to its target capital structure.

Variations in Capital Structures among Firms

As might be expected, wide variations in the use of financial leverage occur both among industries and among the individual firms in each industry. Table 19-8 illustrates this point. Retailers make heavy use of debt, especially short-term debt used to carry inventories. Manufacturing companies as a group use less debt, especially short-term debt. Within manufacturing, small firms with limited access to the stock market employ the most debt, and again the bulk of their liabilities are short-term. The data in the table are not broken down sufficiently to so indicate, but the majority of the debt shown for small manufacturers represents trade credit.

Financing mixes also very widely among manufacturing sectors. Aircraft companies are highly leveraged, borrowing heavily on a short-term basis to finance the construction of airplanes. Because of their

Table 19-8
Capital Components as a Percentage of Total Capital, 1982

	Current Liabilities	Long-Term Debt	Total Liabilities	Equity
Retail trade	29%	29%	58%	42%
Manufacturing (all sizes)	25	26	51	49
Assets under $5 million	35	19	54	46
Assets over $1 billion	24	26	50	50
Selected manufacturing industries				
Aircraft	54	13	67	33
Electrical equipment	34	18	52	48
Steel	22	42	64	36
Drugs	23	19	42	58

Source: Federal Trade Commission, *Quarterly Financial Report*, First Quarter, 1983.

long production cycle, aircraft manufacturers have large work-in-process inventories that must be financed. Aircraft manufacturers receive advances from their customers, and these advances are shown as current liabilities. Like the aircraft companies, manufacturers of electrical equipment also have long construction periods—for example, nuclear reactors take years to build—and short-term credit is often used to finance this construction. The drug companies, on the other hand, do not use much leverage. Their production period is short, and the uncertainties inherent in an industry that is both oriented toward research and development and exposed to lawsuits arising from adverse reactions to its products render the heavy use of leverage unwise.

Summary

In this chapter the concepts of operating leverage, financial leverage, and target capital structure have been discussed. *Operating leverage* refers to the use of fixed costs in operations, and it is related to the firm's production processes. The more operating leverage the firm has, the more risky are its securities, other things held constant.

Financial leverage refers to the use of debt in the capital structure—the more debt the firm employs, the higher its financial leverage. Financial leverage generally raises expected EPS, but it also increases the riskiness of the firm's securities. Because the risk of its stock and bonds increases as the debt/assets ratio rises, the interest rate on debt and the required rate of return on equity will also rise. Thus leverage produces two opposing effects: higher EPS, which leads to a higher stock price, but increased riskiness, which depresses P_0. There is, however, a debt/assets ratio that strikes an optimal balance between these opposing effects; this ratio is called the *optimal capital structure*, and it is the one that maximizes the price of the firm's stock.

Although it is theoretically possible to determine the optimal capital structure, as a practical matter we cannot estimate this structure with precision. Accordingly, financial executives also analyze the effects of different capital structures on interest coverage ratios, which give clues about the probability of bankruptcy. Firms also tend to analyze such factors as sales stability, asset structure, and so on, and the final target capital structure is more judgmental than rigorously determined.

All of the concepts developed in this chapter are both used and extended in Chapters 20 and 21.

Small Business $ $ $ $ $ $ $ $ $

Capital Structure in the Small Firm

Small businesses rely heavily on banks and other suppliers of debt funds for a large portion of their capital. In fact, it has been indicated in earlier chapters that small firms have relatively limited access to the public equity markets, which means that they must turn either to private equity or to debt. As a result, debt financing is very important to small business.

In spite of the importance of debt to small firms, there are a number of factors which may limit the extent to which the owner-manager of a small firm may wish to use the debt markets. These factors include the risk of debt financing to the owner-manager, increased likelihood and relative cost of bankruptcy, and the effect of taxes.

Earlier in the chapter we noted that as financial leverage increases, EPS becomes more sensitive to changes in sales or operating profits. This variability in earnings may be even more important for small firms than for large ones whose securities are widely traded in the capital markets. In fact, some financial theorists argue that, in firms with widely traded stock, additional debt increases expected returns by just enough to offset the added risk that debt entails. Under these hypothesized circumstances there is no optimal capital structure because the value of the firm is unaffected by debt. However, the theory does not hold if a firm's shares are unmarketable or if the owner-managers want to retain their shares of stock in order to maintain control of the firm. Thus the increased variability in earnings per share caused by additional debt is a risk that cannot be transferred to others through the sale of the owner-managers' shares in the capital markets. Therefore owner-managers may be especially sensitive to the level of debt employed.

While debt increases the variability in EPS for any firm, other factors may cause a more pronounced earnings variability in small firms. For example, small firms typically have narrower product lines and smaller customer bases than do larger firms. Since their sales do not represent well-diversified sources of income, there is likely to be greater uncertainty in the earnings of a smaller firm. This increased uncertainty in earnings is a factor that tends to keep the debt level relatively low.

Of course, a small customer base can be an advantage for a firm. If a small firm's key customer is willing to make a long-term commitment to take its output, that commitment would be viewed as a definite plus by a financial institution considering a loan to the firm, assuming the customer has reasonable financial strength. Under normal circumstances, however, a small customer base is a disadvantage because of the increased risk of sudden loss of income.

Bankruptcy costs are thought by many researchers to be a significant factor in limiting the debt used by a firm. Two factors which influence capital structure decisions are: (1) the actual costs of bankruptcy if it occurs and (2) the probability that bankruptcy will occur. As we have already seen, the probability of earnings fluctuation is greater in smaller firms, and greater earnings variability means higher risk of failure. The probability of bankruptcy would therefore normally be higher in a small firm, other things being equal.

In addition to a higher probability of bankruptcy in the smaller firm, there is the problem that some of the costs of bankruptcy are fixed. Although the costs of bankruptcy are normally higher the larger the firm, the costs do not rise proportionately with the size of the firm. As a result, bankruptcy costs tend to be relatively higher in the smaller firm. Therefore these concerns probably reduce the amount of debt financing that managers of small firms would consider optimal.

One of the obvious benefits of debt financing is that the interest payments on debt are tax deductible, making the after-tax cost of debt smaller. However, firms with earnings under $100,000 pay taxes at a lower marginal rate than do firms with earnings over $100,000. For example, a firm earning $250,000 pays taxes at a 46 percent marginal tax rate. A firm with earnings of only $45,000, however, has a marginal tax rate of only 18 percent. The after-tax cost of a 18 percent loan, for example, would be only 9.72 percent to the firm with higher profits, but it would be 14.4 percent to the less profitable firm.

The purpose of this example is not to suggest that higher taxes are beneficial, but rather to indicate that the tax deductibility of interest has a greater advantage to firms with higher marginal tax rates. If most of the debt available in the financial markets is demanded by firms in high tax brackets, that debt may be priced with interest rates that are relatively unattractive to less profitable smaller firms. As a result, the relative desirability of debt may be much less in a smaller firm when the cost of that debt is correctly measured on an after-tax basis.

Of course, there are certain factors that may make debt more attractive to small firms. That small firms have limited access to equity markets has already been mentioned. In addition, a number of programs exist that make it easier for small firms to borrow money. Perhaps the best-known programs to assist small businesses in obtaining debt funds are those of the Small Business Administration (SBA). Although the SBA makes direct loans to small businesses, it also guarantees small-business loans made by commercial banks and small-business investment companies. These loans are generally made on more attractive terms than are conventional loans, and they are made to businesses that would otherwise have difficulty qualifying for loans.

A small business faces an interesting dilemma. Because access to other sources of funds is relatively difficult, the small firm is motivated to make heavy use of debt financing in its capital structure. On the other hand, factors that influence the target level of debt financing generally bias the small firm toward a lower use of debt than would otherwise be indicated. The owner-manager's dilemma is to balance these conflicting pressures in selecting a method of financing the firm. In achieving such a balance, the use of small-business debt sources that are unavailable to larger firms may be a help.

Resolution to Decision in Finance

Is Cities Service Worth the Price?

Armand Hammer acquired Cities Service despite the tremendous financial burden it imposed. In the process, according to some analysts, he ransomed Oxy's earning power well into the future. Oxy's financial problems were compounded by the fact that 1982 was a bad year for virtually all the major oil producers. But with its 1982 earnings dropping to 69 cents per share, Oxy's performance was the worst. By the end of 1982 Oxy was carrying a numbing load of $8.8 billion in debt and preferred stock.

Bludgeoned by huge debts and plunging profits, Hammer was forced to raise money by selling some of Oxy's assets. He was able to make about $3 billion by unloading gas pipelines, refining and marketing operations, gas and oil acreage, coal and chemical properties, and a number of other, smaller units. But some industry experts contended that still wasn't enough to restore Oxy to its pre-acquisition level of performance.

Oxy's most important goal for 1983 was to knock down its debt load from $6.6 billion to $3 billion. In addition, the company promised its bankers that it would retire most of its $2.1 billion in preferred stock, although that would take time. Hammer also believed it was crucial to bolster the price of Oxy's stock. Although he felt that all of Oxy's assets should have made its common stock worth $80 a share, Wall Street was valuing it at only $24.

Despite Hammer's scramble to raise cash, most analysts feared that true progress would be slow in coming to Oxy. The acquisition of

> Cities so drained Oxy's coffers that it had to cut back its oil exploration budget from $1.4 billion in 1982 to only $900 million in 1983. Also clouding the picture was uncertainty about future oil demand and prices.
>
> At the end of 1983 Oxy's capital structure was still in disarray, although company officials were quick to defend their actions and minimize their problems. Most experts agreed that it would take several years before Oxy recovered enough from this acquisition to determine whether it had been worth the price.
>
> Source: "Oxy's Troubled Days," *Dun's Business Month*, February 1983, 58–62; "Armand Hammer's Scramble to Raise Cash," *Fortune*, Mar. 21, 1983, 95–96; and "Behind the Shakeup at Occidental Petroleum," *Business Week*, July 11, 1983, 78–79.

Key Terms. You should be able to define each of the following terms:

Capital structure; optimal capital structure; target capital structure
Financial risk

Financial leverage; degree of financial leverage; total leveraging effect

Questions

19-1 The uncertainty inherent in projections of future operating income is called what?

19-2 "One type of leverage affects both EBIT and EPS. The other type affects only EPS." Explain what the statement means.

19-3 What is the relationship between market (or beta) risk and leverage?

19-4 Why is the following statement true? "Other things being the same, firms with relatively stable sales are able to carry relatively high debt ratios."

19-5 Why do public utility companies usually pursue a different financial policy from that of retail firms?

19-6 Some economists believe that swings in business cycles will not be as wide in the future as they have been in the past. Assuming that they are correct in their analysis, what effect might this added stability have on the types of financing used by firms in the United States? Would your answer be true for all firms?

19-7 Why is EBIT generally considered to be independent of financial leverage? Why might EBIT actually be influenced by financial leverage at high debt levels?

19-8 How might increasingly volatile inflation rates, interest rates, and bond prices affect the optimal capital structure for corporations?

19-9 If a firm went from zero debt to successively higher levels of debt, why would you expect its stock price to first rise, then hit a peak, and then begin to decline?

19-10 Why is the debt level that maximizes a firm's expected EPS generally higher than the debt level that maximizes its stock price?

19-11 In public utility rate cases, a utility's riskiness is a key issue, as utilities are supposed to be allowed to earn the same rate of return on common equity as unregulated firms of comparable risk. The difficulty is in specifying in quantitative terms the riskiness of utilities and nonutilities. Describe how the degree of leverage concepts (DOL, DFL, and DTL) might be used as indicators of risk in a rate case.

Self-Test Problem

ST-1 Suppose Gentry Motors is in this situation: (1) EBIT = $4 million; (2) tax rate = t = 35%; (3) debt outstanding = D = $2 million; (4) k_d = 10%; (5) k_s = 15%; (6) shares of stock outstanding = N_0 = 600,000; and (7) book value per share = $10. Gentry's product market is stable, and it expects no growth, so all earnings are paid out as dividends. The debt consists of perpetual bonds.

    a. What are Gentry's earnings per share (EPS) and its price per share (P_0)?

    b. What are the total assets of the firm (based on book values)?

    c. What is Gentry's weighted average cost of capital, k_a? (The computation of the cost of capital is covered in Chapter 21.)

    d. Gentry can increase its debt by $8 million, to a total of $10 million, using the new debt to buy back and retire some of its shares at the current price. Its interest rate on all debt will be 12 percent (it will have to call and refund the old debt), and its cost of equity will rise from 15 percent to 17 percent. EBIT will remain constant. Should Gentry change its capital structure?

    e. If Gentry did not have to refund the $2 million of old debt, what effect would this have? Assume the new and the still outstanding old debt are equally risky, with k_d = 12%, but the coupon rate on the old debt is 10 percent.

    f. What is Gentry's TIE coverage ratio under the original situation and under the conditions in Part d?

Problems

* **19-1** Harper Transit Corporation has a DOL of 2.0 and its DFL is 3.0. If sales increase by 10 percent, what percentage increase will occur in net income?

* **19-2** Spartan Decorators has a single product which sells for $500. Variable costs per unit are $300 and total fixed costs are $600,000, which includes $100,000 in interest. Spartan plans to sell 3,500 units this year.

    a. What is the firm's DOL?

    b. What is the firm's DFL?

    c. What is the firm's DTL?

19-3 Joseph Black Associates, Inc. has the following characteristics: (1) sales = 5,000 units; (2) sale price per unit = $5; (3) variable cost per unit = $3; (4) fixed cost = $3,000; (5) long-term debt = $1,000; (6) coupon rate on debt = 4%; (7) current earnings per share = $2.00.

---

*Refer to Appendix E for check answers to problems with asterisks.

* **a.** Determine the firm's EPS if sales increase by 25 percent next year. Use the DTL formula as the basis for your computations.
   b. Confirm your answer in Part a with a projected income statement (there are 2,088 shares outstanding). The tax rate is 40 percent.

19-4 Fetzer Electronics can produce small electronic motors by using one of two methods. Variable and fixed operating costs under the Standard and Capital methods are listed below:

	Standard	Capital
Fixed cost	$50,000	$150,000
Variable cost	$3.75	$2.50

Whichever production method is chosen, the motors will sell for $5.00.
   a. Calculate the degree of operating leverage for the Standard and Capital methods at sales of $300,000 and $400,000.
   b. Assume that the Standard and Capital methods can be financed in either of the following ways: (1) no debt; (2) $225,000 of debt at 10 percent. Calculate the DFL for the Standard method at sales of $300,000 and $400,000. The DFLs for the Capital method at these sales levels with debt are 0 and 1.82, respectively.
   c. Calculate the degree of total leverage (DTL) under the Standard method with debt at sales of $300,000 and $400,000. The DTLs for the Capital method at these sales levels are -6.67 and 7.27, respectively.
   d. At the sales level of $300,000 the DTL for the Capital method was negative ($DTL_c = -6.67$). Does a negative degree of leverage imply that an increase in sales will *lower* profits?

19-5 MBA Corporation will begin operations next year for the production of a single product to be priced at $8 per unit. MBA has a choice of two methods of production: Method A, with variable costs of $3 per unit and $400,000 of fixed costs; and Method B, with variable costs of $5 per unit and fixed costs of $200,000.
   * **a.** Compute MBA's contribution margin under each method of production.
   * **b.** What is the breakeven point, in units, for each method?
   c. At what level of sales, in units, would the firm be indifferent between the two production methods with respect to expected operating earnings?

19-6 Suppose some years later MBA (see Problem 19-5) has acquired $1 million in assets and has established a debt ratio of 30 percent. The cost of debt (k_d) to MBA is 10 percent. The sales forecast for the coming year is 150,000 units.
   a. Under which production method would operating profits be most adversely affected if sales did not reach expected levels?
   b. Given the present debt of the firm, which method would produce the greatest percentage increase in earnings per share for a given increase in EBIT?

19-7 Conn's Bolt Company is an all-equity firm with $10 million in assets and 200,000 shares of common stock outstanding. The firm's president, Charlie Conn, is considering an expansion of the facilities which will increase operating profits to $2 million. The cost of the plant expansion is $5 million. The funds may be obtained in one of three ways: (1) Common stock issue at $50 per share, giving 100,000 new shares of common; (2) debt issue, 9 percent coupon rate; or (3) preferred stock issue, 8 percent dividend. The company's tax rate is expected to be 40 percent.

a. Which alternative provides the highest EPS?

b. Conn has determined the P/E multiples of firms with capital structures similar to those proposed:

Financing	P/E Multiple
Equity	12
Debt issue	10
Preferred stock	11

What is the stock price that would be associated with the earnings from each financial plan?

c. How should the firm finance the proposed expansion?

19-8 Hank Bierman and Sid Smidt are planning to start a business to produce insulated window assemblies, utilizing a new process they recently patented. The enterprise is to be called B & S Window Company, and its initial plant will be located in upstate New York. As a result of optimistic reports by builders in the area, local banks and insurance companies are willing to supply the firm with debt capital on reasonably favorable terms. Stock can also be sold to local investors, so financing does not appear to be a problem.

Two production methods are available. Plan A calls for using a minimum amount of automated equipment, renting buildings, and purchasing—rather than manufacturing—major components. Under Plan A fixed costs will be $1.8 million per year, while variable costs will be $70 per window assembly. Plan B calls for more operating leverage: fixed costs will be $4.8 million, but variable costs will be only $40 per unit. Regardless of which production process is used, the estimated sales price is $100 per unit. Fixed costs do not include any interest charges.

Bierman and Smidt are planning to promote their windows on the basis of fuel and air-conditioning cost savings. Although they will advertise for sales in the home improvement and renovation market, the major market will be builders of new homes. Since new home starts are highly cyclical, sales will undoubtedly fluctuate widely. The two partners estimate that the following probability distribution of sales will apply, once the new firm is in full operation:

Probability	Sales in Units	Sales in Dollars
0.10	40,000	$ 4 million
0.15	80,000	8 million
0.75	120,000[a]	12 million

[a]The capacity limit is 120,000 under either production method.

a. Which production plan should Bierman and Smidt choose? To answer this question, calculate the breakeven point and expected EBIT under each plan, then analyze the riskiness of both A and B. Also, you should think about the probable amount of investment needed for each plan, as well as about the probable rate of return on this investment. Note too that the breakeven point can be determined graphically or by use of the equation

$$Q = \frac{F}{P - V},$$

where Q is the breakeven volume, F the fixed costs, and V the variable cost per unit. Finally, in answering this question you need only work with expected sales.

b. Regardless of your conclusion in Part a, assume that Bierman and Smidt decide on Plan B and that they require total capital of $10 million to put the plan into effect. Debt is available according to the following schedule (these rates apply to all the debt raised):

Amount Borrowed	Interest Rate
Up to $1 million	9.50%
$1.1 to $2 million	10.00
$2.1 to $3 million	10.75
$3.1 to $4 million	12.00
$4.1 to $5 million	15.00
$5.1 to $6 million	20.00
$6.1 to $7 million	27.00

Bierman and Smidt plan to invest their own funds in the new company, and also to sell stock to relatives, business associates, and employees. Some shares will also be offered to the public, so there will be a market price for the stock. Based on conversations with their investment bankers, they conclude that their firm's P/E ratio will depend on its debt/assets ratio. Specifically, they think the P/E ratio will vary with debt in accordance with the following schedule:

Debt/Assets	P/E
Up to 20%	10.00×
20.1 to 30%	9.75
30.1 to 40%	9.50
40.1 to 50%	9.00
50.1 to 60%	8.50
60.1 to 70%	7.50

If they want to maximize the price of their firm's stock, what capital structure should Bierman and Smidt choose? Use a 40 percent tax rate in your calculations. Also, assume that any funds not raised by debt will be obtained by selling common stock at a price of $10 per share. Hence, if they decide on a 50 percent debt ratio, they will raise $5 million as debt and $5 million as equity, selling 500,000 shares at $10 each. Disregard flotation costs in this problem. [Hints: (1) You can calculate expected sales and work only with this figure to generate expected EPS. (2) Rather than completing a table such as Table 19-3, you can use this equation to simplify calculations:

$$EPS = [(EBIT - I)(1 - t)]/Shares.$$

(3) Note that this problem gives data on P/E ratios rather than on beta coefficients. Simply multiply calculated EPS values by the given P/E ratios to obtain the expected stock prices.]

c. At the expected sales level, and with your target debt/assets ratio, what is Bierman and Smidt's times-interest-earned ratio?

d. Suppose the debt is in the form of a 5-year term loan. What will be the annual amortization payment (interest plus principal)? Use this to calculate Bierman and Smidt's debt service coverage ratio. (The debt service ratio here is defined as EBIT/amortization payments. Also, DFa for 10.75 percent for 5 years = 3.719.)

e. Suppose this is *your* company and you plan to own 50 percent of the stock. Which capital structure would *you* choose? Would your choice be influenced by your other assets—that is, would it matter if your entire net worth were invested in this company versus a situation where you owned about $10 million of other securities?

Answer to Self-Test Problem

ST-1 a.

EBIT	$4,000,000
Interest ($2,000,000 × 0.10)	200,000
Net before taxes	$3,800,000
Taxes (35%)	1,330,000
Net after taxes	$2,470,000

$$EPS = \$2,470,000/600,000 = \$4.116667.$$
$$P_0 = \$4.116667/0.15 = \$27.44.$$

b.   Total assets = Debt + Equity
= Debt + Book value of equity × Number of shares outstanding
= $2,000,000 + ($10 × 600,000)
= $2,000,000 + $6,000,000
= $8,000,000.

c. $k_a = w_d k_d(1 - t) + w_s k_s$
= (2/8)(10%)(1 - 0.35) + (6/8)(15%)
= 1.63% + 11.25%
= 12.88%.

d.

EBIT	$4,000,000
Interest ($10,000,000 × 0.12)	1,200,000
Net before taxes	$2,800,000
Taxes (35%)	980,000
Net after taxes	$1,820,000

$$\text{Shares bought and retired} = \Delta N = \Delta \text{Debt}/P_0$$
$$= \$8,000,000/\$27.44$$
$$= 291,545.$$

$$\text{New outstanding shares} = N_1 = N_0 - \Delta N$$
$$= 600,000 - 291,545$$
$$= 308,455.$$

$$\text{New EPS} = \$1,820,000/308,455$$
$$= \$5.90.$$

$$\text{New price per share} = P_0 \text{ (new)}$$
$$= \$5.90/0.17$$
$$= \$34.71.$$

Therefore Gentry should change its capital structure.

e. In this case, the company's net income after taxes would be higher by $(0.12 - 0.10)(\$2,000,000)(1 - 0.35) = \$26,000$, because its interest charges would be lower. The new price would be

$$P_0 = \frac{(\$1,820,000 + \$26,000)/308,455}{0.17}$$
$$= \$35.20.$$

In the first case, where the debt had to be refunded, the bondholders were compensated for the increased risk of the higher debt position. In the second case, the old bondholders were not compensated; their 10 percent coupon perpetual bonds would now be worth

$$\$100/0.12 = \$833.33,$$

or $1,666,667 in total, down from the old $2,000,000, or a loss of $333,333. The stockholders would have a gain of

$$(\$35.20 - \$34.71)(308,455) = \$151,143,$$

which would, of course, be at the expense of the old bondholders. (There is no reason to think that bondholders' losses would exactly offset stockholders' gains.)

f.

$$TIE = \frac{EBIT}{I}.$$

$$\text{Original TIE} = \frac{\$4,000,000}{\$200,000} = 20\times.$$

$$\text{New TIE} = \frac{\$4,000,000}{\$1,200,000} = 3.33\times.$$

Selected References

Donaldson's work on the setting of debt targets is old but still relevant:

Donaldson, Gordon, *Corporate Debt Capacity* (Boston: Division of Research, Harvard Business School, 1961).

———, "New Framework for Corporate Debt Capacity," *Harvard Business Review*, March–April 1962, 117–131.

———, "Strategy for Financial Emergencies," *Harvard Business Review*, November–December 1969, 67–79.

Other useful references are:

Caks, John, "Corporate Debt Decisions: A New Analytical Framework," *Journal of Finance*, December 1978, 1297–1315.

Gahlon, James M., and James A. Gentry, "On the Relationship between Systematic Risk and the Degrees of Operating and Financial Leverage," *Financial Management*, Summer 1982, 15–23.

Hamada, Robert S., "The Effect of the Firm's Capital Structure on the Systematic Risk of Common Stocks," *Journal of Finance*, May 1972, 435–452.

Hunt, Pearson, "A Proposal for Precise Definitions of 'Trading on the Equity' and 'Leverage'," *Journal of Finance*, September 1961, 377–386.

Jaedicke, Robert K., and Alexander A. Robichek, "Cost-Volume-Profit Analysis under Conditions of Uncertainty," *Accounting Review*, October 1964, 917–926.

Kelvie, William E., and John M. Sinclair, "New Techniques for Breakeven Charts," *Financial Executive*, June 1968, 31–43.

Masulis, R. W., *The Effects of Capital Structure Change on Security Prices: A Study of Exchange Offers* (Los Angeles: Study Center in Managerial Economics and Finance, UCLA, December 1978).

Raun, D. L., "The Limitations of Profit Graphs, Break-even Analysis, and Budgets," *Accounting Review*, October 1964, 927–945.

Reinhardt, U. E., "Break-Even Analysis for Lockheed's Tri Star: An Application of Financial Theory," *Journal of Finance*, September 1973, 821–838.

Shalit, Sol S., "On the Mathematics of Financial Leverage," *Financial Management*, Spring 1975, 57–66.

The Cost of Capital

Decision in Finance

The New World of Corporate Finance

In 1982, the winds of change once again whistled through Wall Street when the Securities and Exchange Commission adopted the controversial Rule 415, which permits "shelf" offerings of corporate securities. Under Rule 415, companies may register up to two years' worth of securities en masse and then sell them in bits and blocks "off the shelf."

When a company files its 415 registration, it must already have approval for the offering from its board of directors. The board may set in advance the terms and rates acceptable, or it may authorize a subcommittee or individuals to approve each sale off the shelf. The company must name its candidates for underwriter and work out the basic format of the underwriting agreement for the eventual sale, even though the company may not know who the underwriter will actually be on each sale or whether it will in fact use one; it may sell direct. Moreover, a company selling debt may register in the same statement a variety of styles of securities, such as zeros, deep discounts, and straight bonds maturing in anywhere from one to thirty years, without specifying the amount of each type or deciding which type it will sell.

After filing for a specific dollar volume of bonds or number of shares, the company may sell all or part of the issue in several ways: direct to an institution; to an underwriter who in turn markets it to institutions or to retail customers; or through a traditional syndicated sale. The institutional purchaser owns the securities outright, with the attendant market risk, and it can sell them publicly at any time. Thus the company may sell at different prices to different buyers at the same time. And it can pay underwriters varying fees on the same sale.

As you read this chapter, consider the effects that Rule 415 would have on a company's cost of capital. If you were the chief financial officer of a large corporation, would you recommend registering new securities under Rule 415? Why or why not?

See end of chapter for resolution.

The cost of capital is critically important in finance. First, capital budgeting decisions have a major impact on a firm, and proper capital budgeting procedures require an estimate of the cost of capital. Second, many other types of decisions, including those related to leasing, to bond refunding, and to working capital policy require estimates of the cost of capital. Finally, maximizing the value of a firm requires that the costs of all inputs, including capital, be minimized, and to minimize the cost of capital we must be able to calculate it.[1]

The first task of this chapter is to explain the logic of the weighted average cost of capital. Next, we consider the costs of the major components of the capital structure. Third, the individual component costs are brought together to form a weighted average cost of capital. Finally, the relationship between capital budgeting and the cost of capital is discussed.

The Logic of the Weighted Average Cost of Capital

Suppose a particular firm's cost of debt is estimated to be 8 percent, its cost of equity is estimated to be 12 percent, and the decision has been made to finance next year's projects by selling debt. The argument is sometimes made that the cost of capital for these projects is 8 percent, because debt will be used to finance them. However, this position is incorrect. To finance a particular set of projects with debt implies that the firm is also using up some of its potential for obtaining new low-cost debt in the future. As expansion occurs in subsequent years, at some point the firm will find it necessary to use additional equity financing to prevent the debt ratio from becoming too large.

To illustrate, suppose the firm borrows heavily at 8 percent during

---

[1]The cost of capital is also vitally important in regulated industries, including electric, gas, telephone, railroad, airline, and trucking companies. In essence, regulatory commissions seek to measure a utility's cost of capital, then set prices so that the company will just earn this rate of return. If the estimate is too low, then the company will not be able to attract sufficient capital to meet long-range demands for service, and the public will suffer. If the estimate of capital costs is too high, customers will pay too much for service.

1984, using up its debt capacity in the process, to finance projects yielding 9 percent. In 1985 it has projects available that yield 11 percent, well above the return on 1984 projects, but it cannot accept these new projects because they would have to be financed with 12 percent equity money. To avoid this problem, the firm should be viewed as an ongoing concern, and the cost of capital used in capital budgeting should be calculated as a **weighted average,** or **composite,** of the various types of funds it uses.

Basic Definitions

Capital components are the items on the right-hand side of the balance sheet: various types of debt, preferred stock, and common equity. Any net increase in assets must be financed by an increase in one or more capital components.

Capital is a necessary factor of production, and, like any other factor, it has a cost. The cost of each component is defined as the *component cost* of that particular type of capital. For example, if the firm can borrow money at 8 percent, the component cost of debt is defined as 8 percent. Throughout most of this chapter we concentrate on debt, retained earnings, and new issues of common stock. These are the major capital structure components, and their component costs are identified by the following symbols:

k_d = interest rate on the firm's new debt = component cost of debt, before tax.

$k_d(1 - t)$ = component cost of debt, after tax, where t is the marginal tax rate. The term $k_d(1 - t)$ is the debt cost used to calculate the weighted average cost of capital.

k_s = component cost of retained earnings (or internal equity). This k_s is identical to the k_s developed in Chapter 18 and defined there as the required rate of return on common stock.

k_e = component cost of external capital obtained by issuing new common stock. As we shall see, it is necessary to distinguish between equity raised by retaining earnings versus that raised by selling new stock. This is why we distinguish between k_s and k_e.

k_a = an average, or composite, cost of capital. If a firm raises $1 of new capital to finance asset expansion, and if it is to keep its capital structure in balance (that is, if it is to keep the same percentage of debt and equity), then it will raise part of the dollar as debt and part as common equity (with

weighted average, or composite, cost of capital, k_a A weighted average of the after-tax component costs of debt, preferred stock, and common equity.

capital components The items on the right-hand side of the balance sheet: various types of long-term debt, preferred stock, and common equity.

equity coming either as retained earnings or from the sale of new common stock).[2]

These definitions and concepts are explained in detail in the remainder of this chapter.

Minimum Required Return

Any source of funds that the company uses has an implicit cost associated with it. As we learned in the chapter on capital budgeting, the firm raises money to invest in productive assets which provide a cash flow to the firm. The cash flow must cover not only the project's operating expenses but the financial obligations arising from the acceptance of the project as well.

In Chapters 17 and 18 we explored the various forms of return associated with each financing vehicle. With debt financing, the project's cash flow must cover the periodic interest payments. If the company is financed in part with preferred stock, preferred dividends must be paid. Finally, the required return on common stock equity financing must also be met through the project's cash flow. The firm will determine the portion of after-tax earnings which will be paid in the form of dividends to shareholders and the portion which will be reinvested to insure the firm's future growth. Remember, even if a particular project is financed entirely with debt, the appropriate required return for the project is the firm's weighted average cost of capital. Therefore the project's cash flow must be large enough to cover these explicit costs (interest and dividends) as well as implicit costs (earnings retention for growth).

The minimum acceptable rate of return a project can earn is that rate which just satisfies all sources of financing. Perhaps a simple example will clarify our point. Assume that the McIntire Toy Corporation is planning to buy a new plastic molding machine for $800,000. The company will raise funds for the new machine in proportion to its present capital structure—50 percent debt and 50 percent equity. New debtholders will require a 12 percent return, while shareholders expect to receive an 18 percent return on investment. For simplicity's sake, suppose that the cash returns from this project will continue at the current level forever and that all residual earnings will be paid out in the form of dividends. If the company's marginal tax rate is 40 percent, what minimum cash flow after operating expenses must be produced by the project in order to justify the investment? In essence, the question becomes: What return must the project produce in order to satisfy all sources of financing?

---

[2]Firms try to keep their debt and equity in balance, but they do not try to maintain any proportional relationship between the common stock and retained earnings accounts as shown on the balance sheet. Common equity is common equity, whether it is represented by common stock or by retained earnings.

If the project's cash flow must satisfy all sources of financing, it must at least cover the dividend and interest payments required by equity holders and debtholders, respectively. (The company does get a small "break" in the required returns in that interest is a tax-deductible expense.) Therefore the project's **required cash flow** is equal to the amount of financing times its required return:

required cash flow
The amount of a project's financing times the required return for each financing source.

$$
\begin{aligned}
\text{Required cash flow} &= \text{Required after-tax return on debt} \times \text{Amount of} \\
&\quad \text{debt} + \text{Required return on equity} \times \text{Amount} \\
&\quad \text{of equity} \\
&= (.12)(1 - t)(\$400{,}000) + (.18)(\$400{,}000) \\
&= (.12)(1 - .4)(\$400{,}000) + (.18)(\$400{,}000) \\
&= \$28{,}800 + \$72{,}000 \\
&= \$100{,}800.
\end{aligned}
$$

Thus

$$
\begin{aligned}
\frac{\text{Minimum acceptable}}{\text{rate of return}} &= \frac{\text{Required cash flow}}{\text{Investment}} \\
&= \frac{\$100{,}800}{\$800{,}000} \\
&= 12.6\%.
\end{aligned}
$$

As we shall demonstrate with Equation 20-6, the cost of capital for a company is the weighted average of the component cost of each source of capital. In the present example, with a capital structure comprised of 50 percent debt and 50 percent equity,

$$
\begin{aligned}
\text{Cost of capital} &= \text{After-tax cost of debt} \times \text{Proportion of debt in the} \\
&\quad \text{capital structure} + \text{Cost of equity} \times \text{Proportion of} \\
&\quad \text{equity in the capital structure} \\
&= (.12)(1 - .4)(.5) + (.18)(.5) \\
&= .036 + .090 \\
&= .126, \text{ or } 12.6\%.
\end{aligned}
$$

Thus it should be clear that a project's minimum acceptable cash flow is one that just satisfies each of the suppliers of capital; therefore a project's minimum acceptable rate of return is equal to the cost of capital. Although we return to this concept later in the chapter, the reader should be aware at this point that if the project provides a return greater than the cost of capital, the project will have a positive net present value since its returns exceed its minimum requirements.

Now that we have analyzed the basic concept behind the cost of capital, we can evaluate how the cost of each source of capital is computed, and then more formally describe the computation of the cost of capital.

Cost of Debt

The component cost used to calculate the weighted cost of capital is the interest rate on debt, k_d, multiplied by $(1 - t)$, where t is the firm's marginal tax rate:[3]

$$\text{Component cost of debt} = k_d(1 - t). \qquad \textbf{(20-1)}$$

For example, if a firm can borrow at a rate of 14 percent, and if it has a tax rate of 40 percent, then its **after-tax cost of debt** is

after-tax cost of debt,
$k_d(1 - t)$
The relevant cost to the firm for new debt financing since interest is deductible from taxable income.

$$k_d(1 - t) = 14\%(.06) = 8.4\%.$$

The reason for making the tax adjustment is as follows. The value of the firm's stock, which we want to maximize, depends on *after-tax* income. Interest is a deductible expense. The effect of this is as if the taxing authorities were paying part of the interest charges. Therefore, to put the costs of debt and equity on a comparable basis, we adjust the interest rate downward to account for the preferential tax treatment of debt.

The importance of the tax deductibility of interest may be observed below. Suppose a firm with a 50 percent tax rate has the choice of financing with debt or preferred stock. Interest is paid before taxes (thus it is tax deductible), while preferred stock dividends are paid after taxes and therefore are not tax deductible. If we assume the interest or preferred dividend payment is equal to $20, the result is summarized below:

	Debt Option	Preferred Option
EBIT	$100	$100
$-I$	-20	-0
EBT	80	100
$-T$	-40	-50
EAIT	40	50
$-Pfd$	-0	-20
NI	$\underline{\underline{\$40}}$	$\underline{\underline{\$30}}$

---

[3]In our discussion of the required return on equity, flotation costs, or the cost of selling equity through an investment banker, will be an integral part of the *cost of equity*. However, when we evaluate the *cost of debt*, flotation costs will be ignored. The flotation cost for a debt issue, sold through investment bankers in the capital markets, is usually quite low as a percentage of the issue. In fact, most debt is placed directly with banks, insurance companies, pension funds, and the like, and therefore has virtually no flotation cost. Thus, while the costs associated with the sale of both debt and equity by investment bankers are real, only the cost of selling equity will be considered in this chapter.

Note that, due to the tax deductibility of interest, the preferred dividend would have to fall by the amount of the tax subsidy on interest—50 percent—for the net income on the preferred-stock-financed income stream to equal the debt-financed stream's net income. Therefore the effective cost of debt capital to the business is not the interest rate on debt, but rather the after-tax cost determined by Equation 20-1.

The tax deductibility of interest holds not only for businesses but for individuals as well. Individuals may deduct the interest portion of their payments for homes, cars, and other debt-financed assets.

Our primary concern with the cost of capital is to use it in a decision-making process—to determine the minimum acceptable return on new capital budgeting or other investment projects. Thus the appropriate cost of debt is the cost for new borrowing, not the historical interest rates on old, previously outstanding debt. In other words, we are interested in the cost of the next dollar borrowed, or the *marginal* cost of debt. Whether the firm borrowed at a high or low rate in the past is irrelevant for this purpose.

Cost of Preferred Stock

The component **cost of preferred stock, k_p,** that is used to calculate the weighted cost of capital is the preferred dividend, D_p, divided by the net issuing price, P_n, or the price the firm receives after deducting flotation costs:

cost of preferred stock, k_p
The preferred dividend, D_p, divided by the net issuing price, P_n.

$$\text{Component cost of preferred stock} = k_p = \frac{D_p}{P_n}. \qquad \textbf{(20-2)}$$

Equation 20-2 assumes that the dividend from the preferred stock remains constant, that is, that the dividend will always be paid and that the preferred stock is not a participating preferred issue.

Let's suppose that a firm has preferred stock that pays a $12 dividend and sells for $100 per share in the market. If the company issues new shares of preferred, it will incur an underwriting (or flotation) cost of 2.5 percent, or $2.50 per share, so it will net $97.50 per share. Therefore the cost of preferred stock would be 12.31 percent:

$$k_p = \$12.00/\$97.50 = 12.31\%.$$

Equation 20-2 can also be used to determine the cost of preferred stock if an issue is already outstanding. Suppose the price of the stock falls to $80 per share. This is a signal to the firm that investors will no longer accept a return of approximately 12 percent; now they will require a 15 percent return:

$$k_p = \$12.00/\$80.00 = 15\%.$$

Of course, the investors' required return is the firm's cost of capital for that source of financing. Note that no tax adjustments are made when calculating k_p because, unlike interest on debt, dividends are not tax deductible.

Cost of Retained Earnings, k_s

cost of retained earnings, k_s
The rate of return stockholders require on the firm's common stock based on alternative investment opportunities that stockholders could make if no earnings were retained.

The cost of debt is based on the interest rate investors require on debt issues, adjusted for taxes. *The* **cost of retained earnings** *can be defined similarly; it is* **k_s,** *the rate of return stockholders require on the firm's common stock.*[4]

The required rate of return is equal to the riskless rate plus a risk premium: $k_s = R_F + \rho$. For stocks in equilibrium (which is the typical situation), the required rate of return is also equal to the expected rate of return, $\hat{k}_s$. In Chapter 18 we saw that the expected rate of return on a share of common stock depends, ultimately, on the dividends paid on the stock:

$$P_0 = \frac{D_1}{(1 + \hat{k}_s)} + \frac{D_2}{(1 + \hat{k}_s)^2} + \cdots + \frac{D_\infty}{(1 + \hat{k}_s)^\infty}. \qquad \text{(18-1)}$$

Here P_0 is the current price of the stock; D_t is the dividend expected to be paid at the end of Year t; and $\hat{k}_s$ is the expected rate of return. If dividends are expected to grow at a constant rate, then, as we saw in Chapter 18, Equation 18-1 reduces to the following expression:

$$P_0 = \frac{D_1}{\hat{k}_s - g}. \qquad \text{(20-3)}$$

We can solve for $\hat{k}_s$ to obtain the expected rate of return on common equity, which in equilibrium is also equal to the required rate of return:[5]

$$\hat{k}_s = \frac{D_1}{P_0} + \text{Expected g.} \qquad \text{(20-4)}$$

Thus investors expect to receive a dividend yield, D_1/P_0, plus a capital gains yield (a measure of the expected growth in the firm's value), g, for a total expected return of $\hat{k}_s$.

To illustrate, suppose a business, Tubbs Inc., begins to retain some

---

[4]"Retained earnings" for our purpose here refers to that part of current earnings which is not paid out in dividends but, rather, is retained and reinvested in the business.
[5]Note, however, that if a firm's growth rate is not expected to remain constant, then Equations 20-3 and 20-4 will not hold.

earnings rather than paying them all out as dividends. The stock is in equilibrium, it sells for $20.00, the next expected dividend is $1.60, and the expected growth rate is now 7 percent. The firm's expected and required rate of return, hence its cost of retained earnings, is

$$\hat{k}_s = k_s = \frac{\$1.60}{\$20.00} + 7\% = 8\% + 7\% = 15\%.$$

This is the minimum rate of return that management must be able to earn to justify retaining earnings and plowing them back into the business rather than paying them out to stockholders as dividends. Henceforth in this chapter we assume that equilibrium exists and use the terms k_s and $\hat{k}_s$ interchangeably.

The logic behind assigning a cost of capital to retained earnings involves the **opportunity cost** principle. The firm's after-tax earnings literally belong to the stockholders. Bondholders are compensated by interest payments, while earnings belong to the common stockholders and serve to "pay the rent" on stockholders' capital. Management may pay out earnings in the form of dividends, or earnings can be reinvested in the business. *If management decides to retain earnings, there is an opportunity cost involved—stockholders could have received the earnings as dividends and invested these funds in other stocks, in bonds, in real estate, or in anything else. Thus the firm must earn on the retained earnings at least as much as stockholders themselves could earn in alternative investments of comparable risk.*

What rate of return do stockholders expect to earn on equivalent risk investments? The answer is k_s. *Therefore, if the firm cannot invest retained earnings and earn at least k_s, then it should pay these funds to its stockholders and let them invest directly in other assets that do provide this return.*[6]

opportunity cost
The rate of return on the best alternative investment available—the highest return that will *not* be earned if the funds are invested in a particular project.

Finding the Basic Required Rate of Return on Common Equity

As we learned in Chapter 19, the vast majority of all firms in the United States have a debt/equity ratio of less than 1.0. That is, common stock equity typically provides the largest proportion of financing in the firm's capital structure. Unfortunately, the cost of equity is the most difficult of the components of the cost of capital to compute.

---

[6]One complexity in estimating the cost of retained earnings is that dividends and capital gains are taxed differently. Retaining earnings rather than paying them out as dividends can convert ordinary income to capital gains. This point is discussed in Eugene F. Brigham, *Financial Management: Theory and Practice,* 3rd ed. (Hinsdale, IL: Dryden Press, 1982), Appendix 15A.

Other sources of capital have periodic fixed or semifixed payment schedules, as with interest and principal payments on debt or with dividends on preferred stock (which are generally fixed, although there may be a participation feature). Unlike these securities, common stock has no constant payment pattern in either timing or amount for its returns in the form of dividends or market price when sold.

It is obvious by now that the basic rate of return investors require on a firm's common equity, k_s, is a most important yet elusive quantity. This required rate of return is the cost of retained earnings, and it forms the basis for the cost of capital obtained from new stock issues. How is this all-important quantity estimated? While we have assumed that the dividend capitalization model, $D_1/P_0 + g$, is an appropriate means of evaluating the investors' required return on equity, many other models exist, including the following.

The CAPM Approach

The Capital Asset Pricing Model (CAPM) as developed in Chapter 16 can be used to help estimate k_s. To use the CAPM, we proceed as follows:

Step 1 Estimate the riskless rate, R_F, generally taken to be either the Treasury bond rate or the 30-day Treasury bill rate.

Step 2 Estimate the stock's beta coefficient, b, and use this as an index of the stock's risk.

Step 3 Estimate the rate of return on "the market" or on an "average" stock. Designate this return k_M.

Step 4 Estimate the required rate of return on the firm's stock as follows:

$$k_s = R_F + b(k_M - R_F).$$

The value $(k_M - R_F)$ is the risk premium on the average stock, while b is an index of the particular stock's own risk.

To illustrate the CAPM approach, assume that $R_F = 6\%$, $k_M = 10\%$, and $b = 0.7$ for a given stock. The stock's k_s is calculated as follows:

$$k_s = 6 + 0.7(10 - 6) = 6 + 2.8 = 8.8\%.$$

Had b been 1.8, indicating that the stock was riskier than average, k_s would have been

$$k_s = 6 + 1.8(4) = 6 + 7.2 = 13.2\%.$$

It should be noted that while the CAPM approach appears to yield accurate, precise estimates of k_s, there are several problems with the approach.[7]

Bond Yield plus Risk Premium Approach

Although it is essentially an ad hoc, subjective procedure, analysts often estimate a firm's cost of common equity by adding a risk premium of about four percentage points to the interest rate on the firm's long-term debt. For example, if a firm's bonds yield 9 percent, then its cost of equity might be estimated as follows:

$$k_s = \text{Bond rate} + \text{Risk premium} = 9\% + 4\% = 13\%.$$

This risk premium is a judgmental estimate, so the estimated value of k_s is also judgmental.[8]

Which of the methods to determine the cost of equity is correct? The answer is, of course, that all are correct within their limiting assumptions. Then which ones should be used in business situations? Many business firms use all of these methods to approximate the cost of equity. The Du Pont Corporation uses five different methods to evaluate and approximate the cost of equity capital to the firm. Therefore we would suggest that in practical work it is best to use all three of the methods discussed here, and then apply judgment when the methods produce differing results. Managers experienced in estimating equity capital costs recognize that both careful analysis and some very fine judgments are required. *It would be nice to pretend that these judgments are unnecessary and to specify an easy, precise way of determining the exact cost of equity capital. Unfortunately, this is not possible. Finance is in large part a matter of judgment, and we simply must face this fact.*

Cost of Newly Issued Common Stock, or External Equity, k_e

The cost of new common stock, or external equity capital, k_e, is higher than the cost of retained earnings, k_s, because of flotation costs involved in selling new common stock. What rate of return must be earned on funds raised by selling stock in order to make this action worthwhile? To put it another way, what is the cost of new common stock?

cost of external equity, k_e
The cost of retained earnings adjusted for flotation costs.

---

[7]These problems are discussed in Brigham, op. cit., Chapter 5, so we will not belabor the point here.

[8]Analysts who use this procedure often cite studies of historical returns on stocks and bonds and use the difference between the average yield (dividends plus capital gains) on stocks and the average yield on bonds as the risk premium of stocks over bonds. The most frequently cited study is R. G. Ibbotson and R. A. Sinquefield, "Stocks, Bonds, Bills, and Inflation: Year-By-Year Historical Returns (1926–1974)," *Journal of Business*, January 1976.

For a firm with a constant growth rate, the answer is found by applying the following formula:

$$k_e = \frac{D_1}{P_0(1 - F)} + g. \tag{20-5}$$

Here F is the percentage flotation cost incurred in selling the issue, so $P_0(1 - F)$ is the net price per share received by the company when it sells new shares.

Recall that Tubbs Inc. had a required return of 15 percent on its currently issued common stock equity. However, if the firm wishes to issue new equity there will be a flotation cost charged by the investment banker which will affect the cost of equity. If the flotation charge for Tubbs's new issue is 10 percent, the cost of new outside equity is computed as follows:

$$
\begin{aligned}
k_e &= \frac{\$1.60}{\$20.00(1 - 0.10)} + 7\% \\
&= \frac{\$1.60}{\$18.00} + 7\% \\
&= 8.89\% + 7\% \\
&= 15.89\%.
\end{aligned}
$$

Investors require a return on equity shares which consists of a current dividend yield, D_1/P_0, and a growth or capital gains component, g. For Tubbs this required return, k_s, was 15 percent. However, because of flotation costs, the company *must earn more* than 15 percent on funds obtained by selling common stock to provide this 15 percent return. What caused this seeming contradiction? Specifically, the firm will have to provide the $1.60 in dividends next year and maintain a 7 percent growth with $18 a share, not $20. Thus the firm must meet these investor expectations with only 90 percent of the issue, since 10 percent goes to the investment banker for services in selling the stock. Therefore, if Tubbs earns less than 15.89 percent on the new equity-financed project, the investment will be unable to provide the required dividend of $1.60 and the anticipated 7 percent growth. Such a decline in either dividends or growth or both would cause the value of the stock to decline. Conversely, if the project earns more than 15.89 percent, the firm's dividend and/or growth will be larger than required and the price of Tubbs's stock will rise.

Combining Debt and Equity: Weighted Average, or Composite, Cost of Capital, k_a

In Chapter 19 we examined the effects of leverage on the cost of debt, on the cost of equity, and on the market price of a company's stock. We concluded that the optimal mix of securities, or the optimal capital structure, is the one that maximizes the price of the firm's stock, and that a rational firm would use this mix as its *target capital structure*. Furthermore, we noted that the firm should raise new capital in proportion to its target capital structure in order to keep the capital structure on target over time.

The proportions of debt and equity in the target capital structure are used to help calculate the weighted cost of capital for the firm. Remember, the cost that is most important is the cost of the *marginal* or *next* dollar to be raised based on the firm's proportional debt/equity mix. Assume that Wofford's Unfinished Furniture Stores, Inc. has a target capital structure calling for 40 percent debt and 60 percent common stock equity. Other key data are summarized below:

$$P_0 = \$27.50.$$

$D_0 = \$2.00 =$ Dividends per share in the *last* period. (D_0 has already been paid, so an investor purchasing this stock today would *not* receive D_0, but rather would receive D_1, the *next* dividend.)

$$g = 10\%.$$

$$k_s = \frac{D_1}{P_0} + g = \frac{D_0(1 + g)}{P_0} + g$$

$$= \frac{\$2.00(1.1)}{\$27.50} + 0.10 = \frac{\$2.20}{\$27.50} + 0.10$$

$$= 0.08 + 0.10 = 0.18$$

$$= 18\%.$$

$$k_d = 10\%.$$

$$t = 40\% = 0.4.$$

$$k_d(1 - t) = 10\%(0.6) = 6\%.$$

Now suppose the company needs to raise $3 million. To keep its capital structure on target, it must obtain $0.4(\$3,000,000) = \$1,200,000$ as debt and $0.6(\$3,000,000) = \$1,800,000$ as equity. The weighted average cost of the new capital is calculated as follows:

Component	Weight	Component Cost	Product
Debt	0.4	6.0%	2.4%
Equity	0.6	18.0	10.8
		Weighted average cost = k_a =	13.2%

The calculations in the above table can also be thought of in an equation format:

$$k_a = \left(\begin{array}{c} \text{Fraction} \\ \text{of debt in} \\ \text{capital} \\ \text{structure} \end{array}\right)\left(\begin{array}{c} \text{Interest} \\ \text{rate} \end{array}\right)\left(1 - \text{Tax rate}\right) + \left(\begin{array}{c} \text{Fraction} \\ \text{of equity} \\ \text{in capital} \\ \text{structure} \end{array}\right)\left(\begin{array}{c} \text{Cost of} \\ \text{equity} \end{array}\right)$$

$$= w_d(k_d)(1 - t) + w_s(k_s) \qquad \qquad \textbf{(20-6)}$$
$$= 0.4(10\%)(0.6) + 0.6(18\%)$$
$$= 2.4\% + 10.8\%$$
$$= 13.2\%.$$

Using either method, we see that every dollar of new capital consists of 40 cents of debt with an after-tax cost of 6 percent and 60 cents of equity with a cost of 18 percent. The average cost of the whole dollar is 13.2 percent.

Preferred Stock

Wofford's does not use preferred stock. However, if it did, the cost of preferred stock would be included in the calculation of the composite cost of capital as follows:

1. Estimate the component cost of the preferred stock, k_p:

$$k_p = D_p/P_n.$$

Here D_p is the dividend that Wofford's would have to pay on the preferred stock (remember, the dividend is constant and generally not skipped since no common dividends may be paid if preferred dividends are omitted), and P_n is the net (after flotation costs) price per share the company would receive. If $D_p = \$3.25$ and $P_n = \$25$, then

$$k_p = \$3.25/\$25 = 0.13 = 13\%.$$

Since preferred dividends are not deductible, no tax adjustment is needed.

2. Determine the target capital structure percentages, or weights. We assume that Wofford's has decided to use $w_d = 35$ percent debt, $w_p = 10$ percent preferred stock, and $w_s = 55$ percent common stock equity.

3. Combine the component costs with the capital structure weights to determine the weighted average cost of capital, using an expanded version of Equation 20-6. We have already assumed that $k_d = 10\%$, $k_p = 13\%$, and $k_s = 18\%$, so

$$k_a = w_d(k_d)(1 - t) + w_pk_p + w_sk_s$$
$$= 0.35(10\%)(1 - t) + 0.10(13\%) + 0.55(18\%)$$
$$= 0.021 + 0.013 + 0.099 = 0.133$$
$$= 13.3\%.$$

Thus, if Wofford's decided to use preferred stock in addition to debt and common stock, the average cost of each dollar raised would rise slightly to 13.3 percent.

Minimizing the Weighted Average Cost of Capital

A firm that seeks to maximize the price of its stock must also seek to minimize the costs of producing any given level of output. Thus management should try to obtain its required capital at the lowest possible cost, and this amounts to minimizing its weighted average cost of capital.

Table 20-1, which again uses data developed for SCI in Chapter 19, shows how that company's capital structure affects its weighted average cost of capital. At a zero debt ratio, all of SCI's capital is common equity, so $k_a = k_s = 12\%$. When the company begins to use debt, the cost of capital becomes a weighted average of the costs of debt and equity. As the use of debt increases, the weight of debt increases and that of equity decreases.

Notice that k_a declines until the debt/assets ratio hits 40 percent, at which point $k_a = 10.8$ percent. After this point k_a begins to rise. Notice also that SCI's stock price, taken from Table 19-5 and shown in Column 10 of Table 20-1, is maximized at the same 40 percent debt/assets ratio that minimizes k_a. This illustrates a very important point: *the capital structure that minimizes a firm's weighted average cost of capital also maximizes the value of its stock.*

The values in Columns 3, 6, and 9 of Table 20-1 are plotted in Figure 20-1. This type of graph is used often in finance to show pictorially the relationship between each cost component—k_s, k_d, and k_a—and the debt/assets ratio.

Several additional points should be noted regarding Table 20-1 and Figure 20-1:

1. As indicated above, k_s cannot be measured with a high degree of precision. It is difficult to obtain an estimate of k_s for a given capital structure, and even more difficult to estimate the relationship between k_s and the debt/assets ratio. Thus the data contained here should be taken as illustrative, not as representing precise estimates.

2. The costs of debt and equity do rise with increases in the debt ratio, and the weighted average cost of capital does first decline, then rise, as debt is added to the capital structure.

3. The average cost of capital curve seems to be shaped more like a U (or, really, like a shallow bowl) than like a V with a sharp, clearly defined minimum point. Thus relatively small departures from the optimal capital structure will have no significant effect on the firm's cost of capital. For example, if SCI used as little as 30 percent or as much as 50 percent debt, this would not have much effect on either its average cost of capital or its stock price. Furthermore, a relatively flat average

Table 20-1
Calculation of SCI's Average Cost of Capital, k_a, with Different Capital Structures

Debt/ Assets Ratio (1)	Before-Tax Cost of Debt, k_d (2)	After-Tax Cost of Debt, $k_d(1-t)$ (3)	Weight of Debt, w_d (4)	Product: $(3) \times (4)$ (5)	Cost of Equity, k_s (6)	Weight of Equity, w_s (7)	Product: $(6) \times (7)$ (8)	Weighted Average Cost of Capital, $k_a =$ (5) + (8) (9)	Stock Price from Table 19-5 (10)
0%	8.0%	4.80%	0.0	0.00%	12.0%	1.0	12.00%	12.00%	$20.00
10	8.0	4.80	0.1	0.48	12.2	0.9	10.98	11.46	20.98
20	8.3	4.98	0.2	1.00	12.6	0.8	10.08	11.08	21.83
30	9.0	5.40	0.3	1.62	13.2	0.7	9.24	10.86	22.50
40	10.0	6.00	0.4	2.40	14.0	0.6	8.40	10.80	22.86
50	12.0	7.20	0.5	3.60	15.2	0.5	7.60	11.20	22.11
60	15.0	9.00	0.6	5.40	16.8	0.4	6.72	12.12	19.64

Notes:
1. The marginal tax rate is 40 percent.
2. The before-tax cost of debt and the values for k_s are taken from Table 19-5.
3. The cost of capital is minimized, and the stock price is maximized, at a 40 percent debt/assets ratio.

Figure 20-1
Relationship between SCI's Capital Structure and Its Cost of Capital
This figure illustrates how a company's capital structure affects its cost of capital. As debt is added, the weighted average cost of capital (k_a) begins to decline, bottoms out at a debt/assets ratio of 40 percent, and then begins to rise. Stock value peaks at the same 40 percent ratio (Table 20-1), showing that maximum stock value will follow from a capital structure that minimizes a firm's weighted average cost of capital.

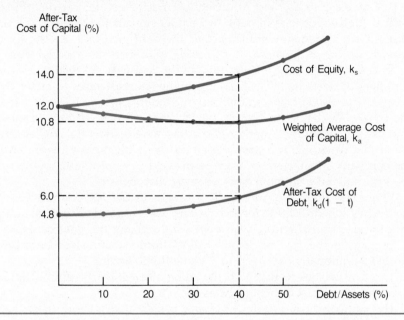

cost of capital curve gives financial managers flexibility in raising new capital—they can sell bonds one year, then stock the next, to take advantage of reduced flotation costs on larger offerings and also to take advantage of relatively favorable conditions in either the stock or the bond markets during a particular year.

Changes in the Cost of Capital

In the previous section we demonstrated that the cost of capital changes as the proportion of debt and equity in the capital structure changes. As a general rule, a different **marginal cost of capital (MCC)**[9] will exist for every possible capital structure; *the optimal capital structure is the one that produces the lowest MCC.* Could Wofford's Unfinished Fur-

marginal cost of capital (MCC)
The cost of obtaining another dollar of new capital; the weighted average cost of capital at a particular dollar value of new capital.

---

[9]Recall that the marginal cost of a dollar is defined as the cost of obtaining another dollar of new capital. For our purposes the terms *marginal* and *weighted average* cost of capital will be used synonymously.

niture Stores raise an unlimited amount of new capital at the 13.2 percent cost as long as its capital structure is maintained at 40 percent debt and 60 percent equity? The answer is *no*. As companies raise larger and larger sums during a given time period, the costs of both the debt and the equity components begin to rise, and as this occurs, the weighted average cost of obtaining new capital rises.

This increase in the cost of capital occurs for several reasons. First, even if the proportions of debt and equity remain the same, the level of interest payments must increase as the debt increases. As the fixed interest payments increase, the financial risk increases, as evidenced by lower coverage ratios. Certainly, as the financial risk increases, the suppliers of debt capital will require higher interest rates to offset the greater risk. Second, generating larger amounts of equity means that the firm will exhaust its internal equity and will have to turn to more expensive new equity. Another factor that would affect the cost of capital is that the firm's risk profile may change with rapid growth, since the company's management may be pressed beyond its capabilities or the firm may take on more risky projects than before.

MCC schedule
A graph or table that relates the firm's weighted average cost of capital to the amount of new capital raised.

Where will these cost increases or breaks in the **MCC schedule** occur? While it is difficult to tell in practice, we can provide some insights into the determination of these points by utilizing the data generated in discussing the cost of capital for Wofford's Unfinished Furniture Stores. Additionally, we need to assume the following:

1. The firm wishes to maintain the same 40%/60% debt/equity capital structure under all financing plans.

2. The company will not invest in any project that is more risky than current projects.

3. Wofford's can borrow up to $8,000 at the current 10 percent interest rate, with additional debt costing 12 percent.

4. The firm has a total of $8,400 in undistributed profits for this period which management has decided to retain rather than use for dividends. (Note that this money was earned this year and not retained previously.)

5. $k_s = D_1/P_0 + g = \$1.80/\$22.50 + 0.10 = 18\%$

$k_e = D_1/P_0(1 - F) + g = \$1.80/\$22.50(1 - 0.08) + 0.10 = 18.7\%$,

where

D_1 = next year's dividend,
P_0 = current common stock price for Wofford's shares,
F = percentage flotation cost for new equity shares,
g = expected growth rate.

6. The marginal tax rate will remain a constant 40 percent for these computations.

Wofford's weighted average cost of capital is calculated in Table 20-2, which first shows the new retained earnings (earnings retained

Table 20-2
Wofford's Marginal Cost of Capital Using:
(1) New Retained Earnings and (2) New Common Stock

Source	Weight	×	Component Cost	=	Product
(1) MCC When Equity Is Obtained Internally (from Retained Earnings)					
Debt	0.4		6.0%[a]		2.40%
Equity	0.6		18.0		10.80
	1.0				13.20%
(2) MCC When Equity Is Obtained Externally (from Sale of New Stock)					
Debt	0.4		6.0%		2.40%
Equity	0.6		18.7		11.22
	1.0				13.62%

[a]Recall that the cost of debt = $k_d (1 - t) = 10\% (.6) = 6\%$.

this year, not in the past) and then the new common stock. We see that the weighted average cost of each dollar, or the marginal cost of capital, is 13.2 percent so long as retained earnings are used, but the average cost jumps to 13.62 percent as soon as the firm exhausts its internal financing and is forced to sell new common stock.

How much new capital can Wofford's raise before it exhausts its retained earnings and is forced to sell new common stock—that is, where will the **break, or jump, in the MCC schedule** occur? The question becomes one of how much *total financing*—debt plus the $8,400 in retained earnings—can be done before retained earnings are exhausted and the firm is forced to sell new common stock. Sixty percent of the total financing will be made with the $8,400 of retained earnings. Therefore, if X equals total financing allowable with no new equity, then

$$0.6X = \text{Retained earnings} = \$8,400.$$

Solving for X, we obtain the **break point:**

$$\text{Break point} = X = \frac{\text{Retained earnings}}{0.6} = \frac{\$8,400}{0.6} = \$14,000.$$

Thus Wofford's can raise $14,000, consisting of $8,400 of retained earnings and $5,600 ($14,000 − $8,400 = $5,600) of new debt supported by these new retained earnings, without altering its capital structure:

40%—new debt supported by retained earnings	$ 5,600
60%—retained earnings	8,400
Total expansion supportable by retained earnings, or break point for retained earnings in the MCC schedule	$14,000

break, or jump, in the MCC schedule
A change in the weighted average cost of capital that occurs when there is a change in a component cost of capital.

break point
The dollar value of new capital raised that corresponds to a jump in the MCC schedule.

We have noted that there will be other possible breaks in the MCC schedule when the cost of any component source of capital changes. One such possible change for Wofford's would be the increase in the cost of debt if more than $8,000 is needed. If additional debt (over the $8,000 level) is required, it can be acquired, but at a cost of 12 percent. This will result in a second break point in the MCC schedule at the level where the $8,000 of cheaper, 10 percent debt is exhausted. At what amount of *total financing* will the 10 percent debt be used up? If we let Y represent the total financing at this second break point, then

$$0.4Y = \$8,000,$$

and, solving for Y, we obtain

$$Y = \frac{10\% \text{ debt}}{0.4} = \frac{\$8,000}{0.4} = \$20,000 = \text{Break point for debt.}$$

Thus there will be another break in the MCC schedule after Wofford's has raised a total of $20,000. As we demonstrated previously, up to $14,000 the MCC is 13.2 percent and just beyond $14,000 the MCC rises to 13.62 percent. Now we see that the MCC rises again at $20,001, to 14.1 percent:

Source	Weight	$\times$	Component Cost	$=$	Product
Debt	0.4		7.2%[a]		2.88%
Equity	0.6		18.7		11.22
	1.0				14.10%

[a]The cost of debt = $k_d (1 - t) = 12\% (1 - 0.4) = 7.2\%$.

In other words, the next dollar beyond $20,000 will consist of 40 cents of 12 percent debt (7.2 percent after taxes) and 60 cents of new common stock (retained earnings were used up much earlier), and this marginal dollar will have an average cost of 14.1 percent.

The effect of this new MCC increase is shown in Figure 20-2. We now have two breaks, one caused by using up all of the retained earnings and the other caused by using up all of the 10 percent debt. With the two breaks, we have three different MCCs: $MCC_1 = 13.2\%$ for the first $14,000 of new capital; $MCC_2 = 13.62\%$ in the interval between $14,000 and $20,000; and $MCC_3 = 14.1\%$ for all new capital beyond $20,000.

There could, of course, be still more break points—for example, debt costs could continue to rise, or the flotation costs on new common

Figure 20-2
**Marginal Cost of Capital Schedule for Wofford's Using Retained Earnings,
New Common Stock, and Higher-Cost Debt**
Even though a business may maintain a constant optimal capital structure, it cannot count
on raising an unlimited amount of new capital at the same cost. For example, Wofford's
can expect to encounter two breaks, or increases, in its marginal cost of capital (MCC).
The first occurs at $14,000 in total financing, when retained earnings are exhausted and
the firm issues new common stock. The second break comes at $20,000, when cost of
debt increases, bringing the MCC to 14.10 percent. A break will thus occur whenever
costs of either debt or equity increase.

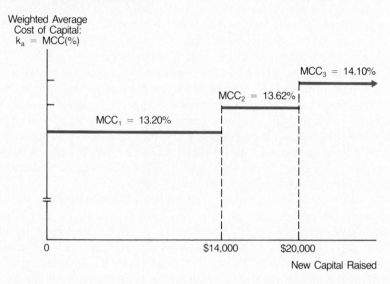

stock could increase above 8 percent as larger amounts of stock are
sold. These changes would cause more breaks in the MCC.

The easiest sequence for calculating MCC schedules is as follows:
1. Identify the points where breaks occur. A break will occur any time
the cost of one of the capital components rises. (However, it is possible
that two capital components could both increase at the same point.)
2. Determine the cost of capital for each component in the intervals
between breaks.
3. Calculate the weighted averages of these costs; the weighted averages are the MCCs in each interval.
Notice that if there are n separate breaks, there will be n + 1 different
MCCs. For example, in Figure 20-2 we see two breaks and three different MCCs.

Before concluding this section, we should note again that a different
MCC schedule would result if a different capital structure were used.
The optimal capital structure produces the lowest MCC.

Combining the MCC and the
Investment Opportunity Schedule (IOS)

Now that we have calculated the MCC schedule, we can use it to determine the discount rate used in the capital budgeting process; that is, *we can use the MCC schedule to find the cost of capital for use in determining projects' net present values (NPVs) as discussed in Chapter 15.*

To understand how the MCC is used in capital budgeting, assume that Wofford's has three financial executives: a financial vice president, a treasurer, and a director of capital budgeting. Of course, if the firm were smaller, the steps we will outline would still be carried out, but by the financial officer—perhaps with the aid of the firm's president—rather than with a staff as in the case of a larger firm.

For Wofford's, the financial vice president first asks the treasurer to develop the firm's MCC schedule, as we have done in Figure 20-2. Next, the financial vice president asks the director of capital budgeting (DCB) to determine the dollar amounts of potentially acceptable projects, using the IRR method (or using the NPV method at a number of different discount rates). The DCB has a listing of all the firm's potential projects, including the cost of each project and its projected annual net cash inflows. This listing is shown in Table 20-3.

The DCB would first calculate each project's IRR as shown in the last column of Table 20-3, then plot the data given there as the **investment opportunity schedule** (IOS) shown in Figure 20-3. The figure also reproduces Wofford's MCC schedule as plotted in Figure 20-2. The IOS shows how much money Wofford's could invest at different rates of return. If the cost of capital were above 17 percent, none of the available projects would have a positive NPV, hence none of them should be accepted. In that case Wofford's would simply not expand. If the cost of capital were 17 percent, Wofford's should take on only Project D, and its capital budget would call for the company to raise and invest $7,000. If the cost of capital were 16 percent, the firm should take only

investment opportunity schedule (IOS)
A listing, or graph, of the firm's investment opportunities ranked in order of the projects' rates of return.

Table 20-3
Potential Capital Budgeting Projects Available to Wofford's

Project	Cost	Annual Inflows	Project Life (Years)	IRR (or Discount Rate at Which NPV = 0)
A	$4,000	$1,137	5	13.0%
B	3,000	721	7	15.0
C	5,000	885	10	12.0
D	7,000	1,950	6	17.0
E	4,000	862	8	14.0
F	5,000	2,226	3	16.0

Figure 20-3
Combining Wofford's MCC and IOS Curves to
Determine Its Optimal Capital Budget

This figure shows how the MCC schedule is used in capital budgeting. The investment opportunity schedule (IOS) indicates how much Wofford's can afford to invest at different rates of return. The two schedules intersect at an MCC of 13.62 percent, indicating the cost of capital that should be used in evaluating projects in capital budgeting. Projects D, F, B, and E, which have returns in excess of the cost of capital, would thus be accepted, making the total optimal capital budget $19,000. Because Projects A and C would have to be financed at 14.10 percent, they should be rejected.

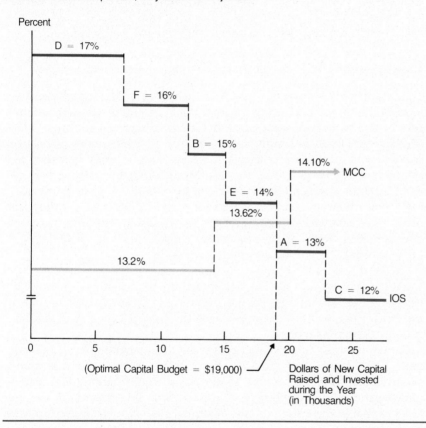

Projects D and F, raising a total of $12,000. Successively lower costs of capital call for larger and larger investment outlays.

Just how far down its IOS curve should the firm go? That is, which of its available projects should it accept? The answer is that the firm *should accept the four projects (D, F, B, and E) which have rates of return in excess of the cost of capital that would be required to finance them.* Projects A and C should be rejected, because they would have to be financed with capital that has a cost of 14.1 percent, and at that cost of capital, A and C have (1) negative NPVs and (2) IRRs that are below their costs of capital. Therefore Wofford's Unfinished Furniture Stores should have a capital budget of $19,000.

In the plotting of the IOS and MCC schedules, their intersection should be noted—in our example the MCC is 13.62 percent at that point. If the firm uses 13.62 percent to evaluate all projects, then Projects D, F, B, and E will be accepted, while A and C will be rejected. Thus *the cost of capital used in the capital budgeting process as discussed in Chapter 15 is actually determined at the intersection of the IOS and MCC schedules. If this intersection rate is used, then the firm will make correct accept/reject decisions, and its level of financing and investment will be optimal. If it uses any other rate, its capital budgeting will not be optimal.*

Summary

This chapter has shown how the MCC schedule is developed and then used in the capital budgeting process. We began by discussing the process of estimating the cost of each capital structure component. The *after-tax cost of debt* is simply $k_d(1 - t)$. The first increment of *common equity* is raised by *retaining earnings*, whose cost, k_s, may be estimated in one of three ways: (1) by the CAPM equation, $k_s = R_F + b(k_M - R_F)$; (2) by the dividend growth model, $k_s = D_1/P_0 + g$; or (3) by adding a risk premium of about 4 percent to the firm's cost of long-term debt. Once retained earnings have been exhausted, the firm must sell new common stock, or *external equity*, whose cost is $k_e = D_1/[P_0(1 - F)] + g$ in the case of a constant-growth stock.

The next task is to combine the component costs to form a *weighted average cost of capital, k_a*. The weights used to develop k_a should be based on the firm's target capital structure. If these weights are used, the stock price will be maximized and the cost of capital will simultaneously be minimized.

Capital typically has a higher cost if the firm expands beyond certain limits. This means that the MCC curve turns up beyond some point. We used the *break point concept* to develop a step-function MCC schedule, which we then combined with the IOS to determine both the optimal capital budget and the cost of capital that should be used in capital budgeting.

The concepts developed here are extended in Chapter 21, where we consider the optimal allocation of current earnings between dividends and retained earnings.

Small Business $ $ $ $ $ $ $ $ $

Cost of Equity Capital for Small Firms

The three techniques for estimating the cost of equity capital that were discussed in this chapter have serious limitations when applied to small firms, increasing the need for the small-business manager to use judgment. The first technique is the application of Gordon's constant-growth model in the formula $D/P + E(g)$, where D is the expected dividend for the next period, P is the current market price, and $E(g)$ is the expected growth rate in dividends. Imagine a small, rapidly growing firm such as Biotechnology General (BTG) discussed in Chapter 18. BTG does not pay dividends, and it will not do so for the foreseeable future. For this firm, then, a constant-dividend-growth model will not be applicable, and in fact it is difficult to imagine any dividend model that would be of practical benefit in such a case.

The second technique is to use the yield on the firm's bonds plus a risk premium of, say, 4 percent. A small firm is unlikely to have a public debt issue outstanding; such debt is highly illiquid and is not normally issued by smaller firms. BTG, for example, has no such debt issue outstanding. Therefore we could not use the bond risk-premium approach for BTG.

The third approach suggested is to use the CAPM to estimate equity capital cost. If the firm's equity is not publicly traded, this approach cannot be used, but it is workable even for relatively small firms that do have publicly traded equity. If the firm has no publicly traded equity, then it can use the so-called "pure-play" technique: find a firm in the same line of business that does have public equity, and estimate the beta of the public firm's stock. As a first approximation, that beta can be used to estimate the cost of equity capital of the nonpublic firm.

To illustrate the pure-play approach, again consider BTG. Since BTG stock was issued very recently, few data are available for estimating BTG's equity beta. But the data that are available for a more established firm, such as Genentech, might give at least an estimate of the beta for the biological and genetic engineering industry. Of course, Genentech's beta would have to be subjectively modified to reflect Genentech's relatively established record and the differences in the nature of the products developed by the two firms.

As long as there are public companies available for comparison and those firms are in similar lines of business, the estimates of their betas can be used in estimating the cost of capital of a firm whose equity is not publicly traded. The resulting equity capital cost estimate would then have to be adjusted upward to reflect a penalty for the illiquidity of the nonpublic firm.

Flotation Costs for Small Issues

When external equity capital is raised, the flotation costs increase the cost of equity capital beyond what it would be for internal funds. These external flotation costs are especially significant for smaller issues and may substantially affect capital budgeting decisions involving external equity funds.

To illustrate this point, consider a

firm that is expected to pay constant dividends forever. In this case, if F is the percentage flotation cost, then the cost of equity capital is $D/[P(1 - F)]$. The higher the flotation cost, the higher the cost of external equity.

How big is F? According to a study made by the Securities and Exchange Commission in 1974, the average flotation cost of large common stock offerings (over $50 million) is only about 4 percent. For a firm that is expected to pay a 20 percent return on equity, that is, $D/P = 20\%$, for a large offering the cost of equity is $20\%/(1 - .04)$, or 20.8 percent.

The SEC's data for small offerings (less than $1 million) suggest that flotation costs for small offerings average about 21 percent. Thus the cost of equity capital in the above example would be $20\%/(1 - .21)$, or about 25.3 percent. Compared to the 20.8 percent for large offerings, it is clear that a small firm will have a considerably higher hurdle rate for the same project than would a large firm. The small firm is therefore at a substantial disadvantage because of the effects of flotation costs.

The Small Firm Effect

A number of researchers have observed that portfolios of small-firm stocks have consistently higher average returns than do portfolios of large-firm stocks. On the surface, it would seem to be beneficial for small firms to appear to produce average returns that are higher than those of large firms. In reality, it is bad news for the small firms. What it means is that the capital market demands higher returns for stocks of small firms than for otherwise similar stocks of large firms. In short, the cost of equity capital is higher for small firms, even ignoring the flotation costs at the time of issuance.

It might be argued that the stocks of small firms are more risky than the stocks of large firms, thereby accounting for the differences in returns. It is true that research usually finds that betas are higher on average for the small firms than for the large firms. However, the larger returns for small firms remain larger even after taking out the effects of the higher risks of small firms—at least the higher risks in observed beta values.

The small-firm effect is an anomaly; that is, it is not consistent with presently available theory. In other words, we don't understand why small firms have higher returns, we just know that they do. Until a satisfactory explanation exists for the small-firm effect, we can say only that the required returns (and cost of equity capital) are greater for small firms than they would be for otherwise similar large firms. The manager of a small firm should take this factor into account in estimating the cost of equity capital. In general, the cost of equity capital appears to be about 4 percent higher per annum for small firms (those with market values of less than $20 million) than for large firms of similar risk characteristics.

Resolution to Decision in Finance

The New World of Corporate Finance

Due to the streamlined procedures it allows for distributing securities, Rule 415 has the potential to save corporate financial officers huge amounts of time and money. Rule 415 can bring big changes to the corporate treasurer's life. It is now possible for him or her to eliminate the uncertainty about total borrowing cost, to sell securities in small pieces at more frequent intervals rather than chance the market with one huge offering on one day, and to slash paperwork and regulatory hassles at the Securities and Exchange Commission and with his or her own company directors, accountants, and lawyers.

These are all possible because decisions the chief financial officer made during the registration period can now be made weeks and even months ahead. Far removed from the pressure-cooker climate of a contemplated offering, the company can prepare a 415 registration before a sale is set or there is any deadline to be met. It may register when it has no intention of selling, perhaps because the market is unfavorable, with the thought of being ready when it improves.

Corporations are finding 415 an especially valuable way to deal with the persistent volatility of the bond market. Rallies have been exceedingly short and infrequent during the past few years. "This year, there hasn't been one that lasted more than a couple of days—if you want to call anything this year a rally," comments Senior Vice President David Lovejoy of Security Pacific Corp. Thus, adds Exxon Assistant Treasurer Allen Harrison, "Rule 415 gives us the opportunity to meet a bid that may not be there 48 hours later."

Lovejoy, who sold the first debt deal under 415, believes that "the main advantage was the favorable rate. We paid 13.90 percent on May 20, when the government rate was 13.60 percent." Rates on a similar issue were close to 15 percent—a full point higher—only a month later, underlining Lovejoy's belief that "I owe it to my shareholders to use 415." Security Pacific also plans to save money by using 415 to make direct sales to institutions, eliminating any underwriter's spread.

The fact that Rule 415 allows companies to bypass investment bankers has brought loud protests from the Wall Street crowd. As a result of 415, a number of corporate issuers have begun to disregard investment banking relationships that have lasted a generation, adding a herd of new underwriters to their stables. Wall Street houses such as Dean Witter Reynolds and Warburg Paribas Becker/A. G. Becker have captured new business.

Regional underwriters have lost out because fewer syndicates are being formed; the steady, lucrative business they had for decades is no longer assured, and they fear for the very existence of their corporate finance departments. If these deteriorate, small, new companies will have a tough time going public.

In fact, 415's advantages are definitely weighted in favor of big companies, particularly those with triple-A and double-A credit ratings and those that are frequent issuers, such as banks, utilities, and credit companies. These borrowers, especially the frequent borrowers, get a big payoff by cutting paperwork costs and hassles and enlarging the number of ideas for financing and selling their securities.

Rule 415 may also be more suited for selling debt than equity because of the different ways the market will be affected. A large debt registration isn't likely to affect borrowing costs, which depend more on prevailing interest rates and credit ratings. But a large stock registration can depress the price of outstanding shares and increase the cost of capital on subsequent sales.

Commissioner John Evans and the free-market thinkers who dominate the SEC these days are aware of 415's negative possibilities for users and investment bankers. But according to their free-market philosophy, if 415 isn't basically advantageous, it won't be used. And if 415 does work, then American corporations will benefit from a less regulated, more efficient, and cheaper market.

Source: Adapted from "The New World of Corporate Finance," by Arlene Hershman. Reprinted with the permission of *Dun's Business Month* (formerly *Dun's Review*), August 1982. Copyright 1982, Dun & Bradstreet Publications Corporation.

Key Terms You should be able to define each of the following terms:

Weighted average, or composite, cost of capital, k_a
Capital components
Required cash flow
After-tax cost of debt, $k_d(1 - t)$
Cost of preferred stock, k_p
Cost of retained earnings, k_s

Opportunity cost
Cost of external equity, k_e
Marginal cost of capital (MCC)
MCC schedule; break, or jump, in the MCC schedule; break point
Investment opportunity schedule (IOS)

Questions

20-1 In what sense is the marginal cost of capital an average cost?

20-2 How would each of the following affect a firm's cost of debt, $k_d(1 - t)$; its cost of equity, k_s; and its average cost of capital, k_a? Indicate by a plus (+), a minus (−), or a zero (0) if the factor would raise, lower, or have an indeterminate effect on the items in question. Assume other things are held constant. Be prepared to justify your answer, but recognize that several of the parts probably have no single correct answer; these questions are designed to stimulate thought and discussion.

	Effect on		
	$k_d(1-t)$	k_s	k_a
a. The corporate tax rate is lowered.	_____	_____	_____
b. The Federal Reserve tightens credit.	_____	_____	_____
c. The firm uses more debt; that is, it increases the debt/assets ratio.	_____	_____	_____
d. The dividend payout ratio is increased.	_____	_____	_____
e. The firm doubles the amount of capital it raises during the year.	_____	_____	_____
f. The firm expands into a risky new area.	_____	_____	_____
g. The firm merges with another firm whose earnings are countercyclical to those of the first firm and to the stock market.	_____	_____	_____
h. The stock market falls drastically, and our firm's stock falls along with the rest.	_____	_____	_____
i. Investors become more averse to risk.	_____	_____	_____
j. The firm is an electric utility with a large investment in nuclear plants. Several states propose a ban on nuclear power generation.	_____	_____	_____

20-3 Suppose a firm estimates its MCC and IOS schedules for the coming year and finds that they intersect at the point 10%, $10 million. What cost of capital should be used to evaluate average-risk projects, high-risk projects, and low-risk projects?

Self-Test Problem

ST-1 Laser Communications, Inc. (LCI) has the following capital structure, which it considers to be optimal:

Debt	25%
Preferred stock	15
Common equity	60
Total capital	100%

LCI's net income expected this year is $17,142.86; its established dividend payout ratio is 30 percent; its tax rate is 40 percent; and investors expect earnings and dividends to grow at a constant rate of 9 percent in the future. LCI paid a dividend of $3.60 per share last year, and its stock currently sells at a price of $60 per share. Treasury bonds yield 11 percent; an average stock has a 14 percent expected rate of return; and LCI's beta is 1.51. (Note: All dollars except per-share figures are in thousands.)

LCI can obtain new capital in the following ways:

Common: New common stock would have a flotation cost of 10 percent for up to $6,000 of new stock, and 20 percent for all common over $6,000.

Preferred: New preferred stock can be sold to the public at a price of $100 per share, with a dividend of $11. Flotation costs of $5 per share would be incurred for up to $3,750 of preferred, while these costs would rise to $10, or 10 percent, on all preferred over $3,750.

Debt: Up to $2,500 of debt can be sold at an interest rate of 12 percent; debt in the range of $2,501 to $5,000 must carry an interest rate of 14 percent; and all debt over $5,000 will have an interest rate of 16 percent.

a. Find the break points in the MCC schedule.
b. Determine the component costs of capital for each capital structure component.
c. Calculate the weighted cost of capital (or the MCC) in the interval between each break in the MCC schedule.

Problems

20-1 Calculate the after-tax cost of debt under each of the following conditions:
   a. Interest rate = 10%, marginal tax rate = 0%.
   b. Interest rate = 10%, marginal tax rate = 40%.
   c. Interest rate = 10%, marginal tax rate = 60%.

20-2 Houston International has an 8 percent, $1,000 par bond issue outstanding with 15 years left to maturity.
   * **a.** If investors require a 10 percent return (yield to maturity), what is the current market price of the bond?
   b. If the company wishes to sell a new issue of equal-risk bonds at par, what coupon rate will the investors require?

20-3 IBEX Corporation has a bond issue outstanding with the following financial characteristics: 15 percent coupon; 10 years to maturity; $1,000 par value; and $1,170 current market price.
   a. Using the formula found in Footnote 7 of Chapter 17, calculate the bond's approximate yield to maturity.
   b. With the information obtained in Part a, determine the bond's exact yield to maturity.
   c. What is the relationship between the yield to maturity on outstanding bonds and the cost of debt for new debt securities the firm wishes to issue?

20-4 Louisiana Electric Utility sold an issue of $8 preferred stock to the public

---

*Refer to Appendix E for check answers to problems with asterisks.

at its par value of $100 several years ago. Since that original sale, the stock's price has dropped to $62.50.

* **a.** What is the current component cost of preferred stock to Louisiana Electric?

  b. If the firm's tax rate is 40 percent, what is the after-tax component cost of preferred stock to Louisiana Electric?

* **20-5** York Industries paid a dividend of $2 per share recently; that is, $D_0 = \$2$. The company's stock sells for $40 per share. The expected growth rate is 10 percent. Calculate York's cost of retained earnings.

20-6 Pennsylvania Petroleum's EPS 5 years ago was $2.7224; its EPS is $4.00 today. The company pays out 40 percent of its earnings as dividends, and the stock sells for $43.20.

  a. Calculate the growth rate. (Assume that the growth rate has been constant over the 5-year period.)

  b. Calculate the *next* expected dividend per share, D_1. ($D_0 = 0.4(\$4) = \$1.60$.) Assume that the past growth pattern will continue.

  c. What is the cost of retained earnings for the firm?

20-7 The E. W. Walker Company's next expected dividend (D_1) is $1.728, its growth rate is 8 percent, and the stock now sells for $43.20. New stock can be sold at a price of $36.72 after flotation costs.

  a. What is Walker's cost of retained earnings?

  b. What is Walker's percentage flotation cost, F?

  c. What is Walker's cost of new common stock, k_e?

* **20-8** Wisconsin Products has the following capital structure: debt, 40 percent; preferred stock, 15 percent; and common stock, 45 percent. The cost of debt is 12 percent, the cost of preferred stock is 14 percent, and the cost of equity is 17 percent. The firm's marginal tax rate is 40 percent. What is the firm's cost of capital?

20-9 Sunshine State Corporation expects earnings of $10 million next year. Its dividend payout is 40 percent, and its debt/assets ratio is 60 percent.

  a. What amount of retained earnings does the company expect next year?

* **b.** At what amount of financing will there be a break point in the MCC schedule if the only equity financing source is retained earnings?

  c. If Sunshine can borrow $4 million at an interest rate of 8 percent, another $4 million at a rate of 9 percent, and additional debt at a rate of 10 percent, at what points will rising debt costs cause breaks in the MCC schedule?

20-10 Seattle Manufacturing's earnings per share have been growing at a steady 8 percent over the last 10 years. The firm's common stock, 140,000 shares outstanding, is now selling for $50 a share, and the expected dividend for next year, D_1, is $2. The current interest on new debt is 8 percent. The firm's marginal tax rate is 40 percent. The firm's capital structure, considered to be optimal, is as follows:

Debt	$ 3,000,000
Common equity	7,000,000
Total capital	$10,000,000

  a. Calculate the after-tax costs of new debt and of common equity, assuming that new equity comes only from retained earnings. Since the historical growth rate is expected to continue, we may calculate the cost of equity as $k_s = D_1/P_0 + g$.

* **b.** Find the marginal cost of capital, again assuming no new common stock is to be sold.

  c. If this year's addition to retained earnings is $280,000, how much can be spent for capital investments before external equity must be sold?

* **d.** What is the marginal cost of capital (cost of funds raised in excess of the amount calculated in Part c) if new common stock can be sold to the public at $50 a share to net the firm $45 a share after flotation costs? The cost of debt is constant.

  e. We have assumed that the capital structure is optimal. What would happen if the firm deviated from this capital structure? Use a graph to illustrate your answer.

20-11 On January 1 the total assets of the Gould Company were $60 million. During the year the company plans to raise and invest $30 million. The firm's present capital structure, shown below, is considered to be optimal. Assume that there is no short-term debt.

Debt	$30,000,000
Common equity	30,000,000
Total capital	$60,000,000

New bonds will have an 8 percent coupon rate and will be sold at par. Common stock, currently selling at $30 a share, can be sold to net the company $27 a share. The stockholders' required rate of return is estimated to be 12 percent, consisting of a dividend yield of 4 percent and an expected growth rate of 8 percent. (The next expected dividend is $1.20, so $1.20/$30 = 4%.) Retained earnings for the year are estimated to be $3 million (ignore depreciation). The marginal corporate tax rate is 40 percent.

  a. Assuming all asset expansion (gross expenditures for fixed assets plus related working capital) is included in the capital budget, what is the dollar amount of the capital budget? (Ignore depreciation.)

  b. To maintain the present capital structure, how much of the capital budget must be financed by common equity?

  c. How much of the new common equity funds needed must be generated internally? Externally?

  d. Calculate the cost of each of the common equity components.

  e. At what level of capital expenditures will there be a break in the MCC schedule?

  f. Calculate the MCC **(1)** below and **(2)** above the break in the schedule.

  g. Plot the MCC schedule. Also, draw in an investment opportunity schedule that is consistent with both the MCC schedule and the projected capital budget. Any IOS that is consistent will do.

20-12 Haslem Enterprises has the following capital structure, which it considers to be optimal under the present and forecasted conditions:

Debt (long-term only)	30%
Common equity	70
Total capital	100%

For the coming year management expects to realize net earnings of $105,000. The past dividend policy of paying out 50 percent of earnings will continue. Present commitments from its banker will allow Haslem to borrow according to the following schedule:

Loan Amount	Interest Rate
$0 to $42,000	8%
$42,001 and above	12

The company's marginal tax rate is 40 percent, the current market price of its stock is $50 per share, its *last* dividend was $1.85 per share, and the expected growth rate is 8 percent. External equity (new common stock) can be sold at a flotation cost of 15 percent. The firm has the following investment opportunities for the next period:

Project	Cost	Annual Cash Flows	Project Life	IRR Schedule[a]
A	$ 75,000	$15,629	8 years	13.0
B	100,000	15,582	10	9.0
C	50,000	15,775	4	
D	25,000	14,792	2	12.0
E	50,000	12,858	6	

[a]IRR schedule is that discount rate at which NPV $\approx$ 0.

Management asks you to help determine what projects (if any) should be undertaken. You proceed with this analysis by answering the following questions posed in a logical sequence:
a. How many breaks are there in the MCC schedule?
b. At what dollar amounts do the breaks occur, and what causes them?
c. What is the weighted average cost of capital, k_a, in each of the intervals between the breaks?
d. What are the IRR values for Projects C and E?
e. Graph the IOS and MCC schedules.
f. Which projects should Haslem's management accept?

Answer to Self-Test Problem

ST-1 a. A break point will occur each time a low-cost type of capital is used up. We establish the break points as follows, after first noting that LCI has $12,000 of retained earnings:

$$\text{Retained earnings} = (\text{Total earnings})(1.0 - \text{Payout})$$
$$= (\$17,142.86)(0.7)$$
$$= \$12,000.$$

Capital Used Up	Break Point Calculation	Break Number
Retained earnings	$BP_{RE} = \dfrac{RE}{\text{Equity fraction}} = \dfrac{\$12,000}{0.60} = \$20,000.$	②
10% flotation common	$BP_{10\%E} = \dfrac{RE + \text{Equity at 10\% flotation}}{\text{Equity fraction}}$	
	$= \dfrac{\$12,000 + \$6,000}{0.60} = \$30,000.$	④
5% flotation preferred	$BP_{5\%P} = \dfrac{\text{Preferred at 5\% flotation}}{\text{Preferred fraction}}$	
	$= \dfrac{\$3,750}{0.15} = \$25,000.$	③
12% debt	$BP_{12\%D} = \dfrac{\text{12\% debt}}{\text{Debt fraction}} = \dfrac{\$2,500}{0.25} = \$10,000.$	①
14% debt	$BP_{14\%D} = \dfrac{\text{12\% debt} + \text{14\% debt}}{\text{Debt fraction}}$	
	$= \dfrac{\$2,500 + \$2,500}{0.25} = \$20,000.$	②

A summary of the break points is as follows:

1. There are three common equity costs and hence there are two changes—and two equity-induced breaks—in the MCC. There are two preferred costs and hence one preferred break. There are three debt costs and hence two debt breaks.

2. The circled numbers in the right column of the table above designate the sequential order of the breaks. They were determined by inspection after the break points were calculated. Note that the second debt break and the break for retained earnings both occur at $20,000.

3. The breaks themselves are summarized below:

Break Number	Total Dollars of Capital Raised	Cause of Break
1	$10,000	Used up 12% debt and therefore had to go to 14% debt.
2	$20,000	Two factors: (1) used up retained earnings and (2) used up 14% debt.
3	$25,000	Used up preferred with F = 5%.
4	$30,000	Used up common with F = 10%.

b. Component costs within indicated total capital intervals:

Retained earnings (used in interval $0–$20,000):

$$k_s = \frac{D_1}{P_0} + g = \frac{D_0(1 + g)}{P_0} + g$$

$$= \frac{\$3.60(1.09)}{\$60} + 0.09$$

$$= 0.0654 + 0.09 = 15.54\%.*$$

Common with F = 10% ($20,000–$30,000):

$$k_e = \frac{D_1}{P_0(1.0 - F)} + g = \frac{\$3.924}{\$60(0.9)} + 9\% = 16.27\%.$$

Common with F = 20% (over $30,000):

$$k_e = \frac{\$3.924}{\$60(0.8)} + 9\% = 17.18\%.$$

Preferred with F = 5% ($0 to $25,000):

$$k_p = \frac{\text{Preferred dividend}}{P_n} = \frac{\$11}{\$100(0.95)} = 11.58\%.$$

Preferred with F = 10% (over $25,000):

$$k_p = \frac{\$11}{\$100(0.9)} = 12.22\%.$$

Debt at k_d = 2% ($0–$10,000):

$$k_d(1 - t) = 12\%(0.6) = 7.20\%.$$

Debt at k_d = 14% ($10,000–$20,000):

$$k_d(1 - t) = 14\%(0.6) = 8.40\%.$$

---

*We could also calculate k_s by the CAPM method:

$$k_s = R_F + b(k_M - R_F) = 11\% + 1.51(14\% - 11\%) = 15.53\%.$$

If the dividend growth model and the CAPM had not given consistent results, further analysis would have been necessary to determine which k_s estimate was better. Here we will use 15.54 percent.

Debt at $k_d = 16\%$ (over \$20,000):

$$k_d(1 - t) = 16\%(0.6) = 9.60\%.$$

c. MCC calculations within indicated total capital intervals:

(1) \$0–\$10,000 (debt = 7.2%, preferred = 11.58%, and RE = 15.54%):

$$MCC = k_a = w_dk_d(1 - t) + w_pk_p + w_sk_s$$
$$= 0.25(7.2\%) + 0.15(11.58\%) + 0.60(15.54\%) = 12.86\%.$$

(2) \$10,001–\$20,000 (debt = 8.4%, preferred = 11.58%, and RE = 15.54%):

$$MCC = k_a = 0.25(8.4\%) + 0.15(11.58\%) + 0.60(15.54\%) = 13.16\%.$$

(3) \$20,001–\$25,000 (debt = 9.6%, preferred = 11.58%, and equity = 16.27%):

$$MCC = k_a = 0.25(9.6\%) + 0.15(11.58\%) + 0.60(16.27\%) = 13.90\%.$$

(4) \$25,001–\$30,000 (debt = 9.6%, preferred = 12.22%, and equity = 16.27%):

$$MCC = k_a = 0.25(9.6\%) + 0.15(12.22\%) + 0.60(16.27\%) = 14.00\%.$$

(5) Over \$30,000 (debt = 9.6%, preferred = 12.22%, and equity = 17.18%):

$$MCC = k_a = 0.25(9.6\%) + 0.15(12.22\%) + 0.60(17.18\%) = 14.54\%.$$

Selected References

The weighted average cost of capital as described in this chapter is widely used in both industry and academic circles. It has been criticized on several counts, but to date it has withstood the challenges. See the following articles:

Arditti, Fred D., and Haim Levy, "The Weighted Average Cost of Capital as a Cutoff Rate: A Critical Examination of the Classical Textbook Weighted Average," *Financial Management*, Fall 1977, 24–34.

Beranek, William, "The Weighted Average Cost of Capital and Shareholder Wealth Maximization," *Journal of Financial and Quantitative Analysis*, March 1977, 17–32.

Boudreaux, Kenneth J., and Hugh W. Long; John R. Ezzell and R. Burr Porter; Moshe BenHorim; and Alan C. Shapiro; "The Weighted Average Cost of Capital: A Discussion," *Financial Management*, Summer 1979, 7–23.

Reilly, Raymond R., and William E. Wacker, "On the Weighted Average Cost of Capital," *Journal of Financial and Quantitative Analysis*, January 1973, 123–126.

Some other works that are relevant are:

Alberts, W. W., and S. H. Archer, "Some Evidence on the Effect of Company Size on the Cost of Equity Capital," *Journal of Financial and Quantitative Analysis*, March 1973, 229–242.

Chen, Andrew, "Recent Developments in the Cost of Debt Capital," *Journal of Finance*, June 1978, 863–883.

Gordon, Myron J., and L. I. Gould, "The Cost of Equity Capital with Personal Income Taxes and Flotation Costs," *Journal of Finance*, September 1978, 1201–1212.

Gordon, Myron J., and P. J. Halpern, "Cost of Capital for a Division of a Firm," *Journal of Finance*, September 1974, 1153–1163.

Myers, S. C., "Interactions of Corporate Financing and Investment Decisions— Implications for Capital Budgeting," *Journal of Finance*, March 1974, 1–25.

Nantell, Timothy J., and C. Robert Carson, "The Cost of Capital as a Weighted Average," *Journal of Finance*, December 1975, 1343–1355.

Additional references on the cost of capital are cited in Chapters 19 and 21, which deal with the effects of financial leverage and dividend policy on the cost of capital.

Determining the Dividend Policy

Decision in Finance

Generous to a Fault?

The late 1970s and early 1980s were difficult years for the U.S. automobile industry. Poor sales caught automakers off guard, and they were left with huge backlogs of inventory. Chrysler's troubles attracted the most publicity, but in 1980 it was the Ford Motor Company that suffered the biggest losses. That year Ford lost almost $3 billion pretax on its North American operations. In that area its losses were 50 percent greater than Chrysler's and 300 percent greater than General Motors'. Only with the help of $600 million in overseas profits and $800 million in tax credits was Ford able to hold its net loss down to $1.5 billion.

Despite its financial difficulties, in 1980 Ford paid dividends of over $300 million to its common stockholders. And it spent heavily for much-needed research and development on new products. To pay its bills, the company drew down its working capital and added $2 billion of debt to its balance sheet.

The outlook for 1981 appeared even worse. Ford had only $200 million in tax credits left to claim, and car sales showed no sign of picking up. So at the end of the first quarter of 1981, Ford's board of directors faced a difficult decision. Should it ask its stockholders to forgo dividends for one quarter or more? Or should it pay its usual quarterly dividend of 30 cents per share (cut from $1 per share the previous July)? With 120 million shares outstanding, the company would need to borrow over $140 million at outrageous interest rates to maintain its usual dividend policy for the entire year. But which was more important in the long run—to avoid further debt or to continue paying dividends?

As you read this chapter, look for the factors that Ford's board should have considered as it reexamined its dividend policy. What course of action would you have recommended? Why?

See end of chapter for resolution.

Dividend policy involves the decision to pay out earnings or to retain them for reinvestment in the firm. Our basic stock price model, $P_0 = D_1/(k_s - g)$, shows that a policy of paying out more cash dividends will raise D_1, which will tend to increase the price of the stock. However, raising cash dividends means that less money is available for reinvestment, and plowing back less earnings into the business will lower the expected growth rate and depress the price of the stock. Thus dividend policy has two opposing effects, and the **optimal dividend policy** is the one that strikes a balance between current dividends and future growth and thereby maximizes the price of the firm's stock.

A number of factors influence dividend policy, among them the differential tax rates on dividends and capital gains, the investment opportunities available to the firm, alternative sources of capital, and stockholders' preferences for current versus future income. The major goal of this chapter is to show how these and other factors interact to determine the optimal dividend policy.

optimal dividend policy
The dividend policy that strikes a balance between current dividends and future growth and thereby maximizes the firm's stock price.

The Residual Theory of Dividends

In the preceding chapters on capital budgeting and the cost of capital, we indicated that generally the marginal cost of capital and investment opportunity schedules must be combined before the cost of capital can be established. In other words, the optimal capital budget, the marginal cost of capital, and the marginal rate of return on investment are determined *simultaneously*. In this section we use this framework to develop what is called the **residual theory of dividends,** which states that a firm should follow these four steps: (1) determine the optimal capital budget, (2) determine the amount of equity needed to finance that budget, (3) use retained earnings to supply this equity to the greatest extent possible, and (4) pay dividends only if more earnings are available than are needed to support the capital budget. The word *residual* implies "left over," and the residual theory states that dividends should be paid only out of leftover earnings.

The basis of the theory is that *investors prefer to have the firm retain and reinvest earnings rather than pay them out in dividends if the return on reinvested earnings exceeds the rate of return the investors could obtain on other*

residual theory of dividends
The theory that dividends paid should equal the excess of earnings over retained earnings necessary to finance the optimal capital budget.

investments of comparable risk. If the corporation can reinvest retained earnings at a 20 percent rate of return, while the best rate stockholders can obtain if the earnings are passed on in the form of dividends is 12 percent, then stockholders would prefer to have the firm retain the profits.

We saw in Chapter 20 that the cost of retained earnings is an *opportunity cost* that reflects rates of return available to equity investors. If a firm's stockholders could buy other stocks of equal risk and obtain a 12 percent dividend-plus-capital-gains yield, then 12 percent is the firm's cost of retained earnings. The cost of new outside equity raised by selling common stock is higher because of the costs of floating the issue.

Most firms have a target capital structure that calls for at least some debt, so new financing is done partly with debt and partly with equity. As long as the firm finances at the optimal point, using the proper amounts of debt and equity, and provided it uses only internally generated equity (retained earnings), its marginal cost of each new dollar of capital will be minimized. Internally generated equity is available for financing a certain amount of new investment; beyond this amount the firm must turn to more expensive new common stock. At the point where new stock must be sold, the cost of equity and consequently the marginal cost of capital rises.

These concepts, which were developed in Chapter 20, are illustrated in Figure 21-1 with data from the Erie Steel Company. Erie has a marginal cost of capital of 10 percent as long as retained earnings are available, but the MCC begins to rise at the point where new stock must be sold. Erie has $60 million of earnings and a 40 percent optimal debt ratio. Provided it does not pay cash dividends, Erie can make net investments (investments in addition to asset replacements financed from depreciation) of $100 million, consisting of $60 million from retained earnings plus $40 million of new debt supported by the retained earnings at a 10 percent marginal cost of capital. Therefore its marginal cost of capital is constant at 10 percent up to $100 million of capital. Beyond $100 million the marginal cost of capital rises as the firm begins to use more expensive new common stock. Of course, if Erie does not retain all of its earnings, the MCC will begin to rise before $100 million. For example, if Erie retained only $30 million, then the MCC would begin to rise at $30 million retained earnings + $20 million debt = $50 million.

Next, suppose Erie's director of capital budgeting constructs an investment opportunity schedule and plots it on a graph. The investment opportunity curves for three different years—one for a good year (IOS$_G$), one for a normal year (IOS$_N$), and one for a bad year (IOS$_B$)—are shown in Figure 21-2. IOS$_G$ shows that Erie can invest more money, and at higher rates of return, than it can when the investment opportunities are as given by IOS$_N$ and IOS$_B$.

Figure 21-1
Marginal Cost of Capital
The marginal cost of capital is the weighted average of the costs of equity (k_s) and debt (k_d), as shown on the left. The MCC will be 10 percent as long as the firm uses only retained earnings for financing. The right side of this figure shows that retained earnings of $60 million, with a 40 percent debt ratio, will allow the firm to raise $100 million at an MCC of 10 percent. Beyond $100 million, new stock must be issued, which means an increase in the cost of equity and a resultant rise in the MCC.

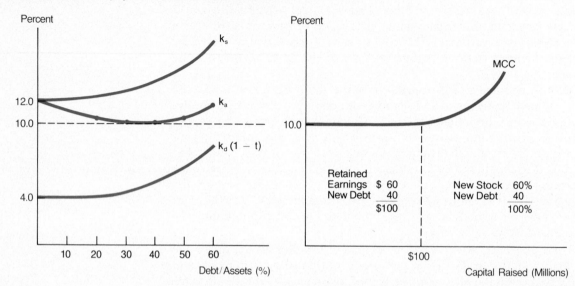

In Figure 21-3 we combine the investment opportunity schedules with the cost of capital schedule. The point where the IOS curve intersects the MCC curve defines the proper level of new investment. When investment opportunities are relatively bad (IOS_B), the optimal level of investment is $40 million; when opportunities are normal (IOS_N), $70 million should be invested; and when opportunities are relatively good (IOS_G), Erie should make new investments in the amount of $150 million.

Consider the situation where IOS_G is the appropriate schedule. Erie has $60 million in earnings and a 40 percent target debt ratio. Thus it can finance $100 million, consisting of $60 million of retained earnings plus $40 million of new debt, at a cost of 10 percent, if it retains all of its earnings. If it pays out part of the earnings in dividends, then it will have to begin using expensive new common stock earlier than need be, so the MCC curve will rise before it otherwise would. *This suggests that under the conditions of IOS_G, Erie should retain all of its earnings. According to the residual theory, its payout ratio should be zero.*

Under the conditions of IOS_N, however, Erie should invest only $70 million. How should this investment be financed? First, notice that if it

Figure 21-2
Investment Opportunity (or IRR) Schedules
Investment opportunity schedules show which new investments are available to a firm at various rates of return. In this figure IOS$_G$ represents a good year, IOS$_N$ a normal year, and IOS$_B$ a bad year. When investment opportunities are good, internal rates of return are higher and Erie can invest larger amounts. When opportunities are poor, as in IOS$_B$, the firm will necessarily curtail its investment plans.

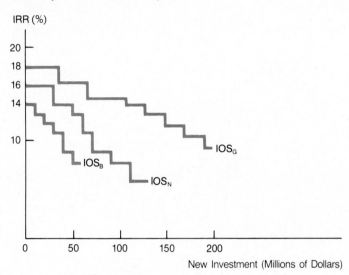

retains the full amount of its earnings, $60 million, it will need to sell only $10 million of new debt. However, if Erie retains $60 million and sells only $10 million of new debt, it will move away from its target capital structure. To stay on target, Erie must finance 60 percent of the required $70 million by equity—retained earnings—and 40 percent by debt; this means retaining $42 million and selling $28 million of new debt. Since Erie retains only $42 million of its $60 million total earnings, it must distribute the residual, $18 million, to its stockholders. Thus its optimal payout ratio is $18 million/$60 million = 30 percent.

Under the conditions of IOS$_B$, Erie should invest only $40 million. Because it has $60 million in earnings, it could finance the entire $40 million out of retained earnings and still have $20 million available for dividends. Should this be done? Under our assumptions, this would not be a good decision, because Erie would move away from its optimal capital structure. To stay at the 40 percent target debt/assets ratio, Erie must retain $24 million of earnings and sell $16 million of debt. When the $24 million of retained earnings is subtracted from the $60 million total earnings, Erie is left with a residual of $36 million, the amount that should be paid out in dividends. Thus the payout ratio as prescribed by the residual theory is 60 percent.

Figure 21-3
Interrelation among Cost of Capital, Investment Opportunities,
and New Investment
A firm's optimal level of new investment can be determined by combining the MCC and
IOS curves. In this figure, for example, the IOS$_N$ curve is crossed by the MCC curve at an
investment level of $70 million. Any investment beyond $70 million, in a normal year,
would generate returns lower than the 10 percent cost of capital and thus should not be
undertaken.

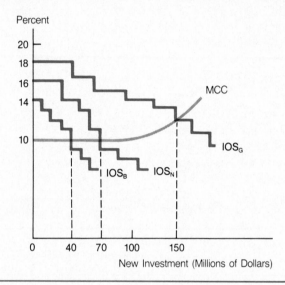

Factors That Influence Dividend Policy

The residual theory of dividends is only a starting point in establishing
a dividend policy. Other factors which influence dividend policy may
be grouped into four broad categories: (1) constraints on dividend payments, (2) investment opportunities, (3) availability and costs of alternative sources of capital, and (4) effects of dividend policy on the required rate of return, k_s. These categories and their factors are
discussed below.

Constraints on Dividend Payments

constraints on dividend
payments
Restrictions or limitations on the
payment of dividends.

1. Bond indentures. Debt contracts generally restrict dividend payment to earnings generated after the loan was granted. Also, debt contracts often stipulate that no dividends can be paid unless the current
ratio, the times-interest-earned ratio, and other safety ratios exceed
stated minimums.

2. Impairment of capital rule. Dividend payments cannot exceed the
balance sheet item "retained earnings." This is a legal restriction called
"the impairment of capital rule," and it is designed to protect creditors.

3. Availability of cash. Cash dividends can be paid only with cash. Thus a shortage of cash in the bank can restrict dividend payments. However, unused borrowing capacity can offset this factor.

4. Penalty tax on improperly accumulated earnings. To prevent wealthy individuals from using corporations to avoid personal taxes, the tax code provides for a special surtax on improperly accumulated income (see Chapter 2). Thus, if the IRS can demonstrate that the dividend payout ratio is being deliberately held down to help stockholders avoid personal taxes, the firm is subject to heavy penalties.

Investment Opportunities

5. Location of the IOS schedule. If the relevant IOS schedule in Figure 21-3 is far to the right, this will tend to produce a low payout, and conversely if the IOS is far to the left. Also, the steeper the slope of the IOS, the more important it is to use the payout prescribed by the residual theory.

6. Possibility of accelerating or delaying projects. If the firm can accelerate or postpone projects, this will permit more flexibility in its dividend policy.

Industry Practice

Dividend Achievers of 1983

By 1983 the recession of the late 1970s and early 1980s had taken its toll on the number of American and Canadian companies with outstanding dividend-growth records.

For the first time since *Dun's Business Month* inaugurated the survey in 1979, there was shrinkage in the ranks of *Top Corporate Performers*— companies that have increased their dividends for at least ten consecutive years; one stumble or one year of flat dividends and they are out.

In 1982, 434 companies met the test. But in 1983 there were only 414, a 4.6 percent decline. Even with the decrease, however, the list was still a solid 78 percent longer than the inaugural one, published in 1979.

In 1983, 63 companies joined the ranks of top performers. Among them were Borden, Inc., Ex-Cell-O Corp., and FMC Corp. But the newcomers were more than offset by the dropouts, as 83 corporations failed to meet the stringent requirements. Among the dropouts were Atlantic Richfield Co., Standard Oil Co. of California, and Warner Communications, Inc.

The best performer of 1983 was RPM, Inc., a producer of specialized protective coatings, fabrics, and wall coverings that increased its dividends at the compound rate of 41.2 percent

Top Corporate Performers

Rank	Company	Where Traded	Current Indicated Dividend	1973 Dividend	Ten-Year Dividend Growth Rate	Recent Stock Price	Current Yield
1	RPM Inc.	OTC	$ .56	$.0142	41.2%	$18	3.1%
2	AAR Corp.	NYSE	.44	.0146	40.6	15¼	2.9
3	Parsons Corp.	NYSE	1.00	.03	40.1	23¾	4.2
4	American States Life Insurance Co.	OTC	.88	.0333	38.7	41½	2.1
5	Hughes Tool Co.	NYSE	.84	.04	35.6	21¼	4.0
6	Keystone International, Inc.	NYSE	.48	.023	35.2	18¼	2.6
7	Service Master Industries, Inc.	OTC	.88	.043	34.4	39¾	2.2
8	Nucor Corp.	NYSE	.32	.015	34.2	38½	0.8
9	Hospital Corp. of America	NYSE	.40	.024	31.9	44¾	0.9
10	Harland (John H.) Co.	NYSE	.76	.05	31.3	39¾	1.9
11	Levi Strauss & Co.	NYSE	1.85	.115	30.9	45½	4.1
12	Schlumberger Limited	NYSE	1.04	.07	30.2	55⅛	1.9
13	Duplex Products, Inc.	ASE	.76	.054	29.9	25¾	3.0
14	Acme Electric Corp.	NYSE	.32	.0237	29.6	11¼	2.8
15	Cameron Iron Works, Inc.	NYSE	.40	.03	29.6[7]	18⅝	2.2
16	Dart & Kraft Inc.	NYSE	3.84	.2888	29.5	71⅜	5.4
17	Rite Aid Corp.	NYSE	.64	.05	29.0	42¾	1.5
18	Pay N Pac Stores, Inc.	NYSE	.56	.04	28.7	18⅜	3.0
19	Grumman Corp.	NYSE	.90	.07	28.4	29¾	3.0
20	Mary Kay Cosmetics, Inc.	NYSE	.12	.01	28.2	20⅜	0.6

during the past decade. Runners-up among the top five were AAR Corp. (40.6 percent compound growth), Parsons Corp. (40.1 percent), American States Life Insurance (38.7 percent), and Hughes Tool Co. (35.6 percent). Interestingly, all of the top five except Parsons were newcomers to the list.

Keystone International, Inc., 1982's leader, dropped to sixth place as its dividend growth slid from 54.2 percent to 35.2 percent; that's still terrific, of course, but not good enough for top honors.

The list of dividend achievers was compiled for *Dun's Business Month* by Moody's Investors Service from the approximately 4,000 companies in its data base. This universe includes all the firms listed on the New York and American Stock Exchanges and all those actively traded on the NASDAQ over-the-counter market.

As an investment guide, *Dun's Top Corporate Performers* list is based on the belief that an investment in a fixed-income security with a substantial current yield does not necessarily provide the highest income over the long run. Not only can investors enjoy a high cash return from a stock that consistently increases its dividend, but they can also receive a kicker in the form of capital appreciation.

For example, the average yield among the 414 companies on the *Top Performers* list in 1983 was 4.5 percent (versus 5.6 percent in 1982). At that

Latest Earnings Per Share	1982 Payout	Annual Sales (Millions)	Net Income (Millions)	Return on Sales	Stockholders' Equity (Millions)	Return on Equity	Fiscal Year
$ .99	40.4%	$ 131.0	$ 7.2	5.5%	$ 48.3	14.9%	5/31/83
.71	60.6	155.0	2.8	1.8	43.2	6.5	5/31/83
1.74	39.5	1,214.0	42.8	3.5	176.8	24.2	12/25/82
3.45	23.2	46.9	7.7	16.4	49.0	15.7	12/31/82
2.65	30.2	1,595.9	147.6	9.3	1,255.9	11.8	12/31/82
1.10	39.5	130.1	17.0	13.1	85.0	20.0	12/31/82
.98	68.4	598.4	21.6	3.6	54.8	39.4	12/31/82
1.59	16.4	486.0	22.2	4.6	202.3	11.0	12/31/82
2.25	13.8	3,539.4	171.9	4.9	1,234.7	13.9	12/31/82
2.04	30.4	160.2	17.1	10.7	76.6	22.3	12/31/82
3.05	54.1	2,572.1	126.6	4.9	970.0	13.1	11/28/82
4.60	20.9	6,283.8	1,349.2	21.5	5,226.4	25.8	12/31/82
2.34	29.1	219.8	9.0	4.1	62.0	14.5	10/31/82
.04	750.0	49.9	0.1	0.3	18.8	0.7	6/30/83
.11	363.6	955.9	3.3	0.3	546.4	0.6	6/30/83
6.40	56.3	9,974.4	350.3	3.5	2,773.5	12.6	12/31/82
2.37	22.4	1,294.7	49.9	3.9	260.7	19.2	2/26/83
.87	55.6	187.3	6.4	3.4	47.4	13.5	2/28/83
3.36	21.6	2,056.7	90.3	4.4	370.8	24.4	12/31/82
1.18	9.3	304.3	35.3	11.6	95.3	37.1	12/31/82

rate, a $10,000 investment would return $450 in dividends compared with interest of $1,278 for a similar investment in a corporate bond, where the recent rate was 12.78 percent.

But the dividend may grow, while interest from the bond remains the same. Thus, using the 14 percent growth rate that prevailed for the average of *Dun's Top Corporate Performers* from 1973 to 1983, the theoretical annual dividend on $10,000 in stocks would rise to $1,463 at the tenth year, overtaking the annual interest from the bonds.

In addition, there is the potential for large capital appreciation on the stock. Based on a projected annual dividend of $2,818 at the fifteenth

year and a continuation of the 4.5 percent yield, the $10,000 investment in stocks could theoretically be worth more than $62,600, a fivefold increase in market value. Even if interest rates were to fall sharply, bonds wouldn't appreciate anywhere near as much.

Viewed another way, the stocks would outperform the bonds in only three years. By then, the stocks could return more than $4,500 ($1,500 in dividends plus $3,000 in appreciation) versus only $3,834 for the bonds.

Source: "Dividend Achievers Suffer First Setback." Reprinted with the permission of *Dun's Business Month* (formerly *Dun's Review*), December 1983. Copyright 1983, Dun & Bradstreet Publications Corporation.

Alternative Sources of Capital

7. Cost of selling new stock. If a firm wishes to finance a given level of investment, it can obtain equity by retaining earnings or by selling new common stock. If flotation costs are high, k_e will be well above k_s, making it much better to finance through retention versus sale of new common stock (see Chapter 20). If flotation costs are low, then dividend policy will be less important. Flotation costs must include underwriting costs and underpricing caused by a downward-sloping demand curve for new stock. Flotation costs differ among firms (for example, they are higher for small firms). Hence the importance of dividend policy and the optimal policy varies among firms.

8. Control. If management is concerned about maintaining control, it may be reluctant to sell new stock, hence may retain more earnings than it otherwise would. This factor is most important for small, closely held firms.

9. Capital structure flexibility. A firm can finance a given level of investment with debt or equity. As we saw above, if stock flotation costs are low, dividend policy is less important because equity can be raised by retaining earnings or by selling new stock. A similar situation holds for debt policy. If the firm is willing to adjust its debt ratio, it can maintain a constant dollar dividend by using a variable debt ratio. The shape of the average cost of capital curve (left panel in Figure 21-1) determines the practical extent to which the debt ratio can be varied. If the average cost of capital curve is relatively flat over a wide range, then dividend policy is less critical than it is if the curve has a distinct minimum.

Effects of Dividend Policy on k_s

10. Capital gains tax rate. Dividends are taxed at federal rates up to 50 percent, plus additional state taxes. The tax on capital gains is generally limited to 28 percent. This makes wealthy investors tend to prefer capital gains to dividends. To the extent that this factor is important, k_s will be smaller the lower the payout, other things held constant. If k_s does vary with the dividend payout, then the MCC curves in Figures 21-1 and 21-3 are not constant as shown, but vary depending on the payout. This could invalidate the residual theory and require more complex decision rules. In general, the optimal payout would be *lower* than that suggested by the simple residual theory.

Large, publicly owned firms have stockholders whose tax brackets range from zero (for some retirees and institutional investors such as pension funds) to about 60 percent (for wealthy individuals). This makes it difficult to accommodate all stockholders and thus creates a problem—for which group of stockholders should dividend policy be set? To the extent that stockholders can shift their investments among firms, a firm can set any specific policy, then have stockholders who do not like this policy sell to other investors who do. Thus the firm will attract a certain *clientele* of stockholders. However, switching may be inefficient because of (1) brokerage costs, (2) the possibility that selling stockholders must pay capital gains taxes, and (3) a possible shortage of investors who like the firm's newly stated dividend policy.

11. Stockholders' desire for current versus future income. Some stockholders desire current income; retired individuals and university endowment funds are examples. Other stockholders have no need for current investment income and simply reinvest any dividends received, after first paying income taxes on the dividend income. If the firm retains and reinvests income rather than paying dividends, those stockholders who need current income will be disadvantaged. They will presumably receive capital gains, but they will be forced to sell off some of their shares to obtain cash. This will involve brokerage costs, which are relatively high unless large sums are involved. Also, some institutional investors (or trustees for individuals) may be precluded from selling stock and then "spending capital." Stockholders who are saving rather than spending dividends will, of course, have to incur brokerage costs to reinvest their dividends. (However, as noted in a later section, many firms today have automatic dividend reinvestment plans which minimize the expense of reinvestment.)

Investors can, of course, switch companies if they own stock in a firm whose dividend policy differs from the policies they desire—this is another example of the **clientele effect.** However, there are costs associated with such changes (brokerage and capital gains taxes), and there may be a shortage of investors to replace those seeking to switch, in which case the stock price may fall and remain low.

clientele effect
The tendency of a firm to attract a certain type of investor according to its dividend policy.

12. Risk of dividends versus risk of capital gains. It has been argued by Gordon that investors regard returns coming in the form of dividends as being less risky than capital gains returns. Others disagree. If someone receives dividends, then turns around and reinvests them in the same firm or one of similar risk, there would appear to be little difference in risk between this operation and having the company retain and reinvest the earnings in the first place. This question has been subjected to statistical studies, but without conclusive results.

13. Information content of dividends. It has been observed that an increase in the dividend (for example, the annual dividend per share is raised from $2 to $2.50) is often accompanied by an increase in the price of the stock, while a dividend cut generally leads to a stock price decline. This suggests to some authors that investors like dividends more than capital gains. However, other authors argue differently. They state that corporations are always reluctant to cut dividends, so firms do not raise dividends unless they anticipate higher, or at least stable, earnings in the future. Thus a dividend increase is a signal to investors that the firm's management forecasts good future earnings. Conversely, a dividend reduction signals that management is forecasting poor earnings in the future. Therefore these authors would claim that rather than indicating a preference for either dividends or earnings, price changes following changes in dividend policy reflect an important **information content** embodied in the dividend announcements. As with many other controversies regarding dividend policy, empirical studies on the topic have been inconclusive. There is clearly some information content in dividend announcements, but it may or may not be the complete explanation for the stock price changes that follow increases or decreases in dividends.

14. Legal listing. New York and certain other important states have a list of stocks of good, solid companies which can be purchased by certain fiduciary institutions—this is called the **legal list.** Institutional investors not subject to the legal list still consider it and often refuse to buy stocks that are not included. Being on the legal list increases the demand for a firm's stock, so companies like to be on it. Since one criterion for inclusion on the legal list is the absence of dividend reductions, companies try very hard to maintain stable dividend policies.

The fourteen points discussed above are considered by financial executives when they are establishing their firms' dividend policies, but the only real generalizations we can make are these:

1. The optimal dividend policy for a firm is influenced by many factors. Some suggest a higher payout than would be called for by the residual theory, while others suggest a lower optimal payout.
2. Much research has been done on dividend policy, but many points are still unresolved. Researchers are far from being able to specify a precise model for establishing corporate dividend policy.

Although no one has been able to construct a usable model for finding an optimal dividend policy, the residual theory does at least provide a good starting point, and we do have a checklist of factors to consider before finalizing the dividend policy. Later in the chapter we return to the process of establishing a dividend policy, but first we must take up three other components of dividend policy—actual payment procedures, stock splits, and stock dividends.

information content of dividends
A theory that investors regard dividend changes as signals of management forecasts.

legal list
A list of securities in which pension funds, insurance companies, and other financial institutions are permitted to invest.

Dividend Payment Procedures

Corporations tend to use one of three major dividend payment procedures. These alternatives are discussed in this section.

Constant, or Steadily Increasing, Dividend per Share

Some firms set a specific annual dividend per share and then maintain it, increasing the annual dividend only if it seems clear that future earnings will be sufficient to allow the dividend to be maintained. A corollary of the policy is this rule: *Avoid ever reducing the annual dividend.* The fact that most corporations do in fact follow, or attempt to follow, such a policy lends support to the information content hypothesis described as Factor 13 in the preceding section.

A stable payment policy is illustrated in Figure 21-4 with data for the Walter Watch Company over a 34-year period. Initially, earnings were $2 and dividends were $1 a share, so the payout ratio was 50 percent. Earnings rose for four years, while dividends remained constant; thus the payout ratio fell during this period. During 1955 and 1956 earnings

Figure 21-4
Walter Watch Company: Dividends and Earnings over Time
Many firms use a stable dividend payment policy, maintaining a specific dividend amount and raising it only if earnings increase on an apparently permanent basis. As shown in this figure, the Walter Watch Company paid dividends of $1.00 beginning in 1950 and maintained it over a 34-year period along with several small dividend increases. Note that a temporary drop in earnings below the dividend level in 1965 did not affect the amount of dividend paid.

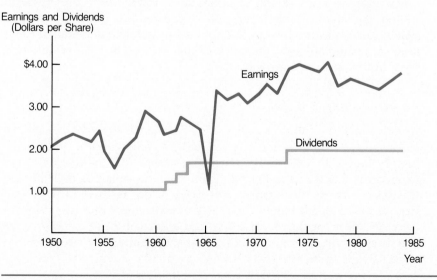

fell substantially; however, the dividend was maintained and the pay-out rose above the 50 percent target. During the period between 1956 and 1960 earnings experienced a sustained rise. Dividends were held constant for a time, while management sought to determine whether the earnings increase would be permanent. By 1961 it was apparent that the earnings gain would be maintained, so dividends were raised in three steps to reestablish the 50 percent target payout. During 1965 a strike caused earnings to fall below the regular dividend. Expecting the earnings decline to be temporary, management maintained the div-idend. Earnings fluctuated on a fairly high plateau from 1966 through 1972, during which time dividends remained constant. A new increase in earnings permitted management to raise the dividend in 1973 to re-establish the 50 percent payout ratio.

A variant of this policy is the "stable growth rate" policy. Here the firm sets a target growth rate for dividends, say, 6 percent per year, and strives to increase dividends by this amount each year. Obviously, earnings must be growing at a reasonably steady rate for this policy to be feasible.

There are several rationales for these policies. First, given the exis-tence of the "information content" idea, a fluctuating payment policy might lead to fluctuating stock prices, which in turn could lead to a high k_s. Second, stockholders who use dividends for current consump-tion want to be able to count on receiving dividends on a regular basis, so irregular dividends might lower demand for the stock. Third, a sta-ble dividend policy is most consistent with the requirements for legal listing. Fourth, even though the optimal payout (in the residual theory sense) might vary somewhat from year to year, delaying some invest-ment projects, departing from the target capital structure during a par-ticular year, or even selling common stock might all be preferable to cutting the dividend or reducing its growth rate. Finally, setting a steady dividend growth rate will confirm investors' estimates of the g factor and thus enhance the price of the stock; that is, investors will think of the stock as a growth stock.

Constant Payout Ratio

A very few firms follow a policy of paying out a constant percentage of earnings. Earnings will surely fluctuate, so following this policy nec-essarily means that the dollar amount of dividends will fluctuate. For reasons discussed in the preceding section, this policy is not likely to maximize a firm's stock price. However, before its bankruptcy Penn Central Railroad did follow the policy of paying out one half its earn-ings: "A dollar for the stockholders and a dollar for the company," as one director put it. Logic like this could drive any company to bank-ruptcy!

Low Regular Dividend plus Extras

The low regular dividend plus a year-end extra is a compromise between the first two policies. It gives the firm flexibility, but it leaves investors somewhat uncertain about what their dividend will be. Still, if a firm's earnings and cash flows are quite volatile, using **extra dividends** may well be its best choice. The directors can set a relatively low regular dividend—low enough that it can be maintained even in low-profit years or in years when a considerable amount of reinvestment is needed—and then supplement it with an extra dividend in years when excess funds are available. General Motors, whose earnings fluctuate widely from year to year, has long followed the practice of supplementing its regular dividend with an extra dividend paid at the end of the year, when its profits and investment requirements are known.

extra dividend
A supplementary dividend paid in years when excess funds are available.

The Actual Dividend Payment

Dividends are normally paid quarterly. For example, AT&T paid dividends of $5.40 during 1983, $1.35 each quarter. In common financial language, we say that AT&T's *regular quarterly dividend* is $1.35 or that its *regular annual dividend* is $5.40. The actual payment procedure is as follows:

1. Declaration date. The directors meet, say on November 15, and declare the regular dividend. On this date the directors issue a statement similar to the following: "On November 15, 1984 the directors of the XYZ Company met and declared the regular quarterly dividend of 50 cents a share, plus an extra dividend of $1.00 a share, payable to holders of record on December 15, payment to be made on January 2, 1985."

declaration date
Date on which a firm's directors issue a statement declaring a regular dividend.

2. Holder-of-record date. At the close of business on the **holder-of-record date,** December 15, the company closes its stock transfer books and makes up a list of the shareholders as of that date. If XYZ Company is notified of the sale and transfer of some stock before 5 P.M. on December 15, the new owner receives the dividend. However, if notification is received on or after December 16, the old stockholder gets the dividend check.

holder-of-record date
The date on which registered security owners are entitled to receive the forthcoming cash or stock dividend.

3. Ex dividend date. Suppose Jean Brown buys 100 shares of stock from John Smith on December 13. Will the company be notified of the transfer in time to list Brown as the new owner and thus pay the dividend to her? To avoid conflict, the stock brokerage business has set up a convention of declaring that the right to the dividend remains with the stock until four business days prior to the holder-of-record date;

ex dividend date
The date on which the right to the current dividend no longer accompanies a stock; for a listed stock this date is four working days prior to the date of record.

on the fourth day before the record date, the right to the dividend no longer goes with the shares. The date when the right to the dividend leaves the stock is called the **ex dividend date.** In this case the ex dividend date is four days prior to December 15, or December 11:

	Dec. 10
Ex dividend date:	Dec. 11
	Dec. 12
	Dec. 13
	Dec. 14
Holder-of-record date:	Dec. 15

Therefore, if Brown is to receive the dividend, she must buy the stock by December 10. If she buys it on December 11 or later, Smith will receive the dividend.

The total dividend, regular plus extra, amounts to $1.50, so the ex dividend date is important. Barring fluctuations in the stock market, we would normally expect the price of a stock to drop by approximately the amount of the dividend on the ex dividend date. Thus, if XYZ closed at $51.50 on December 10, it would probably open at about $50 on December 11.

payment date
Date on which a firm actually mails dividend checks.

4. Payment date. The company actually mails the checks to the holders of record on January 2, the **payment date.**

Dividend Reinvestment Plans

dividend reinvestment plan (DRP)
A plan which enables a stockholder to automatically reinvest dividends received back into the stock of the paying corporation.

During the 1970s most of the larger companies instituted **dividend reinvestment plans, (DRPs),** whereby stockholders can automatically reinvest dividends received in the stock of the paying corporation.[1] *There are two types of DRPs: one involves only stock that is already outstanding, while the other involves newly issued stock.* In either case the stockholder must pay income taxes on the amount of the dividends, even though stock rather than cash is received.

Under the first type of plan the stockholder elects either to continue receiving dividend checks or to have the dividends used to buy more stock in the corporation. If the stockholder elects reinvestment, a bank, acting as trustee, takes the total funds available for reinvestment (less a fee), purchases the corporation's stock on the open market, and allocates the shares purchased to the participating stockholders' accounts

---

[1]See R. H. Pettway and R. P. Malone, "Automatic Dividend Reinvestment Plans," *Financial Management*, Winter 1973, 11–18, for an excellent discussion of the topic.

on a pro rata basis. The transactions costs of buying shares (brokerage costs) are low because of volume purchases, so these plans benefit small stockholders who do not need cash dividends for current consumption.

The other type of DRP provides for dividends to be invested in *newly issued stock; hence these plans raise new capital for the firm.* AT&T, Florida Power & Light, Union Carbide, and many other companies have had such plans in effect, using them to raise substantial amounts of new equity capital. No fees are charged to stockholders, and many companies offer stock at a discount of 5 percent below the actual market price. The companies absorb these costs as a trade-off against flotation costs that would be incurred on stock sold through investment bankers rather than through the dividend reinvestment plans. Discussions with corporate treasurers suggest that many other companies are seriously considering establishing or switching to new-stock DRPs.[2]

Stock Repurchase

As an alternative to cash dividends, a firm may distribute income to stockholders by *repurchasing its own stock.* For example, Gulf Oil announced plans to buy back 10 million shares of its common stock. Gulf's stock was selling for about $30 per share when the repurchase plans were formulated. Subsequently, it rose to $37.50. Gulf's chairman, Jerry McAfee, noted (1) that the stock's book value was $51 per share, and (2) that the replacement value of Gulf's assets was about $130 per share. Thus, in management's view, the stock was underpriced and represented an attractive investment.

Other reasons for distributing corporate income through **stock repurchase** rather than as cash dividends include these: (1) it avoids the high personal tax rate on cash dividends, and (2) it permits those stockholders who want cash to acquire it by selling some of their shares back to the firm, while stockholders who do not want cash may simply keep their shares. Since fewer shares will be outstanding after the repurchase, earnings per share and consequently the price of the remaining shares should increase.

stock repurchase
A means by which a firm distributes income to stockholders by buying back shares of its own stock, thereby decreasing shares outstanding, increasing EPS, and increasing the price of the stock.

---

[2]One interesting aspect of DRPs is that they are forcing corporations to reexamine their basic dividend policies. A high participation rate in a DRP suggests that stockholders might be better off if the firm simply reduced cash dividends, as this would save stockholders some personal income taxes. Quite a few firms are surveying their stockholders to learn more about their preferences and to find out how they would react to a change in dividend policy. A more rational approach to basic dividend policy decisions may emerge from this research.

Also, it should be noted that the 1981 tax law revision permits investors to exempt from taxable income up to $750 of dividends paid by public utilities and reinvested in new-stock DRPs. The purpose of this provision was to help the utilities obtain investment capital.

The principal disadvantages of repurchases are (1) they are usually done on an irregular basis, so a stockholder cannot depend on income from this source, and (2) if regular repurchases were made, there is a good chance that the Internal Revenue Service (or Congress) would rule that the repurchases were simply a tax avoidance scheme and would assess penalty tax rates.

Stock Dividends and Stock Splits

Another aspect of dividend policy is the concept of stock dividends and stock splits. The rationale for stock dividends and splits can best be explained through an example; we use Carter Chemical Company to illustrate.

As Carter Chemical continues to grow and retain earnings, its book value per share will also grow. More important, earnings per share and the market price per share will rise. Suppose only a few thousand shares were outstanding. After some years of growth, each share would have a very high EPS and DPS. If a "normal" P/E ratio were applied to the stock, the derived market price might be so high that few people could afford to buy even one share. This would limit demand for the stock, thus keeping the total market value of the firm below what it would be if more shares, at lower prices, were outstanding.

Although there is little empirical evidence to support the contention,

Stock splits, which increase the number of shares of a company's stock available for ownership, are often reported in the business press. This excerpt from the *Wall Street Journal* announces splits for four different companies and indicates how the split affects expected dividends as well as the value of the stock. Notice that stock splits need not be even, such as 2-for-1; two of these four companies announced 3-for-2 stock splits.

Source: *The* Wall Street Journal, *April 18, 1984, p. 48. Reprinted by permission of The Wall Street Journal, © Dow Jones & Company, Inc., 1984. All rights reserved.*

American Security Corp. declared a 3-for-2 stock split, payable May 25 to shares of record May 4. The bank-holding company said it expects the dividend rate on the new shares will be equivalent, on an adjusted basis, to the 38 cents paid last quarter.

American Precision Industries Inc. directors proposed a 3-for-2 stock split, subject to shareholder approval. Richard Becht, vice president, finance, said the split might help improve trading in the company's shares. The company currently has about 1.8 million shares outstanding. A spokesman said shareholders probably will be asked to vote on the proposal in the current quarter or early in the third quarter. Robert J. Fierle, president, said first-quarter earnings more than tripled to $695,000, or 38 cents a share, from $167,000, or nine cents a share, a year earlier. Sales rose more than 35% to $9.1 million from $6.7 million. Mr. Fierle said the higher profit reflected better margins in the electronics business and sale of an unprofitable business. The Buffalo, N.Y., company makes heat-transfer equipment and electronics parts.

Florida Public Utilities Co. said its shareholders approved a 2-for-1 stock split by approving an increase in authorized common to 1.2 million from 500,000. The split is payable May 1 to stock of record April 20. Par value of the stock will be $1.50 a share; pre-split par value was $3 a share.

Hawaiian Electric Industries Inc. holders approved a 2-for-1 split of common, effective for stock of record May 10. The split will increase to about 15.5 million the company's common shares outstanding. C. Dudley Pratt Jr., president and chief executive officer, said the stock split will provide more market shares for sale to customers of Hawaiian Electric's three utility subsidiaries, who will be offered participation starting next month in a customer stock purchase plan.

there is nevertheless a widespread belief in financial circles that an *optimal price range* exists for stocks. *Optimal* means that, if the price is in this range, the price/earnings ratio will be maximized. Many observers, including Carter Chemical's management, feel that the best range for most stocks is from $20 to $80 per share. Accordingly, if at some future point the price of Carter's stock rose to $80, management would probably declare a 2-for-1 **stock split,** thus doubling the number of shares outstanding, halving the earnings and dividends per share, and thereby lowering the price of the stock. Each stockholder would have more shares, but each share would be worth less. If the post-split price were $40, Carter's stockholders would be exactly as well off as they were before the split. If the price of the stock were to stabilize above $40, stockholders would be better off. Stock splits can be of any size. For example, the stock could be split 2-for-1, 3-for-1, 1.5-for-1, or in any other way.[3]

stock split
An action to increase the number of shares outstanding; e.g., in a 3-for-1 split shares outstanding are tripled and each stockholder receives 3 new shares for each share formerly held.

Stock dividends are similar to stock splits in that they divide the pie into smaller slices without affecting the fundamental position of the company. On a 5 percent stock dividend, the holder of 100 shares would receive an additional 5 shares (without cost); on a 20 percent stock dividend, the same holder would receive 20 new shares; and so on. Again, the total number of shares is increased, so earnings, dividends, and the price per share all decline.

stock dividend
A dividend paid in additional shares of stock rather than cash; involves a transfer from retained earnings to the common stock and paid-in capital accounts.

If a firm wants to reduce the price of its stock, should a stock split or a stock dividend be used? Stock splits are generally used after a sharp price run-up, when a large price reduction is sought. Stock dividends are frequently used on a regular annual basis to keep the stock price more or less constrained. For example, if a firm's earnings and dividends are growing at about 10 percent per year, the price would tend to go up at about that same rate, and it would soon be outside the desired trading range. A 10 percent annual stock dividend would maintain the stock price within the optimal trading range.

The economic effects of stock splits and stock dividends are virtually identical. Even so, the New York Stock Exchange has adopted a rule calling all distributions of stock under 25 percent a *dividend* and a greater than 25 percent distribution a *split,* even if the issuing corporation calls its action something else.

Accountants also treat stock splits and stock dividends somewhat differently. Section 1 of Table 21-1 shows the equity portion of Carter Chemical Company's balance sheet before any action is taken on a stock dividend or split. On a 2-for-1 split, the shares outstanding are doubled and the par value is halved. This treatment is shown in Section 2

---

[3]*Reverse splits,* which reduce the shares outstanding, can even be used; for example, a company whose stock sells for $5 might employ a 1-for-5 reverse split, exchanging 1 new share for 5 old shares and raising the value of the shares to about $25, which is within the optimal range.

Table 21-1
Carter Chemical Company: Stockholders' Equity Accounts, Pro Forma
December 31, 1985

1. *Before a Stock Split or a Stock Dividend:*
   Common stock (60 million shares authorized,
     50 million outstanding, $1 par) $ 50,000,000
   Additional paid-in capital   100,000,000
   Retained earnings   1,850,000,000
     Total common stockholders' equity $2,000,000,000

2. *After a 2-for-1 Stock Split:*
   Common stock (120 million shares authorized,
     100 million outstanding, $0.50 par) $ 50,000,000
   Additional paid-in capital   100,000,000   Changes: Par value/2
   Retained earnings   1,850,000,000
     Total common stockholders' equity $2,000,000,000

3. *After a 20 Percent Stock Dividend:*
   Common stock (60 million shares authorized,
     60 million outstanding, $1 par) $ 60,000,000   + $ 1 per share
   Additional paid-in capital   890,000,000   + $79 per share
   Retained earnings   1,050,000,000   − $80 per share
     Total common stockholders' equity $2,000,000,000   = $ 0 net change per share

of the table, where the only accounting change to Carter's 1985 stock-holders' equity pro forma is the adjustment to the par value of the stock. Had Carter decided to have a larger split, say a 5-for-1 split, we would have only had to divide the par value by 5 to reflect all necessary ac-counting changes. Since we can find the number of shares outstanding by dividing the common stock account by the par value of the stock, the new $0.20 par value and $50 million common stock account would indicate the number of shares had grown fivefold to 250 million shares.

Section 3 of Table 21-1 demonstrates the accounting changes which would occur in the equity section if Carter proceeds with a 20 percent stock dividend rather than the stock split. If Carter's common stock were selling at $80 per share, a 20 percent stock dividend would result in an $800 million transfer (or recapitalization) of funds from retained earnings to the common stock and paid-in-capital accounts. The trans-fer from retained earnings is calculated as follows:

$$\begin{pmatrix} \text{Dollars} \\ \text{transferred from} \\ \text{retained} \\ \text{earnings} \end{pmatrix} = \begin{pmatrix} \text{Number} \\ \text{of shares} \\ \text{outstanding} \end{pmatrix} \begin{pmatrix} \text{Percentage} \\ \text{of the} \\ \text{stock dividend} \end{pmatrix} \begin{pmatrix} \text{Market} \\ \text{price of} \\ \text{the stock} \end{pmatrix}$$

$$= (50 \text{ million})(0.2)(\$80)$$
$$= \$800,000,000.$$

The common stock account would increase by the stock's par value ($1) per share for each of the 10 million new shares issued. The remaining $79 per share (price less par value) is added to the paid-in-capital (or as its older but more descriptive account title was known, capital-in-excess-of-par).

Price Effects

Several empirical studies have examined the effects of stock splits and stock dividends on stock prices.[4] The findings of the Barker study are presented in Table 21-2. When stock dividends were associated with a cash dividend increase, the value of the company's stock 6 months after the ex dividend date had risen by 8 percent. On the other hand, when stock dividends were not accompanied by cash dividend increases, stock values fell by 12 percent, which approximated the percentage of the average stock dividend.

These data seem to suggest that stock dividends are seen for what they are—simply additional pieces of paper—and that they do not represent true income. When they are accompanied by higher earnings and cash dividends, investors bid up the value of the stock. However, when stock dividends are not accompanied by increases in earnings and cash dividends, the dilution of earnings and dividends per share causes the price of the stock to drop by about the same percentage as the stock dividend. The fundamental determinants of price are the underlying earnings and dividends per share.

Table 21-2
Price Effects of Stock Dividends

	Price at Selected Dates (in Percentages)		
	Six Months prior to Ex Dividend Date	At Ex Dividend Date	Six Months after Ex Dividend Date
Cash dividend increase	100	109	108
No cash dividend increase	100	99	88

---

[4]C. A. Barker, "Evaluation of Stock Dividends," *Harvard Business Review*, July–August 1958, 99–144. Barker's study has been replicated several times in recent years, and his results are still valid—they have withstood the test of time. Another excellent study, using an entirely different methodology yet reaching similar conclusions, is that of E. Fama, L. Fisher, M. C. Jensen, and R. Roll, "The Adjustment of Stock Prices to New Information," *International Economic Review*, February 1969, 1–21.

Establishing a Dividend Policy: Some Illustrations

Many factors interact to determine a firm's optimal dividend policy. Moreover, since these interactions are too complex to permit the development of a rigorous model for use as a guide to dividend policy, firms are forced to consider their dividend policies in a relatively subjective manner. Some illustrations of how dividend policies are actually set are given below.

Erie Steel Company

Erie Steel Company analyzed its situation in terms of the residual theory as shown in Figure 21-3. The residual theory suggested a dividend of $1.80 per share during 1985, or a 30 percent payout ratio. Erie's stock is widely held, and a number of tax-exempt institutions are important stockholders. A questionnaire to its stockholders revealed no strong preferences for dividends versus capital gains. Erie's long-range planning group projected a cost of capital and a set of investment opportunities during the next three to five years that are similar to those shown for this year.

Based on this information, Erie's treasurer recommended to the board of directors that it establish a dividend of $1.80 for 1985, payable 45 cents quarterly. The 1984 dividend was $1.70, so the $1.80 represents an increase of about 6 percent. The treasurer also reported to the board that, in the event of an unforeseen earnings downturn, the company could obtain additional debt to meet its capital expenditure requirements. The board accepted the treasurer's recommendation and in December of 1984 declared a dividend of 45 cents per share, payable January 15, 1985. The board also announced its intention of maintaining this dividend for the balance of 1985.

Watkins Electronics

Watkins Electronics has a "residual theory position" that resembles IOS_G in Figure 21-3. This suggests that no dividend be paid. Watkins has, in fact, paid no dividend since its inception in 1972, even though it has been continuously profitable and earnings have recently been growing at a 25 percent rate. Informal conversations with the firm's major stockholders, all of whom are in high tax brackets, suggest that they neither expect nor want dividends—they would prefer to have the firm retain earnings, have good earnings growth, and provide capital gains, which are taxed at relatively low rates. The stock now sells for $106 per share. Watkin's treasurer recommended a 3-for-1 split, no cash dividend, and a future policy of declaring an annual stock dividend geared to earnings for the year. The board of directors concurred.

Midwest Electric Company

Midwest Electric Company has an acute need for new equity capital. The company has a major expansion program underway and absolutely must come up with the money to meet construction payments. The debt ratio is high, and if the times-interest-earned ratio falls any lower, (1) the company's bonds will be downgraded and (2) it will be barred by bond indenture provisions from further debt issues. These facts suggest a cut in dividends from the $2.50 per share paid last year. However, the treasurer knows that many of the stockholders rely on dividends for current living expenses, so if dividends are cut, these stockholders may be forced to sell, thus driving down the price of the stock. This would be especially bad in view of the treasurer's forecast that there will be a need to sell new common stock during the coming year. (New outside equity would be needed even if the company totally eliminated the dividend.) The treasurer is aware that many other utilities face a similar problem. Some have cut their dividends, and their stock prices invariably have fallen by amounts ranging from 30 to 70 percent.

   Midwest's earnings were forecasted to increase from $3.33 to $3.50. The treasurer recommended that the dividend be raised from $2.50 to $2.70, with the dividend increase being announced a few weeks before the company floated a new stock issue. The hope was that this action would cause the price of the stock to increase, after which the company could sell a new issue of common stock at a better price.

North American Oil

North American Oil's 1984 dividend was $2.45 per share, up from $2.30 in 1983. Both dividend figures represented about 50 percent of earnings, and this payout was consistent with a residual theory analysis. The company's growth rate in EPS and DPS had been in the 5 to 10 percent range during the past few years, and management had projected a continuation of this trend. The financial vice president foresaw a cash flow problem in 1985—earnings were projected to increase in line with the historical average, but an especially large number of good investment opportunities (along with some unprofitable but required pollution control expenditures) were expected. A preliminary analysis using the residual theory suggested that the dividend in 1985 should be cut back sharply, if not eliminated.

   The financial vice president quickly rejected this cutback, recommending instead a 6 percent *increase* in the dividend, to $2.60. He noted that the company could easily borrow funds during the coming year to meet its capital requirements. The debt ratio would rise somewhat above the target, but the firm's average cost of capital curve is relatively flat, and cash flows from the 1985 investments should permit a reduction in the debt ratio over the next few years. The vice president felt that it was more important to maintain the steady growth in dividends than to adhere strictly to the target debt ratio.

Summary

Dividend policy involves the decision to pay out earnings or to retain them for reinvestment in the firm. Any change in dividend policy has both favorable and unfavorable effects on the price of the firm's stock. Higher dividends mean higher cash flows to investors, which is good, but lower future growth, which is bad. The optimal dividend policy balances these opposing forces and maximizes the price of the stock.

We identified a number of factors that bear on dividend policy, including these: legal constraints such as bond indenture provisions, the firm's investment opportunities, the availability and cost of funds from other sources (new stock and debt), tax rates, stockholders' desire for current income, and the information content of dividend changes. Because of the large number of factors that bear on dividend policy, and also because of the relative importance of these factors changes over time and across companies, it is impossible to develop a precise, generalized model for use in establishing dividend policy. Firms can, however, consider the *residual theory model*, along with other factors, in reaching a judgment as to the most appropriate dividend policy.

Firms tend to use one of three payment policies: (1) a stable or continuously increasing dollar dividend per share; (2) a low regular dividend plus extras that depend on annual earnings; and (3) a constant payout ratio, which will cause the dollar dividend to fluctuate. Most firms follow the first policy, a few use the second, and almost none use the third. Also, we noted that many firms today are using dividend reinvestment plans to help stockholders reinvest dividends at minimal brokerage costs, and some firms use stock repurchase plans in lieu of increasing cash dividends.

Stock splits and stock dividends were also discussed. Our conclusion was that these actions may be beneficial if the firm's stock price is quite high, but otherwise they have little effect on the value of the firm.

Resolution to Decision in Finance

Generous to a Fault?

Ford Motor Company decided to regard its financial difficulties as merely temporary and, consequently, chose to continue paying quarterly dividends of 30 cents per share. Although all the numbers seemed to indicate that it was unwise to pay a dividend, Ford's board felt that it was crucial to think beyond the balance sheet.

"You would completely change the character of the company if you eliminated the dividend," argued Ford Treasurer John Sagan. "You're no longer an investment-grade stock of any kind [if the dividend is cut out]. You can't willy-nilly raise dividends or eliminate them. You do that, you're a schlock company." And though the dividend amounts to a lot of money in absolute terms, Sagan said, "for a $40 billion company, $140 million isn't that large in the balance."

In addition, there was pride to consider. Ford had consistently paid dividends since 1947, shortly after Henry Ford II seized control of the almost bankrupt company from his grandfather. A return to no dividends could have been interpreted as a signal that things were getting as bad as they were before Henry II took over.

The board also had to weigh how stockholders would be affected by its decision. The Ford family itself would have been hard hit by a no-dividend decision, since it owned 13 million shares of company stock. But even harder hit would have been what the board thought of as the extended Ford Motor Company family. Twenty-seven million shares of Ford—22 percent of the company—were held in employee stock plans. And employees and retirees held many more millions of shares in their own names. Omitting dividends would have inflicted serious hardship on people who had worked loyally for the company and depended on dividends to supplement their pensions and Social Security checks.

In fact, most of Ford's management live in the Detroit area, surrounded by people to whom Ford dividends are an important source of income. As a result, unlike the managers of faceless conglomerates with far-flung holdings, Ford's managers are constantly reminded that their shareholders are living, breathing human beings. This made it even more difficult for the board to eliminate the dividend.

The interests and possible reactions of institutional investors also had to be considered. Such investors, who held almost half of Ford's stock, might have been forced to sell if the dividend had been omitted. "We felt it important to keep some incentive for investors," said one board member.

> Finally, the board took into account the information content embodied in dividend announcements. When a company cuts or forgoes a dividend, its stock price usually declines because the public assumes that management is forecasting poor earnings for the future. Ford wanted to avoid giving such an impression. By eliminating a dividend, "You're telling the public you expect the problem to be long term," said Sagan. "We see this as a valley situation."
>
> Source: Adapted from "Generous to a Fault?" *Forbes*, April 13, 1981, 31–32.

Key Terms You should be able to define each of the following terms:

Optimal dividend policy
Residual theory of dividends
Constraints on dividend payments
Clientele effect
Information content of dividends
Legal list
Extra dividend

Declaration date; holder-of-record date; ex dividend date; payment date
Dividend reinvestment plan (DRP)
Stock repurchase
Stock split; stock dividend

Questions

21-1 As an investor, would you rather invest in a firm that has a policy of maintaining **(a)** a constant payout ratio, **(b)** a constant dollar dividend per share, **(c)** a target dividend growth rate, or **(d)** a constant regular quarterly dividend plus a year-end extra when earnings are sufficiently high or corporate investment needs are sufficiently low? Explain your answer, stating how these policies would affect your k_s.

21-2 How would each of the following changes probably affect aggregate (that is, the averages for all corporations) payout ratios? Explain your answers.
  a. An increase in the personal income tax rate.
  b. A liberalization in depreciation policies for federal income tax purposes, that is, faster tax write-offs.
  c. A rise in interest rates.
  d. An increase in corporate profits.
  e. A decline in investment opportunities.

21-3 What are the pros and cons of having the directors formally announce what a firm's dividend policy will be in the future?

21-4 Most firms would like to have their stock selling at a high P/E ratio and also have an extensive public ownership (many different shareholders). How may stock dividends or stock splits be compatible with these aims?

21-5 What is the difference between a stock dividend and a stock split? As a stockholder, would you prefer to see your company declare a 100 percent stock dividend or a 2-for-1 split? Assume that either action is feasible.

21-6 "The cost of retained earnings is less than the cost of new outside equity capital. Consequently, it is totally irrational for a firm to sell a new issue of stock and to pay dividends during the same year." Is this a true statement? Why or why not?

21-7 Would it ever be rational for a firm to borrow money in order to pay dividends? Explain.

21-8 Union representatives have presented arguments similar to the following: "Corporations such as General Foods retain about one half their profits for financing needs. If they financed by selling stock instead of by retaining earnings, they could cut prices substantially and still earn enough to pay the same dividend to their shareholders. Therefore their profits are too high." Is this a valid statement? Why or why not?

Problems

* 21-1 Utah Mining had net income for 1984 of $5 million.
  a. What was the firm's payout ratio if it paid $3 million in dividends?
  b. If the firm's payout was 25 percent, what was the dividend payment?
  c. If the payout ratio was 40 percent, what was the retention ratio?
  d. In 1983 the firm's payout ratio was 60 percent and $2.5 million was paid in dividends. What was Utah Mining's net income in 1983?

* 21-2 Solectron is expanding the productive capacity of its plant with a $10 million investment. The board of directors approved the expansion under the conditions that (1) the firm would not exceed its current 40 percent debt/assets ratio and (2) the dividend payout ratio would remain at 25 percent. If net earnings are $5 million, how much external equity must the firm seek in the coming year?

21-3 Hannover Entertainment Systems has the following common stock equity accounts on its balance sheet:

Common stock ($2 par)	$ 500,000
Paid-in capital	3,750,000
Retained earnings	10,000,000
Total equity	$14,250,000

The market price of the firm's common stock is $25. Restate the equity accounts of Hannover to reflect a 15 percent stock dividend.

* 21-4 In 1983 Datatec paid dividends of $1,575,000. The firm's net income for 1983 was $5,250,000. For the past 5 years the earnings and dividends have grown at a constant 8 percent rate. However, 1984 was an especially profitable year, with net income totaling $9,450,000. For 1985 Datatec has $7,000,000 of profitable investment opportunities planned. Even so, the surge in earnings enjoyed in 1984 cannot last, and the firm's profits are expected to return to the previous 8 percent stable-growth rate. Calculate the 1984 dividends for Datatec under each of the following dividend policies:

  a. A stable and growing dividend payment.
  b. Stable payout (based on the 1983 payout ratio).

---

*Refer to Appendix E for check answers to problems with asterisks.

    c. Passive residual dividend policy if the firm uses no debt to finance investment opportunities.

    d. Passive residual dividend policy if the firm maintains a 40 percent debt/assets ratio.

21-5 Findlay Trucking has just announced a 4-for-1 stock split. Prior to the split, dividends were $6 per share. The firm plans to pay a dividend of $1.80 per share after the split. What is the percentage increase in the cash dividend that occurs after the split?

21-6 Ohio International Corporation declares a 4 percent stock dividend and a cash dividend of $0.40 per share. The cash dividend is paid on both the old shares and the shares received in the stock dividend. Construct a pro forma balance sheet giving the effect of these actions; use one new balance sheet that incorporates both actions. The stock sells for $25 per share. A condensed version of Ohio International's end-of-year balance sheet (before dividends) is given below:

Cash	$ 50,000,000	Debt	$1,000,000,000
Other assets	1,950,000,000	Common stock (60 million shares authorized, 50 million shares outstanding, $1 par)	50,000,000
		Paid-in capital	200,000,000
		Retained earnings	750,000,000
Total assets	$2,000,000,000	Total claims	$2,000,000,000

21-7 Carolina Tobacco Company has for many years enjoyed a moderate but stable growth in sales and earnings. However, cigarette consumption and consequently Carolina's sales have been declining recently, partly because of a national awareness of the dangers of smoking to health. Anticipating further declines in tobacco sales for the future, Carolina's management hopes eventually to move almost entirely out of the tobacco business and, instead, to develop a new, diversified product line in growth-oriented industries.

    Carolina has been especially interested in the prospects for pollution control devices—its research department has already done much work on the problems of filtering smoke. Right now the company estimates that an investment of $24 million is necessary to purchase new facilities and begin operations on these products, but the investment could return about 18 percent within a short time. Other investment opportunities total $9.6 million and are expected to return about 12 percent.

    The company has been paying a $2.40 dividend on its 6 million shares outstanding. The announced dividend policy has been to maintain a stable dollar dividend, raising it only when it appears that earnings have reached a new, permanently higher level. The directors might, however, change this policy if reasons for doing so are compelling. Total earnings for the year are $22.8 million, common stock is currently selling for $45, and the firm's current leverage ratio (debt/assets ratio) is 45 percent. Current costs of various forms of financing are: new bonds, 7%; new common stock sold at $45 to yield the firm $41; investors' required rate of return on equity, 9%; and tax rate, 50%.

   a. Calculate the marginal cost of capital above and below the point of exhaustion of retained earnings for Carolina, both with and without the dividend.

 * b. How large should Carolina's capital budget be for the year?

   c. What is the appropriate dividend policy for Carolina? How should the capital budget be financed?

   d. How might risk factors influence Carolina's cost of capital, capital structure, and dividend policy?

   e. What assumptions, if any, do your answers to the above make about investors' preferences for dividends versus capital gains, that is, investors' preferences regarding the D_1/P_0 and g components of k?

Selected References

Dividend policy is another area that has been studied extensively by academicians. The first major academic work, and still a classic, is Lintner's analysis of how corporations actually set their dividend payment policies:

Lintner, John, "Distribution of Incomes of Corporations among Dividends, Retained Earnings, and Taxes," *American Economic Review*, May 1956, 97–113.

The effects of dividend policy on stock prices and capital costs have been examined by many researchers. The classic theoretical argument that dividend policy is important, and that stockholders like dividends, was set forth by Gordon, while Miller and Modigliani developed the notion that dividend policy is not important:

Gordon, Myron J., "Dividends, Earnings and Stock Prices," *Review of Economics and Statistics*, May 1959, 99–105.

Miller, Merton H., and Franco Modigliani, "Dividend Policy, Growth, and the Valuation of Shares," *Journal of Business*, October 1961, 411–433.

Many researchers have both extended Gordon's and Miller and Modigliani's theoretical arguments and attempted to test the effects of dividend policy in a variety of ways. Although statistical problems have precluded definitive conclusions, the following articles, among others, have helped to clarify the issues:

Brennan, Michael, "Taxes, Market Valuation, and Corporate Financial Policy," *National Tax Journal*, Spring 1975, 417–427.

Hayes, Linda S., "Fresh Evidence That Dividends Don't Matter," *Fortune*, May 4, 1981, 351–354.

Lewellen, Wilbur G., Kenneth L. Stanley, Ronald C. Lease, and Gary G. Schlarbaum, "Some Direct Evidence on the Dividend Clientele Phenomenon," *Journal of Finance*, December 1978, 1385–1399.

Litzenberger, R. H., and K. Ramaswamy, "The Effect of Personal Taxes and Dividends on Capital Asset Prices: Theory and Empirical Evidence," *Journal of Financial Economics*, June 1979, 163–195.

Mukherjee, Tarun K., and Larry M. Austin, "An Empirical Investigation of Small Bank Stock Valuation and Dividend Policy," *Financial Management*, Spring 1980, 27–31.

Pettit, R. R., "Taxes, Transactions Costs, and the Clientele Effect of Dividends," *Journal of Financial Economics*, December 1977, 419–436.

For an excellent review of both the theoretical and the empirical literature (along with another test of the alternative theories), see:

Vanderheiden, Paul A., *Dividend Level and Variability: Effects on Stock Returns*, Ph.D. dissertation, University of Florida, 1980.

On stock dividends and splits, see:

Baker, W. Kent, and Patricia L. Gallagher, "Management's View of Stock Splits," *Financial Management*, Summer 1980, 73–77.

Copeland, Thomas E., "Liquidity Changes Following Stock Splits," *Journal of Finance*, March 1979, 115–141.

On repurchases, see:

Finnerty, Joseph E., "Corporate Stock Issue and Repurchase," *Financial Management*, Autumn 1975, 62–71.

Stewart, Samuel S., Jr., "Should a Corporation Repurchase Its Own Stock?" *Journal of Finance*, June 1976, 911–921.

Selected Topics in Financial Management

VII

Throughout this text we are developing the basic framework for financial decisions. At this point we still have several important topics to discuss. We have deferred these final topics so that they could be analyzed on an integrated basis through the use of analytical tools developed in earlier chapters. Chapter 22 deals with mergers and acquisitions, Chapter 23 investigates alternatives available to firms in poor financial health, Chapter 24 provides an analytical framework within which to evaluate leases, and Chapter 25 covers international finance.

Mergers

Decision in Finance

The James River Paper Chase

In 1969 Brenton S. Halsey and Robert C. Williams borrowed $1.5 million to buy a small paper company in Richmond, Virginia, and renamed it James River after the body of water on which it was located. But the company name wasn't the only thing Halsey and Williams changed. Until they took over, the plant had produced unbleached paper that sold for about $400 per ton. Convinced that the plant was too small to make money on such commodity paper, the pair converted it to produce paper for automotive oil filters—a specialty product that currently sells for $2,000 per ton. In its first year their new company had revenues of $4 million, and Halsey and Williams figured they were on to something.

Their first plant served as a model for the next 15 acquisitions that Halsey and Williams made. Their strategy was basically simple. They would buy small, inefficient commodity paper mills at bargain prices and convert them to manufacture less competitive and more profitable specialty products. They would consider only operations that could generate a 25 percent rate of return and that required no more than 50 cents of investment per dollar of sales.

This strategy worked perfectly until 1982, when Halsey and Williams encountered an acquisition opportunity that didn't meet all their criteria but seemed too good to pass up. The paper products division of American Can was up for sale. Its $1.1 billion in sales would double James River's size overnight. The catch was that its purchase price was $420 million, while James River's own net worth was only $170 million. James River's balance sheet was already debt-heavy due to its other acquisitions. And the American Can deal would increase debt to 66.5 percent of capitalization and raise the company's interest bill to $77.6 million a year.

> As you read this chapter, look for some of the factors that Halsey and Williams probably took into account as they considered the American Can acquisition. Under what conditions would you recommend that they purchase the new business? Do you think they'd be better off sticking with their already well-proven, winning acquisition strategy?
>
> *See end of chapter for resolution.*

Most corporate growth occurs through *internal expansion*, which takes place when the firm's existing divisions grow through normal capital budgeting activities. However, the most dramatic growth, and often the largest changes in firms' stock prices, are the result of **mergers.** Recently newspapers and business periodicals have reported a large number of business combinations, including that of Du Pont and Conoco, U.S. Steel and Marathon Oil, and many others. For legal purposes there are many important distinctions among the various means by which two or more economic units can combine. Our emphasis, however, is on the fundamental business and financial aspects of mergers and acquisitions.

merger
Any combination that forms one company from two or more previously existing companies.

The Economic Implications of Mergers

The primary motivation for mergers is to increase the value of the combined enterprise. If Companies A and B merge to form Company C, and if C's value exceeds that of A and B taken separately, then **synergy** is said to exist. Synergy has often been described as the "2 plus 2 equals 5 effect." Thus, when synergy exists, the new business entity will be worth more than the simple sum of the merged firms. Such a merger is, of course, beneficial to both A's and B's stockholders. Synergistic effects can arise from three sources: (1) *operating economies* resulting from economies of scale in production or distribution; (2) *financial economies*, including either a higher P/E ratio, a lower cost of debt, or a greater debt capacity; and (3) *increased market power* due to reduced competition. Operating and financial economies are socially desirable, but mergers that reduce competition are both undesirable and illegal.

When two firms begin merger negotiations, or when one firm begins thinking about acquiring another, one of the first considerations is antitrust: Is the Justice Department likely to try to block the merger, and would it be able to do so? If the answer to either part of this question is yes, then chances are high that the merger will be aborted because of the legal expenses involved in fighting the Justice Department.

synergy
The condition wherein the whole is greater than the sum of its parts; in a synergistic merger the postmerger value exceeds the sum of the separate companies' premerger values.

Types of Mergers

Economists classify mergers into four groups: (1) horizontal, (2) vertical, (3) congeneric, and (4) conglomerate. A **horizontal merger** occurs when, for example, one widget manufacturer acquires another, or one retail food chain merges with a second—that is, when one firm combines with another in its same line of business. An example of a **vertical merger** is a steel producer's acquisition of an iron or coal mining firm (a "downstream" merger), or an oil producer's acquisition of a petrochemical company (an "upstream" merger). Congeneric means "allied in nature or action"; hence a **congeneric merger** involves related enterprises but not producers of the same product (horizontal) or firms in a producer-supplier relationship (vertical). Examples of congeneric mergers include banks' acquisitions of leasing companies, as well as insurance companies' takeovers of mutual fund management companies. **Conglomerate mergers** occur when unrelated enterprises combine; Mobil Oil's acquisition of Montgomery Ward illustrates a conglomerate merger.

Operating economies (and also anticompetitive effects) are at least partially dependent on the type of merger involved. Vertical and horizontal mergers generally provide the greatest operating benefits, but they are also the ones most likely to be attacked by the Justice Department. In any event, it is useful to think of these economic classifications when analyzing the feasibility of a prospective merger.

horizontal merger
The combination of two firms that produce the same type of goods or service.

vertical merger
A company's acquisition of one of its suppliers or one of its customers.

congeneric merger
A merger between firms in the same general industry, where the merger partners are neither customers nor suppliers of each other.

conglomerate merger
A merger between companies in different industries.

Procedures for Combining Firms

In the vast majority of merger situations, one firm (generally the smaller of the two) is acquired by another company. Occasionally the acquired firm will initiate the action, but it is much more common for a firm to seek acquisitions than to seek to be acquired. Following convention, we shall call a company that seeks to acquire another the **acquiring company** and the one which it seeks to acquire the **target company.**

Once an acquiring company has identified a possible acquisition, it must establish a suitable price, or range of prices, that it is willing to pay. With this in mind, the acquiring firm's managers must decide how to approach the target company's managers. If the acquiring firm has reason to believe the target company's management will approve the merger, then it will simply propose a merger and hope to work out some suitable terms. Then the two management groups will issue statements to their stockholders recommending that they approve the merger. Assuming that the stockholders do approve, the acquiring firm will simply buy the target company's shares from its stockholders, paying for them either with its own shares (in which case the target company's stockholders become stockholders of the acquiring company) or

acquiring company
A company that seeks to acquire another company.

target company
A company that another firm, generally a larger one, seeks to acquire through merger.

United States Gypsum Company

has acquired

Masonite Corporation

We initiated this transaction and acted as financial advisor to Masonite Corporation.

Goldman, Sachs & Co.

New York   Boston   Chicago   Dallas   Detroit
Houston   Los Angeles   Memphis   Miami
Philadelphia   St. Louis   San Francisco
London   Hong Kong   Tokyo   Zurich

May 15, 1984

Announcements of *friendly mergers*, such as this advertisement in the *Wall Street Journal*, appear frequently in the business press. In this case, managements of both the acquiring company, U.S. Gypsum, and the target company, Masonite, approved the terms of the merger. Goldman, Sachs & Co. is the investment banking firm that handled the merger.

friendly merger
A merger in which the terms are approved by the managements of both companies.

hostile merger (takeover)
A merger in which the target firm's management resists acquisition.

tender offer
The offer of one firm to buy the stock of another by going directly to the stockholders, frequently over the opposition of the target company's management.

with cash. Situations in which the terms of the merger are approved by both management groups are called **friendly mergers.**

Under other circumstances the target company's management may resist the merger. Perhaps it feels that the price offered for the stock is too low, or perhaps the target firm's management simply wants to maintain its independence. In either case the target firm's management is said to be *hostile*, and the acquiring firm must make a direct appeal to the target firm's stockholders. In **hostile mergers, or takeovers,** the acquiring company generally makes a **tender offer,** in which it asks the stockholders of the firm it is seeking to control to submit, or "tender," their shares in exchange for a specified price. The price is generally stated as so many dollars per share of the stock to be acquired, although it can be stated in terms of shares of stock in the acquiring firm. The tender offer is a direct appeal to stockholders, so it need not be approved by the management of the target firm. Tender offers are not new, but the frequency of their use has increased greatly in recent years.

Tenneco Corporation's acquisition of Kern County Land Company can be used to illustrate how a tender offer works. Kern was a relatively old, conservatively managed company whose assets consisted largely of oil properties and agricultural land, together with some manufacturing subsidiaries. Many informed investors believed that Kern's assets had a potential long-term value in excess of its current market price. Occidental Petroleum, a relatively aggressive company, made an investigation of Kern's assets and decided to make a cash tender offer for the stock. At that time Kern's market price on the New York Stock Exchange was about $60 a share, while the price Occidental decided to offer Kern's stockholders was $83.50 a share. According to Kern's management, Occidental's executives got in touch with them over a weekend and stated that a tender offer would be made the following Monday.

Because Occidental's published statements indicated that it felt Kern's low market value was partly the result of an unimaginative management, Kern's executives could anticipate being fired if Occidental's takeover bid were successful. Naturally, they resisted it. Kern's president wrote a letter to the stockholders condemning the merger; the letter was also published as a paid appeal in the *Wall Street Journal*. His position was that Kern's stock was worth more than Occidental Petroleum had offered and that stockholders should not sell out for $83.50.

How would Kern's stockholders react to these statements? In the first place, the stock had been selling at about $60 a share, and they were now offered $83.50 cash per share. With this differential stockholders would certainly accept the offer unless Kern's management could do something to keep the price above $83.50. What Kern did was obtain "marriage proposals" from a number of other companies. Kern's management reported to the newspapers—while Occidental's tender offer was still outstanding—that it had received a substantial number of proposals calling for the purchase of Kern's stock at prices substantially in excess of $83.50. This kept stockholders from tendering to Occidental.

The offer Kern's management finally recommended—and presumably the one giving Kern's stockholders the highest price—was from Tenneco. Tenneco offered one share of convertible preferred stock worth about $105 for each share of Kern's stock. Furthermore, since the merger involved an exchange of stock rather than cash, Kern's stockholders would not have to pay capital gains tax on this stock at the time of the exchange. (Had they accepted Occidental's offer, the difference between $83.50 and the cost of their stock when they purchased it would have been taxable income.) Also, according to newspaper reports, Tenneco planned to keep Kern's existing management after the merger was completed.

Financial Analysis of a Proposed Merger

In theory, merger analysis is quite simple. The acquiring firm simply performs a capital budgeting analysis to determine whether the present value of the expected future income from the merger exceeds the price paid for the target company. The target company's stockholders, on the other hand, should accept the proposal if the price offered exceeds the present value of the firm's expected future cash flows, assuming that it operates independently. However, some difficult issues are involved: (1) it is necessary for the acquiring company to estimate the cash flow benefits that will be obtained from the acquisition; (2) it is necessary to determine what effect, if any, the merger will have on the required rate of return on equity; and (3) having estimated the benefits of the merger, it is necessary for the acquiring and target firms' managers and stockholders to bargain over how to share these benefits.

Operating Mergers versus Financial Mergers

From the standpoint of financial analysis, there are two basic types of mergers:

operating merger
A merger in which the operations of two companies are integrated with the expectation of achieving synergistic benefits.

1. **Operating mergers,** in which the operations of two companies are integrated with the expectation of obtaining synergistic effects.
2. **Pure financial mergers,** in which the merged companies will not be operated as a single unit and from which no operating economies are expected.

Of course, a merger may actually be a combination of these two features.

pure financial merger
A merger in which the merged companies will not be operated as a single unit and from which no operating economies are expected.

The primary benefit from an *operating* merger is higher expected total profits. For example, the combined company may be able to reduce overheads and thereby raise profits. The expected benefits of *financial* mergers are more varied. In one case the target company may have no financial leverage, so the acquiring firm may plan to buy the company, pay for it by issuing debt, and gain market value from the capital structure change. In another instance one of the firms may be so small that its stock is illiquid, its k_s value high, and its P/E ratio low. In such a case the stock will have a low value, and it may represent a bargain purchase for the acquirer. In still other instances one firm may have excessive liquidity, large annual cash flows, and unused debt capacity, while another firm may need financial resources to take advantage of growth opportunities. Control Data's merger with Commercial Credit is a case in point. Control Data needed capital to compete with IBM, while Commercial Credit had large cash reserves and marketable securities that could be converted to cash. Finally, a significant number of mergers are of the "failing firm" or "shotgun marriage" variety designed primarily to avoid the "transactions costs" of bankruptcy. A good example of a failing firm merger was the 1978 merger of Jones & Laughlin and Youngstown Sheet and Tube, two of the top ten steel producers, who were given approval by the Justice Department to combine and form the fourth largest U.S. steel company.

Estimating Future Operating Income

In a pure financial merger the postmerger cash flows are simply the sum of the expected cash flows of the two companies if they operated independently. However, if the two firms' operations are to be integrated, then good projected cash flow statements, which are absolutely essential to sound merger decisions, will be difficult to construct.

The basic rationale for any operating merger is synergy. Del Monte Corporation provides a good example of a series of well-thought-out, successful operating mergers. Del Monte successfully merged and integrated numerous small canning companies into a very efficient, highly profitable organization. It used standardized production techniques to increase the efficiency of all its plants, a national brand name and national advertising to develop customer loyalty, a consolidated distribution system, and a centralized purchasing office that obtained substantial discounts from volume purchases. Because of these economies, Del Monte became perhaps the most efficient and profitable canning company, and its merger activities helped make possible the size that produced these economies. Consumers also benefited because Del Monte's efficiency enabled the company to sell high-quality products at relatively low prices.

An example of poor pro forma analysis that resulted in a disastrous merger is the consolidation of the Pennsylvania and New York Central Railroads. The premerger analysis was highly misleading. It failed to reveal the fact that certain key elements in the two rail systems were incompatible and hence could not be meshed together. Rather than gaining synergistic benefits, the combined system actually incurred additional overhead costs that helped lead to its bankruptcy.

It is impossible to generalize further about the construction of pro forma statements except to say that, in planning operating mergers, the development of these statements is *the single most important aspect* of the merger analysis. In fact, many firms that are actively engaged in mergers have an "acquisition department." These departments evaluate merger candidates and develop pro forma statements which forecast, under varying assumptions, the results of the mergers and evaluate plans for making the projections materialize.

Industry Practice

Do Mergers Make Sense?

Is the merger mania that has gripped corporate America over the past few years paying off? Not according to many of the academics who staff the nation's business and management schools and act as consultants to industry. They deplore Du Pont's $7.5 billion takeover of Conoco, U.S. Steel's $6 billion purchase of Marathon Oil, Fluor Corp.'s $2.2 billion acquisition of St. Joe Minerals, and most of the other big mergers that have made the current boom the most expensive in history. In 1981 alone, U.S. companies spent $82 billion for acquisitions.

The academics contend that most of the current mergers, particularly those of the conglomerate kind, make no real economic or management sense. They are ill-conceived, inadequately planned, and overpriced, they argue. Worse, there is little or no evidence that the primary objectives sought in mergers—greater economies of scale and productivity, increased profitability, and improved stock performance—are being attained to any significant degree. And few companies, the critics add, possess the management skills to blend a large acquired firm into their own operations and run it effectively.

James O'Toole, management professor at the University of Southern California, among others, thinks that Du Pont's takeover of Conoco typifies the largely unjustifiable merger. To begin with, Du Pont probably would not have attempted the acquisition were it not for the chance to play the White Knight in the fierce struggle between Mobil Oil and Seagram to take over Conoco. But by appearing as the good guy, Du Pont rightly figured it could clear the antitrust hurdle and buy Conoco for a price that initially seemed a bargain. It viewed the merger as a relatively cheap means of acquiring a more stable source of petroleum feedstock for its chemical output than foreign oil.

In the end, however, Du Pont paid dearly. When the company entered the takeover battle, Conoco's stock price was $77 a share, substantially below its appraised value of $160 a share. Du Pont, whose own stock was selling at around $51 a share, made an initial bid averaging $79.52 a share. By the time the acquisition was concluded, the offer had soared to $98 a share, and investors had made known their feelings about the merger by chopping more than 10 percent off the price of Du Pont stock, equivalent to an equity loss of $790 million. A year later the market value had fallen another 25 percent, a far steeper decline than that of other chemical companies—and a clear sign that investors were still worried about the effects of the merger.

To pay for Conoco, Du Pont more than tripled its debt to $3.9 billion at a time of towering interest rates, which required about $500 million a year to service. If Du Pont could not sell off sizable Conoco assets to raise funds, analysts point out, the demands of interest costs on cash flow could retard its spending on other promising company operations. The uncertain oil outlook also made Du Pont's purchase price for Conoco look even more unjustifiable.

Du Pont, of course, disagrees with the critics. The company considers the acquisition a long-term investment that will pay off handsomely in time, according to Harold S. May, vice president for corporate studies.

Du Pont paid a high price, May says, because it had wanted an oil company for a long time and feared that waiting for another opportunity to come along might cost it even more; also, it was unable to find another oil company available last year that fitted its needs as well as Conoco. In time, he adds, the synergism of the merger will make itself apparent in improved earnings, and the company will be able to prove the cost advantages of a more stable source of feedstock when its current contracts with suppliers run out.

Meanwhile the critics expect no better results for U.S. Steel and Fluor, among others. Fluor, the nation's second largest engineering and construction firm, expected St. Joe's broad-based minerals business to act as a contracyclical balancing force in its operations. Instead, both its own and St. Joe's businesses have declined in tandem, and analysts foresee only slow growth in each area for some time.

In reaction to the merger, investors ruthlessly reduced Fluor's market value by a whopping 70 percent. And Wall Street showed an equal lack of enthusiasm for the Marathon merger by slicing 45 percent off Big Steel's market price.

As the critics point out, in the rush to acquire natural resource firms, the low market prices of target companies made them attractive initially. But so many players leaped into the fray that the prices were bid up sharply, and in their haste the acquiring companies gave insufficient thought to the outlook for oil and minerals. "Since oil is a depletable resource, they assumed that prices would keep going up,"

says Art Cuse, a Los Angeles merger and acquisition consultant. "But the same thing was said about housing and land, and now their prices are falling."

Academics and others put most of the blame for the merger boom on corporate development executives and investment bankers. According to Richard P. Rumelt, a professor of business strategy at UCLA's Graduate School of Management, staff acquisition specialists try to justify their existence by convincing management of the need to go outside the company to secure future growth and expansion. By presenting various rationales and playing on the ambitions of top officers, they frequently succeed even without the aid of a thorough plan or analysis. "It's a tremendous ego trip for top managers," says Rumelt. "Billions of dollars are involved, so it feels like it's very important, and that's an enormous kick."

Investment bankers, the critics say, have the most basic motive for encouraging mergers: fat fees. Morgan Stanley & Co., for example, collected nearly $15 million for advising Conoco on its takeover. "They get extraordinary fees, so they want to jam companies together as often as they can," Cuse says.

But while the merger specialists and investment bankers prosper, the academics argue, neither stockholders nor the economy has profited from the recent round of mergers. Stockholders of most of the major acquiring firms have lost considerable value in their holdings, and the economy has reaped none of the direct benefits usually claimed for mergers, such as new jobs and lower consumer prices. "That acquiring companies should be so generous and make such unprofitable investments for their stockholders is just not understandable," says Yale economist Paul MacAvoy.

By the mid-1980s, however, many academics expect to see a more traditional view prevailing among corporate leaders. "There's a general reaction beginning to set in among businessmen against the merger trend," says O'Toole. "They are becoming more aware of the poor track record of the recent past and are starting to rekindle the notion that it's time to move away from mergers and get back to the basics."

Source: "Do Mergers Make Sense?" by Thomas J. Murray. Reprinted with the permission of *Dun's Business Month* (formerly *Dun's Review*), October 1982. Copyright 1982, Dun & Bradstreet Publications Corporation.

Postmerger Market Values

Once the postmerger income statement has been estimated, the next step is to project the postmerger market price of the acquiring firm's stock. This, in turn, involves two steps: (1) estimating postmerger earnings per share and (2) estimating the postmerger P/E ratio. Since earnings per share depend on the terms of the merger (how much the acquiring firm pays for the acquired company), this topic is examined next.

Terms of the Merger

The terms of a merger include two important elements: (1) Who will control the combined enterprise? (2) How much will the acquiring firm pay for the acquired company?

Postmerger Control. The employment/control situation is of vital interest when a small, owner-managed firm sells out to a larger concern. The owner-manager may be anxious to retain a high position and also be concerned about keeping operating control of the organization after the merger. Thus these points are likely to be stressed during the merger negotiations. When a publicly owned firm, not controlled by its managers, is merged into another company, the acquired firm's management also is worried about its postmerger position. If the acquiring firm agrees to keep the old management, then management may be willing to support the merger and recommend its acceptance to the stockholders. If the old management is to be removed, then it will probably resist the merger, as Kern's management did in the example described earlier in the chapter.

The Price Paid. The second key element in a merger is the price to be paid for the acquired company—the cash or shares of stock to be given in exchange for the firm. If the merger is to be for cash, the analysis is similar to a regular capital budgeting analysis: the incremental earnings are estimated; a discount rate is applied to find the present value of these earnings; and, if the present value of the future incremental earnings exceeds the price to be paid for the acquired firm, then the merger is approved. If, because of operating economies or financial considerations, the acquired firm is worth more to the acquiring firm than its market value as a separate entity, then the merger is feasible. Obviously, the acquiring firm tries to buy at as low a price as possible, while the acquired firm tries to sell out at the highest possible price. The final price is determined by negotiations, with the side that negotiates better capturing most of the incremental value. *The larger the synergistic benefits, the more room there is for bargaining and the higher the probability that the merger will actually be consummated.*

If the merger calls for an exchange of stock, then the key issue is the **exchange ratio (ER),** which is the number of shares the acquiring firm gives for each of the acquired firm's shares. For example, when Emhart Industries acquired USM, 1.125 shares of Emhart were exchanged for each USM share; thus the exchange ratio was 1.125. The three factors that have the greatest influence on the exchange ratio—current earnings, projected future earnings, and market price—are discussed next.

exchange ratio (ER)
The number of shares the acquiring firm must give for each of the acquired firm's shares.

Earnings per Share. Suppose the acquiring company (Firm A) earns $4.53 per share, while the target company (Firm T) has EPS = $3.49, and the companies are equally risky. On the basis of relative earnings, the exchange ratio would be set at $3.49/$4.53 = 0.77. This means that 77 shares of Firm A's stock would be exchanged for every 100 shares of Firm T's stock. An exchange on this basis would leave each stockholder's postmerger earnings unchanged. For example, the holder of 100 shares of T would receive 77 shares of A. The premerger earnings would have been $100 \times \$3.49 = \$349$, while the postmerger earnings would be $77 \times \$4.53 = \$349$.

Projected Future Earnings. The above situation would be appropriate if (1) there were no synergistic effects and (2) the firms had identical growth rates. However, when the merger is expected to produce higher earnings, or when the firms' EPS growth rates differ, it is more appropriate to set the exchange ratio on the basis of *expected future EPS rather than historic EPS.*

First, consider the same case with no synergy but with the additional information that Firm A has been growing and is expected to continue to grow at a 6 percent rate, while T's growth rate is 4 percent. On the basis of the latest reported earnings, the exchange ratio would be $3.49/$4.53 = 0.77. However, on the basis of next year's projected earnings, the ratio would be $3.49(1.04)/\$4.53(1.06) = \$3.63/\$4.80 = 0.756$. Furthermore, on the basis of earnings 5 years hence, the exchange ratio would be $4.25/$6.06 = 0.701. Thus a problem exists—on the basis of future earnings, the exchange ratio varies depending on how far into the future earnings are projected.

When possible synergistic effects are considered, it becomes even more difficult to use current earnings as a basis for the exchange ratio. Suppose, for example, that Firm A's EPS = $4.53, Firm T's EPS = $3.49, and no growth is expected. If the merger terms are based on relative EPS, then, as we have seen, the ratio will be set at 0.77, and both firms' stockholders will have the same postmerger earnings. Thus EPS for Firm A, the surviving company, will remain at $4.53. However, let us assume that synergistic effects are present, and on the basis of a 0.77 exchange ratio, A's postmerger EPS will rise to $6. This will benefit both T's and A's stockholders—the holder of 100 shares of T will now have earnings of 77 × $6 = $462 versus $349 before the merger, while a 100-share owner of A will have 100 × $6 = $600 versus $453 without the merger.[1]

Market Values. Current and future earnings, risk, growth rates, potential synergistic effects, and a host of other factors are embodied in a firm's market price, so in many respects relative market prices represent the best basis for setting exchange ratios. Suppose, for example, that Firm A sells for $40 per share, while Firm T's current price is $30. On the basis of market values, the exchange ratio would be set at $30/$40 = 0.75.

If no synergistic effects are likely, or if T's synergistic value to potential acquiring firms has already been accounted for in its price, then the actual exchange ratio will probably be based on relative market values. However, if T's price reflects only its "stand alone" value, but the firm could enjoy substantially higher profits if combined with another company, then the actual exchange ratio could be set well above the market value ratio.

Illustration of a Merger Analysis

To illustrate how a merger might be analyzed, consider the proposed merger between Consolidated Enterprises and Target Technology, Inc. Consolidated Enterprises has been growing at a rate of about 5 percent per year, while Target Technology's past and projected future growth rate is 20 percent. Consolidated's total after-tax earnings are $50 million, or $4 for each of its 12.5 million shares; Target's latest earnings were $3 million, or $2 for each of its 1.5 million shares. Consolidated pays a $2 dividend, while Target pays $1 per share. Consolidated's current market price is $30 per share, and Target's is $20 per share.

---

[1]Accordingly, if synergy is anticipated, then A can realistically pay more for T than 0.77 shares, while T's stockholders can accept less than 0.77 shares and still come out ahead. For a discussion of breakeven exchange ratios based on expected EPS, see Eugene F. Brigham, *Financial Management: Theory and Practice*, 3rd ed. (Hinsdale, IL: Dryden Press, 1982), Chapter 20.

When they began considering a possible merger, Consolidated's an-alysts first assumed that no synergistic effects would occur but that the combined companies would grow at a 5.85 percent rate, calculated as follows:

	Total Earnings	Percentage Weights	Growth Rate	Product
Consolidated Enterprises	$50,000,000	0.9434	5%	4.717%
Target Technology	3,000,000	0.0566	20	1.132
	$53,000,000	1.0000		
Weighted average growth rate				5.849%

Next, the Consolidated analysts considered possible exchange ratios (ER). On the basis of *current* earnings, ER = $2/$4 = 0.5 shares of Consolidated given up for each share of Target. On the basis of *future* earnings, the ratio would increase; for example, if earnings projected out 5 years were used, then the exchange ratio would be about 1.0:

$$\text{ER} = (1.20)^5(\$2)/(1.05)^5(\$4)$$
$$= 2.4883(\$2)/1.2763(\$4)$$
$$= \$4.98/\$5.11 = 0.975 \cong 1.0.$$

On the basis of relative market prices, the exchange ratio would be set at $20/$30 = 0.667, and EPS would be $53/[12.5 + (0.667 × 1.5)] = $3.93.

The Consolidated analysts then projected earnings per share for each of the next 5 years under the alternative exchange ratios. This projec-tion was made by first estimating total corporate earnings of the com-bined firm for each year, then dividing by the number of shares out-standing, which differs depending on the exchange ratio used. Figure 22-1 gives a plot of Consolidated's EPS assuming no merger and also assuming a merger based on current market prices. As the graph shows, Consolidated's EPS would decline immediately after the merger, assuming no synergy and a 0.667 exchange ratio, but in the future EPS would grow more rapidly than it would have without the merger.

Using other exchange ratios, other earnings growth rates, and syn-ergistic effects, we could derive many other EPS patterns. Because so many factors are involved, it is difficult to generalize about postmerger earnings per share. However, one important generalization should be made: *If a firm with a high P/E ratio buys a firm with a lower P/E ratio, and the exchange ratio is based on current market prices, then the acquiring firm will obtain an immediate increase in EPS. Conversely, if a low P/E ratio com-pany buys a high P/E firm, there will be an immediate dilution in EPS.* This point is borne out by the Consolidated-Target merger analysis. Consol-

Figure 22-1
EPS Projections for Consolidated Enterprises
In considering a merger, the acquiring company attempts to forecast possible results of
the proposed acquisition. In this figure Consolidated Enterprises projects future earnings
per share resulting from a proposed merger in which stock would be exchanged at a ratio
based on relative market prices. Against this is plotted future EPS if no merger occurs.
With a merger EPS will immediately be diluted because the newly acquired firm has a
higher price/earnings ratio than Consolidated. This dilution is inevitable but short-lived;
2½ years after the merger, EPS will begin to increase faster than it would have without a
merger.

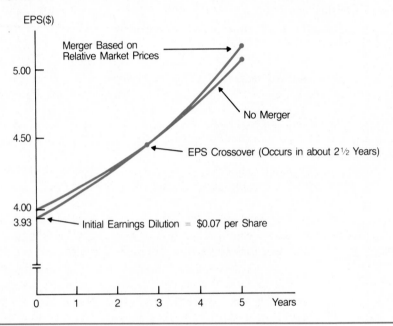

idated had a lower P/E ratio ($30/$4 = 7.5×) than Target ($20/$2 =
10×), and this relationship led to the initial **dilution** in Consolidated's
EPS as shown in Figure 22-1. *In effect, Consolidated diluted its current
EPS in order to obtain a higher future EPS growth rate.*

Target's stockholders will have a higher level of current earnings at
the market value exchange ratio:

Old earnings per 100 shares owned: 100 × $2 = $200.
New earnings per 100 shares   100(0.667)($3.93) = $262.
   formerly owned:

The stockholders will, of course, be giving up some of their future
growth opportunities.

Operating Synergy. The analysis thus far is based on the assumption
of no operating synergies. However, Consolidated and Target may

earnings dilution
The acquisition of a firm with a
high P/E ratio by a firm with a
low P/E ratio, where the
exchange ratio is based on
current market prices.

complement each other. For example, Target's metallurgical scientists may be able to improve Consolidated's product line, or Consolidated's unused plant may be utilized by Target. If synergy does occur, it could partially or completely offset the initial dilution and also result in an increase in the postmerger growth rate.

The Postmerger Market Price: Estimating a P/E Ratio. After developing estimates of the postmerger EPS, the next task is to estimate a P/E ratio and then apply this P/E ratio to the earnings estimate to obtain a *predicted postmerger market price.* The postmerger P/E ratio will reflect investors' estimates of the merged company's risk and growth prospects. If investors feel that Consolidated and Target, as a combined enterprise, will be less risky because of diversification effects, then the P/E ratio may rise. Similarly, if investors think that the postmerger growth rate will be more reflective of Target's situation, this too will enhance the P/E ratio.

The resulting P/E ratio might be the same as Consolidated's old ratio, 7.5 times. If this ratio is applied to an EPS of $3.93, the resulting price is $29.48. In this case Consolidated's postmerger price would have declined from the old $30 level. On the other hand, if investors applied Target's P/E of 10 to the combined company, then the postmerger stock price would be $39.30.

Several points should be clear from this brief discussion. First, Consolidated should acquire Target if and only if the acquisition will raise Consolidated's stock price. Second, the postmerger price will reflect both the final EPS, which will depend on the exchange ratio and on possible synergistic effects, and the final P/E ratio, which will depend on investors' appraisal of the combined firm's risk and growth prospects. If a firm's analysts are good at estimating these factors, they will have a record of good acquisitions; otherwise, their merger program will not be successful.

Effects of Accounting Practices on Reported Profits

Although a detailed discussion of accounting is best left to accounting courses, at least some mention should be made of alternative accounting treatments of merged firms and their effects on reported profits. Mergers are handled in either of two basic ways: (1) as a *pooling of interests* or (2) as a *purchase.* The method used can have a significant effect on the postmerger reported profits, and this in turn can influence the desirability of the merger.

Pooling of Interests

In a **pooling of interests** the consolidated balance sheet is constructed by simply adding together the balance sheets of the merged companies. Table 22-1 shows the essential elements of the consolidated bal-

pooling of interests
An accounting method for combining the financial statements of two firms that merge; the assets of the merged firms are simply added to form the balance sheet of the surviving corporation.

Table 22-1
Pooling of Interests Accounting

	Firm A	Firm B	Merged Firm: A
Current assets	$ 50	$25	$ 75
Fixed assets	50	25	75
Total assets	$100	$50	$150
Debt	$ 40	$20	$ 60
Common equity	60	30	90
Total liabilities and net worth	$100	$50	$150

ance sheet after Firms A and B have merged under a pooling of inter- ests. This final balance sheet holds regardless of how many shares Firm A gave up to acquire Firm B.

Purchase Accounting

purchase
The situation wherein the acquiring firm is assumed to have bought the target company much as it would buy any capital asset.

Under **purchase** accounting the acquiring firm is assumed to have bought the acquired company much as it would buy any capital asset, paying for it with cash, debt, or stock of the acquiring company. If the price paid is exactly equal to the net asset value (total assets minus liabilities), then the consolidated balance sheet is similar to that under pooling. Otherwise there is an important difference. If the price paid exceeds the net asset value, then assets are increased to reflect the price actually paid, whereas if the price paid is less than the net asset value, then assets are written down when preparing the consolidated balance sheet.

Table 22-2 illustrates purchase accounting, using the same data as for the pooled companies. Note that Firm B's net asset value is $30, which is also its reported common equity value. This $30 could reflect the correct market value (which is determined by the firm's earning power), but it could also be more or less than the true value. Three situations are considered. First, in Column 3 we assume that Firm A gives cash or stock worth $20 for Firm B. Thus B was apparently over- valued, and A pays less than B's net asset value. While the overvalua- tion could be in fixed or current assets, we assume that fixed assets are overvalued. Accordingly, we write down both B's fixed assets and its common equity by $10 before constructing the consolidated balance sheet shown in Column 3. Next, in Column 4 we assume that A pays exactly its net asset value for B. In this case pooling and purchase ac- counting would produce identical balance sheets. Finally, in Column 5 we assume that A pays more than net asset value for B: $50 is paid for $30 of net assets. This excess is partly attributed to undervalued assets

Table 22-2
Purchase Accounting

	Firm A (1)	Firm B (2)	Merged Firm: A[a]		
			$20 Paid (3)	$30 Paid (4)	$50 Paid (5)
Current assets	$ 50	$25	$ 75	$ 75	$ 80
Fixed assets	50	25	$ 65[b]	75	80
Goodwill	0	0	0	0	10[d]
	$100	$50	$140	$150	$170
Debt	$ 40	$20	$ 60	$ 60	$ 60
Equity	60	30	80[c]	90	110[e]
	$100	$50	$140	$150	$170

[a]The price paid is the *net* asset value, that is, total assets minus debt.
[b]Assume Firm B's fixed assets are written down to $15 before constructing the consolidated balance sheet.
[c]Firm B's common equity is reduced by $10 prior to consolidation to reflect the fixed asset write-off.
[d]"Goodwill" refers to the excess paid for a firm over and above the appraised value of the physical assets purchased. Goodwill represents payment both for intangibles such as patents and for "organization value" that might arise from having an effective sales force.
[e]Firm B's equity is increased prior to consolidation to reflect the above-book purchase price.

(land, buildings, and machinery, and also inventories worth more because of inflation); to reflect this fact, current and fixed assets are each increased by $5. In addition, we assume that $10 of the $20 excess is due to a superior sales organization or some other intangible factor, and we post this excess as "goodwill." B's common equity is correspondingly increased by $20, and this is reflected in the consolidated common equity account.

Income Statement Effects

There can be a significant difference in reported profits under the two accounting methods. If asset values are increased, this must be reflected in higher depreciation charges (and also in a higher cost of goods sold if inventories were written up). This reduces reported profits. Also, **goodwill** represents the excess paid for a firm over its net asset value. This excess, in turn, is paid because of the acquired firm's superior earning power, which will, presumably, be eroded over time as patents expire, as new firms enter the industry, and so on. Thus the accountants (in Accounting Principles Board Opinion #17) require that goodwill be written off, or amortized with the write-off period corresponding to the expected life of the superior earning power but in no case exceeding 40 years.

Goodwill is certainly not a trivial issue. For example, Philip Morris, Inc. acquired Seven-Up Corporation for a price of $520 million; approximately $390 million of this represented goodwill. Table 22-3 illustrates

goodwill
Intangible asset of a firm established by the excess of the price paid for the going concern over the value of its assets.

Table 22-3
Income Effects of Pooling versus Purchase Accounting

| | Premerger | | Postmerger: Firm A | |
	Firm A (1)	Firm B (2)	Pooling (3)	Purchase (4)
Sales	$100	$50	$150	$150
Operating costs	72	36	108	109[a]
Operating income	$ 28	$14	$ 42	$ 41
Interest (10%)	4	2	6	6
Taxable income	$ 24	$12	$ 36	$ 35
Taxes (50%)	12	6	18	17.5
Earnings after tax	$ 12	$ 6	$ 18	$ 17.5
Goodwill write-off	0	0	0	1[b]
Net income	$ 12	$ 6	$ 18	$ 16.5
EPS[c]	$ 2	$ 2	$ 2	$ 1.83

[a]Operating costs are $1 higher than they otherwise would be to reflect the higher reported costs caused by the physical asset markup at the time of purchase.
[b]$10 of increased goodwill ÷ 10 years = $1 write-off per year.
[c]Firm A had six shares and Firm B three shares before the merger. A gives one of its shares for each of B's, so A has nine shares outstanding after the merger.

the effects of goodwill write-off by showing the income statements for Firms A and B before the merger and for Firm A after the merger. For the purchase we assume that A purchased B for $50, creating $10 of goodwill and $10 of higher physical asset value. Furthermore, we assume that this $20 will be written off over ten years.[2] As Column 4 indicates, writing off goodwill and higher asset values under purchase accounting causes reported profits to be lower than under pooling.

The write-off of goodwill is also reflected in earnings per share. In our hypothetical merger we assume that nine shares exist in the consolidated firm. (Six of these shares went to A's stockholders, three to B's.) Under pooling EPS = $2, while under purchase EPS = $1.83. Furthermore, the greater the amount of goodwill, the larger the write-off and the more significant the dilution in reported earnings per share. This fact causes managers to prefer pooling to purchase accounting.

Requirements for Pooling

Six conditions must be met before the pooling method may be used:
1. The acquired firm's stockholders must maintain an ownership position in the surviving firm.

---

[2]The write-off of goodwill is not a deduction for income tax purposes, but the other excess write-offs are deductible. Also, "negative goodwill" is eliminated at the time of the merger, so negative goodwill cannot be used to increase reported profits in later years.

2. The basis of accounting for the assets of the acquired entity must remain unchanged.

3. Only independent interests may be combined; each entity must have had autonomy for two years prior to the initiation of the plan to combine, and no more than 10 percent ownership of voting common stock may be held as intercorporate investments.

4. The combination must be effected in a single transaction; contingent payouts are not permitted in poolings, but they may be used in purchases.

5. The acquiring corporation may issue only common stock identical to its outstanding voting common stock in exchange for substantially all the voting common stock of the other company; "substantially" is defined as 90 percent.

6. The combined entity cannot dispose of a significant portion of the assets of the combined companies for two years after the merger.

If all of these conditions are met, then the combination is, in a sense, a "merger among equals," and a pooling of interests has occurred. In contrast, a purchase involves (1) new owners, (2) an appraisal of the acquired firm's physical assets with a restatement of the balance sheet to reflect these values, and (3) the possible creation of goodwill.

Holding Companies

Holding companies date from 1889, when New Jersey became the first state to pass a law permitting corporations to be formed for the sole purpose of owning the stocks of other companies. Many of the advantages and disadvantages of holding companies are identical to the advantages and disadvantages of large-scale operations already discussed in connection with mergers and consolidations. Whether a company is organized on a divisional basis or with the divisions kept as separate companies does not affect the basic reasons for conducting a large-scale, multiproduct, multiplant operation. However, the holding company form of large-scale operations has some different advantages and disadvantages from those of completely integrated divisionalized operations.

holding company
A corporation that owns sufficient common stocks of other corporations to achieve working control of those corporations; formed for the sole purpose of owning stocks in other companies.

Advantages of Holding Companies

Control with Fractional Ownership. Through a holding company operation a firm may buy 5, 10, or 50 percent of the stock of another corporation. Such fractional ownership may be sufficient to give the acquiring company effective working control or substantial influence over the operations of the company in which it has acquired stock ownership. Working control is often considered to entail more than 25 percent of the common stock, but it can be as low as 10 percent if the stock is widely distributed. One financier says that the attitude of management is more important than the number of shares owned, adding that "if they think you can control the company, then you do." In addition, control on a very slim margin can be held through friendship with large stockholders outside the holding company group.

operating company
A subsidiary of a holding company; a separate legal entity.

Isolation of Risks. Because the various **operating companies** in a holding company system are separate legal entities, the obligations of any one unit are separate from those of the other units. Catastrophic losses incurred by one unit of the holding company system are therefore not transmitted as claims on the assets of the other units.

Although this is the customary generalization on the nature of a holding company system, it is not completely valid. First, the parent company may feel obligated to make good on the subsidiary's debts, even though it is not legally bound to do so, in order to keep its good name and thus retain customers. Examples of this would include American Express's payment of over $100 million in connection with the salad oil swindle of the 1960s and United California Bank's coverage of its Swiss affiliate's multimillion-dollar losses on cocoa futures in the 1970s. Second, a parent company may feel obligated to supply capital to an affiliate in order to protect its initial investment; General Public Utilities' continued support of its affiliate's Three Mile Island nuclear plant is an example. And third, when lending to one of the units of a holding company system, an astute loan officer may require a guarantee or a claim on the assets of the parent or of other elements in the holding company system. To some degree, therefore, the assets in the various elements of a holding company are joined.

Disadvantages of Holding Companies

consolidated return
An income tax return that combines the income statements of several affiliated firms.

Partial Multiple Taxation. Provided the holding company owns at least 80 percent of a subsidiary's voting stock, the Internal Revenue Service permits the filing of **consolidated returns,** in which case dividends received by the parent are not taxed. However, if less than 80 percent of the stock is owned, returns may not be consolidated, but 85 percent of the dividends received by the holding company may be deducted. With a tax rate of 46 percent, this means that the effective tax rate on intercorporate dividends is 6.9 percent. This partial double taxation somewhat offsets the benefits of holding company control with limited ownership, but whether the penalty of 6.9 percent of dividends received is sufficient to offset other possible advantages is a matter that must be decided in individual situations.

Ease of Enforced Dissolution. It is relatively easy for the U.S. Department of Justice to require dissolution by disposal of stock ownership of a holding company operation it finds unacceptable. For instance, Du

Pont was required to dispose of its 23 percent stock interest in General Motors Corporation, acquired in the early 1920s. Because there was no fusion between the corporations, there were no difficulties, from an operating standpoint, in requiring the separation of the two companies. However, if complete amalgamation had taken place, it would have been much more difficult to break up the company after so many years, and the likelihood of forced **divestiture** would have been reduced.

Leverage in Holding Companies

divestiture
The selling off of an asset or a division by its parent company; if the asset is given to the parent company's stockholders, the divestiture is called a *spin-off*.

The holding company vehicle has been used to obtain huge degrees of financial leverage. In the 1920s several tiers of holding companies were established in the electric utility and other industries. In those days an operating company might have $100 million of assets, financed by $50 million of debt and $50 million of equity. A first-tier holding company might own the stock (its only asset) and be financed with $25 million of debt and $25 million of equity. A second-tier holding company, which owned the stock of the first-tier company, might be financed with $12.5 million of debt and $12.5 million of equity. The system could be extended, but with only two holding companies, we see that $100 million of operating assets are controlled at the top by $12.5 million of equity, and that these assets must provide enough cash income to support $87.5 million of debt. *This holding company system is highly leveraged, even though the individual components have only 50 percent debt/assets ratios.* Because of this *consolidated leverage,* even a small decline in profits at the operating company level could bring the whole system down like a house of cards.

Summary

A merger involves the consolidation of two or more firms. Mergers can provide economic benefits through economies of scale, but they also have the potential for reducing competition, and for this reason they are carefully regulated by governmental agencies.

In most mergers one company (the *acquiring firm*) initiates action to take over another (the *target firm*). The acquiring company must analyze the situation and determine the value of the target company. Often there will be *operating economies*, or *synergistic benefits*, which will raise the earnings of the combined enterprise over the sum of the earnings of the two separate companies. In this circumstance the merger is potentially beneficial to both sets of stockholders, but the two firms' managers and stockholders must agree as to how the net benefits will be shared. This all boils down to how much the acquiring company is willing to pay, either in cash or in shares of its own stock, for the target company. There are various methods for determining an appropriate price.

In a merger one firm disappears. However, an alternative is for one firm to buy all or a majority of the common stock of another and to run the acquired firm as an operating subsidiary. When this occurs, the acquiring firm is said to be a *holding company*. Holding company operations have both advantages and disadvantages. The major advantage is the fact that control can often be obtained for a smaller cash outlay. The disadvantages include tax penalties and the fact of incomplete ownership.

Resolution to Decision in Finance

The James River Paper Chase

Brenton S. Halsey and Robert C. Williams decided to go through with the purchase of American Can's paper products division, primarily due to the synergism they foresaw. The purchase gave them something they badly wanted: a strong presence in consumer paper products that would balance their concentration in industrial specialty products. Industrial paper sales are cyclical and dependent on the economy, so when recession hit, James River's sales were hurt. But consumer products—paper towels and tissues, disposable food and beverage containers, and paperboard packaging—are necessities and are thus recession-proof. Acquisition of the American Can operation, which included the popular Dixie cup line, brought consumer product sales up to 30 percent of James River's total and provided good balance for some of the company's more vulnerable product lines.

The 66.5 percent debt load that the purchase imposed was a formidable burden. But in January 1983 James River decreased its debt ratio to 45 percent by issuing some new stock. Although this is still high in comparison to the industry average of 35 percent, Halsey insists that he isn't concerned and notes that cash flow more than covers interest expenses. "We can use leverage to the benefit of shareholders without a great deal of risk," he says. "So why not use it?"

Based on James River's extraordinary growth through acquisitions, it would be difficult to argue with Halsey. From the tiny paper mill they bought in 1969 Halsey and Williams have built an empire that comprises 23 additional mills, 21,000 employees, and $2.2 billion in sales. Between 1978 and 1983, while other paper products companies were struggling to maintain their market positions, James River's revenues grew at a compound rate of 55.5 percent, making it the country's fourth largest paper products company. Its earnings surged at a compounded 25.5 percent a year and its return on equity stood at 22 percent, in sharp contrast to the industry average of 8 percent.

Looking ahead, Halsey and Williams predict that James River's growth will slow somewhat, and they figure that acquisitions will account for only around 20 percent of its revenue increases. Nonetheless, they predict that revenues will pass $3 billion by 1988 and expect that earnings will rise 20 percent a year until then.

Source: "James River: The Paper Chase Pays Off," *Dun's Business Month*, December 1983, 48–49.

Key Terms You should be able to define each of the following terms:

Merger
Synergy
Horizontal merger; vertical merger;
  congeneric merger; conglomerate
  merger
Acquiring company; target company
Friendly merger; hostile merger
  (takeover)
Tender offer
Operating merger; pure financial
  merger

Exchange ratio (ER)
Earnings dilution
Pooling of interests; purchase
Goodwill
Holding company; operating
  company
Consolidated return
Divestiture

Questions

22-1 Four economic classifications of mergers are *horizontal, vertical, conglomerate,* and *congeneric.* What is the significance of these terms in merger analysis with regard to **(a)** the likelihood of Justice Department intervention and **(b)** possibilities for operating synergy?

22-2 Firm A wants to acquire Firm B. Firm B's management thinks the merger is a good idea. Might a tender offer be used?

22-3 What is the difference between operating mergers and pure financial mergers?

22-4 Several years ago the SEC and the New York Stock Exchange each issued a set of rulings on disclosure of information which, in effect, required that firms disclose that they have entered into merger discussions as soon as they start such discussions. Since the previous procedure had been to delay disclosure until it was evident that there was a reasonably good expectation the merger under discussion would actually go through (and not to bring the matter up at all if the merger died in the early stages), it can safely be predicted that, in a statistical sense, a larger percentage of prospective mergers will be abandoned in the future than in the past.

a. Why do you think the new rulings were put into effect?

b. Will the new rulings have any adverse effects? Why?

22-5 Philip Morris, Inc. recently acquired Seven-Up Corporation for $520 million. Seven-Up had a book value of equity of $130 million. Do you think Philip Morris's management would prefer to treat the merger as a pooling or as a purchase? Would your reaction be the same if the book value had been $520 million and the price paid $130 million?

22-6 Two large, publicly owned firms are contemplating a merger. No operating synergy is expected, but returns on the two firms are not perfectly positively correlated, so σ_{EBIT} would be reduced for the combined corporation. One group of consultants argues that this risk reduction is sufficient grounds for the merger. Another group thinks that this type of risk reduction is irrelevant because stockholders could already hold the stock of both companies and thus gain the risk reduction benefits of merger. Whose position is correct?

Problems

* 22-1 The Hilltop Hotels are negotiating a merger with the Doze Inn Motel chain. Consider the following table:

	EPS	D_0	g	P_0	Number of Common Shares
Hilltop	$3.00	$1.50	8%	$53.55	5 million
Doze Inn	1.00	0.90	3	11.61	1 million

Establish the appropriate exchange ratio:

a. Based on current EPS.

b. Based on EPS in 5 years.

c. Based on current market values.

22-2 Morris Sisters' Cafeterias hopes to acquire Davidson's Cafeterias through a merger. Davidson's management will consider the offer only if the price is high and management can stay on in its present capacity. Morris Sisters' expects to gain operating efficiency from the merger through purchasing, advertising, and distribution economies. It estimates that if the two chains had been operating jointly during the year which just ended, earnings would have totaled $21 million. The most recent financial information on the two firms is summarized below:

	EPS	DPS	g	P_0	Number of Shares
Morris Sisters'	$2.50	$2.00	6%	$40	6 million
Davidson's	1.80	0.90	2	18	2 million

---

*Refer to Appendix E for check answers to problems with asterisks.

a. Calculate the exchange ratio based on **(1)** market values and **(2)** most recent earnings per share.

* **b.** How many shares can Morris Sisters' give Davidson's and still maintain its current EPS? Assume combined earnings will be $21 million.

* **c.** What is the exchange ratio indicated in Part b?

d. Irrespective of your answers in Parts a and c, assume that Morris Sisters' agrees to a 1-for-1 exchange of shares. Calculate the expected postmerger EPS.

e. Calculate the premerger P/E ratio for each firm.

f. Assume a postmerger P/E ratio of 14. Now calculate the expected postmerger market price and compare it with Morris Sisters' premerger price. Should Morris Sisters' acquire Davidson's?

g. Now assume the merger did not affect Morris Sisters' P/E ratio; that is, it remains at its current level. Under these conditions, would you approve the merger?

22-3 Fairchild Industries has agreed to merge with Berry Products. The following financial information applies to the firms before the merger:

	Total Earnings	Number of Shares	P/E Ratio
Fairchild	$1,500,000	500,000	18
Berry	2,000,000	2,000,000	20

Berry will buy Fairchild with a 4-for-1 exchange of stock. Earnings will remain at the premerger level.

a. What will be the effect on EPS for the Berry stockholders?

b. What will be the effect on EPS for the premerger Fairchild stockholders?

22-4 The Reilly Group plans to merge with MBI. The following financial information is available for each firm. All dollar amounts are in millions.

	MBI	Reilly Group
Sales	$500	$150
Net income	$ 75	$ 15
Shares outstanding	25 million	10 million
P/E ratio	12	8

* **a.** Compute the premerger earnings per share and the stock price for each firm.

b. The Reilly Group stockholders will receive 0.5 shares of MBI for each share of Reilly they currently hold. Assuming no immediate changes in the premerger sales and margin, what will sales, net income, and earnings per share be after the merger?

* **c.** If expected gains from the merger cause MBI's postmerger P/E ratio to increase to 15, what is the new stock price?

22-5 Beti's Boutique wishes to acquire Jan's Jeans for $250,000. Beti expects the incremental earnings to be $45,000 for 10 years. She has also calculated her marginal cost of capital for this investment to be 12 percent. Conduct a capital budgeting analysis for Beti to determine whether or not she should purchase Jan's shop.

22-6 Southern Bakery is being acquired by the Royal Crumb Cookie Company. Their premerger balance sheets are as follows:

Southern Bakery

Current assets	$ 750	Debt	$ 875
Fixed assets	1,125	Common equity	1,000
Total assets	$1,875	Total liabilities and net worth	$1,875

Royal Crumb Cookie Company

Current assets	$1,500	Debt	$2,000
Fixed assets	1,625	Common equity	1,125
Total assets	$3,125	Total liabilities and net worth	$3,125

    a. Construct the postmerger balance sheet for Royal Crumb Cookie Company, assuming the acquisition is a pooling of interests.

    b. Assume the merger in Part a was a purchase rather than a pooling of interests. Royal Crumb bought Southern for $2,000. Now construct the postmerger balance sheet.

    c. Southern's and Royal Crumb's premerger income statements are shown below. Calculate postmerger net income and EPS for both purchase and pooling. Assume a 1-for-1 stock exchange was made and that goodwill will be written off over a 25-year expected life.

	Southern	Royal Crumb
Sales	$750	$1,300
Operating costs	488	830
Operating income	$262	$ 470
Interest	100	200
Taxable income	$162	$ 270
Taxes	81	135
Earnings after taxes	$ 81	$ 135
Goodwill write-off	0	0
Net income	$ 81	$ 135
Common shares	60	100
EPS	$1.35	$ 1.35

Selected References

Brenner, Menachem, and David H. Downes, "A Critical Evaluation of the Measurement of Conglomerate Performance Using the Capital Asset Pricing Model," *Review of Economics and Statistics*, May 1979, 292–296.

Elgers, Pieter T., and John J. Clark, "Merger Types and Shareholder Returns: Additional Evidence," *Financial Management*, Summer 1980, 66–72.

Firth, Michael, "The Profitability of Takeovers and Mergers," *Economic Journal*, June 1979, 316–328.

Gahlon, James M., and Roger D. Stover, "Diversification, Financial Leverage, and Conglomerate Systematic Risk," *Journal of Financial and Quantitative Analysis*, December 1979, 999–1013.

Hong, Hai, G. Mandelker, and R. S. Kaplan, "Pooling versus Purchase: The Effects of Accounting for Mergers on Stock Prices," *Accounting Review*, January 1978, 31–47.

Kummer, Donald R., and J. Ronald Hoffmeister, "Valuation Consequences of Cash Tender Offers," *Journal of Finance*, May 1978, 505–516.

Mueller, Dennis C., "The Effects of Conglomerate Mergers: A Survey of the Empirical Evidence," *Journal of Banking and Finance*, December 1977, 315–347.

Myers, Stewart C., "Introduction: A Framework for Evaluating Mergers," in *Modern Developments in Financial Management*, ed. Stewart C. Myers (New York: Praeger, 1976).

Salter, Malcolm S., and Wolf A. Weinhold, "Diversification via Acquisition: Creating Value," *Harvard Business Review*, July–August 1978, 166–176.

Shrieves, Ronald E., and Donald L. Stevens, "Bankruptcy Avoidance as a Motive for Merger," *Journal of Financial and Quantitative Analysis*, September 1979, 501–515.

Steiner, Peter O., *Mergers: Motives, Effects, Policies* (Ann Arbor, MI: University of Michigan Press, 1975).

Bankruptcy and Reorganization

Decision in Finance

Don Lennox's Tough Decisions

In 1979, When Don Lennox joined International Harvester as President Archie McCardell's special assistant, he felt his timing was perfect. Harvester was enjoying its best year ever: it earned $369 million on $8.4 billion in sales, and that fall its stock hit an all-time high of $45 a share. Under the circumstances it would have been hard for Lennox to foresee the woes that would shortly befall his new employer. But between 1980 and 1983 Harvester piled up $3 billion in losses while its stock tumbled as low as $3 a share.

Some say that IH's financial troubles began with a long and bitter 1980 strike that cost the company $500 million. But others trace the problems back farther and deeper. They contend that over the years Harvester management had become too complacent, reticent to make any decision that would rock the status quo. While its executives enjoyed high salaries and rode around in chauffeured limousines, Harvester tolerated inefficient production plants, bought off its unions with high wage scales, and offered a level of job security that could be sustained only by steadily rising profits and sales. In fact, despite its seemingly bright performance, Harvester failed to earn a high enough return on equity during most of its glory years. So the company was more vulnerable than even its insiders realized, and when trouble struck, many Wall Streeters predicted that IH was a goner.

In May 1982 the IH board of directors ousted Archie McCardell, who had since become chairman, and turned the company over to Louis W. Menk, an outside director and retired head of Burlington Northern Railroad Company. Menk, in turn, asked Lennox to become president. Stunned by the axing of McCardell, his friend and former boss, Lennox nonetheless accepted the challenge of turning the company around

663

from the brink of bankruptcy. "That same night," Lennox says, "I sat down and made a two-page list of things I thought needed to be done, regardless of who had a personal stake in them."

As you read this chapter, consider the courses of action available to Don Lennox. Which would you suggest that he include on his list? Why?

See end of chapter for resolution.

Thus far this text has dealt with issues faced by growing, successful enterprises. However, many firms encounter financial difficulties, and some actually fail. An understanding of business failures, their causes, and their possible remedies is important to financial managers of successful as well as potentially unsuccessful firms, for the managers of the successful firms must know their rights and how to enforce them. There are several instances in which the failure of another firm affects a successful one: (1) sales and profits are lost when a major customer fails; (2) the flow of incoming materials is interrupted when a supplier fails; and (3) an increased share of the market becomes available when a competitor fails. At the same time the financial manager of a failing firm must know how to ward off total collapse and thereby minimize losses. Such an ability often means the difference between loss of the firm versus rehabilitation and eventual success.

Failure

Failure can be defined in several ways, depending on the problems involved or the situation facing the firm. To distinguish among them, it is necessary to define the following terms:

economic failure
The condition in which a firm's revenues do not cover its total cost, including its cost of capital.

Economic failure Failure in an economic sense signifies that a firm's revenues do not cover its total costs, including its cost of capital.

business failure
The condition in which a business has terminated with a loss to creditors.

Business failure This term is used by Dun & Bradstreet, which is the major compiler of failure statistics, to include any business that has terminated with a resultant loss to creditors.[1]

insolvency
The inability to meet maturing debt obligations.

Technical insolvency A firm can be considered technically insolvent if it cannot meet its current obligations as they fall due. Technical insolvency denotes a lack of liquidity and may be only temporary.

This chapter was coauthored by Arthur L. Herrmann of the University of Hartford.

[1]Dun & Bradstreet, Inc., *The Business Failure Record* (New York: updated annually).

Insolvency in bankruptcy A firm is insolvent in bankruptcy when its total liabilities exceed the fair valuation of its assets. This is usually a more serious condition than technical insolvency, and it often leads to liquidation of the firm.

Bankruptcy This is a legal term. Although many people use the term *bankrupt* to refer to any firm that has "failed," a firm is not legally bankrupt unless it has failed according to criteria established by the Federal Bankruptcy Act and has been adjudged bankrupt by a federal court. Bankruptcy is a legal procedure, carried out under special courts of law, for liquidating or reorganizing a business. It can be either **voluntary,** in which case the debtor petitions the court, or **involuntary,** in which case the creditors petition the court and prove that the debtor is not paying debts as they mature.

insolvency in bankruptcy
A more serious condition than technical insolvency, when a firm's total liabilities exceed the value of its total assets.

bankruptcy
A legal procedure for formally liquidating a business, carried out under the courts of law.

voluntary bankruptcy
Bankruptcy in which the debtor petitions the court.

involuntary bankruptcy
Bankruptcy in which the creditors petition the court and prove that the debtor is not paying debts as they mature.

Causes of Failure

The causes of financial failure are numerous, and they vary from situation to situation. However, it is useful to isolate the major underlying causes in order to avoid them if possible, or to correct them in the event a reorganization is necessary. A recent Dun & Bradstreet compilation assigned percentage values to these causes as follows:[2]

Cause of Failure	Percentage of Total
Management incompetence	45.6%
Lack of managerial experience	12.5
Unbalanced experience in finance, sales, production, and so on	19.2
Lack of experience in product line	11.1
Neglect	0.7
Disaster	0.5
Fraud	0.3
Reason unknown	10.1
	100.0%

Management incompetence includes the effects of recessions and unfavorable industry trends. This placement is logical, since managements should plan ahead and be prepared for both booms and recessions. Financial difficulties are usually the result of a series of errors, misjudgments, and interrelated weaknesses that can be attributed directly or indirectly to management, and signs of potential financial distress are often evident before the firm actually fails. Research to isolate and identify the causes of business failure, and thus to predict or pre-

---

[2]Dun & Bradstreet, Inc., *The Business Failure Record* (New York: 1983), 12.

vent it, is extremely important. A number of financial remedies are available to management when it becomes aware of the imminence or occurrence of insolvency. These remedies are described later in this chapter.

The Failure Record

How widespread is business failure in the United States? In Table 23-1 we see that a fairly large number of businesses fail each year, although the failures in any one year are not a large percentage of the total business population. In 1981, for example, there were 16,794 business failures (as defined by Dun & Bradstreet), but this was only 0.61 percent of all business firms. It is interesting to note that while the failure rate per 10,000 businesses fluctuates with the economy, the average liability per failure has tended to increase over time. This is due both to increased price levels and to an increase in the number of multimillion-dollar bankruptcies in recent years (see Table 23-2). While the list of firms in Table 23-2 was compiled relatively recently, it is unfortunately

Table 23-1
Historical Failure Rate: Experience of U.S. Businesses

Years	Number of Failures	Average Failure Rate (per 10,000 Concerns)	Average Liability per Failure
1857–1968 (average per year)	11,233	87	$ 28,292
1900–1968 (average per year)	13,659	70	32,889
1946–1968 (average per year)	11,089	42	61,101
1959–1969 (average per year)	13,881	54	84,724
1970	10,748	44	175,638
1971	10,326	42	185,641
1972	9,566	38	209,099
1973	9,345	36	245,912
1974	9,915	38	307,937
1975	11,432	42	383,152
1976	9,628	35	312,762
1977	7,919	28	390,872
1978	6,619	24	355,946
1979	7,564	28	352,637
1980	11,742	42	394,744
1981	16,794	61	414,147
1982	25,346	89	NA
1983	31,334	110	NA

Sources: Edward I. Altman, *Corporate Bankruptcy in America* (Lexington, MA: Heath Lexington Books, 1972); Dun & Bradstreet, Inc., *The Business Failure Record* (1984), and *The Monthly Failure Report* (May 1976).

Table 23-2
The Ten Biggest Bankruptcies as of October 1982

	Liabilities	Date
Penn Central Transportation Co.	$3.3 billion	June 1970
Wickes	2.0 billion	April 1982
Itel	1.7 billion	January 1981
Braniff Airlines	1.1 billion	May 1982
Manville Corp.	1.1 billion	August 1982
W. T. Grant Co.	1.0 billion	October 1975
Seatrain Lines	785 million	February 1981
Continental Mortgage Investors	607 million	March 1976
United Merchants & Manufacturing	552 million	July 1977
AM International	510 million	April 1982

Source: Edward I. Altman, *Corporate Financial Distress* (New York: Wiley, 1983), 2.

incomplete. Among the larger, better-known additions to this list are Continental Airlines, The Charter Company, and Baldwin-United Corp. This list of bankrupt companies might have been even larger if companies such as Chrysler and International Harvester had been unable to reorganize outside the bankruptcy courts.

Although bankruptcy is more frequent among smaller firms, it is clear from Table 23-2 that large firms are not immune to bankruptcy. These data actually understate the financial problems among larger firms because, as Altman notes, mergers or governmental intervention are generally used as an alternative to outright bankruptcy except in cases of fraud or where the failing company is too large to be absorbed by another firm. The decision to give federal aid to Chrysler is one excellent illustration. Also, in recent years the Federal Home Loan Bank System has arranged the absorption of several very large "problem" savings and loan associations by sound institutions, and the federal banking authorities have done the same thing for banks. Several U.S. government agencies, principally the Defense Department, were able to bail out Lockheed when it otherwise would have failed, and the shotgun marriage of Douglas Aircraft and McDonnell was designed to prevent Douglas's failure. Merrill Lynch took over Goodbody & Company, which would otherwise have gone bankrupt and would have frozen the accounts of its 225,000 customers while the bankruptcy settlement was worked out. This would have panicked investors across the country, so the New York Stock Exchange member firms put up $30 million as an inducement to get Merrill Lynch to keep Goodbody from folding. Similar instances could be cited in other industries.

Why do government and industry seek to avoid bankruptcy among larger firms? There are many reasons. In the case of the financial institutions, the main one is to prevent an erosion of confidence. With Lockheed and Douglas, the Defense Department wanted not only to maintain viable suppliers but also to avoid disrupting local communities. Even when the public interest is not at stake, the fact that bankruptcy is a very expensive process gives private industry strong incentives to avoid out-and-out bankruptcy. The costs and complexities of bankruptcy are discussed in subsequent sections of this chapter, but first some less formal and less expensive remedies and legal actions are examined.

Industry Practice

The Big Bankruptcy Scare

Even without the urgency of scare headlines, the events were frightening enough. During 1982, a wave of bankruptcies rolled across the land. There was Lionel Corp. Then AM International, Saxon Industries, and Wickes Corp. Then Braniff and Penn Square Bank. Then Nucorp. And these were just the more prominent firms. There were thousands of lesser-known companies, with thousands more still to come.

The effect of all this on the companies, employees, and stockholders involved was devastating enough. But for the country as a whole, there was a greater fear. The questions these bankruptcies bring to mind are terrifying.

Will another major airline fail and put its employees on the street, cutting down their buying power and felling in the process the myriad local restaurants, dry cleaners, and other small businesses that the employees patronized, plus the S&Ls that hold their mortgages?

Will another Penn Square Bank surprise the financial community, jar credit unions, and precipitate a liquidity crisis at major banks?

Will negotiations with Poland to restructure its billion-dollar borrowings fall apart and U.S. banks sustain ruinous loan losses?

The economy appears fragile at many key points. And often it is not the Chrysler that everybody expects to go belly up that does, but some unexpected company from left field, a Penn Central or W. T. Grant. Between the known and the unknown potential bankruptcies, everybody is understandably nervous.

Business bankruptcies also heighten the potential for bank failures, and one bank failure could set off a chain reaction to other banks. A Penn Square exposes weaknesses in Continental Illinois' lending procedures; a Drysdale Securities publicizes the sloppiness in Chase Manhattan Bank's credit checking. Suddenly, the spread between the Treasury bill rate and the bank CD rate widens as investors perceive a growing risk in owning bank paper. Since the banks run on constant transfusions of short-term money, they are imperiled if their ability to sell CDs is reduced or lost.

At the same time, depositors worry whether their money is safe.

What are the facts behind these fears?

No doubt, business failure statistics in 1982 "were alarming," notes Vice President Rowena Wyant of Dun & Bradstreet's Business Economics Division. D&B defines a failure as a business closing its doors and causing a loss to its creditors. D&B collects information on 2.8 million firms, excluding farms and financial, real estate, and professional businesses. In one week in June 1982, 532 of these companies failed, the highest weekly total in 50 years. And the number of failures in the first half of 1982 was 11,948, higher than any comparable period since 1933 and up 45 percent from 1981's first half.

Small businesses dominate the reckoning, but the headline-making losses are from big businesses. Among petitioners at the bankruptcy bar this year, Wickes Corp. left its short-term creditors holding the bag for the largest amount—$2 billion; then Braniff Airlines, $1.1 billion; AM International, $510 million; Saxon Industries, $461 million; and Lionel Corp., $165 million.

Big numbers and spiraling percentage increases are disturbing, but they are not so awful when measured against a $3 trillion economy. Even 1982's failure record was estimated at barely more than half the Great Depression peak.

Furthermore, the popular perception of a major bankruptcy tripping off additional bankruptcies and eventually sending the GNP skidding is the opposite of what business cycle studies show, according to Professor Victor Zarnowitz of the University of Chicago's Graduate School of Business. Bad economic times make business failures rise, he says, "not the other way around." Even when fail-ures increase and more large companies fail, the business cycle expert adds, "they are not a strong determining factor in business cycles; they are the consequences and the results more than the determinant."

Since the Great Depression, the potential for snowballing bankruptcies of all kinds has been substantially diminished. Organizations such as the FDIC, the Fed, and the farm agencies have provided a safety net in times of stress, and their performance has generated confidence in the system.

Moreover, the attitude in Washington today toward business failure is very different than in the 1930s. If business bankruptcies appear to threaten vital interests, Congress is likely to make the government a lender of last resort, as it did with Lockheed, Chrysler, and New York City.

The fact—or at least the strong belief among experts—that bankruptcies do not cause depressions is certainly reassuring. But important questions still remain. Are bankruptcies ultimately beneficial to the economy? Or do they do more harm than good? To no one's surprise, economists disagree.

"I certainly don't regard bankruptcy *per se* as a good thing," Nobel laureate Milton Friedman told *Dun's Business Month*. "Still, the effect on the economy is not often what people fear. A Chrysler bankruptcy would have increased the efficiency of American automakers because assets would have fallen into better hands. If Chrysler could have stayed alive without government bailouts, fine. It is better to permit companies to go bankrupt than to prevent them by government subsidy."

That about sums up the argument of those who have been tabbed the "economic Darwinists."

In each business cycle, free-market economists argue, failure guarantees the continuing revitalizing of capitalism because only the fit survive. Long-term secular development—the progress of technology, for example—also requires that some businesses fail, a process economist Joseph Schumpeter labeled "creative destruction. . . . It is what capitalism consists in and what every capitalist concern has got to live in."

Disputing such sanguine views are the economists who believe that the economic and social costs of bankruptcy far outweigh its efficiency benefits—and therefore that the government should take a hand in ameliorating the situation. For example, economics professor Robert Lekachman of New York's Herbert Lehman College admits that he came down reluctantly on the side of bailing out Chrysler after he weighed the social and financial cost of keeping Chrysler alive against the additional burdens of welfare, unemployment insurance and food stamps that would have resulted from throwing the company into bankruptcy. Wharton Econometric Forecasting's F. Gerard Adams, who also approved the Chrysler move, comments: "Here was a case where a lot of people said, 'Let them go broke We will be better off.' But by providing Chrysler with the means of staying in business, we ended with what seems a more efficient and viable company—and that is the counter-argument to the economic Darwinist."

Although these economists may not agree about whether a particular company should be bailed out, they agree that the losses resulting from business bankruptcies go beyond the companies involved to the economy as a whole. The whole industry loses, according to Washington University's Hyman Minsky. In the case of airlines, Braniff's bankruptcy decreased the value of all airline assets. "The value of the airplanes they owned went down, and therefore their ability to borrow to buy new planes declined," he says. The impact was felt by the aviation manufacturers as well. "The ability of Boeing to sell 767s diminished," he says. Finally, Minsky speculates that Braniff's bankruptcy was a factor in McDonnell Douglas's decision not to invest in a new airplane.

Allen Sinai of Data Resources, Inc. agrees that the major effect of bankruptcies is to lower asset values, increase borrowing costs, discourage the banks from lending because their costs of money rise and, finally, to depress capital spending.

These widely diverging and firmly held opinions about bankruptcies may be confusing, but there's an encouraging conclusion to be drawn from it all. The disagreement stems largely from the fact that so few bankruptcy waves have occurred in recent history. Economists do not have enough episodes with which to construct mathematically based models measuring the impact of these events. Lacking a statistical record, each side in the debate attacks the other with theory and anecdotal evidence. Neither can prove the other wrong.

But that is not a bad situation. If anything, the absence of statistical proof is strong evidence that the safeguards erected over the years against a severe downward spiral—with bankruptcies feeding on a contraction which in turn feeds on bankruptcies—are working.

Source: Adapted from "Bankruptcy Scare" by Arlene Hershman with Marilyn Wilson and G. Bruce Knecht. Reprinted with the permission of *Dun's Business Month* (formerly *Dun's Review*), September 1982. Copyright 1982, Dun & Bradstreet Publications Corporation.

Extension and Composition

In the case of a fundamentally sound company whose financial difficulties appear to be temporary, the creditors generally prefer to work directly with the company and help it recover and reestablish itself on a sound financial basis. Such voluntary plans usually involve *extension*, which postpones the date of required payment of past-due obligations, and *composition*, by which the creditors voluntarily *reduce* their claims on the debtor. Both procedures are designed to keep the debtor in business and to avoid court costs. Although creditors do not obtain immediate payment and may still suffer losses, they often recover more money, and sooner, than if one of the formal procedures had been followed. Also, chances are good that a customer will be preserved.

The start of an extension or a composition is a meeting between the failing firm and its creditors. The creditors appoint a committee consisting of four or five of the largest creditors, plus one or two of the smaller ones. This meeting is typically arranged and conducted by an adjustment bureau associated with the local credit managers' association.[3] Once the decision has been reached that the case can be worked out, the bureau assigns investigators to make an exhaustive report. Then the bureau and the creditors' committee use the facts of the report to formulate a plan for adjustment of claims. Another meeting between the debtor and the creditors is then held in an attempt to work out an extension or a composition, or a combination of the two. Several meetings may be required to reach final agreements.

At least three conditions are usually necessary to make an extension or a composition feasible: (1) the debtor must be a good moral risk, (2) the debtor must show an ability to make a recovery, and (3) general business conditions must be favorable to recovery.

Creditors prefer **extension** because it provides for payment in full. The debtor buys current purchases on a cash basis and pays off the past balance over an extended time. In some cases creditors may agree not only to extend the time of payment but also to subordinate existing claims to vendors extending new credit during the period of the extension. The creditors must have faith that the debtor will solve its problems.

In a **composition** a reduced cash settlement is made. Creditors receive in cash from the debtor a uniform percentage of the amounts owed them. The cash received, which may be as low as ten cents on

extension
An informal method of reorganization in which the creditors voluntarily postpone the date of required payment on past-due obligations.

composition
An informal method of reorganization in which creditors voluntarily reduce their claims on the debtor firm.

---

[3]There is a nationwide group called the National Association of Credit Management, which consists of bankers and industrial companies' credit managers. This group sponsors research on credit policy and problems, conducts seminars on credit management, and operates local chapters in cities throughout the nation. These local chapters frequently operate adjustment bureaus.

the dollar, is taken as full settlement of the debt. Bargaining will take place between the debtor and the creditors over the savings that result from avoiding costs associated with the bankruptcy: costs of administration, legal fees, investigators, and so on. In addition to escaping such costs, the debtor gains in that the stigma of bankruptcy may be avoided; as a result the debtor may be induced to part with most of the savings that result from avoiding a formal bankruptcy.

Often the bargaining process will result in a compromise involving both an extension and a composition. For example, the settlement may provide for a cash payment of 25 percent of the debt immediately, plus 6 future installments of 10 percent each, for a total payment of 85 percent. Installment payments are usually evidenced by notes, and creditors will also seek protective controls.

These voluntary settlements are informal and simple. They are also relatively inexpensive because investigative, legal, and administrative expenses are held to a minimum. Thus voluntary procedures result in the largest return to creditors. In addition, the almost-bankrupt business may be saved to continue as a future customer. One possible disadvantage is that the debtor is left to manage the business. This situation may result in an erosion of assets, but there are numerous controls available to protect the creditors. It should also be noted that small creditors may play a nuisance role by insisting on payment in full. As a consequence, settlements typically provide for payment in full for claims under $500 or $1,000. If a composition is involved and all claims under $500 are paid, all creditors will receive a base of $500 plus the agreed-upon percentage for the balance of their claims.

Reorganization

reorganization
The financial restructuring of a firm to reflect its assets' current market value; under reorganization the firm continues to exist.

If the situation is such that informal procedures are not feasible, then it may become necessary to use more formal procedures. The first of these is a **reorganization,** which is a court-approved attempt to keep a company alive by changing its capital structure. It is like composition or extension, but the legal formalities are much more involved. Regardless of the legal procedure followed, reorganization processes have certain features in common.

1. The firm is insolvent either because it is unable to meet cash obligations as they come due (technical insolvency) or because claims on the firm exceed its assets (insolvency in bankruptcy). Hence some modifications in the nature or amount of the firm's obligations must be made—fixed charges must be reduced. The procedure may include scaling down interest charges, converting short-term debt into long-term debt, converting debt into common stock, or simply writing off some claims against the company.

2. New funds must be raised for working capital and for property rehabilitation, because firms in financial trouble almost always let their properties run down, and they generally deplete their liquid assets.

3. The operating and managerial causes of the difficulty must be discovered and eliminated.

The procedures involved in a reorganization are highly legalistic and are, in fact, thoroughly understood only by attorneys who specialize in bankruptcy and reorganization. However, there are certain general principles of which all financial managers should be aware. As noted above, a reorganization requires a scaling down of claims, and in any reorganization two conditions must be met: (1) the scaling down must be fair to all parties, and (2) there must be a reasonably high probability of successful rehabilitation and profitable future operations. These are the standards of *fairness* and *feasibility*, which are analyzed further later in the chapter.

Federal Bankruptcy Laws

Bankruptcy proceedings begin when a debtor is unable to meet scheduled payments to creditors, and these central issues arise:

1. Is the inability to meet scheduled debt payments a temporary problem of technical insolvency or is it a permanent problem caused by asset values falling below debt obligations?

2. If basic long-run asset values have truly declined, then economic losses have occurred. In this event who shall bear the losses? Two theories exist: (1) the **absolute priority doctrine,** which states that claims must be paid in strict accordance with the priority of each claim, regardless of the consequence to other claimants, and (2) the **relative priority doctrine,** which is more flexible and which gives a more balanced consideration to all claimants.

3. Is the company "worth more dead than alive," that is, would the business be more valuable if it were maintained and continued in operation or if it were liquidated and sold off in pieces? Under the absolute priority doctrine, liquidations are more likely because this generally permits senior creditors to be paid off sooner, but often at the expense of junior creditors and stockholders. Under the relative priority doctrine, senior creditors are more likely to be required to wait for payment in order to increase the chances of providing some value to junior creditors and stockholders.

4. Who should control the firm while it is being liquidated or rehabilitated? The existing management may be left in control, or a *trustee* may be placed in charge of operations.

These are the issues that are addressed in the federal bankruptcy statutes.

Our bankruptcy laws were first enacted in 1898, were modified substantially in 1938, and then were changed radically in the **Bankruptcy Reform Act of 1978.** The 1978 act was designed primarily to streamline and speed up proceedings, and it also represented a shift from the absolute priority doctrine toward the relative priority doctrine. (These doctrines should be thought of as a continuum, not as absolute

absolute priority doctrine
The doctrine that states that claims must be paid in strict accordance with the priority of each claim, regardless of the consequence to other claimants.

relative priority doctrine
A flexible approach to the priority of creditors' claims, giving balanced consideration to all claimants.

Bankruptcy Reform Act of 1978
Legislation enacted to speed up and streamline bankruptcy proceedings.

points. The new law represents a movement along the continuum, not a jump from one polar position to the other.) During the 1970s, as bankruptcies became larger and more complex, it was simply taking too long to conclude bankruptcy proceedings, so Congress acted to speed things up.

The new bankruptcy law consists of eight odd-numbered chapters. (The even numbers were eliminated by Congress in the rewrite.) Chapters 1, 3, and 5 contain general provisions applicable to the other chapters. Chapter 7 governs liquidations; Chapter 9 provides for financially distressed municipalities; **Chapter 11** is the business reorganization chapter; Chapter 13 covers the adjustment of debts for "individuals with regular income"; and Chapter 15 sets up a system of trustees who help administer the new act. All bankruptcy cases filed after October 1, 1979 are governed by this new code.

Chapter 11
The chapter of the Bankruptcy Reform Act of 1978 that outlines the procedure for business reorganization.

Prior to passage of the new bankruptcy act, reorganizations in bankruptcy were of two types: either Chapter XI proceedings, which were voluntary reorganizations originated by the existing management, or Chapter X proceedings, which were involuntary, were originated by creditors, and called for a court-appointed trustee to restructure completely the finances of the firm or else to liquidate it. Long, drawn-out court fights occurred over whether the proceedings should be under Chapter X or Chapter XI.

The new bankruptcy code combines the old Chapters X and XI into a single procedure (the new Chapter 11) which is more flexible and which provides more scope for informal negotiations between a company and its creditors and stockholders. Under the new act a case is started by the filing of a petition with the bankruptcy court. The petition may be either voluntary or involuntary; that is, it may be filed either by the firm's management or by its creditors. A committee of unsecured creditors is then appointed by the court to negotiate with management for a reorganization, which may include the restructuring of debt and other claims against the firm. A trustee may be appointed by the court if it is in the best interests of the creditors and stockholders; otherwise the existing management may stay in office. Under the new Chapter 11, if no fair and feasible reorganization can be worked out, the firm will be liquidated under the procedures spelled out in Chapter 7 of the act.

Financial Decisions in Reorganization

liquidation
Dissolution of a firm through the sale of its assets.

When a business becomes insolvent, a decision must be made whether to dissolve the firm through **liquidation** or to keep it alive through *reorganization*. Fundamentally, this decision depends on a determination of the value of the firm if it were rehabilitated versus the value of the assets if they were sold off individually. The procedure that promises higher returns to the creditors and owners will be adopted. Often the greater indicated value of the firm in reorganization, compared with its value in liquidation, is used to force a compromise agreement among the claimants in a reorganization, even when each group feels that its relative position has not been treated fairly in the reorganization plan. Both the SEC and the courts are called upon to determine the *fairness* and the *feasibility* of proposed plans of reorganization.

Standard of Fairness

The basic doctrine of fairness states that claims must be recognized in the order of their legal and contractual priority. Carrying out this concept of fairness in a reorganization involves the following steps:
1. Future sales must be estimated.
2. Operating conditions must be analyzed so that the future earnings on sales can be predicted.
3. The capitalization rate to be applied to these future earnings must be determined.
4. This capitalization rate must be applied to the estimated future earnings to obtain an indicated value for the company.
5. Provision for distribution to the claimants must then be made.

The meaning and content of these procedures may best be set out by the use of an example of reorganization involving the Edison Paper Corporation. Table 23-3 gives Edison's balance sheet as of March 31,

standard of fairness
In bankruptcy or reorganization, claims must be recognized in the order of their legal and contractual priority.

Table 23-3
Edison Paper Corporation: Balance Sheet,
March 31, 1984 (Millions of Dollars)

Assets	
Current assets	$ 3.50
Net property	12.50
Miscellaneous	0.70
Total assets	$16.70
Liabilities and Capital	
Accounts payable	$ 1.00
Taxes	0.25
Notes payable	0.25
Other current liabilities	1.75
7½% first-mortgage bonds, due 1995	6.00
9% subordinated debentures, due 1990[a]	7.00
Common stock ($1 par)	1.00
Paid-in capital	3.45
Retained earnings	(4.00)
Total liabilities and capital	$16.70

[a]These debentures are subordinated to the notes payable.

1984. The company had been suffering losses running to $2.5 million a year, and, as will be made clear below, the asset values in the March 31, 1984 balance sheet are overstated. Since the firm was insolvent, it filed a petition for reorganization, under Chapter 11 of the Bankruptcy Act, with a federal court. The court, in accordance with the law, appointed a disinterested trustee. On June 13, 1984 the trustee filed with the court a plan of reorganization, which was subsequently analyzed by the SEC.

The trustee found that the company could not be internally reorganized and concluded that the only feasible program would be to combine Edison Paper with an established producer of paper containers and wrappers. Accordingly, the trustee solicited the interest of a number of paper companies. Late in July 1984 National Paper Company showed an interest in Edison Paper. On August 3, 1984 National Paper made a formal proposal to take over Edison Paper's $6 million of 7½ percent first-mortgage bonds, to pay the $250,000 taxes owned by Edison Paper, and to pay 40,000 shares of National Paper common stock to the company. Since the stock had a market price of $75 a share, the value of the stock was equivalent to $3 million. Thus National Paper was offering $3 million, plus the $6 million loan takeover and the $250,000 taxes—a total of $9.25 million on assets that had a net book value of $16.7 million.

Trustee's Plan. The trustee's plan, based on 40,000 shares at $75 equaling $3 million, is shown in Table 23-4. As in all Chapter 11 plans, the

Table 23-4
Edison Paper Corporation: Trustee's Plan

Prior Claims	Amount	Receives
Taxes	$ 250,000	Cash paid by National Paper
Mortgage bonds, 7½%, 1995	6,000,000	Bonds assumed by National Paper

Trustee's plan for remainder of claims:
Valuation based on 40,000 shares at $75 equals $3 million, or 30 percent of $10 million liabilities.

Other Claims	Original Amount	30% × Amount of Claim	Claim after Subordination	Number of Shares of Common Stock
Notes payable	$ 250,000	$ 75,000	$ 250,000	3,333
General unsecured creditors	2,750,000	825,000	825,000	11,000
Subordinated debentures	7,000,000	2,100,000	1,925,000	25,667
	$10,000,000	$3,000,000	$3,000,000	40,000

secured creditors' claims are paid in full (in this case the mortgage bonds are taken over by National Paper). However, the total claims of the unsecured creditors equal $10 million, with only $3 million available. Thus each claimant would be entitled to receive 30 percent before the adjustment for subordination. Before this adjustment holders of notes payable would receive 30 percent of their $250,000 claim, or $75,000. However, the debentures are subordinated to the notes payable, so an additional $175,000 must be transferred to notes payable from the subordinated debentures. In the last column of the lower portion of Table 23-4 the dollar claims of each class of debt are restated in terms of the number of shares of National Paper common stock received by each class of unsecured creditors.

The Securities and Exchange Commission evaluated the proposal from the standpoint of fairness. The SEC began by estimating the value of Edison Paper (Table 23-5). After a survey and discussion with various experts, it arrived at estimated sales of $25 million a year. It further estimated that the profit margin on sales would equal 6 percent, thus giving indicated future earnings of $1.5 million a year.

The SEC analyzed P/E ratios for comparable paper companies and arrived at 8 times future earnings for a capitalization factor. Multiplying 8 by $1.5 million gave an indicated total value of the company of

---

Table 23-5
Edison Paper Corporation: SEC Evaluation

Estimated sales of Edison Paper Corporation	$25,000,000 per year
Earnings at 6 percent of sales	1,500,000
Value with P/E ratio of 8 times earnings	12,000,000
Mortgage bonds assumed	6,000,000
Net value	$16,000,000

Claims	Amount	Claim	Claim after Subordination
Taxes	$ 250,000	$ 250,000	$ 250,000
Notes payable	250,000	143,750	250,000[a]
General unsecured creditors	2,750,000	1,581,250	1,581,250
Subordinated debentures (subordinate to notes payable)	7,000,000	4,025,000	3,918,750[a]
Totals	$10,250,000	$6,000,000	$6,000,000
Total available	$ 6,000,000		
Percentage claims[b]	57.5%		

[a]Notes payable must be satisfied before subordinated debentures receive anything.
[b]($6,000,000 − $250,000)/($10,250,000 − $250,000).

$12 million. Since the mortgage bonds assumed by National Paper totaled $6 million, a net value of $6 million was left for the other claims. This value is double that of the 40,000 shares of National Paper stock offered for the remainder of the company. Because the SEC felt that the value of these claims was $6 million rather than $3 million, it concluded that the trustee's plan for reorganization did not meet the test of fairness. Note that under both the trustee's plan and the SEC plan the holders of common stock were to receive nothing, which is one of the risks of ownership, while the holders of the first-mortgage bonds were to be paid in full.

National Paper was told of the SEC's conclusions and asked to increase the number of shares it offered. National Paper refused, and no other paper company offered to acquire Edison Paper. Because no better alternative offer could be obtained, and the only alternative to the trustee's plan was liquidation, National Paper's proposal was accepted despite the SEC's disagreement with the valuation.

Standard of Feasibility

standard of feasibility
A test made by the SEC during a reorganization to determine whether fixed charges would be covered by earnings, and hence whether the reorganized company will be viable.

The primary test of feasibility in a reorganization is whether the fixed charges after reorganization will be adequately covered by earnings. Adequate coverage generally requires an improvement in earnings or a reduction of fixed charges, or both. Among the actions that must generally be taken are the following:
1. Debt maturities usually must be lengthened, and some debt converted into equity.
2. When the quality of management has been substandard and inadequate for the task, a new team must be given control of the company.
3. If inventories have become obsolete or depleted, they must be replaced.
4. Sometimes the plant and the equipment must be modernized before the firm can operate and compete successfully on a cost basis.
5. Reorganization may also require an improvement in production, marketing, advertising, and other functions.
6. It is sometimes necessary to develop new products or markets to enable the firm to move from areas where economic trends are poor into areas with more potential for growth or at least stability.

To illustrate how the feasibility tests are applied, let us refer again to the Edison Paper Corporation example. The SEC observed that in the reorganization National Paper Company would take over the properties of the Edison Paper Corporation. It judged that the direction and aid of National Paper would remedy the production deficiencies that had troubled Edison Paper. Whereas the debt/assets ratio of Edison Paper had become unbalanced, National Paper went into the purchase with only a moderate amount of debt. After consolidation National Paper's total debt would be approximately $17.5 million versus total assets of more than $63 million, or a very reasonable debt ratio of about 28 percent.

National Paper's net income before interest and taxes had been running at a level of approximately $15 million. The interest on its long-term debt would be $1.5 million and, taking short-term borrowings into account, would total a maximum of $2 million a year. The $15 million profit before interest and taxes would therefore provide a 7.5 times coverage of fixed charges; this exceeds the norm of 5 times for the industry.

Notice that the question of feasibility would have been irrelevant (from the standpoint of the SEC) if National Paper had offered $3 million in cash rather than in stock, and had it offered to pay off the bonds rather than take them over. It is the SEC's function to protect the interests of Edison Paper's creditors. Since they are being forced to take common stock in another firm, the SEC must look into the feasibility of the transaction. If National Paper had made a cash offer, however, the feasibility of its own operation after the transaction was completed would have been none of the SEC's concern.

Liquidation Procedures

Liquidation can occur in two ways: (1) through an *assignment*, which is a liquidation procedure that does not go through the courts, or (2) through a formal *bankruptcy* carried out under the jurisdiction of a special court. Liquidation should occur when the business is worth more dead than alive, or when the possibilities of restoring profitability are so remote that the creditors run a high risk of loss if operations are continued.

Assignment

Assignment is an informal procedure for liquidating debts, and it usually yields creditors a larger amount than they would receive in a formal bankruptcy. An assignment calls for title to the debtor's assets to be transferred to a third person, known as an *assignee* or *trustee*. The assignee is instructed to liquidate the assets through a private sale or a public auction, and then to distribute the proceeds among the creditors on a pro rata basis. The assignment does not automatically discharge the debtor's obligations. However, the debtor may write on the check to each creditor the requisite legal language to make endorsement of the check acknowledgment of full settlement of the claim.

Assignment has some advantages over bankruptcy through the courts, which involves more time, legal formality, and expense. The assignee has more flexibility in disposing of property than does a bankruptcy trustee. Action can be taken sooner, before the inventory be-

assignment
An informal procedure whereby a third party liquidates the firm's assets and distributes the proceeds to the creditors.

comes obsolete or the machinery rusts, and, since the assignee is often familiar with the channels of trade in the debtor's business, better results may be achieved. However, an assignment does not automatically result in a full and legal discharge of all the debtor's liabilities, nor does it protect the creditors against fraud. Both of these problems can be overcome by formal bankruptcy proceedings, which are discussed in the following section.

Liquidation in Bankruptcy

The Federal Bankruptcy Act serves three important functions during a liquidation: (1) it provides safeguards against fraud by the debtor; (2) it provides for an equitable distribution of the debtor's assets among the creditors; and (3) it allows insolvent debtors to discharge all their obligations and to start new businesses unhampered by a burden of prior debt. However, liquidation is time-consuming, it can be costly, and it results in the loss of the business.

Priority of Claims on Distribution of Proceeds in a Bankruptcy

The order of priority of claims in bankruptcy under Chapter 7 of the 1978 act is as follows:

1. *Secured creditors, from the proceeds of the sale of specific property pledged for a lien or a mortgage.* If the proceeds from the sale of property do not fully satisfy the secured creditors' claims, the remaining balance is treated as a general creditor claim. See No. 8 below.

2. *Trustee's costs to administer and operate the bankrupt estate.*

3. *Expenses incurred after an involuntary case has begun but before a trustee is appointed.*

4. *Wages due workers if earned within three months prior to the filing of the petition in bankruptcy.* The amount of wages is not to exceed $2,000 per person.

5. *Claims for unpaid contributions to employee benefit plans.* These claims, plus wages in No. 4, are not to exceed the $2,000 per wage earner limit.

6. *Unsecured claims for customer deposits, not to exceed a maximum of $900 per individual.*

7. *Taxes due the United States, state, county, and any other government agency.*

8. *General or unsecured creditors.* Trade credit, unsecured loans, the unsatisfied portion of secured loans, and debenture bonds are classed as general creditors. Holders of subordinated debt also fall into this category, but they must turn over required amounts to the holders of senior debt.

9. *Preferred stock.*

10. *Common stock.*

To illustrate how this priority of claims works out, consider the balance sheet of Wallace, Inc., shown in Table 23-6. Assets total $90 million. The claims are indicated on the right-hand side of the balance sheet. Note that the debentures are subordinated to the notes payable to banks.

Now assume that the assets are sold. The assets as reported in the balance sheet in Table 23-6 are greatly overstated—they are, in fact, worth less than half of the $90 million at which they are carried. The following amounts are realized on liquidation:

Current assets	$28,000,000
Net property	5,000,000
Total receipts	$33,000,000

The order of priority for payment of claims is shown in Table 23-7. The first mortgage is paid from the net proceeds of $5 million from the sale of fixed property, leaving $28 million available to other creditors. Next come the fees and expenses of administration, which are typically about 20 percent of gross proceeds; in this example they are assumed to be $6 million. Next in priority are wages due workers, which total $700,000. The total amount of taxes to be paid is $1.3 million. Thus far, the total of claims paid from the $33 million is $13 million, leaving $20 million for the general creditors.

Table 23-6
Wallace, Inc.: Balance Sheet

Current assets	$80,000,000	Accounts payable	$20,000,000
Net property	10,000,000	Notes payable (due bank)	10,000,000
		Accrued wages, 1,400 at	
		$500	700,000
		U.S. taxes	1,000,000
		State and local taxes	300,000
		Current debt	$32,000,000
		First mortgage	6,000,000
		Second mortgage	1,000,000
		Subordinated debentures[a]	8,000,000
		Long-term debt	$15,000,000
		Preferred stock	2,000,000
		Common stock	26,000,000
		Paid-in capital	4,000,000
		Retained earnings	11,000,000
		Total equity	$43,000,000
Total assets	$90,000,000	Total claims	$90,000,000

[a]Subordinated to $10 million notes payable to the First National Bank.

Table 23-7
Wallace, Inc.: Order of Priority of Claims

Distribution of Proceeds on Liquidation
1. Proceeds of sale of assets $33,000,000
2. First mortgage, paid from sale of net property   5,000,000
3. Fees and expenses of administration of
   bankruptcy   6,000,000
4. Wages due workers earned 3 months prior to
   filing of bankruptcy petition   700,000
5. Taxes   1,300,000
6. Available to general creditors $20,000,000

Claims of General Creditors	Claim (1)	Application of 50 Percent (2)	After Subordination Adjustment (3)	Percentage of Original Claims Received (4)
Unsatisfied portion of first mortgage	$ 1,000,000	$ 500,000	$ 500,000	92
Unsatisfied portion of second mortgage	1,000,000	500,000	500,000	50
Notes payable	10,000,000	5,000,000	9,000,000	90
Accounts payable	20,000,000	10,000,000	10,000,000	50
Subordinated debentures	8,000,000	4,000,000	0	0
	$40,000,000	$20,000,000	$20,000,000	56

Notes:
1. Column 1 is the claim of each class of creditor. Total claims equal $40 million.
2. From Line 6 in the upper section of the table we see that $20 million is available. This sum, divided by the $40 million of claims, indicates that general creditors will receive 50 percent of their claims. This is shown in Column 2.
3. The debentures are subordinated to the notes payable. Four million dollars is transferred from debentures to notes payable in Column 3.
4. Column 4 shows the results of dividing the Column 3 figure by the original amount given in Table 23-6, except for the first mortgage, where $5 million paid on sale of property is included. The 56 percent total figure includes the first-mortgage transactions; that is, ($20,000,000 + $5,000,000) ÷ ($40,000,000 + $5,000,000) = 56%.

The claims of the general creditors total $40 million. Since $20 million is available, claimants would each receive 50 percent of their claims before the subordination adjustment. This adjustment requires that the subordinated debentures turn over to the notes payable all amounts received until the notes are satisfied. In this situation the claim of the notes payable is $10 million, but only $5 million is available; the deficiency is therefore $5 million. After transfer by the subordinated debentures of $4 million, there remains a deficiency of $1 million, which will be unsatisfied.

Note that 90 percent of the bank claim is satisfied, whereas only 50 percent of other unsecured claims will be satisfied. These figures illustrate the usefulness of the subordination provision to the security to which the subordination is made. Since no other funds remain, the claims of the holders of preferred and common stocks are completely wiped out.

Studies of the proceeds in bankruptcy liquidations reveal that unsecured creditors receive, on the average, about 15 cents on the dollar, while common stockholders generally receive nothing.

Summary

The major cause of business failure is incompetent management. Bad managers should, of course, be removed as promptly as possible, but if failure has occurred, a number of remedies are open to the interested parties.

The first question to be answered is whether the firm is better off "dead or alive"—whether it should be liquidated and sold off piecemeal or be rehabilitated. Assuming the decision is made that the firm should survive, it must be put through what is called a *reorganization*. Legal procedures are always costly, especially in the case of a business failure. Therefore, if it is at all possible, both the debtor and the creditors are better off if matters can be handled on an informal basis rather than through the courts. The informal procedures used in reorganization are (1) *extension*, which postpones the date of settlement, and (2) *composition*, which reduces the amount owed.

If voluntary settlement through extension or composition is not possible, the matter is thrown into the courts. If the court decides on reorganization rather than liquidation, it will appoint a trustee (1) to control the firm going through reorganization and (2) to prepare a formal plan for reorganization. The plan, which for large firms must be reviewed by the SEC, must meet the standard of *fairness* to all parties and be *feasible* in the sense that the reorganized enterprise will stand a good chance of surviving instead of being thrown back into the bankruptcy courts.

The application of standards of fairness and feasibility developed in this chapter can help determine the probable success of a particular plan for reorganization. The concept of fairness involves the estimation of sales and earnings and the application of a capitalization rate to earnings to determine the appropriate distribution to each claimant.

The feasibility test examines the ability of the new enterprise to carry the fixed charges resulting from the reorganization plan. The quality of management and the company's assets must be assured. Production and marketing may also require improvement.

Finally, where liquidation is regarded as the only solution to the debtor's insolvency, the creditors should adopt procedures that will net them the largest recovery. *Assignment* of the debtor's property is the cheaper and the faster procedure. Furthermore, there is more flexibility in disposing of the debtor's property and thus providing larger returns. *Bankruptcy* provides formal procedures for liquidation to safeguard the debtor's property from fraud. It also provides equitable distribution to the creditors. Nonetheless, it is a long and cumbersome process, and unless the trustee is closely supervised by the creditors, the debtor's property may be poorly managed during bankruptcy proceedings. The debtor does, however, obtain a full legal release from liability.

Resolution to Decision in Finance

Don Lennox's Tough Decisions

Don Lennox's list of things that needed to be done to save International Harvester contained ten items. The first was to sell IH's construction equipment business. The second was to get rid of six Cadillacs and drivers. Others involved some of Archie McCardell's pet projects. Lennox knew he would have to step on some toes, but he saw harsh actions as the only way to save as many jobs as possible in the long run.

Menk and Lennox began their reform in the executive suite, cutting out layers of staff as well as the limos and other luxuries that management had long enjoyed. This set the stage for a massive campaign to cut operating expenses, spearheaded by the sale of the construction equipment unit to Dresser Industries. Lennox also sold off over a dozen other businesses, including axles and transmissions, airliner tow trucks, off-highway haulers, turbines, and the Scout four-wheel drive jeep. And he got the company out of life insurance and numerous joint ventures, such as mining.

Within 18 months of McCardell's departure, Lennox had cut Harvester's overhead by $1 billion by selling off unprofitable businesses, consolidating operations, closing down plants, and slashing the payroll by two thirds, to 32,000 people. By the end of 1983, Lennox had radically downsized IH from the $8.4 billion company it had been in 1979 to a $4 billion company. He then turned his attention to rebuilding the company's two main markets: medium- and heavy-duty trucks and farm equipment.

Despite the unpleasantness of the task, Lennox was willing to make the brutal cutbacks necessary to insure Harvester's survival. But just as crucial was the support of lenders, equipment dealers, suppliers, and stockholders, who endured IH's massive restructuring and reinvestment program. "The key thing," said a source close to Harvester, "is that no one wants Harvester to go under, and therefore it's not going to go under until we run out of money through bad luck or a miscalculation of some kind."

Proof of this statement can be found in the fact that Harvester's 200 lenders approved its 1983 refinancing package two months ahead of the required deadline. Under the plan $505 million of the company's $3.5 billion term debt would be turned into convertible preferred stock and $100 million in new equity would be issued. As a result, Harvester's debt service would be reduced by 25 percent, or $60 million.

With recovery predicted for trucking and farm equipment sales, Lennox believes that the restructured International Harvester is well positioned to profit. Although it's still too soon to tell, Harvester's proponents claim that it has gained from its adversity. Having sold off its sidelines and cut its unit costs, it's now leaner—and probably meaner—than most of its competitors.

Source: Adapted from "Can Don Lennox Save Harvester?" *Business Week*, Aug. 15, 1983, 80–84; "Lean, Mean, and Lucky to Be Alive," *Financial World*, Dec. 31, 1983, 26–27; and "International Harvester Lives!" *Fortune*, Dec. 26, 1983, 64–70.

Key Terms You should be able to define each of the following terms:

Economic failure; business failure; insolvency; insolvency in bankruptcy; bankruptcy

Voluntary bankruptcy; involuntary bankruptcy

Extension; composition

Reorganization; liquidation

Absolute priority doctrine; relative priority doctrine

Bankruptcy Reform Act of 1978; Chapter 11

Standard of fairness; standard of feasibility

Assignment

Questions

23-1 "A certain number of business failures is a healthy sign. If there are no failures, this is an indication (a) that entrepreneurs are overly cautious, and hence not as inventive and as willing to take risks as a healthy, growing economy requires; (b) that competition is not functioning to weed out inefficient producers; or (c) that both situations exist." Is this a true statement? Why or why not?

23-2 How could financial analysis be used to forecast the probability of a given firm's failure? Assuming that such analysis is properly applied, could it always predict failure?

23-3 Why do creditors usually accept a plan for financial rehabilitation rather than demand liquidation of the business?

23-4 Would it be possible to form a profitable company by merging two companies, both of which are business failures? Explain.

23-5 What is the difference between a reorganization and a bankruptcy?

23-6 Would it be a sound rule to liquidate whenever the liquidation value is above the value of the corporation as a going concern? Discuss.

23-7 Why do liquidations usually result in losses for the creditors or the owners, or both? Would partial liquidation or liquidation over a period limit their losses? Explain.

23-8 Are liquidations likely to be more common for public utility, railroad, or industrial corporations? Why?

Problems

23-1 The financial statements of the Carleton Publishing Company for 1983 follow. A recapitalization plan is proposed in which each share of the $6 preferred stock will be exchanged for one share of $2.40 preferred stock (stated value, $37.50) plus one 8 percent subordinated income debenture (stated principal, $75). The $10.50 preferred stock would be retired from cash.

    * **a.** Show the pro forma balance sheet (in millions of dollars) giving effect to the recapitalization and showing the new preferred stock at its stated value and the common stock at its par value.

    b. Present the pro forma income statement (in millions of dollars carried to two decimal places).

    * **c.** How much does the firm increase income available to common stock by the recapitalization?

    d. How much larger are the required pre-tax earnings after the recapitalization compared with the situation before the change? Required earnings are the amount that is just enough to meet fixed charges (debenture interest and/or preferred stock dividends).

**Carleton Publishing Company: Balance Sheet,
December 31, 1983 (Millions of Dollars)**

Current assets	$120	Current liabilities	$ 42
Investments	48	Advance payments for subscriptions	78
Net fixed assets	153	Reserves	6
Goodwill	15	$6 preferred stock, $112.50 par	
		(1,200,000 shares)	135
		$10.50 preferred stock, no par	
		(60,000 shares, callable at $150)	9
		Common stock, $1.50 par (6,000,000	
		shares outstanding)	9
		Retained earnings	57
Total assets	$336	Total claims	$336

---

*Refer to Appendix E for check answers to problems with asterisks.

Carleton Publishing Company: Consolidated Statement of Income and Expense, Year Ended December 31, 1983 (Millions of Dollars)

Operating income		$540.0
Operating expense		516.0
Net operating income		$ 24.0
Other income		3.0
Other expense		0.0
Earnings before income tax		$ 27.0
Income tax at 50 percent		13.5
Income after taxes		$ 13.5
Dividends on $6 prior preferred stock	$7.2	
Dividends on $10.50 preferred stock	0.6	
Income available for common stock		7.8
		$ 5.7

  * e. How is the debt/assets ratio affected by the recapitalization? (Debt includes advances for subscriptions.)

  f. Would you vote for the recapitalization if you were a holder of the $6 prior preferred stock?

23-2 At the time it defaulted, Rexford Forge had net current assets valued on its books at $20 million and net fixed assets valued at $25 million. At the time of final settlement its debts were as follows:

Current liabilities	$12 million
First-mortgage bonds	10 million
Second-mortgage bonds	5 million
Debenture bonds	4 million

None of the current liabilities have preferences in liquidation as provided for in the bankruptcy laws, and none have been secured by pledge of assets.

  Assume that the amount shown for each of the four classes of liabilities includes all unpaid interest to the date of settlement. The fixed assets were pledged as security for the first-mortgage bonds and repledged for the second-mortgage bonds. Determine the appropriate distribution of the proceeds of liquidation under the following conditions:

  a. Liquidation of current assets realizes $18 million, and $7 million is obtained from fixed assets.

  b. Liquidation of current assets realizes $9 million, and $4 million is obtained from fixed assets.

23-3 Brosky Distribution Systems is bankrupt and the assets of the firm are being sold to satisfy the claims of the firm's creditors. The firm's balance sheet is reproduced on the next page.

Brosky Distribution Systems: Balance Sheet (Thousands of Dollars)

Current assets	$20,000	Accounts payable	$ 5,000
Net fixed assets	2,500	Notes payable (due bank)	2,500
		Accrued wages	175
		U.S. taxes	250
		State and local taxes	75
		Current debt	$ 8,000
		First mortgage	$ 1,500
		Second mortgage	250
		Subordinated debentures[a]	2,000
		Long-term debt	$ 3,750
		Preferred stock	$ 500
		Common stock	6,500
		Paid-in capital	1,000
		Retained earnings	2,750
		Total equity	$10,750
Total assets	$22,500	Total claims	$22,500

[a]Subordinated to $2,500,000 notes payable to bank.

Unfortunately, the trustees found the firm's assets were greatly overstated. The following amounts (in thousands of dollars) were realized after liquidation:

Current assets	$7,000
Net fixed assets	1,250
Total receipts	$8,250

The fees and expenses directly associated with the bankruptcy were $1.5 million. Determine the appropriate distribution of the proceeds of liquidation for Brosky. How much will the preferred and common shareholders receive after the creditors have been paid?

Selected References

Altman, Edward I., *Corporate Financial Distress* (New York: Wiley, 1983).

Altman, Edward I., "Bankruptcy and Reorganization," in *Financial Handbook* (New York: Wiley, 1981), Chap. 35.

Altman, Edward I., "Financial Ratios, Discriminant Analysis and the Prediction of Corporate Bankruptcy," *Journal of Finance*, September 1968, 589–609.

Altman, Edward I., R. G. Haldeman, and P. Narayanan, "Zeta Analysis: A New Model to Identify Bankruptcy Risk of Corporations," *Journal of Banking and Finance*, June 1977, 29–54.

Altman, Edward I., and Arnold W. Sametz, *Financial Crises: Institutions and Markets in a Fragile Environment* (New York: Wiley, 1977).

Collins, Robert A., "An Empirical Comparison of Bankruptcy Prediction Models," *Financial Management*, Summer 1980, 52–57.

Dun & Bradstreet, Inc., *The Business Failure Record* (New York: updated annually).

Harris, Richard, "The Consequences of Costly Default," *Economic Inquiry*, October 1978, 477–496.

Miller, Danny, "Common Syndromes of Business Failure," *Business Horizons*, December 1977, 43–53.

U.S. Department of Commerce, *Survey of Current Business* (Washington, DC: updated monthly).

Warner, Jerold B., "Bankruptcy Costs: Some Evidence," *Journal of Finance*, May 1977, 337–347.

Leasing

Decision in Finance

Sandy's Gamble

When McDonnell Douglas Corporation launched its DC-9-80 commercial twinjet in 1977, everyone was sure they had a winner. Although its base price was about the same as a Boeing 727, the fuel-efficient Super 80 cost about 30 percent to 40 percent less per seat-mile to operate. In the cost-conscious airlines industry, this was expected to give McDonnell Douglas a strong competitive advantage.

By summer 1982 the promise of the Super 80 had yet to be realized, however. Total sales amounted to only 115 planes, and there were 17 planes built or half-built that had no buyers. The problem, realized McDonnell Douglas Chairman Sanford McDonnell, lay not in the planes but in the airlines industry itself. The grim fact was that McDonnell's potential customers were simply too broke to buy planes on their own account.

Sandy McDonnell faced three tough choices. He could close down the Long Beach, California, plant where the planes were built, which would disperse 16,000 trained workers and leave the company holding millions of dollars' worth of useless aircraft parts. He could go on manufacturing costly planes without advance orders and continue trying to sell them in a depressed market. Or he could find a way to help his customers finance the planes that they needed and wanted but couldn't afford.

As you read this chapter, consider how leasing could solve the problems of both McDonnell Douglas and the commercial airlines. What kind of lease would be most beneficial to all parties? Why?

See end of chapter for resolution.

Firms generally own fixed assets and report them on their balance sheets, but it is the *use* of buildings and equipment that is important, not their ownership per se. One way of obtaining the use of facilities and equipment is to buy them, but an alternative is to lease them. Prior to the 1950s leasing was generally associated with real estate—land and buildings. Today, however, it is possible to lease virtually any kind of fixed asset, and in 1984 about 20 percent of all new capital equipment acquired by businesses was financed through a lease arrangement.

Conceptually, as we show in this chapter, leasing is quite similar to borrowing, so leasing provides financial leverage. In effect, a lease is a type of debt.[1] Leasing takes several different forms, the three most important of which are (1) *sale and leaseback* arrangements, (2) *service leases*, and (3) straight *financial or capital leases*.

Sale and Leaseback

sale and leaseback
An operation whereby a firm sells land, buildings, or equipment to a financial institution and simultaneously leases the property back for a specified period under specific terms.

Under a **sale and leaseback** arrangement, a firm owning land, buildings, or equipment sells the property to a financial institution and simultaneously executes an agreement to lease the property back for a specified period under specific terms. The financial institution could be an insurance company, a commercial bank, a specialized leasing company, or an individual investor. The lease is an alternative to a mortgage.

lessee
The party leasing a property.

lessor
The owner of a property to be leased.

Note that the seller, or **lessee,** immediately receives the purchase price put up by the buyer, or **lessor.** At the same time the seller-lessee retains the use of the property. This parallel to borrowing is carried over to the lease payment schedule. Under a mortgage loan arrangement, the financial institution would receive a series of equal payments just sufficient to amortize the loan and to provide the lender with a specified rate of return on investment. Under a sale and leaseback arrangement, the lease payments are set up in exactly the same manner—the payments are sufficient to return the full purchase price to the investor, plus a stated return on the investment.

Service Leases

service lease
A lease under which the lessor maintains and services the asset; also called an *operating lease*.

A **service lease,** sometimes called an *operating lease,* provides for both *financing* and *maintenance.* IBM is one of the pioneers of the service lease contract. Computers and office copying machines, together with automobiles and trucks, are the primary types of equipment involved in service leases. These leases ordinarily call for the lessor to maintain

---

[1]Some instructors will prefer to cover this chapter immediately after Chapter 17, which deals with long-term debt. If this is done, it will be necessary to discuss separately the after-tax cost of debt.

and service the leased equipment, and the cost of the maintenance is built into the lease payments.

Another important characteristic of service leases is the fact that they are frequently *not fully amortized*. In other words, the payments required under the lease contract are not sufficient to recover the full cost of the equipment. However, the lease contract is written for a period considerably shorter than the expected life of the leased equipment, and the lessor expects to recover all costs either in subsequent renewal payments or through sale of the leased equipment.

A final feature of service leases is that they frequently contain a *cancellation clause* giving the lessee the right to cancel the lease and return the equipment before the expiration of the basic lease agreement. This is an important consideration to the lessee, for it means that the equipment can be returned if it is rendered obsolete by technological developments or is simply no longer needed.

Financial Leases

A **financial lease,** sometimes called a *capital lease,* is one that (1) does *not* provide for maintenance service, (2) is *not* cancelable, and (3) *is* fully amortized (that is, the lessor receives rental payments equal to the full price of the leased equipment). The typical arrangement involves the following steps:

financial lease
A lease that does not provide for maintenance service, is not cancelable, and covers the entire expected life of the equipment; also called a *capital lease.*

Step 1 The firm that will use the equipment (the lessee) selects the specific items it requires and negotiates the price and delivery terms with the manufacturer.

Step 2 The user firm then arranges with a bank or a leasing company (the lessor) to buy the equipment from the manufacturer or the distributor. When the equipment is purchased, the user firm simultaneously executes an agreement to lease the equipment from the financial institution. The terms of the lease call for full amortization of the financial institution's investment, plus a rate of return on the unamortized balance close to the percentage rate the lessee would have to pay on a secured term loan. For example, if the lessee would have to pay 10 percent for a term loan, then a rate of about 10 percent would be built into the lease contract. The lessee is generally given an option to renew the lease at a reduced rental on expiration of the basic lease. However, the basic lease usually cannot be canceled unless the financial institution is completely paid off. Also, the lessee generally pays the property taxes and insurance on the leased property. Since the lessor receives a return *after,* or *net of,* these payments, this type of lease is often called a "net, net" lease.

Industry Practice

Why Sale-Leasebacks Are Booming

What do Gibson Greeting Cards, U.S. Steel, Heekin Can, Seamen's Bank for Savings, and the *New York Daily News* have in common? They're tapping a hidden source of dollars: their own properties. Recession-pinched profits and embarrassingly illiquid balance sheets are forcing more companies to resort to sale-leasebacks. The trend goes beyond the well-known deals with headquarters buildings: companies are also unlocking the equity tied up in plants and warehouses by selling and leasing them back.

An estimated 20 percent of all corporate assets lies in real estate, and with inflation boosting the value of those assets, some companies may be sitting on gold mines. Showing those inflated values is impossible, however, because companies must report real estate assets at cost minus depreciation. But the same properties can be sold at market prices, boosting net worth dramatically.

The basic strategy is well established; Integrated Resources, Inc. has arranged sale-leasebacks for more than 800 properties valued at $3.8 billion in 14 years. Publicly registered or privately placed limited partnerships acquire the real estate. Then, through "net-lease deals," corporate tenants start paying rent but continue paying maintenance costs and property taxes.

Boosting Earnings

A key benefit to real estate investors is the tax deduction that comes from depreciation. Property owners deduct the cost of a building from taxable income, thereby increasing cash flow. But this benefit also has the effect of reducing reported earnings. For those companies that sell and lease back properties, the benefits of boosting earnings outweigh those of depreciation.

By selling real estate, a corporation is effectively selling tax benefits, for which investors often pay a premium. The seller gets a break on the rent, which is generally lower than what the payments for alternative financing—a mortgage—would be. Benjamin V. Lambert, president of Eastdil Realty Inc., which arranges sale-leasebacks, says that this could be as beneficial as lopping 1.5 percentage points off a mortgage interest rate.

Since operating leases are off-balance-sheet financing, the seller's debt-to-equity ratio is improved, enhancing borrowing capacity. Says Richard H. Ader, executive vice president at Integrated Resources: "The only corporations that would not look into sale-leaseback as an alternative method of financing are those that have excess cash."

In an innovative use of sale-leasebacks, Wesray Corp., the investment company headed by former Treasury Secretary William E. Simon, sold real estate of companies it purchased in order to help finance the buy-outs. As part of its leveraged buy-out of Heekin Can, Inc., Wesray sold 3 factories last December for $21 million to a partnership managed by W. P. Carey & Co., an investment banking firm. A similar deal, yielding $35 million, was worked out early last year

when Wesray acquired Gibson Greeting Cards, Inc. from RCA Corp.

"Expertly Opportunistic"

The tenants, Gibson and Heekin,
have 20-year leases, which will be adjusted every 5 years. Carey collects
rent owed the limited partnerships,
whose investors are now getting a
9 percent return. Carey's chairman,
William P. Carey, says investors are
looking for "income that is sheltered
from taxation, safety inherent in long-
term net leases, and appreciation in
value of the property."

Simon is parlaying his experience in
sale-leasebacks into a new venture,
teaming up with Eastdil Realty to

form a $250 million investment pro-
gram for pension funds. Eastdil Corporate Partners' goal is to use pension
fund assets to buy properties that will
be leased back to corporate tenants.
There have been no takers in the first
four months of the offer, but, says Simon: "We have lots of interested people. Real estate is an excellent investment. And with many institutions
overextended today, you can be ex-
pertly opportunistic in the real estate
field."

Financial leases are almost the same as sale and leaseback arrangements, the major difference being that the leased equipment is new
and the lessor buys it from a manufacturer or a distributor instead of
from the user-lessee. A sale and leaseback may, then, be thought of as
a special type of financial lease. Both sale and leaseback arrangements
and financial leases are analyzed in the same manner.

Internal Revenue Service Requirements for a Lease

The full amount of the annual lease payment is a deductible expense
for income tax purposes *provided the Internal Revenue Service agrees that a
particular contract is a genuine lease and not simply an installment loan called
a lease*. This makes it important that a lease contract be written in a
form acceptable to the Internal Revenue Service. The following are the
major factors that are examined to determine whether a given contract
is likely to be classified as a bona fide lease transaction from the standpoint of the IRS:

1. The term, or years involved in the lease, must be less than 75 percent of the life of the asset; otherwise the lease is likely to be regarded
as a sale for tax purposes.

2. The rent must provide a reasonable rate of return to the lessor in
relation to rates of return on loans.

3. The renewal option must be bona fide, and this requirement can
best be met by giving the lessee the first option to meet an equal bona
fide outside offer.

4. There should be no repurchase option; if there is, the lessee should merely be given parity with an equal outside offer.

The reason for the IRS's concern about these factors is that without restrictions a company could set up a "lease" transaction calling for very rapid payments, *which would be tax deductions.* The effect would be to depreciate the equipment over a much shorter period than its useful life. For example, if a $200,000 printing press with a 20-year life were leased for 3 years, then purchased under a purchase option for $1 or renewed for $1 a year, this would have the same cash flow effect as depreciating the press in 3 years rather than over 20 years.

Effects of Leasing on a Firm's Balance Sheet

Leasing is often called **off-balance-sheet financing,** because, under certain conditions, neither the leased assets nor the liabilities under lease contracts appear on a firm's balance sheet. This point is illustrated in Table 24-1 by the balance sheets of two hypothetical firms, A and B. Initially, the balance sheets of both firms are identical, and they both have debt ratios of 50 percent. Next, each firm decides to acquire assets costing $100. Firm A borrows $100 to make the purchase, so both an asset and a liability go on its balance sheet, and its debt ratio is increased to 75 percent. Firm B leases the equipment. The lease may call for fixed charges as high as or even higher than the loan, and the obligations assumed under the lease can be equally or more dangerous from the standpoint of financial analysis, but the firm's debt ratio will remain at 50 percent.

To correct this problem, the Financial Accounting Standards Board issued FASB #13, which requires that, for an unqualified audit report, firms entering into financial (or capital) leases must restate their balance sheets to report the leased asset under fixed assets and the present value of the future lease payments as a debt.[2] This process is called **capitalizing the lease,** and its net effect is to cause Firms A and B to have similar balance sheets, both of which will, in essence, resemble the one shown for Firm A.

The logic behind FASB #13 is as follows. If a firm signs a lease contract, its obligation to make lease payments is just as binding as are payments under a loan agreement—the failure to make lease payments can bankrupt a firm just as fast as the failure to make principal and interest payments on a loan. Therefore, for all intents and purposes, a financial lease is identical to a loan. This being the case, if a firm signs a lease agreement, this has the effect of raising its effective debt ratio

off-balance-sheet financing
Financing wherein for many years neither the leased assets nor the liabilities under the lease contract appeared on the lessee's balance sheet; problem corrected by FASB #13.

capitalizing the lease
Incorporating the lease provisions into the balance sheet by reporting the leased asset under fixed assets and reporting the present value of future lease payments as debt; required by FASB #13.

---

[2]FASB #13, "Accounting for Leases" (November 1976). This document spells out in detail the conditions under which the lease must be capitalized and the procedures for capitalizing it.

Table 24-1
Balance Sheet Effects of Leasing

Before Asset Increase			After Asset Increase								
Firms A and B			Firm A, Which Borrows and Purchases				Firm B, Which Leases				
Total assets	$100	Debt $ 50 Equity 50 $100	Total assets	$200		Debt $150 Equity 50 $200	Total assets	$100		Debt $ 50 Equity 50 $100	

and changing its true capital structure. Therefore, if the firm had previously established a target capital structure, and if there is no reason to think that the optimal capital structure has changed, then using lease financing requires additional equity support in exactly the same manner as does debt financing.

If disclosure of the lease in our Table 24-1 example were not made, then Firm B's investors could be deceived into thinking that its financial position is stronger than it really is. Thus, even before FASB #13 was issued in 1976, firms were required to disclose the existence of long-term leases in footnotes to their financial statements. At that time it was debatable whether or not investors recognized fully the impact of leases and, in effect, would see that Firms A and B were in essentially the same financial position. Some people argued that leases were not fully recognized, even by sophisticated investors. If this were the case, then leasing could alter the capital structure decision in a really significant manner—a firm could increase its true leverage through a lease arrangement with a smaller effect on its cost of conventional debt (k_d) and on its cost of equity (k_s). These benefits would accrue to existing investors at the expense of new investors who were, in effect, deceived by the fact that the firm's balance sheet did not reflect its true liability situation.

The question of whether investors were truly deceived was debated but never resolved. Those who believe strongly in efficient markets thought that investors were not deceived and that footnotes were sufficient, while those who question market efficiency thought that leases should be capitalized. FASB #13 represents a compromise between these two positions, though one that is tilted heavily toward those who favor capitalization.

A lease is classified as a capital lease, and hence capitalized and shown directly on the balance sheet, if one or more of the following conditions exist:
1. Under the terms of the lease, ownership of the property is effectively transferred from the lessor to the lessee.

2. The lessee can purchase the property at less than its true market value when the lease expires.

3. The lease runs for a period equal to or greater than 75 percent of the asset's life. Thus, if an asset has a 10-year life and the lease is written for 8 years, the lease must be capitalized.

4. The present value of the lease payments is equal to or greater than 90 percent of the initial value of the asset, less any tax credit taken by the lessor.[3]

These rules, together with strong footnote disclosure rules for operating leases, should certainly be sufficient to insure that no one will be fooled by lease financing, and thus that leases will be regarded as debt and will have the same effects as debt on k_d and k_s. Therefore leasing is not likely to permit a firm to use more financial leverage than could be obtained with conventional debt.

Evaluating Lease Proposals

In the typical case the events leading to a lease arrangement follow the sequence described below. There is a great deal of uncertainty regarding the theoretically correct way to evaluate lease versus purchase decisions, and some very complex decision models have been developed to aid in the analysis. However, the simple **lease evaluation** analysis given here is accurate enough for most decisions.

lease evaluation
The analysis of the firm's cash flows under lease or purchase to determine the lower present value of costs.

1. The firm decides to acquire a particular building or piece of equipment; this decision is based on regular capital budgeting procedures. The decision to acquire the machine is not at issue in the typical lease analysis—this decision was made previously as part of the capital budgeting process. In a lease analysis we are concerned simply with whether to obtain the use of the machine by lease or by purchase. However, if the effective cost of the lease is substantially lower than the cost of debt—and, as explained later in this chapter, this could occur for a number of reasons, including the situation where the lessor is able to use the investment tax credit but the lessee is not—then the cost of capital used in capital budgeting would have to be recalculated and, perhaps, projects formerly deemed unacceptable might become acceptable.

2. Once the firm has decided to acquire the asset, the next question is how to finance its acquisition. Well-run businesses do not have excess cash lying around, so new assets must be financed in some manner.

3. Funds to purchase the asset could be obtained by borrowing, by retaining earnings, or by selling stock, or the asset could be leased.

---

[3]The discount rate used to calculate the present value of the lease payments must be the lower of (1) the rate used by the lessor to establish the lease payments (this rate is discussed later in the chapter) or (2) the rate of interest the lessee would have to pay for new debt with a maturity equal to that of the lease.

As indicated at the beginning of this chapter, a lease is comparable to a loan in the sense that the firm is required to make a specified series of payments and that failure to meet these payments can result in bankruptcy. Thus the most appropriate comparison is between lease financing and debt financing. The lease versus borrow-and-purchase analysis is illustrated with data on the Carter Chemical Company. The following conditions are assumed:

1. Carter plans to acquire equipment with a cost of $11,111,111, delivered and installed.

2. An investment tax credit of $1,111,111, which is approximately 10 percent, applies. Thus the net financing required if Carter borrows and purchases is $10,000,000.

3. Carter can borrow the required $10,000,000 on a 10 percent loan to be amortized over 5 years. Therefore the loan will call for payments of $2,637,965.60 per year, calculated as follows:

$$\text{Payment} = \frac{\$10,000,000}{\text{DFa }(10\%, \text{ 5 years})} = \frac{\$10,000,000}{3.7908} = \$2,637,965.60$$

4. The equipment will definitely be used for 5 years, at which time its estimated salvage value is $715,000. If the operation is profitable, Carter will continue to use the equipment. If not, the equipment will be sold, presumably at its estimated salvage value.

5. Carter can lease the equipment for 5 years at a rental charge of $2,791,670 per year, but the lessor will own it at the expiration of the lease. (The lease payment schedule is established by the potential lessor, and Carter can accept it, reject it, or negotiate). If Carter plans to continue using the equipment, a purchase arrangement will have to be negotiated with the lessor. We assume that Carter will be able to buy the equipment at its estimated salvage value, $715,000.

6. The lease contract calls for the lessor to maintain the equipment. If Carter borrows and purchases, it will have to bear the cost of maintenance, which will be performed by the equipment manufacturer at a contracted cost of $500,000 per year.

7. The equipment falls in the ACRS 5-year-class life, and for this analysis we assume that Carter's effective tax rate is 40 percent. Also, note that the depreciable basis is the original cost less one half of the ITC, or $11,111,111 − $555,556 = $10,555,555.

Table 24-2 shows the steps involved in the analysis. Columns 2 through 10 are devoted to the costs of borrowing and purchasing. Within this set Columns 2 through 5 give the loan amortization schedule; Column 6 shows the maintenance expense; and Column 7 gives depreciation charges. Tax-deductible expenses—interest, maintenance, and depreciation—are summed and shown in Column 8, while Column 9 gives the taxes saved because Carter has these deductions. Column 10 summarizes the preceding columns and gives the annual net

Table 24-2
Carter Chemical Company: Lease versus Purchase Analysis
(Thousands of Dollars)

Applicable to Net Cost of Owning

Loan Amortization Schedule

Year (1)	Total Payment (2)	Interest (3)	Amortization Payment (4)	Remaining Balance (5)	Maintenance Cost (6)	Depreciation (7)
1	$ 2,638	$1,000	$ 1,638	$8,362	$500	$ 1,583
2	2,638	836	1,802	6,560	500	2,322
3	2,638	656	1,982	4,578	500	2,217
4	2,638	458	2,180	2,398	500	2,217
5	2,638	240	2,398	0	500	2,217
5[a]	—	—	—	—	—	
	$13,190	$3,190	$10,000			$10,556

[a]Two lines are shown for Year 5 in order to account for the salvage value, $715,000.

Notes:

1. The net advantage to leasing could be calculated by subtracting Column 11 from Column 10, then discounting these differences. This procedure is more efficient, hence preferable in actual practice, but the procedure used here is better for explanatory purposes.
2. Leases often involve payments at the *beginning* of the period rather than at the end. Also, a down payment may be required under either the lease or the loan. In either event, it would be necessary to set up a "0" year to show payments made at time zero.
3. Students may wish to review the construction of loan amortization tables in Chapter 14.

cash outflows Carter will incur if it borrows and purchases the equipment.

The lease payments are $2,791,670 per year; this rate, which includes maintenance, was established by the prospective lessor and offered to Carter. If Carter accepts the lease, the full $2,791,670 will be a deductible expense, so the after-tax cost of the lease will be calculated as follows:

$$\text{After-tax cost} = \text{Lease payment} - \text{Tax savings}$$
$$= \text{Lease payment} - (\text{Tax rate})(\text{Lease payment})$$
$$= \text{Lease payment}(1 - \text{Tax rate})$$
$$= \$2,791,670(1 - 0.4)$$
$$= \$1,675,000.$$

This amount is shown in Column 11, Years 1 through 5.

Notice that the last entry in Column 11, the $715,000 shown under Year 5, represents the $715,000 expected Year 5 purchase price. We include this amount as a cost of leasing on the assumption that Carter

Tax-Deductible Expense = 3 + 6 + 7 (8)	Tax Savings = (0.4)(8) (9)	Cash Outflow If Owned = 2 + 6 − 9 (10)	Applicable to Lease		Comparative Costs	
			Lease Cost after Tax = (1 − 0.4) (Lease Cost) (11)	DFs for 6% (12)	Present Value of the Cost of Owning = 10 × 12 (13)	Present Value of the Cost of Leasing = 11 × 12 (14)
$3,083	$1,233	$1,905	$1,675	0.9434	$1,797	$1,580
3,658	1,463	1,675	1,675	0.8900	1,491	1,491
3,373	1,349	1,789	1,675	0.8396	1,502	1,406
3,175	1,270	1,868	1,675	0.7921	1,480	1,327
2,957	1,183	1,955	1,675	0.7473	1,461	1,252
			715	0.7473	—	534
					$7,731	$7,590

Net advantage to leasing = $7,731 − $7,590 = $141

will want to continue the operation and thus will be forced to purchase the equipment from the lessor. If we assume that the operation will not be continued, then we would put the $715,000 into Column 10 as an inflow; that is, it would have a minus sign.

The next step is to compare the net cost of owning with the net cost of leasing. However, we must first put the annual cash flows of leasing and borrowing on a common basis. This requires converting them to present values, which brings up the question of the proper rate at which to discount the costs. In Chapter 16 we saw that the more risky the cash flow, the higher the discount rate used to find present values. This principle, observed in our discussion of capital budgeting, applies to lease analysis as well. Just how risky are the cash flows under consideration here? Most of them are relatively certain, at least compared to the types of cash flow estimates that were developed in capital budgeting. For example, the loan payment schedule is set by contract, as is the lease payment schedule. The depreciation expenses are also established and not subject to change, and the $500,000 annual maintenance cost is fixed by contract as well. The tax savings are somewhat uncertain, but they will be as projected so long as Carter's effective tax rate remains at 40 percent. The residual value is the least certain of the cash flows, but even here Carter's management is fairly certain it will want to acquire the property, hence will incur the $715,000 outlay in Year 5.

Since the cash flows under the lease and the borrow-and-purchase alternatives are both relatively certain, they should be discounted at a relatively low rate. Most analysts recommend that the company's cost of debt be used, and this rate seems reasonable in this instance. Furthermore, since all the cash flows are on an after-tax basis, *the after-tax cost of debt, which is 6 percent, should be used.* Accordingly, we multiply the cash outflows in Columns 10 and 11 by the 6 percent DFs given in Column 12. The resulting present values are shown in Columns 13 and 14; when these columns are summed, we have the net present values of the costs of owning and leasing. The financing method that produces the smaller present value of cost is the one that should be selected. The example shown in Table 24-2 indicates that leasing has the advantage over buying: the present value of the cost of leasing is $141,000 less than that of buying. In this instance it is to Carter's advantage to lease.

Factors That Affect Leasing Decisions

The basic method of analysis set forth in Table 24-2 is sufficient to handle most situations. However, certain factors warrant additional comment.

Estimated Residual Value

residual value
The market value of a property at the end of its lease term.

It is important to note that the lessor owns the property at the expiration of a lease. The value of the property at the end of the lease is called its **residual value.** Superficially, it would appear that where residual values are large, owning would have an advantage over leasing. However, this apparent advantage of owning is subject to substantial qualification. If residual values are large, as they will be for certain types of equipment and also if land is involved, competition between leasing companies and other financial sources, as well as competition among leasing companies themselves, will force leasing rates down to the point where potential residual values are fully recognized in the lease contract rates. Thus the existence of residual values on equipment is not likely to result in materially lower costs of owning.

Increased Credit Availability

Leasing is sometimes said to have an advantage for firms seeking the maximum degree of financial leverage. First, it is frequently stated that firms can obtain more money for longer terms under a lease arrangement than under a secured loan agreement for the purchase of a specific piece of equipment. Second, since some leases do not appear on the balance sheet, lease financing has been said to give the firm a stronger appearance in a *superficial* credit analysis and thus to permit the firm to use more leverage than it could use if it did not lease.

There is probably some truth to these claims for smaller firms. However, now that large firms are required to capitalize major leases and report them on their balance sheets, this point is of questionable validity for them.

Investment Tax Credit and Accelerated Depreciation

The investment tax credit, discussed in Chapter 2, can be taken only if the firm's profits and taxes exceed a certain level. If a firm is unprofitable, or if it is expanding so rapidly and generating such large tax credits that it cannot use them all, then it may be worthwhile for it to enter a lease arrangement. Here the lessor (a bank or leasing company, or a wealthy individual) will take the credit and give the lessee a corresponding reduction in lease charges. Railroads and airlines have been large users of leasing for this reason in recent years, as have industrial companies faced with particular situations. Anaconda, for example, financed most of the cost of a $138 million aluminum plant through a lease arrangement. Anaconda had suffered a $358 million tax loss when Chile expropriated its copper mining properties, and the carryforward of this loss would hold taxes down for years. Thus Anaconda could not use the tax credit associated with the new plant. By entering a lease arrangement, Anaconda was able to pass the tax credit on to the lessors, who in turn gave Anaconda lower lease payments than would have existed under a loan arrangement. Anaconda's financial staff estimated that financial charges over the life of the plant would be $74 million less under the lease arrangement than under a borrow-and-purchase plan.

Accelerated depreciation has the same type of effect as the tax credit. A firm that is suffering losses and not paying taxes cannot benefit from accelerated depreciation on new equipment. However, if the equipment is sold to a lessor who is in a high tax bracket, then the tax advantage of accelerated depreciation can be captured, and part of it can be returned to the lessee in the form of lower rental payments.

Tax considerations—the investment tax credit and accelerated depreciation—are probably the dominant motives behind most financial leases that are written today.

Summary

This chapter has analyzed the three major types of leases: (1) *service leases,* (2) *sale and leaseback plans,* and (3) *financial leases for new assets.* Service, or operating, leases provide both for the financing of an asset and for its maintenance, while both sale and leaseback plans and regular financial leases provide only financing and are alternatives to debt financing.

Financial leases (and sale and leaseback plans) are evaluated by a cash flow analysis. We start with the assumption that an asset will be acquired, and that the acquisition will be financed either by debt or by a lease. Next, we develop the annual net cash outflows associated with each financing plan. Finally, we discount the two sets of outflows at the company's after-tax cost of debt and choose the alternative with the lower present value of costs.

Leasing sometimes represents off-balance-sheet financing, which permits firms to obtain more financial leverage if they employ leasing than if they use straight debt. This was formerly cited as a major reason for leasing. However, today taxes are the primary reason for the growth of financial leasing. Leasing permits the tax shelters (deductible expenses and the ITC) to be transferred from the user of an asset to the supplier of capital, and if these parties are in different tax brackets, both can benefit from the lease arrangement.

Resolution to Decision in Finance

Sandy's Gamble

By tradition, airplane manufacturers have always insisted on selling their products either directly to the airlines or to leasing companies that then lease to the carriers for 15 years or longer. But Sandy McDonnell decided to break that tradition with short-term, fly-before-buy leasing deals that he hoped to convert to sales when the economy improved.

McDonnell's first customer, in October 1982, was American Airlines, which took a 5-year lease on 20 DC-9-80s, with the option of a 13-year extension. The plan called for American to make lease payments of about $180,000 per plane per month—roughly what the interest would have been on the original price. And to sweeten the deal, the airlines would run virtually no risk: it would have no cash tied up in down payments, and on 30 days' notice, it could return the planes for a penalty of less than $2 million per plane. McDonnell worked out similar deals with TWA and Alitalia shortly thereafter.

Leasing was a daring route for Sandy McDonnell to take. He had to raise around $450 million to fund production and finance ownership on the American and TWA deals. McDonnell Douglas itself put up about 75 percent of the money, while its suppliers, such as engine-maker Pratt & Whitney, put up the rest. The net effect of the leasing deals would depress McDonnell Douglas's earnings for at least 3 years. But from Sandy McDonnell's point of view, that was a necessary price to pay for all the benefits the company would receive.

Most important was the fact that the leasing deals filled the production lines and averted the plant shutdown that everyone had dreaded. In the process they attracted new interest in the company's products, squelched rumors that McDonnell Douglas might abandon the commercial airplane market, and instilled confidence that the DC-9-80 would not become obsolete for at least 5 years. The leases also created goodwill because they enabled airlines to acquire the efficient planes they needed but couldn't afford to buy or lease conventionally.

Of course, the biggest risk to McDonnell Douglas is that the planes might be returned. But the company is sure that once the airlines fly the planes, they'll like them and keep them. Even if American does return its planes after 5 years, it will have paid between 25 percent and 40 percent of their cost and McDonnell Douglas will have depreciated them to less than market value. "We're strong enough financially to get them all back," says a company official.

Although the leases may penalize McDonnell Douglas's short-term profits, they may ensure the viability of the company that Sandy McDonnell's uncle founded over 45 years ago. It's still too soon to predict the final outcome of Sandy's gamble, but you have to give him and his board credit for courage, innovation, and farsightedness.

Source: Adapted from "Sandy's Gamble," *Forbes,* Dec. 20, 1982, 79–85; and "A Leasing Plan to Keep Jet Production Rolling," *Business Week,* Oct. 11, 1982, 34–35.

Key Terms You should be able to define each of the following terms:

Sale and leaseback; service, or operating, lease; financial, or capital, lease
Lessee; lessor

Off-balance-sheet financing
Capitalizing the lease
Lease evaluation
Residual value

Questions

24-1 Distinguish between operating leases and financial leases. Would you be more likely to find an operating lease employed for a fleet of trucks or for a manufacturing plant?

24-2 Would you be more likely to find that lessees are in high or low income tax brackets as compared to lessors?

24-3 Commercial banks moved heavily into equipment leasing during the early 1970s, acting as lessors. One major reason for this invasion of the leasing industry was to gain the benefits of accelerated depreciation and the investment tax credit on lease equipment. During this same period commercial banks were investing heavily in municipal securities, and they were also making loans to real estate investment trusts (REITs). In the mid 1970s these REITs got into such serious difficulty that many banks suffered large losses on their REIT loans. How could its investments in municipal bonds and REITs reduce a bank's willingness to act as a lessor?

24-4 One alleged advantage of leasing voiced in the past is that it kept liabilities off the balance sheet, thus making it possible for a firm to obtain more leverage than it otherwise could have. This raised the question of whether or not both the lease obligation and the asset involved should be capitalized and shown on the balance sheet. What are the pros and cons of capitalizing leases and the related assets?

24-5 Suppose there were no IRS restrictions on what constituted a valid lease. Why should some restrictions be imposed? Explain in a manner that a legislator might understand.

24-6 What are the advantages and disadvantages of leveraged leases from the standpoint of **(a)** the lessee, **(b)** the equity investor in the lease, and **(c)** the supplier of the debt capital?

24-7 Suppose Congress enacted new tax law changes that would (1) permit equipment to be depreciated over a shorter period, (2) lower corporate tax rates, and (3) increase the investment tax credit. How would each of these potential changes affect the relative volume of leasing (versus conventional debt) in the U.S. economy?

Problems

* **24-1** University Leasing, Inc., which specializes in business financing in the Minneapolis–St. Paul area, is setting up a financial lease with Memorial Stadium, Inc. The lease will cover ice machines, pizza ovens, popcorn poppers, and cola dispensers which have a total cost of $200,000. The lease runs for 5 years. What is the annual lease payment based on a 9 percent interest rate? (Nine percent is simply the rate used to establish the lease payments. It is not the rate of return to the lessor.)

* **24-2** Refer to Problem 24-1. What would the annual lease payment be if University Leasing required lease payments to be made at the beginning of the year rather than at the end of the year? Note: Only 5 payments will be made.

24-3 Two furniture manufacturing companies, Henri-Don and Roy Hill, began operations with identical balance sheets. A year later both required additional manufacturing capacity at a cost of $50,000. Henri-Don obtained a 5-year, $50,000 loan at an 8 percent interest rate from its bank. Roy Hill, on the other hand, decided to lease the required $50,000 capacity from Furniture Financers for 5 years at 8 percent. The balance sheet for each company, before the asset increases, follows:

---

*Refer to Appendix E for check answers to problems with asterisks.

		Debt	$ 50,000
		Equity	100,000
Total assets	$150,000	Total claims	$150,000

a. Show the balance sheets for both firms after the asset increase, and calculate each firm's debt ratio.

b. Show how Roy Hill's balance sheet would look immediately after the financing if it capitalized the lease.

c. Would the rate of return on (1) assets and (2) equity be affected by the choice of financing? How?

✳ 24-4 Hogan Leasing Supply has been approached by Mallory Construction to arrange lease financing for $8 million in equipment. The lease would cover a 10-year period. The assets are expected to have little or no value at the end of the lease. The machinery is eligible for an investment tax credit (ITC) of 10 percent.

If Mallory proposes a lease payment of $1,500,000 at the end of each of the next 10 years, what rate of return would Hogan earn? Assume that Hogan depreciates the assets on a straight line basis, utilizes the ITC immediately, and has a marginal tax rate of 40 percent.

24-5 Refer to Problem 24-4. If the assets are 5-year-class property for tax purposes and ACRS is used to depreciate the machinery, what is the impact on NPV of the lease for Hogan? No computations are necessary.

24-6 Green Gardens, a manufacturer of lawn care and gardening products, has decided to expand production of its gardening tools division. The equipment necessary for expanded production can be either purchased or leased. The purchase plan requires Green Gardens to obtain a loan of $100,000 at a 10 percent interest rate, the loan to be amortized in level payments over a 5-year period. The lease provides $100,000 worth of equipment for 5 years, with the payment ($25,046) based on an 8 percent interest rate. If the equipment is acquired through the borrow-and-purchase arrangement, maintenance costs of $4,000 per year must be borne by Green Gardens. However, the lessor will assume these costs if Green Gardens decides to lease. As a proprietorship, Green Gardens is taxed at Joe Green's personal income tax rate of 20 percent.

The equipment will be depreciated by the ACRS method (5-year class), and it is expected to have a $25,000 salvage value after 5 years. It is assumed that Green Gardens will purchase the equipment at the expiration of the lease for $25,000. The lessor is Rachel Walsh, the famous actress, whose marginal income is taxed at a combined federal and state rate of 70 percent. She could invest the $100,000 in taxable investments with risk similar to the lease yielding 10 percent before tax. The same depreciation schedule would apply for either Miss Walsh or Mr. Green.

a. Develop an exhibit analyzing Green Gardens' lease-versus-purchase alternatives following the format of Table 24-2. (Use DFa = 3.7908 to calculate the loan payment, and round to the nearest dollar.)

b. Suppose that a 10 percent ITC applies; that, because of his low taxes and investment tax credits on other investments, Mr. Green cannot use it; and, further, that Miss Walsh can. How could this fact affect Mr. Green's cost analysis? No calculations are necessary.

Selected References

Athanasopoulos, Peter J., and Peter W. Bacon, "The Evaluation of Leveraged Leases," *Financial Management*, Spring 1980, 76–80.

Bower, Richard S., "Issues in Lease Financing," *Financial Management*, Winter 1973, 25–34.

Dyl, Edward A., and Stanley A. Martin, Jr., "Setting Terms for Leveraged Leases," *Financial Management*, Winter 1977, 20–27.

Gaumnitz, Jack E., and Allen Ford, "The Lease or Sell Decision," *Financial Management*, Winter 1978, 69–74.

Gordon, Myron J., "A General Solution to the Buy or Lease Decision: A Pedagogical Note," *Journal of Finance*, March 1974, 245–250.

Idol, Charles R., "A Note on Specifying Debt Displacement and Tax Shield Borrowing Opportunities in Financial Lease Valuation Models," *Financial Management*, Summer 1980, 24–29.

Levy, Haim, and Marshall Sarnat, "Leasing, Borrowing, and Financial Risk," *Financial Management*, Winter 1979, 47–54.

Lewellen, Wilbur G., Michael S. Long, and John J. McConnell, "Asset Leasing in Competitive Capital Markets," *Journal of Finance*, June 1976, 787–798.

Miller, Merton H., and Charles W. Upton, "Leasing, Buying, and the Cost of Capital Services," *Journal of Finance*, June 1976, 761–786.

Olsen, Robert A., "Lease versus Purchase or Lease versus Borrow: Comment," *Financial Management*, Summer 1978, 82–83.

Perg, Wayne F., "Leveraged Leasing: The Problem of Changing Leverage," *Financial Management*, Autumn 1978, 47–51.

Roberts, Gordon S., and Arthur C. Gudikunst, "Equipment Financial Leasing Practices and Costs: Comment," *Financial Management*, Summer 1978, 79–81.

International Financial Management

Decision in Finance

Sri Lanka: Playing the Incentive Game

In 1977, Sri Lankans voted their socialist government out of office and installed a regime committed to free-market principles. The goal of newly elected president Junius R. Jayawardene: attract foreign investment to create jobs, to earn foreign exchange, and to bring in technology to get the country moving again.

But persuading foreign companies to build factories on the small island country in the Indian Ocean proved to be a difficult task. Sri Lanka, formerly called Ceylon, had a terrible image in the international business community due to its socialist past. In addition, because the socialist government had preferred to spend its money on food and other consumer subsidies, the island lacked the transportation and communications networks that industry depends on. Consequently, despite the nation's high literacy rate (88 percent) and exceptionally low wages ($35 per month average), businesses continued to put Sri Lanka at the bottom of their priority lists.

President Jayawardene knew that he couldn't solve his country's economic problems overnight. But he was committed to making the fastest progress possible. He decided to devise a package of incentives to lure foreign investors to Sri Lanka. And to improve his nation's image and visibility, he created the Greater Colombo Economic Commission, whose principal job is to court foreign businesspeople.

As you read this chapter, consider the incentives that President Jayawardene could offer to improve his country's climate for foreign investment. Do you think that the decision makers at large corporations are likely to be swayed by the investment incentives offered by a small, less-developed country like Sri Lanka? Why or why not?

See end of chapter for resolution.

Almost 25 percent of U.S. manufacturing firms' assets are located abroad, and a similar percentage of their income is derived from foreign sources. Furthermore, international investment is growing more rapidly than domestic investment for American firms in the aggregate. This growth, which is highlighted in the left panel of Figure 25-1, has been caused primarily by the high rates of return available on foreign investments, especially in developing nations, as shown in the right panel.

multinational corporation
A firm that operates in two or more countries.

parent company
The base company of a multinational corporation.

A firm that operates in two or more nations is defined as a **multinational corporation.** Such a corporation typically has a base company in one country (the **parent company**) and operates branches and subsidiaries throughout the world. Its shares are normally owned mostly, if not entirely, by residents of the parent company's country. Although there has been much talk recently in the United States about foreigners, especially those from the OPEC countries, buying control of U.S. real estate and corporations, the fact of the matter is that multinational companies based in the United States invest far more money abroad than do those based in any other country. In fact, the United States has more assets abroad than do Britain, Japan, West Germany, Canada, and Switzerland combined. General Electric has television assembly plants in Mexico, South Korea, and Singapore; IBM has computer hardware manufacturing and servicing subsidiaries in many parts of Europe and the Far East; Caterpillar produces tractors and farm equipment in the Middle East, Europe, the Far East, and Africa. U.S. executives increasingly travel and live abroad, and U.S. multinational corporations have come to exert significant economic and political influence in many parts of the world.

Companies actually move into multinational operations for a number of specific reasons. First, a good many of the present U.S. multinational firms commenced their international operations because raw materials were located abroad; this is true of oil, mining, and some food processing companies. Other firms expanded overseas in order to obtain an outlet for their finished products. Frequently, the latter firms first set up sales offices, and then developed manufacturing plants when it became clear that the market would support such plants. Still other firms have moved their manufacturing facilities overseas in order to take advantage of low production costs in cheap labor areas; the electronics and textile companies are good examples. Finally, banks, accounting firms, and other service corporations have expanded overseas both to better serve their primary customers and to take advantage of profitable new investment opportunities.

The study of multinational finance takes traditional managerial finance as its starting point, and then builds on the models of capital

---

This chapter was coauthored by Professor Hai Hong of the University of Singapore.

Figure 25-1
Overseas Investment by U.S. Corporations and Rates of Return on This Investment in Different Countries
Foreign investment by U.S. business has grown exponentially since 1950, as illustrated in Graph a. Graph b shows the high rates of return fueling this investment, particularly in less-developed countries.

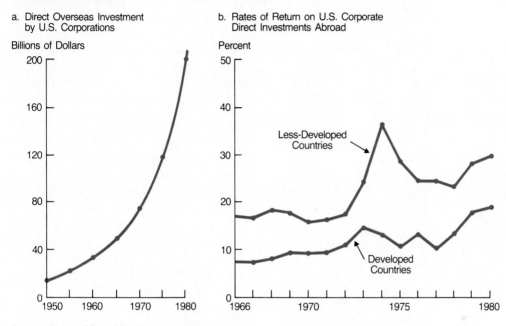

a. Direct Overseas Investment by U.S. Corporations

b. Rates of Return on U.S. Corporate Direct Investments Abroad

Source: *Survey of Current Business,* various issues.

budgeting, cost of capital, and working capital management discussed earlier in this book. However, multinational financial management must also take into account international differences in financial markets and institutions. Accordingly, this chapter is divided into four major sections: (1) foreign exchange rates and the international monetary system, (2) procedures for analyzing foreign investments, (3) financial management of foreign assets, and (4) international capital markets.

Exchange Rates and the International Monetary System

An **exchange rate** specifies the number of units of a given currency that can be purchased for one unit of another currency. Exchange rates for the leading trading partners of the United States appear in the financial sections of newspapers each day. See, for example, the rates given for September 8, 1983, as shown in Table 25-1.

exchange rate
The number of units of a given currency that can be purchased for one unit of another currency.

Table 25-1
Illustrative Exchange Rates, September 8, 1983

	U.S. Dollars Required to Buy One Unit of Foreign Currency (1)	Number of Units of Foreign Currency per U.S. Dollar (2)
British pound	$1.4920	0.6702
Canadian dollar	0.8127	1.2305
Dutch guilder	0.3342	2.9922
French franc	0.1242	8.0525
Greek drachma	0.0108	92.5926
Indian rupee	0.0981	10.1937
Italian lira	0.000627	1,594.8963
Japanese yen	0.004089	244.5586
Mexican peso	0.00662	151.0574
Norwegian krone	0.1342	7.4510
Saudi Arabian riyal	0.2874	3.4795
Singapore dollar	0.4675	2.1390
South African rand	0.8900	1.1236
Spanish peseta	0.00658	151.9757
Swedish krona	0.12658	7.9000
Swiss franc	0.45998	2.1740
West German mark	0.37358	2.6768

Note: Column 2 equals 1.0 divided by Column 1.

Recent History of the World Monetary System

fixed exchange rate system
The world monetary system in existence prior to 1971 under which the value of the U.S. dollar was tied to gold and the values of the other currencies were pegged to the U.S. dollar.

From the end of World War II until August 1971, the world was on a **fixed exchange rate system** administered by the International Monetary Fund (IMF). Under this system the U.S. dollar was linked to gold ($35 per ounce), and other currencies were then tied to the dollar. Exchange rates between other currencies and the dollar were controlled within narrow limits. For example, in 1964 the British pound was fixed at 2.80 dollars for 1 pound, with a 1 percent permissible fluctuation about this rate:

	Value of the Pound (Exchange Rate in Dollars per Pound)
Upper limit (+ 1%)	2.828
Official rate	2.800
Lower limit (− 1%)	2.772

Fluctuations in exchange rates tend to occur because of changes in the supply of and demand for dollars, pounds, and other currencies.

These supply and demand changes have two primary sources. First, changes in the demand for currencies depend on changes in imports and exports of goods and services. For example, U.S. importers must buy British pounds to pay for British goods, while British importers must buy U.S. dollars to pay for U.S. goods. If U.S. imports from Britain were to exceed U.S. exports to Britain, then there would be a greater demand for pounds than for dollars; this would drive up the price of the pound relative to that of the dollar. In terms of Table 25-1, the dollar cost of pounds might rise from $1.4920 to $2.0000. The U.S. dollar would be said to be *depreciating,* while the pound would be *appreciating.* In this example the root cause of the change would be the U.S. **deficit trade balance** with Britain. Of course, if U.S. exports to Britain were greater than U.S. imports from Britain, then Britain would have a deficit trade balance with the United States.[1] (Still, under the old fixed rate system, the change in relative currency values was subject to the artificial 1 percent limit.)

deficit trade balance
A country's trade balance resulting from an excess of its imports over its exports.

Changes in the demand for a currency, and hence exchange rate fluctuations, also depend on capital movements. For example, suppose interest rates in Britain were higher than those in the United States. To take advantage of the high British interest rates, U.S. banks, corporations, and even sophisticated individuals would buy pounds with dollars, and then use those pounds to purchase high-yielding British securities. These purchases would tend to drive up the price of pounds.[2]

Prior to 1972 these fluctuations were kept within the narrow 1 percent limit by regular intervention of the British government in the market. When the value of the pound was falling, the Bank of England

---

[1] If the dollar value of the pound moved up from $1.49 to $2.00, this increase in the value of the pound would mean that British goods would now be more expensive in the U.S. market. For example, a box of candy costing 1 pound in England would rise in price in the United States from $1.49 to $2.00. Conversely, U.S. goods would be cheaper in England. For example, the British could now buy goods worth $2.00 for 1 pound, whereas before the exchange rate change, 1 pound would buy merchandise worth only $1.49. These price changes would, of course, tend to *reduce* British exports and *increase* imports, and this, in turn, would lower the exchange rate because people in the United States and other nations would be buying fewer pounds to pay for English goods. However, in the old days the 1 percent limit severely constrained the market's ability to reach an equilibrium between trade balances and exchange rates.

[2] Such capital inflows would also tend to drive down British interest rates. If rates were high in the first place because of efforts by the British monetary authorities to curb inflation, then the international currency flows would have helped thwart that effort. This is one of the reasons why domestic and international economics are so closely linked.

A good example of this occurred during the summer of 1981. In an effort to curb inflation, the Reagan administration pushed U.S. interest rates to record levels. This, in turn, caused an outflow of capital from European nations to the United States. The Europeans were suffering from a severe recession and wanted to keep interest rates down in order to stimulate investment, but the U.S. policy made this difficult because of the ease of international capital flows.

devaluation
The process of officially reducing the value of a country's currency relative to other currencies.

revaluation
The process of officially increasing the value of a country's currency relative to other currencies.

floating exchange rates
Exchange rates not fixed by government policy but allowed to float up or down in accordance with supply and demand.

managed floating system
A system in which major currency rates move with market forces, unrestricted by any internationally agreed-upon limits.

would step in and buy pounds, offering gold or foreign currencies in exchange. These government purchases would push up the pound rate. Conversely, when the pound rate was too high, the Bank of England would sell pounds. The central banks of other countries operated similarly. Of course, a central bank's ability to control its exchange rate was limited by its supply of gold and foreign currencies.

With the approval of the IMF, a country could **devalue** its currency—which means to officially lower its value relative to other currencies—if it experienced persistent difficulty over a long period in preventing its exchange rate from falling below the lower limit, and if its central bank was running out of the gold and other currencies which could be used to buy its own currency and thus prop up its price. For just these reasons the British pound was devalued from $2.80 per pound to $2.50 per pound in 1967. This lowered the price of British goods in the United States and elsewhere and raised the prices of foreign goods in Britain, thus stopping the deficit British trade balance which had been putting pressure on the pound in the first place. Conversely, a nation with an export surplus and a strong currency might **revalue** its currency upward, as West Germany did twice in the 1960s.

Today's Floating Exchange Rate System

Devaluations and revaluations occurred only rarely before 1971. They were usually accompanied by severe international financial repercussions, partly because nations tended to postpone these needed measures until economic pressures had built up to explosive proportions. For this and other reasons the old international monetary system came to a dramatic close in the early 1970s, when the U.S. dollar, the foundation upon which all other currencies were anchored, was cut loose from gold and, in effect, allowed to "float."

Under a system of **floating exchange rates,** currency prices are allowed to seek their own levels without much governmental intervention. The present world monetary system is known as a **managed floating system:** major world currency rates move (float) with market forces, unrestricted by any internationally agreed-upon limits. However, the central bank of each country does intervene in the foreign exchange market, buying and selling its currency to smooth out exchange rate fluctuations to some extent. Each central bank also tries to keep its average exchange rate at a level deemed desirable by its government's economic policy. This is important, because exchange rates have a profound effect on the levels of imports and exports, which in turn influence the level of domestic employment. For example, if a country were having a problem with unemployment, then its central bank might encourage a *decline* in the value of its currency. This would cause its goods to be cheaper in world markets and thus stimulate exports, production, and domestic employment. Conversely, the central

Figure 25-2
Changes in the Values of Marks, Yen, and Pounds Relative to the Value of the Dollar, 1962–1982.

Prior to 1971 world currencies were narrowly controlled and changes in relative values were minimal. Since 1971 currencies have been allowed to float, resulting in marked fluctuations in values. As this figure shows, the mark and yen have increased in value relative to the dollar, while the pound has generally decreased. These fluctuations are due to the relative economic strengths and inflation rates of the four countries.

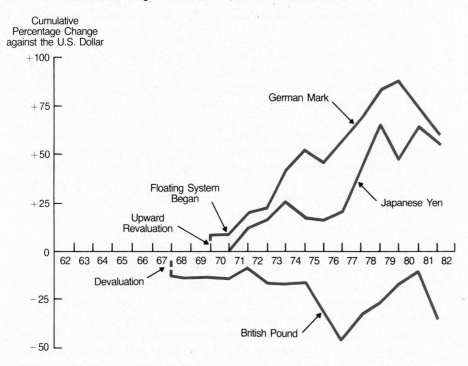

Source: *International Financial Statistics*, various issues.

bank of a country that is operating at full capacity and experiencing inflation might try to raise the value of its currency in order to reduce exports and increase imports. However, under the current floating rate system, such intervention can affect the situation only temporarily—market forces will prevail in the long run.

Figure 25-2 shows how German marks, Japanese yen, and British pounds moved in comparison to the dollar from 1962 to 1982. Until 1971, when the fixed rate system was terminated, rates were quite stable. The pound's fluctuations against the dollar were too small to even show up on the graph prior to 1967, when a devaluation occurred. The mark was revaluated in 1969. The yen was stable until 1971, when the dollar was allowed to float. The pound has drifted down, although it did rise from 1977 through 1980 as a result of exports of North Sea oil.

The yen and the mark rose against the dollar during the 1970s, although recently they have fallen. The root cause of these divergent trends has been the strengths of the British, German, and Japanese economies relative to that of the United States, and the relative inflation rates in the four countries. This point is discussed in detail in a later section.

Trading in Foreign Exchange

Importers, exporters, and tourists, as well as governments, buy and sell currencies in the foreign exchange market. For example, when a U.S. trader imports automobiles from West Germany, payment will probably be made in German marks. The importer buys marks (through its bank) in the foreign exchange market, much as one buys common stocks on the New York Stock Exchange or pork bellies on the Chicago Mercantile Exchange. However, while stock and commodity exchanges have organized trading floors, the foreign exchange market consists of a network of brokers and banks based in New York, London, Tokyo, and other financial centers. Most buy and sell orders are conducted by cablegram and telephone.[3]

Spot Rates and Forward Rates

spot rate
The effective exchange rate for a foreign currency for delivery on (approximately) the current day.

The exchange rates shown earlier in Table 25-1 are known as **spot rates,** which means the rate paid for delivery of the currency "on the spot" or, in reality, two days after the day of the trade. For most of the world's major currencies, it is also possible to buy (or sell) currency for delivery at some agreed-upon future date, usually 30, 90, or 180 days from the day the transaction is negotiated. This rate is known as the **forward exchange rate.** For example, if a U.S. firm must make payment to a Swiss firm in 90 days, the U.S. firm's treasurer can buy Swiss francs today for delivery in 90 days, paying the 90-day forward rate. Forward rates are exactly analogous to futures prices on commodity exchanges, where contracts are drawn up for wheat or corn to be delivered at agreed-upon prices at some future date.

forward exchange rate
An agreed-upon price at which two currencies are to be exchanged at some future date.

premium on forward rate
The difference between the forward exchange rate and the lower spot rate.

discount on forward rate
The difference between the spot rate and the lower forward exchange rate.

When the forward rate is *above* the current spot rate, the forward rate is said to be at a **premium;** conversely, when the forward rate is *below* the spot rate, it is said to be at a **discount.** Table 25-2 shows forward rates for British pounds and Swiss francs on September 8, 1983, along with spot rates from Table 25-1, which have been included for comparison. Note that forward rates on both pounds and francs sell at a premium. The reason for this premium will be explained shortly.

---

[3]For a more detailed account of foreign exchange trading and money market instruments for financing foreign trade, see Rita M. Rodriguez and E. Eugene Carter, *International Financial Management* (Englewood Cliffs, NJ: Prentice-Hall, 1979), Chapters 5 and 6.

Why do individuals and corporations buy or sell forward currencies? The main reason is that forward markets provide protection against future changes in exchange rates. For example, suppose that on September 8, 1983 a U.S. jeweler buys watches from a Swiss manufacturer for 1 million Swiss francs. Payment is to be made in Swiss francs 90 days after the goods are shipped, or on December 7, so the Swiss firm is extending trade credit for 90 days. The Swiss franc has been strong recently, and the U.S. firm is afraid that the trend will continue. If the franc appreciates rapidly, more dollars will be required to buy the million francs, and the profits on the watches will be lost. Still, the U.S. firm does not want to forgo the free trade credit, so it protects itself by buying 1 million 90-day-forward francs for $0.46661 × 1,000,000, or $466,610. When payment comes due on December 7, regardless of the spot rate on that day, the U.S. firm can obtain the needed Swiss francs at the agreed-upon price. The U.S. firm is said to have *covered its trade payables*.

Inflation, Interest Rates, and Exchange Rates

Relative inflation rates, or the rates of inflation in foreign countries compared to that at home, have many implications for multinational financial decisions. Obviously, relative inflation rates will greatly influence production costs at home and those abroad. Equally important, they have a dominant influence not only on relative interest rates but also on exchange rates. Both relative interest rates and exchange rates influence the methods chosen by multinational corporations for financing their foreign investments, and both of these factors have a major impact on the profitability of foreign investments.

The currencies of countries with higher inflation rates than that of the United States tend over time to depreciate against the dollar. Some countries where this is the case are Britain, Italy, Mexico, and all the South American nations. On the other hand, the currencies of countries such as West Germany, Switzerland, and Japan, which have had

Table 25-2
Illustrative Spot and Forward Exchange Rates, September 8, 1983

	British Pounds	Swiss Francs
Spot rate	$1.4920	$0.45998
30-day forward	1.4923	0.46221
90-day forward	1.4936	0.46661
180-day forward	1.4955	0.47314

Source: *The Wall Street Journal*, Sept. 8, 1983.

less inflation than the United States, have appreciated relative to the dollar. *In fact, a foreign currency will, on average, depreciate at a percentage rate approximately equal to the amount by which its inflation rate exceeds our own.*[4]

Relative inflation rates are also reflected in interest rates. The interest rate in any country is largely determined by its inflation rate; this point was made in Chapter 5. Therefore countries currently experiencing higher rates of inflation than the United States also tend to have higher interest rates, while the reverse is true for countries with lower inflation rates.

It is tempting for the treasurer of a multinational corporation to borrow in countries with the lowest interest rates. However, this is not always the best strategy. For example, suppose interest rates in West Germany are lower than those in the United States because of Germany's lower inflation rate. A U.S. multinational firm could save interest by borrowing in Germany, but the German exchange rate can be expected to appreciate in the future, causing annual interest and principal payments on this debt to cost an increasing number of dollars over time. Thus the lower interest rate could be more than offset by losses from currency appreciation. Similarly, one should not expect multinational corporations to avoid borrowing in a country like Brazil, where interest rates are very high, because future depreciation of the Brazilian cruzeiro might well make such borrowing relatively inexpensive.

Procedures for Analyzing Potential Foreign Investments

Although the same basic principles of investment analysis apply to both foreign and domestic operations, there are some key differences. First, *cash flow analysis is much more complex for overseas investments.* Most multinational firms set up a separate subsidiary in each foreign country in which they operate. *The relevant cash flows are the dividends and royalties repatriated by each subsidiary to the parent company. These cash flows must be converted to the currency of the parent company and thus are subject to future exchange rate changes.* In other words, General Motors' German subsidiary may make a profit of 100 million marks in 1982 and again in 1983, but the value of these profits to GM will depend on the dollar/mark exchange rate: How many *dollars* is 100 million marks worth?

---

[4]This is known as the Purchasing Power Parity Theorem. Some recent studies have shown that this theorem holds quite well over the long run (5 years or more), but over the short run the relationship is much less accurate. This is because factors other than inflation are also important in the short run, especially the activities of the national governments in trying to support their exchange rates at some desired levels. Some evidence on this is given in R. Aliber and C. Stickney, "Accounting Exposures of Foreign Exchange: The Long and the Short of It," *Accounting Review*, January 1975, 44–57.

Industry Practice

The World Woos U.S. Business

When word got out that Portland, Oregon's Hyster Co. would build a $100 million factory in Europe to make materials-handling systems, representatives of various foreign governments rushed to contact the company. They wanted Hyster to know that they would not only welcome such a facility, but were prepared to offer some valuable incentives, from red-tape cutting to cash grants, to get it.

Taking into account such factors as market accessibility, economic stability, and labor quality, Hyster eventually narrowed the list of contenders to Ireland and Northern Ireland. Then, last spring, after some hard bargaining with both countries, it settled on a site near Dublin. Among the attractions: a government pledge to pick up the tab for employee training; a generous research and development grant; and a maximum income tax rate of 10 percent, guaranteed through the year 2000.

To the delight of American executives, this kind of international corporate courting is becoming increasingly popular these days. Plagued by high unemployment and troublesome trade deficits that seem to resist internal solutions, both developing and developed nations are pursuing foreign investment with unprecedented fervor.

From France and Indonesia to Luxembourg and Israel, governments are increasing their promotion budgets and fielding teams of sales representatives to hammer home the advantages of building factories, offices, and research centers within their borders. To reinforce these messages, many are offering liberal financial inducements, from land at bargain-basement prices to low-interest loans—concessions that can add millions of dollars to a company's bottom line. According to a recent study by the plant site consulting firm Fantus Co., a subsidiary of the Dun & Bradstreet Corp., such investment incentives are currently offered by at least 70 countries.

For some countries, particularly less-developed ones like India, China, and Jamaica, the wooing of American industry contrasts sharply with earlier policies that shunned multinational corporations as evil forces of economic imperialism. That's all changed now, thanks to high energy prices, a worldwide recession, and the fact that borrowed funds are now more difficult to come by and much more expensive. Rare is the political leader who does not now understand that his continued tenure in office will be affected by his country's economic health. Indian Prime Minister Indira Gandhi, who seems to have gone out of her way in the past to irritate such American companies as International Business Machines and Coca-Cola, planned her 1982 U.S. visit partly to publicize the easing of her country's investment laws. And Guinea's president, Ahmed Sékou Touré, until recently one of the world's most virulently anticapitalist rulers, appeared at a Chase Manhattan Bank forum in New York not long ago to proclaim his conversion to the ethic of private development.

Ireland, more than any other country, has helped change attitudes toward foreign investment. Once regarded by many as an industrial no-man's land, Ireland 15 years ago adopted a generous package of tax breaks and other concessions for companies willing to build or expand their facilities there. On top of its 10 percent maximum income tax rate and 100 percent training grants, the government is empowered to make capital grants of up to 50 percent of the cost of fixed assets, loan guarantees, and interest subsidies. It now devotes about 11 percent of its capital budget to this purpose.

The effort has paid off. Since 1970, American companies, ranging from Ford and General Electric to Hallmark Cards and Apple Computer, have invested about $3.6 billion in Ireland, transforming it from a predominately agricultural society into one of Europe's healthiest industrial economies. In 1981, in the face of stagnant world trade, Ireland increased exports of goods by an impressive 11 percent in real terms.

The Irish lesson has not been lost on governments elsewhere. South Korea, Greece, and South Africa, to name a few, now offer incentives that, while no match for Ireland, have attracted many corporations. A number of governments, including Turkey, Zaire, and Sri Lanka, have retained such Wall Street investment bankers as Lehman Brothers, Kuhn Loeb, and Morgan Stanley to analyze their investment appeal and develop incentive packages to overcome their weaknesses.

Others are enlisting banks and other highly visible private institutions to use their contacts and influence to intermediate with potential investors. Both Chase Manhattan and Citibank regularly organize invest-ment seminars on behalf of their client countries.

Officials of other, less-developed nations have flocked to a program organized by the United Nations that teaches them how to sell potential investors on their countries. The United Nations also provides them with an office and staff and organizes seminars.

Although some efforts have been made to catalogue various investment incentives, determining exactly which countries offer what and under what conditions is virtually impossible. It is generally agreed in the industrial development business, however, that countries tend to prefer one or more of the following five types of concessions:

1. Industrial parks are particularly common in advanced industrial countries where there is a scarcity of choice sites for free-standing plants, and in poorer sections of less-developed countries like Mexico and Jordan, where adequate roads and utilities are not always available. Some governments, like West Berlin, heavily subsidize these sites by leasing them to companies at below-market rates, while other exempt them from property taxes.

2. Cash grants, because of the cost involved, tend to be found in more-developed countries like Luxembourg, Italy, and Greece, and are often designed to overcome a liability, such as a shortage of skilled workers. Because of this, such funds are usually earmarked for specific purposes, such as training or construction in depressed areas. The Netherlands, for example, pays a fixed sum toward job education, and Northern Ireland provides grants for both training and plant construction.

3. Tax breaks can take the form of ex-

emptions, credits, or accelerated depreciation. The first is by far the most common, and, because they require little cash outlay, all are widely used by developing countries such as Jamaica, Barbados, Sri Lanka, and Egypt.

4. Loan subsidies, which include both guarantees and below-market rates, are offered mainly by moderately and highly developed countries such as Norway, Canada, and West Germany, which can afford them. Like grants, they are often earmarked for specific purposes, such as export financing or industrial machinery.

5. Training programs differ from training grants in that they are administered by the host government, which recruits, screens, and trains individual workers for industrial jobs. Except for a few states in the United States, such programs are rare.

To be sure, few such incentives are available to all comers; many are awarded on a case-by-case basis in negotiations between government and company representatives. Electronics, pharmaceutical, petrochemical, and machinery companies are in great demand, especially among the traditionally developed countries of Europe and the newly developed Asian ones like Taiwan, Hong Kong, Korea, and Singapore. Meanwhile, Malaysia, Indonesia, the Philippines, and Sri Lanka are hustling for the low-wage assembly jobs that others are losing.

Exactly what role these inducements should play is a matter of debate among experts. Some argue that executives too often let fat incentives distract them from other economic considerations.

Others, however, insist that incentives are too often ignored until late in the game, even though they can have a major impact on a project's economic viability. President Theodore Levine of New York's Development Counsellors International, which advises countries on incentive packages, points out that concessions won now may affect the bottom line for years to come, and argues that companies should put more emphasis on getting them. After all, he says, "This is a swell time to drive a bargain."

Source: Adapted from "The World Woos U.S. Business" by Niles Howard with Henriette Sendee. Reprinted with the permission of *Dun's Business Month* (formerly *Dun's Review*), November 1982. Copyright 1982, Dun & Bradstreet Publications Corporation.

Dividends and royalties are normally taxed by both foreign and domestic governments. Furthermore, a foreign government may restrict the amount of the cash flows that may be **repatriated** to the parent company. For example, some governments place a ceiling, stated as a percentage of the company's net worth, on the amount of cash dividends that may be paid by a subsidiary to its parent company. Such restrictions are normally intended to force multinational firms to reinvest earnings in the foreign country, although restrictions are sometimes imposed to prevent large currency outflows which might destabilize exchange rates.

In addition to the complexities of the cash flow analysis, *the cost of capital may be different for a foreign project than for an equivalent do-*

repatriation of earnings
Restriction on the amount of cash flows that may be directed from a foreign subsidiary to its parent company.

mestic project because foreign projects may be more or less risky. A higher risk could arise from two primary sources—(1) exchange risk and (2) sovereign risk—while a lower risk might result from international diversification.

exchange risk
The risk that the basic cash flows of a foreign project will be worth less in the parent company's home currency.

Exchange risk refers to the fact that exchange rates fluctuate. This increases the inherent uncertainty about cash flows to the parent. In other words, foreign projects have an added risk element relating to what the basic cash flows will be worth in the parent company's home currency. As we shall see later, it is often possible to "hedge" against exchange rate fluctuations, but it may not be possible to hedge completely, and, in addition, the costs of hedging must be added to the basic cost of capital.

sovereign risk
The risk of expropriation of a foreign subsidiary's assets by the host country and of unanticipated restrictions on cash flows to the parent company.

Sovereign risk refers both to the possibility of expropriation and to unanticipated restrictions of cash flows to the parent company, such as tighter controls on repatriation of earnings or higher taxes. The risk of expropriation of U.S. assets abroad is small in traditionally friendly and stable countries such as Britain or Switzerland. However, in the East European countries and in most parts of the developing world of Latin America, Africa, and the Far East, the risk may be substantial. Recent expropriations include those of ITT and Anaconda in Chile, Gulf Oil in Bolivia, Occidental Petroleum in Libya, International Petroleum in Peru, and many companies in both Cuba and Iran.

The combined impact of exchange and sovereign risks, as well as such normal risk factors as the stability and predictability of product markets, labor supplies, and governmental regulations, can be summarized as the "investment climate" of a foreign country. A survey of the investment climates in countries all over the world, which appeared in a leading Japanese business journal, is shown in Table 25-3. The countries are rated in descending order from AAA to B, in much the same way that Moody's rates corporate bonds for risk of default. These ratings, or other procedures as established by an individual multinational corporation, may be used as a basis for estimating the costs of capital for capital budgeting purposes in each country in which the firm operates.

Although exchange and sovereign risks would typically increase the cost of capital of foreign projects as compared with domestic ones, the benefits of *international diversification* may tend to lower the cost of capital for a foreign project. Operating conditions in the United States and foreign nations are not perfectly correlated—international economies are, to some extent, similar to the situation shown in Figure 16-3 in Chapter 16—so the returns on a corporation's portfolio of assets may be more stable if it is diversified internationally. More will be said about international diversification later in the chapter, but it can have the effect of holding down the cost of capital on foreign capital budgeting projects.

Table 25-3
The Risks of Foreign Investments in Various Countries

	Sociopolitical and Investment Climate	Risk Rating		Sociopolitical and Investment Climate	Risk Rating
West Germany	94	AAA	Brazil	77	BBB
United States	95	AAA	Mexico	76	BBB
Canada	91	AA	Malaysia	64	BBB
France	90	AA	Indonesia	65	BBB
Australia	83	AA	Philippines	68	BBB
Sweden	90	AA	Argentina	70	BB
Netherlands	90	AA	Chile	79	BB
Saudi Arabia	83	AA	Kenya	72	BB
Belgium	94	A	Pakistan	63	BB
Spain	83	A	South Korea	54	BB
Britain	87	A	Peru	60	BB
New Zealand	83	A	Thailand	54	BB
Italy	78	A	Egypt	30	BB
Singapore	80	BBB	India	23	B
Portugal	79	BBB			

Note: Iran was listed as an A-rated country in 1977; its rating has been lowered greatly.
Source: *Nikkei Business*, reprinted in the *Far Eastern Economic Review*, Mar. 18, 1977, 88.

An Illustration of Multinational Capital Budgeting

The principles of capital budgeting in a multinational setting can be illustrated by International Electronics Corporation's (IEC's) analysis of a proposed plant in Bratina to assemble television sets for sale in Bratina and other South American countries. If the plant is built, a new IEC subsidiary will be incorporated in Bratina. It will be financed only with common stock, all of which will be owned by the parent firm.

The cost of capital used to analyze the plant was established by the methods described in Chapter 20 and is assumed to be 15 percent. Bratina has a 20 percent corporate income tax, and there is no withholding tax on dividends paid.

While there are no restrictions on earnings repatriations, depreciation cash flows may not be repatriated except when the company is liquidated or sold. The investment, to be made in January 1986, consists almost entirely of plant and equipment, and the cost will be 50 million Bratinian cruzes. Because of the nature of the television industry and the Bratinian market, IEC bases its analysis on a time horizon of only 5 years. At the end of the 5 years (in 1990), it is assumed that the operation will have a terminal value of 25 million cruzes. Table 25-4 summarizes the projected income statements.

Table 25-4
Projected Cash Flows, 1986–1990 (Millions of Bratinian Cruzes)

	1986	1987	1988	1989	1990
Revenues	50.0	55.0	60.0	65.0	70.0
Operating cost	30.0	30.0	35.0	35.0	40.0
Depreciation	5.0	5.0	5.0	5.0	5.0
Income before tax	15.0	20.0	20.0	25.0	25.0
Bratinian tax	3.0	4.0	4.0	5.0	5.0
Net income	12.0	16.0	16.0	20.0	20.0
Earnings repatriated	12.0	16.0	16.0	20.0	20.0
U.S. tax	4.5	6.0	6.0	7.5	7.5
After-tax cash flow	7.5	10.0	10.0	12.5	12.5

The parent corporation receives a *tax credit* from the U.S. government for taxes paid by its subsidiary to the foreign government. The amount of the credit depends on the dividend payout ratio of the subsidiary. With a 100 percent payout policy, which the Bratinian subsidiary will follow, the parent corporation pays the difference between the U.S. tax rate (assumed to be 50 percent) and the Bratinian tax rate of 20 percent. Thus the U.S. tax each year amounts to an additional 30 percent of the net income for that year. For example, in the 1986 column of Table 25-4 we see that if the subsidiary earned 15 million cruzes before tax, it would pay a Bratinian tax of 20 percent, or 3 million cruzes, and a U.S. tax of $50 - 20 = 30\%$, or 4.5 million cruzes.

Since the cash flows from depreciation cannot be repatriated until the company is liquidated at the end of 1990, they will be invested in Bratinian government bonds to earn tax-exempt interest at the rate of 8 percent. The accumulated and interest-compounded depreciation

Table 25-5
Depreciation Cash Flows

Year of Depreciation	Amount (Millions of Cruzes)	Future Value Interest Factor at 8 Percent	Terminal Value in 1990 (Millions of Cruzes)
1986	5.0	1.3605	6.802
1987	5.0	1.2597	6.299
1988	5.0	1.1664	5.832
1989	5.0	1.0800	5.400
1990	5.0	1.0000	5.000
			Total 29.333

Table 25-6
Cash Flows to Parent Company and the Parent's NPV

	Cash Flows (Millions of Cruzes) (1)	Exchange Rate (2)	Cash Flows (Millions of Dollars) (3)	DF at 15 Percent (4)	PV of Cash Flows (Millions of Dollars) (5)
1986	7.500	5.00	$ 1.500	0.8696	$ 1.304
1987	10.000	5.25	1.905	0.7561	1.440
1988	10.000	5.51	1.815	0.6575	1.193
1989	12.500	5.79	2.159	0.5718	1.235
1990	66.833	6.08	10.992	0.4972	5.465

Total $10.637

Less initial investment of 50 million
cruzes at 5 cruzes per dollar =   (10.000)
NPV of project = $ 0.637

cash flow at the termination of the project is shown in Table 25-5 to be 29.333 million cruzes.

The next steps in the analysis are (1) to convert the annual cash flows from cruzes to dollars and (2) to find the net present value of the project. These steps are shown in Table 25-6. Column 1 gives the annual cash flows in cruzes. In 1986 through 1989 dividends represent the only cash flow, but the 1990 cash flow of 66.833 million cruzes consists of dividends (12.5 million cruzes), the estimated sale price of the fixed assets (25 million cruzes), and the interest-accumulated depreciation cash flows (29.333 million cruzes).

The estimated exchange rates are shown in Column 2. The current rate, 5 cruzes to the dollar, is expected to hold during 1986, but the cruze is expected to depreciate thereafter at a rate of 5 percent per year.

Dividing the cash flows in cruzes (Column 1) by the exchange rates (Column 2) gives the expected cash flows in dollars as shown in Column 3. The dollar cash flows are converted to a present value basis in Column 5, and the sum of the annual PV cash flows is $10.637 million. By subtracting the initial cost of the project, $10 million, from the PV of the inflows, we obtain the project's NPV, $637,000. Since its NPV is positive, the project should be accepted.[5]

Strategic Considerations in Analyzing Foreign Investments

Although we have emphasized the *financial* aspects of foreign investments, nonfinancial or *strategic* considerations often dominate the decision. For example, if Ford were to set up production in Peru, General

---

[5]The project's IRR is 16.9 percent, which exceeds the 15 percent cost of capital, so the IRR criterion also indicates acceptance.

Motors might feel compelled to do the same in order not to lose its position in the South American automobile market. Similarly, many U.S. companies are establishing operations in Hong Kong, not so much because of the profit prospects of a Hong Kong branch but, rather, to be in a position to move rapidly if China is opened to U.S. firms on a wide scale. Because of many unknown economic factors in foreign investment, top management may not trust the "numbers" and may decide that it simply cannot sit idly by while a major competitor expands and preempts a potentially important market. Under these circumstances financial analysis is used only as a rough screening device to eliminate ventures that are obviously unprofitable.[6]

The political ramifications of foreign investment are another strategic consideration. In recent years labor unions have increasingly opposed U.S. multinational investments abroad. The unions and their supporters in Congress claim that such investments "export" U.S. jobs and capital—U.S. citizens lose jobs to foreigners who work for U.S. subsidiaries abroad, and the outflow of U.S. dollars to finance the investments tends to weaken the dollar in foreign exchange markets. Regardless of the merits of such criticisms, a multinational corporation's management must weigh carefully the investment benefits to the company versus possible reprisals against domestic operations by labor unions or unfriendly politicians.

Sources of Funds for Foreign Investments

In the IEC example above we assumed that the foreign subsidiary would obtain all of its capital as common equity supplied by the parent. Several other sources of funds exist, including (1) sale of common stock to local residents, (2) borrowing from local banks, and (3) borrowing in world financial markets.

Selling common stock to residents of foreign countries has both advantages and disadvantages. For example, it can result in loss of control of the subsidiary if the parent company owns less than 50 percent of the shares. Some countries require majority ownership by local residents. This allows them to have some control over major decisions made by corporations operating within their boundaries, and it also enables them to retain part of the companies' profits. However, this is not necessarily bad from the point of view of the multinational corporation—local participation may be a desirable feature in countries with less stable governments, since it provides an incentive for the local res-

---

[6]See A. Yair, *The Foreign Investment Decision Process* (Boston: Harvard Business School, Division of Research, 1966); and A. Stonehill and L. Nathanson, "Capital Budgeting and the Multinational Corporation," *California Management Review*, Summer 1968. An excellent survey of motives for foreign investments may be found in G. Ragazzi, "Theories of the Determinants of Foreign Investments," *IMF Staff Papers*, March 1966.

idents to exert pressure against the threat of expropriation or other interference. Similar protection is obtained by borrowing funds in the subsidiary's country. If the subsidiary company is highly leveraged and obtains this debt from local sources, expropriation will result in only minimal losses to the parent.

Aside from protecting against expropriation, borrowing locally may be advantageous if local sources of funds in the foreign country offer attractive interest rates. In comparing foreign and domestic interest rates, however, one must be careful to take into account expected future changes in the exchange rate. As was pointed out earlier, a country with interest rates lower than those in the United States has a currency that is likely to appreciate, causing the number of dollars required to meet interest and principal payments to increase over time and to offset the lower foreign interest rate.

The decision to use local or parent country financing necessarily depends in part on projections of future trends in foreign exchange rates. Because such projections are not always accurate, using foreign debt may be more risky than using domestic debt. With the growth of multinational corporations and the uncertainties of world inflation and floating rates, corporate treasurers are making increasing use of expertise offered by commercial bankers, who make such projections and advise firms on the best way to meet their foreign currency requirements. It should come as no surprise to learn that their international divisions have been among the fastest-growing departments of the larger banks in recent years.

Management of Foreign Assets

The *Wall Street Journal* recently reported that TRW, a major aerospace and electronics conglomerate, was losing $300,000 in earnings every time the German mark moved up 1 percent against the dollar. This happened because TRW's West German subsidiary had about $30 million worth of debt denominated in marks. Since the interest and principal on the debt had to be paid in marks, a 1 percent appreciation of the mark meant that, in terms of U.S. dollars, the company had to pay more dollars to buy the marks needed to service the debt. For example, suppose the average exchange rate of marks for dollars was 0.516 dollars per mark in November, but it appreciated by 1.36 percent to 0.523 dollars per mark by December. The mark debt account of TRW would therefore appear as follows:

Month	Mark Rate ($/Mark)	Debt in Marks	Debt in Dollars
November	0.516	72,115,384	$37,211,538
December	0.523	72,115,384	37,716,346
		Increase in dollar value of debt	$ 504,808

translation gain or loss
The gain or loss resulting from translating financial statements from a foreign subsidiary's currency to the parent company's currency.

monetary assets
Assets in the form of cash, marketable securities, and accounts receivable that are held by a firm.

net monetary position
The difference between the monetary assets held by a firm and its owed money denominated in a foreign currency.

exchange rate exposure
Exposure to losses due to fluctuating exchange rates.

The increase in the dollar equivalent of foreign debt is reported as an *income loss item* under accounting standards introduced in 1981 by the Financial Accounting Standards Board (FASB #52). Such a loss is known as a **translation loss,** since it arises from "translating" financial statements from a foreign currency to U.S. dollars.[7]

Had TRW held only **monetary assets** (defined as cash, marketable securities, and accounts receivable) denominated in marks, its position would have been reversed: an appreciation of the mark would have produced a **translation gain,** while a depreciation would have led to losses. Had TRW both held monetary assets and owed money denominated in marks, then the difference between these two items would be its **net monetary position.** The net position indicates whether or not the company will have a translation gain or loss as a result of exchange rate fluctuations, that is, whether the company has **exchange rate exposure.**

Companies like TRW operate on a worldwide basis, and they have positive net monetary positions in some countries and negative positions in others. Thus TRW might have translation losses in West Germany but translation gains in other countries, and its consolidated, or corporate, position could show either a gain or a loss. *Under FASB #52, the net corporate translation gain or loss must be reported through the income statement for the period in which the exchange rate change occurs.* For firms with large foreign operations but whose subsidiaries do not operate in a self-contained manner, translation losses can significantly lower earnings per share and thus have an adverse effect on stock prices. Therefore multinational corporations have devised a number of ways to minimize the likelihood of translation losses. These techniques are discussed in the following paragraphs.

Foreign Exchange Exposure

As noted earlier, an exposure to losses due to changing exchange rates is called *exchange rate exposure.* It exists whenever the amounts of monetary assets and liabilities denominated in each foreign currency are not in exact balance. Monetary instruments like TRW's debt are obviously exposed, as are monetary assets such as cash held as marks.

---

[7]FASB #52, which is a modification of FASB #8 (1976), makes a distinction between foreign operations that are relatively complete, self-contained, and integrated into a foreign country versus foreign operations that are more in the nature of an extension of the parent's domestic operations. For self-contained subsidiaries, translation gains and losses are reported as adjustments to the equity section of the balance sheet; thus these gains and losses are not reflected in the parent's reported net income. For subsidiaries which are not self-contained, as we assume to be the case for TRW, translation gains and losses are flowed directly through to the parent's net income. This point is also discussed later in the chapter, in the section entitled "FASB #52."

Nonmonetary assets can also be exposed. For example, if the French subsidiary of Goodyear carries an inventory of tires in Paris, the dollar value of these tires could change if the French franc is depreciated. The actual change in the tires' value will depend on where they are sold and on the contracts governing these sales. If all the tires are to be shipped to the United States at a predetermined dollar price, then a French devaluation would cause no loss in real value. But if the tires are to be sold to French consumers at a fixed French franc price, the dollar value of the inventory would fall. If the sales price is not fixed, and if the weakening of the franc results in a rise in French consumer prices, then the tires may be sold at franc prices high enough to produce the same number of dollars as was anticipated before the devaluation. We see, then, that the effect of depreciation on the dollar value of nonmonetary assets is difficult to determine.

If a multinational firm's income is to be reported properly to investors, the effects of changes in the value of assets and liabilities must be analyzed properly. Yet, since it is extremely difficult to determine the effects of changes in currency values on assets such as tires, finding the proper reporting method is a complex, difficult task.

nonmonetary assets
Those assets with implied, rather than stated, monetary values, such as inventories and fixed assets.

FASB #52

In late 1981 the Financial Accounting Standards Board revised its old FASB #8, which dealt with the method of accounting for foreign currency translations, with the issuance of **FASB #52.** FASB #52 came about as a result of criticism from the business community of FASB #8, under which certain accounts such as sales were translated at current exchange rates, whereas other accounts such as cost of goods sold and depreciation were translated at the exchange rate that existed at the time inventory or fixed assets were purchased (the "historic" exchange rate). This inconsistency caused large variations in the reported income of multinational corporations whenever exchange rate fluctuations occurred, even though real economic income had not changed.

FASB #52 contains the following features:

FASB #52
The requirement of the Financial Accounting Standards Board which states that translation gains or losses must be reported at the current exchange rate for that period.

1. All translations occur at the *current exchange rate* as of the date a financial statement is prepared. Thus the term *historic exchange rate* no longer is meaningful.
2. In preparing the parent company's consolidated balance sheet, the foreign subsidiary's balance sheet (all assets and liabilities) is translated into U.S. dollars at the current exchange rate.
3. For the consolidated income statement, revenues and expenses (including the cost of goods sold) are translated at the average exchange rate that prevailed during the reporting period (for example, a quarter for a quarterly earnings report).
4. The cumulative effects of exchange rate changes on the value of a

parent company's investment in a foreign subsidiary are reported by the parent in the notes to its financial statements. For example, suppose the German subsidiary of a U.S. firm had, on January 1, 1985, (1) assets valued at 100 million dollars or 200 million marks, (2) liabilities denominated in marks with a value of 50 million dollars or 100 million marks, and (3) a net worth of 50 million dollars or 100 million marks, all based on an exchange rate of 1 dollar to 2 marks. Now suppose that during 1985 the value of the mark doubled, to 1 dollar to 1 mark. The subsidiary's new net worth, under FASB #52, would be $200 million assets − $100 million debt = $100 million net worth versus the previous $50 million. The $50 million increase in net worth would not be reported as income, but it would be reported as a note or in some other form in the 1985 annual report. Continuing, if the mark depreciated during 1986, a negative net worth effect would be shown as a note in the 1986 annual report, along with the cumulative effect of 1985 plus 1986. This cumulation would continue until the German subsidiary was liquidated or it was agreed (by the firm's management and auditors) that the valuation change was permanent.

Of course, these provisions *do not* apply to companies whose foreign operations are not conducted through fully integrated and self-contained subsidiaries. Such companies must still worry about exchange rate fluctuations causing volatility of the parent company's reported income.

hedging exchange rate exposure
The process of protecting a firm against loss due to future exchange rate changes.

Hedging Exchange Rate Exposures

Suppose the financial manager of a multinational corporation has an estimate of the firm's exchange exposure in each country in which it operates nonintegrated subsidiaries. What actions can be taken to reduce the exposure? Consider our previous example of TRW's debt of 72 million German marks. If the financial manager fears an appreciation of the mark, all of TRW's German debt could be retired and replaced by borrowing in U.S. dollars. However, this would be desirable only if dollar funds were available at acceptable interest rates. Alternatively, the financial manager could use *forward contracts* in the foreign exchange market.

In November the spot rate on marks was 0.516 dollars per mark, and the 30-day forward rate was 0.518 dollars per mark. To see how forward contracts can be used to protect against exchange rate risk, suppose that in late November TRW's financial manager is worried about the mark's appreciating by December 31. TRW could enter into a contract to buy marks on December 31 at the forward price, 0.518 dollars per mark. Suppose that by December 31 the spot price had risen to 0.523. TRW could buy marks at the contractual price of 0.518, sell them at the higher spot price of 0.523, and earn a profit of $360,577:

On December 31 the forward contract becomes due:

Buy 72,115,384 marks at the agreed-upon price of $0.518/mark	$37,355,769
Sell 72,115,384 marks at the spot price of $0.523/mark	37,716,346
Profit in dollars	360,577

This profit would largely offset the $504,808 increase in TRW's German debt as previously computed. The difference of $144,231 is TRW's *hedging cost*.

A number of other methods of hedging against losses of different types of liabilities and assets are available, but to discuss them would go well beyond the scope of this book. The important points, for our purpose, are (1) fluctuating exchange rates can cause earnings fluctuations for multinational corporations, but (2) for a price the financial manager can sometimes buy protection against this risk in the form of various types of hedges. In a world of floating exchange rates, managing assets and liabilities located all across the globe presents quite a challenge. The financial manager at corporate headquarters must not only anticipate currency realignments in each country but also coordinate hedging strategies in all these countries.

International Capital Markets

Direct foreign investment by U.S. multinational corporations is one way for U.S. citizens to invest in world markets. Another way is to purchase stocks, bonds, or various money market instruments issued in foreign countries. U.S. citizens actually do invest substantial amounts in the stocks and bonds of large corporations in Europe, and to a lesser extent in the Far East and South America. They also buy securities issued by foreign governments. Such investments in foreign capital markets are known as *portfolio investments* (and are distinguished from *direct investments* by U.S. corporations in physical assets).

Eurodollars

Whenever a U.S. dollar is placed in a time deposit in a European bank, including a European branch of a U.S. bank, a **Eurodollar** is created. For example, Eurodollars would be created if a French wine exporter received a $100,000 payment (in dollars) for a shipment to the United States and then deposited the check in a Paris bank's time deposit (rather than exchanging the dollars for francs). Eurodollars are also created when a U.S. resident places dollar time deposits in any commercial bank located in Europe.

Eurodollars are used to conduct transactions throughout Europe—indeed, throughout the world. U.S. firms, including banks, borrow in the Eurodollar market, as do Japanese, South American, and African

Eurodollar
A U.S. dollar on deposit in a foreign bank—generally, but not necessarily, a European bank.

firms. It is estimated that the total quantity of Eurodollars in 1982 approximated $300 billion, but no one knows the exact figure.

Eurodollar Interest Rates

Eurodollars are always held in interest-bearing accounts. Thus the French wine-exporting firm would receive interest on its deposit balances. The interest rate paid on these deposits depends (1) on the bank's lending rate, as the interest a bank earns on loans determines its willingness and ability to pay interest on deposits, and (2) on rates of return available on U.S. money market instruments, for if rates in the United States are above Eurodollar deposit rates, these funds will be sent back and invested in the United States, while if Eurodollar deposit rates are significantly above U.S. rates, more dollars will be sent to Europe, and this inflow will drive rates there down.

International Bond Markets

foreign bond
A bond sold by a foreign borrower but denominated in the currency of the country in which it is sold.

Eurobond
A bond sold in a country other than the one in whose currency the bond is denominated.

The Eurodollar market is essentially a short-term market—most loans and deposits are for less than one year. However, there are also two important types of international bond markets: foreign bonds and Eurobonds. **Foreign bonds** are bonds sold by a foreign borrower but denominated in the currency of the country in which the issue is sold. Examples would include a U.S. firm selling a bond denominated in Swiss francs in Switzerland, or a Canadian government bond denominated in dollars floated in the United States. The term **Eurobonds** is used to designate any bond sold in some country *other than* the one in whose currency the bond is denominated. Examples would include a British firm's issue of pound bonds sold in France, a Ford Motor Company issue denominated in dollars and sold in West Germany, or a German firm's sale of mark bonds in Switzerland.

Over half of all Eurobonds are denominated in dollars; bonds in German marks and Dutch guilders account for most of the rest. Although centered in Europe, Eurobonds are truly international. Their underwriting syndicates include investment bankers from all parts of the world, and the bonds are sold to investors not only in Europe but also in such faraway places as Bahrain and Singapore. Thus multinational corporations, together with international financial institutions and national governments, play an important role in mobilizing capital in all parts of the world to finance production and economic growth. For better or for worse, this has resulted in great interdependence among world economies.

Summary

As the world economy becomes more integrated, the role of multinational firms is ever increasing, and new companies are joining the ranks of the multinationals every day. Although the same basic principles of financial management apply to multinational corporations as to domestic ones, the financial manager of a multinational firm faces a much more complex task. The primary problem, from a financial standpoint, is the fact that cash flows must cross national boundaries. These flows may be constrained in various ways, and, equally important, their value in dollars may rise or fall depending on exchange rate fluctuations. This means that the multinational manager must be constantly aware of the many complex interactions among national economies and the effects of these interactions on multinational operations.

World capital markets allow people from different countries to invest in the productive resources of other countries. U.S. citizens buy the stocks and bonds of foreign corporations, and foreigners in turn buy U.S. securities. More efficient investments are possible for everyone due to the diversification opportunities offered through these markets.

Because of the central role of the U.S. dollar in international commerce, large markets have developed for U.S. dollar deposits (Eurodollars) and dollar-denominated bonds (Eurobonds) in Europe and Asia. These markets represent important sources of capital for multinational corporations.

Financial management in a multinational firm is both important and challenging. The risks of international operations are high, but so are the potential rewards. In a world economy that grows more interdependent each year, the multinational manager can look forward to an ever-expanding role in corporate decision making.

Resolution to Decision in Finance

Sri Lanka: Playing the Incentive Game

In the beginning, the Greater Colombo Economic Commission's task of attracting foreign investment to Sri Lanka was indeed formidable. One of its biggest challenges was to persuade businesspeople that the new government was trustworthy, stable, and eager to help. To reassure businesses that their investments are safe, the GCEC publicizes the fact that the rights of foreign investors are guaranteed in Sri Lanka's constitution so that even if the government changes, the policy endures.

In addition, the GCEC tries to overcome investors' fears of government intervention and delay by constantly demonstrating its ability to insulate investors from bureaucracy. During delicate investment negotiations, GCEC representatives make on-the-spot decisions and answer right away, instead of asking for postponements to consult with their home government.

Such tactics have gained the Sri Lankans great respect in the international business community. Says Tony Braughton, Motorola's regional director for Asia, "In our negotiations, we were very impressed with the GCEC people. They think like businessmen. And they do their homework well. They understand that each additional cost, even one cent, makes you that much less competitive."

In fact, Motorola was so impressed with the GCEC that it built a $22 million factory in Sri Lanka. According to Braughton, the country's incentives were "among the best in the world." They included unlimited repatriation of profits, freedom from restrictions on equity, tax holidays for a minimum of seven years, and government training for workers.

Sri Lankan officials are also pleased with the way their program is working. Prior to Jayawardene's election, unemployment was more than 20 percent, and there was only slight economic growth. By 1982, unemployment was down to 13 percent. Furthermore, in the four years between 1978 and 1981, real growth averaged an impressive 6.5 percent. This turnabout was due primarily to the government's decision to cut taxes and import duties and to redirect subsidies from consumers to producers, most notably by ending subsidized food rations for everybody. The major contribution of foreign investment has been in generating employment—23,000 jobs directly and hundreds, if not thousands, more indirectly.

Consultants, such as Sam Passow of Business International, describe Sri Lanka's incentives as exceedingly generous. But the Sri Lankans do not feel they are giving anything away blindly. "They know how much foreign investment can do for a country," says Braughton. "The spin-offs are enormous. The incentives are just practical."

Source: Adapted from "Sri Lanka's Turnaround: How One Country Plays the Incentive Game." Reprinted with the permission of *Dun's Business Month* (formerly *Dun's Review*), November 1982. Copyright 1982, Dun & Bradstreet Publications Corporation.

Key Terms You should be able to define each of the following terms:

Multinational corporation; parent company
Exchange rate; fixed exchange rate system; floating exchange rate; managed floating system

Repatriation of earnings
Exchange risk; sovereign risk
Translation gain or loss; exchange rate exposure; FASB #52

Deficit trade balance
Devaluation; revaluation
Spot rate; forward exchange rate
Premium on forward rate; discount
   on forward rate

Monetary assets; nonmonetary
   assets; net monetary position
Hedging exchange rate exposures
Eurodollar; foreign bond; Eurobond

Questions

25-1 Under the fixed exchange rate system, what was the currency against which all other currency values were defined?

25-2 Exchange rates fluctuate under both the fixed exchange rate and floating exchange rate systems. What, then, is the difference between the two systems?

25-3 If the French franc depreciates against the U.S. dollar, can a dollar buy more or fewer French francs as a result?

25-4 If the United States imports more goods from abroad than it exports, foreigners will tend to have a surplus of U.S. dollars. What will this do to the value of the dollar with respect to foreign currencies? What is the corresponding effect on foreign investments in the United States?

25-5 Why do U.S. corporations build manufacturing plants abroad when they could build them at home?

25-6 Most firms require higher rates of return on foreign projects than on identical projects located at home. Why?

25-7 What is a Eurodollar? If a French citizen deposits $10,000 in Chase Manhattan Bank in New York, have Eurodollars been created? What if the deposit is made in Barclay's Bank in London? Chase Manhattan's Paris branch?

25-8 Explain how, under FASB #52, the financial statements of foreign subsidiaries are consolidated into the statements of their U.S. parent companies. What effect does the method used to translate foreign currencies into U.S. dollars have on the parent's reported net income?

Problems

* **25-1** If British pounds sell for $1.70 (U.S.) per pound, what should dollars sell for in pounds per dollar?

* **25-2** Suppose 1 French franc could be purchased in the foreign exchange market for 20 U.S. cents today. If the franc appreciated 10 percent tomorrow against the dollar, how many francs would a dollar buy tomorrow?

* **25-3** In March 1984 the exchange rate between U.S. dollars and the French franc was fr. 8 = $1, and the exchange rate between the dollar and British pound was £1 = $1.50. What was the exchange rate between francs and pounds?

25-4 Look up the same three currencies in the foreign exchange section of a current issue of the *Wall Street Journal*. What is the current exchange rate between francs and pounds?

---

*Refer to Appendix E for check answers to problems with asterisks.

25-5 Table 25-1 lists foreign exchange rates for September 8, 1983. On that day how many dollars would be required to purchase 1,000 units of each of the following: Indian rupees, Italian lira, Mexican pesos, and Saudi Arabian riyals?

25-6 Look up the same four currencies in the foreign exchange section of a current issue of the *Wall Street Journal*.

  a. What is the current exchange rate for changing dollars into 1,000 units of rupees, lira, pesos, and riyals?

  b. What is the percentage gain or loss between the September 8, 1983 exchange rate and the current exchange rate for each of the currencies in Part a?

25-7 New York Imports, Inc. has agreed to buy 12,000 cases of French wine for 10 million francs at today's spot rate. The firm's financial manager, Frank O'File, has noted the current spot and forward rates given below:

	U.S. Dollar/Franc	Franc/U.S. Dollar
Spot	.1250	8.0000
30-day forward	.1243	8.0450
60-day forward	.1229	8.1400
90-day forward	.1212	8.2500

On the same day Mr. O'File agrees to purchase 12,000 more cases of wine in 3 months at the same price of 10 million francs.

  * **a.** What is the price of the wine, in U.S. dollars, if it is purchased at today's spot rate?

  * **b.** What is the cost, in dollars, of the second 12,000 cases if payment is made in 90 days and the spot rate at that time equals today's 90-day forward rate?

  c. If Mr. O'File is concerned with the dollar losing value relative to the franc in the next 90 days, what can he do to reduce his exposure to exchange risk?

  d. If he does not hedge his exposure to exchange risk, and the exchange rate for the French franc is 7.77 to $1 in 90 days, how much will he have to pay for the wine (in dollars)?

* **25-8** After all foreign and U.S. taxes, a U.S. corporation expects to receive 2 pounds of dividends per share from a British subsidiary this year. The exchange rate at the end of the year is expected to be $1.80 per pound, and the pound is expected to depreciate 5 percent against the dollar each year for an indefinite period. The dividend (in pounds) is expected to grow at 10 percent a year indefinitely. The parent U.S. corporation owns 10 million shares of the subsidiary. What is the present value of its equity ownership of the subsidiary? Assume a cost of equity capital of 12 percent for the subsidiary.

25-9 You are the financial vice president of International Widgets, Inc., headquartered in Miami, Florida. All shareholders of International Widgets live in the United States. Earlier this month you obtained a loan of 10 million Canadian dollars from a bank in Toronto to finance the construction of a new plant in Montreal. At the time the loan was received, the exchange rate was 78 U.S. cents to the Canadian dollar. By the end of the month it has unexpectedly dropped to 74 cents. Has your company made a gain or loss as a result, and by how much?

25-10 The Smith-Capone Corporation of Chicago manufactures typewriters for the world market. In early 1984 the company's board of directors requests the international planning department of the company to evaluate a proposal for setting up a wholly owned subsidiary in Paralivia, a country of 50 million people in South America. The subsidiary will make typewriters for the Paralivian market. Paralivia is a rapidly developing country which has effectively invested its rich oil revenues to support a growing industrial economy. Currently it imports all of its typewriters from abroad, and Smith-Capone is expected to capture a large portion of this market.

Political sentiment in Paralivia regarding foreign investments has been somewhat lukewarm because such investments have overtones of foreign economic control. Not long ago the government passed a law requiring all foreign investments to pass to local ownership after 6 years or less. Paralivia recently adopted a parliamentary system of government after 20 years of military dictatorship under General Francisco, but the transition of power was peaceful. Gordon Lidder, chairman of the board of Smith-Capone, has expressed concern about the stability of the new government, but "usually reliable" CIA sources indicate that the government has popular support and is unlikely to be toppled for at least 5 to 10 years.

The following financial information on the proposed project is available:

Paralivian currency: Because the inflation rate in Paralivia is about 5 percent higher than that in the United States, the Paralivian *ringo* is expected to depreciate relative to the dollar by about 5 percent a year. In 1985, when the investment will be made, the exchange rate is expected to be 2 ringos per dollar.

Investment: The estimated investment to be made in 1985 is 60 million ringos in inventory, plant, and equipment. The parent corporation, Smith-Capone, will provide all the capital in the form of equity in the subsidiary. The project will begin to generate earnings in 1986. At the end of 6 years (in 1991) all plant and equipment will be sold to the Paralivian government for 20 million ringos. This amount of money, plus all accumulated cash, will be repatriated as a liquidating dividend.

Repatriation: Only dividends may be repatriated by the subsidiary to the parent company. Cash flows from depreciation may not be repatriated except as part of the liquidating dividend in 1991. However, these cash flows can, in the meantime, be invested in local money market instruments to yield a 15 percent tax-free return.

Taxes: The Paralivian corporate income tax rate is 25 percent. There is also a 10 percent withholding tax on dividends. The U.S. tax rate is 50 percent on the gross earnings of the foreign subsidiary. However, the parent company gets a tax credit for taxes already paid to foreign governments. In the case of the liquidating dividend, the tax treatment is quite different. The Paralivian government will not tax this dividend. Smith-Capone has obtained a ruling from the Internal Revenue Service of the United States that the liquidating dividend will not be taxed by the U.S. government either.

Cost of capital: Based on the sovereign and exchange risk characteristics of Paralivia, Smith-Capone gives Paralivia a BB rating and requires a rate of return of 20 percent on equity.

Projected demand, costs, and exchange rates:

Year	Demand for Typewriters (Thousands)	Price (Ringos)	Unit Variable Operating Cost (Ringos)	Exchange Rate (Ringos per Dollar)
1986	50	1,000	400	2.1
1987	55	1,000	420	2.2
1988	60	1,100	440	2.3
1989	70	1,100	460	2.4
1990	80	1,200	490	2.5
1991	90	1,200	540	2.6

Fixed cost: Depreciation expense is 10 million ringos per year. Consider this to be the only fixed cost of the project.

Use the information given above to answer the following questions:
a. Excluding the liquidating dividend, what is the estimated after-tax dividend received by the parent company each year?
b. What is the estimated liquidating dividend? (Remember that blocked depreciation flows are reinvested at 15 percent.)
c. What is your recommendation for the project? (Consider its NPV and specify any other relevant considerations.)

Selected References

Useful texts and other books that describe international financial management in some detail include, among others, the following:

Aggarwal, Raj Kumar, *The Management of Foreign Exchange: Optimal Policies of a Multinational Company* (New York: Arno, 1980).

Aliber, Robert Z., *Exchange Risk and Corporate International Finance* (New York: Wiley, 1978).

Eiteman, David K., and Arthur I. Stonehill, *Multinational Business Finance* (Reading, MA: Addison-Wesley, 1979).

Lessard, Donald R., ed., *International Financial Management, Theory and Application* (New York: Warren, Gorham & Lamont, 1979).

Rodriguez, Rita M., and E. Eugene Carter, *International Financial Management* (Englewood Cliffs, NJ: Prentice-Hall, 1979).

For more on capital budgeting by multinational firms, see:
Oblak, David J., and Roy J. Helm, Jr., "Survey and Analysis of Capital Bud-

geting Methods Used by Multinationals," *Financial Management*, Winter 1980, 37–41.

Shapiro, Alan C., "Capital Budgeting for the Multinational Corporation," *Financial Management*, Spring 1978, 7–16.

Papers dealing with exchange rate risk include the following:

Calderon-Rossell, Jorge R., "Covering Foreign Exchange Risks of Single Transactions," *Financial Management*, Autumn 1979, 78–85.

Eaker, Mark R., "Covering Foreign Exchange Risks: Comment," *Financial Management*, Winter 1980, 64–65.

Feiger, George, and Bertrand Jacquillat, "Currency Option Bonds, Puts and Calls on Spot Exchange and the Hedging of Contingent Foreign Earnings," *Journal of Finance*, December 1979, 1129–1139.

Goodman, Stephen H., "Foreign Exchange-Rate Forecasting Techniques: Implications for Business and Policy," *Journal of Finance*, May 1979, 415–427.

Regarding decisions as to the use of financing outside the parent company's home country, see:

Eaker, Mark R., "Denomination Decision for Multinational Transactions," *Financial Management*, Autumn 1980, 23–29.

Folks, William R., Jr., and Ramesh Advani, "Raising Funds with Foreign Currency," *Financial Executive*, February 1980, 44–49.

Severn, Alan K., and David R. Meinster, "The Use of Multicurrency Financing by the Financial Manager," *Financial Management*, Winter 1978, 45–53.

Other recent works of interest include these:

Elliott, J. W., "The Expected Return to Equity and International Asset Prices," *Journal of Financial and Quantitative Analysis*, December 1978, 987–1002.

Meadows, Edward, "How the Euromarket Fends Off Global Disaster," *Fortune*, Sept. 24, 1979, 122–135.

Shapiro, Alan C., "Financial Structure and Cost of Capital in the Multinational Corporation," *Journal of Financial and Quantitative Analysis*, June 1978, 211–226.

Appendixes

Appendix A*

interest factors

Future Value of $1 at the End of n Periods: IF = (1 + k)ⁿ

Future Value of \$1 at the End of n Periods: $IF = (1 + k)^n$

Period	1%	2%	3%	4%	5%	6%	7%	8%	9%	10%
1	1.0100	1.0200	1.0300	1.0400	1.0500	1.0600	1.0700	1.0800	1.0900	1.1000
2	1.0201	1.0404	1.0609	1.0816	1.1025	1.1236	1.1449	1.1664	1.1881	1.2100
3	1.0303	1.0612	1.0927	1.1249	1.1576	1.1910	1.2250	1.2597	1.2950	1.3310
4	1.0406	1.0824	1.1255	1.1699	1.2155	1.2625	1.3108	1.3605	1.4116	1.4641
5	1.0510	1.1041	1.1593	1.2167	1.2763	1.3382	1.4026	1.4693	1.5386	1.6105
6	1.0615	1.1262	1.1941	1.2653	1.3401	1.4185	1.5007	1.5869	1.6771	1.7716
7	1.0721	1.1487	1.2299	1.3159	1.4071	1.5036	1.6058	1.7138	1.8280	1.9487
8	1.0829	1.1717	1.2668	1.3686	1.4775	1.5938	1.7182	1.8509	1.9926	2.1436
9	1.0937	1.1951	1.3048	1.4233	1.5513	1.6895	1.8385	1.9990	2.1719	2.3579
10	1.1046	1.2190	1.3439	1.4802	1.6289	1.7908	1.9672	2.1589	2.3674	2.5937
11	1.1157	1.2434	1.3842	1.5395	1.7103	1.8983	2.1049	2.3316	2.5804	2.8531
12	1.1268	1.2682	1.4258	1.6010	1.7959	2.0122	2.2522	2.5182	2.8127	3.1384
13	1.1381	1.2936	1.4685	1.6651	1.8856	2.1329	2.4098	2.7196	3.0658	3.4523
14	1.1495	1.3195	1.5126	1.7317	1.9799	2.2609	2.5785	2.9372	3.3417	3.7975
15	1.1610	1.3459	1.5580	1.8009	2.0789	2.3966	2.7590	3.1722	3.6425	4.1772
16	1.1726	1.3728	1.6047	1.8730	2.1829	2.5404	2.9522	3.4259	3.9703	4.5950
17	1.1843	1.4002	1.6528	1.9479	2.2920	2.6928	3.1588	3.7000	4.3276	5.0545
18	1.1961	1.4282	1.7024	2.0258	2.4066	2.8543	3.3799	3.9960	4.7171	5.5599
19	1.2081	1.4568	1.7535	2.1068	2.5270	3.0256	3.6165	4.3157	5.1417	6.1159
20	1.2202	1.4859	1.8061	2.1911	2.6533	3.2071	3.8697	4.6610	5.6044	6.7275
21	1.2324	1.5157	1.8603	2.2788	2.7860	3.3996	4.1406	5.0338	6.1088	7.4002
22	1.2447	1.5460	1.9161	2.3699	2.9253	3.6035	4.4304	5.4365	6.6586	8.1403
23	1.2572	1.5769	1.9736	2.4647	3.0715	3.8197	4.7405	5.8715	7.2579	8.9543
24	1.2697	1.6084	2.0328	2.5633	3.2251	4.0489	5.0724	6.3412	7.9111	9.8497
25	1.2824	1.6406	2.0938	2.6658	3.3864	4.2919	5.4274	6.8485	8.6231	10.834
26	1.2953	1.6734	2.1566	2.7725	3.5557	4.5494	5.8074	7.3964	9.3992	11.918
27	1.3082	1.7069	2.2213	2.8834	3.7335	4.8223	6.2139	7.9881	10.245	13.110
28	1.3213	1.7410	2.2879	2.9987	3.9201	5.1117	6.6488	8.6271	11.167	14.421
29	1.3345	1.7758	2.3566	3.1187	4.1161	5.4184	7.1143	9.3173	12.172	15.863
30	1.3478	1.8114	2.4273	3.2434	4.3219	5.7435	7.6123	10.062	13.267	17.449
40	1.4889	2.2080	3.2620	4.8010	7.0400	10.285	14.974	21.724	31.409	45.259
50	1.6446	2.6916	4.3839	7.1067	11.467	18.420	29.457	46.901	74.357	117.39
60	1.8167	3.2810	5.8916	10.519	18.679	32.987	57.946	101.25	176.03	304.48

*Appendix A corresponds to Table A-3 on the laminated card inserted in the book. In the equation in Appendix A, IF means the same as FVIF$_{k,n}$ on the insert card.

Period	12%	14%	15%	16%	18%	20%	24%	28%	32%	36%
1	1.1200	1.1400	1.1500	1.1600	1.1800	1.2000	1.2400	1.2800	1.3200	1.3600
2	1.2544	1.2996	1.3225	1.3456	1.3924	1.4400	1.5376	1.6384	1.7424	1.8496
3	1.4049	1.4815	1.5209	1.5609	1.6430	1.7280	1.9066	2.0972	2.3000	2.5155
4	1.5735	1.6890	1.7490	1.8106	1.9388	2.0736	2.3642	2.6844	3.0360	3.4210
5	1.7623	1.9254	2.0114	2.1003	2.2878	2.4883	2.9316	3.4360	4.0075	4.6526
6	1.9738	2.1950	2.3131	2.4364	2.6996	2.9860	3.6352	4.3980	5.2899	6.3275
7	2.2107	2.5023	2.6600	2.8262	3.1855	3.5832	4.5077	5.6295	6.9826	8.6054
8	2.4760	2.8526	3.0590	3.2784	3.7589	4.2998	5.5895	7.2058	9.2170	11.703
9	2.7731	3.2519	3.5179	3.8030	4.4355	5.1598	6.9310	9.2234	12.166	15.916
10	3.1058	3.7072	4.0456	4.4114	5.2338	6.1917	8.5944	11.805	16.059	21.646
11	3.4785	4.2262	4.6524	5.1173	6.1759	7.4301	10.657	15.111	21.198	29.439
12	3.8960	4.8179	5.3502	5.9360	7.2876	8.9161	13.214	19.342	27.982	40.037
13	4.3635	5.4924	6.1528	6.8858	8.5994	10.699	16.386	24.758	36.937	54.451
14	4.8871	6.2613	7.0757	7.9875	10.147	12.839	20.319	31.691	48.756	74.053
15	5.4736	7.1379	8.1371	9.2655	11.973	15.407	25.195	40.564	64.358	100.71
16	6.1304	8.1372	9.3576	10.748	14.129	18.488	31.242	51.923	84.953	136.96
17	6.8660	9.2765	10.761	12.467	16.672	22.186	38.740	66.461	112.13	186.27
18	7.6900	10.575	12.375	14.462	19.673	26.623	48.038	85.070	148.02	253.33
19	8.6128	12.055	14.231	16.776	23.214	31.948	59.567	108.89	195.39	344.53
20	9.6463	13.743	16.366	19.460	27.393	38.337	73.864	139.37	257.91	468.57
21	10.803	15.667	18.821	22.574	32.323	46.005	91.591	178.40	340.44	637.26
22	12.100	17.861	21.644	26.186	38.142	55.206	113.57	228.35	449.39	866.67
23	13.552	20.361	24.891	30.376	45.007	66.247	140.83	292.30	593.19	1178.6
24	15.178	23.212	28.625	35.236	53.108	79.496	174.63	374.14	783.02	1602.9
25	17.000	26.461	32.918	40.874	62.668	95.396	216.54	478.90	1033.5	2180.0
26	19.040	30.166	37.856	47.414	73.948	114.47	268.51	612.99	1364.3	2964.9
27	21.324	34.389	43.535	55.000	87.259	137.37	332.95	784.63	1800.9	4032.2
28	23.883	39.204	50.065	63.800	102.96	164.84	412.86	1004.3	2377.2	5483.8
29	26.749	44.693	57.575	74.008	121.50	197.81	511.95	1285.5	3137.9	7458.0
30	29.959	50.950	66.211	85.849	143.37	237.37	634.81	1645.5	4142.0	10143.
40	93.050	188.88	267.86	378.72	750.37	1469.7	5455.9	19426.	66520.	*
50	289.00	700.23	1083.6	1670.7	3927.3	9100.4	46890.	*	*	*
60	897.59	2595.9	4383.9	7370.1	20555.	56347.	*	*	*	*

*IF > 99,999.

Appendix B*

Present Value of $1: DF = $1/(1 + k)^n$

Period	1%	2%	3%	4%	5%	6%	7%	8%	9%	10%
1	.9901	.9804	.9709	.9615	.9524	.9434	.9346	.9259	.9174	.9091
2	.9803	.9612	.9426	.9246	.9070	.8900	.8734	.8573	.8417	.8264
3	.9706	.9423	.9151	.8890	.8638	.8396	.8163	.7938	.7722	.7513
4	.9610	.9238	.8885	.8548	.8227	.7921	.7629	.7350	.7084	.6830
5	.9515	.9057	.8626	.8219	.7835	.7473	.7130	.6806	.6499	.6209
6	.9420	.8880	.8375	.7903	.7462	.7050	.6663	.6302	.5963	.5645
7	.9327	.8706	.8131	.7599	.7107	.6651	.6227	.5835	.5470	.5132
8	.9235	.8535	.7894	.7307	.6768	.6274	.5820	.5403	.5019	.4665
9	.9143	.8368	.7664	.7026	.6446	.5919	.5439	.5002	.4604	.4241
10	.9053	.8203	.7441	.6756	.6139	.5584	.5083	.4632	.4224	.3855
11	.8963	.8043	.7224	.6496	.5847	.5268	.4751	.4289	.3875	.3505
12	.8874	.7885	.7014	.6246	.5568	.4970	.4440	.3971	.3555	.3186
13	.8787	.7730	.6810	.6006	.5303	.4688	.4150	.3677	.3262	.2897
14	.8700	.7579	.6611	.5775	.5051	.4423	.3878	.3405	.2992	.2633
15	.8613	.7430	.6419	.5553	.4810	.4173	.3624	.3152	.2745	.2394
16	.8528	.7284	.6232	.5339	.4581	.3936	.3387	.2919	.2519	.2176
17	.8444	.7142	.6050	.5134	.4363	.3714	.3166	.2703	.2311	.1978
18	.8360	.7002	.5874	.4936	.4155	.3503	.2959	.2502	.2120	.1799
19	.8277	.6864	.5703	.4746	.3957	.3305	.2765	.2317	.1945	.1635
20	.8195	.6730	.5537	.4564	.3769	.3118	.2584	.2145	.1784	.1486
21	.8114	.6598	.5375	.4388	.3589	.2942	.2415	.1987	.1637	.1351
22	.8034	.6468	.5219	.4220	.3418	.2775	.2257	.1839	.1502	.1228
23	.7954	.6342	.5067	.4057	.3256	.2618	.2109	.1703	.1378	.1117
24	.7876	.6217	.4919	.3901	.3101	.2470	.1971	.1577	.1264	.1015
25	.7798	.6095	.4776	.3751	.2953	.2330	.1842	.1460	.1160	.0923
26	.7720	.5976	.4637	.3607	.2812	.2198	.1722	.1352	.1064	.0839
27	.7644	.5859	.4502	.3468	.2678	.2074	.1609	.1252	.0976	.0763
28	.7568	.5744	.4371	.3335	.2551	.1956	.1504	.1159	.0895	.0693
29	.7493	.5631	.4243	.3207	.2429	.1846	.1406	.1073	.0822	.0630
30	.7419	.5521	.4120	.3083	.2314	.1741	.1314	.0994	.0754	.0573
35	.7059	.5000	.3554	.2534	.1813	.1301	.0937	.0676	.0490	.0356
40	.6717	.4529	.3066	.2083	.1420	.0972	.0668	.0460	.0318	.0221
45	.6391	.4102	.2644	.1712	.1113	.0727	.0476	.0313	.0207	.0137
50	.6080	.3715	.2281	.1407	.0872	.0543	.0339	.0213	.0134	.0085
55	.5785	.3365	.1968	.1157	.0683	.0406	.0242	.0145	.0087	.0053

*Appendix B corresponds to Table A-1 on the laminated card inserted in the book. In the equation in Appendix B, DF means the same as $PVIF_{k,n}$ on the insert card.

Period	12%	14%	15%	16%	18%	20%	24%	28%	32%	36%
1	.8929	.8772	.8696	.8621	.8475	.8333	.8065	.7813	.7576	.7353
2	.7972	.7695	.7561	.7432	.7182	.6944	.6504	.6104	.5739	.5407
3	.7118	.6750	.6575	.6407	.6086	.5787	.5245	.4768	.4348	.3975
4	.6355	.5921	.5718	.5523	.5158	.4823	.4230	.3725	.3294	.2923
5	.5674	.5194	.4972	.4761	.4371	.4019	.3411	.2910	.2495	.2149
6	.5066	.4556	.4323	.4104	.3704	.3349	.2751	.2274	.1890	.1580
7	.4523	.3996	.3759	.3538	.3139	.2791	.2218	.1776	.1432	.1162
8	.4039	.3506	.3269	.3050	.2660	.2326	.1789	.1388	.1085	.0854
9	.3606	.3075	.2843	.2630	.2255	.1938	.1443	.1084	.0822	.0628
10	.3220	.2697	.2472	.2267	.1911	.1615	.1164	.0847	.0623	.0462
11	.2875	.2366	.2149	.1954	.1619	.1346	.0938	.0662	.0472	.0340
12	.2567	.2076	.1869	.1685	.1372	.1122	.0757	.0517	.0357	.0250
13	.2292	.1821	.1625	.1452	.1163	.0935	.0610	.0404	.0271	.0184
14	.2046	.1597	.1413	.1252	.0985	.0779	.0492	.0316	.0205	.0135
15	.1827	.1401	.1229	.1079	.0835	.0649	.0397	.0247	.0155	.0099
16	.1631	.1229	.1069	.0930	.0708	.0541	.0320	.0193	.0118	.0073
17	.1456	.1078	.0929	.0802	.0600	.0451	.0258	.0150	.0089	.0054
18	.1300	.0946	.0808	.0691	.0508	.0376	.0208	.0118	.0068	.0039
19	.1161	.0829	.0703	.0596	.0431	.0313	.0168	.0092	.0051	.0029
20	.1037	.0728	.0611	.0514	.0365	.0261	.0135	.0072	.0039	.0021
21	.0926	.0638	.0531	.0443	.0309	.0217	.0109	.0056	.0029	.0016
22	.0826	.0560	.0462	.0382	.0262	.0181	.0088	.0044	.0022	.0012
23	.0738	.0491	.0402	.0329	.0222	.0151	.0071	.0034	.0017	.0008
24	.0659	.0431	.0349	.0284	.0188	.0126	.0057	.0027	.0013	.0006
25	.0588	.0378	.0304	.0245	.0160	.0105	.0046	.0021	.0010	.0005
26	.0525	.0331	.0264	.0211	.0135	.0087	.0037	.0016	.0007	.0003
27	.0469	.0291	.0230	.0182	.0115	.0073	.0030	.0013	.0006	.0002
28	.0419	.0255	.0200	.0157	.0097	.0061	.0024	.0010	.0004	.0002
29	.0374	.0224	.0174	.0135	.0082	.0051	.0020	.0008	.0003	.0001
30	.0334	.0196	.0151	.0116	.0070	.0042	.0016	.0006	.0002	.0001
35	.0189	.0102	.0075	.0055	.0030	.0017	.0005	.0002	.0001	*
40	.0107	.0053	.0037	.0026	.0013	.0007	.0002	.0001	*	*
45	.0061	.0027	.0019	.0013	.0006	.0003	.0001	*	*	*
50	.0035	.0014	.0009	.0006	.0003	.0001	*	*	*	*
55	.0020	.0007	.0005	.0003	.0001	*	*	*	*	*

*The factor is zero to four decimal places.

Appendix C*

Sum of an Annuity of \$1 per Period for n Periods: $\text{IFa} = \sum_{t=1}^{n} (1 + k)^{n-t} = \dfrac{(1 + k)^n - 1}{k}$

Number of Periods	1%	2%	3%	4%	5%	6%	7%	8%	9%	10%
1	1.0000	1.0000	1.0000	1.0000	1.0000	1.0000	1.0000	1.0000	1.0000	1.0000
2	2.0100	2.0200	2.0300	2.0400	2.0500	2.0600	2.0700	2.0800	2.0900	2.1000
3	3.0301	3.0604	3.0909	3.1216	3.1525	3.1836	3.2149	3.2464	3.2781	3.3100
4	4.0604	4.1216	4.1836	4.2465	4.3101	4.3746	4.4399	4.5061	4.5731	4.6410
5	5.1010	5.2040	5.3091	5.4163	5.5256	5.6371	5.7507	5.8666	5.9847	6.1051
6	6.1520	6.3081	6.4684	6.6330	6.8019	6.9753	7.1533	7.3359	7.5233	7.7156
7	7.2135	7.4343	7.6625	7.8983	8.1420	8.3938	8.6540	8.9228	9.2004	9.4872
8	8.2857	8.5830	8.8923	9.2142	9.5491	9.8975	10.259	10.636	11.028	11.435
9	9.3685	9.7546	10.159	10.582	11.026	11.491	11.978	12.487	13.021	13.579
10	10.462	10.949	11.463	12.006	12.577	13.180	13.816	14.486	15.192	15.937
11	11.566	12.168	12.807	13.486	14.206	14.971	15.783	16.645	17.560	18.531
12	12.682	13.412	14.192	15.025	15.917	16.869	17.888	18.977	20.140	21.384
13	13.809	14.680	15.617	16.626	17.713	18.882	20.140	21.495	22.953	24.522
14	14.947	15.973	17.086	18.291	19.598	21.015	22.550	24.214	26.019	27.975
15	16.096	17.293	18.598	20.023	21.578	23.276	25.129	27.152	29.360	31.772
16	17.257	18.639	20.156	21.824	23.657	25.672	27.888	30.324	33.003	35.949
17	18.430	20.012	21.761	23.697	25.840	28.212	30.840	33.750	36.973	40.544
18	19.614	21.412	23.414	25.645	28.132	30.905	33.999	37.450	41.301	45.599
19	20.810	22.840	25.116	27.671	30.539	33.760	37.379	41.446	46.018	51.159
20	22.019	24.297	26.870	29.778	33.066	36.785	40.995	45.762	51.160	57.275
21	23.239	25.783	28.676	31.969	35.719	39.992	44.865	50.422	56.764	64.002
22	24.471	27.299	30.536	34.248	38.505	43.392	49.005	55.456	62.873	71.402
23	25.716	28.845	32.452	36.617	41.430	46.995	53.436	60.893	69.531	79.543
24	26.973	30.421	34.426	39.082	44.502	50.815	58.176	66.764	76.789	88.497
25	28.243	32.030	36.459	41.645	47.727	54.864	63.249	73.105	84.700	98.347
26	29.525	33.670	38.553	44.311	51.113	59.156	68.676	79.954	93.323	109.18
27	30.820	35.344	40.709	47.084	54.669	63.705	74.483	87.350	102.72	121.09
28	32.129	37.051	42.930	49.967	58.402	68.528	80.697	95.338	112.96	134.20
29	33.450	38.792	45.218	52.966	62.322	73.639	87.346	103.96	124.13	148.63
30	34.784	40.568	47.575	56.084	66.438	79.058	94.460	113.28	136.30	164.49
40	48.886	60.402	75.401	95.025	120.79	154.76	199.63	259.05	337.88	442.59
50	64.463	84.579	112.79	152.66	209.34	290.33	406.52	573.76	815.08	1163.9
60	81.669	114.05	163.05	237.99	353.58	533.12	813.52	1253.2	1944.7	3034.8

*Appendix C corresponds to Table A-4 on the laminated card inserted in the book. In the equation in Appendix C, IFa means the same as $\text{FVIFA}_{k,n}$ on the insert card.

Number of Periods	12%	14%	15%	16%	18%	20%	24%	28%	32%	36%
1	1.0000	1.0000	1.0000	1.0000	1.0000	1.0000	1.0000	1.0000	1.0000	1.0000
2	2.1200	2.1400	2.1500	2.1600	2.1800	2.2000	2.2400	2.2800	2.3200	2.3600
3	3.3744	3.4396	3.4725	3.5056	3.5724	3.6400	3.7776	3.9184	4.0624	4.2096
4	4.7793	4.9211	4.9934	5.0665	5.2154	5.3680	5.6842	6.0156	6.3624	6.7251
5	6.3528	6.6101	6.7424	6.8771	7.1542	7.4416	8.0484	8.6999	9.3983	10.146
6	8.1152	8.5355	8.7537	8.9775	9.4420	9.9299	10.980	12.135	13.405	14.798
7	10.089	10.730	11.066	11.413	12.141	12.915	14.615	16.533	18.695	21.126
8	12.299	13.232	13.726	14.240	15.327	16.499	19.122	22.163	25.678	29.731
9	14.775	16.085	16.785	17.518	19.085	20.798	24.712	29.369	34.895	41.435
10	17.548	19.337	20.303	21.321	23.521	25.958	31.643	38.592	47.061	57.351
11	20.654	23.044	24.349	25.732	28.755	32.150	40.237	50.398	63.121	78.998
12	24.133	27.270	29.001	30.850	34.931	39.580	50.894	65.510	84.320	108.43
13	28.029	32.088	34.351	36.786	42.218	48.496	64.109	84.852	112.30	148.47
14	32.392	37.581	40.504	43.672	50.818	59.195	80.496	109.61	149.23	202.92
15	37.279	43.842	47.580	51.659	60.965	72.035	100.81	141.30	197.99	276.97
16	42.753	50.980	55.717	60.925	72.939	87.442	126.01	181.86	262.35	377.69
17	48.883	59.117	65.075	71.673	87.068	105.93	157.25	233.79	347.30	514.66
18	55.749	68.394	75.836	84.140	103.74	128.11	195.99	300.25	459.44	700.93
19	63.439	78.969	88.211	98.603	123.41	154.74	244.03	385.32	607.47	954.27
20	72.052	91.024	102.44	115.37	146.62	186.68	303.60	494.21	802.86	1298.8
21	81.698	104.76	118.81	134.84	174.02	225.02	377.46	633.59	1060.7	1767.3
22	92.502	120.43	137.63	157.41	206.34	271.03	469.05	811.99	1401.2	2404.6
23	104.60	138.29	159.27	183.60	244.48	326.23	582.62	1040.3	1850.6	3271.3
24	118.15	158.65	184.16	213.97	289.49	392.48	723.46	1332.6	2443.8	4449.9
25	133.33	181.87	212.79	249.21	342.60	471.98	898.09	1706.8	3226.8	6052.9
26	150.33	208.33	245.71	290.08	405.27	567.37	1114.6	2185.7	4260.4	8233.0
27	169.37	238.49	283.56	337.50	479.22	681.85	1383.1	2798.7	5624.7	11197.9
28	190.69	272.88	327.10	392.50	566.48	819.22	1716.0	3583.3	7425.6	15230.2
29	214.58	312.09	377.16	456.30	669.44	984.06	2128.9	4587.6	9802.9	20714.1
30	241.33	356.78	434.74	530.31	790.94	1181.8	2640.9	5873.2	12940.	28172.2
40	767.09	1342.0	1779.0	2360.7	4163.2	7343.8	22728.	69377.	*	*
50	2400.0	4994.5	7217.7	10435.	21813.	45497.	*	*	*	*
60	7471.6	18535.	29219.	46057.	*	*	*	*	*	*

*IFa > 99,999.

Appendix D*

Present Value of an Annuity of $1 per Period for n Periods: $DFa = \sum_{t=1}^{n} \frac{1}{(1 + k)^t} = \frac{1 - \dfrac{1}{(1 + k)^n}}{k}$

Number of Periods	1%	2%	3%	4%	5%	6%	7%	8%	9%
1	0.9901	0.9804	0.9709	0.9615	0.9524	0.9434	0.9346	0.9259	0.9174
2	1.9704	1.9416	1.9135	1.8861	1.8594	1.8334	1.8080	1.7833	1.7591
3	2.9410	2.8839	2.8286	2.7751	2.7232	2.6730	2.6243	2.5771	2.5313
4	3.9020	3.8077	3.7171	3.6299	3.5460	3.4651	3.3872	3.3121	3.2397
5	4.8534	4.7135	4.5797	4.4518	4.3295	4.2124	4.1002	3.9927	3.8897
6	5.7955	5.6014	5.4172	5.2421	5.0757	4.9173	4.7665	4.6229	4.4859
7	6.7282	6.4720	6.2303	6.0021	5.7864	5.5824	5.3893	5.2064	5.0330
8	7.6517	7.3255	7.0197	6.7327	6.4632	6.2098	5.9713	5.7466	5.5348
9	8.5660	8.1622	7.7861	7.4353	7.1078	6.8017	6.5152	6.2469	5.9952
10	9.4713	8.9826	8.5302	8.1109	7.7217	7.3601	7.0236	6.7101	6.4177
11	10.3676	9.7868	9.2526	8.7605	8.3064	7.8869	7.4987	7.1390	6.8052
12	11.2551	10.5753	9.9540	9.3851	8.8633	8.3838	7.9427	7.5361	7.1607
13	12.1337	11.3484	10.6350	9.9856	9.3936	8.8527	8.3577	7.9038	7.4869
14	13.0037	12.1062	11.2961	10.5631	9.8986	9.2950	8.7455	8.2442	7.7862
15	13.8651	12.8493	11.9379	11.1184	10.3797	9.7122	9.1079	8.5595	8.0607
16	14.7179	13.5777	12.5611	11.6523	10.8378	10.1059	9.4466	8.8514	8.3126
17	15.5623	14.2919	13.1661	12.1657	11.2741	10.4773	9.7632	9.1216	8.5436
18	16.3983	14.9920	13.7535	12.6593	11.6896	10.8276	10.0591	9.3719	8.7556
19	17.2260	15.6785	14.3238	13.1339	12.0853	11.1581	10.3356	9.6036	8.9501
20	18.0456	16.3514	14.8775	13.5903	12.4622	11.4699	10.5940	9.8181	9.1285
21	18.8570	17.0112	15.4150	14.0292	12.8212	11.7641	10.8355	10.0168	9.2922
22	19.6604	17.6580	15.9369	14.4511	13.1630	12.0416	11.0612	10.2007	9.4424
23	20.4558	18.2922	16.4436	14.8568	13.4886	12.3034	11.2722	10.3711	9.5802
24	21.2434	18.9139	16.9355	15.2470	13.7986	12.5504	11.4693	10.5288	9.7066
25	22.0232	19.5235	17.4131	15.6221	14.0939	12.7834	11.6536	10.6748	9.8226
26	22.7952	20.1210	17.8768	15.9828	14.3752	13.0032	11.8258	10.8100	9.9290
27	23.5596	20.7069	18.3270	16.3296	14.6430	13.2105	11.9867	10.9352	10.0266
28	24.3164	21.2813	18.7641	16.6631	14.8981	13.4062	12.1371	11.0511	10.1161
29	25.0658	21.8444	19.1885	16.9837	15.1411	13.5907	12.2777	11.1584	10.1983
30	25.8077	22.3965	19.6004	17.2920	15.3725	13.7648	12.4090	11.2578	10.2737
35	29.4086	24.9986	21.4872	18.6646	16.3742	14.4982	12.9477	11.6546	10.5668
40	32.8347	27.3555	23.1148	19.7928	17.1591	15.0463	13.3317	11.9246	10.7574
45	36.0945	29.4902	24.5187	20.7200	17.7741	15.4558	13.6055	12.1084	10.8812
50	39.1961	31.4236	25.7298	21.4822	18.2559	15.7619	13.8007	12.2335	10.9617
55	42.1472	33.1748	26.7744	22.1086	18.6335	15.9905	13.9399	12.3186	11.0140

*Appendix D corresponds to Table A-2 on the laminated card inserted in the book. In the formula in Appendix D, DFa means the same as $PVIFA_{k,n}$ on the insert card.

Number of Periods	10%	12%	14%	15%	16%	18%	20%	24%	28%	32%
1	0.9091	0.8929	0.8772	0.8696	0.8621	0.8475	0.8333	0.8065	0.7813	0.7576
2	1.7355	1.6901	1.6467	1.6257	1.6052	1.5656	1.5278	1.4568	1.3916	1.3315
3	2.4869	2.4018	2.3216	2.2832	2.2459	2.1743	2.1065	1.9813	1.8684	1.7663
4	3.1699	3.0373	2.9137	2.8550	2.7982	2.6901	2.5887	2.4043	2.2410	2.0957
5	3.7908	3.6048	3.4331	3.3522	3.2743	3.1272	2.9906	2.7454	2.5320	2.3452
6	4.3553	4.1114	3.8887	3.7845	3.6847	3.4976	3.3255	3.0205	2.7594	2.5342
7	4.8684	4.5638	4.2883	4.1604	4.0386	3.8115	3.6046	3.2423	2.9370	2.6775
8	5.3349	4.9676	4.6389	4.4873	4.3436	4.0776	3.8372	3.4212	3.0758	2.7860
9	5.7590	5.3282	4.9464	4.7716	4.6065	4.3030	4.0310	3.5655	3.1842	2.8681
10	6.1446	5.6502	5.2161	5.0188	4.8332	4.4941	4.1925	3.6819	3.2689	2.9304
11	6.4951	5.9377	5.4527	5.2337	5.0286	4.6560	4.3271	3.7757	3.3351	2.9776
12	6.8137	6.1944	5.6603	5.4206	5.1971	4.7932	4.4392	3.8514	3.3868	3.0133
13	7.1034	6.4235	5.8424	5.5831	5.3423	4.9095	4.5327	3.9124	3.4272	3.0404
14	7.3667	6.6282	6.0021	5.7245	5.4675	5.0081	4.6106	3.9616	3.4587	3.0609
15	7.6061	6.8109	6.1422	5.8474	5.5755	5.0916	4.6755	4.0013	3.4834	3.0764
16	7.8237	6.9740	6.2651	5.9542	5.6685	5.1624	4.7296	4.0333	3.5026	3.0882
17	8.0216	7.1196	6.3729	6.0472	5.7487	5.2223	4.7746	4.0591	3.5177	3.0971
18	8.2014	7.2497	6.4674	6.1280	5.8178	5.2732	4.8122	4.0799	3.5294	3.1039
19	8.3649	7.3658	6.5504	6.1982	5.8775	5.3162	4.8435	4.0967	3.5386	3.1090
20	8.5136	7.4694	6.6231	6.2593	5.9288	5.3527	4.8696	4.1103	3.5458	3.1129
21	8.6487	7.5620	6.6870	6.3125	5.9731	5.3837	4.8913	4.1212	3.5514	3.1158
22	8.7715	7.6446	6.7429	6.3587	6.0113	5.4099	4.9094	4.1300	3.5558	3.1180
23	8.8832	7.7184	6.7921	6.3988	6.0442	5.4321	4.9245	4.1371	3.5592	3.1197
24	8.9847	7.7843	6.8351	6.4338	6.0726	5.4510	4.9371	4.1428	3.5619	3.1210
25	9.0770	7.8431	6.8729	6.4642	6.0971	5.4669	4.9476	4.1474	3.5640	3.1220
26	9.1609	7.8957	6.9061	6.4906	6.1182	5.4804	4.9563	4.1511	3.5656	3.1227
27	9.2372	7.9426	6.9352	6.5135	6.1364	5.4919	4.9636	4.1542	3.5669	3.1233
28	9.3066	7.9844	6.9607	6.5335	6.1520	5.5016	4.9697	4.1566	3.5679	3.1237
29	9.3696	8.0218	6.9830	6.5509	6.1656	5.5098	4.9747	4.1585	3.5687	3.1240
30	9.4269	8.0552	7.0027	6.5660	6.1772	5.5168	4.9789	4.1601	3.5693	3.1242
35	9.6442	8.1755	7.0700	6.6166	6.2153	5.5386	4.9915	4.1644	3.5708	3.1248
40	9.7791	8.2438	7.1050	6.6418	6.2335	5.5482	4.9966	4.1659	3.5712	3.1250
45	9.8628	8.2825	7.1232	6.6543	6.2421	5.5523	4.9986	4.1664	3.5714	3.1250
50	9.9148	8.3045	7.1327	6.6605	6.2463	5.5541	4.9995	4.1666	3.5714	3.1250
55	9.9471	8.3170	7.1376	6.6636	6.2482	5.5549	4.9998	4.1666	3.5714	3.1250

Appendix E
Answers to Selected End-of-Chapter Problems

2-2	$67,150	**8-3d**	2.1	**11-1b(1)**	$1,500,000
2-4a	$71,750	**8-3e**	5.14%	**11-1b(2)**	−$6,500,000
2-4b	$9,200	**8-4**	4.167%	**11-4b**	$164,400
2-4c	$1,380	**8-5**	$480,000	**11-6**	9.6%; 9.3%
		8-6	−$720,000		
4-1b	$50,000,000	**8-7a**	$10,800,000		
4-2b	$640,000,000	**8-7d(1)**	−$4,511,500 (surplus)	**12-1a**	28 days
		8-8b	$720,000	**12-1b**	$46,666.76
		8-9b	25%	**12-2**	$36,666.74
5-1a	12.3%; 10.1%; 10.57%; 10.95%;	**8-9c**	Total assets = $86,976,000	**12-3**	75 days
	11.3%; 11.4%; 11.45%			**12-4a**	$18,000
				12-4b	$9,525
6-2	$60	**9-1b**	Firm B	**12-4c**	$2,200
6-4	CS = $11,000,000; P-I-C =	**9-1c**	$400,000	**12-4d**	$6,275
	$19,500,000; R.E. = $53,000,000	**9-2a**	40,000	**12-5a**	500 pounds
6-6	$1,312,000	**9-2b**	$600,000	**12-5b**	10 orders
6-7a	No change in assets or claims	**9-2c**	5	**12-5c**	250 pounds
6-7b	$700,000 increase in assets and	**9-3a**	60,000	**12-7b**	21 days
	debt	**9-3b**	$900,000	**12-7c**	$29,166.69
		9-3c	7	**12-7d**	27 days
7-1	43 days	**9-4a**	$2,500,000	**12-7e(1)**	756 kegs
7-2	Utilization = 4; utilization period	**9-4b**	8	**12-7e(2)**	13.23 orders
	= 90 days	**9-4c**	80% increase	**12-7e(3)**	378 kegs
7-3	40 days	**9-5**	$5.50		
7-4	14.9%			**13-1a**	28.8%
7-6	60% debt			**13-1b**	108%
7-7	2.448%	**10-1a**	$400,000	**13-1c**	7.2%
7-8	$1,250,000	**10-1b**	$255,000	**13-5a**	14.5%
		10-3a	CR = 1.6; NWC = $3,750,000;	**13-5b**	15%
			ROE = 14.67%	**13-5c**	13.9%
8-2a	$170,000	**10-3b**	CR = 2.0; NWC = $6,250,000;	**13-5d**	18%
8-2b	$45,000 internally; $125,000		ROE = 14%	**13-7**	14.4%
	externally	**10-5a**	$I_x = 6.67$	**13-8**	13.58%
8-2c	60% debt	**10-5b**	$I_xP = 54$ days	**13-12a**	$150,000
8-2d	1.69	**10-5c**	ACP = 70 days	**13-13a**	60 days
8-2e	4.5%	**10-5d**	8.04%	**13-13b**	14.4%
8-3a	$45,000	**10-6a**	$100,000	**13-14a(1)**	18.18%
8-3b	$45,000 internally; zero exter-	**10-6b**	$125,000	**13-14a(2)**	12.68%
	nally	**10-6c**	9.47%		
8-3c	54.3%				

14-2a	$1,628.90	**17-2b**	12.93%	**21-1c**	60%
14-2c	$613.90	**17-2c**	14%	**21-1d**	$4,166,667
14-3a	7 years	**17-3**	$1,226.03	**21-2**	$2,250,000
14-3b	5 years	**17-5a(1)**	12%	**21-4a**	$1,701,000
14-5a	$6,144.60	**17-5a(2)**	6%	**21-4b**	$2,835,000
14-5c	$5,000	**17-6a**	$875.15	**21-4c**	$2,450,000
14-7	$1,527.40			**21-4d**	$5,250,000
14-8a	15%	**18-1**	$21.25	**21-7b**	$33,600,000
14-11	20%	**18-2**	$42.80		
14-12	10–12%	**18-3**	$45.80	**22-1a**	0.3333
14-15a	$24,840.75	**18-5a**	$D_1 = \$2.625$; $D_2 = \$2.756$;	**22-1b**	0.2630
			$D_3 = \$2.894$	**22-1c**	0.2168
15-3b	$20,537.66	**18-5b**	$6.838	**22-2b**	2,400,000 shares
15-3c	20%	**18-5d**	$52.50	**22-2c**	1.2
15-4a	$3,612.70	**18-7**	$20.45	**22-4a**	$EPS_{MBI} = \$3$; $P_{MBI} = \$36$;
15-4b	14%	**18-9a**	$18.17		$EPS_{RG} = \$1.50$; $P_{RG} = \$12$
15-6c	$IRR_s = 21.5\%$; $IRR_L = 15.3\%$			**22-4c**	$45
15-7b	$NPV_x = \$2,650.50$; $NPV_y =$	**19-1**	60%		
	$2,189.30	**19-2a**	3.5	**23-1a**	$TA = \$327,000,000$
15-7c	$IRR_x \approx 18\%$; $IRR_y \approx 15\%$	**19-2b**	2	**23-1c**	$1.32
15-8a	$113,077	**19-2c**	7	**23-1e**	D/TA (before) $= 35.7\%$; D/TA
		19-3a	$2.72		(after) $= 64.2\%$
16-1a	$NPV_A = \$3,001.87$; $NPV_B =$	**19-5a**	A = $5; B = $3		
	$5,731.58	**19-5b**	$Q_A = 80,000$; $Q_B = 66,667$	**24-1**	$51,417.85
16-3a	$10,805			**24-2**	$47,173.15
16-3b	15%	**20-2a**	$847.89	**24-4**	9.4%
16-5a	($855.58)	**20-4a**	12.8%		
16-5b	$3,960.58	**20-5**	15.5%	**25-1**	0.5882 pounds per dollar
16-7a	12%	**20-8**	12.63%	**25-2**	4.546 francs
16-7b	14%	**20-9b**	$15,000,000	**25-3**	12 francs = 1 pound
16-7c	18%	**20-10b**	9.84%	**25-7a**	$1,250,000
16-9a	16.5%	**20-10d**	10.15%	**25-7b**	$1,212,121.21
				25-8	$514,290,000
17-1a	$35.71	**21-1a**	60%		
17-2a	10%	**21-1b**	$1,250,000		

Appendix F
Selected Equations

Chapter 5

$$k = k^* + IP + DP + LP + MP.$$

Chapter 6

$$EPS = \frac{\text{Net income after tax}}{\text{Shares outstanding}}.$$

$$DPS = \frac{\text{Dividends paid to common shareholders}}{\text{Shares outstanding}}.$$

Chapter 7

$$\frac{\text{Current}}{\text{ratio}} = \frac{\text{Current assets}}{\text{Current liabilities}}.$$

$$\frac{\text{Quick}}{\text{ratio}} = \frac{\text{Current assets} - \text{Inventory}}{\text{Current liabilities}}.$$

$$\frac{\text{Fixed assets utilization}}{\text{(or turnover)}} = \frac{\text{Sales}}{\text{Net fixed assets}}.$$

$$\frac{\text{Inventory utilization}}{\text{(or turnover)}} = \frac{\text{Sales}}{\text{Inventory}}.$$

$$ACP = \frac{\text{Receivables}}{\text{Sales per day}} = \frac{\text{A/R}}{\text{Sales/360}}.$$

$$\frac{\text{Total assets utilization}}{\text{(or turnover)}} = \frac{\text{Sales}}{\text{Total assets}}.$$

$$\frac{\text{Profit}}{\text{margin}} = \frac{\text{Net profit after taxes}}{\text{Sales}}.$$

$$\frac{\text{Debt}}{\text{ratio}} = \frac{\text{Total debt}}{\text{Total assets}}.$$

$$ROA = \frac{\text{Net profit after taxes}}{\text{Total assets}}.$$

$$TIE = \frac{\text{EBIT}}{\text{I}}.$$

$$ROE = \frac{\text{Net profit after taxes}}{\text{Common equity}}.$$

$$\text{P/E ratio} = \frac{\text{Price per share}}{\text{Earnings per share}}.$$

$$\text{M/B ratio} = \frac{\text{Price per share}}{\text{Book value per share}}.$$

$$ROE = ROA \times \frac{\text{Assets}}{\text{Common equity}}.$$

$$ROA = \frac{\text{Profit}}{\text{margin}} \times \frac{\text{Total assets}}{\text{utilization}}.$$

$$BEP = \frac{\text{EBIT}}{\text{Total assets}}.$$

Chapter 8

$$EFN = A/S(\Delta S) - L/S(\Delta S) - MS_1(1 - d).$$

Chapter 9

$$\text{Breakeven } Q = \frac{F}{P - V}. \qquad DOL = \frac{Q(P - V)}{Q(P - V) - F}.$$

Chapter 12

$$\Delta I = (ACP_N - ACP_0)(S_0/360) + [ACP_N(\Delta S/360)].$$

$$\Delta P = \Delta S - (B_N S_N - B_0 S_0) - k(\Delta I).$$

$$EOQ = \sqrt{\frac{2FS}{CP}}.$$

Chapter 13

$$\text{Percentage cost} = \frac{\text{Discount percent}}{100 - \text{Discount percent}} \times \frac{360}{\text{Days credit is outstanding} - \text{Discount period}}.$$

$$\text{Effective rate of interest on simple interest loan} = \frac{\text{Interest}}{\text{Amount borrowed}}.$$

$$\text{Effective rate of interest on discounted loan} = \frac{\text{Interest}}{\text{Amount borrowed} - \text{Interest}}.$$

$$= \frac{\text{Interest rate (\%)}}{1.0 - \text{Interest rate (fraction)}}.$$

$$\text{Approximate effective rate of interest on installment loan} = \frac{\text{Annual interest}}{\text{Loan amount} \div 2}.$$

$$\text{Effective rate of interest on compensating balance loan} = \frac{\text{Interest rate (\%)}}{1.0 - \text{Compensating balance fraction}}.$$

$$\text{Discount loan with compensating balance} = \frac{\text{Interest rate (\%)}}{1.0 - \text{Stated interest rate (fraction)} - \text{Compensating balance (fraction)}}.$$

Chapter 14

$$FV = PV(IF). \qquad IF = (1 + k)^n.$$

$$PV = FV(DF). \qquad DF = [1/(1 + k)^n] = (1/IF).$$

$$FVa = Pmt(IFa). \qquad IFa = \frac{(1 + k)^n - 1}{k}.$$

$$PVa = Pmt(DFa). \qquad DFa = \frac{1 - \dfrac{1}{(1 + k)^n}}{k}.$$

Chapter 15

$$\text{NPV} = \sum_{t=1}^{n} \frac{CF_t}{(1 + k)^t} - C \qquad \text{IRR: } \sum_{t=1}^{n} \frac{CF_t}{(1 + r)^t} - C = 0.$$

$$= \sum_{t=1}^{n} CF_t(DF) - C. \qquad \sum_{t=1}^{n} CF_t(DF) - C = 0.$$

Chapter 16

$$1 + k_n = (1 + k_r)(1 + i). \qquad k = R_F + b(k_M - R_F).$$

$$\text{NPV} = \sum_{t=1}^{n} \frac{CF_t}{(1 + k_n)^t} - C. \qquad \hat{k} = \sum_{i=1}^{n} P_i k_i.$$

$$\text{NPV} = \sum_{t=1}^{n} \frac{RCF_t}{(1 + k_r)^t} - C. \qquad \sigma = \sqrt{\sum_{t=1}^{n} (k_i - \hat{k})^2 P_i}.$$

Chapter 17

$$V = \sum_{t=1}^{n} I\left(\frac{1}{1 + k_d}\right)^t + M\left(\frac{1}{1 + k_d}\right)^n$$

$$= I(DFa) + M(DF).$$

$$\text{Approximate YTM} = \frac{I + (M - V)/n}{(M + V)/2}.$$

$$P_p = \frac{D}{k_p}.$$

$$\text{FCC} = \frac{\text{EBIT} + \text{Lease payments}}{I + \text{Lease payments} + \dfrac{\text{Sinking fund payments}}{1 - t}}.$$

Chapter 18

$$D_t = D_0(1 + g)^t.$$

$$P_o = \frac{D_1}{k_s - g}.$$

Appendix 18A

$$V_w = (P_0 - P_s)\,(N).$$

Chapter 19

$$DTL = \frac{Q(P - V)}{Q(P - V) - F - I}. \qquad DFL = \frac{EBIT}{EBIT - I}.$$

$$DTL = (DOL)(DFL).$$

$$EPS_1 = EPS_0[1 + (DTL)(\%\Delta S)]. \qquad EPS = \frac{(EBIT - I)(1 - t)}{Shares\ outstanding}.$$

Chapter 20

$$k_d\ after\text{-}tax = k_d\ (1 - t). \qquad k_e = \frac{D_1}{P_0(1 - F)} + g. \qquad k_s = \frac{D_1}{P_0} + g.$$

$$k_p = D_p/P_n. \qquad k_a = w_d(k_d)(1 - t) + w_s(k_s\ or\ k_e) + w_p(k_p).$$

$$Break\ point = \frac{\$\ of\ low\text{-}cost\ capital}{\%\ of\ this\ type\ of\ capital}.$$
$$in\ capital\ structure$$

Glossary

ABC system A system of modifying EOQs and inventory levels according to monitored inventory usage rates.

absolute priority doctrine The doctrine which states that claims must be paid in strict accordance with the priority of each claim, regardless of the consequence to other claimants.

accelerated cost recovery system (ACRS) A depreciation system that permits assets to be written off over periods generally much shorter than their operating lives.

account receivable A balance due from a debtor on a current account.

accruals Continually recurring short-term liabilities, such as accrued wages, accrued taxes, and accrued interest.

acquiring company A company that seeks to acquire another company.

add-on interest Interest calculated and added to funds received to determine the face amount of an installment loan.

after-tax cost of debt, $k_d(1 - t)$ The relevant cost to the firm for new debt financing, since interest is deductible from taxable income.

aging schedule A report showing how long accounts receivable have been outstanding; it gives the percentage of receivables now past due and the percentage past due in specific past periods.

amortization schedule A schedule that shows precisely how a loan will be repaid; it gives the payment required on each specific date and a breakdown of each payment showing how much of it

constitutes interest and how much constitutes repayment of principal.

amortize To liquidate on an installment basis. An amortized loan is one in which the principal amount of the loan is repaid in installments during the life of the loan.

amortized loan A loan in which the principal amount is repaid in installments during the life of the loan.

annual report A report, issued annually by corporations to their stockholders, containing basic financial statements and management's opinion of operations and future prospects.

annuity A series of equal payments or receipts for a specified number of periods.

annuity due A series of payments of a fixed amount for a specified number of periods where the payments occur at the beginning of the period.

arrearage An unpaid dividend on preferred stock.

asked price The price at which a dealer or specialist in securities will sell shares of stock out of inventory.

asset management ratios Set of several ratios, including inventory utilization, average collection period, and total assets utilization, which are designed to measure how effectively the firm's assets are being managed.

assets All things to which the firm holds legal claim.

assignment An informal procedure whereby a third party liquidates the firm's assets and distributes the proceeds to the creditors.

average collection period (ACP) The ratio computed by dividing average daily credit sales into accounts receivable to find the number of days' sales tied up in receivables.

average tax rate The tax rate determined by dividing taxes paid by taxable income.

balance sheet A statement of the firm's financial status at a specific point in time.

bankruptcy A legal procedure for formally liquidating a business, carried out under the courts of law.

Bankruptcy Reform Act of 1978 Legislation enacted to speed up and streamline bankruptcy proceedings.

basic earning power ratio The ratio of operating profits to assets. This ratio indicates the power of the firm's assets to generate operating income.

beta coefficient A measurement of the extent to which the returns of a given stock move with the stock market.

beta risk The risk of a firm measured from the standpoint of an investor who holds a highly diversified portfolio.

bid price The price that a dealer or specialist in securities will pay for a stock.

blanket inventory lien A claim on all inventories of a borrower.

Blue Sky Laws State laws that prevent the sale of securities having little or no asset backing.

Board of Governors of the Federal Reserve System Seven-member decision-making authority of the Fed.

bond A long-term debt instrument.

bond ratings Ratings assigned to bonds based on the probability of their firms' default. Those bonds with the smallest default probability are rated AAA and carry the lowest interest rates.

bracket creep An upward change in tax bracket that occurs when progressive tax rates combine with inflation to cause a greater portion of each taxpayer's income to be taxed.

break, or jump, in the MCC schedule A change in the weighted average cost of capital that occurs when there is a change in the component cost of capital.

break point The dollar value of new capital raised that corresponds to a jump in the MCC schedule.

breakeven point Level of operations wherein neither profits nor losses are incurred.

business failure The condition in which a business has terminated with a loss to creditors.

business risk The risk associated with future operating income.

bylaws A set of rules for governing the management of a company.

call provision A provision in a bond contract that gives the issuer the right to redeem the bonds under specified terms prior to the normal maturity date.

capital account The account that represents a bank's total assets less its liabilities.

Capital Asset Pricing Model (CAPM) A model based on the proposition that any stock's required rate of return is equal to the riskless rate of return plus the stock's risk premium.

capital assets Assets with a life of more than one year that are not bought or sold in the ordinary course of business, such as stocks, bonds, and real estate.

capital budgeting The process of analyzing projects and deciding whether an investment should be made.

capital components The long-term items on the right-hand side of the balance sheet: various types of long-term debt, preferred stock, and common equity.

capital gain The profit from the sale of a capital asset.

capital gains yield The capital gain during any one year divided by the beginning price.

capital intensity ratio The amount of assets required per dollar of sales (A/S).

capital loss The loss from the sale of a capital asset for less than its purchase price.

capital market The financial market in which funds are borrowed or lent for long periods.

capital structure The percentage of each type of capital used by the firm—debt, preferred stock, and common equity.

capitalizing the lease Incorporating the lease provisions into the balance sheet by reporting the leased asset under fixed assets and reporting the present value of future lease payments as debt, as required under conditions spelled out in FASB #13.

cash account The account that represents a bank's vault cash and funds required to be kept on deposit with the Federal Reserve.

cash discount A reduction in price given for early payment.

cash flow The actual net cash that flows into or out of the firm during a specified period.

certificate of deposit (CD) A receipt for funds deposited for a specified time and interest rate.

Chapter 11 The chapter of the Bankruptcy Reform Act of 1978 that outlines the procedure for business reorganization.

charter A formal legal document that describes the scope and nature of a corporation and defines the rights and duties of its stockholders and managers.

clientele effect The tendency of a firm to attract a certain type of investor according to its dividend policy.

collateral Assets that are used to secure a loan.

collection policy Procedures that a firm follows to collect past-due accounts.

company risk That part of a security's risk associated with random events. Such risk can be eliminated by proper diversification.

comparative ratio analysis The analysis based on a comparison of a firm's ratios with those of other firms in the same industry.

composition An informal method of reorganization in which creditors voluntarily reduce their claims on the debtor firm.

compounding The arithmetic process of determining the final value of a payment or series of payments when compound interest is applied.

computerized inventory control system Inventory control through the use of computers to indicate order points and to adjust inventory balances.

congeneric merger A merger between firms in the same general industry, where the merger partners are neither customers nor suppliers of each other.

conglomerate merger A merger between companies in different industries.

consolidated return An income tax return that combines the income statements of several affiliated firms.

constraints on dividend payments Restrictions or limitations on the payment of dividends.

consumer revolving credit interest Interest calculated monthly on the outstanding balance of a consumer credit card account.

contribution margin The difference between sales price per unit and variable costs per unit.

conversion price, P_c The effective price paid for common stock when the stock is obtained by converting either convertible preferred stocks or convertible bonds.

conversion ratio, R The number of shares of common stock that may be obtained by converting a convertible bond or share of convertible preferred stock.

convertible bond A security that is convertible into shares of common stock.

convertible securities Bonds or preferred stocks that are exchangeable at the option of the holder for common stock of the issuing firm.

corporate risk The risk that relates to the probability that a project will incur losses that will destabilize profits or, at worst, cause bankruptcy. Sometimes referred to as *total risk.*

corporation A legal entity created by a state, separate and distinct from its owners and managers, having unlimited life, easy transferability of ownership, and limited liability.

cost of capital The discount rate that should be used in the capital budgeting process.

cost of external equity, k_e The cost of retained earnings adjusted for flotation costs.

cost of preferred stock, k_p The preferred dividend, D_p, divided by the net issuing price, P_n.

cost of retained earnings, k_s The rate of return stockholders require on the firm's common stock based on alternative investment opportunities available to stockholders if no earnings were retained.

costly trade credit Credit taken in excess of the free trade credit period, thereby forfeiting the discount offered.

coupon rate The stated rate of interest on a bond.

coverage The measure of a firm's ability to meet interest and principal payments. Times interest earned is the most common coverage ratio.

credit period The length of time for which credit is granted.

credit policy Basic decisions that determine a firm's credit period, credit standards, collection procedures, and discounts.

credit standards Standards that stipulate the minimum financial strength of acceptable credit customers.

current ratio The ratio computed by dividing current assets by current liabilities.

debenture A long-term debt instrument that is not secured by a mortgage on specific property.

debt ratio The ratio of total debt to total assets.

declaration date The date on which a firm's directors issue a statement declaring a regular dividend.

default risk The risk that a borrower will not pay the interest or principal on a loan.

default risk premium (DP) The difference between the interest rate on a Treasury bond and that on a corporate bond.

deficit trade balance A country's trade balance resulting from an excess of its imports over its exports.

degree of financial leverage The percentage change in earnings available to common shareholders that is associated with a given percentage change in earnings before interest and taxes.

degree of operating leverage (DOL) The ratio of the percentage change in operating income to the percentage change in sales.

demand deposits Transaction deposits at commercial banks that are available on demand, usually through a check.

Depository Institutions Deregulation and Monetary Control Act of 1980 Act that eliminated many of the distinctions between commercial banks and other depository institutions.

depreciation The systematic distribution of the cost or value of equipment charged off over either its estimated useful life or its IRS-determined tax life.

devaluation The process of officially reducing the value of a country's currency relative to other currencies.

discount bond A bond that sells below its par value which occurs when the coupon rate is lower than the going rate of interest.

discount on forward rate The difference between the spot rate and the lower forward exchange rate.

discount rate The interest rate used in the discounting process. Also, the interest rate charged by the Fed for loans of reserves to depository institutions.

discounted cash flow (DCF) techniques Methods of ranking investment proposals, including the internal rate of return method and net present value method.

discounted interest Interest calculated on the face amount of a loan and deducted in advance.

discounting The process of finding the present value of a series of future cash flows. Discounting is the reverse of compounding.

divestiture The selling off of an asset or a division by its parent company. If the asset is given to the parent company's stockholders, the divestiture is called a *spin-off*.

dividend payout ratio The percentage of earnings paid out in dividends.

dividend policy Determination of the percentage of current earnings to be paid out as dividends to stockholders.

dividend reinvestment plan (DRP) A plan that enables a stockholder to automatically reinvest dividends received back into the stock of the paying corporation.

dividend yield The ratio of the current dividend to the current price of a share of stock.

Du Pont System A system of analysis designed to show the relationships among return on investment, asset turnover, and profit margin.

earnings dilution The acquisition of a firm with a high P/E ratio by a firm with a low P/E ratio, where the exchange ratio is based on current market prices. The acquiring firm is diluting its current EPS in order to obtain a higher future EPS growth rate.

earnings per share (EPS) The net income of the firm divided by the number of shares of common stock outstanding.

economic failure The condition in which a firm's revenues do not cover its total cost, including its cost of capital.

economic ordering quantity (EOQ) The optimal (least-cost) quantity of inventory that should be ordered.

Economic Ordering Quantity (EOQ) Model Formula for determining the order quantity that minimizes the total inventory cost: $EOQ = \sqrt{2FS/CP}$.

efficient capital market Market in which securities are fairly priced in the sense that the price reflects all publicly available information on each security.

equity Money supplied by the firm's owners.

Eurobond A bond sold in a country other than the one in whose currency the bond is denominated.

Eurodollar A U.S. dollar on deposit in a foreign bank—generally, but not necessarily, a European bank.

ex dividend date The date on which the right to the current dividend no longer accompanies a stock. For a listed stock this date is four working days prior to the date of record.

excess capacity Capacity that exists when an asset is not being fully utilized.

exchange rate The number of units of a given currency that can be purchased for one unit of another currency.

exchange rate exposure Exposure to losses due to fluctuating exchange rates.

exchange ratio (ER) The number of shares the acquiring firm must give for each of the acquired firm's shares.

exchange risk The risk that the basic cash flows of a foreign project will be worth less in the parent company's home currency.

expected rate of return The rate of return expected to be realized from an investment; the mean value of the probability distribution of possible returns.

extension An informal method of reorganization in which the creditors voluntarily postpone the date of required payment on past-due obligations.

external funds needed Funds that must be acquired by a firm through borrowing or by selling new stock.

extra dividend A supplementary dividend paid in years when excess funds are available.

factoring A method of financing accounts receivable under which a firm sells its accounts receivable to a financial institution.

FASB #52 The requirement of the Financial Accounting Standards Board which states that translation gains or losses must be reported at the current exchange rate for that period.

federal funds market The market in which depository institutions lend reserve funds among themselves for short periods of time.

Federal Open Market Committee (FOMC) Committee of the Federal Reserve System that has responsibility for open-market operations.

Federal Reserve System The chief regulator of the banking system in the United States.

finance Evaluation and acquisition of productive assets, procurement of funds, and disbursement of profits.

financial intermediaries Specialized financial firms that facilitate the transfer of funds from savers to those who need capital.

financial lease A lease that does not provide for maintenance service, is not cancelable, and covers the entire expected life of the equipment; also called a *capital lease.*

financial leverage The extent to which fixed-income securities (debt and preferred stock) are used in a firm's capital structure.

financial management The acquisition and utilization of funds to maximize the efficiency and value of an enterprise.

financial risk The portion of total corporate risk over and above the basic business risk that results from using debt.

financial service corporations Institutions whose services include a wide variety of financial operations, usually including banks, S&Ls, investment banking, insurance, pension plans, and mutual funds.

first-in, first-out (FIFO) Inventory valuation method which assumes that production process inventory will be used in the same order in which it was received.

five C's of credit Factors used to evaluate credit risk: character, capacity, capital, collateral, and conditions.

fixed assets utilization The ratio of sales to fixed assets; also known as *fixed assets turnover.*

fixed costs Costs that do not vary with the level of output.

fixed exchange rate system The world monetary system in existence prior to 1971 under which the value of the U.S. dollar was tied to gold and the values of the other currencies were pegged to the U.S. dollar.

floating exchange rates Exchange rates not fixed by government policy but allowed to float up or down in accordance with supply and demand.

floating rate bond A bond whose interest rate fluctuates with shifts in interest rates.

flotation cost The cost of issuing new stocks or bonds.

foreign bond A bond sold by a foreign borrower but denominated in the currency of the country in which it is sold.

formula, or exercise, value The theoretical value of a warrant if it were exercised today; the actual value is determined in the marketplace.

forward exchange rate An agreed-upon price at which two currencies are to be exchanged at some future date.

founders' shares Classified stock that has sole voting rights and restricted dividends; it is owned by the firm's founders.

free trade credit Credit received during the discount period.

friendly merger A merger in which the terms are approved by the managements of both companies.

funded debt Long-term debt.

future value (FV) The amount to which a payment or series of payments will grow by a given future date when compounded at a given interest rate.

goodwill Intangible asset of a firm established by the excess of the price paid for the going concern over the value of its assets.

hedging exchange rate exposure The process of protecting a firm against loss due to future exchange rate changes.

holder-of-record date The date on which registered security owners are entitled to receive the forthcoming cash or stock dividend.

holding company A corporation that owns sufficient common stocks of other corporations to achieve working control of those corporations. It is formed for the sole purpose of owning stocks in other companies.

horizontal merger The combination of two firms that produce the same type of goods or service.

hostile merger (takeover) A merger in which the target firm's management resists acquisition.

improper accumulation Earnings retained by a business for the purpose of enabling stockholders to avoid personal income taxes.

income bond A bond that pays interest to bondholders only if the interest is earned.

income statement A statement summarizing the firm's revenues and expenses over an accounting period.

incremental analysis An analysis to determine the increase or decrease in both sales and costs associated with a given easing or tightening of a credit policy.

incremental future cash flow The net cash flow attributable to an investment project.

incremental profit The difference between incremental sales and incremental costs.

indenture A formal contract between the issuer of a bond and the bondholders.

indexed tax rate Provision which ties tax rates to inflation (or other index) to prevent bracket creep.

inflation An increase in the volume of money and credit relative to the available supply of goods, resulting in a rise in the general level of prices.

inflation premium (IP) A premium for anticipated or expected inflation that investors add to the pure rate of return in order to protect the investor's purchasing power.

information content of dividends The theory that investors regard dividend changes as signals of management forecasts.

insiders Officers, directors, and major stockholders of a company who might be able to take advantage of their position to profit in their companies' stocks at the expense of their stockholders.

insolvency The inability to meet maturing debt obligations.

insolvency in bankruptcy A more serious condition than technical insolvency, when a firm's total liabilities exceed the value of its total assets.

interest rate The price paid by borrowers to lenders for the use of funds.

interest rate risk The risk to which investors are exposed due to changing interest rates.

internal rate of return (IRR) The rate of return on an asset investment, calculated by finding the discount rate that equates the present value of future cash flows to the cost of the investment.

inventory management The balancing of a set of costs that increase with larger inventory holdings with a set of costs that decrease with larger holdings.

inventory utilization The ratio of sales to inventories; also known as *inventory turnover*.

inverted yield curve A downward-sloping yield curve.

investment banking house A financial firm that underwrites and distributes new investment securities and that helps businesses obtain financing.

investment opportunity schedule (IOS) A listing, or graph, of the firm's investment opportunities ranked in order of the projects' rates of return.

investment outlay Funds expended for fixed assets of a specified project plus working capital funds expended as a result of the project's adoption.

investment tax credit (ITC) A specified percentage of the cost of new assets that business firms can deduct as a credit against their income taxes.

involuntary bankruptcy Bankruptcy in which the creditors petition the court and prove that the debtor is not paying debts as they mature.

last-in, first-out (LIFO) Inventory valuation method that assumes that the most recently received inventory will be the first used.

lease evaluation The analysis of the firm's cash flows under lease or purchase to determine the lower present value of costs.

legal list A list of securities in which pension funds, insurance companies, and other financial institutions are permitted to invest.

lessee The seller leasing a property.

lessor The owner of a property to be leased.

liabilities All the legal claims held against the firm by nonowners.

line of credit An arrangement whereby a financial institution commits itself to lend funds up to a specified maximum amount during a specified period.

liquid asset An asset that can be readily converted to spendable cash.

liquidation Dissolution of a firm through the sale of its assets.

liquidity The ability to sell an asset at a reasonable price on short notice.

liquidity premium (LP) A premium added to the equilibrium interest rate on a security that cannot be converted to cash on short notice.

liquidity ratio The relationship of a firm's cash and other current assets to its current obligations.

long-term gain or loss Gain or loss from the sale of an asset held for more than six months.

"lumpy" assets Those assets that cannot be acquired smoothly but require large, discrete additions.

managed floating system A system in which major currency rates move with market forces, unrestricted by internationally agreed-upon limits.

margin requirement The maximum percentage of the purchase price of a security that can be borrowed.

marginal cost of capital (MCC) The cost of obtaining another dollar of new capital; the weighted average cost of capital at a particular dollar value of new capital. The MCC increases as more and more capital is raised.

marginal cost of capital (MCC) schedule A graph or table that relates the firm's weighted average cost of capital to the amount of new capital raised.

marginal tax rate The tax applicable to the last unit of income.

market risk That part of a security's risk that cannot be eliminated by diversification. It is measured by the beta coefficient.

market value ratios The ratios that relate a firm's stock price to its earnings and book value per share.

maturity risk premium (MP) A premium for the risk to which investors are exposed due to the length of a security's maturity.

measuring risk Determining the amount of risk on the assumption that the tighter the probability distribution of expected future returns, the smaller the risk of a given investment.

merger Any combination that forms one company from two or more previously existing companies.

monetary assets Assets in the form of cash and marketable securities that are held by a firm.

money market The financial market in which funds are borrowed or lent for short periods.

money market fund A mutual fund that invests in short-term, low-risk securities and that allows investors to write checks against their accounts.

mortgage bond A pledge of designated property (real assets) as security for a bond.

multinational corporation A firm that operates in two or more countries.

mutual fund A corporation that invests the pooled funds of savers, thus obtaining economies of scale in investing and reducing risk by diversification.

Net monetary position The difference between the monetary assets held by a firm and its owed money denominated in a foreign currency.

net present value (NPV) A method of ranking investment proposals. The NPV is equal to the present value of future returns, discounted at the marginal cost of capital, minus the present value of the cost of the investment.

net working capital Current assets minus current liabilities.

net worth The capital and surplus of the firm—common stock, paid-in capital, and retained earnings.

New York Stock Exchange; American Stock Exchange The two major U.S. security exchanges.

nonmonetary assets Those assets with implied, rather than stated, monetary values, such as inventories and fixed assets.

"normal" yield curve An upward-sloping yield curve.

NOW (Negotiable Order of Withdrawal) account A form of savings account that allows withdrawal by check.

off-balance-sheet financing Financing wherein for many years neither the leased assets nor the liabilities under the lease contract appeared on the lessee's balance sheet. The Financial Accounting Standards Board issued FASB #13 to correct this problem.

offering price The price at which common stock is sold to the public.

open-market operations The purchase and sale of U.S. Government securities by the Federal Reserve System.

operating company A subsidiary of a holding company; a separate legal entity.

operating income Earnings before interest and taxes (EBIT).

operating leverage The extent to which fixed costs are used in a firm's operation.

operating merger A merger in which the operations of two companies are integrated with the expectation of achieving synergistic benefits.

opportunity cost The rate of return on the best alternative investment available—the highest return that will *not* be earned if the funds are invested in a particular project.

optimal capital structure The capital structure that balances risks and returns to maximize stock price and minimize the cost of capital.

optimal dividend policy The dividend policy that strikes a balance between current dividends and future growth and thereby maximizes the firm's stock price.

option A contract giving the holder the right to buy or sell an asset at some predetermined price within a specified period of time.

order point Point at which stock on hand must be replenished.

organized security exchanges Formal organizations having tangible, physical locations and conducting auction markets in designated ("listed") securities.

over-the-counter market All facilities that provide for trading in unlisted securities—those not listed on the organized exchanges.

paid-in capital The funds received in excess of par value when the firm sells stock for the first time, that is, in the primary market.

par value The nominal or face value of a stock or bond.

partnership An unincorporated business owned by two or more persons.

payback (or payback period) The length of time required for cash flows to return the cost of an investment.

payment date Date on which a firm actually mails dividend checks.

percentage of sales method A method of forecasting financial requirements by expressing various balance sheet items as a percentage of sales and then multiplying these percentages by expected future sales to construct pro forma balance sheets.

pledging of accounts receivable Short-term borrowing from financial institutions where the loan is secured by accounts receivable; also called *discounting of accounts receivable.*

pooling of interests An accounting method for combining the financial statements of two firms that merge. The assets of the merged firms are simply added to form the balance sheet of the surviving corporation.

portfolio theory The theory that deals with the selection of optimal portfolios—those that provide the highest possible return for any specified degree of risk.

post-audit A comparison of the actual and expected results for a given capital project.

preemptive right A provision contained in the corporate charter and bylaws that gives holders of common stock the right to purchase on a pro rata basis new issues of common stock (or securities convertible into common stock).

preferred stock A long-term equity security paying a fixed dividend.

premium The amount that a bond sells for above its par value which occurs when the coupon rate is above the going rate of interest.

premium on forward rate The difference between the forward exchange rate and the lower spot rate.

present value (PV) The value today of a future payment or series of payments, discounted at the appropriate discount rate.

price/book ratio The ratio of a stock's market price to its book value. Also called market/book ratio.

price-earnings (P/E) ratio The ratio of price to earnings; shows how much investors are willing to pay per dollar of profits.

primary markets The markets in which newly issued securities are bought and sold for the first time.

prime rate A published rate of interest that commercial banks charge very large, strong corporations.

pro forma statement A financial statement that shows how an actual statement will look if certain specified assumptions are realized; used to forecast financial requirements.

probability distribution A listing of all possible outcomes or events, with a probability (the chance of the event's occurrence) assigned to each outcome.

production opportunity The return available within an economy from investment in productive (cash-generating) investments.

profit margin on sales Profit per dollar of sales, computed by dividing net income after taxes by sales.

profit maximization The maximization of the firm's net income; does not consider risk or timing of earnings and thus is not an appropriate standard for financial decisions.

profitability ratios The ratios that show the combined effects of liquidity, asset management, and debt management on operating results.

progressive tax A tax that requires a higher percentage payment on higher incomes. In 1984 the personal income tax in the United States, which goes from a rate of 11 percent on its lowest increments of income to 50 percent on the highest increments, is progressive.

promissory note A document specifying the amount, percentage interest rate, repayment schedule, and other terms and conditions of a loan.

proprietorship A business owned by one individual.

prospectus A document issued for the purpose of describing a new security issue and the issuing company. A "red herring," or preliminary prospectus, may be distributed to potential buyers prior to approval of the registration statement by the Securities and Exchange Commission (SEC). The SEC examines prospectuses to insure that statements contained in them are not false or misleading. After the registration has been reviewed by the SEC, the securities, accompanied by the prospectus, may be offered for sale.

proxy A document giving one person the authority or power to act for another. Typically, the authority in question is the power to vote shares of common stock.

proxy fight An attempt by a person, group, or company to gain control of a company by getting the stockholders to vote a new management into office.

purchase The situation wherein the acquiring firm is assumed to have bought the target company much as it would buy any capital asset.

pure financial merger A merger in which the merged companies will not be operated as a single unit and from which no operating economies are expected.

quick (acid test) ratio The ratio computed by deducting inventories from current assets and dividing the remainder by current liabilities.

rapid depreciation methods Depreciation methods that write off the cost of an asset at a faster rate than the write-off under the straight line method.

rate of return, k The rate of interest offered by or required of an investment.

ratio analysis Analysis of the relationships among financial statement accounts.

real rate of return The real, default-free rate of interest that produces a balance between the supply of and demand for capital.

real, risk-free rate of interest The rate of interest on default-free U.S. Treasury securities less the expected inflation rate.

recession A period of slack economic activity usually having two or more consecutive quarters in which real output declines.

red-line method An inventory control procedure wherein a red line drawn around the inside of an inventory-stocked bin indicates the order point level.

registration statement A statement of facts filed with the SEC about a company planning to issue securities.

regular annuity A series of payments of a fixed amount for a specified number of periods where the payments occur at the end of the period; also called *deferred annuity*.

relative priority doctrine A flexible approach to the priority of creditors' claims, giving balanced consideration to all claimants.

reorganization The financial restructuring of a firm to reflect its assets' current market value. Under reorganization the firm continues to exist.

repatriation of earnings Cash flow, usually in the form of dividends or royalties, from a foreign branch or subsidiary to the parent company. A foreign government may restrict the amount of the cash flows that may be repatriated.

replacement decision The decision to replace an existing asset that is still productive with a new one; an example of mutually exclusive projects.

required cash flow The amount of a project's financing source times the required return for each source of funds.

required rate of return The minimum rate of return on common stock that stockholders consider acceptable.

required reserves The minimum reserves that a bank must hold as vault cash or reserve deposits with the Federal Reserve.

residual theory of dividends The theory that dividends paid should equal the excess of earnings over retained earnings necessary to finance the optimal capital budget.

residual value The value of a property at the end of its lease term.

restrictive covenant A provision in a bond indenture or term loan agreement that requires the bond issuer to meet certain stated conditions.

retention rate The percentage of earnings retained after payment of dividends.

return on common equity (ROE) The ratio of net profit after taxes to common equity; measures the rate of return on stockholders' investment.

return on total assets (ROA) The ratio of net income after taxes to total assets.

revaluation The process of officially increasing the value of a country's currency relative to other currencies.

revolving credit agreement A formal line of credit extended to a firm by a bank.

rights offering A securities flotation offered to existing stockholders.

risk The probability that actual future returns will be below expected returns.

risk-free rate, R_F The rate of return on short-term Treasury securities, which have no default risk and no maturity premiums.

risk premium, RP The difference between the required rate of return on a particular risky asset and the rate of return on a riskless asset with the same expected life.

safety stocks Additional inventories carried to guard against changes in sales rates or production/shipping delays.

sale and leaseback An operation whereby a firm sells land, buildings, or equipment to a financial institution and simultaneously leases the property back for a specified period under specific terms.

sales (demand) forecast Forecast of unit and dollar sales for some future period. Generally, sales forecasts are based on recent trends in sales plus forecasts of the economic prospects for the nation, region, industry, and so forth.

seasonal dating Procedure for setting effective invoice dates for discounts to induce customers to buy early.

secondary markets The markets in which stocks are traded after they have been issued by corporations.

secondary reserves Excess reserves invested by banks in marketable securities.

secured loan A loan backed by collateral.

Securities and Exchange Commission (SEC) The U.S. Government agency that regulates the issuance and trading of stocks and bonds.

security agreement A standardized document that includes a description of the specific assets pledged for the purpose of securing a loan.

Security Market Line (SML) The line that shows the relationship between risk and rate of return for individual securities.

selling group A group of stock brokerage firms formed for the purpose of distributing a new issue of securities.

service lease A lease under which the lessor maintains and services the asset; also called an *operating lease.*

short-term gain or loss Gain or loss from the sale of an asset within six months of the time it was purchased.

simple interest Interest calculated on funds received and paid on maturity of a loan.

sinking fund A required annual payment designed to retire a bond or a preferred stock issue.

social responsibility The concept that businesses should be responsible to some degree for the welfare of society at large.

sovereign risk The risk of expropriation of a foreign subsidiary's assets by the host country and of unanticipated restrictions on cash flows to the parent company.

spontaneously generated funds Funds that arise automatically from routine business transactions such as accrued wages or trade credit.

spot rate The effective exchange rate for a foreign currency for delivery on (approximately) the current day.

spread The difference between the price a security dealer offers to pay for securities (the "bid" price) and the price at which the dealer offers to sell them (the "asked" price).

standard deviation, σ A statistical measurement of the variability of a set of observations.

standard of fairness In bankruptcy or reorganization, the concept that claims must be recognized in the order of their legal and contractual priority.

standard of feasibility A test made by the SEC during a reorganization to determine whether fixed charges would be covered by earnings, and hence whether the reorganized company will be viable.

statement of changes in financial position A statement reporting the firm's sources of financing and the uses of those funds over an accounting period.

statement of retained earnings A statement reporting that portion of earnings not paid out in dividends. The figure that appears on the balance sheet is the sum of retained earnings for each year of the company's history.

stock dividend A dividend paid in additional shares of stock rather than cash; involves a transfer from retained earnings to the common stock and paid-in capital accounts.

stock repurchase A means by which the firm distributes income to stockholders by buying back shares of its own stock, thereby decreasing shares outstanding, increasing EPS, and increasing the price of the stock.

stock split An action taken to increase the number of shares outstanding; e.g., in a 3-for-1 split shares outstanding are tripled and each stockholder receives 3 new shares for each share formerly held.

stockholder wealth maximization The appropriate goal for management decisions; considers the risk and timing associated with increasing earnings per share in order to maximize the firm's stock price.

straight line method The cost of an asset divided by its estimated life.

Subchapter S The section of the Internal Revenue Code that allows certain small business corporations to be taxed as either proprietorships or partnerships rather than as corporations.

subordinated debenture A bond having a claim on assets only after the senior debt has been paid off in the event of liquidation.

synergy The condition wherein the whole is greater than the sum of its parts. In a synergistic merger the postmerger earnings exceed the sum of the separate companies' premerger earnings.

takeover The acquisition of one firm by another over the opposition of the acquired firm's management.

target capital structure The point at which a firm's value is maximized.

target company A company that another firm, generally a larger one, seeks to acquire through merger.

tax loss carry-back and carry-forward Corporate losses that can be carried back or carried forward to offset taxable income.

tender offer The offer of one firm to buy the stock of another by going directly to the stockholders, frequently over the opposition of the target company's management.

term loan A loan, generally obtained from a bank or insurance company, with a maturity greater than one year.

term structure of interest rates The relationship between yields and maturities of securities.

time preferences for consumption The preferences of consumers for current consumption as opposed to saving for future consumption.

times interest earned (TIE) The ratio of earnings before interest and taxes to interest charges; measures the ability of the firm to meet its annual interest payments.

total assets utilization The ratio that measures the turnover of all of a firm's assets, computed by dividing sales by total assets.

total leveraging effect The combination of operating leverage and financial leverage that results in a magnified effect of a small change in sales on the firm's earnings per share.

trade credit Interfirm debt arising through credit sales and recorded as an account receivable by the seller and as an account payable by the buyer.

translation gain or loss The gain or loss resulting from translating financial statements from a foreign subsidiary's currency to the parent company's currency.

trend analysis The analysis of a firm's financial ratios over time to determine the improvement or deterioration of a financial situation.

trust receipt An instrument acknowledging that the borrower holds certain goods in trust for the lender.

trustee The representative of bondholders who acts in their interest and facilitates communication between them and the bond issuer.

two-bin method An inventory control procedure wherein the order point is reached when one of two inventory-stocked bins is empty.

underwriting syndicate A syndicate of investment firms formed to spread the risk associated with the purchase and distribution of a new issue of securities.

Uniform Commercial Code A system of standards that simplifies the procedure for establishing loan security.

variable costs Costs that vary with the level of output.

venture capital Risk capital supplied to small companies by wealthy individuals, partnerships, or corporations, usually in return for an equity position in the firm.

vertical merger A company's acquisition of one of its suppliers or one of its customers.

voluntary bankruptcy Bankruptcy in which the debtor petitions the court.

warehouse financing A way in which inventory is supervised as collateral for a loan.

warrant An option to buy a stated number of shares of common stock at a specified price.

weighted average cost of capital, k_a A weighted average of the after-tax component costs of debt, preferred stock, and common equity.

window dressing Use of certain techniques to make a financial statement look better to credit analysts.

working capital A firm's investment in short-term assets—cash, marketable securities, inventory, and accounts receivable.

working capital management The administration, within policy guidelines, of current assets and current liabilities.

working capital policy Basic policy decisions regarding target levels for each category of current assets and for the financing of these assets.

yield curve The graph of the relationship between the yields and maturities of a group of equal-risk securities. Often Treasury securities are used since their risk varies only with their term to maturity.

yield to maturity (YTM) The rate of return earned on a bond if it is held to maturity.

zero coupon bond A bond that pays no annual interest but sells at a discount below par and therefore provides compensation to investors in the form of capital appreciation.

Index

ABC system, **307**
Abnormal yield curve, **109**
Absolute priority doctrine, **673**
Accelerated cost recovery system (ACRS), **147**–150
  straight line option for, 149–150
Accelerated leasing, 703
Accounts payable, 127, 320
  (*See also* Trade credit)
Accounts receivable, 126, **290**
  aging schedule for, 299
  cost of financing, 348
  evaluation of financing, 348
  financing by factoring, 337–338, 345, 346–347
  financing by pledging, 336–337, 345, 346
  future use of financing of, 348–349
  potential profit in carrying, 298
  small businesses factoring, 337–338
  small businesses pledging, 336–337
  (*See also* Credit policy)
Accruals, 127, 192, **320**
Acid test (quick) ratio, **158**
Acquiring company, **637**–638
Add-on interest, **331**
After-tax cost of debt, **570**–571
Aging schedule, **299**
Alabama Power Company, 63–64
American Can Company (paper products division), 635–636(DIF), 656–657(DIF)
American Stock Exchange (AMEX), 47(DIF), **59**, 69–70(DIF)
American Telephone and Telegraph, 189(DIF), 206–207(DIF)
Amortization schedule, **372**
Amortize, **461**
Amortized loans, **371**–372
Annual inflation rates, and long-term interest rates, 102

Annual report, **120**–121, 124–125
  analysis of, 155–156
Annuity, **364**
  deferred, 364
  discount factor on, 365, 367, 370, 746–747
  future compound value of, 365
  future value interest factor for, 365, 744–745
  future value of, 364–366
  present value of, 366–368
  regular, 364
Annuity due, **364**
Annuity tables, 744–747
Arrearage, **483**
Asked price, **60**–61
Asset management ratios, **158**–160
  average collection period, 159–160
  fixed assets utilization, 160
  inventory utilization, 158–159
  total assets utilization, 160
Assets, **126**
  fixed, 126
  foreign (*See* Foreign asset management)
  lumpy, 204
  monetary, 728
  nonmonetary, 729
Assignment, **679**–680
Automobile industry, changes in, resulting in lowered breakeven point, 221–222
Average collection period, 159–**160**
Average tax rate, **28**–29

Balance sheet, **125**–129
  effect of leasing on, 696–698
  pro forma, 190, 191, 192–193, 196
Baldwin-United Corporation, 23(DIF), 42–43(DIF)
Banking system (*See* Commercial banks)
Bank loans (*See* Short-term bank loans)

Note: Boldface terms in the index refer to key terms in the text and the boldface number refers to the page on which the key term is defined. (DIF) refers to Decision in Finance and Resolution to Decision in Finance; (SB) to Small Business sections; and (IP) to Industry Practice.

Bankruptcy, 665
  and absolute priority doctrine, 673
  deliberate, 292–293
  economists' reactions to, 668–672
  insolvency in, 665
  involuntary, 665
  priority of claims in, 680–683
  and relative priority doctrine, 673
  and small businesses, 555
  voluntary, 665
  (*See also* Failure; Liquidation;
  Reorganization)
Bankruptcy costs, relationship with taxes
  and value of the firm, 546–547
Bankruptcy laws, 673–674
Bankruptcy proceedings, 680–683
Bankruptcy Reform Act of 1978, 673–678
  Chapter 11 of, 674
Basic earning power ratio, 161–162, **164**
Berkshire Hathaway, 119(DIF), 137–138(DIF)
Beta risk, 441–446
  versus corporate risk, 444–446
Bid price, 60–61
Biotechnology General Corporation, 493–
  494(DIF), 508–509(SB), 510(DIF), 589(SB)
Blanket inventory lien, 349
Blue Sky Laws, 66
**Board of Governors of the Federal Reserve
  System, 85**
Board Products Corporation, 18–19(SB)
Bond markets, 62–64
  international, 732
Bond rating, 100, 468–477
  changes in, 472
  coverage ratios used in, 472–473, 476–477
  factors used in, 469
  importance of, 470
  relationship with yield, 470–471, 473
Bond valuation, 477–482
Bonds, 461–468
  advantages and disadvantages of, 484–485
  call provision of, 463–464, 524
  convertible, 466, 523–529
  coupon rate on, 462
  debenture, 465
  discount, 481
  floating rate, 466
  foreign, 732
  income, 466
  junk, 474–476
  mortgage, 464–465
  par value of, 466
  premium, 481
  rating of (*See* Bond rating)
  repayment provisions for, 462–464
  and restrictive covenants, 464
  sinking fund to retire, 462–463
  subordinated debenture, 465
  types of, 464–468
  valuation of, 477–482
  yield to maturity of, 481–482
  zero coupon, 466–468
Bottom line, 124
Bracket creep, 30
Break in the MCC schedule, 583–585
Break point, 583
Breakeven analysis, 218–225
  for evaluation of new products and
  expansion, 224–225
    for measuring responsiveness of profits to
    changes in sales, 225
    practical uses of, 224–225
    problems in, 223–225
Breakeven point, 218–224
Business decisions, and interest rates, 110–
  112
Business failure, 664
  (*See also* Failure)
Business organization, forms of:
  corporation, 26–27
  limited partnership, 25
  partnership, 24–25
  proprietorship, 24
  Rand D limited partnership, 40–41
Business risk, 225–226
  analysis of, 229
  and operating leverage, 227
Bylaws, 26

Call provision, 463–464, **524**
Capital, cost of (*See* Cost of capital)
Capital account, 79, 81
Capital Asset Pricing Model (CAPM), 433–
  466
Capital assets, 30
Capital budgeting, 386–404
  capital projects for, 387–388
  and cost of capital, 386
  classifying capital projects, 388–389
  effects of inflation on, 422–425
  estimating cash flows for, 389–391
  evaluating capital projects for (*See* Capital
    project evaluation)
  evaluating risk in, 418–446 (*See also* Risk)
  illustrated, 400–401
  multinational, 723–726
  post-audit for, 403–404
  replacement decisions in, 418–422
  risk analysis in, 441–446
  in the small firm, 447–449
  steps in, 386–387
Capital components, 567
Capital formation process, 55
Capital gain, 30–31
  taxes paid on, 31, 39–40
Capital gains yield, 498
Capital intensity ratio, 202
Capital lease, 693, 695
Capital loss, 30
  tax benefits of for small businesses, 40
Capital markets, 51
  international, 731–732
Capital project evaluation, 392–399
  internal rate of return (IRR) method, 395–
  399, 413–416
  net present value (NPV) method, 394–
  395, 413–416
  payback method, 392–393
Capital projects:
  classifying, 388–389
  evaluating (*See* Capital project evaluation)
  ideas for, 387–388
Capital requirements:
  effect of dividend policy on, 202
  and profit margin, 202
  relationship with growth in sales, 198–203
Capital sources, influencing dividend policy,
  612

Capital structure, 534
  and mergers, 549–550
  in the small firm, 554–556
  variations among firms, 552–553
Capital structure decisions, factors
  influencing, 550–552
Capitalizing the lease, 696
Carborundum Company, 3(DIF), 20–21(DIF)
Cash, 126, 260
  marketable securities substituting for, 274
  reasons for holding, 260–261
Cash account, 81
Cash budget, 261–263
Cash discounts, 297–298
Cash flow, 129, 390
  estimating for capital budgeting, 389–391
Cash flow analysis, and liquidity, 547–549
Cash flow cycle, 129–130
Cash management, 260–273
  cash budget in, 261–263, 265–266
  compensating balances in, 261, 270–271
  float used in, 269–270
  increasing efficiency of, 266–273
  matching costs and benefits of, 270
  in multidivisional firm, 272
  overdraft systems for, 271–272
  precautionary balances in, 260, 274
  risks in, 263–264
  slowing check payment as an option, 267–
    269
  speculative balances in, 260
  speeding check deposit as an option, 267–
    269
  synchronizing cash inflows and outflows,
    266–267
  target cash balances in, 272
  transactions cash balances in, 260
  trends in, 263–264
Certificate of deposit (CD), 77, 80, 280
Chapter 11, 674
Charter, 26
Check clearing, 267–269
Chrysler Corporation, 224, 241
Cities Service, 533(DIF), 556–557(DIF)
Clientele effect, 613
Collateral, 328, 335
Collection policy, 297
Commercial banks:
  advertising by, 80
  balance sheet for, 77
  capital accounts held by, 79, 81
  cash accounts held by, 81
  certificates of deposit issued by, 77, 80
  choosing, for a loan, 326–327
  demand deposit creation by, 82–84
  demand deposits in, 77
  as financial intermediaries, 56–57
  reasons for failure, 78–79
  sources and uses of funds, 77, 79, 81–82
  (See also Short-term bank loans)
Commercial paper, 279
  for short-term financing, 333–334
Common stock:
  flotation stock for, 504
  investment bankers selling, 503, 506
  issuing, 503–507
  offering price for, 504, 506
  prospectus for, 503
  registration statement for, 503

  rights offering of, 503
  selling groups for, 506
  small businesses offering, 508–509
  types of, 496–497
  underwriting syndicates for, 506
  valuation of, 497–503
Common stock valuation, 497–503
  during constant growth, 500–503
  expected dividends as basis for, 498–500
  terms used in, 498
Company risk, 435
Compaq Computer Corporation, 70(SB)
Comparative ratio analysis, 171–172
Compensating balances, 261, 270–271
  raising effective interest rates, 332–333
Composite costs of capital, 566–567, 576–
  581
  minimizing, 579, 581
Composition, 671–672
Compounding, 357–359
Computerized financial planning models,
  204–205
Computerized inventory control systems,
  307
Congeneric merger, 637
Conglomerate merger, 637
Conoco, 642–643(IP)
Consolidated corporate tax returns, 36, 654
Consolidated return, 36, 654
Constraints on dividend payments, 608–609
Consumer credit markets, 51
Consumer revolving credit interest, 332
Contribution margin, 219
Conversion price, 523
Conversion ratio, 523
Convertible bonds, 466, 523–529
Convertible securities, 523–529
  advantages of, 524
  call provision of, 524
  conversion price of, 523
  conversion ratio for, 523
  decisions on use of, 525–528
  disadvantages of, 525
  reporting earnings when outstanding,
    528–529
Corporate income taxes:
  consolidated returns for, 36, 654
  on dividend and interest income, 31, 34
  double taxation, 30
  effect of depreciation on, 36, 146–147
  effect of interests and dividends paid by
    corporation, 34–35
  and improper accumulation, 35–36
  and investment tax credit, 36–37
  reasons for variation in, 32–33
  tax loss carry-back and carry-forward, 35
Corporate risk, 444
  versus beta risk, 444–446
Corporation, 26–27
  bylaws for, 26
  charter for, 26
  reasons for organizing as, 26–27
  taxation of (See Corporate income taxes)
Cost of capital, 386, 566–588
  changes in, 581–586
  components of, 570–576
  marginal, 581
  for small businesses, 589–590
Cost of debt, 570–571

Cost of external equity, 575-576
Cost of new common stock, 575–576
Cost of preferred stock, 571–572
Cost of retained earnings, 572–573
    effect of dividend policy on, 612–614
Cost recovery (*See* Depreciation)
Costly trade credit, 325
Coupon rate, 64, 462
Coverage, 472–473, 476–477
Credit period, 291, 294
Credit policy, 290–291, 294–300
    cash discounts in, 297–298
    collection policy as part of, 297
    credit period, 291, 294
    credit standards for, 294–297
    effectiveness of, 298–300
    five C's of credit, 294–295
    illustrated, 316–317
    incremental analysis for, 291
    potential profit in carrying accounts
    receivable, 298
Credit quality, measuring, 294–295
Credit reporting agencies, 295, 296–297
Credit standards, 294–297
Credit unions, 57
Current assets, impact on risk and return,
    241–243
Current ratio, 157–158

Debenture, 465
Debt:
    combined with equity, 576–581
    cost of, 570–571
Debt management ratios, 161–163
    basic earning power, 161–162
    debt ratio, 163
    rate of return on equity, 161–162
    times interest earned, 163
Debt ratio, 163
Declaration date, 617
Default risk, 100–101, 276–277
Default risk premium (DP), 100–102, 103,
    107
Deferred annuity, 364
Deficit trade balance, 713–714
Degree of financial leverage, 543–545
Degree of operating leverage, 230–231
Del Monte Corporation, 641
Demand deposit creation, 82–84
Demand deposits, 77
Demand forecast, 190
Depository Institutions Deregulation and
    Monetary Control Act of 1980, 85
Depreciation, 36, 123, 126, 132–133
    accelerated cost recovery system method
    for, 147–150
    double declining balance method for, 143–
    145
    effect of, on reported income, 142–150
    effect of, on taxes paid, 36, 145–146
    methods after 1981, 147–150
    methods before 1981, 142–147
    methods compared, 143, 144
    role of, 131–133
    straight line method, 143, 144
    sum-of-years'-digits method, 145
Devaluation, 714
Discount bonds, 481

Discount factor, 360–361, 363, 742–743
    for an annuity, 365, 367, 370, 746–747
Discount on forward rate, 716
Discount rate, 88–89, 396
    compared with Treasury bill rate, 89
Discounted cash flow (DCF) techniques,
    394
Discounted interest, 331
Discounting, 360–362
Discounts, cost of not taking, 321–325
Divestiture, 655
Dividend expected, 498
Dividend and interest income:
    taxation of, for corporations, 31, 34
    taxation of, for individuals, 30
Dividend payment procedures, 615–618
    constant or increasing, 615–616
    constant payout ratio, 616
    declaration for, 617
    ex dividend date for, 617–618
    holder-of-record date for, 617
    low regular, plus extras, 617
    payment date, 618
Dividend payments, constraints on, 608–609
Dividend payout ratio, 193
Dividend performance, 609–611
Dividend policy, 14, 604–626
    effect on cost of retained earnings, 612–
    614
    effect on financial requirements, 202
    establishing, 624–626
    factors influencing, 608–609, 612–614
    influenced by constraints on dividend
    payments, 608–609
    influenced by investment opportunities,
    609
    influenced by sources of capital, 612
    optimal, 604
    reinvestment plans, 618–619
    stock dividend, 620–623
    stock repurchase, 619–620
    stock split, 620–623
Dividend reinvestment plan (DRP), 618–
    619
Dividends, residual theory of, 604–608
Dividend yield, 498
Double declining balance method of
    depreciation, 143–145
Double taxation of corporate income, 30
Du Pont Company, 642–643(IP)
Du Pont equation, 167
Du Pont system, 166–171

Economic failure, 664 (*See also* Failure)
Earnings, timing of, 12
Earnings dilution, 648
Earnings before interest and taxes (EBIT),
    123, 225, 227, 228
Earnings per share (EPS), 12
    before and after merger, 645
    effect of financial leverage on, 536–539
    and stockholder wealth maximization, 12,
    14
Econometric models, 194–195
Economic ordering quantity (EOQ), 303
Economic ordering quantity model, 303–
    304
Efficient capital market, 64–65

Equity, 127
combined with debt, 576–581
stockholders', 127–129
Equity multiplier, 167, 170
Erie Steel Company, 624
Eurobonds, 732
Eurodollar bank time deposits, 280
Eurodollar interest rates, 732
Eurodollars, 731–732
Ex dividend date, 617–**618**
Excess capacity, 202–**203**
Exchange rate, 711–712
fixed system for, 712
floating, 714–716
forward, 716
and inflation and interest rates, 717–718
spot, 716
Exchange rate exposure, 728–729
hedging, 730–731
Exchange ratio (ER), 645
Exchange risk, 722
Exercise value, 529
Expected rate of return, 427–**429**, **498**
Extension, 671
External equity, cost of, 575–576
External funds needed, 200, 199–201, 202
(*See also* Capital requirements)
Extra dividend, 617

Factoring, 345, 346–347
for small businesses, 337–338
Failure:
of banks, 78–79
causes of, 665–666
composition to deal with, 671–672
definition of terms, 664–665
extension to deal with, 671
occurrence of, 666–668
reorganization to deal with, 672–673, 674–679
(*See also* Bankruptcy)
FASB #52, 729–730
Federal funds market, 79
Federal income tax system, 29–38
consolidated returns by holding companies, 654
and corporations (See Corporate income taxes)
individual income taxes, 28–31
and small businesses, 37–38, 39–40
and Subchapter S corporations, 37–38, 39–40
Federal Open Market Committee (FOMC), 85–86, 90
Federal Reserve Board, 75(DIF), 92(DIF)
Federal Reserve System, 84–91
Board of Governors of, 85
discount rate charged by, 88–89
effect of policy on interest rates, 108–109
Federal Open Market Committee of, 85–86, 90
open-market operations controlled by, 85–86, 89–91
organization and structure of, 85–86
reserve requirements of, 86–88
tools of, 86–91
Finance, 4
history of, 4–5
place in business organization, 7–9

Financial analysis:
of a proposed merger, 640–641, 644–649
(*See also* Ratio analysis)
Financial asset markets, 51
Financial forecasters, 194–195
Financial forecasting:
computerized planning models for, 204–205
percentage of sales method, 190–203
when balance sheet ratios are subject to change, 203–204
Financial intermediaries, 54, 53–58
classes of, 56–58
functions of, 52–56
regulation of, 58
Financial lease, 693, 695
Financial leverage, 161–163, **534**–546
combined with operating leverage, 545–546
degree of, 543–545
effect of, on expected earnings per share, 536–539
effect of, on stock prices, 539–542
Financial management, 7
growth of, 4–5
increasing importance of, 5, 6–7
international (*See* International financial management)
interrelationship with other areas, 6–7
planning and control in, 5
in small businesses, 18–20
and social responsibility, 14–16
and stockholder wealth maximization, 9–12, 14
Financial markets, 50–52
importance of efficiency in, 52
types of, 51–52
Financial planning, 201
Financial quotations, 61–62
Financial ratios:
projected, 196–198
(*See also* Ratio analysis)
Financial requirements (*See* Capital requirements)
Financial requirements, forecasting (*See* Forecasting financial requirements)
Financial risk, 534
Financial service corporations, 58, 52–53
Financial statements:
annual report, 120–121, 124–125
balance sheet, 125–129
effect of trade credit on, 323–325
falsifying, 153–154, 176–177
importance of, 154
income statement, 121–124
interpretation of, 154–173 (*See also* Ratio analysis)
projected, 196–198
sources and uses of funds statement, 131–136
statement of changes in financial position, 131–136
statement of retained earnings, 130–131
window dressing techniques, 173
Financing strategies, for working capital, 243–249
Firm, goals of (*See* Goals of the firm)
First-in, first-out (FIFO), 150–151
Five C's of credit, 294–295

Fixed assets utilization ratio, 160
Fixed costs, 218–219
Fixed exchange rate system, 712
Float, 269–270
Floating exchange rates, 714–716
Floating rate bond, 466
Flotation costs, 504
  for small businesses, 589–590
FOMC (See Federal Open Market
  Committee)
Ford Motor Company, 603–604(DIF), 627–
  628(DIF)
Forecasting financial requirements:
  computerized planning models for, 204–
  205
  percentage of sales method, 190–203
  when balance sheet ratios are subject to
  change, 203–204
Foreign asset management, 727–731
  accounting for, 729–730
  FASB #52, 729–730
  hedging exchange rate exposure, 730–731
  monetary and nonmonetary assets, 728–
  729
Foreign bonds, 732
Foreign investment, 718, 721–727
  analyzing, 718, 721–722
  exchange risk in, 722
  management of assets, 727–731
  repatriation of earnings, 721
  sources of funds for, 726–727
  and sovereign risk, 722
  (See also International financial
  management)
Formula value, 520
Forward exchange rate, 716–717
Founder's shares, 496
Free trade credit, 325
Friendly merger, 638
Funded debt, 460
Future compound value of an annuity, 365
Future value, 356–359
  of an annuity, 364–366
  versus present value, 362–364
Future value interest factor, 358–359, 363,
  740–741
  for an annuity, 365, 744–745
Future value tables, 740–741, 744–745
Futures markets, 51

General Electric Company, 385(DIF),
  405(DIF)
Goal setting in small businesses, 19–20
Goals of the firm, 9–12, 14–16
Goodwill, 651–652
Gordon model, 501
Growth, in sales, relationship with capital
  requirements, 198–203
Growth rate, 498
Gulf Oil Corporation, 11

Hedging exchange rate exposure, 730–731
High Tech Electronic Software, 41(SB)
Holder-of-record date, 617
Holding companies, 653–655
  advantages of, 653–654
  control with fractional ownership in, 653–
  654
  disadvantages, 654–655

isolation of risks in, 654
  leverage in, 655
  operating companies as part of, 654
Horizontal merger, 637
Hostile merger (takeover), 638

Improper accumulation, 35–36
Income bonds, 466
Income statement, 121–124
  effect of accounting methods on, 651–652
Incremental analysis, 291
Incremental future cash flow, 420
Incremental profit, 291
Indenture, 462
Indexed tax rate, 29–30
Individual income taxes, 28–31
  on capital gains, 30–31
  on dividend and interest income, 30
Industry averages, 157–158, 172
Inflation, 101
  effects on capital budgeting decisions,
  422–425
  and interest and exchange rates, 717–718
  and interest rates, 101–103
Inflation premium (IP), 101, 103, 104
Information content of dividends, 614
Insiders, 65
Insolvency, 644
Insolvency in bankruptcy, 655
Interest rate, 96
  and business decisions, 110-112
  determining, 370–371
  effect of default risk on, 100–101
  effect of Federal Reserve policy on, 108–
  109
  effect of inflation on, 100–103
  effect of opportunity risk premium on,
  106–107
  effect of production opportunities on, 96–
  97, 99
  effect of time preferences for consumption
  on, 96–97, 99
  and inflation and exchange rates, 717–718
  influence of recessions on, 109–110
  and liquidity premium, 103
  long-term, and annual inflation rate, 102
  nominal, 97–98
  real 97–98, 99, 101
  real, default-free, 103
  and stock prices, 112
  on term loans, 461
  term structure of, 103–106
Interest rate risk, 107, 277
  effect on yield curve, 108
Internal rate of return (IRR), 395–399
  computer solutions to, 399
  conflict with present net value when
  comparing projects, 413–416
  with constant cash inflows, 396–397
  trial and error method, 397–399
International bond markets, 732
International Business Machines, 95(DIF),
  113–114(DIF), 274
International capital markets, 731–732
  Eurodollar interest rates, 732
  Eurodollars, 731–732
International financial management, 710–732
  analyzing foreign investments, 718, 721–
  722

multinational capital budgeting illustrated, 723–726
multinational corporations in, 710–711
sources of funds, 726–727
International Harvester, 663–664(DIF), 684–685(DIF)
International industrial development, 719–721
International monetary system, 711–718
    and deficit trade balances, 713–714
    exchange rates, 711–712, 714–718
    fixed exchange rate system, 712
    floating exchange rates, 714–716
    recent history of, 712–714
    trading in foreign exchange, 716
Inventory control systems, 306–307
    ABC system, 307
    computerized, 307
    red-line method, 306–307
    two-bin method, 307
Inventory financing, 349–352
    blanket inventory lien for, 349
    trust receipts as security, 349
    warehouse financing, 350–352
Inventory management, 300–308
    control systems for, 306–307
    economic ordering quantity model for, 301–304
    effect of inflation on, 308
    safety stocks in, 304–306
Inventory utilization ratio, 158–159
Inventory valuation:
    effect on reported income, 150–151
    methods compared, 151
Inverted yield curve, 109
Investment banking groups, 506–507
Investment banking house, 54–55
Investment opportunities, influencing dividend policy, 609
Investment opportunity schedule, 586, 606–607
    combining with marginal cost of capital, 586–588
Investment outlay, 392
Investment tax credit (ITC), 36–37
    and leasing, 703
Involuntary bankruptcy, 665

James River Paper Company, 635–636(DIF), 656–657(DIF)
Junk bonds, 474–476
J. Walter Thompson, 259(DIF), 281–282(DIF)

Kennecott Copper Company, 3(DIF), 20–21(DIF)
Kern County Land Company, 639–640

Last-in, first-out (LIFO), 150–151
Lease evaluation, 698–702
Leasing, 692–703
    and accelerated depreciation, 703
    effect on firm's balance sheet, 696–698
    estimating residual value, 702
    evaluating proposals for, 698–701
    factors affecting decisions, 702–703
    financial lease form of, 693, 695
    increasing credit availability by, 702–703
    Internal Revenue Service requirements for, 695–696
    and investment tax credit, 703
    sale and leaseback form of, 692, 694–695
    service lease form of, 692–693
Legal listing, 614
Lessee, 692
Lessor, 692
Leverage:
    financial, 161–163
    in holding companies, 655
    operational, 226–231
Liabilities, 127
Life insurance companies, 57
Limited partnership, 25
LIN Broadcasting Corporation, 49(DIF), 71–72(DIF)
Line of credit, 329
Liquid asset, 103
Liquidation, 674
Liquidation procedures, 679–683
    assignment, 679–680
    liquidation in bankruptcy, 680–683
Liquidity, 27
    of assets, 126
    and cash flow analysis, 547–549
Liquidity (marketability) risk, 277
Liquidity premium (LP), 103
Liquidity ratios, 157–158
    current ratio, 157–158
    quick (acid test) ratio, 158
Local markets, 51
Lockbox plan, 267, 268
Long-term financing (See Bonds; Capital structure; Common stock; Financial leverage; Preferred stock)
Long-term gain or loss, 30
Lotus Development Corporation, 70(SB)
"Lumpy" assets, 204

Managed floating system, 714
Margin requirements, 65
Marginal cost of capital (MCC), 581, 604–606
    combined with investment opportunity schedule, 586–588
Marginal cost of capital (MCC) schedule, 581–585
    break or jump in, 583–584
Marginal tax rate, 28
Market/book (M/B) ratio, 165–166
Market price, postmerger, 649
Market risk, 435 (See also Beta risk)
Market value:
    effect of merger on, 646
    postmerger, 644
Market value ratios, 165–166
    market/book ratio, 165–166
    price/earnings ratio, 165
Marketability (liquidity) risk, 277
Marketable securities, 126, 274–280
    certificates of deposit, 280
    commercial paper, 279
    default risk of, 276–277
    Eurodollar bank time deposits, 280
    factors influencing choice of, 276–278
    government, 279
    interest rate risk of, 277
    liquidity risk of, 277
    money market mutual funds, 280
    nongovernment, 279–280

Marketable securities, *(continued)*
  purchasing power risk of, 277
  returns on, 277–278
  strategies for, 275–276
  substituting for cash, 274
  as temporary investment, 274–275
  types of, 278–280
Maturity risk premium (MP), 106–**107**
McDonnell Douglas Corporation, 691(DIF),
  704–705(DIF)
Measuring risk, **429**–432
Merged firms, effect of accounting
  treatments on reported profits, 649–653
Mergers, 636
  and capital structure, 549–550
  congeneric, 637
  conglomerate, 637
  discussion of, 642–644
  economic implications of, 636
  effect on market values, 646
  and exchange ratio for stock, 645
  financial analysis of, 640–641, 644–649
  financial analysis illustrated, 646–649
  friendly, 638
  goodwill write-offs, 651–652
  horizontal, 637
  hostile (takeover), 638
  income statement effects of accounting
    methods, 651–652
  operating, 640
  operating and pure financial compared,
    640–641
  pooling of interests accounting for, 649–
    650, 652–653
  and postmerger control, 644
  predicting postmerger market price, 649
  price negotiation, 644–645
  procedures for, 637–640
  and projected future earnings, 645–646
  purchase accounting for, 650–651
  pure financial, 640
  pure financial and operating compared,
    640–641
  terms of, 644–646
  vertical, 637
  (See also Holding companies)
Merrill Lynch, 95(DIF), 113–114(DIF)
Midwest Electric Company, 625
Minimum required return, 568–569
Monetary assets, 728
Money market funds, 58
Money market mutual funds, 280
Money markets, 51
Mortgage bonds, 464–465
Mortgage markets, 51
Multinational capital budgeting, illustrated,
  723–726
Multinational corporation, 710–711
Mutual funds, 57–58
Mutual savings banks, 57

National markets, 51
Near-cash reserves, 279
Net monetary position, 728
Net present value (NPV), 394
  conflict with internal rate of return when
    comparing projects, 413–416
  in replacement decisions, 421–422
Net working capital, 133, 240

Net worth, 127–129
New York Stock Exchange (NYSE), 49(DIF),
  59–60, 61, 63, 71–72(DIF)
  bonds listed by, 63
Nominal interest rates, 97–98
Nominal rate of return, 423–424
Nonmonetary assets, 729
Normal profits, 14–15
"Normal" yield curve, 109
North American Oil, 625–626
Northwestern National Bank, 319(DIF), 338–
  340(DIF)
Northwestern Steel and Wire, 289(DIF),
  309(DIF)
NOW (Negotiable Order of Withdrawal)
  account, 77

Occidental Petroleum, 533(DIF), 556–
  557(DIF), 639
Off-balance-sheet financing, 696
Offering price, 504, 506
Open-market operations, 85–86, 89–91
Operating companies, 654
Operating costs and expenses, 123
Operating income, 225
  estimating for a proposed merger, 641
Operating lease, 692–693
Operating leverage, 226–231
  and business risk, 227
  combined with financial leverage, 545–546
  controlling, 231
  degree of, 230–231
Operating merger, 640
Operating revenues, 123
Operations analysis, 218–231
  (See also Breakeven analysis; Business risk;
    Operating leverage)
Opportunity cost, 573
Optimal capital structure, 534
Optimal dividend policy, 604
Option, 519
Organizational structure, place of finance in,
  7–9
Organized security exchanges, 59
Osborne Computer Corporation, 70(SB)
Overdraft systems, 271–272
Over-the-counter (OTC) market, 49(DIF),
  59, 60–61, 71–72(DIF)

Paid-in capital, 128
Par value, 128, 466
Parent company, 710
Parker Pen Company, 217(DIF), 232(DIF)
Partnership, 24–25
  limited, 25
Passbook savings accounts, 77
Payback period, 392
Payment date, 618
Peabody Coal Company, 3(DIF), 20–21(DIF)
Pension funds, 57
PepsiCo, 153–154 (DIF), 176–177(DIF)
Percentage of sales method, 190–203
Peterson, James, 217, 232
Physical asset markets, 51
Pledging of accounts receivable, 345, 346
  for small businesses, 336–337
Pooling of interests, 649–650
  conditions for, 652–653

Portfolio risk, 433–437
Portfolio theory, 432–446
  beta in, 437–438, 441–444
  company risk in, 435
  market risk in, 435
  portfolio risk in, 433–435
Post-audit, 403–404
Postmerger market values, 644
Precautionary balances, 260, 274
Preemptive right, 495
Preferred stock, 482–483
  advantages and disadvantages of, 484–485
  arrearage on, 483
  cost of, 571–572
Premium (bond), **481**
Premium on forward rate, 716
Present value (PV), 360–362
  of an annuity, 366–368
  of an uneven series of receipts, 368–370
  versus future value, 362–364
Present value tables, 742–743, 746–747
Price/earnings (P/E) ratio, 165
Price of stock, 498
Primary markets, 51
Prime rate, 330
Pro forma balance sheets, 190, 191
  steps in construction, 192–193, 196
Pro forma statements, 190, 191
  steps in construction, 192–193, 196
Probability distribution, 277, 426
  continuous, 429
Production opportunities, 96–97, 99
Professional debtors, 292–293
Profit margin, and need for external funds, 202
Profit margin on sales, 164, 166–167
Profit maximization, 12
Profitability ratios, 164–165
  basic earning power, 164
  profit margin on sales, 164, 166–167
  return on common equity, 165
  return on total assets, 164
Progressive tax, 28
Projected financial statements and ratios, 196–198
Projected future earnings, after a merger, 645–656
Promissory note, 329
Proprietorship, 24
Prospectus, 503
Proxy, 495
Proxy fight, 11, 495
Proxy resolutions, 13
Purchase accounting, 650–651
Purchasing power risk, 277
Pure financial merger, 640

Quick (acid test) ratio, 158

Rapid depreciation methods, 142
Rate of return, 356
  expected, 427–429, 498
  finding, 573–575
  nominal, 423–424
  real, 423–424
  relationship with risk, 439–441
  required, 498
Rate of return on assets, 167, 170

Rate of return on equity (ROE), 161–162
Ratio analysis, 154–173
  asset management ratios, 158–160
  average collection period, 159–160
  basic earning power ratio, 161–162, 164
  comparative, 171–172
  current ratio, 157–158
  debt management ratios, 161–163
  debt ratio, 163
  Du Pont system, 166–171
  fixed assets utilization ratio, 160
  industry average figures for, 157–158, 172
  inventory utilization ratio, 158–159
  limitations of, 172–173
  liquidity ratio, 157–158
  market/book ratio, 165–166
  market value ratios, 165–166
  price/earnings ratio, 165
  profit margin on sales ratio, 164
  profitability ratios, 164–165
  projected ratios, 196–198
  quick (acid test) ratio, 158
  rate of return on equity, 161–162
  return on common equity, 165
  return on total assets, 164
  for small businesses, 174–176
  times-interest-earned ratio, 163
  total assets utilization ratio, 160
  trend analysis, 166
Real, default-free rate of interest, 103
Real interest rates, 97–98, 99, 101
Real rate of return, 99, 101, 423–424
Recession, 109–110
Red-line method, 306–307
Regional markets, 51
Registration statement, 503
Regular annuity, 364
Remaining disbursements, 123
Reorganization, 672–673
  financial decisions in, 674–679
  standard of fairness for, 675–677
  standard of feasibility for, 677–679
Relative priority doctrine, 673
Repatriation of earnings, 721
Replacement decisions, 418–422
  effect of accounting treatments on, 649–653
  when comparing projects with unequal lives, 421–422
Required cash flow, 569
Required rate of return, 498
Required reserves, 86–88
Residual theory of dividends, 604–608
Residual value, 702
Resource poverty in small businesses, 18–19
Restrictive covenants, 464
Retained earnings, 128
  cost of, 572–573
  effects of dividend policy on costs of, 612–614
  improper accumulation of, 35–36
  statement of, 131
Retention rate, 199
Return, impact of current assets on, 241–243
Return on common equity (ROE), 165
Return on total assets (ROA), 164
Revaluation, 714
Revolving credit agreement, 329
Rights offering, 503

Risk, 12–14, **425**–426
  beta, 441–446
  business, 225–226, 227, 229
  corporate, 444–446
  financial, 534
  impact of current assets on, 241–243
  market, 435
  measuring, 429–432
  relationship with rate of return, 439–441
  standard deviation as a measure of, 429–432
Risk-free rate, 107
Risk premium, 107–108
Risk/return trade-off, 67

Safety stocks, 304–306
Sale and leaseback, 692, 694–695
Sales (demand) forecast, 190
Salomon Brothers, 95(DIF), 113–114(DIF)
Savings and loan associations, 57
Seasonal dating, 298
Secondary markets, 51–52, 506–507
Secondary reserves, 84
Secured loans, 335
Securities and Exchange Commission (SEC), 61
  regulation of outstanding securities by, 65
  regulations for new issues, 64–65
Security agreement, 335
Security exchanges, 59–60
Security Market Line (SML), 439–441, 444
Security markets:
  American Stock Exchange, 47(DIF), 59, 69–70(DIF)
  bond market, 62–64
  and efficient capital markets theory, 66–67
  New York Stock Exchange, 49(DIF), 59–60, 62, 63, 71–72(DIF)
  organized security exchanges, 59–61
  over-the-counter, 59, 60–61
  risk/return trade-off in, 67
  SEC regulation of, 64–65
  state regulation of, 65–66
  stock market, 58–62
  stock market reporting system, 61–62
Selling group, 506
Service lease, 692–693
Sevin Rosen Partners, 70–71(SB)
Short-term bank loans, 326–332
  add-on interest on, 331
  applying for, 327–328
  collateral needed for, 328
  choosing a bank for, 326–327
  compensating balances required for, 329
  cost of, 330
  discounted interest on, 331
  effective interest rates when compensating balances apply, 332–333
  lines of credit for, 329
  maturity of, 328
  and prime rate, 330
  promissory notes for, 328
  revolving credit agreement for, 329–330
  simple interest on, 330–332
Short-term credit:
  advantages and disadvantages of, 248–249
  compared with long-term, 248–249
  to finance assets, 246–247

Short-term financing:
  accruals, 127, 192, 320
  commercial paper, 279, 333–334
  of receivables, 345–349 (*See also* Accounts receivable)
  security used in, 335, 345–352
  short-term bank loans (*See* Short-term bank loans)
  trade credit (*See* Trade credit)
Short-term gain or loss, 30
Simple interest, 330–331
Sinking fund, 462–463
Small businesses:
  capital budgeting in, 447–449
  capital structure in, 554–556
  cost of equity capital for, 589–590
  factoring receivables by, 337–338
  financial management in, 18–20
  flotation costs for, 589–590
  goal setting in, 19–20
  pledging receivables by, 336–337
  R and D limited partnerships for, 40–41
  raising equity capital for, 508–509
  ratio analysis for, 174–176
  resource poverty in, 18–19
  risk capital for, 68–71
  section 1244 stock provisions, 39–40
  Subchapter S tax status for, 39–40
  tax treatment of capital losses for, 40
  taxation of, 37–38, 39–40
  and venture capital industry, 69–71
  working capital for, 251–252
Small firm effect, 590
Social responsibility, 13, **14**–16
  need to enforce, 15
  and stock price maximization, 15–16
Sole proprietorship, 24
Sources and uses of funds statement, 131–136
Sovereign risk, 722
Speculative balances, 260
Spontaneously generated funds, 192
Spot markets, 51
Spot rate, 716–717
Spread, 504
Standard deviation, 429–433
Standard of fairness, 675–677
Standard of feasibility, 678–679
Statement of changes in financial position, 131–136
  preparing, 133–136
Statement of retained earnings, 131
Stock dividends, 621, 620–623
  price effects of, 623
Stock exchanges, 59–69 (*See also* American Stock Exchange; New York Stock Exchange)
Stock market, 58–64
  bonds traded on, 62–64
  over-the-counter market, 60–61
  regulation of, 64–66
  reporting for, 61–62
  stock exchanges, 59–60
  (*See also* American Stock Exchange; New York Stock Exchange)
Stock price maximization, and social responsibility, 15–16
Stock prices:
  effect of financial leverage on, 539–542

and interest rates, 112
Stock repurchases, 619–620
Stock splits, 621, 620–623
  price effects of , 623
Stockholder wealth maximization, 9–12, 14
  and earnings per share, 12, 14
  financial manager's options for, 12, 14
  reasons for, 9–12
  (*See also* Stock price maximization)
Stockholders' equity, 127–128
Stockholders' legal rights and privileges,
  494–497
  control of the firm, 494–495
  purchase of stock, 495–496
Straight line method of depreciation, 143,
  144
Subchapter S, 37–38, 39–40
Subordinated debenture, 465–466
Sum of an annuity, table for, 744–745
Sum-of-years'-digits method of depreciation,
  145
Synchronized cash flows, 266–267
Synergy, 636, 641

Takeover, 638
Target capital structure, 535
Target cash balance, 272
Target company, 637–638
Tax loss carry-back and carry-forward, 35
Taxes:
  relationship with bankruptcy costs and
    value of the firm, 546–547
  (*See also* Federal income tax system)
Tender offer, 11, 638
Tenneco Corporation, 639–640
Term loans, 460–461
  advantages of, 461
  amortization of, 461
  interest rate on, 461
Term structure of interest rates, 103–106
Time preferences for consumption, 96–97,
  99
Time value of money, 356–375
  and amortized loans, 371–372
  determining interest rates, 370–371
  future value, 356–359
  future value of an annuity, 364–366
  present value, 360–362
  present value of an annuity, 366–368
  present value of an uneven series of
    receipts, 368–370
  present value versus future value, 362–
    364
Times-interest-earned (TIE) ratio, 163, 548–
  549
Total assets utilization ratio, 160
Total leveraging effect, 545
Total risk (*See* Corporate risk)
Trade credit, 320–325
  components of, 325
  cost of, 321–323
  costly, 325

effect on financial statements, 323–325
  free, 325
Transactions balances, 260
Transfer of capital, 54–56 (*See also* Financial
  intermediaries)
Translation gain, 728
Translation loss, 728
Treasurer, responsibilities of, 7–9
Treasury bill rate, compared with discount
  rate, 89
Trend analysis, 166
Triple taxation, 34
Trust receipt, 349
Trustee, 462
Two-bin method, 307

Underwriting syndicates, 506
Uniform Commerical Code, 335
United States Steel, 459–460(DIF), 485–
  486(DIF)

Valero Energy Corporation, 417(DIF), 450–
  451(DIF)
Value of the firm, relationship with taxes
  and bankruptcy costs, 546–547
Variable costs, 218–219
Venture capital, 69–71
Vertical merger, 637
Voluntary bankruptcy, 665

Warehouse financing, 350–352
  acceptable products for, 351
  advantages and disadvantages, 352
  cost of, 352
Warrant, 519–523
  decisions on use of, 525–528
  formula (exercise) value of, 520
  price of, 520–522
  reporting earnings when outstanding,
    528–529
  used in financing, 522–523
Watkins Electronics, 624
Wedtech Corporation, 239(DIF), 253(DIF)
Weighted average cost of capital, 566–567,
  576–581
  minimizing, 579, 581
Window dressing, 173
Working capital, 240–250
  for small businesses, 251–252
Working capital management, 240–241
  combining current asset and liability
    decisions, 249–250
  financing strategies, 243–249
Working capital policy, 240–241
  effect on rates of return, 241–243
World markets, 51

Yield curve, 104–106
  effect of interest rate risk on, 108
  normal and abnormal, 109
Yield to maturity (YTM), 481–482

Zero coupon bonds, 466–468